Introduction to Medieval Europe, 300–1500

Introduction to Medieval Europe, 300–1500 provides a comprehensive survey of this complex and varied formative period of European history. Covering themes as diverse as barbarian migrations, the impact of Christianisation, the formation of nations and states, the emergence of an expansionist commercial economy, the growth of cities, the Crusades, the effects of plague, and the intellectual and cultural life of the Middle Ages, the book explores the driving forces behind the formation of medieval society and the directions in which it developed and changed. In doing this, the authors cover a wide geographic expanse, including Western interactions with the Byzantine Empire and the Islamic world.

Now in full colour, this second edition contains a wealth of new features that help to bring this fascinating era to life, including:

- A detailed timeline of the period, putting key events into context
- Primary source case boxes
- Full colour illustrations throughout
- New improved maps
- A glossary of terms
- Annotated suggestions for further reading

The book is supported by a free companion website with resources including, for instructors, assignable discussion questions and all of the images and maps in the book available to download, and for students, a comparative interactive timeline of the period and links to useful websites. The website can be found at **www.routledge.com/cw/blockmans**.

Clear and stimulating, the second edition of *Introduction to Medieval Europe* is the ideal companion to the study of Europe in the Middle Ages at undergraduate level.

Wim Blockmans is Professor Emeritus of Medieval History at the University of Leiden.

Peter Hoppenbrouwers is Professor of Medieval History at the University of Leiden.

Praise for this edition

'*Introduction to Medieval Europe* provides an excellent overview into the fascinating world of the Middle Ages. It covers issues such as mentalities of men and women as well as giving an insight into the world of medieval politics. Included is a thought-provoking chapter on continuities which provides a new framework for the understanding of a world distant to us both in time and place.'

Thomas Småberg, *Malmö University, Sweden*

'This is an extraordinarily wide-ranging introduction, covering Europe in its broadest sense from the British Isles to Turkey. It not only explains the political, intellectual and religious developments that occurred between the late Roman period and the Reformation but it also gives an insight into what life must have been like for most people. An essential first port of call for anyone wishing to understand the Middle Ages.'

Jonathan Harris, *Royal Holloway University, UK*

'The particular strength of this new edition of *Introduction to Medieval Europe, 300–1550* is the authors' ability to trace the development and transformation over time of large scale social, economic, and religious structures and mentalities. How did pagans become Christians? How did slaves and peasants become serfs? How did armed horsemen become knights? Few if any other textbooks at this level can offer students such a sure guide along the path to understanding how the outlines of medieval society took shape.'

Sean Field, *University of Vermont, USA*

'This commendably clear and concise overview of the medieval period should be essential reading for all students coming to the subject for the first time. The coverage of social, economic and intellectual themes is particularly strong. Readers will appreciate the profusion of maps, diagrams and other illustrations which buttress the text.'

Simon Barton, *University of Exeter, UK*

'In their new edition on the Middle Ages, Blockmans and Hoppenbrouwers offer a rich, accessible, and valuable resource for students and lecturers of medieval history alike. With its expanded list of tables, figures, illustrations, color maps, primary source boxes, and annotated bibliographies, this revised text is a must-have for anyone interested in the formation of pre-modern Europe. Through a careful re-organization of materials and an extended treatment of the period along sensible thematic and chronological lines, this work will continue to reign among the leading introductory surveys on the medieval world.'

Kriston Rennie, *University of Queensland, Australia*

'In the crowded field of historical surveys of medieval Europe, Blockmans and Hoppenbrouwers have managed to produce something distinctive and original. Their book gives a clear, well-written overview of the political, social, economic and artistic developments in these important centuries with helpful explanations of technical terms and good suggested further reading. Eastern Europe is given full weight and thoughtful illustrations give valuable insights into a culture more visual than literate. But more than this the authors demonstrate why medieval Europeans deserve to be studied, their influence on later times and different places, how many of our own preoccupations derive from theirs. Blockmans and Hoppenbrouwers make the European Middle Ages not just fascinating, but relevant as well.'

Andrew Roach, *University of Glasgow, UK*

'This is a work that helps its reader to grasp the defining contours of medieval history, without being subjected to a whirlwind of narrative detail. It is refreshing in its pan-European scope, bringing Lithuania to stand alongside France, and in its effective location of key issues in broader frameworks of change and continuity. Most of all, it treats the alterity of the Middle Ages on its own terms – and explains just what it is that makes understanding that fundamentally different world quite so interesting and worthwhile.'

Stephen Mossman, *University of Manchester, UK*

Introduction to Medieval Europe, 300–1500

Second Edition

Wim Blockmans and Peter Hoppenbrouwers

Routledge
Taylor & Francis Group

LONDON AND NEW YORK

First published in 2002 in the Dutch language as 'Eeuwen des Onderscheids: Een geschiedenis van middeleeuws Europa' by Prometheus

English translation, 'Introduction to Medieval Europe 300–1550' first published in 2007 by Routledge

This second edition published 2014
by Routledge
2 Park Square, Milton Park, Abingdon, Oxon OX14 4RN

and by Routledge
711 Third Avenue, New York, NY 10017

Routledge is an imprint of the Taylor & Francis Group, an informa business

Publication of the first edition was made possible with the financial support from the Foundation for the Production and Translation of Dutch Literature.

British Library Cataloguing in Publication Data
A catalogue record for this book is available from the British Library

Library of Congress Cataloging in Publication Data
Blockmans, Willem Pieter.
   [Eeuwen des onderscheids. English]
   Introduction to medieval Europe 300-1500 / Wim Blockmans and Peter Hoppenbrouwers. — Second edition.
      pages cm
   Includes bibliographical references and index.
   First published in 2002 in the Dutch language as "Eeuwen des Onderscheids: Een geschiedenis van middeleeuws Europa" by Prometheus. English translation, "Introduction to Medieval Europe 300–1550" first published in 2007 by Routledge."
   1. Middle Ages. 2. Europe—History—476-1492. 3. Civilization, Medieval.
   I. Hoppenbrouwers, P. C. M. II. Title.
   D117.B5413 2013
   940.1—dc23   2013022937

ISBN: 978-0-415-67586-4 (hbk)
ISBN: 978-0-415-67587-1 (pbk)
ISBN: 978-1-315-85761-9 (ebk)

Typeset in Stone Serif
by Keystroke, Station Road, Codsall, Wolverhampton

Contents

Illustrations

Figures

Tables

Maps

Boxes

Illustration acknowledgements

Plates

1.1 Statue of the Tetrarchs, 300–315 CE. © 2013 Photo Scala, Florence.
1.2 Detail from the Peutinger Table. © Austrian National Library Picture Archives, Vienna.
1.3 Seigneur Julius mosaic © 2013 DeAgostini Picture Library/Scala, Florence.
1.4 Arles arena, sixteenth century. © 2013 Photo The Print Collector/Heritage-Images/Scala, Florence.
2.1 The Book of Kells c.800. © The Board of Trinity College, Dublin, Ireland/The Bridgeman Art Library.
3.1 The symbolic sealing of a contract between king and vassal. Archives Départ. des Pyrénées-Orientales, Perpignan, France/Giraudon/The Bridgeman Art Library.
3.2 Viking burial ship. © Werner Forman Archive/Viking Ship Museum, Bygdoy.
3.3 Moorish stronghold and city walls, Obidos, Portugal. © Photolocation 3/Alamy.
4.1 Enamelled altar showing the parable of the vineyard. © 2013 Photo Scala, Florence – courtesy of the Ministero Beni e Att. Culturali.
4.2 Girding on a knight's sword. © The British Library Board.

5.1 Silvester, bishop of Rome, baptises Emperor Constantine. © The Art Archive/Alamy.
5.2 Harold swears his oath as successor to Edward the Confessor, Bayeux Tapestry. © akg-images/Erich Lessing.
5.3 Murder of Thomas Becket. © The British Library Board.
5.4 The castle of Montsó. © imagebroker/Alamy.
6.1 The abbey of Cluny. © Bibliothèque nationale de France.
6.2 The forge at the abbey of Fontenay, Burgundy. © Ian Dagnall/Alamy.
6.3 St Francis supports the Church: fresco by Giotto. © 2013 Photo Scala, Florence.
7.1 Depiction of the cruel habits of Tartars in a Western chronicle. © Master and Fellows of Corpus Christi College, Cambridge.
7.2 The fortress Krak des Chevaliers, Syria. © Grzegorz Japol – Fotolia.com.
7.3 Earthenware representing travellers on the Silk Road. © Images & Stories/Alamy.
7.4 The drapery market at Bologna in the fifteenth century. © Roger-Viollet/Topfoto.
8.1 Mappa mundi, Hereford Cathedral. © akg-images/North Wind Picture Archives.
8.2 Title page of *Margarita Philosophica*. © akg-images.

8.3 Astronomical clock. © De Agostini Picture Library/A. Dagli Orti/The Bridgeman Art Library.

9.1 Ypres drapers' hall and belfry. © incamerastock/Alamy.

9.2 Fresco from the meeting room of the Council of Nine Governors, Siena. © 2013 Photo Scala, Florence.

9.3 Towers in San Gimignano, Tuscany. © SOPA RF/SOPA/Corbis.

9.4 Venice as the largest and wealthiest medieval metropolis. Venice 1565, by Bolognino Zaltieri. akg-images/ullstein bild.

10.1 Mural painting depicting the *danse macabre*. © Artaud Frère, Rue de la Métallurgie, 44470 Carquefou- Nantes, France. Yvan Travert/akg-images.

10.2 Rebel peasants. © Private Collection/Archives Charmet/The Bridgeman Art Library.

10.3 Distribution of bread to the poor. © 2013 DeAgostini Picture Library/Scala, Florence.

11.1 Jaume I, count of Barcelona and king of Aragon, oversees justice. © The J. Paul Getty Museum, Los Angeles, Ms Ludwig XIV 6 fol. 72v.

11.2 Ceremonial session of the two Houses of Parliament in 1523. © 2011 Her Majesty Queen Elizabeth II/The Bridgeman Art Library.

12.1 Statue of Pope Boniface VIII, *c*.1300 on show on the façade of the Palazzo Pubblico of Bologna, Museo Civico Medievale. © Museo Civico Medievale, Bologna, Italy/Giraudon/The Bridgeman Art Library.

12.3 Well of Life. Photograph © National Gallery in Prague 2013.

12.4 Episodes from the lives of hermits, Fra Angelico. © 2013 The Museum of Fine Arts, Budapest/Scala, Florence.

12.5 Purgatory. © Musée Condé, Chantilly, France/The Bridgeman Art Library.

Unnumbered plates

Ivory diptych at Monza © 2013 White Images/Scala, Florence.

Suevi skull. © Stiftung Schleswig-Holsteinische Landesmuseen Schloss Gottorf, Schleswig.

Sutton Hoo. © The Trustees of the British Museum.

Jelling rune stones and church. Permission for reproduction granted to Peter Hoppenbrouwers. © Jelling Bogtrykkeris Forlag, Jelling, Denmark.

Burial with master and slave from Stengrade, Denmark, from p. 55, *The Vikings*, Else Roesdahl, translated by Susan M. Margeson and Kirsten Williams, Allen Lane, Penguin Books 1992, © Else Roesdahl 1987. This translation © Susan M. Margeson and Kirsten Williams, 1991.

Lord of rings: three gold bracteates. © National Museum of Denmark.

Reliquary depicting Charlemagne conquering Pamplona from Santiago de Compostela © 2013 DeAgostini Picture Library/Scala, Florence.

Medieval ploughs. © Musée de la Tapisserie, Bayeux, France/With special authorisation of the city of Bayeux/Giraudon/The Bridgeman Art Library.

Altar frontal, Nidaros cathedral, Norway. © akg-images/Interfoto.

Man with wounds from the surgical manual, *Surgical Treatment for Blows, Stab and Gunshot Wounds*. From Shipperges, p. 115. Wellcome Library, London.

Christine de Pizan writing in her study, *Oeuvres* offered to Queen Isabeau in 1407, London, British Library. © The British Library Board.

Karlstein Castle, exterior © Siloto/Alamy.

Introduction

The Middle Ages as a period in European history

Try to imagine a world in which:

- population density at its highest level was less than that of present-day Russia, without the latter's infrastructure
- medical knowledge was appalling, which meant that most people died young and had to live with serious physical suffering
- people, consequently, lived under a demographic 'high-pressure' regime, which means that only by maximising fertility were they able to keep ahead of mortality
- there was an abundance of young people
- infrastructure (roads, bridges) and means of transportation were of poor quality/primitive, so
- few people ever travelled far – hence, geographical scope and the mental outlook of most people were narrow
- economic production was overwhelmingly agricultural
- as a result, most people were peasants who lived in small villages
- technological development and mechanisation of human labour were very limited
- the Christian religion informed practically every aspect of daily life
- most people did not have any formal education, and were unlikely to be able to read or write.

Welcome to the Middle Ages! The Middle Ages are not just a straightforward part of world history taking place all over the globe. According to long-accepted agreement among historians, adopted by standard university curricula and standard textbooks all over the world, the Middle Ages are a period in Europe's past that roughly covers the millennium between 500 and 1500 CE. Nowadays, the term 'medieval', with 'feudal' used as a regular alternative, often represents something backward and barbaric, which then is contrasted with more splendid cultures that preceded and followed the Middle Ages. Where did such ideas come from?

The terms 'Middle Ages', 'humanism' and 'Renaissance'

In fourteenth-century Italy, poets and scholars who considered themselves **humanists**, that is, lovers of Greek and Roman Antiquity, for the first time expressed the belief that they were at the threshold of a new era of intellectual brilliance that would stand out sharply against the darkness of preceding centuries. The term *tenebrae* ('darkness') came from the pen of Francesco Petrarca (Petrarch) (1304–1374), the famous poet who spoke of the interim period between classical Antiquity and his own time as *media tempestas*, *media aetas*, *media tempora* ('the period in-between') – all terms with a decidedly negative connotation. For intellectuals after Petrarch this 'middle period' was nothing but an unfortunate intermezzo, which was on the verge of eventually turning into a new golden age inspired by classical culture. The expression *medium aevum* ('Middle Age') was given official status much later, in 1678 to be precise, when Du Cange published his two-volume *Glossarium* of Latin words used in that period that deviated from their classical meaning. Several decades later the German professor of history Kristoph Keller (Christophorus Cellarius) presented the first academic textbook on the history of the Middle Ages under the title *Historia Medii Aevi* ('History of the Middle Age'). It covered the period from Emperor Constantine the Great (306–337) to the Fall of Constantinople (1453). Soon, this became generally accepted methodology in university courses on history.

Since 'Middle Ages' is a humanist construct, the success of the concept is no doubt connected to the significant development of the system of Latin schools and grammar schools for secondary education. This was where humanistic ideas fully came into their own, since the study of the classical languages Latin and Greek formed the basis of the curriculum. It was hoped that through the study of the biographies of famous men and of the history of ancient culture, including poetry and rhetoric, new generations would be elevated to the idealised image of the heroes of Antiquity. Besides, until well into the nineteenth century Latin remained the language of university education, so that every intellectual was immersed in Antiquity by an active knowledge of its most important cultural carrier – language.

From the seventeenth century onwards, there was a renewed interest in the medieval period in Catholic countries in particular, and there were even specific institutes founded to study the Middle Ages. By contrast, in most of the Protestant world the Middle Ages were often overlooked as an academic subject, with the emphasis instead being placed on all the good that had been achieved since the Reformation. The religious divisions between intellectuals from the early modern ages thus perpetuated for ideological reasons the dividing line in history that humanists had drawn primarily on the basis of cultural-historical (literary, artistic) considerations.

In the course of the nineteenth century historical studies developed into a scholarly discipline. As more university professorships were introduced which continued to accept the humanist dividing line just discussed, newly founded learned societies and professional journals followed, and medieval history developed into a distinctive historical specialism with its own research agenda and its own methodology. Sometimes they were supported by national governments with national agendas. The awe-inspiring source text edition project known as the *Monumenta Germaniae Historica* ('Monuments of German History'), still very much alive, was a co-initiative of Freiherr Vom Stein (1757–1831), a Prussian state minister in the confused years of the Napoleonic wars. Initially, the aim of his private academic enterprise was to find support in the Germanic medieval past for the German nobility's political importance, but soon after Stein's death the revived Prussian state started to fund the *Monumenta* with different ideological intentions in mind: the sources of medieval history should disclose the original character and rationale of the German nation, destined to be restored in all its glory (under Prussian leadership, of course). An equally ambitious, state-sponsored project, although with a less overtly nationalist objective, was the Rolls Series, initiated in the 1850s. It was aimed at publishing new, scholarly reliable editions of all 'the chronicles and memorials of Great Britain and Ireland during the Middle Ages'.

In consolidating this situation, in which medieval history had carved out a field for itself, Jacob Burckhardt's *Die Kultur der Renaissance in Italien* ('The Civilisation of the Renaissance in Italy') played a key role. The phenomenal success of this book, which appeared in 1860, can be explained by the elegance with which the author re-formulated the historical myth imposed upon everyone who had enjoyed more than just an elementary education: the myth that a few generations of Italian intellectuals and artists had – through a truly cultural revolution – freed Europe from the stifling bonds of a society that was all oriented towards collective activity and in which every aspect of life on earth was focused on life after death. '**Renaissance**' literally means 'rebirth', and that rebirth refers to the restoration of ancient ideas and ideals as these were evoked in imitations of classical literature or of (supposedly) classical forms and models in buildings, paintings and sculptures. Actually, the first person to use the term 'Renaissance' in that sense, the Florentine painter and architect Giorgio Vasari (1511–1574), explicitly indicated his visionary predecessor, Giotto di Bondone (*c.*1267–1337) as the uncontested harbinger of this classicist movement. Compared with the loaded concept of 'Renaissance', 'humanism' seems more neutral and therefore easier to deal with. Strictly speaking, humanism refers to a philological procedure consisting of two parts: on the one hand, of attempts to unearth more ancient texts by intensive research in libraries; and on the other hand, of philological efforts to establish a version of those texts that resembles the original as closely as possible. In addition to this, however, humanism,

as its name betrays, has a more general and certainly vaguer meaning – that of an intellectual search more focused on the 'human factor' and of greater interest in the human individual and his intentions and emotions.

Burckhardt concentrated chiefly on this second meaning and elevated one subjective observation about Italian culture in the late Middle Ages – the increased appreciation for individual human achievement – to a key element in the process of revolutionary change that he detected. Since then, Burckhardt's view has been criticised and qualified from various angles. According to the Dutch historian Johan Huizinga, in his *Waning of the Middle Ages* (1919), the courtly culture of the Low Countries and northern France in the fifteenth century revealed a nostalgia for the more recent past rather than an aversion to it, or to a nostalgia that reached back to classical Antiquity – the nostalgia that pervaded the Italian Renaissance. Other critics pointed to a number of 'renaissances before the Renaissance' that had similar humanist features to the Italian Renaissance. The most important were the Carolingian Renaissance and the twelfth-century Renaissance.

As for the religious Reformation of the first half of the sixteenth century, the other main marker of the early modern age, we shall demonstrate that from a theological and institutional point of view it did almost naturally follow on from a long series of reform movements that began in the eleventh century. Its defining function is thus as debatable as that of the terms 'Renaissance' and 'humanism'. Nevertheless, the educational establishment in Protestant countries subsequently promoted the Middle Ages in stark contrast to later times, in order to stress their singularity.

The Middle Ages: continuity and change; sub-periodisation; types of medieval societies

Now that we know where the term 'Middle Ages' comes from, and why it has remained in use in history books and history lessons, the question arises whether there is any point in continuing to use it other than for didactic convenience. Are we still convinced that the changes that took place in European society in the decades around 1500 were fundamental enough to justify a fault line in history? In the 1970s there was a tendency to answer that question in the negative by pointing out that the basic economic and social realities, including most people's living conditions, did not alter substantially before the Industrial Revolution, as sustained economic growth remained out of reach. But the logical conclusion of carving out a new era in history, the Pre-industrial Age, encompassing the centuries between 1000 and 1800, somehow never made it, maybe because of an unwillingness to accept economic processes as the principal determining factor in history. Neither did attempts at spreading out Late Antiquity over the fifth to ninth centuries as a long-winded transformation of the Roman world. Most specialists stick to the idea that indisputable continuities, especially in the East where the Roman Empire formally continued to exist until 1453, were more than adequately counterbalanced by sweeping changes in the social and economic order as well as in politics and religious culture to justify the start of a new historical era.

So, in a way, the Middle Ages have made a comeback in professional history. This is accompanied by new research, clearly inspired by social anthropology and cultural history, to redefine the individual, distinctive character of the medieval period. At the same time it has remained important to stress how much modern Europe owes to its medieval past. So many institutions and ideas that are generally regarded as essential to both the structure of modern European societies and the mental outlook of European people go back to the formative centuries before 1500 – think of parliaments, corporations, universities, local communal self-government, the separation of secular state and organised religion, and capitalist enterprise. In our book we have tried to do justice to

both viewpoints: on the one hand, to accentuate the medieval world's otherness and singularity; on the other hand, to describe that same world as our ancestors' time-space, while avoiding teleological fallacy – the world in which we live and the life that we cherish were not predestined by its medieval past, but that world would have looked quite different without it.

Besides, static features do not make history; history by definition is a process of continuity and change over time. What changes within the chronological boundaries of the Middle Ages have been so fundamental that all aspects of society were affected by them? Among such transformations we mention the following:

- the weakening and disappearance of the Roman Empire in the West, with its centralised imperial bureaucracy, its homogenous administrative structure centred on *civitates*, and its subordinate system of production and distribution
- the constitution of Christendom as the overriding religious and ideological superstructure of European society
- relatively large-scale migrations of multi-ethnic barbarian groups, followed by the formation of proto-national 'regnal communities' (Reynolds 1997) within the former frontiers of the western Roman Empire
- enlargement of agricultural production within the framework of various types of significant aristocratic landownership, which preconditioned long-term population growth and urbanisation on a wide scale, supported by commercialisation and economic expansion, partly along capitalist lines
- the development of regular long-distance overseas trade reaching out to North Africa and Asia
- the virtual disappearance of slavery of Christians in Christian society, and other forms of unfree personal status in the most urbanised regions, which
- allowed the emergence of the commoner, the

ordinary free man in possession of basic rights in towns, villages and states, the cornerstone of late medieval society

■ the evolution of dynastic monarchies based on personal bonds into dynastic monarchies and a wide variety of institutionalised states

■ the rationalisation and partial secularisation of the worldview and the view of mankind

■ the development of an individualised spirituality, also among the great masses of the faithful

■ successive revolutionary changes in written communication in the twelfth and fifteenth centuries.

We agree with the defenders of the concept of pre-industrial societies that after the sixteenth century until the Industrial Revolution there were quantitative but not qualitative changes in these transformations. The distinction between the late Middle Ages and early modern history does not rest on fundamental differences according to type of society or on radical breaks in social developments. Major processes, such as urbanisation and the secularisation of the worldview, ran a continuous course from the eleventh century to the end of the *Ancien Régime*, or even until now. Much of what is new, 'modern' in the early modern period goes back to the later Middle Ages.

In short: in this book we use the term 'Middle Ages' both for pragmatic reasons and because we think it has intrinsic merit in the sense that the millennium between 500 and 1500 contains enough distinctive and interesting processes of historical change to set it apart from the period that preceded it and the period that followed.

Cultural diversity

Europe's geographical variety and its relative lack of large open plains is a natural phenomenon that has most certainly contributed to the long survival of widely differing cultures. Even in the twentieth century, despite the strongly homogenising effects of Church and state institutions, the transport revolution and mass media, we can identify a multitude of regional cultures that are apparent in their own organisation of material life, in their own customs and concepts and in their own languages or dialects. With the current trend towards globalisation it is not easy for us to realise that until the eighteenth century the horizon of most Europeans did not extend beyond the place where they lived or the region where they were born. This does not mean that nobody ever travelled, or that there was no mobility, or that there were no large-scale migrations; it was just that these were relatively uncommon. Normally, people remained for the most part tied to a particular area; this naturally resulted in considerable differences in economic development and cultural outlook.

Major coordinating intellectual, constitutional or religious constructions such as the Church, kingship and state, with which we are nowadays familiar, or which a highly developed elite devised at the time, were far removed from everyday experience at the local and regional level. This was certainly a hindrance to the efforts at unification made by the higher political authorities. For us as historians, the same local diversity and changeability make it extremely problematic to write a comprehensive cultural history of the Middle Ages that would cover all of Europe over more than a thousand years. This has not prevented us, however, from clarifying important cultural phenomena in the successive political, socio-economic, and religious chapters that are the backbone of this book. In that respect, culture, in its broadest sense of those variegated channels through which people give symbolic meaning to existence, has been provided for.

Which Europe?

As we mentioned in the beginning, the historical term 'Middle Ages' by definition only has meaning in a European context, so there is no point

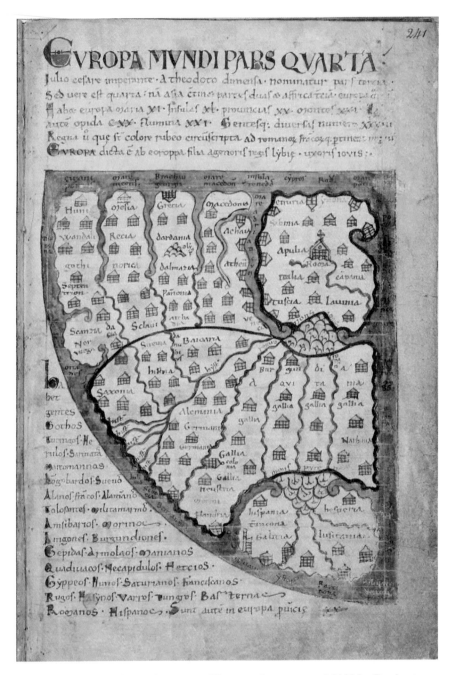

PLATE 0.1 The oldest known independent map of Europe, drawn around 1121 by Lambert, canon in Saint-Omer, in his richly illustrated encyclopedia *Liber Floridus*. Europe is seen as a quarter of the world; a circular *mappa mundi* shows in the upper left part Asia, Egypt, Arabia and Ethiopia, with Paradise on top, beyond India. The Danube, the Rhine and the Rhône can be distinguished, as well as the Alps and the Pyrenees as boundaries to the Italian and Iberian peninsulas; Rome is marked with a cross on a major building. Empirical data are ordered within an overall idealistic worldview, from the Huns and Germanic peoples top left, to Greece, Germany and Gaul, all with their regions.

in accusing medievalists of a Eurocentric bias. Neither are we enthusiastic about the idea – often enough aired – of exporting the medieval label to areas outside Europe ('medieval China', 'medieval Islam'). Yet we also have to admit that the geographically defined continent of Europe does not provide in all respects the most appropriate spatial framework for our considerations. For the clerical literate elite in the medieval period itself the demarcation of their world lay naturally at the frontiers of Christendom, which had run over to Asia and Africa. At the same time, even in the fourteenth century the Christian mission had not yet reached all the lands that make up the European continent. It means that we shall have to assume expansive core areas which in some way or other asserted their superiority, often through conquest but also through peaceful cultural transfer. It also means that those core areas will get more attention than the (shrinking) peripheries.

Seen from this perspective there can be no doubt about the head start enjoyed by the Mediterranean world. Even after the decline of the Roman Empire, the losses caused by the barbarian invasions and the disruption that may at first have been created by the Arab conquests, there was still considerably more wealth and potential for development available in southern Europe than in the north. The region was nourished by the sustained economic and cultural exchanges that were springing up between Christians and Muslims in the Middle East, Iberia, Sicily and southern Italy. By presenting the Mediterranean area as an economic and cultural zone of contact and transit we prevent medieval Europe from turning in on itself, so to speak.

From the thirteenth century onward more and more Europeans crossed the frontiers of the continent of Europe. Overland journeys were made all over Asia to examine the possibilities for direct commercial links with China and India and, of course, for the further propagation of the Catholic faith. In 1291 two Genoese brothers by the melodious name of Vivaldi sailed through the Straits of Gibraltar, 'westwards to India'. It is not known whether they found America, or indeed any other part of the world, for nothing more was heard of them. But their brave initiative sprang from a tremendous drive for expansion, which their fellow Genoese, Christopher Columbus, would emulate with greater success, though with resources not much technically improved, 201 years later.

A comparable culture driven by expansion lay at the other extreme of the continent – that of the Vikings. The lead that early medieval Scandinavia had acquired in a number of respects compared with eastern and north-west Europe resulted in remarkable journeys of discovery to all corners of the world, in commercial ties with Byzantium and central Asia, and in the settlement of its people in Iceland, Greenland, North America, Russia, Britain, Ireland and Normandy. From the eleventh century, however, the expansion stagnated. Its demographic potential was apparently exhausted, and its technical advantage had been matched. The northern (and later Norman) elements were assimilated into the diverse receiving cultures without leaving any dominant trace. By contrast, the Mediterranean expansion that, viewed economically, continued until the sixteenth century, shows that it was based on far firmer foundations.

The Europe that we shall study therefore corresponds only partially to the geographical concept of the continent. On the one hand, we see large areas on its western, northern and, in particular, eastern peripheries that were only integrated later and superficially into the developments in the south and west (Christianisation, expansion and intensification of agriculture, commercialisation, urban growth, consolidation of states). On the other hand, we cannot entirely understand the dynamism emanating from southern Europe without seeing it in relation to relatively advanced regions outside Europe, especially in North Africa and the Middle East.

From scarcity to hegemony

No clairvoyant making a prediction in 1400 about which part of the world would dominate in the future would ever have mentioned Europe. The continent had just lost one-third of its population through a succession of plague epidemics; its religious leaders were involved in painful schisms; the Ottoman Turks were trampling over the remains of the Byzantine Empire in the Balkans; the kings in the West were at war with each other and exhausting their resources; peasants and townspeople were rising up in great numbers against the lords who oppressed them.

The clairvoyant would more probably have named the Mongol conqueror Timur the Lame, Tamerlane, as the future world leader. In the preceding years, Timur had established his iron authority over the enormous region stretching from the Caucasus to the Indus. He had conquered great cities like Baghdad, Edessa, Isphahan, Ankara, Aleppo, Damascus and Delhi. Perhaps our clairvoyant would have foretold the sudden death of this despot in 1405, putting an end to the Mongol terror. The seer may well have considered the flourishing dynasties in the Muslim sultanates of Granada, Egypt and Tunis, but he would have hesitated, for they were quarrelling among themselves and were thus not very stable, despite the glories of their courts and mosques. He might have expected the Ottoman power to expand further into the Balkans and central Europe, and to conquer Syria and Egypt, but in his day all this was still speculative.

In the end, however, he would surely have chosen the Chinese Empire, consolidated as an administrative structure since the second century BCE. Did it not encompass an area as large as western Europe, cities with several hundred thousand inhabitants, very productive agriculture and a highly developed administrative system? The Chinese had for centuries surpassed the Europeans with their technical and organisational capacities; long before 1300 they already had iron tempered with coke, gunpowder, the ship's com-pass, the rudder and printed paper money issued in the emperor's name. They undertook journeys of discovery and commercial expeditions along the coast of India as far as East Africa. There was busy shipping in the China Sea and the Bay of Bengal; large numbers of Chinese traders dealing in high-quality goods were established in foreign ports. If there were ever to be a dominant world power it would have to be China – that is what any sensible person must have thought in 1400. Yet things turned out differently: eventually, between 1000 and 1900, Europe moved from its backward position to the forefront.

In what way was Europe different from its eminent precursors? The distinction lies in the strong drive for expansion to other parts of the world. First and foremost, Europe gained an essential technical advantage over the rest of the world in the fourteenth century through the development of firearms. Advances in shipbuilding and navigational techniques brought possibilities of sailing the oceans on an unprecedented scale. The key question, then, is how this technical lead was managed once it had been achieved.

The most important difference between Europe, China and all the other highly developed regions of the world lies in the fact that there was no unitary authoritative structure in Europe. At the beginning of the fifteenth century, Chinese voyages of discovery along the coast of East Africa could easily have meant that not Vasco da Gama but a Chinese admiral, Zheng He, would already have sailed round the Cape of Good Hope by 1435. But in 1434 the Chinese imperial court decreed that no more exploratory expeditions should be undertaken. The capital of the Ming dynasty had just been moved to Beijing so that the threat from the Mongols in the north could be better resisted. The capital's food supply was assured by the completion of the Grand Canal, some 1,500 kilometres in length, which was opened in 1411 and connected the old capital, Hangzhou, with Tianjin near Beijing. This achievement required a gigantic undertaking by a state that had to establish priorities in its territory with a population that was as large as Europe's.

No single European body had at its disposal the possibilities of organising such an enormous concentration of resources to implement state decisions or completely suppress commercial initiatives. There would always be another leader ready to venture an experiment. The dozens of kingdoms, hundreds of autonomous principalities, prince-bishoprics, city-states and free peasant republics, all of which governed small parts of Europe, found themselves in a constant state of rivalry, and often at full-blown war. Moreover, no single political unit was able to establish its authority permanently. Despite all the resulting devastation, the attempts to expand the means of exercising power were a stimulus to innovation. The Chinese Empire, on the other hand, was mainly occupied in preserving its internal stability. This did not preclude growth, but it was focused on internal production and marketing. Agricultural land was expanded through reclamation, and natural resources were exploited further. China's future would lie in the north-west, in the vast expanses of Xinjang, bordering the Mongolian steppe. Sea-borne trade and industrial production were no longer favoured. Imperial rule was not restricted to the political sphere. It also controlled religion and the economy, so that it resembled a totalitarian system.

In Europe, by contrast, the religious and political spheres became more clearly separated in the later Middle Ages. Before then popes and emperors had struggled in vain to achieve supremacy, thus only proving that a truly universal European power did not exist. A relatively autonomous third power appeared in some regions during the Middle Ages: that of the towns. Towns in Europe, unlike those in other parts of the world, enjoyed an administrative and legal autonomy that expanded as the town grew and the local ruler became relatively weaker. This enabled commercial and industrial enterprise to grow without insurmountable restrictions being imposed by Church or secular authorities. They often threw

up obstacles and tried to take as large a share as possible of the profits from trade. If they went too far, however, capital would take flight to a safer place where it could then grow further.

In this way the segmentation of power over a variety of political units and an independent Church created the unique situation which gave rise to commercial capitalism. This largely autonomous method of organising trade is aimed primarily at making as large a profit as possible, through a constant search for the most lucrative combinations of production factors, for methods of risk-reduction, and for the re-investment of profits in further expansion. Other motives – political, ethical and religious – were subordinated to these goals. It grew into a dynamic market system that was not limited to a particular area of authority but everywhere seized the opportunity to pursue profits. This exercise of power in the political, legal, religious and economic field gave merchants and entrepreneurs in Europe chances that elsewhere were often frustrated by authoritarian religious and secular rulers. And for the same reasons Europe was more open to foreign innovations than any other culture.

Medievalism

'Medievalism' is currently used as a conceptual shorthand for all sorts of conscious references to the Middle Ages in modern culture, including popular culture. Medievalism in that sense originated in the early nineteenth century, when ideologies again started to play an important part in the view of the past. If, in the period of classicism, medieval cathedrals and monasteries had been allowed to fall into disrepair or even to be destroyed on purpose, as happened during the French Revolution, from the 1820s it again became fashionable to build in the Gothic style and even to try to improve upon medieval builders. In France, the architect Eugène Viollet-le-Duc (1814–1879) got involved in a great number of the most influential restoration projects, such as those of the church at Vézelay in Burgundy – one of the points of departure of the First Crusade – the Notre Dame cathedral in Paris, the royal basilica of Saint-Denis north of Paris and the medieval city of Carcassonne in the Languedoc. In his view, restoration meant 'to re-establish a building to a finished state which may in fact never have actually existed at any given time'. This vision was strongly opposed by the visionary art critic and draughtsman John Ruskin (1819–1900). For Ruskin, restoration implied the preservation of the status quo at the time of his intervention. He also propagated that, in designing new buildings, the neo-Gothic style should not be the preserve of Catholic churches but should also be applied in Protestant and secular architecture. His ideas received warm support from, among others, the famous restoration architect Sir George Gilbert Scott (1811–1878), who was in charge of the restoration of the marvellous abbey of Tewkesbury in Gloucestershire – still today the fitting location for an annual medieval festival.

The highest stone towers built in Europe in the nineteenth century were those of the Gothic revival cathedrals in Ulm and Cologne. The newly built Houses of Parliament in London and Budapest are neo-Gothic gems, as are the town halls of Vienna and Munich. The past was thus coloured according to the preferences of the following centuries. In these cases, choosing the Gothic style meant a reference to the medieval origins of parliamentarianism and civic rights with the aim of enhancing the prestige of the newly emerging constitutional, liberal and national states. After having been neglected or even execrated for centuries, the Middle Ages – that is, the image constructed of them – were now extolled.

The idealistic representation of the Middle Ages found its clearest expression in the architecture of churches. Until deep into the twentieth century, entirely new buildings were erected in neo-Romanesque or neo-Gothic style, to enhance the particularity of churches in a modernist environment. In midtown New York, the harmoniously neo-Gothic Catholic St Patrick's cathedral was built between 1858 and 1865; the spires were finished in 1888. That same year, the Episcopal diocese of New York planned its new cathedral, St John the Divine. This building was to arise sixty blocks farther north in a more traditional Byzantine-Romanesque style. After completion of the central dome in 1909 the sponsors suddenly decided to change to a High Gothic French-styled design. When it was opened in 1941, the nave was one of the largest in the world. However, up to the present day, the cathedral remains unfinished with two half-grown spires in the west front and a strange unachieved mishmash in the crossing. To make the situation even more medieval, between 1922 and 1930 the huge Riverside Church, a refined imitation of the cathedral of Chartres, was built on a picturesque site just a few blocks further away. In this curious duel fought by means of medieval symbolism in the then most modern city in the world, the sponsorship of John D. Rockefeller Jr. proved far more effective than the believers' donations to St John the Divine.

In literature, Romantic authors like Walter Scott, Heinrich Heine and Victor Hugo seized eagerly upon medieval stories to present the greatness of a medieval past, in contrast to the rationalism of the Enlightenment and the French revolutionaries. Projected on to this past were conservative values such as kingship, Church and nobility, and a corporative social order, but also liberal ones such as civic freedom and national character, depending on what was required. Musicians used the newly edited medieval sources as basic material for the scenarios of widely applauded operas. Giuseppe Verdi (1813–1901) was an influential Italian composer who systematically chose historic themes to disseminate a nationalistic message in his divided country, the northern provinces of which were under Austrian rule until 1866. Many of his operas dealt with medieval themes, from his very first, *Oberto, conte di Bonifacio* (1837–1838) to his last, *Falstaff*

(1889–1893). His contemporary Richard Wagner (1813–1883) used various Norse sagas as well as the epic poem *Das Nibelungenlied* as the basis for his series of operas *Der Ring des Nibelungen* ('The Ring of [the] Nibelung').

Medieval inspiration continued to function during the twentieth century in various popular domains. Oxford professor of English literature J.R.R. Tolkien (1892–1973) was a specialist in early Germanic literature and mythology, especially the Anglo-Saxon epic *Beowulf*. Here (as well as in Wagner's operas) he found inspiration for his best-selling novels *The Hobbit* (1937) and, especially, *The Lord of the Rings* trilogy (1954–1955), which are among the most widely read books on earth. Recently, these were turned into blockbuster movies and mega-selling computer games. Meanwhile, *Beowulf* itself provided the material for several movies, as did other heroes and heroines from medieval history, legendary (King Arthur, Robin Hood) or real (Alexander Nevskij, William Wallace, Jeanne d'Arc, King Henry II and Eleanore of Aquitaine, Chinggis Khan). Time and time again, historical novels and historical movies that make use of the Middle Ages prove that the medieval period is a great source of base material for fascinating fiction, but also that medieval history – like all history – can be easily abused to support nationalistic claims.

The book's arrangement

In our presentation of medieval history in this book the transformations that we listed in the beginning are important themes, although for the sake of clear arrangement we chose to start from the traditional tripartition: the early Middle Ages (covering the years 300–1000), the central Middle Ages (1000–1300) and the late Middle Ages (1300–1500). Within each part there are chapters on political, economic and social, and religious and cultural aspects. We have opted for a periodisation in which emphasis is placed on transitions rather than sharp breaks, on processes of far-reaching change within which elements of the old society exist alongside the new. Three themes that overlapped the latter two sub-periods (together the second half of the Middle Ages), namely the start of European expansion, the astonishing intellectual accomplishments, and urbanisation and the constitution of urban society are treated in separate chapters between the central and late Middle Ages sections. This gives a total number of twelve chapters, which coincides with twelve course weeks in many academic history curricula.

Part I

The early Middle Ages, 300–1000

1 The end of the Roman Empire in the West

Every day, one of the most powerful images of Late Antiquity is passed almost unnoticed by thousands of tourists strolling around Venice's San Marco Square. It is the Philadelphion (lit. 'brotherly love'), the reddish porphyry statue of the tetrarchy, the 'college of the four rulers', that was cut for the **Emperor** Diocletian's palace at Nicomedia (Asia Minor). In 293, Diocletian had decided that the Roman Empire had become too big and too complex to be ruled by one man alone. He made a division in two parts, East and West, each to be ruled by two emperors: one with the superior rank of *augustus*, the other with the lower rank of *caesar*. Diocletian understood that such a rule by four could only work if the tetrarchs were strongly committed to each other and their common cause. Therefore, as first *augustus* of the East, he gave his daughter in marriage to his *caesar*, Galerius, while his colleague in the West, Maximian, did the same honour to his *caesar*, Constantius Chlorus. This close, yet hierarchical, bond between the four tetrarchs is perfectly expressed in the Philadelphion. Each of the two *augusti* clasps his arm protectively around his junior co-emperor, like a father does to a son. The

PLATE 1.1 Statue of the tetrarchs, 300–315 CE

caesars are indeed represented as young men – which neither of the two in reality was at that time. All four are look-alikes, a purposeful *similitudo* ('similarity') that stresses the unity and harmony, the strength and determination of the imperial junta.

With the installation of the tetrarchy, Diocletian intended to firmly restore peace, unity and prosperity to the Roman Empire after decades of turmoil and civil war. The third century, in particular its middle part, had been beset with all sorts of crises: large-scale barbarian invasions, renewed Persian attacks on the eastern border, mutinies in the army, followed by an avalanche of military coups, massive fall in population, economic decline, impoverishment of the countryside, widespread epidemic disease and rampant inflation following the virtual collapse of the imperial silver coinage. None of these plagues was really new but their accumulated mix proved disastrous, and they were able to accumulate because the Roman superstate and its army failed to secure the peaceful conditions and political stability necessary for recovery.

So, the task imposed upon the four rulers was immense. By the beginning of the fourth century the Roman Empire, although its borders had already retreated, was still impressive. It measured about 4.5 million square kilometres, extending over more than 30 present-day states. To get from one end to the other took the average traveller almost three months over land, even if he made use of the network of paved roads with a total length of around 90,000 kilometres. There were 50–60 million inhabitants belonging to many races and speaking many languages, but all had been considered Roman citizens – provided they were free persons – since 212. Between 10 and 20 per cent of them lived in cities, the largest of which were metropolises of more than 100,000 inhabitants – Rome still the largest of all with an estimated population of more than half a million. The entire Roman army was about that size too, while between 25,000 and 35,000 state officials

PLATE 1.2 'All roads lead to Rome.' Detail from the Peutinger Table, a copy of a third-century Roman map of roads and watercourses, named after the humanist Conrad Peutinger. Towns and rivers are particularly recognisable.

were on the state's payroll – very few people to control and defend a territory and a population of such a size. That is why modern historians are quite divided over the usefulness and the effects of the tetrarchy's crisis management. There are those who say that during, if not already before, the crisis of the third century the Roman Empire went into steep demographic and economic decline, never to find its way back again. Others argue that, after decline, real recovery followed; that there is no reason to think that the Age of Constantine, in terms of population size and prosperity, was inferior to the Age of Trajan.

Governing an empire

Government structure and bureaucracy

To cope with the problems, Diocletian took a number of measures in addition to the introduction of collegiate imperial government. He carried through an administrative reorganisation under which the Empire was divided into two halves, four prefectures (e.g. Gaul, including Britain and Iberia), fourteen dioceses (e.g. Egypt) and 114 provinces (e.g. Africa). Each province was subdivided into *civitates* or (local) districts, which consisted of an urban centre (sometimes also called *civitas*, although more usually *municipium*, *urbs* or *oppidum*) and a rural territory (*ager*) that could extend over hundreds of square kilometres. In addition, there were the two urban prefectures of Rome and Constantinople. Furthermore, a first attempt was made to codify Roman law; the tax system was streamlined and tax collection more rigidly organised; monetary reforms were undertaken (the number of mints was increased and several imperial coins were re-valued) and prices were set at a maximum by law; conformity to state religion was demanded of all citizens. All these measures betray Diocletian's deeper concerns: to provide for law and order; to secure the state's tax income; to contain economic vagaries; to enforce

religiously sanctioned loyalty to the state. To manage this state intervention on every hierarchical level, the imperial bureaucracy was vastly extended and members of the senatorial order were more often than before appointed to high offices in the upper levels of imperial administration. The number of senators was more than doubled in the course of the fourth century till it reached about 2,000 at the accession of Emperor Theodosius in 378.

Because all state officials had to be rewarded for their services, the process of bureaucratisation opened the way not only to some measure of administrative sophistication and efficiency, but also to extensive job-hunting, power broking, leapfrogging and corruption. On paper, everything was neatly, almost militaristically, organised. In real life things were slightly different. Although lip service was paid to professional competence based on formal training, more often family connections, family networking, seniority, money and, in particular, imperial discretion determined who could enter civil service or who was promoted. The only thing the emperor could do was to limit the tenure of high officials to prevent them from building up local clienteles.

Emperor and court

The emperor and his court were at the top of government. This summit was quadrupled under the tetrarchy, but soon the tetrarchy and its underlying aim of non-hereditary collegiate rule proved to be an anomaly. It hardly survived the voluntary retirements of Diocletian and Maximian in 305, mainly because, predictably, most of the *augusti* and *caesars* appointed wanted to be succeeded by their sons or favourites, and most were not prepared to share power with others. The project ended in 324, when Constantine, son of Constantius Chlorus, finally had his last rival killed, and became the sole ruler of the Roman Empire. When soon afterwards he considered re-installing tetrarchical government, it was meant to be strictly a family business to be run by his four sons. This plan failed even before it was executed because of violent competition among the (half-)brothers, and it all ended in monarchy again, first of Constantine's third son, Constantius II (337–361), and then of his nephew Julian (361–363), the last emperor of Constantine's dynasty. When two years later a high-ranking officer, Valentinian, was declared emperor by the army, he was pressed to share imperial power with his brother, Valens. This arrangement set the model for dyarchy rather than tetrarchy, and would lead to the final division of the Roman Empire into an eastern and a western half. Valentinian also stood at the base of the last great imperial dynasty of Antiquity, known as the Valentinian-Theodosian dynasty. It produced emperors without interruption, in the male and female line, until 455.

The emperor's power could well be described as absolute. Long before they converted to Christianity, Roman emperors enjoyed a semi-divine status, and long afterwards they continued to promote themselves as the embodiment of eternal law and divine providence, if not as the personal vicegerents of Christ on earth. Constantius II used to sign imperial ordinances with 'My Eternity'. His public appearances were choreographed with precision, and soaked with elaborate, orientalising ceremonies of sanctity. Everything around the emperor was sacred, even the stables where his horses were kept. All such lofty rituals were intended to distance the ruler from his subjects. In reality, the emperor's position was more ambivalent. He was seen both as a demi-god and as the *primus inter pares* among the Roman citizens. This meant that no emperor could get away with disregarding his ordinary subjects altogether. Carefully staged 'baths in the crowd' were made part of imperial ceremonies, and, besides instilling awe and terror, emperors had to display a willingness to grant clemency and favours. This meant that the imperial court attracted a ceaseless flow of petitioners and

embassies, usually with the express purpose of redressing decisions taken on a local level.

When not campaigning, the emperor was permanently surrounded by a swarm of women (empresses, princesses, mistresses), friends, eunuchs and other members of the *sacrum cubiculum* (the emperor's inner household); their influence was difficult to measure. Others, in particular scions of powerful families, were attached to the emperor's court on purpose, to spend considerable time under the eyes of the ruler and the handful of high court officials who surrounded him. It happened to Constantine who, as a young man, spent many years at the court of Diocletian in Nicomedia.

The enormous expansion of imperial bureaucracy further down also created problems for the emperors, who found themselves caught between their desire for autocratic rule and the necessity to delegate. Roman emperors could not make use of Orwellian means of mind control; on the contrary, they always ran the risk of being misinformed or of being kept ignorant. Despite the Empire's excellent diplomatic and postal service (the *cursus publicus*), and a sophisticated system of so-called agents *in rebus* (about 1,200 messengers with special instructions who roamed the Empire and acted as the emperor's eyes and ears), the impact of orders given by the court could easily peter out with the increase of the vast distances they had to travel. Even the symbolical omnipresence of the emperor in statues and on coins, or in the use of his names and titles in documents and inscriptions, could not alter that. The emperor always had to reckon with autonomist tendencies among far-away administrators who could easily fall prey to local interests. The real art of governing the Roman Empire, besides controlling the army, was to forge 'a working relationship between key members of the departments of central government and key figures in the revenue-producing local communities' (Heather 2005).

Local government

Local government was concentrated in the urban centres of the civitates, and was led by a city council or **curia**. Its members, called *curiales* or *decuriones*, were invariably recruited from the prosperous local elite. They did not just serve as councillors out of an unselfish commitment to the public cause, but also to exhibit their respectability and gain the opportunity to move up in the expanding state bureaucracy, at which many succeeded. In local affairs, city councils could operate with a large degree of autonomy, also thanks to their own revenues from local taxes and civic estates, ranging from shops to farms and grazing lands in the countryside. But the councils did play a leading part in the governance of the Empire as well. They organised the assessment and collection of direct state taxes (see below), provided for law courts and were responsible for the upkeep of public infrastructure (roads, bridges, aqueducts) and the maintenance of the *cursus publicus* within their district's territory. In the countryside, villages had headmen and, increasingly, local clergy and monks for contact with the authorities, but they rarely seem to have acquired administrative autonomy.

Quite apart from the prerequisites of all such administrative duties, many *curiales* were prepared to pay out of their own pockets for games, shows and free opening hours in the public baths or to sponsor the embellishment of their beloved town with forums, temples, statues, basilicas, arches, porticoes, baths, circuses, theatres or amphitheatres. Monuments of this kind, and the ceremonies, rituals and entertainments that were staged there, went to the heart of both civilised Roman lifestyle and the deeply felt need to openly express loyalty to the Roman order and its first protector, the emperor.

The loss of this monumental splendour, and the 'disappearance of comfort' (Ward-Perkins 2005) that inevitably went with it, can only partly be blamed on the barbarian invasions, although these certainly did not help with their preservation. There were two more important factors. One was the advance of Christianity with its anti-secular cultural ideals. Christian leaders strongly opposed pagan luxury and pagan entertainment. Bishop Isidore of Seville, in the early seventh century, warned his flock that they should stay away from 'the madness of the circus, the immorality of the theatre, the cruelty of the amphitheatre, the atrocity of the arena and the luxury of the games' – which also suggests that all these attractions were still available in southern Spain at that time. So, this point should not be pushed too far. Moreover, enormous amounts of money, confiscated from funds related to the old public cults in now pagan temples, were spent on the building of churches that still looked very much like pagan basilicas. The other factor seems to have been more ponderous, and is related to the steady disappearance of the classical city councils during the fourth century. There were a number of reasons for this. One was a growing interest among urban elites to acquire positions in the imperial bureaucracy or the clerical hierarchy of the Christian Church, rather than in local city government. It seems that the position of *curialis* had become less attractive mainly because Diocletian's fiscal reforms had made local tax collection less lucrative and more risky. In the other direction, city politics started to become more and more dominated by another kind of people, the ultra-rich *honorati* ('honourable men'), most often wealthy landowners from the senatorial order. In addition, city government was increasingly led by new types of officials who were appointed from above and who had titles such as *defensor*, *protector*, *curator* or, most importantly, *comes* (*civitatis*). They would preside over city councils and courts of justice, and as a rule, were assisted in the exercise of their duties by the local bishop who, as the leader of the Christian community of a *civitas*, demanded a say in its politics.

All these developments diminished the political and social importance of the old-style *curiales*, as well as the city councils' pivotal role in

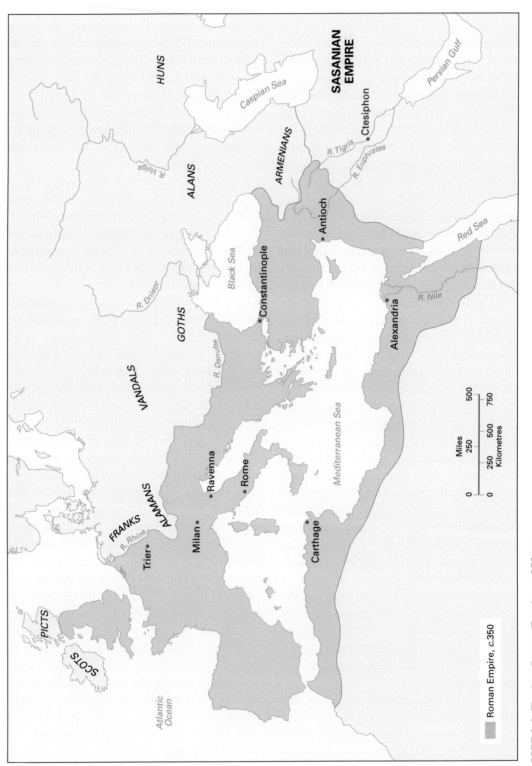

MAP 1.1 The late Roman Empire, c.350 CE

the upholding of classical civic culture. Although the emperors tried to stop this process and the draining of town councils by passing imperial edicts in which curial duties were made obligatory for wealthy citizens, or, later on, decurion status was made hereditary, these had little effect on the ground. In the course of the fifth and sixth centuries curial government virtually came to an end and the old city councils were replaced by smaller, mixed and informal bodies, consisting of both *honorati* and *curiales* under the leadership of **counts** and bishops. This was not just exchanging one oligarchy for another. Unlike the old curiae, the new governing elites were not constitutionally defined, and their members did not recognise a collective responsibility for their administrative dealings, let alone accept any financial liability. In short, the breakdown of the old-style city councils meant the disappearance of a type of corporate government of well-to-do citizens, bound by a collective commitment to their city and the state, that for centuries had been the cornerstone of Roman power and Roman civilisation. It was also the kiss of death for the 'competitive munificence' (Liebeschuetz 2001) that had ensured the monumental grandeur of so many Roman cities.

Taxation and fiscal policy

If the higher purpose of the Roman state was to provide its citizens with peace, legal certainty, justice and prosperity, the most important means that stood at its disposal to reach – and secure – these goals were taxation and the army. It has been calculated that about 5 per cent of the Empire's GNP went on tax payments (normal for developed pre-industrial states or underdeveloped modern countries), and that well over half of the total tax revenues were spent on the army. So, the Empire's survival crucially depended on the smooth running of the fiscal machinery.

Diocletian carried through a number of drastic reforms of the two general flat taxes that already existed and which brought in the bulk of the tax revenues, that is to say, the *iugatio* or land tax (from *iuger*, the standard area measure) and the *capitatio* or poll tax/head tax (from *caput*, 'head'). First, he joined these two taxes together into one undivided tax, known as *iugatio-capitatio* or (in Greek) *syntheleia*. Second, he standardised and refined the assessment basis. Third, he standardised to five years the time interval between the censuses that were conducted to assess individual tax payers' tax liability. Fourth, he introduced the so-called indiction (from *indictio* or 'notification'), to be understood as the public announcement of the total amount of taxes that each province had to pay yearly. Fifth, he had the reassessment intervals of indiction and census synchronised. This meant that every five years – in 312 prolonged to every 15 years – new censuses were conducted and a new indiction was established on the basis of census data.

The smooth execution of all such measures depended very much on the enthusiastic cooperation of city councils. An important task of the *curiales* was the assessment of individual tax payers and the organisation of the actual tax collection. This would not have made them popular with everybody, but on balance such activities must have been profitable.

Two aims of Diocletian's tax reforms had been the reduction of the tax burden and a greater equality in tax liability (Diocletian had printed *AEQUITAS* ['equality'] on his coins), but two others were uniformity and simplicity. Because the latter two led to more efficient tax collection, widespread dissatisfaction sprang up. Diocletian and his successors countered this by taking legal measures to make hereditary the status of three social parties that were closely involved in the taxation process. In addition to the *curiales* as tax collectors, these were the *corporati* (members of the urban corpora, the Roman precursors of the medieval trade and craft **guilds**) and the so-called *coloni* (peasants who were settled on the estates of large landowners) as sizeable groups of tax payers that could be registered relatively easily. However, in the longer term, such measures did not work for lack of control.

Typically, the *iugatio-capitatio*, if paid in kind (which was perfectly acceptable), was often referred to as *annona*, which was actually the word for the steady supply of grain (and other basic foodstuffs) from the Empire's three major 'granaries' – the provinces of Egypt and Africa (present-day Tunisia), and the isle of Sicily – to the two major receivers of state benefit in kind: the army and the proletariats of Rome and Constantinople. The *annona* is the foremost example of the heavy involvement of the Roman state in the Roman economy – another one would be state control over (physical) markets. Specialists are divided as to whether this was a curse or a blessing for the private sector of the Roman economy. Adherents of the curse point out that both the establishment of production and dis- tribution systems by the state and over-regulation dislocated the market and stifled economic initiative. Supporters of the blessing, such as David Mattingly, argue that 'trade under state contract' generated certain economies of scale by 'cross-subsidizing the transport of other com- modities and [by] stimulating demand in civil markets'. In favour of the latter opinion is the reintroduction of a strong standardised gold coin, first under Diocletian (the *aureus*) and then under Constantine (the *solidus*). Gold coins were used in the state's payments to the military, but probably also in dealings between the state and private long-distance wholesale trade.

Collapse of the *annona* – for whatever reason – had two major consequences: the existing size of armies was endangered and the viability of the Empire's two metropolises ceased. When this hap- pened, Rome's population dropped very quickly, from around half a million by about 400 to no more than 30,000–50,000 by the middle of the sixth century. The turning point had been the conquest of the African province by the Vandals in the 430s. The conquest of Egypt by the Arabs two hundred years later had less dramatic effects on the population size of Constantinople because that city had access to the rich arable lands of the Black Sea area.

The Roman army and the frontier

Roman rule rested on military power. In the later Roman period the army's role became even more

PLATE 1.3 Rural scenes around a North African villa, *c*.400, depicted on the so-called Seigneur Julius mosaic.

pronounced. Whereas for a long time Roman emperors had first of all been civilians who, at best, had revealed themselves as competent leaders of military campaigns, in the third century this was turned around: most of the many emperors from that period started as career generals and took imperial power thanks to army backing. This military competence of emperors, and their personal involvement in army operations, would only recede after the death of Theodosius the Great in 395. He was succeeded by his two sons, Arcadius, emperor of the East, and Honorius, emperor of the West, who were notoriously unsoldierly figures. It may be no coincidence that during their reign the Roman Empire reeled, and fell in the West.

During the late imperial period, the Roman army underwent a number of fundamental changes. First of all, towards the end of the third century the Romans switched to what modern military historians have called a new 'Grand Strategy'. They no longer chose to defend the Empire at its frontiers with legions stretched along the whole length of the *limes* or border. The new plan was to distinguish between border troops (*limitanei, ripenses*) and mobile field armies (*comitatenses*), stationed in large garrison towns a good distance from the *limes*. The biggest advantage was a greatly improved utilisation of the main armies' radius of action, both against incursions from outside and against internal unrest or rebellion. The disadvantage was that the border could be easily penetrated, certainly by small raiding parties. The Romans tried to overcome the problem by forming human buffer zones where groups of barbarians were allowed to settle in the thinly populated demilitarised zones inside the *limes*. In exchange, they had to defend these areas as Roman allies. This happened on a small scale until about halfway through the fourth century. After that, so-called *foedera* (literally meaning 'treaties'; the singular form is *foedus*) were entered regularly by sizeable groups of barbarians who formally submitted but then acquired allied status for limited periods of time or for specific campaigns, in which they could operate fairly independently under their own commanders. At a later stage *foedus* came simply to mean a mercenary's contract. There was no formal submission and no connection with border defence. Moreover, these contracts entitled the *foederati* to standard military payment. In order to secure this payment, their leaders tried to obtain a high Roman military rank. One warlord who operated in this way in the later years of the western Empire was Childeric, the father of the Frankish king Clovis. Childeric called himself *rex* (king), but in addition bore the Roman rank of *magister militum* (general).

The growing importance of *foedera* for maintaining Roman order was not an isolated phenomenon, and that brings us to our second point: the increase in the Roman army's size, from an estimated 375,000 at the beginning of the third century to around half a million in the middle of the fourth century. Because the Empire's population during the same period more likely shrank than grew, and the willingness of Roman (male) citizens to sign up for service in the legions did not change, the consequence was that a growing number of soldiers had to be recruited abroad, among foreigners, whom the Romans, with a mixture of contempt and disapproval, called 'barbarians'. This certainly fitted into a long tradition that went back to the glorious days of the Republic, but now the barbarisation of the army went much further in two, related, respects. First, foreign soldiers in the late imperial period were employed in all kinds of army units. They could be assigned to field armies, usually to special barbarian infantry or cavalry units, that had standardised ethnic names (e.g. 'the Armenians'); to territorial troops stationed at the border, either by incorporation into regular border legions (*limitanei, ripenses*) or as so-called *laeti*, i.e. peasant settlers who if need be served as lightly armed garrison troops. Second, more barbarian military men than before succeeded in joining elite units and working their way up to the highest positions in the army. Many generals who played key roles in the dramatic events of 'the period of migrations' were themselves of foreign extraction or else second-generation immigrants. If we count the Isaurians of Asia Minor as 'barbarians' – as many contemporary authors did – then for the first time in 474 a barbarian general, Zeno, became the formally recognised emperor of the Empire in the East, and managed to stay in power for seventeen years. Antipathy to barbarian immigration and the barbarisation of the army was greater in the East than in the West, and concentrated in the upper echelons of the civil administration into which far fewer barbarians had penetrated. Referring to the dominant position of Gothic mercenaries and their powerful commanders in the military defence of Greece and Asia Minor by the end of the fourth century, Senator Synesius of Cyrene called it 'folly to use wolves as watchdogs'.

Economic structure and prosperity

The willingness of thousands of foreigners, especially from the north, to join the Roman army certainly had an economic motivation as well. It is tempting to draw a comparison between the Roman *limes* in the north and the Mexican–American border of today. In both situations, a substantial difference in prosperity on either side of the border set in motion similar push-and-pull factors. Mexicans are drawn into the United States by the existence of a large demand for cheap labour, and they are 'pushed' out of Mexico by poverty, insecurity and violence, largely caused by competition between gangs over the domination of the extremely lucrative drugs market that caters for users in the United States. Similarly, in the later Roman period, barbarians from the north were drawn in massive numbers into the Roman Empire by the existence of a large demand for soldiers, and they were 'pushed' out of their native countries by poverty and violence, caused by competition between warlords over the profits of the raiding and trading over the border – or of the wheeling and dealing with Roman authorities, who in their relations with barbarians used clever divide-and-rule diplomacy, and quickly changed alliances. Political unrest in the most densely populated area of the *limes*, the upper and middle Rhine and the upper and middle Danube, was thus fed gradually over the centuries. It resulted in a regular regrouping of the barbarian confederations outside the borders of the Empire, in a growing migration pressure and often in violent raids too. The massive 'ritual dumps' of hundreds of weapons (whose bearers had been killed in battle or ritually executed) in the peat bogs of Jutland and Schleswig-Holstein provide grim evidence of the endemic raiding and warfare in the northern border regions of the Roman Empire. They show better than anything else how in the first century CE a society of peaceful farmers increasingly became a society geared to war.

The deeper cause of all this, the big difference in prosperity on either side of the border, is the best proof of the Roman Empire's unrivalled success as a state. Still, this requires some explanation because, at first sight, the economic structure of the Empire was not unlike that of the northern barbarian world: both were overwhelmingly rural and in both, agriculture was by far the most important sector of economic production.

The big achievement of the Roman economy had been its ability to find an outlet for low-value/high-quality non-staple food (such as wine, olive oil and *garum* – fish sauce, Antiquity's ketchup) as well as standardised non-food products (such as pottery) to mass markets that could be remote from the production areas. This would have been impossible without a relatively large degree of interregional 'connectivity', which was furthered not only by the Empire's natural advantage of being draped around a gigantic water highway (the Mediterranean) and its superb network of roads, but also by at least three other factors: long-lasting internal peace, legal certainty in doing business and a large demand from cities and army. This can only have further stimulated efficiency, specialisation and the expansion of employment in supplier companies (think of the mass production of packing material, such as amphoras), in transport (ships, carts, pack animals), in finishing, brokerage and retailing, in construction works, etc. It also obliges us to consider a readjustment of the traditional picture of Roman cities as merely 'consumer cities', inhabited by wealthy – and idle – people living off their private means. On the contrary, many cities must have been bustling with commercial and manufacturing activities. The only downside of this highly commercialised and specialised economy was that it made regional economies whose prosperity depended on exports vulnerable to reductions of demand in distant markets as a consequence of circumstances over which they had no control.

The barbarian world of the north

By contrast, the rural society and agrarian economy of the people living in the densely forested plains and mountains that extended north of the northern frontier (*limes*) of the Roman Empire were much simpler. They mostly consisted of peasants who practised subsistence agriculture and who lived in small villages controlled by native warrior aristocracies. The degree of commercialisation was low – but probably significantly higher near the Roman frontier than further away from it – and, even if the names and locations of some marketplaces beyond the frontier are known, settlements that could be called towns must have been rare.

In Late Antiquity, the northern frontier (outside Britain) by and large coincided with the courses of the rivers Rhine and Danube. Ancient geographers roughly divided the barbarians who lived there into Celts and Germans; only in the sixth century would the Slavs be added as a third category. What was meant by these names, and what type of subcategories they covered, changed over time. While Greek and Roman authors from the first century BCE, on vague grounds and with little consistency, started to distinguish 'Germans' from 'Celts', it was Julius Caesar who invented a homeland for the former. Caesar wanted to separate by a forbidding physical borderline – the mighty river Rhine – one group of barbarians, the Gauls (Celts), from another, even more ferocious, group, the Germans. Caesar's Germany was subsequently immortalised on the marble map of the world that was commissioned by the Roman general Marcus Vipsanius Agrippa (d.12 BCE) as the area enclosed by the northern seas and the rivers Rhine, Danube and Vistula. This would also provide the geographical framework for *Germania*, the standard work on the northern barbarians in later Antiquity, which was written shortly before the year 100 CE by the senator and historian Publius Cornelius Tacitus. Quite confusingly, with the development of comparative linguistics in the eighteenth century, the classical ethnographic indications Celts, Germans and Slavs were maintained and re-used as labels for the classification of North European language groups that all belonged to the same, Indo-European, language family. Then, rather precipitately, archaeologists turned these linguistic families into 'cultures', which does not make much sense scientifically. Certainly with respect to Germany, also the name of a modern state, confusion was now complete, but not in a harmless way. The equating of modern Germany with either classical ethnographic *Germania* or with the vast area in which Germanic languages were spoken, or had once been spoken, provided German nationalism under the Nazi regime with dangerous 'historical' claims to *Lebensraum* far beyond the German borders. The perceived pan-Celtic and pan-Slav cultures have been similarly exploited for nationalistic purposes.

Latin authors called the subdivisions of Germans, Celts and Slavs *populi* or *gentes*, which modern scholars translate as peoples, nations or tribes. This also leads to confusion, for the meanings such terms have in modern social sciences or in common parlance do not necessarily coincide with the meanings that the original classical words had in their time. For instance, in modern anthropology 'a people' is an ethnic group, to be defined as an enduring community with its own culture. An essential feature is that its members are conscious of their collective identity. This consciousness is expressed in its own proper name or ethnonym, and in the awareness of a shared past (real or not) and a common destiny. But because of this subjective and constructivist character of ethnicity, it is hardly possible to determine whether named barbarian groups in Late Antiquity actually were 'peoples' in the modern anthropological sense. People in the past are only comprehensible to archaeologists, historians and linguists in so far as their doings have materialised in objects, texts or linguistic remnants. Moreover, as the story of the 'Suevian knot' shows (see Box 1.2), it is not always simple to establish to what extent and under which circumstances such remnants 'produced' ethnic meaning.

The word 'tribe' should be avoided outright, as this is a term modern anthropologists apply to small egalitarian communities in which an economic basis for elite domination is still lacking. As far as we are able to tell, most barbarian groups at the time of the migrations did not correspond to this definition. They were at least one rung higher on the ladder of societal complexity, that of **chiefdoms**. Chiefdoms are characterised by the formation of local elites, in this case warrior aristocracies, who are able to use force when necessary to defend their position of power. To achieve this they must have at their disposal armed followers and allies whose loyalty can be ensured through material favours. This again presupposes a steady supply of either war booty or agricultural surpluses that will reach the hands of the leaders and will be converted into prestige goods (weapons, jewels, horses) valued by their warriors or allies. Roman sources use the term *comitatus* to denote the armed retinues of barbarian warlords, but the modern German translation **Gefolgschaft** is more popular. The rise

of *Gefolgschaften* fits perfectly in the process of the militarisation of the northern barbarian world described above.

One cluster of barbarian peoples may have reached a stage of societal complexity beyond that of chiefdom: the early state. These were the peoples known under the umbrella name of 'Goths'. In the third and fourth centuries they had formed a number of stable kingdoms north of the lower reaches of the Danube, the Dniester and the Dniepr, an area covered by the present-day states of Romania, Moldova and Ukraine. It still is a matter of heated debate whether these Goths originated from Scandinavia, as historians in the sixth century started to tell, or whether Gothic identity was entirely the product of confederative unification of barbarian chiefdoms north of the lower Danube and along the north-western shores of the Black Sea at the beginning of the third century CE. Whatever the case, there is no doubt that the Goths spoke a Germanic language, whose grammar and vocabulary are well known thanks to fragments of a Gothic Bible that had been translated from the Greek by a missionary known as Ulfilas (or Wulfila in Gothic) around the middle of the fourth century. From the moment the Goths appear in Roman history, they had an ambiguous relationship with the Empire. On the one hand, we see many Goths take service in the Roman army, and make money and if possible a career in the Roman Empire; on the other hand, the reinforcement of Gothic power north of the Danube led to them probing Roman strength by way of attacks and invasions in Greece and Asia Minor around the middle of the third century.

But the Roman Empire was not the only opponent the Goths had to deal with. Their geographical location meant not only that the Gothic kingdoms were the neighbours of steppe nomads living in the vast steppe area that stretched from the Danube delta to the Altaic mountains, but that some of them also occupied land that was suitable for nomadic herding. It put them in a dangerous – because competitive –

position. In Late Antiquity, the nomads of the Pontic-Caspian steppe, known under collective names as Scythians, Sarmatians and Alans, spoke Indo-European languages that were related to Iranian, which means that they had been 'native' to the area for a long time. This quickly changed around the middle of the fourth century, when new groups of nomads from further east, who spoke Altaic languages of the Turkic or Mongol type, penetrated, and soon dominated, the western steppes. This was a momentous, if not revolutionary, development in world history, with major consequences for what happened in central Asia and the Middle East, and also central and eastern Europe, during the medieval period. While the relationships of the 'Iranic' steppe nomads with sedentary empires in central Asia and Europe always had been generally peaceful, and never led to serious attacks on, let alone to long-term occupation of, territory that belonged to such empires, this would alter completely when Turkic-Mongol nomads took over the western steppes. On the whole, they were far more aggressive in their contacts with the sedentary world, and their aggression often paid off because of their capacity to build up large confederations, which sometimes developed state-like features, under strong leaders from powerful families. Under such circumstances nomadic forces could turn into redoubtable fighting machines, which made optimal use of the nomads' superior horsemanship and competence in the martial arts, especially their extreme agility and their ability to fire arrows from horseback. The results were impressive. Shortly after 1500, the entire Middle East, including Egypt, as well as the larger part of present-day south-east Europe, Afghanistan, Pakistan and India were ruled by dynasties that originated from Turkic-Mongol steppe nomads, while two European kingdoms (Hungary and Bulgaria) also had nomadic origins. More than a thousand years earlier, the first nomadic confederation of Turkic-Mongol origins had expanded its power over the western steppes and seriously threatened stability in the adjacent polities, the Gothic kingdoms to

start with. These were the Huns, *bipedes bestiae* ('two-legged beasts'), according to one Roman historian.

The collapse of the Roman order in the West

In 376 a large group of Tervingi, a major subdivision of the Goths who lived north of the lower Danube, asked Roman authorities in Thrace for permission to cross the Danube and enter the Empire's territory. The traditional story is that they were fleeing the Huns who, after their sudden appearance on the western steppes, had attacked the Goths and caused such panic among them that the Goths, in great fear, had turned to flight in huge numbers. On further consideration, a connection between the 'invasion of the Huns' in the Pontic steppes and the 'flight of the Goths' is less straightforward, if only because the kingdom of the Tervingi did not border the Pontic steppe directly. Besides, at that point in time, the Huns may already have been active there for several decades. More likely, therefore, is that the admission of large numbers of Goths into the Empire was the result of peace negotiations with imperial authorities that had been going on ever since 369, when the Tervingian Goths had been finally defeated by the Romans after a protracted war.

With hindsight one could say that, by allowing the Goths to cross the Danube, the self-declared descendants of King Priam had hauled in another Trojan horse. Partly, this was their own fault. Local authorities who had to deal with the stream of refugees were not up to the task. Because of their bad treatment the Goths rose in revolt and soundly defeated the army of the eastern emperor Valens at Adrianople (present-day Edirne) in 378. From that point on, the East had a 'Gothic problem': what to do with a large and coherent group of refugees that had its own, fearsome, army? For decades, politicians and imperial authorities in Constantinople remained indecisive about the best solution: give the Goths land to settle in a remote border area or make use of their military abilities and offer them *foedera*? Far more than the Donau crossing or the battle of Adrianople, the fact that the Gothic problem, which was a problem of the East, was not resolved was decisive in setting in motion a series of tragic events.

The start of these events has to be placed in 394, when Emperor Theodosius the Great gained victory over a usurper in the West mainly thanks to Gothic troops. But because he did not sufficiently compensate the heavy losses his Goths had suffered, this led to long-lasting resentment. The Gothic mercenaries found a new leader in Alaric, a young man of noble birth. After Alaric had invaded Greece and ransacked Athens, his Gothic army settled in Epirus, right on the border of the eastern and western empires. Emperor Arcadius, Theodosius's son and successor in the East, then pacified the Goths by granting them the status of *foederati* and awarding Alaric the title of general. But when the payments that went with this status stopped being made, Alaric decided not to invade Greece again, because at that moment anti-Gothic sentiments in the East had risen to fever pitch and ended in a frightful day of reckoning in the streets of Constantinople. Under these circumstances, Alaric thought it wiser to attack Italy, the heart of the western Empire. With that action, which took place in 401–402, Alaric exported the 'Gothic problem', which had emerged in the East and until then had stayed there, to the West. And while the Gothic problem would fade away in the eastern Empire, it would become a crucial element in the fall of the Roman Empire in the West.

Once in Italy, the Gothic army was defeated twice by Flavius Stilicho, the commander-in-chief of the western armies, but Stilicho omitted to finish the job and put an end to Gothic military adventures. Probably, the *generalissimo* had a hidden agenda: with the aid of Alaric's mercenaries he hoped to acquire a firm foothold in the Balkans from which to expand his influence to the East. Whatever he had in mind, history

would prove the consequences disastrous. With Alaric still alive and active in the Balkans, Stilicho had to face the outcome of another event of major significance, which took place in central Europe. The Huns, masters of the Pontic steppe for decades, now, shortly after 400, expanded their power over the semi-steppe lands of the Carpathian Basin (the Hungarian Alföld or puszta), which was only separated from the two Roman provinces of Pannonia by the river Danube. This was the only region in the western part of the European continent suitable to a nomadic way of life, and therefore was often chosen as a basis of operation by nomads from the Pontic steppe who wanted to intensify their contacts (commercial and warlike) with the European sedentary world. It was no accident that the expansion of Hunnic power over the Alföld coincided with the rise of autocratic rulership within the Hunnic confederation.

The arrival of the Huns in central Europe must have caused major distress among the populations that were living in this area. Many were resigned to their fate, or allied themselves with their new masters, which added to existing tensions in the area. Others – in particular war bands under local leaders – must have decided to move away in a western or southern direction, causing further turmoil when they invaded lands that were not uninhabited, and threatening the frontier of the Roman Empire. The final result was the formation of two large multi-ethnic confederations of barbarian warriors and their families that were keen to invade the Roman Empire. The first to do so was led by a Gothic chieftain called Radagais. He forced himself into Italy from the north-east at the end of the year 405. To confront the invaders, Stilicho had to move troops from the Rhine frontier to Italy, and although Stilicho once again triumphed on the battlefield, there was little he could do when in the last days of the year 406, the second confederation that had been built up in central Europe crossed the frozen Rhine near Mainz. It consisted of three main ethnic components – Vandals, Suevi and Alans – but is

BOX 1.1 A VANDAL SAVES ROME: FLAVIUS STILICHO (*c*.365–408)

The ivory diptych in the cathedral treasure of Monza shows Flavius Stilicho (*c*.365–408), in military dress, with his wife Serena and their son Eucherius on his left. The panel was made in 396, or shortly afterwards, on the occasion of the appointment of the minor Eucherius to a high public office.

As the son of a Vandal king, Stilicho was called *semibarbarus* (half-barbarian). Under Emperor Theodosius he had a brilliant military career which ended in his appointment as commander-in-chief (*magister utriusque militiae*) of the Roman legions in the West. Stilicho was a prop and stay to Theodosius. His consort Serena was a niece of Theodosius, who had adopted her as his daughter and entrusted his youngest son, Honorius, to her care. Before this Theodosius had 'recommended' (*commendati*) to Stilicho Honorius and his older brother Arcadius, who would succeed him as emperors of the western and eastern parts of the Empire respectively. This is why Arcadius and Honorius are depicted on Stilicho's shield. Stilicho allied himself even more closely to the imperial family by marrying off his daughter Maria to Honorius, while he intended his son Eucherius to wed Honorius' sister Galla Placidia. Through all these alliances not only did Stilicho feel connected to the imperial family by right and reason, he clearly also cherished imperial ambitions for his own son.

From the imperial palace in Ravenna Stilicho played a tragic key role in a crucial episode in Roman history. When Stilicho refused to transfer the provinces of Illyria and Africa from the western to the eastern Empire, Arcadius sent Alaric and his Gothic army to Italy. Stilicho defeated Alaric a number of times, and it remains a mystery why he allowed the Gothic army to remain intact. Shortly afterwards, the large-scale invasion of Italy by a new Gothic confederation led by Radagais obliged Stilicho to pull his troops out of Gaul in 406. Although Radagais' army was crushed at Fiesole, Gaul was weakened militarily and the great coalition of Vandals, Suevi and Alans, which had crossed over the frozen Rhine near Mainz towards the end of 406, could thrust deep into Gaul without meeting much opposition. Both events seriously weakened the Roman grip on the West.

Vague plans to reunite both parts of the Empire after the death of Arcadius in 408 led to Stilicho's downfall, because Honorius suspected Stilicho of wanting to put his own son, Eucherius, on the throne in Constantinople. The rebellion of a Roman army which had been brought together in Pavia in the summer of 408 in preparation for an expedition to Gaul brought discredit to Stilicho. He sought refuge in Ravenna where he and his followers were brutally murdered on Honorius's orders.

Claudian, an Egyptian-born poet and protégé of Stilicho's wife, sang the praises of Stilicho in countless panegyrics. He gave Stilicho his image as saviour of Rome: *restituit Stilico cunctos tibi, Roma, triumphos* ('Stilicho has given all your triumphs back to you, Rome'), runs one of his verses. After the death of Claudian in 404 Stilicho had a collection made of all the poems eulogising himself; they were an important means of propaganda for the general.

Sources: Santo Mazzarino, *Stilicone. La crisi imperiale dopo Teodosio* (Rome: Signorelli, 1942); Alan Cameron, *Claudian: Poetry and Propaganda at the Court of Honorius* (Oxford: Clarendon Press, 1970).

generally known as the Vandal confederation or Vandal army. In the following years, this Vandal army would traverse Gaul from north to south relatively unhindered, wreaking havoc and destruction. It crossed the Pyrenees in 409 to take possession of large parts of the Iberian peninsula during the decades that followed. The chaos that was caused in Gaul by the Vandal invasion led to various revolts and coup d'états by ambitious generals and senators in the north-western provinces. One of the results was the total withdrawal of Roman troops from Britain.

On top of all this, the untimely death of the eastern emperor, Arcadius, in 408 led to a nasty power struggle in Italy between Stilicho and Arcadius' brother Honorius, the emperor in the West. Both hoped to reap profit from the precarious situation in Constantinople. Neither would succeed but in the process Honorius had Stilicho murdered. Many of Stilicho's loyal troops, for fear of being massacred, fled to the Balkans and joined the army of Alaric. Soon after, Alaric invaded Italy once more, where he tried to wring major benefits – again, the rank of general for himself, land on the Balkans for his soldiers – from Honorius, who had entrenched himself in his impenetrable capital, Ravenna. Because of Honorius's repeated refusal to give in, Alaric laid siege to Rome several times. In August 410, the city was captured and sacked for three days, an event that came as a shock at the time. Among the spoils was Honorius' elder half-sister, Galla Placidia, who later would marry Alaric's successor, Athaulf. On his way to his next target, the rich island of Sicily, Alaric died in Calabria in 411. The Gothic army then turned on its heels. After having been deployed by the Roman authorities as *foederati* in Spain, the Goths were assigned the province of Aquitania to settle, where in 418 they created their own kingdom with the city of Toulouse as its capital. To distinguish the Goths settled in Aquitaine from the Goths who were living in the East or in the Hunnic Empire, modern authors call the former Visigoths or Western Goths, and the latter Ostrogoths or Eastern Goths, although these names were only introduced much later, in the second half of the sixth century, by Jordanes, who wrote the first history of the Goths.

The Gothic settlement in Aquitaine can be seen as the conclusion of a double helix of events which we have no trouble in calling the fall of the Roman Empire in the West: one that started with Alaric's first departure for Italy, the other with the Hunnic conquest of the Alföld. Its essence was the loss of control over the Roman frontier in the north by the imperial government in the West, followed by the collapse of central authority over large parts of the western Empire (including their tax flows). As a consequence, a number of autonomous 'states-within-the state' emerged, some under the leadership of Roman generals or senators, others ruled by barbarian kings. By 420 this process had gained an unstoppable momentum; even to contemporary observers its irreversibility must have been clear: at least in the West, the Roman Empire was gone, and it would not return.

One other sign was the withdrawal of the Roman legions from Spain at about the same time

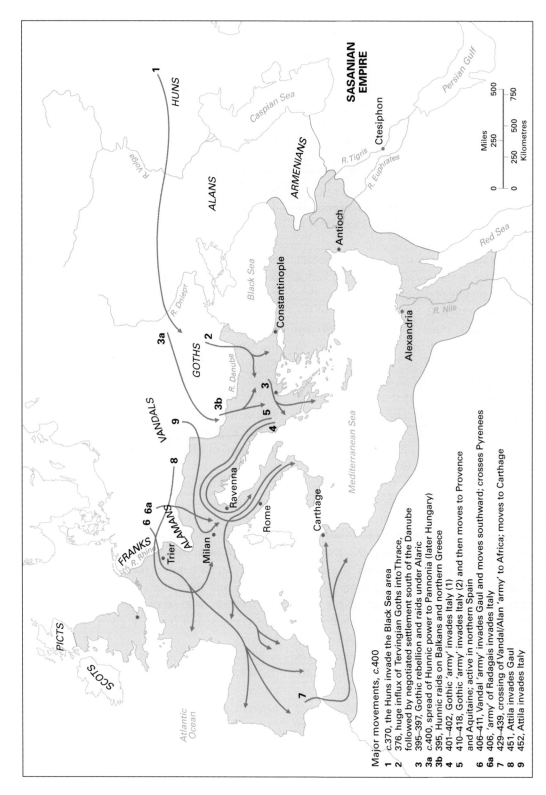

Major movements, c.400

1 c.370, the Huns invade the Black Sea area
2 376, huge influx of Tervingian Goths into Thrace,
   followed by negotiated settlement south of the Danube
3 395–397, Gothic rebellion and raids under Alaric
3a c.400, spread of Hunnic power to Pannonia (later Hungary)
3b 395, Hunnic raids on Balkans and northern Greece
4 401–402, Gothic 'army' invades Italy (1)
5 410–418, Gothic 'army' invades Italy (2) and then moves to Provence
   and Aquitaine; active in northern Spain
6 406–411, Vandal 'army' invades Gaul and moves southward; crosses Pyrenees
6a 406, 'army' of Radagais invades Italy
7 429–439, crossing of Vandal/Alan 'army' to Africa; moves to Carthage
8 451, Attila invades Gaul
9 452, Attila invades Italy

MAP 1.2 Major movements of militarised barbarian groups around 400 CE

as the (Visi)goths arrived in Aquitania. The power vacuum left behind gave the Vandal army the opportunity to partition Iberia among its various ethnic sections. This did not go without continual struggles, in which the Visigoths intervened as well. Visigothic power in Spain would only expand after 429, when allegedly 80,000 Vandals and Alans – men, women and children – crossed from Spain to Africa on the invitation of a rebel general. Within ten years they ruled as lords and masters in North Africa. The power of this hundred-year Vandal-Alan empire was concentrated in the old Punic capital, Carthage, close to modern Tunis.

Of all the significant movements of barbarians that took place in the so-called Migration Period between the middle of the fourth and the middle of the sixth century, the 'epic journeys' of the Gothic and Vandal armies just described still form the episodes that most fire the imagination. In fact they were exceptional. The journeys of the Gothic army did not even follow an invasion, but were a movement that started and ended inside the Empire. Also a sort of journey, but less well known, is the 'wandering' of the Burgundians. In the first quarter of the fifth century these barbarians originating from central Europe created a legendary kingdom along the middle Rhine, near to where Mainz and Worms are situated. Apparently this was soon seen as a threat to Roman authority because other *foederati* were sent to deal with them, first the Visigoths, then the Huns. The confrontation between Huns and Burgundians must have left a deep impression for it provided source material for one of the great medieval epic texts, the *Nibelungenlied*, which was first written down in lower Austria in about 1200. With their power in the middle Rhine area broken, the Burgundians started drifting again. Within the framework of new *foederati* agreements, in 443 Flavius Aetius, the commander of the remaining Roman legions in the West, gave them permission to settle in the middle Rhône region and around Lake Geneva. From there they took control of the low, north-western part of

present-day Switzerland. In 534, this second kingdom of Burgundy was conquered by the Franks.

The later Migration Period

Most migratory movements in the Migration Period did not have this character of a journey that lasted for years. The Alamans, together with the Franks, both vague ethnic indicators, provide a good example of northern barbarians who took decades, if not centuries, to gradually extend their area of settlement from over the Rhine frontier into the Empire. This process cannot be followed precisely but it must have been aimed both at colonisation by peasant settlers and at territorial power by leading warlords among them, who at times operated as Roman *foederati*. By the end of the Migration Period the Alamans were named as the inhabitants of the upper Rhine area and the adjoining part of modern south Germany. The Salian Franks had become the masters of present-day northern France by the third quarter of the fifth century.

The migrations of north German and south Scandinavian barbarians to England were halfway between outright invasion and the colonisation of a neighbouring region. The real settlements of these groups date from the beginning of the fifth century when the Romans withdrew their regular troops from England and left the defence against barbarians from Ireland and Scotland, including the Picts, in the hands of the Angles, Saxons, Jutes and Frisians from the continental North Sea coastal areas, who, again, were often invited for that purpose and formally given the status of *foederati*.

New, dramatic, changes threatened to occur in the West when Hunnic power reached its zenith under Attila, who was sole khan of the Huns between 444/445 and his death in 453. At first, Attila seemed to be satisfied with following an outer frontier strategy that was solely directed at the eastern Empire. This meant that he did not aspire to conquer Roman territory, but to blackmail the imperial authorities in Constantinople into paying him large amounts of gold under threat of invasion, which was indeed carried out on several occasions. Attila initially limited his interference with politics in the western Empire to offering his warriors for hire as mercenaries, preferably on the basis of *foederati* agreements. Hunnic military assistance was often invoked by the western emperor's court at Ravenna, which around the middle of the fifth century was dominated by Flavius Aetius. In his youth, Aetius had spent many years as a hostage at the Hunnic court, which gave him easy access to leading Huns. In spite of that, in 451, for reasons that are not entirely clear, Attila decided to invade the western Empire to plunder northern Gaul. He was met by Aetius and his Visigothic allies near Châlons sur Marne, at a place called the Catalaunian Fields. Here, one of the legendary battles of Late Antiquity took place. Its outcome, after a day of fierce fighting, was a draw. One year later, Attila tried his luck again, this time to invade Italy. He was stopped by famine and malaria, which disrupted the logistics of his operation. Attila returned to the Alföld, where 'the scourge of God' died in 453. After his death, none of his many sons succeeded in being recognised as sole ruler. In no time at all, Hunnic power collapsed.

A completely new phase in the history of the migrations was ushered in when, in 476, there was no further appointment of a separate emperor for the western part of the Empire and power was taken by Odoacer, a general of barbarian origins, who did not style himself emperor but *rex gentium* ('king of [both] peoples', i.e. Romans and barbarians). This situation again confirmed the fiction of a Roman Empire undivided, with a sole emperor in Constantinople. The holder of that highest office, Zeno (474–491), seized the opportunity to turn fiction into reality and to restore effective Roman authority in the West, beginning with Italy and Rome itself. Zeno cleverly persuaded Theoderic the Amal, the leader of rebellious Ostrogothic troops, stationed near Constantinople, to undertake a campaign of con-

quest in Italy. This campaign has too easily been taken for another 'barbarian invasion', which it was not; it was a military expedition within the Roman Empire by an army of mercenaries that had been recruited within the Empire and whose commander acted on behalf of the emperor. Theoderic's expedition became a complete success. He took Ravenna, and killed Odoacer. Then, however, instead of returning Italy as a province to his principal, Theoderic established a royal regime that lasted from 493 to 526.

Although Theoderic did his utmost to make it look as if the emperor in Constantinople had delegated this royal authority to him, his de facto independence and the growing power of his kingdom made further East Roman intervention in Italy inevitable. This resulted in the devastating Gothic wars (535–554). Among the barbarian *foederati* employed by the Byzantine authorities during this conflict were the Langobards, or Lombards. Yet the major invasion of Italy by a large Lombard army in 568 was not the result of a direct request from the emperor in Constantinople. The background to the incursion remains something of a mystery but was connected with the appearance of a new confederation of nomads in the Pontic steppes and the Alföld. These Avars most probably originated in the Far East and were a remnant of the Joujan, who in this period lost their predominant position on the Mongolian steppes to a new strong power in central Eurasia: the Göktürk or 'Blue Turks'. The Lombards, whose homelands were in present-day Hungary and Slovenia, had apparently concluded a treaty of non-aggression with the Avars, only to then begin a war against the Gepids, at that time the most powerful people in the area. It is possible that as a consequence of this treaty the Lombards departed for Italy en masse immediately after their total victory over the Gepids.

Within a few years the Lombards had subjected large parts of Italy, though not all the territories adjoined each other. In fact three centres of power were created: in the north Friuli and the Po valley (which would be called Lombardy after the

Lombards) with Pavia as the royal seat; and in the Apennines the '**dukedoms**', or vicegerencies, of Spoleto and Benevento. These two dukedoms were almost always as good as independent of the kings in Pavia, yet were never recognised as kingdoms. The rest of the peninsula remained in Byzantine hands.

The final phase of the period of migrations began shortly after the Lombard invasion in Italy and was similarly connected to the expansion of the power of the Avars and the weak defence of the European part of the Byzantine Empire. In about 570 Slavic-speaking groups under the control of the Avars from the region of the lower Danube attacked Greece and the Balkans. Originally marauding raids, these incursions continued at frequent intervals for about fifty years and gradually acquired the nature of aggressive migrations with the aim of permanent settlement. The Slavs were given every opportunity for this since the Byzantines had long neglected the Danube border while they were entangled in exhausting wars against the Persians in the East. In the circumstances the emperors could do little but accept the situation and implement a policy of accommodation. This included sending missionaries to the Slav communities in Byzantine territory. Later, Byzantine policies became far more aggressive, leading to a series of wars of submission and the deportation of large groups of Slavs to the interior of Asia Minor.

Barbarian ethnogenesis

The major barbarian groups involved in the events of the Migration Period were invariably provided with general labels such as Franks, Alamans, Goths or Huns. Most of these names were umbrella ethnic terms that were used by contemporary authors for the sake of convenience. When sources sometimes go into more detail about, for instance, the actual composition of barbarian armies, it appears that most of them must have been multi-ethnic confederations,

which constantly changed composition, because, as time went on, many must have left or died, while, vice versa, numbers were replenished with new allies. The Langobard army that invaded Italy in 568 was described as a *multitudo vulgi promiscui* ('a multitude of mixed people[s]'), among whom were mentioned, in addition to the Lombards themselves, Saxons, Gepids, Bulgars, Sarmatians, Pannonians, Suevi and Noricans. However, if such highly dynamic multi-ethnic confederations lasted long enough, they could grow into new peoples, each with their own new identity, which for a more or less significant part was grafted on to the culture of the dominant – often name-giving – group within the original confederation. This presupposes that elements of that culture were consciously perpetuated by a 'tradition-carrying kernel' over a long period of time. The classic example of this process of **ethnogenesis** ('birth of a people') is presented by the Goths. According to modern analysts, there will have been little genetic, or even linguistic, agreement between the Tervingian Goths who left their homelands in the lower Danube region in 375 and the Visigoths who established the Toulousan kingdom almost half a century later. But the Gothic name had remained, and for many specialists in Migration Period history this proves that at least the kings of Toulouse and their aristocratic followers 'for ancestral, social and military reasons [still] thought of themselves as Goths' (Harries 1994). Similar processes of ethnogenesis must also have been at work within the other types of barbarian migrations that we distinguished above.

The barbarian kingdoms in the West

Whoever compares the map of Europe in about 200 with one of about 500 cannot fail to be impressed at the successes achieved by the barbarians. Where once the Romans held sway from the Irish Sea in the north-west to the mouth of the Danube in the south-east, barbarian kingdoms

BOX 1.2 HAIRSTYLE AS AN ETHNIC MARKER? THE SUEVIAN KNOT

Classical writers often clearly attributed typical external features to certain barbarian 'peoples', as the following fragment from Chapter 38 of Tacitus's *Germania* shows:

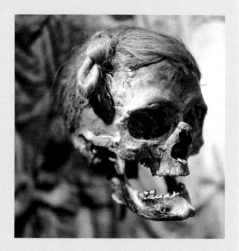

> Now it is time to speak of the Suevi, who unlike the Chatti or Tencteri do not constitute an individual tribe: they occupy the greater part of Germania, divided among nations with names of their own, although all are called Suevi in common.
>
> It is characteristic of the tribe to dress their hair on the side and bind it up tight in a knot. This distinguishes the Suevi from the other Germani, and their free-born from their slaves. Among other tribes, whether through some kinship with the Suevi or, as often happens, through imitation, this also occurs, but infrequently and only in youth, whereas among the Suevi it continues until the hair turns grey; they draw back their bristling hair and often tie it on the very top of their heads. The leading men have an even more ornate style.

Images of barbarian warriors on triumphal columns and the discovery of a skull with the hair preserved in a peat bog in Schleswig-Holstein confirm the accuracy of Tacitus' description. Yet specialists hesitate to see a Suevian in every description, image or discovery of a head with a hair-knot. Tacitus's text gives reason enough for such caution. Historical-ethnographic research reinforces this. It teaches us that clothing, tattoos and hairstyles were sometimes intended as ethnic distinctions, but they may also indicate age, social status or political persuasion or, trivially enough, may just have been in fashion at the time. All these functions then are also subject to changes in time and geographical space. So it may very well be that the hairstyle that was perhaps typical for the Suevi of the first century later spread to other barbarian groupings outside the Roman Empire or even – why not? – to the Romans themselves. There are striking examples of the 'barbarian look' being adopted in the Roman Empire. In the fifth and sixth centuries it was fashionable for young men in Constantinople to wear their hair in the Persian or Hunnish mode: the hair was shaved high at the front and allowed to hang in thin strands to below the shoulder at the back. It is doubtful whether all Persians and Huns wore their hair in this way. According to the Greek Priscus, who visited the court of Attila as a diplomat, the khan of the Huns wore his hair short, more in the style of the Romans.

Source: The passage from *Germania* is taken from the English translation, with introduction and commentary by J.B. Rives (Oxford: Clarendon Press, 1999), p. 92. For discussion on hairstyle as an ethnic marker at the time of the peoples' migrations see Walter Pohl, 'Telling the difference: signs of ethnic identity' in Walter Pohl and Helmut Reimitz (eds), *Strategies of Distinction: The Construction of Ethnic Communities, 300–800* (Leiden: Brill, 1998), pp. 17–69.

had now been established throughout western and southern Europe. Kingship thus became the dominant form of government in the Middle Ages. With respect to its continuity two tendencies can be discerned: one to hereditary succession and the formation of a dynasty, the other to election by the most important aristocrats. Neither principle was applied in its purest form; there was always a mixture. The Visigoths mostly held to the electoral system, the Franks to that of hereditary succession through one family. The view that kingdoms could be divided up was never entertained either. A reign was shared on occasion, for example between father and son, or between two brothers, but mostly that did not lead to a division of the territory. The Frankish Merovingians form an exception in this respect. Between the sixth and eighth centuries there were normally two or three Frankish kingdoms side by side, often ruled by brothers.

The Roman contribution to the 'production' of barbarian kingdoms in the Migration Period cannot be underestimated. Barbarian leaders looked up to the Roman Empire and saw Roman recognition as a clear legitimisation of their own power. Some even tried to link themselves with the imperial family through marriage. Kings like Theoderic the Amal, Sigismund of Burgundia and Clovis continually showed that in their own perception they were part of the Roman order. Although boasting of descending from an age-old Gothic royal family, the Amals, Theoderic repeatedly called his Italian kingdom *res publica Romana* ('a Roman state') and condescendingly addressed his fellow-princes as barbarians. Sigismund spoke of himself as a 'soldier of the Emperor'. After his victories over the Visigoths in 507 and 508 Clovis held triumphal feasts at which, following old Roman custom, he dressed in purple. And even a century and a half later the Visigothic king of Spain, Recceswinth (653–672), seems to have consciously modelled himself on his great idol, Emperor Justinian.

In addition to a Roman-imperial one, most barbarian kingdoms immediately acquired a Christian patina. Kings were gladly seen as shepherds to whom their people were entrusted as a flock of sheep. The most important duty of the king was to protect his subjects from the sins endangering the eternal salvation of their souls. Unlike the clergy, who shared this main task, the king could – or even had to – act firmly if necessary. Of course the king himself had to be the very model of Christian virtue, a true *princeps religiosus* (religious prince).

The most extensive of the new barbarian kingdoms was without doubt that of the Visigoths. At the end of the fifth century their power stretched from the Loire in the north and the Rhône in the east to the southernmost tip of the Iberian peninsula. Only after the Visigoths had been forced to give up the greater part of south Gaul following their crushing defeat by Clovis near Vouillé in 507 did they really manage to consolidate their control over the whole of the Iberian peninsula. Apart from the military successes of King Leovigild (569–586), this was mainly due to the conversion of his son Reccared (586–601) from Arianism to Catholicism. These two factors caused the process of political, social and cultural integration between the descendants of the barbarian invaders and the native Ibero-Roman population to gain momentum. In 711 the Gothic kingdom in Spain came to an abrupt end. A large Muslim army under the command of Tariq ibn Zeyad crossed over from Morocco ('Gibraltar' comes from *djebel al'Tariq*, 'Tariq's mountain') and crushed the Spaniards near Jerez de la Frontera. Within a few years the greater part of the peninsula was in Muslim hands.

The kingdoms of the Burgundians in the Rhône valley and Savoy, of the Vandals in North Africa and of the Ostrogoths in Italy were more short-lived. The first was conquered by the Franks in 534, as we have already seen. The second was recovered by the emperor in Constantinople after a brief campaign in 533, about a hundred years after the Vandal confederation had crossed into North Africa and taken possession of its rich grain-producing coastal lands. Various eastern Roman

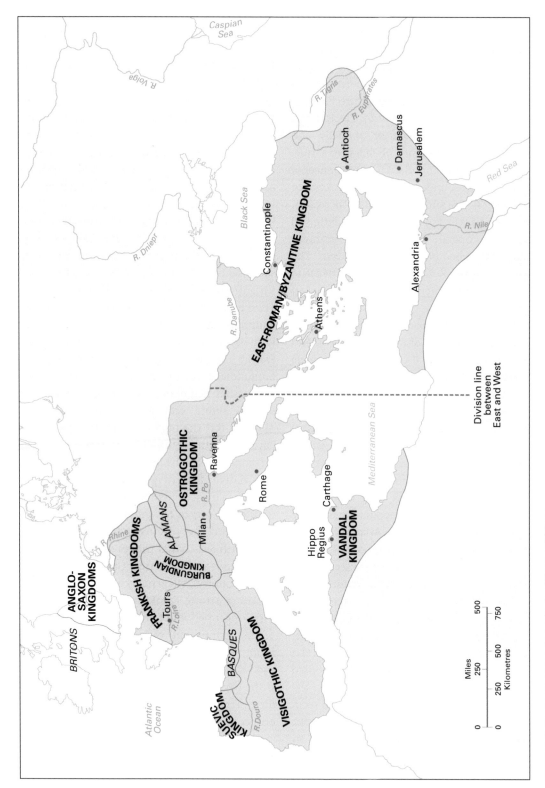

MAP 1.3 Barbarian kingdoms in the West, c.525 CE

emperors had tried to drive the Vandals out of their African province in the second half of the fifth century, but in vain, because the Vandals succeeded in becoming a formidable sea power.

Quite a lot is known about the government of the Ostrogoths over Italy thanks to the *Variae*, a collection of state papers, edited by Cassiodorus, a son of the Roman governor of Sicily and Calabria in the later years of Odoacer's rule. Cassiodorus held the important post of chancellor a number of times under Theoderic the Amal or the Great (493–526) and his immediate successors. From the *Variae* it appears that Theoderic did his utmost to operate a dictatorial government over Italy, modelled on the Roman pattern. The cooperation of the Roman aristocracy, tried and tested in classical officialdom, was essential in this. In return, Theoderic protected Italy by taking the two open land approaches to the peninsula – West Pannonia (modern Slovenia) in the east and Provence in the west. He also attempted to wrestle Spain from the Visigoths. Theoderic's kingdom collapsed soon after he died during the disastrous 'Gothic wars' with the east Roman emperor.

The Lombard invasion that followed would not have improved the situation for quite a while. Still, for centuries the Lombards had lived near the Pannonian frontier, and must have been quite familiar with Roman culture long before 568. They merged with the Italian population, because by no means all Lombards were Arians (just as by no means all Italians were orthodox). A visible proof of successful integration can be seen in the spread and persistence of Lombardic names while, conversely, Lombard as a spoken language rapidly gave way to proto-Italian. There is admiration for the legislative activities of the Lombard kings, and even if one always has to look through the idealised image and ideological charge presented by early medieval law codes, they also reflect the desire of the new rulers to enlarge the legal security of their subjects, much after Roman example. Finally, the Lombards were able to maintain an urban society in north Italy even though they did not have an urban background themselves. The

Lombard territories were governed from the urban centres of the old *civitates* by **dukes** who were assisted by officials named *gastalds*, and, on the local level, by *sculdais* (Latin: *sculteti*).

No less astonishing than the rapid fall of the kingdom of the Ostrogoths was the rapid rise of the kingdom of the Salian Franks. During the fifth century there had been various Frankish warlords between Cologne and Paris who assumed the title of 'king', but their authority did not stretch far. Among them was Childeric, whose power base was in Tournai, but who often operated far beyond and in the service of the Romans. After Childeric's death in 481, his son Clovis extended his power in the north of Gaul, but his major successes came later in life. After his defeat of the Visigoths in 507 he took possession of Aquitaine. Then followed merciless campaigns in which he eliminated a number of rival kingdoms in the Rhineland, including that of the Ripuarian Franks around Cologne. The kingdom of the Burgundians was annexed under Clovis's successors. Other neighbours were forced to accept a satellite status, such as the kingdoms of the Alamans (on the upper Rhine), the Bavarii (cf. Bavaria) and the Thuringi (cf. Thuringia). This was accompanied by the appointment of a Frankish or a native duke or governor. Sometimes the dependence was limited to the payment of annual tribute as a sort of recognition of Frankish overlordship. In other regions, such as Brittany, Frisia (the North Sea coastal fringes of the present-day Netherlands and Germany), Gascony (the French Basque country), but actually also Aquitaine, short phases of strong Frankish influence alternated with longer periods of virtual autonomy.

The picture that we have of Great Britain in about 500 is very diffuse. The groups of Angles and Saxons who had come to England as *foederati* at the beginning of the fifth century had settled there permanently and interbred with the Roman-British population. The invaders were so dominant that they were able to impose their own language. Even so, large parts of Great Britain remained outside the reach of Anglo-Saxon settlement, and this explains why the Celtic language has been preserved in Cornwall, Wales and (parts of) Scotland. In the part of England under the control of the continental barbarians many small 'kingdoms' (or chiefdoms?) were created, which were constantly at war with each other. They eventually grew into seven larger units: Essex, Sussex and Wessex – the kingdoms of the East, South and West Saxons respectively – Kent, East Anglia, Mercia and Northumbria. Of these seven, Mercia – which we must place in the present-day Midlands – was by and large the most important during the early Middle Ages. This meant that for longer periods some or all of the six other kingdoms recognised the supremacy of Mercia, at least in name. The best-known king of Mercia is Offa (757–796), whose name lives on in the new coins he had minted, in the customary laws (**dooms**) that he had collected and recorded and in the impressive earthwork (Offa's Dyke) that he apparently had built, either as a defence or simply as a marker, on the border between Mercia and Wales, for a distance of more than 110 kilometres. Offa maintained regular diplomatic contact with the court of Charlemagne, which indicates that Anglo-Saxon England was by no means isolated from the continent.

The nature of barbarian settlement

Whether they had entered the Roman Empire as peasant colonists or as war bands in search of booty or employment as mercenaries, the barbarian newcomers were small minorities – anywhere between 1 and 10 per cent of the total native populations, depending on the type of migration. Burgundian law had a fitting name for the Burgundian immigrants: *faramanni*, '[fellow] travellers'. At times the newcomers formed such a small group that they could not immediately hold effective control over the territory they claimed to have subjected. They entrenched themselves in central strongholds, whence in the early years they terrorised the native large landowners. In areas where the Roman taxation system was still functioning, barbarian newcomers, during the earliest stage of settlement, may have satisfied themselves with the appropriation of shares in the tax revenue. But the general impression is certainly that the leaders soon started to take possession of land, that is, estates belonging to the fisc (imperial lands) or to great senatorial families owning land all over the Empire, to start with. For the mass of the native peasants – slaves or other – working the land, not much would have changed.

Segregation or integration?

It has long been thought that the barbarian minorities did everything in their power to keep themselves separate from the native population in order to limit the number of people who could share in the advantages of their newly won position. Segregation could have happened in four ways: by forbidding mixed marriages, by closing the army (and the use of weapons) to natives, by introducing the principle of personal ethnic law and by consciously adhering to Arianism, a heretical movement inside Christianity. In recent times there has been serious doubt, not only about the feasibility of implementing strict segregation on an ethnic, functional and religious basis, but also about the will of barbarian kings to remain separate.

Of the methods of segregation just mentioned, personal ethnic law – the principle of treating each individual in a polity according to the (customary) law of the ethnic group in which he is born, which implies the use of separate law codes for all recognised ethnic communities within one state – is the most problematic. The impression is that although barbarian rulers were not in favour of legal segregation, they had to accept a dual legal system in the beginning because those seeking justice appealed to their own traditional legal rules: the barbarian newcomers to their customary law, the native Romans to written Roman law.

The practical solutions that were found to cope with the problem this posed to the administration of justice implied that native populations were granted personal law rights when dealing with private law cases in which both parties were 'Roman' (native), while the 'barbarian' law of the new rulers was given territorial validity in dealing with criminal cases as well as with private lawsuits in which at least one party was 'barbarian' (allochtonous). The problem gradually faded as the different population groups increasingly mixed. This mixing could only have been prevented by a rigid enforcement of a ban on mixed marriages. Such a ban did exist in Visigothic Spain in the first half of the sixth century, but it was only in that place and at that time, and the background is obscure. In Spain the opposition between Arians and Catholics remained real and acute until 589; longer than anywhere else. In other barbarian kingdoms it either did not exist at all (in Frankish Gaul since Clovis), or it did not run along the dividing line between barbarian newcomers and native populations (in Ostrogothic Italy), or it was insignificant. The Lombard rulers in Italy, for example, never made an issue of religious convictions.

All in all, the evidence for a consciously sought segregation is meagre. Only for a short time after gaining power in a particular region was segregation sometimes an option, but this was dictated by the barbarian leaders' desire to guarantee material rewards for their warriors and to put matters on a permanent basis, not by a deliberate policy of apartheid. Ethnic sentiments were only played to in specific circumstances. On the other hand, the evidence for integration is stronger and more plentiful. Archaeologically, it is difficult to distinguish between barbarian invaders and native populations soon after the arrival of the former, which points to a rapid acculturation. Also, in many places, the barbarians abandoned their own language rapidly and easily: the Visigoths and Suevi in the Iberian peninsula, the Burgundians in Savoy and Provence, the Franks in Gaul and the Lombards in Italy all gave up their Germanic languages for regional Romance lan-

guages, just as the Avars and the Bulgarians exchanged their Altaic languages for Slavic ones. Only the Germanic invaders in England, the Franks in the area between the lower Rhine and northern Gaul, the Alamans in the upper Rhine area and lower Switzerland, Slavic settlers in the Balkans and, at a later stage, the Magyars in Hungary, all immigrants, succeeded in making their language the dominant one in regions which were once for some length of time part of the Roman Empire. In the Alps interesting mixing zones emerged, where two languages continued to exist side by side. The durability of this form of integration can be seen in the fact that the linguistic boundaries of Europe today essentially date back to those outlined above.

Proto-nation formation

Outside Italy integration of foreign minorities and native majorities contributed to the creation of a new consciousness of supra-local solidarity, of the idea that natives and newcomers together formed one people. Where this consciousness was strongly politicised – which in this context means closely linked with kingship – we can talk of proto-nation formation. Visigothic Spain is an early example of this: here, in seventh-century literary and legal sources, *rex, gens et patria Gothorum* becomes the standard formula to refer to the 'king, people and homeland of the Spaniards', regardless of their ethnic origins. Some decades later the Roman name 'Hispani' replaced the word 'Gothi' for Spaniards, while henceforth 'Gothi' was mainly used to refer back to the historical barbarians who had conquered Spain in a past that was almost mythical even at that time.

In other barbarian kingdoms it was the name of the invaders that persisted as a proto-national point of reference. Such was the case in Burgundia and Francia, the kingdoms of the Burgundians and Franks, and eventually also in Anglia, the collective name for the kingdoms of the Anglo-Saxons in England. At the same time,

Burgundians, Franks and Angles became the usual names for all the inhabitants, whether their origin was barbarian/foreign or native. This re-branding of old names was even linked to the conscious presentation of the new Franks and Angles as a chosen 'people' or 'race', comparable to the Jewish people from Exodus or the Trojan wandering refugees after the fall of their city: they were seen as a large pseudo-family with a shared past, its own identity and a common destiny within the framework of either secular Roman or Christian salvation history. Of course, such ideas were strongly supported (if not entirely developed) by a kingdom's own, proto-national, church, and not just by paying lip service. In many barbarian kingdoms prayers were said and masses held for the safety and success of the king and the 'national' (royal) army in times of war.

When considering this type of proto-nation formation in the early Middle Ages we must, of course, expel any notion of modern national consciousness, which is why we use the word 'proto'. We just do not know how deep feelings ran that were aired in lofty and learned writings destined for the king and the social elite. Neither did the barbarian kings possess the military or communications facilities to fully and continuously control the vast territories over which their power extended in name. For this reason, whether they liked it or not, they always had to accept a large degree of local and regional autonomy. Under weak kings or in peripheral regions, there were plenty of opportunities to strengthen old regional traditions.

Balance: the end of Roman civilisation?

Did the fall of the Roman Empire in the West also mark the end of Roman civilisation in the West? One is easily inclined to think it did because archaeology does not lie. What could better illustrate the end of a civilisation than the astounding impoverishment of its material culture? Nothing crafted in the sixth and seventh centuries could equal the superb urban planning and construction of roads, harbours, aqueducts and drains of the Roman age; nothing compares to the magnificent public and private buildings of that time, to their refined house design, their decorations, their utensils, their tableware. Typically, none of the new 'capitals' of the barbarian kingdoms that took shape in the course of the fifth and sixth centuries (Toulouse, Paris, Toledo, Pavia) succeeded in coming anywhere near the exterior splendour and the high level of public conveniences of the old Roman capitals.

Yet, there are three asides to be made here. The first is that this impoverishment of material culture cannot have been caused by barbarian invasions alone. Barbarian settlement was not by definition a 'bad thing', as is demonstrated by the flourishing of the agrarian economy in the African province under Vandal rule. Moreover, a certain decline in public building is also observable in those regions of the eastern Empire that did not suffer at all from barbarian invasions, such as Syria and Egypt. So, apparently, there were other factors at stake. We have already pointed out two: the disappearance of classical city councils, responsible for public infrastructure and building, and the penetration of world-averse Christian ethics.

The second aside is prompted by the consideration that loss of luxury and monumentality does not say all about average human well-being on a more elementary level. It was not all roses in the Roman world, and indeed proportionally more people may have been better fed in the early Middle Ages than they had been during the later Roman Empire. And thirdly, neither did the demise of conveniences and comfort imply the death of Roman civilisation in terms of ideals and ideas. On the contrary, in a sense, Rome's appeal proved to be eternal. Throughout the Middle Ages, and long after, Roman ideas on government and law, on science and literature continued to exert a compelling force on the imagination and activities of the upper strata of society in western Europe. Every ruler who felt in any way superior to his rivals, from the barbarian kings of the early Middle Ages through Charlemagne, Frederick II, Charles V, Napoleon and Mussolini, adorned himself with the symbols of the Roman emperors. But there is more to it than that. The sheer fact that today we know so much more of Roman history than of any other ancient civilisation in the world is proof of an avid interest of generations of inquisitive men in the Middle Ages, who thought it worthwhile to copy and study, again and again, the intellectual legacy of 'the Greeks and the Romans'. Most of them were monks or clergy, that is to say, they belonged to the Christian Church. Seen from that perspective one could say that the Church took responsibility for the preservation of classical culture, and it did so largely because the Church itself was an important relic of that culture. That also explains its use of all the instruments that were indispensable for the conservation of secular public authority: the art of writing, a universal language, professionalism in administration and written law, and a stable organisation with fixed territorial divisions.

However, these three asides being made, there is no escape from the conclusion that the rift between the classical civilisation of Late Antiquity and the world of barbarian kingdoms in the West was far more fundamental than the transition from east Roman to Greek-Byzantine in the East, or even than the transition from Greek-Byzantine to Arab in those parts of the eastern Empire that were lost to the Arab-Muslim conquerors around the middle of the seventh century (see Chapter 2). Decisive in the end were the disintegration of Roman government and the downturn of the landowning elite, which, voluntarily or under constraint, had to make room for martial newcomers. Both had a destructive effect on the strong administrative links – including a regular tax flow – that had always existed between countryside and town.

Under these circumstances phenomena that occurred both in the East and in the West, such as demographic crises and a certain tendency to ruralisation, had a far bigger impact in the West than they had in the East. For example, after the eastern Mediterranean had been hit by two natural disasters in succession – the catastrophic crop failures in two consecutive years following the tremendous eruption of the Krakatoa volcano on the isle of Java in March 535 and the outbreak of a lethal plague epidemic in 542 – demographic recovery must have been remarkable. Especially in Syria and Egypt, both agriculture and villages seem to have grown and flourished as never before. It even led to a certain monumentalisation

PLATE 1.4 In the late Empire and the early Middle Ages, Roman cities lost their function and shrank to small dimensions. This implied a shift of the dwellers' cultural preferences and the magnificent ancient buildings fell into ruin. Typically, the arena in Arles became filled with medieval houses, as shown in this woodcut from the sixteenth century.

of the countryside, because many wealthy land-owners had splendid rural villas built, and in addition invested some of their wealth in new monasteries.

Conversely, population decline in the West was more lasting and more far-reaching. An extreme example is the countryside surrounding the city of Rome, which was depopulated almost as fast as the city's population size went down. The political chaos and the lengthy loss of public government at the local level led to a more radical type of economic and social ruralisation than arose in the East. No later than the fifth century large agricultural estates, *latifundia*, encompassing hundreds of hectares, formed the heart of society in the former western Empire. The old senatorial class had used its political clout to obtain fiscal privileges for itself. Senatorial estates enjoyed a status of **immunity**, where the power of the dwindling state could not reach. The great landowners, with their large numbers of dependent peasants, could defend themselves better in times of uncertainty and danger than ordinary, self-employed individuals. They assumed military styles and their central buildings became fortresses, and in this way they were able to organise an armed defence against roving gangs. Lack of safety persuaded many originally free peasant smallholders to place themselves under the protection of these powerful landlords. Sometimes this happened by way of a formal transaction known as *precaria* (literally meaning 'request'), in which the peasant relinquished his land and paid a fee in recognition to the landlord. In return he retained the right to use the land. Many others acquired the status of *colonus*, which tied them to a piece of land that the landowner allowed them to work in exchange for part of the produce and often also specified services. So we can see how, in the West, economic and social relationships that were created out of the ruins of the late Empire would become characteristic features of the early Middle Ages (see Chapter 3).

The survival of the Roman Empire in the East

In 324, Emperor Constantine had Byzantium, the unassuming capital of his only remaining rival, Licinius, razed to the ground and then measured anew and rebuilt stone by stone. The inauguration ceremony presented this rebuilding symbolically as the refounding of Rome, although now a manifestly Christian Rome. Byzantium's strategic location midway between the Rhine and the Euphrates, and on the narrow passage that connected Europe and Asia, the Mediterranean Sea to the Black Sea, made it more suitable than Rome as a centre of government. That is why Constantine moved his court to Byzantium, soon called Constantinople ('Constantine's city').

The emperors of the fourth century did everything possible to give their new capital some of the aura of Rome. Constantine himself and his son Constantius II (337–361) started an ambitious programme of construction in which monumental Christian buildings had a central place right from the beginning, but at the same time the public amenities that were so characteristic of Roman urban culture – palaces, forums, statues, baths, theatres, racecourses – were enlarged and improved. The ceremonial heart of the city lay directly on the Bosporus: it was formed by the great imperial palace, the racecourse (Hippodrome), the two main churches of the Holy Apostles and Saint Eirene, the large forum of Constantine and the most important government buildings, including the Silention basilica, the superb hall of the imperial palace in which the emperors made their solemn pronouncements. The population increase of Constantinople was contrary to the depopulation of Rome. While Rome must have had just under 500,000 inhabitants in about 400, by the middle of the sixth century there were no more than 30,000 left. Constantinople, with an estimated population of 250,000 in Theodosius's time, had by the later date grown into a metropolis of about half a million people. This number dropped later and

Constantinople was never as populous as Rome had been during the Principate, but throughout the Middle Ages it remained by far the largest city in Europe.

Justinian

After 476 the eastern Roman emperors laid claim to the recovery and restoration of the Empire, *renovatio imperii*, from Byzantium and with authority over Rome. The man who really gave shape to this was Justinian (527–565), an ambitious and zealous character from a family of upstart peasants. His policy of renewal had three cornerstones: the recovery of the regions which had been lost; the clarification and codification of Roman law; and the establishment of orthodox religious unity. In the beginning this policy proved to be very successful, but in about 550 it started to go wrong and the gulf between ideal and reality widened.

Justinian tackled the wars of reconquest shrewdly. In order to avoid a war on two fronts he first of all negotiated a long-term truce with the Sasanian rulers of Persia, the most formidable of the enemies of the eastern Roman Empire. Then an expeditionary force successfully attacked the lands of the Vandals in North Africa and Byzantine armies gained a firm foothold on the east coast of Spain. But Justinian underestimated the strength of the kingdom of the Ostrogoths in Italy. Two exhausting wars of attrition, which started in 535 and together would last for almost twenty years, plunged Italy into acute misery. To make matters worse, the greater part of the territorial gains made by the Byzantines were nullified through the Lombard invasion of 568. What, for the time being, was left of Byzantine possessions in Italy comprised a number of important coastal cities (Venice, Bari, Amalfi, Naples); the islands of Sicily, Sardinia and Corsica; parts of Apulia and Calabria; and the wider surroundings of Rome and Ravenna that were interconnected by a territorial corridor through

the Apennine mountains. Ravenna became the seat of the Byzantine governor or *exarch*, who was only driven out by the Lombards in the middle of the eighth century. Taken together, Justinian's attempts to restore Roman rule in the West by military means can only be seen as a failure. Besides, they were extremely costly, and this compelled Justinian to substantially lower the pay of the regular border troops – allegedly 225,000 men. Henceforth, these soldiers had to rely more on what the land attached to their units produced.

The second cornerstone of the imperial restoration, the clarification and codification of Roman law, was far more successful and lasted considerably longer (see Box 1.3). Even if in Late Antiquity it was no longer the 'people of Rome', represented by the Senate, but the emperor, who 'by God's grace' was considered to be the only source of justice and law, Justinian chose to anchor his project in what was called the 'honourable authority of tradition'. That is why the *Corpus Iuris Civilis* made him more than just a virtuous emperor who took seriously his royal responsibility to dispense justice. This self-same administrative act linked him directly with the deep-rooted foundations of Roman authority. Yet, whereas its predecessor, the *Codex Theodosianus* of about 440, was widely used in the barbarian West, the *Corpus Iuris Civilis* proved to be less usable in the East, because fewer and fewer people, intellectuals included, spoke or wrote Latin. Although its rulers and inhabitants persisted in referring to themselves as *Romaioi* (Romans), and Arabs and Turks similarly still spoke of *Rum*, the Byzantine Empire was rapidly becoming Hellenised. Not until the end of the ninth century did a more-or-less complete Greek translation of the *Corpus Iuris Civilis* appear.

The third aspect of Justinian's *renovatio imperii*, the establishment of religious unity, likewise appealed to a long Roman tradition, the interweaving of state affairs and (state) religion. In that tradition, the emperor also was the religious leader. Since Constantine, this had meant that it was the

BOX 1.3 ROMAN LAW

The actual work on Justinian's codification was carried out by a special commission consisting of jurists attached to the imperial court or to one of the two most renowned schools of law in the Empire, at Beirut and Constantinople. The work was completed within a surprisingly short time. In its entirety it was known as the *Corpus Iuris Civilis* ('Body of Civil Law'), but in fact it was made up of three very different parts. The *Codex Justinianus* contains all the imperial edicts from Hadrian (117–134) until the year 533. This part was intended to replace older, less complete compilations such as the *Codex Theodosianus* which dated from about 440. A separate supplement, the *Novellae Constitutiones*, known as *Novellae*, with additions from after 533, appeared later. The largest part of the *Corpus* is formed by the *Digesta* (*Pandectès* in Greek), an extensive selection of legal commentaries by 39 well-known Roman lawyers from the Roman imperial age. The last part, although more modest in size, was perhaps the most influential. It is called *Institutiones* and was intended as a manual for law students or as a reference book for practising lawyers. *Institutiones* looks most like a statute book, a systematic survey of rules of law, which actually are concerned solely with private law. The speed with which a codification of laws of such high quality was compiled is proof that the government apparatus of the eastern Empire set great store by a legal training. From the late Middle Ages onwards the *Corpus Iuris Civilis* would be a major influence on legal concepts and the administration of justice in the West.

As far as private law was concerned Roman law offered many ways of enabling individuals to secure property rights, to dispose of possessions by testament, to enter freely into contracts, and by which the rights of women and minors were protected. The *Codex Justinianus* recognised the statute of the legal person through which collectivities (*universitates* in Latin) such as guilds and local communities were able to assert their rights. Civil and criminal procedures were laid down precisely, so that individual litigants could appeal to them, even against the power of the state. On the other hand, during the compilation many centuries-old provisions were revised in light of the new relationships in the eastern Empire where the emperor and his officials exerted sovereign power over legislation, the administration of justice, government, tax law and the conduct of war. In Justinian's *Corpus Iuris Civilis* we find the principles that 'the ruler is not bound by the law' and that 'what pleases the ruler has the force of law', to which later monarchs with absolutist tendencies gladly appealed.

emperor's duty to lead the Christian Church and to defend it from internal and external enemies. In this way the expedition against the Vandals was consciously promoted as a holy war against heretics because the Vandals were Arians, and Arianism had been decreed a heresy (Chapter 2). To crown his solidarity with the Christian faith, and as an expression of his primacy in the ecclesiastical hierarchy, he had the Church of the Holy Wisdom (Hagia Sophia in Greek) in Constantinople rebuilt after a fire into the largest and most majestic church in Christendom.

Implosion and consolidation

The Byzantine attempts to hold off external threats met with varying degrees of success. The rule of Emperor Heraclius I (610–641) can be called tragic in that respect. In 615–616 Heraclius was close to a total surrender to Shah Khusro of the Persian Empire. But in the following decade, thanks to cutting costs and taxing wealth on an unprecedented scale, and after having found a new ally in the Göktürk masters of the central Asian steppes, Heraclius turned the tide and gained a spectacular victory over the Sasanians in 627. Less than ten years later, Fortune's wheel swung back again. This time the Byzantines suffered a humiliating defeat at the hands of the Arabs (636). Syria and Palestine were lost forever, and Egypt followed shortly after Heraclius's death.

Demographic crisis and loss of territory had serious consequences for the Byzantine economy and society, and for the administrative and military organisation of the Empire. During the seventh century the Byzantine economy showed clear signs of contraction. For that reason, the army and bureaucracy were drastically reduced in size: the army from a total of some 330,000 men in the days of Justinian to an estimated 80,000 in about 740, the central civil service in Constantinople from 2,500 at the beginning of the sixth century to just 600 in the eighth century. Furthermore, a number of important reforms in taxation, military organisation and imperial bureaucracy were implemented under Heraclius and his grandson and successor, Constans II (641–668). In rural areas responsibility for the payment of taxes came to rest directly on farming communities and their leaders. The new taxes were paid mostly in gold. In this way the vital monetary link between the subjects/tax payers on the one hand and (professional) soldiers and public servants on the other could remain intact.

In the same period the army was completely remodelled. Since the days of Diocletian and Constantine, the soldiers, partly conscripts, partly professionals, had been divided among field army units and stationary frontier troops. Now, in agreement with the dimensions of a much smaller empire, a new division was made in four large army corps or *themes*, all of which were stationed in Asia Minor, the largest and richest region that the Byzantine Empire still possessed. A fifth *theme*

was similar to a marine corps and was based in naval units in the Aegean Sea. At a later stage, additional *themes* were established to protect the remaining Byzantine regions in the western part of the Mediterranean. The continuing threat from the Arabs, who in 717–718 laid siege to Constantinople itself, and from domestic conspiracies against the emperor, persuaded Constantine V (741–775) to create six elite units of special forces, known as *tagmata*, which were well paid and closely linked to the emperor. They consisted of 18,000 men – on paper anyway – many of them cavalry. This meant that in times of crisis the emperor would be much better prepared. Very soon, however, a new danger loomed on the horizon: the *tagmata* commanders determined who would become emperor. The solution to this problem was the formation, in the course of the ninth century, of an imperial bodyguard of handpicked men, some of them barbarians. Before the year 1000 the *theme* armies, in their old form, had had their day. After that, in newly conquered regions, purely military districts were established with their own, continuously active troops, whose *strategoi* (commanders) were directly responsible to the emperor. These new-style *themes*, however, were considerably smaller than the old ones.

Renewed expansion

For the time being, military successes were small, such as the reconquest, shortly after 800, of the western part of the Peloponnese, which had been thoroughly 'Slavicised' during the preceding two centuries. After the repossession entire Slav communities were deported and replaced by indigenous Greeks. Further expansion even in Greece was mainly precluded by the rising power of the Bulgars, originally Turkic steppe nomads who had invaded the lower Danube region around 665 and established an autonomous khanate. This new Bulgarian state steadily expanded southwards and westwards until at its largest it encompassed not only modern Bulgaria but also all of Macedonia and major parts of present-day Serbia and Albania. The Bulgarian capital, Pliska, was built far south of the Danube on former Byzantine territory.

It was not until the end of the ninth century that the tide began to turn: although most of Sicily had fallen to the Muslims, the Byzantine position in mainland Italy and Anatolia was strengthened. The major conquests that followed in the tenth century were in part made possible by the weakening of Byzantium's traditional enemies (notably the Muslim rulers in the Middle East) and in part the result of reasonable political stability in Byzantium itself. An effective balance was found between hereditary monarchy and army intervention in matters of state, an almost unavoidable feature of a relatively centralised state which made high demands on the army. This balance meant that the highest military commanders showed restraint in 'correcting' weak emperors or filling power vacuums, notably created when an emperor died before his son had attained his majority, but at the same time they kept a finger on the pulse. This turned the court into a shadow world where behind the fairy-tale scene the air was thick with plots and the protagonists regularly disappeared into the wings.

Throughout the tenth century there were really only two emperors: Constantine VII (913–959) and his grandson Basil II (963–1025). The former reigned first under the regency of the patriarch of Constantinople, and then under that of his mother, the courtesan Zoë, 'of the coal-black eyes' (*Karbonopsina*). After that, for nearly twenty-five years, he had to put up with the career general Romanus Lekapenos as co-emperor beside him. To distinguish him from Lekapenos, Constantine was given the surname Porphyrogenitus ('he who was born to the purple', i.e. the purple curtains of the imperial childbed) meaning that he was the lawful hereditary monarch. Under Basil II the generals Phocas and Tzimisces forced their way one after the other – and after the latter had had the former liquidated – into the role of co-emperor.

These arrangements had a good and a bad side. Lekapenos, Phocas and Tzimisces were all very capable soldiers who, thanks to their position, could pursue their military ambitions. Lekapenos put heavy pressure on the Bulgarian Empire which had flourished remarkably under the powerful khan Symeon (893–927) and his successors. Phocas annexed Cilicia (the south-eastern corner of Asia Minor), Armenia and the islands of Crete and Cyprus, and through his conquest of Antioch acquired a bridgehead in northern Syria. Tzimisces chased the Russians out of Bulgaria, started to occupy Bulgarian Thrace and reduced the Arab emirates of Aleppo and Mosul in the north of Mesopotamia to Byzantine vassal states. The downside of the generals' high-handed actions was that rivalry and self-interest all too easily resulted in internal squabbles. This is what happened after the death of Tzimisces in 976. Thirteen years of civil war followed, which only came to an end when the young Basil II finally managed to take control. The alliance that Basil made with Vladimir, the Russian ruler of Kiev, was of particular importance in this struggle for power.

On the military front Basil scored many successes. He completed the conquest of Bulgaria, with a cruelty that exceeded even the norms of the time, earning him the soubriquet 'the slayer of the Bulgars'. The small Christian kingdoms to the south of the Caucasus, such as Georgia, were brought under Byzantine rule more or less by force. And, lastly, Basil strengthened the Byzantine presence in southern Italy. Only his efforts to recover Sicily from the Muslims came to nothing.

The renewed Byzantine expansion was accompanied by the strengthening of the army, and in particular of the tactical importance of the cavalry. Cavalry units were more heavily armed and were given more important offensive duties, while the infantry was trained to protect the cavalry from counter-attack by taking up a square formation on the battlefield. These army reforms went hand in hand with legislation on recruitment and costs. Basil introduced the principle of

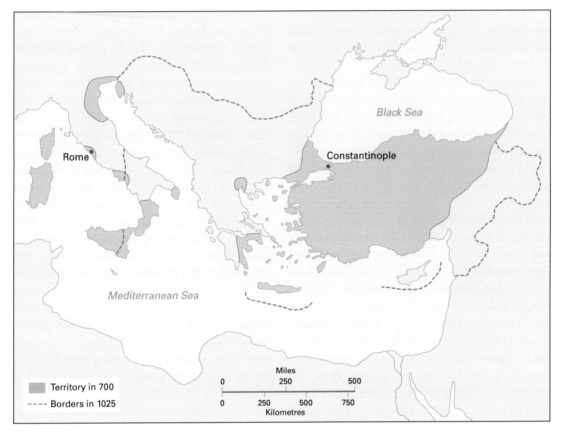

MAP 1.4 The Byzantine Empire, *c.*700 and *c.*1025

subsidiary fiscal solidarity. This meant that larger landowners were obliged to take on the fiscal responsibilities (not the land) of small farmers in the same village who were in financial difficulties. The maintenance costs of the heavily armed cavalrymen, who had to have more than one horse each at their disposal and who needed costly weapons and equipment, were apportioned over certain pieces of land. The owners of that land were then jointly responsible for the maintenance of one cavalryman.

When Basil II died in 1025 Byzantium was once again a major power. The Empire was certainly twice as large as it had been in the eighth century. Basil reigned supreme from the Straits of Messina to the east coast of the Black Sea.

Points to remember

- The fact that the Roman Empire collapsed in the West at the beginning of the fifth century was rather coincidental; ironically, the direct problems that caused the fall of the Empire in the West originated in the East.

- The 'fall' of the Roman Empire in the West has to be understood as the collapse of Roman government structure at local and provincial levels, and especially of its sophisticated tax system. The main catalysts were the lengthy 'journeys' of the Gothic and Vandal armies, and the expansion of Hunnic power over central Europe during the first two decades of the fifth century.

- The irreparable collapse of the Roman tax

system implied that state power in the new barbarian kingdoms of the West had to be built on a different foundation, which was the possession of land (see further Chapter 3).

- The groups of 'barbarians' (foreigners) that were most dramatically involved in the so-called Migration Period had in common that they were multi-ethnic war bands that preferred to operate as Roman federate allies (*foederati*), because that ensured them of pay.
- Everywhere, the barbarian invaders or immigrants were tiny minorities that in the longer run were forced to integrate into the native populations. Historians of that time sometimes presented this process of integration as the creation of a new people with a double origin, one native-Roman, the other foreign-barbarian.
- The fall of the Roman Empire in the West also meant the end of Roman civilisation, especially in terms of loss of high-quality material prosperity and comfort.
- The Roman Empire fell, yet survived: in the West as a guiding political ideal and a cultural model, in the East in reality, although with a profoundly changed appearance as to its size, ethnic composition, language, and cultural orientation. For that reason, it is better to speak of the (Greek-)Byzantine Empire after the sixth century.

Suggestions for further reading

Heather, Peter (2005), *The Fall of the Roman Empire: A New History of Rome and the Barbarians* (Oxford: OUP). Detailed but balanced narrative of the Migration Period which awards barbarian groups, defined rather by military and political leadership than by ethnicity, their proper place in Late Antique history, with surprising new attention to the role played by the Huns.

Liebeschuetz, J.H.W.G. (2001), *The Decline and Fall of the Roman City* (Oxford/New York: OUP). Masterly analysis of arguably the most important aspect of the transformation of the Roman world: the decline and transformation of the classical Roman city (*civitas*), of civic government, and of the ideals of citizenship and civic culture that were closely connected with them.

Mitchell, Stephen (2007), *A History of the Later Roman Empire, AD 284–641* (Oxford/Malden MA: Blackwell). Up-to-date overview of the history of the Roman Empire (East and West) that ranges over the first two centuries of the early medieval period. Although its focus is on political and institutional history it also has adequate chapters on Christianisation and on economic and social structures.

Pohl, Walter, and Helmut Reimitz (eds) (1998), *Strategies of Distinction: The Construction of Ethnic Communities, 300–800* (Leiden: Brill Academic Publishers). Volume with excellent articles on the ethnic factor in the 'barbarian migrations' of the Migration Period and the constitution of regnal communities after the Migration Period, with much attention given to constructivist and historical-legalist positions.

Sarris, Peter (2011), *Empires of Faith: The Fall of Rome to the Rise of Islam, 500–700* (Oxford: OUP). In spite of its title this book offers more of a comprehensive treatment of what happened in the territories of the western and eastern Roman empires respectively and their neighbours (such as the Persians) between 500 and 700 than a comparison between the post-Roman world in the West and the rise of Islam in the East.

2 The establishment of two world religions: Christianity and Islam

The Christian Church in the transition from Antiquity to the Middle Ages

Late Antiquity was a time of great religious ferment. Many people turned away from the fossilised worship of the innumerable gods of the classical Greco-Roman and eastern pantheons. They sought contact with the philosophical currents which inclined towards the belief in one divine power, such as Neoplatonism, or with mystical sects which guaranteed personal contact with a humane deity. Those religions that brought a message of individual salvation and rebirth after death were especially popular. That message was – and is – central to the Christian religion, which originated as a Jewish sect. For Christians, Jesus of Nazareth, who lived in Palestine under the rule of the Emperors Augustus and Tiberius, was not only the Messiah (literally meaning 'anointed', *christos* in Greek), the saviour of the people of Israel promised to the Jews, but even the son made flesh of the only God. His resurrection from death on the cross opened, for the faithful, the way to their own victory over death and to eternal salvation.

Yet, this sort of conviction was by no means unique at the time. What made Christianity so different was its universal appeal and its ethics. The ethics were based on a virtuous commandment to unselfish love of one's neighbour (*caritas*), especially the weaker members of society, for which nothing should be expected in return. The universal appeal of the early Christian Church is expressed in the adjective 'catholic', coming from the Greek word for 'general'. The Church was thus in principle open to everyone, whatever their sex, origin or legal status. This ideal of **'Catholicism'** probably stemmed from the fact that the earliest Christian communities were rooted in the urban middle classes; enlargement of their recruitment base meant reaching out to both the wealthy and the poor, and to all sorts of people, independent of their ethnic background.

The only other ancient religion with universal pretensions was Judaism itself. In the struggle for followers Christianity scored an important victory even before the fourth century, when it appropriated the most important collection of Jewish religious texts. These texts, *tanach* in Hebrew, deal with the relationship between Jahweh, the one true God, and the people of Israel. It was translated into Greek during the third century BCE and was then known as the *Septuagint*, but we always refer to it as the 'Old Testament'. At the same time a new, supplementary written tradition took shape, built up around the four Gospels, reports of the life and teachings of Jesus of Nazareth that were written down within a few generations of his death. Together with a selection of letters and accounts of the activities of his most important followers, the apostles, and with an enigmatic vision of the end of the world, the 'Apocalypse' or 'Revelation' of John of Patmos, the Gospels form the 'New Testament' – in other words the New Covenant of God with the new Israel, the Christian Church. The claim behind this was clear: God's chosen people were no longer the Jews but the Christians.

The Jews, on the other hand, were harassed by the Roman authorities from the beginning of the third century, although they had long enjoyed legal privileges. This took on more discriminatory forms after Christianity had been officially permitted in 311. Jews were not allowed to marry Christians, for example, nor could they keep Christian slaves. All over the Empire, many synagogues were destroyed. In the early Middle Ages further anti-Judaism was held in check by an attitude that can best be described as one of repressive, strictly limited toleration. This was based on the ideas of Paul the Apostle and leading Church Fathers such as Augustine and Pope Gregory the Great. They were convinced that through their treatment of Christ the Jews had followed the path of evil, but that they would eventually turn again to God. Until that time came, the Jews who lived among Christians could hold up a negative mirror, so to speak. Systematic persecution of the Jews was only very sporadic in the early Middle Ages; it occurred in Visigothic Spain in the first half of the seventh century. Under the Emperor Justinian, pagans, Jews and other religious minorities were under constant pressure to convert. Heraclius even made baptism obligatory after his conquest of Jerusalem. In the Carolingian Empire the Jews were placed under the direct protection (*tuitio*) of the king.

Whether the Christians would have managed to become the dominant religious group inside the Roman Empire through their own efforts, we shall never know. Constantine's mysterious conversion on the eve of the battle of the Milvian Bridge (312) – a year after Christianity had officially been tolerated – instantly altered everything, however contrived it may appear to our eyes. Politically speaking, it was very clever of Constantine to proceed with such caution. He did not want to offend Italy's powerful senatorial elite under any circumstances. So while he favoured the Church on the one hand, on the other he remained openly associated with the old state religion which focused on the worship of the invincible sun god (*Sol Invictus*). The assimilation of this god with Christ can still be seen in our Christmas, for 25 December counted as the birthday of the Unconquered Sun. In the year 321 Constantine also introduced the 'venerable day of the Sun' (Sunday) as a compulsory, weekly day of rest. Outside the Church the Emperor never showed himself as a Christian prince. For his entire life Constantine remained *katechumen*, a Christian-in-preparation. He was only baptised on his deathbed.

The religious sympathies of Constantine's successors also fluctuated; Christianity did not become the state religion until the reign of Theodosius I (379–395). The whole process was not without consequences. The number of Christians rose rapidly in the fourth century: from 5–10 per cent of the total population of the Roman Empire in around 300, to an estimated 50 per cent in about 400. The success also had a downside. The once-suspect, closed, regularly

BOX 2.1 CONSTANTINE: THE CAREFUL CONSTRUCTION OF IMAGE

It is difficult to get through to the real historical figure of Emperor Constantine. This is for two major reasons. One is the fact that of his two biographers, one, Eusebius of Caesarea, who met the emperor on several occasions in person, was as fanatic a pro-Constantinian Christian as the other, Eunapius, a contemporary – and admirer – of Emperor Julian, was an anti-Constantinian pagan. Whereas Eusebius presents Constantine as a perfect, saintly ruler, to Eunapius he was an evil-minded loser. The second reason is Constantine himself, who, in whatever light he is placed, must have been a shrewd and calculating politician, who cared very much about his 'image'. This repeatedly led to historical fact-bending. For example, Constantine demonstrably lied about his age after he had come to power and set himself up as the leader of the Christian community, in order to avoid being held in any way responsible for, or seen as approving of, the 'Great Persecution' of Christians that was launched by Emperor Diocletian in 302–303, when Constantine (who by then was already in his thirties) had stayed at Diocletian's court awaiting his appointment as *caesar*.

Constantine's modern biographer, Timothy Barnes, has uncovered a number of other deliberate distortions of historical truth, instigated by Constantine, that reveal the emperor's ruthlessness. His official rehabilitation of Emperor Maximian hides the fact that he actually had forced him to commit suicide in 310. Maximian's son, Maxentius, was denounced for his hatred of Christians and for moral depravity, while in fact he had been quite tolerant towards Christians. The famous battle of the Milvian Bridge at the gates of Rome on 28 October 312 in which Maxentius was beaten and killed was upgraded from a minor military engagement with a certain outcome to a major and decisive clash. In the same vein, Licinius, *augustus* of the East (308–324) and Constantine's last rival in his struggle for supreme rule, was depicted as a persecutor of Christians, which gave Constantine a *casus belli* to finally defeat and depose his colleague in 324. In reality, Constantine had been trying to discard Licinius long before and not primarily out of religious motives.

Furthermore, in 326, Constantine, possibly on the instigation of his second wife, Fausta, had his eldest son by his first marriage, the *caesar* Crispus, tried and promptly executed, and then erased from official history. When the falsity of her accusations came to light, Fausta may have killed herself in desperation, but it was rumoured that Constantine was behind his consort's death as well.

Constantine's conversion to Christianity remains notoriously obscure; from early on Christian authors connected this to a dream that Constantine had on the eve of the battle at the Milvian Bridge. In this dream, (the Christian) God had promised Constantine victory if he would fight under the sign of the cross. More plausibly, as the German historian Peter Weiss has argued, Constantine witnessed a solar halo when marching his legions south in the neighbourhood of a famous temple of the sun-god Apollo at Grand in the Vosges hills near Toul. Solar halos can produce all kinds of cross-shaped reflections within a circle of light. Such an experience better explains why for the rest of his life Constantine kept mixing up in his mind the figures of Christ and Late Antique representations of the 'eternal sun' – among whom was Apollo. This has had momentous repercussions until today, because, in the West, Sunday, as the 'day of the lord', is considered a day of rest and one of the most important holidays on the calendar, Christmas, is celebrated on 25 December because under Constantine it was determined that Christ had been born on the day on which in Late Antiquity the yearly rebirth of the Unconquered Sun was celebrated. Until that time, early Christian communities had celebrated the birth of Christ on Epiphany – the recognition of the child Jesus as God by the Magi (6 January).

Constantine remains an enigmatic figure. He was the only one who left the deadly snakepit of the tetrarchy alive and unscathed. By implication he was a ruthless man who, if necessary, showed no mercy, not even towards his closest family. Constantine's Christianity may be tinged with doubt; he certainly was no saint – and has never been recognised as such.

Source: Timothy Barnes, *Constantine: Dynasty, Religion and Power in the Later Roman Empire* (Malden MA/Oxford: Wiley-Blackwell, 2011) (Blackwell Ancient Lives).

persecuted sect emerged in the fourth century as an aggressive and triumphalist movement with a militant side and a growing intolerance towards other faiths. Throughout the fourth century there still was massive opposition to Christianity. The Christians tried to overcome this resistance by using every possible means of persuasion, from kindness to force. The latter could include verbal aggression, intimidation or ridiculing heathen customs, but the Christians did not shrink from using crude physical violence against heathen shrines, including the famous temples of Serapis in Alexandria and of Zeus Marnas in Gaza. Such targeted and humiliating destruction was certainly intended to persuade non-Christians that their gods were non-gods. Why otherwise would they allow the violent desecration of their holy places? It was a fairly successful ploy which was later enthusiastically copied by missionaries operating in the heathen world of the northern barbarians. The fury of the Christian aggression increased under Theodosius, and now the intolerance did not stop at material damage. Soon after 400 the first heathen martyrs fell: one of them was the Alexandrian philosopher Hypatia, who was stoned to death by Christians for her Neoplatonist ideas – even though the Christian religion was itself permeated with them. All this inevitably ended in active persecution by state authorities, which reached its miserable nadir in the East

in the second half of the sixth century under Emperor Justinian and his successors.

Various reasons have been advanced to explain this remarkable change of mood. The ever broader support from secular authorities which soon turned into openly favouring Christians while non-Christians were excluded from government office generated a triumphalist attitude among members of the Christian elite. They started to call themselves *militantes pro Deo* ('those who want to fight for God'). More harmless but even so quite radical was the qualification *filii ecclesiae* ('sons of the Church') attached to motivated Christians in general who were convinced that God required more from them than just quiet prayer. In their view, the Church was still under threat, and not surprisingly an important ingredient of the new mood was an obsession with pollution and purity; as we shall see, it completely permeated the rapid expansion of the Church in Roman Africa.

The success of Christianity was further strengthened by three more institutional factors which determined the direction in which the Christian Church would develop in the following centuries: first, the leading role that the emperor and the bishop of Rome (the pope) each demanded for himself; second, the rapidly growing wealth of the Church; and finally, its tight organisation in **bishoprics**, grafted on to the basic units of civil government of Late Antiquity, the *civitates*.

The relationship between emperor and pope

According to both Judeo-Christian and Islamic tradition all legitimate authority derives directly from God, and so the highest office-holder is answerable to God alone. This belief is called theocratic. In the Latin-Christian Middle Ages the theocratic idea of authority was behind three different perceptions about the relationship between worldly power and spiritual authority. In the **caesaropapist** perception, which fitted perfectly with the ancient Roman view of emperorship, the highest secular ruler was *ex officio* the head of the Church. In contrast the **hierocratic** view attributed a universal primacy to the highest spiritual authority on earth, in this case the pope. A compromise was formed by dualism, which considered secular power and spiritual authority as two separate, autonomous spheres.

Constantine and Theodosius, and their successors as emperors of the Roman or Byzantine Empire, always considered themselves the undisputed leaders of the Christian Church. They did not think of themselves as just ordinary, secular people, but as sacred beings, earthly extensions of the divine king in heaven. Their task was thus not only to lead the Church and defend it from external enemies, but also to guard the contents of religious doctrine. As early as 314 – two years after his conversion – Constantine had called a council in Arles to pass judgement on the North African Donatists. The beliefs of the barbarian kings in the West in fact did not differ fundamentally from those of the emperor in Constantinople. They too looked upon themselves as *rex et sacerdos* ('king and priest'), as leaders of the Christian community, who were intermediaries between clergy and people (*mediator cleri et plebes*), and whose authority originated directly from God.

Although the caesaropapist position was also brought up openly for discussion by other bishops, including Ambrose of Milan (374–397), it was the popes as bishops of Rome who quickly took the lead in the matter. At the end of the fifth century Gelasius I (492–496) formulated an apparent compromise, known as the 'doctrine of the two swords'. It connects the underlying idea of a clear division of powers, each of which would operate autonomously in its own sphere – dualism – with the conviction that, in the final analysis, spiritual authority was superior to secular power, because 'at the Last Judgment it [would be] the task of the priests to render account for the behaviour of kings'. This addition would give radical popes in the eleventh and twelfth centuries a basis for a hierocratic reinterpretation of the doctrine of the two swords.

In the West the struggle for the highest power in the world had an entirely different, more tangible character from that in the East. There, the conflict came to a head in an unequal struggle between the emperor and the patriarch of Constantinople; in the West in a titanic battle between the (German) emperor and the pope. When the emperor of Constantinople lost effective control over Rome and central Italy at the beginning of the eighth century it also signified the end of his authority over the pope. Three matters further deepened the rift between emperor and pope at the time: first, the Byzantine encroachment on the Roman Church's considerable possessions in southern Italy and Sicily; second, the preference of a number of stubborn emperors for iconoclasm, an obnoxious heresy (see below) in the eyes of the popes; and third, the threat to the interests of the Church of Rome in central Italy from the Lombards, against which the emperor could not offer sufficient protection.

For all these reasons the popes went in search of a new ally and protector, and this they found in about 750 in the Franks. First, Pope Zacharias (741–752) recognised the Carolingian mayor of the palace, Pippin the Short, as the lawful successor to the Merovingian kingdoms. A few years later Pippin intervened in Italy in favour of the pope (see Chapter 3). The most significant, direct result of this was the formal recognition by the Franks of what the popes for some decades had

MAP 2.1 The beginnings of the Papal State, 700–800

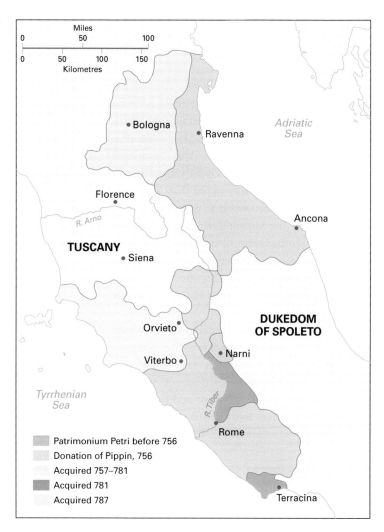

called *res publica Sancti Petri* (lit. 'the state of St Peter') and which, for the sake of convenience, we shall call the Papal State. This had for a long time been only vaguely defined, and was actually a conglomerate of lordship rights around the two territorial cores on which the Byzantine Exarchate of Ravenna was originally based – the regions round Rome (Latium) and Ravenna (Romagna and the Anconan Marches), which were linked to each other by a narrow corridor through the Apennines. With the coronation of Charlemagne in 800, the popes ended their practice of dating all their documents sent to western bishops and rulers by the regnal year of the emperor in Constantinople, which had been the last symbolic recognition by the popes of their former lord and master.

The alliance between the pope and the Carolingians most certainly contributed to the growing alienation between the Church in the East and in the West, although questions of dogma were always the root cause of real schisms. However, after every schism the dialogue was renewed. Attempts to reunite the Churches of the East and West very nearly succeeded in 1450, but the Fall of Constantinople three years later put an end to all illusions.

Material wealth, accumulation and distribution

A second factor in the success of the Christian Church was doubtless its enormous wealth, which accumulated rapidly in the centuries following Constantine's conversion. In the Byzantine Empire as early as the sixth century the Church in its entirety was probably richer than the state. The rapid increase in wealth at that time was in part thanks to the appropriation of the riches from pagan shrines, and in part thanks to rich gifts from emperors and prosperous individuals who believed that the uncertain fate of their soul after death would be helped by their good works in their lifetime.

Recently, the ancient historian Peter Brown (2012) has stressed the novelty of this arrangement, which linked together the sometimes incredibly huge private fortunes of wealthy benefactors, the care of the poor and the fate of the soul. When alive, Jesus had warned the rich that 'it [would be] easier for a camel to go through the eye of a needle than for a rich man to enter the kingdom of heaven' (Matthew 19:24). Now, wealthy people started to see ostentatiously giving away all that they owned, and turning abstemious, as an escape route from eternal damnation. The major object of this explosion of charity was not so much the poor in general as the 'holy poor', that is to say, the monks, whose austere and ascetic lifestyle seemed to come closest to the life that Jesus and his apostles had led. In the end, every gift to the Church was technically seen as a gift to the poor and therefore a gift to Christ.

With its wealth the Christian Church held a key position in the social redistribution of income through different forms of social charity (care of the poor, the sick, widows and orphans). Its wealth thus gave the Church not only political power but, more especially, moral authority in broad (under)layers of the populations of the

great cities of Late Antiquity. The *diaconiae* ('deaconries') are a good example; these were established by the popes in Rome and other large cities, such as Ravenna and Naples, when the authority of Byzantium was failing. They were a sort of welfare centre, staffed by monks, where the needy could get bread and a bath.

When we talk about the wealth of the Church we must remember that the Catholic Church as an umbrella association of believers did not have a central treasury. Its wealth was in the hands of the separate institutions that constituted the Church – bishoprics, parish churches, monasteries and so forth. The further growth of this multiple institutional capital came from two directions. The most important of these was the ceaseless flow of gifts from members of the aristocracy. They very soon took to building a church or monastery on their own land out of their own pocket, preferably provided with rich altar plate and real relics. They arranged the appointment of a priest or abbot or abbess themselves. And of course they were keen to be buried there, so that after death they would be close to the saint to whom their church was dedicated and whose holy relics were supposed to radiate favourably. If they had founded a monastery, the monks living there were expected to commemorate them in their prayers which were thought to be answered by God willingly thanks to the purity of their lifestyle. This phenomenon of private foundation, which was very widespread in the early Middle Ages, is known as the proprietary church system. Pope Gelasius I (492–496) had already spoken out against its proliferation in Italy, but this proved to be of no avail. Because people of aristocratic origin filled all the important positions in the Church, German historians refer to the early medieval Church as *Adelskirche*, meaning 'a Church of and mostly for the aristocracy' (Fletcher 1997).

The motives behind the foundation of proprietary churches or monasteries were many and varied. First and foremost, this generous action assured the founders of the salvation of their soul.

The possession of a church or a monastery also gave them prestige, and not infrequently it generated income for them. Moreover, the proprietary church system enabled aristocratic families to keep family property undivided and out of the eager hands of kings by attaching it to a religious foundation they owned.

The wealth of the Church was also fed from below, or rather by the free peasants. This took place through the levying of **tithes**, a sort of tax on agricultural produce, based on the Old Testament commandment to make a yearly gift of one-tenth of all the yields of the land to God. Exhortations to pay the tithe appear in council resolutions as early as the sixth century, but the tithe only became compulsory in (Christian) Europe in the course of the ninth and tenth centuries. At the same time it was given a more specific allocation. Normally one-quarter was for the bishop and the remaining three-quarters went to the maintenance of the (parish) clergy, the local poor and church building. Now and then this development encountered fierce opposition, not only from the peasants, but also from influential clerics such as Alcuin of York, Charlemagne's adviser, who in about 800 openly opined that 'it was better to neglect the tithe than to lose the faith'. Alcuin's fears were not ungrounded. The introduction of the tithe undermined the already precarious rural life of the early Middle Ages considerably, especially as most of the tithes did not end up in the hands of the groups for which they were intended. Usually the noble owners of churches and monasteries appropriated the largest share of the tithes connected to them.

Church organisation

The clergy and its tasks

By Late Antiquity, the Christian Church was already excellently organised, and this would remain so despite public administration shrinking so severely during the early Middle Ages that it was barely able to function beyond the local area.

This good organisation had its origins in the fact that the Christian Church had a professional, hierarchically organised clergy, *clerus* (literally 'the elected ones'), early on. Its primary task was to lead the 'flock' of believers along the dangerous narrow path to eternal salvation. In the early Middle Ages the clergy had no fewer than eight levels of holy orders: four lower ones, of which that of exorcist (expeller of evil spirits) was surely the oddest, and four higher ones: subdeacon, deacon, priest and bishop. Originally, in the higher orders only the bishops had doctrinal authority, which means the competence to explain the teachings of the Church. Initially only bishops and priests were allowed to administer the **sacraments**; the deacons and subdeacons could only assist them.

A person who wanted to enter the clergy first had to shave the crown of his head (tonsure). Then he had a sort of candidate status, during which period he fell directly under the authority of the bishop. Like the ordained clergy, the candidate enjoyed all the privileges belonging to the clerical state. The most important of these were the *privilegium fori* and the *privilegium immunitatis*. The first meant that clerics did not have to obey a summons to a secular court of law and only had to answer for their (criminal) deeds to a Church court. The second brought with it **exemption** from every fiscal or military obligation in the public domain. Although both privileges dated from the fourth century they were only described with legal precision in the twelfth century, when **canon law** was finally systematised.

A fundamental task of the higher clergy was, as we have said, the administration of the sacraments. By sacraments we mean the visible signs (*signa*), established by Christ himself, of the personal bond between God and the faithful. Since the twelfth century it has been generally accepted that this sacramental bond signifies the bestowal of God's grace. The number of sacraments was then also fixed at seven. The most important ones are the **Eucharist**, baptism and confession.

The Eucharist, meaning 'thanksgiving' and often also called the 'holy mass', is the collective commemoration by a Church community of the Last Supper that Christ shared with his apostles shortly before his redeeming crucifixion. In time, the mass was sometimes given a utilitarian character when it was offered to ask for a special favour – a good harvest or a fruitful marriage, for example. Baptism was the 'sacrament of initiation' that was consciously presented as a rebirth, where the baptismal waters washed away the new Christian's original sin with which mankind had been burdened since Adam, the first man, had fallen from grace. Because every sin committed after baptism could only be atoned for by very strict penance, many aspiring Christians waited to be baptised until they were on their deathbed. In the early Middle Ages the reasoning was reversed and it became customary for babies to be baptised shortly after birth so that the powers of evil could not take hold over them. At first the confession of faith was made by the parents, but for practical reasons it was soon done by sponsors or godparents, usually close relatives or social relations – godparenthood became the ideal means to reinforce social bonds within small-scale communities. Sponsors are first mentioned in the sermons of Caesarius of Arles in the first half of the sixth century.

These changes in the sacrament of baptism prompted changes in the way in which the sacrament of penance – better known as the confession – was administered. Every grave sin committed after baptism required expiation through Christ. This was the purpose of confession. It began with the confession of guilt by the sinner, and was followed by forgiveness (absolution) and the imposition of a penalty (penance) by the administrator of the sacrament. In the beginning confession and penance took place in public, and the penalties imposed were extremely heavy. Under the influence of monastic practice public confession was gradually replaced by private,

aural confession. Here the repentant, obedient 'son' whispered his sin in the ear of his 'father' confessor; the penance imposed remained secret. Sometime after the eleventh century it also became the task of the father confessor to help the sinner disclose his sins by asking direct questions. This gave the confession the character of a systematic soul-searching, which had to bring the sinner not only to an admission of what he had done wrong but, more importantly, to an understanding of his sins, and thus to repentance.

Higher-ranking ordained clerics had to be well informed about the complicated rituals and formulas surrounding the sacraments as well as about the Church ceremonies in which they took place. These can be summarised under the term 'liturgy', from the Greek *leitourgia*, meaning 'service'. Priests and bishops also had to be able to explain Bible texts in a discourse or sermon during the service, which meant that higher-ranking clerics had to be better educated than the lower-ranking, although our expectations of their education should not be too high. This is obvious from the complaints made about the aptitude of the clergy at ecclesiastical councils and in programmes for reform. St Boniface, the famous missionary and archbishop of Mainz (674–754), once grumbled about priests in Bavaria who uttered the baptismal formula thus: *baptizo te in nomine patria et filia* ('I baptise you in name: the fatherland and the daughter') instead of the correct *in nomine patris et filii [et spiritus sancti]* ('in the name of the Father, the Son [and the Holy Ghost]').

The overall impression we receive of the early medieval clergy is quite ambiguous, however. On the one hand, it was a long time before the high moral demands made of the clergy were taken seriously. In Late Antiquity discussion about moral standards centred on the celibacy of the higher-ranking clerics, who, after all, performed sacred acts, and in the view of Late Antiquity had therefore to be pure, undefiled by sexuality. Some, like Augustine, wanted to go further and pleaded for the celibacy of the clergy in general. In practice that proved not to be feasible. Even in the deeply

Christian eastern Roman Empire of Justinian, only bishops had to live in celibacy; married men could be ordained as priests, but unmarried priests, once ordained, could not then marry. In the West all the rules were far slacker. It was not until the great movement for reform in the eleventh century that the guidelines were sharpened (see Chapter 6). Clerical celibacy did then, finally, become the rule in the West, although not in the East.

On the other hand, the shining example of Augustine, who led a communal life with the priests and deacons attached to his cathedral church at Hippo Regius, was followed on a wide scale. The extension of liturgical tasks, with choral prayer in particular, and the gradual Christianisation of the countryside required increasing numbers of clerics in higher orders. Many of them lived together in communities or *monasteria* that were set up around cathedrals and other important places of worship, ranging from churches provided with baptisteries and churches where important relics were kept to churches with *hospitia*, shelters for travellers, pilgrims, invalids and otherwise destitute people, attached to them. They were then known as 'canonical clerics', or simply '**canons**', because they were deemed to abide strictly by the Church's rules of conduct (*canones*). Yet, their way of life differed from that of monks in several essential points; canons did not take monastic vows and they were allowed to have personal possessions. Evidently this created difficulties in differentiating between canons and monks, and in distinguishing canonical monasteries from monasteries of monks. This, and the prejudice that many canons lived too unruly lives, gave rise to a reform movement in the Carolingian period which set both objections right (see below).

Church hierarchy: episcopate and diocese

The bishops were undoubtedly the pivot on which the organisation of the Church revolved. Their jurisdiction was called a 'diocese' or bishopric. In Late Antiquity the borders of a diocese usually coincided with those of the *civitas*, the basic unit of Roman civil administration, which was basically an urban core with a surrounding (rural) district. Accordingly, the density of bishoprics in the Mediterranean region was far greater than in western Europe, where *civitates* dating from Roman times were smaller and had often disappeared. Overall, there may have been around 2,000 bishoprics in the late Empire. The popes showed restraint in increasing that number, because the Council of Sardica had decided in 343 that only cities of some importance could be an episcopal see, 'lest the name of a bishop and his authority be taken too lightly' (*ne vilescat nomen episcopi et auctoritas*). In the fourth century, most bishops were recruited from the municipal elites of the Roman Empire, which implied a high social status, wealth, a thorough education and administrative experience. Members of the senatorial class – the highest level of Late Antique society – were more reluctant to take up the office of bishop, with the exception of those in Gaul. Sidonius Apollinaris (*c*.430–489), bishop of Clermont-Ferrand, and Alcimus Avitus (*c*.470–518), bishop of Vienne, are cases in point. Both were scions of the highest-ranking families of Gaul, and both were related to the briefly reigning Emperor Avitus (455–456), but whereas Sidonius was elected bishop after a career as an official, Avitus succeeded his father who had also been bishop of Vienne.

With their great authority the bishops fulfilled a key function in the transition from Antiquity to the Middle Ages in two respects. They represented the Christian Church and its values at the local and regional level and they made an important contribution to secular public administration. The Emperor Constantine allowed bishops to preside over civil lawsuits, and he acknowledged by law their notarial authority as trustworthy persons who were entitled to witness the liberation of slaves, to organise care for orphans and to take part in the distribution of imperial subsidies to the poor. By using Latin, an archaic language not spoken in the streets but used only by the clergy, in standardised procedures of writing, enriched by the legal traditions of the ancient world, bishops and their servants were the true heirs of Roman professional bureaucracy. As dignitaries of the Church they had five important tasks:

1   They guarded **orthodoxy** and correct religious practice. To that end, they actively exercised doctrinal authority by preaching, taking part in synods and sometimes by writing scholarly Bible interpretations or treatises on Christian doctrine or morality.

2   Bishops ensured that Church rules and orders were applied correctly and, when necessary, issued new regulations.

3   Bishops ordained clerics and had immediate supervision over the clergy and monasteries in their dioceses.

4   Bishops administered justice: *ratione personae* ('because of the [status of the] person') over members of the clergy, and *ratione materiae* ('because of the [nature of the] matter') over Church affairs, beliefs and Christian morality (including everything related to marriage and sexuality). From Late Antiquity officials with the title of 'archdeacon' ('arch' comes from the Greek prefix *archi-*, meaning 'first' or 'most important') took the place of the bishops in their judicial function.

5   Bishops administered the property attached to the bishopric, but were also expected to be generous in the distribution of charity.

Metropolitans and archbishops, patriarchs and pope

The idea that bishops of large cities had a higher status than others was already prevalent in the fourth century. They were called metropolitans. During the seventh and eighth centuries the metropolitan gradually lost status to the archbishop. Originally this was an honorary title given by popes to bishops with a special, important

assignment not without its dangers – that of spreading the Christian faith among the heathen. The first to receive this title was Augustine, a monk sent from Rome to England in 597 to convert the Anglo-Saxons. He became archbishop of Canterbury. More than a century later the first Anglo-Saxon missionaries on the continent likewise received the archepiscopal dignity. Under Charlemagne archbishoprics increasingly began to resemble Church provinces comprising various dioceses.

Another hierarchic layer had been formed above the metropolitans, that of the patriarchs or 'arch-fathers', the honorary title which was used during the Council of Nicaea (325) for the bishops of the four most important cities of the Christian Roman Empire – Rome, Constantinople, Alexandria and Antioch; in 451 Jerusalem was added to these. In time, the inevitable struggle for the top ranking broke out between the patriarchs of Rome and Constantinople. The patriarch of Rome – the pope – won the struggle with flying colours. Apart from Rome's enormous prestige the victory was mainly due to the special place that the Eternal City occupied in Christian sacred history. Had not Peter, the principal apostle, to whom Christ himself – according to the Gospel of St Matthew (16:18–19) – had said 'Thou art Peter, and upon this rock [*petros* in Greek means 'stone' or 'rock'] I will build my church', died a martyr's death in Rome? And was it not written in the same text that Christ had given Peter 'the keys of the kingdom of heaven', and that whatever Peter arranged on earth should so prevail in heaven? By now consistently presenting Peter as the first bishop of Rome and themselves as his successors, powerful popes such as Damasus I (366–384) and Leo the Great (440–461) were able to establish the primacy of Rome over the Christian Church.

From early on the popes gave credence to their claims by stimulating the worship of Peter's grave in Rome. For a long time there was uncertainty about its exact position, but it was finally located on the Vatican, a low hill on the far side of the Tiber. Not long after Emperor Constantine's death

St Peter's cult was moved to a modest burial chapel on that spot. It was soon extended into a large basilica, the predecessor of the great St Peter's that we still admire today. Curiously enough, the Vatican did not become the pope's residence. Instead, Constantine had a new palace and church built on imperial ground to the east of Rome, far away from the Vatican: the Lateran.

In the Byzantine Empire, the emperors maintained their superior, caesaropapist position vis-à-vis the patriarch of Constantinople, just as it had always been since Late Antiquity. Nepotism, in the literal sense, frequently led to the appointment of the Emperor's cousin as patriarch, and the heads of new dynasties Basil I (867–886) and Romanos I (920–944) even appointed their sons. In the tenth century, the emperor granted the new diocese of Bulgaria the right to elect its own primate without the interference of the patriarch of Constantinople. This *autoképhalia* ('[the right to] appoint its own head') initiated the tradition in the eastern Church of national patriarchates, which marks a clear difference from the Roman Church in the West.

Parishes

In the early Middle Ages the organisation of the Church was not yet crystallised below the level of the bishoprics. In those few cities of any size with a busy church life, such as Rome, districts with their own church and their own priests came into existence quite early on. Normally we call these constituent parts of bishoprics 'parishes'. The formation of parishes in the country was a very gradual development, more or less simultaneous with the further expansion of the Christian faith over rural areas (*paganus*, literally meaning 'country-dweller', was for a long time synonymous with 'heathen'). In Gaul, for example, the first country parishes, served by their own permanent, resident priests, came into being in the course of the fifth century; by 600 their number

totalled 200. It was not until the ninth century that Gaul, by then often referred to as 'Francia', had a cohesive network of country parishes.

Church councils

The Catholic Church was probably the first organisation in the West to have a real conference culture, and this, too, contributed to its internal unity. In the early Christian period the bishops regularly met to discuss matters of faith and organisation. The tradition became firmly rooted under Constantine and his successors. The emperors, who continued to see themselves as the supreme heads of Christianity, convened meetings of bishops on several occasions; these were known as '**synods**' or '**councils**'. They were often regional meetings, but sometimes bishops from all over the Empire were invited; this was then called an 'ecumenical council', from the Greek *oikoumenè*, meaning 'the whole (civilised) world'. These ecumenical councils took important decisions on both doctrine and ethics, which had a major influence on the further development of the Church. The creed or final statement of the Council of Nicaea of 325 added to its definition of the holy trinity the well-known formulation that the Church was one, holy, catholic and apostolic (*una, sancta, catholica et apostolica*).

Nicaea was a town in Asia Minor where initially many such ecumenical councils took place. From the sixth century they were more often held in Constantinople, generally in the imperial palace. The first general Church council to be held in the Lateran in Rome was that of 649. This was also the first council convened by the pope and not by the emperor. The second council at Nicaea in 787 was the last attended by bishops from both the East and the West.

The custom of regularly calling regional synods was continued in the new barbarian kingdoms in the West. It was the kings who organised the meetings and who were committed to executing the decisions reached. Normally, practical matters concerning Church discipline and organisation came up for discussion, far more often than questions of dogma. In the Carolingian Empire in particular synods were used to enforce reforms of the clergy and the monasteries. Between the Concilium Germanicum of 742, conducted by that 'indefatigable quibbler' Boniface, archbishop of Mainz, and the great reforms of 816–817 under the rule of Emperor Louis the Pious, it seemed as if a permanent reformation was taking place in the Frankish Church. The two most important targets were the monasteries of monks, which time and again were told that they must adopt the Benedictine Rule, and the canonical clergy, who were also exhorted to follow well-defined rules, preferably in the context of a formal association or '**chapter**'. Laypeople did not escape the reforming zeal either. On several occasions new rules relating to marriage and divorce were formulated. What is particularly striking in all this is that the Carolingian rulers also promulgated measures for Church reform through capitularies, ordinary edicts issued by the secular administration.

Orthodoxy and heterodoxy

Doctrinal discussions about the nature of God

One of the most important tasks of the councils was to decide what exactly Christian doctrine should contain. There was no discussion about the sacred texts on which it had to be based. First of all there was the Bible: but how should what was written in the Bible be understood? A contemporary of Jesus himself, a Jewish philosopher by the name of Philo who lived in Alexandria, had indicated that the Bible should be interpreted on three different levels: historical, moral and allegorical. This view was later accepted by the early Christians, but of course it did not make Bible exegesis any easier, if only because for them there were two sets of texts, the Old and the New Testament. Church leaders, who enjoyed

an exceptional reputation for explaining the Bible and the will of God expressed in it, were quickly seen as authorities, as a source of religious doctrine. They were honoured with the title Fathers of the Church, and the Greek and the Roman Church each had its own roll. In the Roman Church this had four names. The saintly bishops of Milan and Hippo Regius (Ambrose and Augustine), and Jerome, were more or less contemporaries, living in about 400. Two centuries separated them from the fourth, the only pope in the illustrious company, Gregory the Great (590–604). Jerome, an Istrian who settled in Palestine, produced a new Latin translation of the Old and New Testaments with the help of Greek and Hebrew text material. This translation is known in the various surviving early medieval editions as the 'Vulgate'. It was to remain the standard Bible text until the end of the Middle Ages.

Besides the Bible and the works of the Church Fathers the reports (*acta*) and decisions (*canones*) of the ecumenical councils were given the status of authoritative texts early on. Finally, there is the interesting question of the extent to which pronouncements of the pope in Rome had doctrinal authority (in other words, were by definition **orthodox**). This was not yet the case in the early Middle Ages, as is evident from the infamous condemnation of Honorius I at the sixth ecumenical council, held at Constantinople in 680. In the course of time the pope's competence to create binding rules was generally accepted, although the pope only 'gave law' in reaction to explicit questions put to him. To issue general, anticipatory rulings in the modern sense of the word has remained the prerogative of ecumenical councils.

Of the four Latin Church Fathers it was Aurelius Augustinus (354–430) – St Augustine – bishop of Hippo Regius (present-day Annaba in Algeria), who undoubtedly had the most far-reaching influence on the intellectual culture of the Middle Ages. After the Bible his work – almost 240 tracts and countless letters and sermons – was the most widely read, cited and commented-on text material in the Middle Ages. His most famous works are *Confessiones* ('Confessions') and *De civitate Dei* ('On the City of God'). The former is not so much an autobiography as a uniquely frank account of Augustine's long search for the one true God. One half of *De civitate Dei* is a lengthy theological proof of the superiority of Christianity over both Neoplatonism and the old Roman state religion; the other half tells the story of Christianity as a spiritual community. As a leitmotiv Augustine uses the image of two cities over which mankind is divided: the earthly city (*civitas terrena*) represents the leaning towards the ungodly world, selfishness, materialism and disdain for God; on the other hand, the city of God (*civitas Dei*) stands for what is good, selfless and spiritual, in short for the true love of the true God. The first city cannot simply be identified with the secular state or with the heathen world, or the second with the people of Israel and later the Christian Church. When the Church was faced with a great influx of believers after Constantine's conversion, it became by definition a 'mixed body' (*corpus permixtum*). For Augustine, the 'city of God' is therefore a city in the making, whose true, legitimate citizens will only emerge triumphant after the Last Judgement.

The most influential Father of the eastern Church was John Chrysostom (c.349–407), who was born in Antioch. As a young man, he became a hermit. For two years, he never lay down and scarcely slept, his sole purpose being to memorise the whole Bible. His ascetic lifestyle did not however lead to a life in seclusion. Chrysostom means 'the golden mouthed' in Greek, which refers to John's great qualities as a rhetorician. Many of his homilies or sermons were written down by assistants and disseminated. In them he attempts to explain the Bible to a lay public, and also as a practical guide to leading a Christian life. But as a priest in Antioch, a hotspot of worldly temptation, John also fulminated against the tendency of Christians to participate in pagan amusements such as horse races and theatre, or

in Jewish festivals and observances. In 398 he was elevated to the position of archbishop of Constantinople. In that capacity, he harmonised the Eucharistic liturgy, which was to become the standard in the eastern Christian Churches up to the present day. He also set out to reform the clergy. However, his own firm attitude and sober lifestyle were unwelcome at the imperial court and among the high clergy, who could not cope with a hermit who loudly aired admonitions such as 'Of all wild animals, none can be found as harmful as women'. In 403, the archbishop was exiled, despite popular protest and the occurrence of an earthquake, which was immediately seen as the sign of God's displeasure.

The relative openness with which the early medieval Church discussed the content of its doctrine also had its dangers. It exposed all the deep internal differences of opinion which threatened the unity of the Church. The Greek word for heresy, *heresia*, literally means 'choice'; indeed, in any religion, attempts to formulate dogmas – doctrines which, once accepted, are inviolable – demand that choices be made, and, as a result, the denunciation as heresy of the rejected options. According to Augustine *heretici* (heretics) could therefore never be heathens. Heretics were Christians who resisted the correct dogma. Late Antiquity was teeming with heretics. At the beginning of the fifth century Epiphanius, bishop of Cyprus, drew up a list of eighty heresies which he expressly repudiated. His colleague Philastrius, bishop of Brescia, came to almost twice that number in about the same period! No wonder that quarrels abounded, certainly in the eastern Church with its long tradition of rational philosophy, borrowed from the Greeks, which attempted to define absolutely everything, including the indefinable.

The pre-eminent example of the indefinable, the subject of passionate discussion in the East, was the nature of God. From the outset Christianity was presented as a monotheistic religion; there was just one God, who in the New Testament is manifest in three forms: Father, Son

(Jesus Christ) and Holy Ghost. What exactly was the relationship between the three? Christ was especially difficult to fathom, because according to the Bible he was the word of the Father made 'flesh' – so a human being. Some thought that Christ had just one nature: the **Monophysites** (*mono-physis* means 'one nature') believed this nature to be divine, the Nestorians, on the other hand, believed that it was human. Later, concessions were made to the Monophysites by suggesting that Christ had both natures but just one will. Even subtler was Arianism, a doctrine named after Arius, an Alexandrian priest who lived at the beginning of the fourth century. He recognised the divine nature of Christ, but did not consider him equal to God the Father because the Father had procreated the Son and must, therefore, have more substance. At the Council of Chalcedon (451), none of these views was accepted as orthodox. Orthodoxy was – and is – the dogma of the 'holy trinity', the 'three-in-one': God is three godlike persons, who are essentially equal, but of whom just one – Christ – has two natures, one human and one divine.

In the end, several of the heterodoxies just mentioned would survive for many centuries as the standard beliefs of Christian minorities spread over Asia and Africa, such as the Monophysite communities in Armenia, Syria and Egypt (where the Coptic Church originated), and the Nestorians in Iran and central Asia.

The heterodoxies of Donatus and Pelagius

What we probably find more attractive nowadays are two heresies about which we know a lot from the writings of Augustine, who fiercely challenged both of them: Donatism and Pelagianism. In Donatism – the movement was inspired by Bishop Donatus of Carthage (*c*.350) – the idea of purity was central. Bishops and priests who had forsaken their faith in the last great persecutions under Diocletian were considered unclean. Sacraments

administered by them were of no value. The true Church was a community of untainted people, of saints; the self-appointed Catholic Church was in fact the 'synagogue of Satan'. Contrary to this, Augustine always defended the view that the Church derived its sanctity from the intrinsic value of the sacraments, and not from the moral qualities of the clergy who administered them. More generally, he wanted the earthly Church to be open for everyone who wanted to believe. Therefore, the ecclesiastical community was of necessity a reflection of earthly society in all its imperfections. For Augustine the Church contained 'both the corn and the chaff'. They would only be separated on God's threshing floor at the Last Judgement.

Augustine's condescending condemnation of Donatist views is misleading because Donatism was no small affair. Around 400 about half of the 560 bishops in the Roman province of Africa were Donatists; that Augustine's view of the Catholic Church prevailed in the end was not self-evident.

Augustine's clash with Pelagius had a different background. Pelagius was a British monk who had gone to Rome at the end of the fourth century, where he achieved guru status in the highest circles. Augustine was drawn into discussion with the Pelagians by one of his correspondents. Pelagius and he differed especially in their view of the scope of man's free will and of divine grace. The monk argued that through God's grace every individual was free to choose between good and evil, between 'a new life in Christ' and the rejection thereof – with all the resulting implications. It is fair to say that Pelagius, like a socialist *avant la lettre*, fully recognised that someone's freedom of choice could be severely curtailed by social circumstances. Hence his appeal to the elite to combine their pursuit of moral refinement with taking initiatives to improve living conditions for those who were less well off by voluntarily renouncing their wealth – a free choice to do good! Economic and social inequality, according to Pelagius and his followers, was the cause of poverty: 'get rid of the rich and poverty will vanish' was one of their slogans. In Augustine's view so much responsibility for mankind went too far. Since the Fall mankind had been tainted with original sin, which baptism washed away only temporarily. When the sick had been healed by a physician, could they not fall sick again? In everyday life every person's will was fettered by selfishness, intemperance and pride. 'Get rid of pride, and wealth will do no harm' was his answer to the Pelagian slogan. For Augustine divine mercy was not then the gift of moral freedom, but liberation from the chains of sinfulness.

An important question, then, is on whom God confers grace, and whether God has made his choice beforehand. On this point Augustine wanted to believe the seemingly impossible: that absolute divine predestination and human free will existed side by side. The dogma of an absolute predestination, which preordained many to evil and to eternal damnation, was rejected at the Synod of Orange in 529 as being a 'fatalistic conviction' (*fatalis persuasio*). After that, the belief that in his predestination God had already taken man's individual conduct into account came to prevail.

The iconoclast controversy

Some heterodox beliefs continued to exist because rulers were openly sympathetic to them. Constantine's son and successor, Constantius II (337–361), supported Arianism, whereas Justinian's wife, Theodora, was in favour of Monophysitism. But by far the fullest imperial support was given to the last, great heterodoxy of the early Middle Ages, iconoclasm ('[the] destruction of images'). Since the end of the sixth century the fast-growing popularity of the devotion to icons and relics in the Byzantine Empire had roused the opposition of conservative Christian communities in Syria and Anatolia, where the making of images of God and the saints was seen as an infringement of the second of the Ten Commandments.

This view was reinforced by the enormous success of Islam, which also forbade images of God and the prophets. For the deeply Christian Byzantine Empire, the enormous losses of territory to the Arab conquerors of the Middle East appeared as the loss of God's benevolence – just as the repulsion of the Arab fleet that attacked Constantinople in 717 thanks to the deployment of 'Greek fire' (an explosive mixture of petroleum and potassium) was interpreted as the return of divine support. The new emperor, Leo III (717–741), used this sign to motivate and unify his beleaguered subjects, and then also permitted the bishops to destroy images in their churches out of fear that God might again desert his flock if they continued their idolatry.

From that point on, the question of devotion to images was one that divided the Byzantine Empire for almost a century and a half, from the beginning of the eighth to the middle of the ninth century. Iconoclasm was the orthodoxy for two rather long periods: the first between 730 and 780 under the rule of the successful Anatolian general Leo the Isaurian and his son, Constantine V, 'with the shit name' (*Kopronymos*), as his opponents called him; the second between 813 and 843. In the latter period, successive patriarchs convincingly argued in favour of the worshipping of images as being definitely orthodox. After that the Byzantines renounced iconoclasm for good. In the medieval West neither iconoclasm nor its counterpart ever caught on. Roman opinion has always been that a distinction should be made between the pictorial representation and the person represented. The latter could be worshipped, but not the former. The portrayal of saints had first and foremost a didactic purpose in a world where few people could read and write: 'The written word is for the literate', Pope Gregory the Great once wrote in a letter to the bishop of Marseilles, 'what the image is for the illiterate . . . for in the image even the ignorant can see what they must imitate'.

Saints and miracles

The early Christian Church owed a significant part of its strength and authority to the fact that it had been regularly persecuted and there had been many martyrs, determined witnesses who had shown their willingness to die for their faith (martyr literally means 'witness'). From the beginning martyrs had been venerated as saints, and their deaths were annually commemorated at their graves. When Christianity was elevated to become a state religion, this veneration only increased. Believers saw the holy martyrs as symbols of already-won victories of the spirit over the body, of courage over fear and, above all, of life over death. The mortal remains of the martyrs were a means of coming into personal contact with the divine, who might respond by working miracles through his saints. And if the morally perfect part of the earthly existence of these saints could not be exactly imitated it still served as an ethical guideline. When in time it became impossible to build every church over a martyr's grave, the solution was either to venerate the saint through a painted or sculptured image or to distribute the saint in parts. The first martyr to be 'dismantled' in this way was St Stephen, who was stoned to death soon after the crucifixion of Christ in Jerusalem, and whose grave was discovered in 415. Soon there was a buoyant market for relics (the tangible physical remains or personal possessions of a saint), and we know that important monasteries in the Frankish kingdoms, such as those at Saint Riquier, Sens and Chelles, treasured hundreds of relics, all carefully documented, and ranging from scraps of the robe of the Virgin Mary, pieces of Jesus' crib and all sorts of body parts of any one of the apostles to leftovers of manna from the exodus of the Jewish people out of Egypt.

At the beginning of the fourth century, when the persecutions had come to an end, the question arose of how members of the Christian community should then make their mark in order to be recognised as 'saintly'. The ambitions in this direction of one specific group, the monks, who considered themselves model witnesses of the faith were never generally accepted. In the end the practice developed in the East was very different from that in the West. In the East a reputation for exceptional virtue was sufficient for a person to be recognised as a saint; social background played no part. In the West, on the other hand, it was mainly abbots, bishops and devout ladies of aristocratic origin to whom this honour fell. It was generously allocated by the local Church communities and bishops, without any authorisation from a general council or pope. The strict procedure of **canonisation**, as it is still practised today, was only fully developed in the pontificate of Gregory IX (1227–1241).

In the early medieval West, the veneration of saints was further promoted by the fact that Christ was still primarily associated with his divine nature. In this way the role of saints as mediators between a highly exalted, inaccessible God and ordinary believers grew. Because saints were supposed to go directly to heaven, where they were sitting at the right hand of God, they were preferential advocates for the prayers of the faithful. Such mediation was seen not just in the area of spiritual support, but more especially for the acquisition of physical and material assistance. There were even some rather comical rituals in which images of saints were punished like naughty dolls if they failed to deliver. At other times devout donors did not hesitate to take back their offerings in anger when the hoped-for divine intervention did not take place. Seen from this perspective, early medieval hagiolatry formed a perfect link with the sort of barter relationships that were characteristic for the functioning of aristocratic networks in the early Middle Ages (see Chapter 3).

Real saints had contact with God through visions (just like ordinary believers could meet saints in dreams) and showed their special relationship with Him by performing miracles, which were all the more convincing when they surpassed the laws of nature. Miracles – or more probably tales of miracles – which proved the omnipotence of the Christian God could be used as propaganda in spreading the faith, even though missionaries realised that it was better not to exaggerate. Adam of Bremen, who wrote a history of the archbishopric of Bremen-Hamburg in the eleventh century, in looking back to the Christianisation of the area, dryly observed that heathens too could create the illusion of a wonder. Was not the conversion of a pagan soul to the Christian faith the only miracle that really mattered?

For less sophisticated people, miracles facilitated the transition from animistic and magical beliefs to the Christian faith with its highly abstract theology. Miracles and visions became fixed ingredients in the biographies or *vitae* of saints. These were always written in Latin from which we may infer that they were intended primarily for a public of clerics and monks. Nevertheless, *vitae* form an important literary genre with a fairly fixed pattern. A model was supplied by Sulpicius Severus who shortly after 400 wrote the much admired *vita* of Martin of Tours (316–397), a soldier from Pannonia who had become a monk after his retirement in Gaul and then was elected bishop of Tours. *Lives* such as the one of Martin presented saints as inspired, charismatic men and women of God, who led exemplary lives and, if necessary, could bring about God's miraculous intervention. A central point is often formed by the conversion (*conversio*, literally meaning 'turning round') of the protagonist who, after an originally sinful life, receives a sign from God, repents and thereafter offers his life to the service of God. Compilations of saints' lives were rapidly produced, and bishops and priests could draw upon them when preparing edifying sermons. The *Liber vitae patrum* ('Book of Lives of the Saints'), a collection put together by Gregory, bishop of Tours (539–594), enjoyed wide popularity in the early Middle Ages.

Monasticism

It has been suggested, and not without reason, that in the early Middle Ages it was the monks, not popes and bishops, who were the most important role models in Christianity. The roots of Christian monasticism reach back to at least the third century. At that time there were believers in Egypt and Syria who had completely withdrawn from the world in order to concentrate on the spiritual and the divine, hoping in this way to bring about their own personal salvation and that of their fellow Christians. Some of these 'monks' sought their asceticism in solitude (the Greek *monachos* literally means 'living alone'); others gave form to their ideal in small, like-minded communities; while still others preferred a middle ground. Probably the most spectacular ostentation of the first type of piety was given by Simeon Stylites ('the [saint] man on the column') (*c*.390–459), who stood in prayer for 37 years on top of a 60-foot column of an old pagan temple near the main road from Antioch to the Euphrates. Due to the wide renown of this heroic feat, Simeon's self-chosen desert soon dissolved into the spectacle of crowds of admirers who paid a visit to receive the holy man's blessings and, in so doing, may have viewed him as a vital link between the world of the old gods now gone and the new faith that had been imposed upon them.

The second model, which for convenience we will call the monastic life, prevailed in the West, although the first form never quite disappeared. In part monastic life fitted in with the ancient (Stoic) ideal of achieving wisdom and spiritual freedom by disengaging from material and physical needs. Apart from that it clearly had its own character, linked to Christian values. By abandoning the world and worldly things monks considered themselves the only Christians capable of preserving the grace-giving action of the sacraments of the Church – baptism, in particular – during life. Ordinary believers lapsed immediately into new sins.

The growing significance of monasteries and the monastic way of life for early medieval culture and intellectual training also had the effect that monastic ideals and rules became the standard against which all society was measured. In this connection the religious historian R.A. Markus (1990) has spoken of a gradual 'de-secularisation' of Western culture as a result of the suffocating influence of the monastic ideals of world renunciation, spiritual contemplation and sexual abstinence.

Originally the Church authorities looked upon monks as neither clerics nor ordinary laypeople. For Augustine, both clerics and monks were servants of God (*servientes Deo*) and therefore deserved the same legal status and treatment. This view led to the convergence of clerics and monks into one 'clerical estate', a tendency which was reinforced when many monks were eventually ordained as clerics and monasteries were often given tasks in the field of spiritual care. The position of women was still complicated; they could not enter the priesthood but were allowed to become nuns or **canonesses**, at first only when advanced in years, later at marriageable age. Nuns and canonesses were given a special ordination and enjoyed the same legal privileges as clerics and monks.

In the first centuries of the Middle Ages monasticism was far from being organised and well structured. It embraced a motley collection of stylites, herbivores, obscure sects with strange names such as 'Those who never sleep', as well as communities of more than a thousand members, all of which were difficult to regulate. For rural people, in particular, monks formed an alternative source of spiritual authority over which the Church had little control. As the communal form gradually began to predominate, some sort of order came into being. Specifically the Church tried to provide rules for monastic communities or to grant official authority to those rules already in existence. The foundation of new communities and the appointment of abbots were also made subject to the approval of the bishops.

A considerable number of monastic rules have survived. In the West especially, these resembled

precepts or sets of instructions. Matters such as obedience to the abbot, communal activities such as prayer, eating and fasting, and acceptable conduct were described clearly and precisely. But there was great diversity because influences were felt from many directions. In Gaul/Francia, where more than two hundred new monasteries were founded in the seventh century alone, we can distinguish several great monastic traditions side by side.

The most influential was that of the Benedictines. They took their name from Benedict of Norcia (c.485–c.560), the founder of three monasteries in Italy, including that of Monte Cassino, high on its ridge between Rome and Naples. The Benedictine Rule is in fact no more than an adaptation of an extensive and rather strict monastic rule composed at the beginning of the sixth century by a man whom we know only as *Magister*, the master. Benedict toned it down somewhat. His monks were not allowed personal belongings. They were not permitted to leave the monastery (the rule of *stabilitas loci*, 'permanency of residence'). They had to live chaste lives and obey the abbot, the head of the monastic community, unconditionally. Obedience was seen as a religious exercise, an exercise in absolute compliance with God's will, as Christ had complied. This was even harder for the monks and nuns of the early Middle Ages, most of whom were members of aristocratic families accustomed to command rather than to obey. The abbot was enjoined to observe moderation in asserting his authority and to listen to what his 'brothers' had to say.

In general Benedictine Rule can be summed up in the double command to 'work and pray' – although that prayer was also called work, the doing of God's work (*opus Dei*). The Master had laid down a strict daily routine, which Benedict refined into a set programme of singing and reading at fixed times (the Hours). The other forms of work soon came to imply intellectual work only, studying, writing or teaching.

Benedict's Rule owed its enormous popularity to support from two sides. First, in about 600

Pope Gregory the Great showed himself to be a tireless propagandist of Benedict's life and works. Next, Church reformers, such as Boniface and Chrodegang of Metz, working in the Frankish Empire in the eighth century, pressured monastic communities into following the *regula Benedicti*. The Rule was also introduced fairly generally outside the Frankish Empire. This does not mean that the monasteries that followed the Benedictine Rule as yet had formed an 'order' in the sense of a congregation with a coordinating organisation. Monastic orders in that sense only came into existence in the eleventh century.

Typical of a second important monastic tradition in the West, Irish monasticism, was the *peregrinatio*, which literally means a 'stay in foreign parts' or 'exile'. Instead of remaining inside the monastic community Irish monks went out into the wider world to preach Christianity and to found new monasteries. In this way they gave tangible form to the metaphor that, for a real Christian, life on earth is no more than a sojourn among strangers, an exile that will only end with the beginning of eternal life. Besides, leaving one's own community voluntarily could be interpreted as choosing social death for the sake of one's faith, and thus as a form of martyrdom. On the way the Irish monks founded monastic communities where possible, naturally in remote places that were difficult to reach, like Iona and Lindisfarne, situated respectively on islands off the west coast of Scotland and the east coast of England.

The Irish monks wandered around the continent too. In about 590 Columbanus, a monk

PLATE 2.1 The winged symbols of the Four Evangelists mark the introductory page to the Gospel of St Matthew in the Book of Kells. This is the most brilliantly illuminated Celtic manuscript, created in around 800 in the abbey of Iona (western Scotland) and in the Irish Kells, to which monastery the monks had fled from Viking raids. Ten of its 340 folios are full-page pictures in vibrant colours, combining Christian iconography with swirling motifs and interlacing patterns in the insular tradition. These recur in the interlinear ornamentation and the decorated initials. In addition to the Latin texts of the four Gospels, the manuscript contains tables of concordances between the Gospels and summaries of their narratives. The book illustrates the riches of Irish monastic life.

from the monastery of Bangor (not far from modern Belfast) arrived in Gaul. In the following years he journeyed through the Vosges and northern Italy, founding the renowned **abbeys** of Luxeuil and Bobbio. His immediate involvement in the establishment of other monasteries cannot always be proved, but there is no doubt about the Irish influence on Frankish monasticism. It ensured, amongst other things, that cloistered communities were no longer generally situated in or near urban settlements, but often far away in desolate areas.

The practice of the monastic rules was a fairly casual affair, for monasteries formed part of the aristocratic world. This meant, for example, that visitors came and went freely, that monasteries often accommodated important guests and their retinues, and that monks and abbots sometimes surrendered cheerfully to worldly pleasures, such as hunting. In the early Middle Ages monasteries were also used as prisons to confine – either temporarily or permanently – important officials and noble spouses who had fallen from favour, unwanted pretenders to a throne, deposed kings or others who might be considered a danger to the state. Exceptions can be found especially in the East, where monasteries that were strictly secluded from the outside world were always held in high esteem. Examples include the monasteries and ascetic communities concentrated on the peninsula of Mount Athos in northern Greece. In 883, the Byzantine Emperor Basil I granted them total **immunity** from the intervention of military or civil officials, and even the peasants and shepherds living in the neighbourhood had to keep their distance from the monks. In return, the monks '[would] pray for the emperor and the whole world'. Even today, the Mount's immunity is constitutionally guaranteed.

Spreading the faith

Missions and conversion

Christianity is a religion that has always aimed at expansion, at converting others who do not yet share the true faith. This missionary urge is anchored in the Gospels. According to St Matthew, Jesus of Nazareth sent his twelve disciples out as messengers or apostles with the words, 'And as ye go, preach, saying, "The kingdom of heaven is at hand"' (Matthew 10:7). The task of conversion was thus clearly connected with the expectation that the end of time was close by. Jesus added threatening words that cast an ominous shadow over how conversion to Christianity would take place: 'But whosoever shall deny me before men, him will I also deny before my Father who is in heaven.' And, 'Think not that I came to send peace on the earth: I came not to send peace, but the sword.'

Until 311 this missionary zeal was not so urgent. Only later, when Christians were allowed to express their faith openly, did the mission become serious. In the view of Augustine it was explicitly not to be limited to the civilised world of the Roman Empire. The heathen barbarians beyond the borders should also learn the Truth. At the same time Augustine was against forceful conversion. A firm hand could only be used to return heretics and schismatics to the bosom of Mother Church; unbelievers had to be persuaded.

But how should these things be accomplished? Bishops were appointed to Christian communities outside the *limes* only at their own request. This must have happened in the area of the Goths to the north of the Black Sea and in modern-day Armenia and Georgia (in the beginning of the fourth century, the king of Armenia would become the first head of state to convert to Christianity), but also in far-flung regions such as Yemen and Ethiopia. Better known is the case of Ireland, where conversion must have started in about 450 by the half-legendary St Patrick, who was born in the north of Britannia and was abducted and sold as a slave by Irish marauders when a young boy. After six years he escaped and came into contact with Christianity in Gaul. Eventually he returned to the 'island at the end of the world' to bring the new faith to his former captors. Whether the story is true or not, in the early Middle Ages the Christian faith and Church organisation in Ireland took on their own, fascinating forms which were closely connected to the numerous clan-kingdoms of Ireland's characteristic social and political structure. The strict ascetic monasticism caught on, and instead of bishoprics, it was the monasteries that became the centres of Church life. One consequence of this was that abbots, not bishops, emerged as the real leaders in the early Irish Church. Irish bishops generally lived as monks in monasteries, where they were subject to the authority of the abbots.

Elsewhere, the barbarian invasions caused a temporary retreat of Christianity. We see this in fairly large towns on or close to the *limes*, border forts on the Rhine–Moselle–Meuse frontier such as Cologne, Mainz, Trier and Tongeren/Maastricht. As early as the fourth century these were home to a Christian community with its own bishop, but they would disappear for a long period from the beginning of the fifth century. In spite of this, most barbarian invaders converted to Christianity amazingly quickly – the Goths even before 400 – although it was often to the unorthodox Arian faith. The fact that Clovis, king of the Franks, converted to Catholicism in the beginning of the sixth century is seen by many, even today, as an example of astonishing political insight, although little is known about his motives. Clovis may well have realised that it would be impossible to rule Gaul without the support of the Gallo-Roman senatorial elite. This elite was Catholic – anti-Arian – and controlled the allocation of the bishoprics that were so important for the civil administration.

In at least one respect Clovis's conversion to Catholicism was tied closely to *Gefolgschafts*-thinking: all warriors of a lord's retinue were expected to follow the example of their leader.

Conversion was not just an individual act of faith, but a collective action within a system of clientage. One variant of this was that individual converts considered that their entire household (*familia*) had been converted. This meant that thousands of slaves and serfs were automatically counted as Christians after the conversion of their aristocratic masters or after they had been handed over to a Church institution. Whatever they or the 'ordinary free Frank' might have thought about Christianity had nothing to do with it. With the baptism of Clovis the Franks had become Catholic – in the eyes of many modern historians too! Excavations of early medieval burial grounds and saints' lives show how gradually the Christianisation of Frankish Gallo-Roman society took hold. Even 150 years after Clovis' death, missionaries were still active in the area close to the late king's centre of power at Tournai.

This pattern of conversion of an elite followed by a far more gradual, general conversion to Christianity was often repeated in the barbarian kingdoms of the early Middle Ages. Kings and their aristocratic elites opted for Christianity out of political opportunism when they were in danger of succumbing to hostile, external pressures or when they wanted to make advantageous alliances. Conversion thus began as often with diplomatic negotiations – not infrequently after a defeat on the battlefield – as with the work of missionaries.

It was more alarming when military conquest and missionary zeal went hand in hand. In particular the missions of conversion from the Frankish kingdoms were accompanied by brute force aimed at expanding Frankish authority. An alarming portent can be found in the *vita* of St Amandus, who followed the Frankish armies of Dagobert I (623–639) into the Basque country and over the Danube into the Slav lands as a missionary. Barely a century later the renewed drive for expansion under the Pippinid or Carolingian mayors of the palace led to a harsh policy of systematic, military subjection and forced conversions. The first victims were the Frisians and Saxons living north and east of the Rhine.

BOX 2.2 CONVERSION AS A DOUBLE INSURANCE

Anglo-Saxon England became acquainted with Christianity from two directions: from the south (Kent), through the Roman mission of Augustine of Canterbury; and from the north, through the missionary activities of Irish monks. The history of this process presents numerous examples of conversions connected with the hope of success in wars. It did not always immediately produce sincere Christians, as the example of Redwald, king of East Anglia shows. According to the Anglo-Saxon historian and monk, the Venerable Bede (*c.*672–735), after his conversion Redwald continued to worship the old gods, a double insurance policy often pursued at that time. It made it possible to postpone making a definite choice until one's deathbed, and sometimes the old gods were given the benefit of the doubt. The discovery of

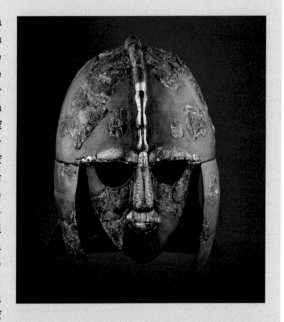

Redwald's grave at Sutton Hoo has provided dazzling proof of this. As was the custom among many heathen barbarians in the north, Redwald had all his belongings buried with him, a treasure of inconceivable wealth, piled up in a fully rigged wooden ship. No true Christian would have done that, because he lived in the certainty that his body had no further value after death and thus would not need sustenance. A true Christian would have found it more prudent to aid the salvation of his own soul by leaving money or goods to a church, monastery or the poor. We should be careful, however, with such generalising interpretations; giving burial gifts remained common practice in aristocratic circles until the eighth century, and the Church was not against it in principle. Burial gifts were perhaps a reflection of social prestige rather than of conceptions of life after death.

Source: Tom Williamson, *Sutton Hoo and its Landscape: The Context of the Monuments* (Oxford: Windgather Press, 2008).

Here the work of conversion was undertaken by Anglo-Saxon monks. Like the Irish they had a missionary zeal and were surely still aware of their ethnic proximity to the inhabitants of the North Sea lands. Willibrord, the 'apostle of the Frisians' (658–739), concentrated on the coastal areas of the northern Netherlands. He immediately tied his fate as missionary to that of the Pippinid rulers, who wanted to subdue the Frisians by force of arms. Willibrord sought authorisation from the pope, and was appointed archbishop of the Frisians with Utrecht as his seat. After repeated attempts by the Frisians to turn the tide, their resistance was finally broken by Charles Martel. The conversion of the Saxons followed a similar pattern. The chief initiator was Winfrid, a monk from near Southampton, who is better known as St Boniface. He, too, carried out his missionary work with a papal mandate as well as under the special protection of the Franks. In 745 the pope appointed him archbishop of Mainz, in the area east of the middle Rhine, where he had already been active for years, and where in 744 he had founded the monastery of Fulda on land donated to him by Carloman, son of Charles Martel. The Carolingians sometimes delayed the mission work, however, and as Boniface could do nothing without the military support of the Franks, the mission in Saxony did not progress. How superficially the new faith penetrated becomes apparent from a depressingly long list of thirty superstitions and heathen practices (*superstitiones et paganiae*) which was drawn up in those years by a person close to the archbishop. He eventually had more success in Bavaria. In the end, the tireless Boniface was killed by robbers in 754, at the age of eighty, while travelling on official business in the north of Frisia, which was still half-pagan.

The recalcitrant Saxons were only really 'converted' when Charlemagne decided to subdue them by military means soon after he became king. At first this seemed an easy undertaking, because after a couple of campaigns he advanced into the Saxon heartland at the source of the Lippe where he set up the royal residence (*palts*) of Paderborn. After they had been subjected the Saxons promised to convert to Christianity. However, they soon started to rebel, spurred on by a new leader, Widukind. When Widukind was defeated, Charlemagne spared his life on condition that he consented to be baptised. Charlemagne himself stood as godfather at the baptismal font; this was not out of kindness, but a public gesture to make it clear that Widukind could count on his special protection and would be, at the same time, entirely at the king's 'fatherly' mercy. There are many similar examples, especially in Anglo-Saxon England, where royal godfathers were quite common. Charlemagne's son, Louis the Pious, was godfather at the baptism of the claimant to the Danish throne, Harald Klak,

in 826, and the Byzantine emperor Michael III stood godfather to Boris, khan of the Bulgars, in 865.

Further rebellions followed in Saxony, and these long hindered the missionary work. For the first time there were signs that the aristocracy's switch to Christianity did not automatically cause the widespread baptism of ordinary free people – quite the contrary. The conversion of the elite was apparently seen as an expression of a pro-Frankish policy, and thus as a betrayal of the Saxon cause. Altogether several decades went by before Christianity made much headway in Saxony. It raised the question in Church circles of whether the use of force was expedient in spreading the true faith. Important advisers to Charlemagne, such as Alcuin of York, were adamantly against it. In Alcuin's view the acceptance of Christianity must be born of an inner conviction; force and violence were entirely wrong. This standpoint became official Carolingian policy after the subjection of the Avars in the years after 796. Consequently, the Avars were not converted to Christianity very quickly.

Another strategy often used, and which was applied in Saxony as well as in Bavaria and Carinthia, regions where Christianity had been introduced in the eighth century, was to use native-born missionaries, often the sons of noblemen who had been sent to Francia as hostages. The important monastery of Corvey, on the upper Weser, for example, was founded by Saxon missionaries who had been brought up in the Neustrian abbey of Corbie (Corvey means 'new Corbie'). Another missionary to the Saxons and Frisians, Liudger, was a Frisian by birth who had been educated in Utrecht and York. In 805 he became the first bishop of Münster and was the forefather of a remarkable 'priestly dynasty'. For many generations, his descendants held the combined positions of abbot of Werden and bishop of Münster and Halberstadt.

The first attempts to convert Scandinavia to Christianity date from the reign of Louis the Pious, who sent missionaries to Denmark and

Sweden. The newly established double arch-bishopric of Bremen-Hamburg was the base of operations, but the campaign soon foundered. This is not surprising as it was precisely at this time that the Vikings set out on their marauding expeditions to western Europe. The earliest missions to convert the Danes should be seen partly in this context. The Carolingians probably hoped to avert the threat of Viking attacks by intervening in the domestic politics of the Viking kings. It did not bring them much success. It was not until the tenth century that new attempts would be made to bring Christianity to Scandinavia and to those groups of Vikings who had settled in Francia, England and Ireland.

The definitive conversion of Scandinavia itself was driven by the new fervour of the German kings of the Ottonian dynasty. The king of Denmark converted in about 960. In the eleventh century his grandson, Cnut, was already reputed to be the ideal Christian monarch. In Denmark, by far the most powerful of the Scandinavian kingdoms, Christianity spread above all because the kings saw that their conversion brought them impressive military and political success, such as the conquest of England. Naturally they attributed this to the good fortune which Christ had brought them, the *gipta Hvítakrists* ('luck of the white Christ') in Old Danish. In Denmark there soon developed a Danish *Adelskirche* with a proprietary church system, based entirely on the German model.

The spread of Christianity in Scandinavia, just as everywhere else in Europe, showed a considerable delay between the conversion of kings and aristocratic elites on the one hand – for Norwegians and Swedes alike dating from about 1000 – and the conversion of the common people on the other. Heathen rituals were held at the great pre-Christian shrine of Uppsala until well into the twelfth century. They did not stop until 1164 when the bishop of Sigtuna moved his seat to Uppsala and was promoted to archbishop. By then Christianity had penetrated into the remotest corners of medieval Europe. The first

bishopric in Iceland, Skálaholt, was established around the middle of the eleventh century. Greenland followed soon after 1125.

The same German fervour that initiated the permanent process of the conversion of Denmark should also be seen as being behind the Christianisation of the Wends, the common collective name for the Slavic-speaking peoples east of the Elbe. This did not happen under the guidance of native kings but rather followed the pattern of the conversion of the Franks and Saxons: a joint missionary offensive with attempts at military subjection. Ironically enough the Saxons played an important role in this. They suffered a major reversal when the Wends rebelled in 983 and Hamburg was reduced to ashes. It would be nearly two centuries before the Wends finally accepted Christianity. A combination of three factors proved to be decisive for the final success: crusade, colonisation and the foundation of monasteries. When, in 1147, the aristocracies of Saxony and Denmark appeared unwilling to take part in the Second Crusade to the Holy Land as long as the heathens were still in their own back yard, so to speak, Pope Eugene III labelled as crusades what in fact were nothing more than marauding raids into Slavonic territory. At the same time the German colonisation of thinly populated areas to the east of the Weser, Elbe and Oder got under way, and the Wendish frontier became studded with monasteries, belonging in particular to the new, highly motivated new monastic orders of the Cistercians and Premonstratensians (see Chapter 6).

From the very beginning the situation in the central Slavonic region was quite different. Unlike the politically divided north, two large territorial principalities, Bohemia and Poland, had been established there quite early on. German influence was strong but no attempt was made at political and military subjugation. The conversion of the first Bohemian princes is shrouded in legend, but can safely be placed at the beginning of the tenth century: the bishopric of Prague was established before 967. The conversion of Poland was undertaken from Bohemia, a major role being played by the first non-German bishop of Prague, Vojtech-Adalbert. This eccentric character spent more time in Italy than in Bohemia, much to the displeasure of his ecclesiastical superior, and perished while preaching among the Prussians, a Baltic people. Just a few years later he was revered as a holy martyr in Gniezno, the centre of the first Polish archbishopric.

During missionary work among the southern Slavonic peoples in the second half of the ninth century another problem arose: competition between the Carolingian and the Byzantine Empire. In the struggle for power that ensued after Charlemagne's destruction of the kingdom of the Avars, two key players, the prince of Moravia and the khan of Bulgaria, tried to gain support sometimes from the Eastern Franks, sometimes from Constantinople. Religious conversion was always a condition of support. Two Byzantine missionaries, the brothers Cyril and Methodius from Thessaloniki, had the lead on the Eastern Franks in the decades after 860, not only because they spoke the Slav language (the Eastern Frankish missionaries working in the area generally did too) but also because they were the first to put the spoken Slavonic language into writing (Cyrillic). In that way the Bible and other essential liturgical texts could be written in Slavonic. This considerably improved the missionaries' means of communication. The rival Eastern Frankish missionaries found however that a Bible in the vernacular bordered on heresy. The quarrel ended in compromise: the pope approved the use of Slavonic as a language of the Church, the Church of Bulgaria came under the authority of the patriarch of Constantinople, and the Church of Moravia and Pannonia (respectively the regions north of Vienna and the western part of modern Hungary) under Rome.

Missionaries from the West did not benefit immediately from this arrangement because soon after 900 Moravia and Pannonia were overrun by the pagan Magyars. When the Magyars were Christianised the whole story was repeated. The first Magyar rulers to convert were baptised in Constantinople, a logical consequence of the anti-Bulgarian alliance they had made with the Byzantines in about 950. For similar reasons the princes of the Russian Empire of Kiev followed in the wake of the Greek Church. However, it was the German kings who subdued the Magyars in battle, after which Hungary finally came into the Latin-Roman Church. Just as had happened in Norway and Denmark, the appeal of Christianity in Hungary was consciously increased by making one of their own kings a saint. In Hungary this happened immediately with the first Catholic Magyar prince, Waik, who received the baptismal name of Stephen and had the air of saintliness about him throughout his life. He was venerated everywhere very soon after his death in 1038.

Thus by about the middle of the eleventh century, more than eight hundred years after the conversion of Constantine, almost all Europe, or at least its ruling elites, had converted to Christianity. Just two groups of peoples were still unconverted: the Balts (a non-Slavonic-speaking group of peoples which includes Prussians, Latvians and Lithuanians) and the (non-Indo-European) Estonians and Finns. Other missionaries followed Adalbert of Prague, but met with equally little success in the inaccessible region of impenetrable forests on the south-eastern shores of the Baltic Sea. Not until well into the fourteenth century could Christianity take root in the Baltic lands, but the laborious attempts at conversion had been given a cruel charter in 1171 with the promulgation of the **bull**, *Non parum animus noster*. In this bull the pope determined that the struggle against the heathens in the north would forever be on an equal footing with the struggle against the Muslims. In practice it meant that the nobility of western Europe were licensed to hunt down the Balts wherever and whenever they wanted. In spite of the successes of the military Teutonic Order, however, which extended its violent activities into the Baltic region after 1230, the indigenous rulers did not allow themselves to be completely overwhelmed. Just as everywhere else in medieval Europe earlier, Christianity could not triumph here until the indigenous aristocracy showed themselves prepared, for whatever reasons, to be receptive to the new faith.

Christianisation and syncretism

The centuries-long monopoly of Christian historians on the historiography of the Middle Ages created an erroneous picture of the Christianisation of Europe, which needs to be adjusted. Not only did the conversion process take place more slowly than is often thought, it also worked out imperfectly. In this connection it is useful to make a distinction between delayed social and delayed mental penetration. By the former we mean that Christianity reached the masses later than the elites; by the latter, that the faith of the believers was for a long time superficial and directed towards externals. Internalisation required intensive pastoral support, which for a long time was either absent or of a dubious quality. The first hesitant attempts to raise the consciousness of ordinary believers date from the Carolingian period and were aimed mainly at moral improvement rather than religious instruction. Similar initiatives were also seen outside the Carolingian Empire, in the England of Alfred the Great (871–899) and the Asturias of Alfonso III (866–910).

One of the first obstacles was that almost all texts essential for a deeper knowledge of the faith – foremost the Bible – were written in Latin. In Anglo-Saxon England text material in the vernacular became sparsely available in the second half of the seventh century; in the Carolingian Empire that did not happen till after 800. A famous early example of an edifying text in the vernacular is the *Heliand*, an epic story of the life of Christ in Old High German, which dates from between 825 and 850. Yet the Church continued to predominantly use Latin until the thirteenth century.

No wonder, then, that generations of missionaries, village priests and bishops failed to root out pre-Christian practices. They certainly tried hard enough. One favoured method was the merciless destruction of cult places, such as the *Irminsul* (literally, 'Pillar of the firmament'), the great holy tree of the Saxons, which must have stood in a forest near Ober-Marsberg in Westphalia, before Charlemagne had it cut down in 772. The Church always had a rather ambivalent attitude to the use of force to spread Christianity. The advice that Gregory the Great gave to his missionaries in England in 601 is typical: destroy the images in heathen shrines, but convert the shrines themselves into churches. One of Gregory's successors, Pope Boniface IV (608–615), himself set a good example by rededicating the famous Pantheon in Rome as the church that it still is today: Santa Maria Rotonda. Charlemagne was buried in an antique sarcophagus with an image of the Rape of Proserpina, who was now seen as a Christian symbol for the hope of resurrection. Countless missionaries and temporal rulers copied these illustrious examples, outside the early Roman Empire as well, where church density was far lower. The cathedral of Uppsala in Sweden stands on the site of an important pre-Christian shrine, and that of Vilnius in Lithuania had a heathen predecessor that was probably built as late as the first half of the fourteenth century.

The cultic re-use of these holy places proved the superiority of the Christian God could be shown, and at the same time it could be seen as a token of respect for the losers. The latter was all the more important because pre-Christian shrines fulfilled a central function in ancestor-worship and were, therefore, an essential identity-defining element in local or regional communities. The *vé* at Jelling in Denmark (see Box 2.3) shows how complicated the interpretation of such rededication can be. It is for this reason that in recent years, particularly under the influence of cultural anthropology and comparative religious studies, a history of Christianity approached purely and simply from a Christian perspective is considered to be a pointless exercise. Current interpretations rather depart from the concept of **syncretism**, the

BOX 2.3 A PAGAN SHRINE SUPPLANTED: FROM *VÉ* TO CHURCH IN JELLING

One of the most interesting archaeological sites in Denmark is in the little town of Jelling in Jutland. In the middle of a large open space are two man-made mounds of about 11 metres high with a small whitewashed church in between them. In the tenth century Jelling was the residence of at least two kings of Denmark: Gorm the Elder (d.940) and his son, Harald Bluetooth (c.935–987). The runic inscriptions on two richly decorated (and once coloured) granite stones standing near the church attest to this. On the smallest is written: KING GORM PLACED THIS COMMEMORATIVE STONE HERE IN REMEMBRANCE OF HIS WIFE THYRA, THE GRACE OF DENMARK ('Danabod', the oldest reference to Denmark in Denmark itself). The inscription on the larger stone reads: KING HARALD PLACED THIS MONUMENT HERE IN MEMORY OF HIS FATHER GORM AND HIS MOTHER THYRA, THE HARALD WHO UNITED

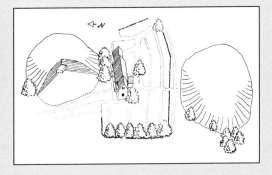

ALL DENMARK AND NORWAY AND WHO MADE THE DANES CHRISTIANS. There is no reason to doubt the veracity of these short statements. We know from another source that Harald Bluetooth's authority stretched over a large part of modern Denmark, and that he moved his permanent residence from Jelling to Roskilde. It has also been established that Harald was baptised by a German missionary called Popo. The decorated figures on the large stone at Jelling depict a Christ triumphant who has defeated (heathen) Evil in the form of two intertwined monsters.

In the first 'national' history of Denmark, the chronicle of Saxo Grammaticus which was completed in about 1200, it was already assumed that the two mounds at Jelling were indeed the graves of Gorm and Thyra. Archaeological excavations to verify the assumption did not take place until the nineteenth century. Then it was found that one mound contained the remnants of an empty wooden double grave and the other mound . . . nothing at all. At least, that was what was believed for almost a century. Then, in 1941, new excavations brought to light the remains of a platform constructed of wooden posts, which had possibly once served as the base of a watchtower. Even more sensational were the findings from the excavations under the little Romanesque church in Jelling, which must have been built in about 1100. Under the church appeared to be the remains of no fewer than three earlier wooden churches, the oldest of which dates from the time of Harald Bluetooth. A burial chamber was revealed under the choir, containing the skeleton of a man of about fifty years of age. It was concluded from the rather disorderly position of the skeleton that this had been a reburial. It is generally assumed that Gorm's body was moved from his pagan grave in the hill to the Christian church after the conversion of his son Harald. But where is Thyra?

This is one of the riddles that Jelling poses. The other relates to the discovery of a large triangular space, bounded by large stones and situated partly under the church and partly under the graveless mound. There is no doubt that this is the remains of a pre-Christian place of worship, or *vé*. Its exact function and its relationship to the burial grounds, which are also pre-Christian, still remain a mystery. The last excavations took place in 2006; these uncovered the remnants of a palisade and of a large ship burial. The Jelling memorial has been on UNESCO's list of World Heritage Sites for many years.

Sources: Johannes Brøndsted, *The Vikings* (Harmondsworth: Penguin, 1965), pp. 293–297; Leif Ingvorsen, *Jelling in the Viking Age* (Jelling n.d.); the illustrations were also taken from this publication, by permission of Jelling Bogtrykkeris Forlag in Jelling. http://whc.unesco.org/en/list/697/video.

functional fusion of old and new religious representations. The designation of time – a religiously loaded subject – provides a good example. Throughout Europe the designation of the days of the week and the months of the year are of pre-Christian origin. Only our calendar of years and holidays has been completely Christianised, with certain notable exceptions including Christmas (already mentioned), and the midwinter and midsummer celebrations. The midwinter feast was a barbarian adaptation of the Roman feast of Saturnalia (the feast of Saturn, the god of seed-time), which in turn was of Etruscan origin. The pagan midsummer feast was given a Christian make-over as the feast-day of St John the Baptist (24 June), but it is still abundantly celebrated in its pre-Christian form in unimpeachably Christian countries such as Norway and Sweden.

A second aspect of syncretism relates to the tolerated identification of heathen gods and practices with Christian saints and rites. In Brittany the exceptional devotion to St Anne appears to date directly from the Celtic or even pre-Celtic worship of a 'mother goddess of the earth' called Ane. In the same region, until well into the nineteenth century, mothers of twins directed their prayers to St Gwen Teirbron, a Celtic fertility goddess whose likeness, to the discomfort of many a village priest, was conspicuous for the three prominently displayed breasts. Finally, a certain degree of religious ambiguity was accepted

for a long time. Christian Anglo-Saxon kings continued to trace their ancestry back to Woden – until the eighth century when someone hit on the brilliant idea of dropping Woden's divine status and tracing his ancestry back to Adam, the first man. At different locations in Scandinavia soapstone moulds have been found in which both a crucifix and a Thor-hammer could be cast.

Similar processes of syncretism were facilitated because many early medieval Christian practices were soaked in magic. Who cared about the difference between the healing effects of holy relics or of talismans and amulets? Valuable caskets have been excavated in which they were kept side by side. Certainly the parish priest, with whom the majority of believers came into contact, worked in this semi-magical world. Only with the pursuit of the ideals of the eleventh-century reform movement were the priests forced to follow the Church's moral line; their duties were increasingly limited to administering the sacraments and hearing simple catechisms (see Chapter 6). Only then did Catholic priests become 'sacramental priests' more than local sorcerers. Even after that, the Church was only partially successful in reaching the masses and impressing upon them its dogmas, moral precepts and rituals. Long after the Middle Ages Argus-eyed priests gazed in puzzlement at the veneration of a holy greyhound near Lyons, of a hunting goddess with bear-claws instead of hands in the Dolomites, bulls offered in sacrifice in Scotland and numerous pilgrimages to holy wells, streams, lakes, trees and forests in Wales and Cornwall, all barely understood witnesses to a world that had gone, but also silent protests against an invader, against a strange religion that had been imposed from outside.

The Arab conquests and the establishment of Islam

At about the same time as the Lombards entered Italy and groups of Slavs swarmed over the Balkans, Mohammed (c.570–632) was born in Mecca on the west of the Arabian peninsula. Almost everything we know of him is from Arabic tradition, which was only written down a century after the Prophet's death, with all the potential for inaccuracy in interpretation that such delay can entail. According to this tradition, in later life Mohammed had visions in which God (Allah) revealed his will to him. On Allah's orders Mohammed spread the revelation and became Allah's Prophet. This caused tension in Mecca, and Mohammed and his followers fled northwards to Medina, an event which marks the beginning of the Islamic era (622). Seven years later he returned to Mecca and assumed power. Support for him grew rapidly all over south and west Arabia. Under his first successors (caliphs) the authority of Mecca expanded with incredible speed. It was first directed at the north and east of the Arabian peninsula and the neighbouring desert regions between the 'fertile crescent' where many Arab Bedouin roamed about. In the year 637 the Byzantines and Persians suffered humiliating defeats against Arab armies at the Yarmuk river (south of Damascus) and al-Qaddisya (near Kufa on the Euphrates) respectively. This opened the way for the Arab conquest of Palestine, Syria and Iraq. A few years later the Byzantines were easily driven out of Egypt. Raids and expeditions into Iran and North Africa were undertaken from these new bases. Within a hundred years of Mohammed's death, Arab power stretched from Spain in the west to the Indus delta and Kyrgyzstan

in the east, where in 751 the Arab conquerors met with, and defeated, an advance army of the Chinese Tang emperor. Shortly after 660 the Arab capital had been moved from Mecca to Damascus, the seat of the caliphs of the Umayyad family. This move was of enormous importance for Arabic culture, which was now exposed to considerable Syrian and Persian influences.

Along with the Arab conquests went the spread of Islam, Mohammed's new religion, which literally means 'subjection [to the will of God]'. Christianity and Islam share three important dogmas with the Jewish religion: belief in one (male) God, knowledge of whom can only be obtained through revelation in a holy book; belief in a life after death, after a final judgement where God separates the good from the bad; and the conviction that the profession of the true faith contributes to individual salvation in the life hereafter. Also, in all three religions faith contains not only metaphysical ideas but a clear view of life and the world as well. (Orthodox) Jews and Muslims go furthest in this: for them, all of life – internal and external, private and public – is impregnated with religion, and ethical precepts and courses of action for individual dealings in the political, economic and social fields are borrowed from religion. Strictly speaking, Islam makes no distinction between secular and religious law: Islam has only *sharia*, the body of regulations for living, held to be in accordance with God's will. Islam similarly makes no distinction, at least in theory, between secular and spiritual authority. In the early Middle Ages the caliph, as direct successor of the Prophet, was both head of state and leader of the Islamic religious community (*umma* in Arabic; compare with the Christian *ecclesia*). The *umma* dwelt in the 'House of Islam' (*Dar al-Islam*) which was rigidly divided from the hostile outside world, the 'House of War' (*Dar al-Harb*). Thus Islam created for the first time in Arab society a focus of strong loyalty above and beyond the clan or the grouping of kinship. Without this new bond the spectacular Arab conquests would have been inconceivable.

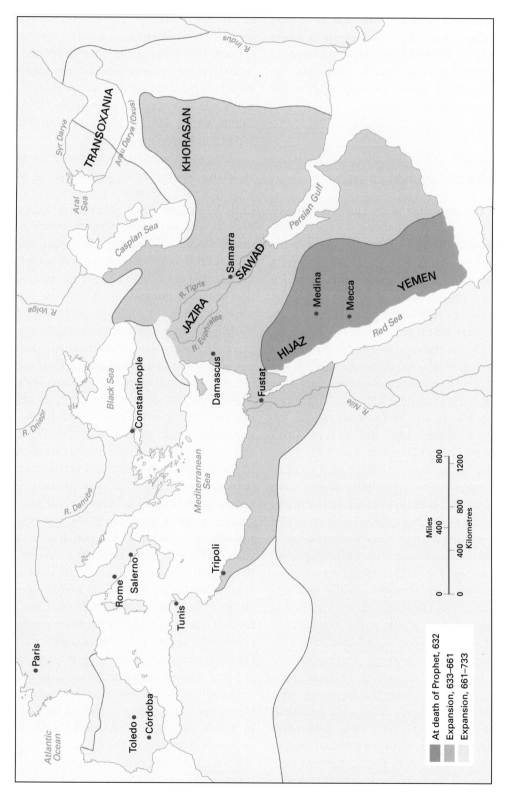

MAP 2.2 The rise of the Arab Empire, 632–733

From the very beginning Islam had its own book, the Qur'an (*Qur'ân* means 'what has been recited'), the record of Allah's revelation to the Prophet Mohammed. According to the Arab tradition, the text of the Qur'an was laid down in its present, definitive form around 650. Several of the 114 chapters or *suras* stress that Allah revealed himself to Mohammed in Arabic. For orthodox Muslims this meant until recently that the Qur'an could only be read, listened to, recited and reproduced in Arabic. This resulted in a wide dissemination of Arabic as a 'higher' language in lands where Arabic was not and is not spoken at all. The Qur'an was translated into Latin shortly before 1150. Not much later, Peter the Venerable, abbot of the famous Benedictine abbey at Cluny, prided himself on the fact that he had read the Qur'an, and during the late Middle Ages there was for some time a centre for Qur'anic studies in Barcelona. Of course, this was not entirely out of purely academic interest but rather under the motto, 'know your enemy so that you can better fight him'.

In addition to the Qur'an, Islam recognises various other sources of religious authority. The most important of these form the *sira* or official biography of Mohammed and the so-called hadith, a body of sayings and deeds ascribed to the Prophet himself. They were collected and memorised during his lifetime by the 'Companions', the people close to him. Then for centuries they were passed down by word of mouth in unbroken chains (*asānīd* or *sanad*) from generation to generation, so that there were eventually tens of thousands of hadith in circulation. In about 850 two revised compilations were put into writing, quite independently of each other, which since then have become the standard corpus. Taken together, the *sira* and the hadith comprise the *sunnat al-Nabi* ('customs of the Prophet'), *soenna* for short, whence derives 'Sunni' for those who hold to the *soenna*.

Unlike Catholic Christianity Islam does not have a hierarchic clergy. In principle the establishment of what is true has been made dependent on individual exegesis and even nowadays,

competent teachers of the Qur'an enjoy great social respect in Muslim communities. On the other hand, the danger of confusion and heterodoxy is inherent in the same principle. Islam has countered that with the formation of a limited number of recognised schools of exegesis, the *madhhab*. The same is true for another important aspect of Islamic religious studies, the *fiqh* ('meditation'), which deals with the study of Islamic law.

The ethical aspects of Islam are rigorously elaborated and explicitly bound to the notion of God. Some Orientalists, therefore, refer to Islam as 'orthopractical' rather than 'orthodox'. The religious-ethical duties are described simply and precisely. The five so-called 'pillars of the faith' are central: (1) the public confession of the belief in Allah and his Prophet; (2) regular recital of prayers; (3) giving alms to the poor; (4) fasting in the month of Ramadan; and (5) making a pilgrimage to Mecca at least once in a lifetime. Among the less precisely described obligations is *jihad*. It is often translated as a 'holy war', but it literally means 'effort' or 'striving', defined as the 'effort to spread the laws of Allah and Islam over the earth'. Force of arms is just one of the instruments through which this duty of effort can be fulfilled. There are also innumerable instructions relating to everyday life. Because this changes with time and differs according to culture, more enlightened Islamic scholars have advocated that a distinction be made between sacrosanct dogmas and religious precepts on the one hand and adaptable rules for moral living and social intercourse on the other.

Despite its emphasis on tradition, universality, comprehensiveness and ethical pragmatism, Islam has not succeeded in keeping *Dar al-Islam* one and undivided. The most important split dates from the problematical years following the Prophet's death in 632, when a significant minority was in favour of the succession of Ali, a first cousin of Mohammed who was also married to his daughter, Fatima. Eventually, Ali was made caliph, but the seeds of discord had been sown, and a hard core of malcontents was formed who believed that only Ali and his descendants could be the true heirs to the Prophet. By the end of the ninth century, this resulted in the formation of a broad separatist movement, the 'party of Ali', (*shi'at 'Ali* in Arabic), whose adherents were called Shi'ites and which had, and still has, a particularly large following in Iraq and Iran. The Shi'ites do not reject the *soenna*, but they have their own tradition and their own spiritual leader appointed by Allah himself, the Imam, who must be a direct descendant of one of the two sons of Ali. There were more splits within Shi'ism, even before 1500. The so-called 'Twelvers' only recognised the authority of twelve Imams, whose graves (for example, at Nadjaf and Kerbela in Iraq) are the most holy objects of pilgrimage and prayer. According to the Twelvers the twelfth Imam, or Mahdi, is immortal. This Mohammed al-Muntazar disappeared around 875 and has lived in hiding ever since. One day he will reveal himself and reclaim his authority over the true Islam, unsullied by Sunni blemishes. A second breakaway movement, the Ismaili, named after Ismail, the son of the sixth Imam, Jafar al-Sadiq (*c.*760), was created by the desert Bedouin of Syria and north Arabia who were dissatisfied with the rule of the Abbasids.

But the problems that accompanied the rapid Arab expansion were not only caused by questions of succession and religious dissent. Most were related to the control of the enormous area that the Arab armies had conquered. As the Arab population was small there could be no question of intense territorial occupation and thus, if they did not return home, the Arab warriors established themselves in towns and villages as a ruling upper class. In that respect the Arab conquests resembled those of the northern barbarians in some parts of Europe. But there are also substantial differences. The Arabs exposed themselves to social and cultural integration far more slowly than the barbarians in the West. Initially, the Arabs did not impose their religion, Islam, on the conquered populations. They strove rather to retain their ethnic purity, and in all probability

for a long time succeeded in this. In contrast, the Arabs learnt a lot about local government and administration from the Byzantines and Persians. No barbarian kingdom in the West came close to the highly developed administrative system in the Arab Empire.

In order to support themselves the Arab soldier-immigrants in the conquered regions of the Middle East received an allowance from the taxes that the subjected peoples had to raise. The inequality in the fiscal treatment of Arab and non-Arab Muslims was a particular cause of tension. Arabs were not required to pay taxes although they were obliged to give alms (Arabic, *sadaqa*), officially for the poor. Non-Arab converts paid a heavy land and poll tax, and in that respect were treated no differently from those who had not converted. This situation was ended at the beginning of the eighth century when Arab and non-Arab Muslims were treated alike for tax purposes – which greatly encouraged conversion to Islam. But the Arab upper class continued to monopolise military and administrative power, and this finally became unacceptable to the native elites. Abu-Abbas al-Saffah, scion of another house of Mecca that was related to the Prophet, took advantage of this disaffection to stir up rebellion against the Umayyads in the north-east of Iran. The rising was successful and led to the establishment in 750 of the caliphate of the Abbasids, who had a new capital built on the Tigris – Baghdad – that would grow into one of the largest cities in the world.

The Abbasids pursued a rigorous policy of centralisation which led to even more bureaucracy. The policy stood or fell by the effectiveness of the means of exercising power that the caliphs had at their disposal, in particular military support from the Iranians who had helped the Abbasids gain control. Regional separatism lay dormant everywhere. At the beginning of the ninth century things started to go wrong and a long period of civil war and revolts broke out. One consequence was that the Sawad, the fertile southern part of Mesopotamia where Baghdad itself was situated, fell into serious economic decline, threatening the caliphs' most important source of income. Some caliphs tried to turn the tide by taking reformative measures. Al-Mutasim (833–842) was the first to experiment with armies composed of non-Arab warriors from distant border territories (Turks, Armenians, Kurds, Berbers). This was the beginning of what was to be a long tradition in the Islamic world, where the nucleus of the army consisted increasingly of non-Arab elite corps, and it would not be long before the commanders of these corps became part of the ruling elite. As in medieval Europe this development was connected to the professionalisation of warfare and the growing importance of cavalry. Turkish nomads and Berber Bedouin were particularly sought after, because they were excellent, tough horsemen. During the tenth century the Arabic system of *mamluks* (slaves) came into being: mounted soldiers of non-free status were placed in moderate-sized companies under their own commander, who paid them and whom they had to obey. A second measure intended to deal with the crisis was the issue of what is known as *iqta*. These were contracts in which the state revenues (taxes, domain produce, etc.) within a certain district were lent for a short period to a person of high standing, who during that period exercised both civil and military authority in that area. In exchange, the holder of the *iqta,* if he held a military command, had to pay his troops from the proceeds.

After the first quarter of the tenth century not much authority remained with the caliph of Baghdad. His military commander-in-chief was now in charge and took the title *amir al-umara* (literally meaning 'leader of leaders'). From the second half of the tenth century this position was practically monopolised by the Buyids, a family originating south of the Caspian Sea but which had created its own kingdom in west and central Iran. The Buyids probably encouraged the Islamic Shi'ite tradition, thus lending valuable support to the development of Shi'ism into a real force within the Islamic faith. This led to a sharpening of religious differences in Iraq, because the caliphs tended to take the side of the Sunnis.

The fact that the Buyids were able to create their own kingdom was symptomatic of the collapse of the united Arab Empire – which in fact already had a precedent in 750 when the last of the Umayyads fled from Damascus to Spain, where the dynasty would remain in power for many centuries without paying much heed to Baghdad. In the tenth century numerous small principalities in the Middle East, which were still more or less loyal to the caliph, worked themselves loose from Baghdad. The Arabs no longer imposed themselves on the vast area that they had once conquered. From then on Islam was the unifying force, while the Arab language remained in use in prayer and administration.

In the border area of the north, in particular, political fragmentation resulted in a serious weakening of the military; the small kingdoms of Armenian, Georgian and Kurd rulers bore the brunt respectively of renewed Byzantine aggression and of Turkish nomads who at the beginning of the eleventh century left the Caspian steppe and pushed into eastern Iraq and Anatolia by way of Turkmenistan. On the other hand, the regionalism brought opportunities for the formation of strong, new cores, as the rise of the Fatimids shows. The Fatimids were the descendants of a Syrian leader from an Ismaili Shi'ite sect, who had proclaimed himself Imam shortly before 900. Soon afterwards he fled to Ifriqiya (approximately modern-day Tunisia) where the Ismaili movement had more followers than in Syria. With the support of the Kutama Berbers, who wanted nothing to do with the Arab elite, the Fatimids seized power and proclaimed themselves caliphs. Since the Umayyad ruler in Spain had reacted by doing the same, from that point on there were three caliphs. From Ifriqya the Fatimids extended their power through attacks on the Maghreb and Egypt. They conquered Egypt in 969, where they built a new capital, al-Qahira (Cairo, which literally means 'the victorious'), just four kilometres north of Fustat, the former capital of the Abbasid province of Egypt.

From Egypt the Fatimids finally advanced on Palestine and their homeland Syria. By then it had become evident that they must strengthen the military basis of their power; this they did chiefly through the *mamluk* system. The Fatimids remained in power until the middle of the eleventh century in spite of some eccentric caliphs. Among them was al-Hakim (996–1021), a dangerous psychopath whose reign of terror lasted for 25 years. His name was always uttered with loathing in the West, for in 1009 he plundered Jerusalem and destroyed the Holy Sepulchre.

The strength of the Fatimids lay in their enormous prestige; because of it succession was never a problem. Unlike the Abbasids they allowed family members to share the power as little as possible, so that the caliph would never suffer competition from his kin. They also had a tolerant attitude towards religion, never attempting to make Egypt a Shi'ite state. Finally, Egypt enjoyed great prosperity under the Fatimids. Cairo became an important transit market for trade between the Indian and African worlds on the one hand and the Mediterranean on the other. The Azhar mosque, the building of which started shortly after 969, soon developed into a great centre of learning. By the eleventh century Baghdad was no longer the beating heart of the Islamic world: Cairo had taken its place.

Because of the similarities between the three monotheistic religions, Jews and Christians – the 'peoples of the Book' as they were often called – were generally tolerated in the Islamic world. There was little pressure to immediate conversion – from that perspective the high-speed spread of Islam in the trail of Arab conquests is as illusory as the Christianisation of barbarian Europe. Islam was the religion of only a tiny minority in the Near East. In the cities, the Muslim communities were dwarfed by the civilian populations among whom they lived as a dominant military elite. The Arab leaders imported slaves on a massive scale, especially from central Asia. Thanks to the practice of concubinage and polygamy, the children of female slaves grew up in an entirely Arab and Muslim environment. Nevertheless, the Arabs had no choice but to tolerate to some extent and within narrow limits the existing religions in their conquered territories. Even under this 'sort of religious and social apartheid' (Brown 2012), Christians enjoyed a better position under Muslim rule than Muslims did in the Christian world. In medieval Europe, Christians saw Islam not as a new religion but as a reprehensible aberration of their own faith. This negative perception later expanded: then 'the sect of Mohammed' was not just seen as a heresy, but also as a punishment from God, a terrible affliction which, through their own fault, Christians had to suffer in the long progress to the Last Judgement.

Points to remember

- The early medieval period saw the firm establishment of two world religions: Christianity and Islam. Both were closely related to Judaism. Both were also at the same time activist, often militant movements and open, non-exclusive communities.
- Three important factors behind the success of the Church in the early medieval period were its close association to secular rulers, its virtual monopoly on literacy and its institutional wealth, which had three main sources: imperial and royal funds, donations by rich believers who wanted to secure eternal salvation by giving to the 'poor' and tithes paid by the peasant populations.
- Christian bishops were key figures in the often chaotic early medieval world; they were not only leaders of local churches, but they also were essential for the upkeep of secular governance.
- Christian kings in the early Middle Ages had a caesaropapist conception of royal authority, that is, they regarded themselves as the leaders of the Church in their kingdom.
- Countless examples of syncretism prove that the Christian faith in the early Middle Ages

took shape in a confrontational mixture of top-down imposition of dogma, ritual and moral admonition, and bottom-up attachment to local traditions with respect to the supernatural.

- In the early stages of Christianisation monks, as reputed 'holy men', were essential intermediaries between the organised Church and local religious cultures.
- Early Christianity's model of sanctity was provided by the martyrs of the faith. After the persecutions of Christians had stopped, two groups claimed the inheritance of the 'holy martyrs': first and foremost the monks (by heroic withdrawal from the world), but also the bishops (as leaders who set an example of virtuous Christian behaviour in the world).
- Most of the time, Christianisation was not a neutral, purely missionary activity; more often it went hand in hand with political deals or with attempts by secular rulers at military conquest.
- The spread of Islam followed in the wake of the remarkable, Islam-inspired Arab conquests. Consequently, the fundamental openness of Islam was initially hampered by Arab racism, which was only broken in the middle of the eighth century with the Abbasid revolution.
- In the Muslim world no distinction of principle is made between political and religious leadership, or between secular and religious law.

Suggestions for further reading

Brown, Peter (2012), *Through the Eye of a Needle: Wealth, the Fall of Rome, and the Making of Christianity in the West, 350–550 AD* (Princeton/Oxford: Princeton University Press, 2012). Sublime examination of the roots of the crucial relationship between the wealth of the Christian Church and the Christian idea about eternal salvation, which marked the victory of Christianity in the West in the centuries after Constantine.

Dunn, Marilyn (2000), *The Emergence of Monasticism: From the Desert Fathers to the Early Middle Ages* (Oxford/Malden MA: Blackwell). Succinct and useful survey of the early history of monasticism, with due attention given to the main monastic traditions that took shape in the West (including Ireland and England), as well as to the role of women.

Fletcher, Richard (1997), *The Conversion of Europe: From Paganism to Christianity 371–1386 AD* (London: Harper Collins). Robust attempt at covering, region by region, the entire history of Europe's Christianisation until the late fourteenth century. Its focus is on the conversion process and the establishment of churches and basic ecclesiastical institutions. It has less to say about the internalisation of the Christian faith.

Kennedy, Hugh (2004; 2nd revised edition), *The Prophet and the Age of the Caliphates: The Islamic Near East from the Sixth to the Eleventh Century* (London/New York: Routledge). Remains to date the standard treatment in English of the rise of Islam, the Arab conquests, and the establishment of the Arab Muslim caliphate until the beginning of the eleventh century.

Macmullen, Ramsay (1997), *Christianity and Paganism in the Fourth to Eighth Centuries* (New Haven/London: Yale University Press). Elegant, well-written discussion of the confrontation between Christianity and pre-Christian religions in the late and post-Roman world. Its keyword is assimilation rather than syncretism.

3 The powerful and the poor: society and economy in the Frankish kingdoms and beyond

The turbulence of the Migration Period and the great epidemics of plague in the sixth century left behind a western world that was emptier and more desolate than it had been in the later years of the Roman Empire. Soil research shows that in many parts of Europe the forests increased during the fifth and sixth centuries, as did various forms of pastoralism. A large number of archaeological findings point to a sharp fall in settlement density. Estimates of overall population decline in post-Roman Gaul, Italy and Spain were in the order of 50 per cent, and some remote and forested areas, such as the Ardennes, may even have lost all their population for a while. It is important to realise how much this affected the so-called land–labour ratio. Because there was plenty of land, to become a large landowner was less of a problem than to bring land to productive value, for which scarce labour was indispensable. Therefore, the real challenge for the mighty

few was to control the labour of the majority poor rather than to grab land. By and large they succeeded in attaining that goal. First of all, in the long run – that is to say, seen over the half millennium covered by the early medieval period – peasants lost a significant amount of their hold on land in favour of aristocratic large landowners (including kings and ecclesiastical institutions). Specialists on the period do not hesitate to speak of a complete transformation of the dominant mode of production: from a peasant mode to a 'feudal' or aristocratic mode. Its essence was a substantial increase in the transfer of agrarian surpluses from peasants to aristocratic lords under non-economic (non-commercial), 'political' pressure. However, and this will be the second major point to be made in this chapter, this transformation was not a bad thing in many respects. It did create the seed-bed for substantial demographic and economic growth. For many years the entire period from 500 to 1000 was depicted as a time of demographic stagnation, but that view has been revised. Nowadays, one tends to think in terms of a slow but sure recovery that started in the West around the beginning of the seventh century. A cautious estimate suggests that the population of western Europe doubled between 600 and 1000 from about 12 million to 24 million. During the same period, a remarkable recovery of commercial exchange is visible, even if this took the form of long-distance trade within trade networks of low complexity, primarily aimed at providing a small elite with expensive prestige objects.

The key to our understanding of this transformation was the collapse of the Roman tax state. Despite attempts by the stronger of the barbarian kings to maintain taxation, all had failed by the end of the sixth century. This failure had severe consequences. To begin with, in early medieval kingdoms there was no room for a Roman-style professional army, civic infrastructure, lavish court, sizeable bureaucracy or large cities with proletarian populations that had to be fed on state expenses. This also meant that alternative solutions had to be found for creating a 'public order'. An obvious one was to involve wealthy people with authority in public government without necessarily paying them, or even just to privatise certain aspects of public government on a local level; another was to impose on all adult free subjects public obligations in such areas as (para)military service, maintenance of vital infrastructure and participation in local government and jurisdiction. One can easily be sceptical about the viability of arrangements of that kind, but some early medieval polities were remarkably successful in upholding a public order without having regular tax revenues at their disposal, not only relatively centralised monarchies like the Frankish kingdoms, but also the extraordinary, headless 'Free State' Iceland, which took shape after the North Atlantic island had been colonised by Norwegian settlers in the last decades of the ninth century (see below). The

drawback was that in these practically tax-free polities the social elite had to obtain income in other, more direct, and sometimes forcible and arbitrary ways: from booty, tribute, labour or land rent. The effects for the direct producers, overwhelmingly peasants in early medieval societies, could diverge widely: in sparsely populated areas with low aristocratic presence hardly, if any, surplus had to be handed over to whatever overlord there was – which could even lead to an extension of leisure. At the other extreme were those peasants who were tied to the land of powerful landlords who could exact heavy payments and services.

Warlords and landlords

The early medieval aristocracy

Early medieval Europe was a peasant society dominated by a warrior aristocracy, that is to say, by a social elite that thought of itself as superior to ordinary people only because of its blood, its wealth and its reputation in battle, and for all these reasons claimed a 'natural' disposition to lord over others. Whether or not to term this aristocracy a 'nobility' is primarily a question of definition. References to early medieval aristocrats point variously to prominence (*procures*, the princes), wealth (*divites*, the rich), political and military power (*potentes*, the powerful) and freedom-independence (*liberi*). All these qualities were held to be transferable. They were thus seen to be attributes of families rather than of individuals. But birth alone was not enough. Aristocratic qualities had to be proved and constantly re-affirmed, and aristocratic preponderance had to be expressed in the possession of lordship, either as 'senior' over (other) free men or as master of all sorts of dependent people and slaves. In that sense, throughout the whole of the Middle Ages, nobility was always a combination of birth, wealth, achievement and lifestyle.

Society was less aristocratic in the first half of the early Middle Ages than it had been before or would (again) become afterwards. At the same time it was more aristocratic – and aristocratic in a different way – in the barbarian kingdoms on former Roman territory than in the Celtic, Scandinavian and Slav lands beyond the old Rhine–Danube frontier. Of the 'supraregional imperial aristocracy of service' with its 'mandarin life-style' (Sarris 2011) that ruled the later Roman Empire, not much was left in the sixth century. Their successors in the barbarian kingdoms of the West had a different outlook. Like before, illustrious descent, landed wealth, the exercise of public offices, and strong and continuous personal links to king and court as the main avenue to further accumulation of wealth and political influence (also called **Königsnähe**, lit. 'closeness to the king') had remained the mainstay of aristocratic power. But there were two notable differences as well that found their origins in the specific circumstances of the Migration Period. One was the military background of a large number of the new leading families while at the same time a Roman-style military organisation was absent. This meant that the core of early medieval armies consisted of the personal retinues of wealthy aristocrats, who as a result had a decidedly militaristic outlook. The other was the crucial importance of the Church and its clergy for the functioning of public governance, in particular at the local level. Consequently, aristocratic families in the early medieval West had to divide their interests between the military and civil-ecclesiastical ranges of influence, which gave them a double-edged, if not schizophrenic, quality. Not surprisingly, the early Middle Ages produced both martial heroes of epic dimension and numerous aristocratic saints (*Adelsheiligen* in German).

Of all the early states on former Roman territory, the Merovingian kingdoms of Frankish Gaul fit this prototype best. Powerful families had possessions and political interests everywhere, but the concentration of aristocratic estates was largest in the Paris basin, where in the Merovingian period the economic and social difference between aristocrats and peasants was already immense. In Lombard Italy, on the other hand, the aristocracy was far more localised and, in addition, city-based. Consequently, towns from early on became centres of political and social power that extended over the countryside. At the same time, the Lombard aristocracy was, on average, less wealthy than its Frankish counterpart, and high status was derived from office-holding rather than ancestry. By implication, in Italy ordinary free men with landed possessions of modest size retained a stronger social and economic position. Aquitaine and Visigothic Spain had an intermediate position. Classical, less martial, Roman traditions for aristocratic wealth and lifestyle were better maintained there, while at the same time aristocratic power, as in Italy, was more localised than north of the Loire river.

By contrast, the barbarian world beyond the borders of the former Roman Empire had preserved more of its prehistoric character of small-scale, thinly populated chiefdom societies, of which the free peasant was the backbone but whose most conspicuous features were local warlords and their *Gefolgschaften*. Such personal retinues of warriors were called *lið* in early medieval Scandinavia, and *druzhina* in Slavic languages. The intimacy of the relationship between chief and followers can be sampled in the Old English epic poem *Beowulf*, which probably originated around 800 in the Anglo-Saxon kingdom of Mercia. When the eponymous hero, at the beginning of the tale, arrives at the court of Hrodgar, king of the Geats (Jutes?), he enters a conveniently arranged, even somewhat cosy, universe, centred around the royal 'hall' – more a decorated barn than a palace – where the king's retainers are received and fed and where his wife, the queen, politely passes around mead and beer. Such a structure could only remain intact in its purest form when scale of recruitment and scale of action were small, and when there were always wars to wage. In general, and tautologically, only war could give warriors a raison d'être (including a living) and only war could keep in place the system of gift-exchange and redistribution of wealth that was central to the functioning of the early medieval type of aristocratic society (see below). But one only has to compare the royal hall of Yeavering (Northumbria) – which had a wooden theatre in Roman style, nonetheless – with Charlemagne's palaces at Aachen and Ingelheim to feel the difference in splendour and scope of ambition between the world of barbarian warlords in the north and the world of 'civilised', but no less warlike, kings in the south.

Although sparse written sources are quick to qualify the warlords of northern and central Europe as 'kings' or 'dukes', the extent of their power was really quite limited. In Celtic Wales, there would have been four greater and seven smaller 'kingdoms' by the seventh century, while early medieval Ireland famously had 150 *túatha* ('peoples') that corresponded with as many kingdoms, ruled by *rí* ('kings'), who at times were subordinated to powerful men claiming to be 'great king' (*riuri*), 'king of great kings' (*ri riuirech*) or 'high king' (*ard rí*). In chiefdom societies of that scale, the social and legal distance between aristocrats and common free men were not unbridgeable. In Anglo-Saxon England ordinary free men (*ceorls*) sometimes had the same *wergeld* – the compensation money that had to be paid for killing or severely injuring a person – as (ordinary) noblemen (*thegns*); all depended on their respective wealth, and a point could be reached at which a *ceorl* was openly recognised as a *thegn*. But things changed fast in the seventh century. Numismatic evidence indicates that Anglo-Saxon England had a positive balance of payments with continental Francia. It means that its rural economy produced surplus (including metals and woollen textiles) that could be tapped and traded, and the Anglo-Saxon elite profited visibly, as can be seen in a number of hoards and treasures from this time.

The huge part of central and eastern Europe where people who spoke Slav and Baltic languages lived remains far more obscure. The archaeological traces they left – in so far as they can be identified as Slav or Baltic – betray a simple, rather primitive material culture and a flat society with little social articulation. In his description of the Slav groups that turned up at the Danube frontier around the middle of the sixth century, the Greek historian Procopius even uses the word 'democracy': that would have been how the Slavs ruled themselves, although towards their enemies they were extremely cruel and murderous. Early Slav settlements had simple buildings: sunken-floored huts, undefined pit-houses and a 'generally nondescript material culture' (Barford 2001). Relics of rites and religion clearly point to polytheistic convictions, including the still immensely popular vampire-myth, that were reinforced when conversion to Christianity led to replacing cremation of dead bodies by inhumation. The earliest traces of settlement enclosures and wooden strongholds date back to the seventh century. They are indicative of a gradual increase in the range of political action and the extent of social unrest that went with it. At that point in time the first Slav warlords appear in written sources, such as 'king' Samo, the leader of a successful Slav revolt against the Avars in 623. He was of Frankish origin and established a strong, supra-local lordship that existed for no less than about four decades.

Arguably the most exciting experiment in creating *ex nihilo* a new society and a new state took place far beyond the former frontier of the Roman Empire, in Iceland. Iceland was colonised by Norsemen from Norway and the British Isles in the decades after 870. In this desolate environment, a relatively flat and egalitarian society of (predominantly) free peasants (*bœndr*) took shape without the aid of a social blueprint or Christian ideology. They were led by an aristocracy of local chieftains called *goðar* (singular *goði*), whose most important function was more political than military, but who did not have a fixed district; followers of various *goðar* in the same area usually lived interspersed. Neither in wealth nor in social distinction did *goðar* differ very much from their constituents, and in principle, any free man could become a *goði* just as he had been free in his choice of to which *goði* he was going to give suit. To become *goði* one just had to bind (which often meant: 'to buy') a certain number of supporters. Because the *goðar* were responsible for organising local *things* (courts of justice), they played a key part in the settlement of disputes and conflicts, and redistributed part of their wealth through acts of hospitality, loans, gift-giving and public feasts. However, for specific activities, such as the common use of grazing land and the organisation of local poor relief, separate and self-governing local communities existed apart from the *goðar*. Iceland did not have a king or any other overlord formally until 1262–1264, when the 'period of the Free State' ended, and the king of Norway was recognised as lord of Iceland. Despite being a headless polity, and although armed violence certainly was not absent, Free State Iceland did not have an army (there were no enemies!); there were no real wars, no pitched battles, no military campaigns, no large-scale destructions. The only tax *bœndr* paid to *goðar* was called the *thingfararkaup* ('payment for travelling to the *thing*/court'), a yearly remuneration of the *goðar*'s expenses to visit the Althing, Iceland's general assembly. One of the reasons behind Iceland's success as a state was its extreme legalism: everything had to be done in strict accordance with precisely defined rules, which led to 'a self-limiting pattern of state formation' (Byock 2001).

Honour and blood

In early medieval Europe, honour was an important concept, whose essence was the recognised value of a family – more so than of an individual – within a larger society that always had to be defended, no matter what the cost. There is no reason to suppose that honour in this sense only counted for the social elite, but obviously the stakes of defending family honour were much higher for aristocrats than for peasants. This appears most clearly from cases of homicide and grave physical injury. Then the families of a victim felt not only justified but also duty-bound to compensate for the harm done by inflicting commensurate damage on the perpetrator or a member of his family of equal standing. In principle, early medieval law allowed them to do so, provided they had a free status. However, more often than actually taking vengeance, with its risk of retaliation leading to an endless cycle of feuding, families of victims chose to have their damage compensated with a payment of money known as **wergeld** (literally 'man money'). To determine the exact amount of *wergeld* that had to be paid by the perpetrator and his relatives to the victim (if still alive) and his family, there were long price lists that took account of variables such as the sex and legal status of victims, and the nature of the injury inflicted. Once *wergeld* had been duly paid the families of perpetrator and victim were expected to be reconciled and live in friendship, because they had no reason to reproach each other any longer. Peace then reigned between them; if this peace was broken the king imposed harsh punishments.

This highly institutionalised system of compensatory payments indicates two things. One is that homicide and inflicting grave physical injury were not necessarily seen as crimes that should be dealt with by punishing the perpetrator, and him alone. Rather, they were subjected to a symbolical transaction between kin groups; the aim was to restore honour by letting the perpetrator and his relatives publicly pay off vengeance. The other thing is that precisely the survival of countless detailed regulations with regard to wergeld payments suggests that acts of violence that could lawfully arouse retaliation were normally expected to be settled in public law courts. In that situation, blood vengeance, even in a headless state such as Iceland, 'became an option rather than a duty' (Byock 2001). In the Carolingian Empire, taking vengeance was actually forbidden by law in 779.

The position of ordinary free men

In the absence of state institutions supported by tax flows, non-aristocratic, free, able-bodied men had two public obligations which in the Roman Empire had been delegated to professionals: military service and attendance at public courts of justice. In addition, local communities were responsible for the upkeep of what was left of public infrastructure (roads and bridges, in particular). For a long time after the Migration Period some sort of general conscription continued to exist in the barbarian kingdoms of the West. In Lombard Italy, this maintained its (nominally) ethnic basis into the eighth century in the sense that non-Lombard free men were not called to arms. The armies of the Frankish and Visigothic kingdoms around 600 seem to have been built up of free landowners who were all considered to be 'Franks' and 'Goths' respectively whatever their ethnic background, around a core of royal and aristocratic retinues. Under the Carolingians the mobilisation of ordinary free men for the royal levy was further reduced. Charlemagne's yearly campaigns against increasingly distant enemies lasted for months and generally took place in the busiest, and most critical, part of the agrarian year. On top of this all warriors had to bring horses and provide their own supplies during the campaigns. At the beginning of the ninth century Charlemagne took steps to limit military service for ordinary free men. After that, only those who owned more than a certain amount of land had to join the army in person: free peasants who had less land either took turns at military service or were jointly responsible for equipping a warrior. Alternatively, service could be bought off by paying compensation money, called *haribannus* ('army money'), which originally must have been a penalty for non-attendance. Only when the Empire itself was invaded did the entire able-bodied male population have to take up arms in defence of the community. A similar system was introduced in Anglo-Saxon England at about the same time.

Gradually, war was again becoming a matter for well-trained specialists, who had to have the resources to devote themselves full-time to the practice of arms, to breed and feed a number of horses, and to purchase expensive weapons and armour.

We can see a parallel development in the administration of justice in the Carolingian Empire. The Franks originally required all free men to attend all sessions of the public court of justice (*mallus*) in their county, even if they were not involved in a suit. At the same time, the formulation of verdicts now came into the hands of small, permanent benches of judges known as *scabini* (aldermen) – not to be confused with their namesakes in later medieval towns; as far as we know, the Carolingian *scabini* were always aristocrats and dealt with cases coming from a wide area, usually a whole county.

Joining the army and attending court sessions were not only cumbersome (and dangerous) obligations; they also attributed honour to ordinary free men and they provided them with suitable venues to mobilise patronage of the powerful (and there are examples of free peasants who belonged to the clientele of an aristocrat). From that perspective, the discharge of public duties meant the loss of a chance of upward mobility. Characteristically, after that point in time, ordinary free men in Carolingian sources are often referred to as *pauperi* ('poor men'), not necessarily because of their poverty, but because of their powerlessness. In addition to this dichotomic division into *liberi* ('free men' but meaning aristocrats) and *pauperi*, a fixed tripartition in 'estates' (*ordines* in Latin) was becoming increasingly evident: there were people who prayed (clerics), people who fought and people who did manual work. There was no doubt that peasants – free or not – belonged to the third category and no longer to the second. The first texts in which this comes to the fore are the monk Heiric of Auxerre's *Miracula Sancti Germani* ('Miracles of St Germain', *c*.870), and the Anglo-Saxon translation of Boethius' *De consolatione filosofiae* ('The Consolation of Philosophy'), made for King Alfred the Great of Wessex (871–899).

Tenancy, serfdom and slavery

This gradual social degradation of ordinary free men was further reinforced by the fact that many of them were, or ended up as, tenants of aristocratic large landowners. As we saw, in the course of the early Middle Ages more of the wealth of kings, aristocrats and religious institutions (bishoprics, abbeys) was tied up in large landownership. Consequently, more peasants became enmeshed in a tenurial relationship with the social elite. Early medieval tenancy is in no way to be compared with modern leasehold, in which the lease price is ultimately determined by the law of supply and demand, and both lessor and lessee are free to end their purely contractual relationship. Early medieval tenancy was different in two essential ways. First, the nature and weight of the rent (as the neutral designation of the recompense given by the peasant to his landlord) varied widely because they were determined by the arbitrary decision of landlords who could, or could not, consider ingrained local custom. Consequently, the terms of tenancy even on one and the same holding could vary widely, as could the nature of the rent: labour rent, rent in kind or rent in coin all depended on the needs of the landlord and the topographical structure of his estates.

It is possible to distinguish long-term trends in tenancy as well. On most large estates in Merovingian Gaul, peasant tenants received small parcels of land against rent in kind. Labour services were still absent, which is a sign of extensive land use. Only the eighth century saw a return to more intensification. Landlords started to reserve parts of their estates for direct exploitation ('**demesnes**') and demand labour services of their tenants to work the demesne. This was partly the consequence of the relative shortage of labour, and partly linked to the regular expeditions of large armies that needed to be fed. Because of the shortage of labour, powerful lords tried to tie tenant-peasants to the land, which meant that they were not free to leave. Being tied to the land of a powerful man (or ecclesiastical institution) implied a further measure of personal dependency that would be totally unacceptable in modern leasehold relationships: medieval landlords administered justice (to some degree) over their tenants, that is to say, they normally settled disputes and punished small breaches of local custom. It is difficult to gauge the basis of these rights: probably, aristocrats (meaning 'better men') just thought of themselves as having a natural right to 'lord over' ordinary people. In this connection German historians speak of **Grundherrschaft**, which, by stressing the old 'lordship' part, has a completely different connotation from the modern English 'landlord[ship]'. By modern standards private interests and elements of the exercise of public authority were inextricably linked with these lordly rights.

Because extant sources very much favour the social elite it is extremely difficult, even for the relatively well-documented Carolingian Empire, to determine what percentage of the free peasantry ended up losing its freedom because they became tenants of aristocratic lords. Free men could voluntarily submit themselves and their land to powerful lords because they needed protection. Conversely, there must have been plenty of opportunities for aristocrats to take over plots of land of free commoners. All we can say is that substantial numbers of small peasants lost their freedom in the course of the early Middle Ages because they became tied to the land of large landowners and, through that, subordinated to these landlords' power. Peasant-tenants with such a status are usually called serfs (or **villeins**) in modern literature, which is a translation of *servi* in the sources of the time, the classical Latin word for slaves.

However, medieval serfs can be compared to the slaves of Antiquity just as little as they can be compared to modern leaseholders. This is not to say that there were no slaves in the early Middle

Ages. On the contrary, slavery was an institution that was present everywhere, both inside and outside former Roman territory – even on Iceland. The interminable petty warfare between warlords, however, and the yearly campaigns kings undertook against foreign enemies ensured a constant supply of human cattle in the slave markets of western Europe. Slaves were just about the only export article of any value in the thriving Christian trade with the Islamic world. In time the region occupied by the still pagan Slavs was the major source, hence the word 'slave', a dubious honour in naming, in which the Celtic Britons were ahead of the Slavs (in early medieval times 'briton' was another word for 'slave'). The great slave markets then moved eastwards, to towns such as Mainz and Prague, with Venice as their main outlet on the Mediterranean. In addition to these organised man-hunts the slave population was replenished by those wretches who through poverty or debt were forced to sell themselves or their children, or who were enslaved as a punishment.

Another misconception is that the early Christian Church spoke out explicitly against the institution of slavery. That, too, is incorrect. The Church Fathers in fact considered slavery to be proof of the great wickedness of those who found themselves in that deplorable situation. Important dignitaries and institutions of the Church themselves possessed large numbers of slaves. The Church was clearly morally ambiguous in the matter, however, and Christianity did indeed contribute to the radical disappearance of slavery from Christian Europe. From the beginning Christianity had welcomed the unfree. Even though slaves were looked upon as second-class Christians who were not allowed to hold priestly office, for example, they were nonetheless members of the Christian community, fellow Christians and thus fellow men. This sort of reasoning was an enormous advance on the ancient view of slaves as beasts or machines. *Instrumentum vocale*, 'tool-with-a-voice', was a common classical designation for a slave.

Following that, Church leaders took over certain Stoic ideas concerning slavery. One of these ideas was that although the institution of slavery may have been unavoidable, that in itself was no reason to treat slaves inhumanely; another, that regularly manumitting slaves contributed to an individual's moral edification. Many abbots, bishops and devout noblewomen enhanced their saintliness through the formal liberation of slaves. Finally, from the eighth century onwards, Church leaders started to prohibit outright the sale of Christian slaves to pagans, but the fact that such appeals were repeated time and again during the eighth and ninth centuries creates the impression that they were not immediately effective. Implicitly, the Church allowed slave holding by Christian owners, who would not endanger the slaves' religion.

Still, even if slavery did not disappear immediately and completely, certain socio-cultural and economic factors contributed to a relative improvement in the treatment of slaves. The major incentive was no doubt an economic one: the structural labour shortage in a situation of low population density. On the one hand, this scarcity led to the accelerated spread of labour-saving technology, such as water-mills – an invention of the first century before Christ – which relieved slave labour, and to some extent made it unnecessary. On the other hand, the landowning elite found it extremely convenient to bring as much as possible of the land on their estates under cultivation and to keep it so. One method of doing this was to give a slave a small plot of land with a small house on an estate. By this upgrading in the socio-economic position of slaves the difference between slaves and other peasants settled on estates tended to become blurred.

Large landownership and manorialism

In the early medieval Frankish kingdoms, large landownership could be huge. Bertrand, scion

BOX 3.1 MASTER AND SLAVE EVEN UNTIL DEATH

In the second decade of the tenth century Ibn Fadhlan, an envoy of the caliph of Baghdad, made a journey through the Volga region where he came into contact with a group of Vikings (*Rus*). Never had he come across filthier people amongst all of Allah's creatures: 'They do not wash even after they have relieved nature or had sex, nor do they clean themselves after they have eaten.' The tall, fair-haired men were tattooed from head to toe, always carried arms and shamelessly copulated in public with slave-girls. Ibn Fadhlan also witnessed the funeral preparations of a dead chief:

> When a chief dies his slaves and servants are asked who is prepared to follow him into death. Whoever volunteers cannot go back on the decision. In this case a woman volunteered. She was treated with much respect while preparations for the cremation went ahead. On the day of the cremation the chief's boat was pulled up on to land and the people walked around it muttering all sorts of words. An old woman who was called the 'Angel of Death' placed a bier covered in rugs and cushions on the boat. She was responsible for all the preparations. The dead body, which had been kept in a burial pit for ten days, was brought out and dressed in splendid robes made especially for the occasion. Then this corpse was stood among the cushions in the tent that had been erected on the ship over the bier. The dead chief was provided with alcoholic drink, food, aromatic herbs and all his arms. Then a dog, two horses, two cows, a cock and a hen were killed and placed on the ship.
>
> The woman who was going to die went to all the tents in the camp and had sex with the owner of each tent, who then said: 'Tell your lord and master that I do this out of affection for him.' Then she completed various rituals. A circle of warriors lifted her up three times above something resembling a door post. The first time she said, 'Look, I see my father and mother'; the second time, 'I see all my dead kinsfolk together'; and the third time, 'I see my master sitting in paradise; it is green and beautiful there, he is surrounded by men and slaves and he is calling me. Lead me to him.' Then she killed a chicken and was taken to the ship where she removed all her jewellery, drained two goblets and sang a song. Finally she was taken to the tent of her dead master, and when she hesitated she was roughly pushed inside by the Angel of Death. Six warriors followed her in and had sex with her. Then she was placed next to her master and killed. Two of the warriors held her feet, two her hands, and two strangled her with a cord, while the Angel of Death stabbed her repeatedly in the breast until she gave up the ghost. The dead chief's closest relatives set fire to the firewood under the boat. Others threw flaming branches on to the fire and within an hour everything had been burnt. Then

they covered the remains with earth and on the hill they put a post with the name of the chief and the name of their king, who dwelt in the fortified place called Kyawh (Kiev).

Ibn Fadhlan's description of the Vikings' barbaric appearance and their customs clearly contains a number of stereotypes from ancient geography. But archaeological finds in Scandinavia have confirmed several of the unlikely sounding details from the story of the cremation. The graves of men of high status often contain double interments of master and slave, as can be seen in the sketch of the contents of a double grave found near Stengade on the Danish island of Langeland. The left-hand skeleton must be that of the master, the right-hand one that of the slave who, voluntarily or not, followed him in death, because the head of the right-hand skeleton had been severed from the body and the feet had probably been tied together. A long spear had been laid diagonally across both bodies.

Source: Text fragments from Ibn Fadhlan and illustration of the Stengade grave from Else Roesdahl, *The Vikings* (London: Penguin, 1998), pp. 34, 54–55 and 157, illustration by permission of Penguin Books, London. For a broader context, see Nizar F. Hermes, *The 'European' Other in Medieval Arabic Literature and Culture: Ninth–Twelfth Century AD* (New York: Palgrave Macmillan, 2012).

of a powerful family in Merovingian Gaul and bishop of Le Mans between 585 and 616, owned close to 300,000 hectares of land, an incredible quantity. For Charlemagne's empire there are more figures available, which tell us that in around 800 the largest abbeys were supposed to own between 3,000 and 8,000 mansi or tenant holdings – which on average, as we shall see, had something like 12 hectares of arable – middle–large abbeys between 1,000 and 2,000, and small abbeys between 300 and 400. In the same period royal vassals, that is to say, important lay aristocrats, would own between 30 and 200 peasant holdings, while a legal provision of 806 mentions the possession of 12 mansi as a minimum for sending a fully armed horseman to war.

The way in which large landownership was organised is much debated. Were large landowners predominantly owners of a myriad scattered smallholdings or were their possessions concentrated in so-called *villae* – whose meaning in early medieval documents can be both 'estate' and 'village' (two terms that are not mutually exclusive anyway)? Specialists take a middle course: really large landowners, like Bertrand of Le Mans, owned both: entire villas *and* numerous scattered small-holdings over a wide area. Another extremely rich large landowner, named Abbo, left in his last will of 739 landed possessions scattered over an area of 34,500 km^2 to the monastery of Novalesa on the Italian side of Mont Cenis.

Still, the prevalent idea has long been that the Carolingian rulers purposefully promoted a policy of having the landed possessions of large landowners, first of all the kings themselves and ecclesiastical institutions that were closely connected to them, systematically organised in concentrated, so-called bipartite **estates** or manors (*curtes* or *villicationes* in Latin), hence the term **manorial system**. These were large landed properties with a clear administrative and residential centre, known as *sala* (hall), *curia* (court) or *casa indominicata* (house of the lord). The arable lands and the meadows of a bipartite manor were divided into two parts, which were generally not equal in size. The part that the lord kept for himself, or 'in demesne', was called the lord's land (*terra indominicata*), and the part that was given to peasant-tenants in hereditary possession was known as the (peasant) holdings' land (*terra* *mansionaria*). In addition, the tenants had a limited right to use the often extensive *inculta* (woods or other waste lands) and water resources (lakes, brooks, etc.) that made part of their estate. A considerable part of what was given in return for the possession of these holdings took the form of labour service (*opera*, i.e. 'works') which the serfs who owned a farmstead (*servi casati*) supplied to cultivate the lord's land, often together with serfs who did not have a farmstead (*servi non casati*) and real slaves (*mancipia*) of the lord of the estate. Whatever the exact arrangement, the new, and innovative, element in estate management was the labour services of servile peasant-tenants.

The arable land belonging to the tenant holdings varied in size, and could be anything from less than 5 to 30 hectares. The highest figure is less than it seems, because in remote or marginal areas, much of the land lay fallow every year and the actual yields were shockingly low. Some estates, such as those of the abbey of Saint Bertin near Calais, still had some sort of standard-sized mansi of about 12 hectares around the middle of the ninth century. But, twenty years earlier, the arable fields of the free peasant holdings on the well-documented *villae* of the abbey of Saint-Germain-des-Prés around Paris already varied widely in size as a consequence of subdivision, ranging in measure from around 4.5 to more than 16 hectares.

Not every farmstead was taxed with the same labour services and dues. A distinction was frequently made between 'free holdings' (*mansi ingenuiles*) and 'unfree holdings' (*mansi serviles*), probably stemming from differences in the legal status of the original peasant-owner. Free holdings were generally larger and burdened less heavily than the unfree. But other aspects are not very clear. Free peasants could own unfree holdings while, vice versa, serfs sometimes had free holdings, so there was no one-to-one relationship between the legal position of tenants and the legal status of their holdings.

Why the Carolingian rulers insisted on the creation of such bipartite estates is not altogether clear. They may just have wanted to bring more order to a chaotic world by promoting a system of estate management that implied control over masses of peasants or, alternatively, to better control the powerful, not the poor, by acquiring a better idea of the extent and distribution of aristocratic and ecclesiastical wealth. Maybe the whole policy was aimed primarily at the management of royal and ecclesiastical estates, which had a key function in the upholding and organisation of what central royal power there was: the royal court, the royal palaces and the royal army and its leading warriors.

Whatever the case, one has to keep in mind that the Carolingian Empire was not entirely covered with bipartite estates. As a matter of fact, the classic, bipartite, manorial system, as sketched above, was neither the only form of estate organisation nor the one that was most widespread. It was particularly evident in the region between the Rhine and the Seine basin, where large landownership was often concentrated, making possible the formation of very extensive estates. But this type of estate organisation was rare east of the Rhine, in Lombard Italy, and probably also south of the Loire, while it was virtually absent in peripheral areas such as Catalonia. There, most land-users were small free peasants, while large-scale properties were still often exploited exclusively through the use of slave labour. In the Papal States and the Byzantine parts of southern Italy, including Sicily, large landowners from early on preferred indirect exploitation. In that case plots of land were leased out in hereditary tenure to peasants who were often tied to the land, and who can thus be considered as serfs, but who did not have to provide regular labour services. In Anglo-Saxon England, on the other hand, a form of estate management took shape that was quite similar to the bipartite manor of the Carolingian heartlands, from which it was probably copied. On such estates serf-like tenants, called *geburi* in Anglo-Saxon, had holdings for which they owed labour services.

Modern evaluations of the manorial system as a whole have varied considerably. The pessimists point in particular to the low yields compared with the relatively high costs of transport and supervision; the optimists to an interplay between the spread of the manorial system and slow demographic and economic expansion. Indeed, data on the size of families on peasant farms point to population pressure at the beginning of the ninth century. The more than 1,450 peasant families living on the manors of Saint-Germain-des-Prés at the beginning of the ninth century consisted of between five and nine members each, depending on the size of their farm. And peasants on thirteen estates of the abbey of Saint-Victor at Marseilles had on average five or six children who survived the vulnerable early years of life. That is why the reclamation and cultivation of land was generally started from overpopulated estates. At that point a certain amount of division of labour and specialisation, such as winegrowing, became feasible. That must have raised productivity and invited commercialisation, and some such estates even expanded into real towns: Liège is a prime example. Similarly, population increase on manors may have stimulated an increased use of expensive capital goods, such as mills, iron ploughs and horses for traction. These were all assets that increased output but were out of reach for free small peasant owners.

This argument has been broadened by the British historian Chris Wickham (2005), who argued that a gradual growth of agrarian production during the Carolingian age, resulting from new forms of tenancy, provided the Frankish aristocracy with new leverage to acquire wealth after military expansion had come to a standstill. This wealth from land generated a remarkable increase of elite demand which was the driving force for further economic growth and growing economic complexity. To be a landlord proved to be even more profitable than to be a warlord.

Trade and gift-exchange

Reciprocity and redistribution

Life for early medieval peasants was precarious by definition. Land productivity was low, and due to the absence of modern pesticides and insecticides there was always the danger of crop failure which could easily turn into famine when regional trade was not able to mitigate a sharp decline of local supply. That is why early medieval agriculture had many features of a 'moral economy', an economy where mutual sharing and reciprocity ('you scratch my back, I'll scratch yours') played an important part. Agricultural settlements in the early Middle Ages were so small (between five and ten farms), and so isolated, that mutual cooperation and support were essential conditions for survival. Dealings and transactions in a moral economy are less chaotic and primitive than we tend to think. Reciprocity is only possible when there are clear, socially and culturally rooted norms for division and redistribution.

Non-commercial values were also dominant in the management of estates. It has been rightly stressed that, as far as sources allow us to see, neither aristocratic nor ecclesiastical large landowners ran their estates with a profit-maximising business model in the back of their minds. The old idea of carefully nourished self-sufficiency should not be totally discarded, or the idea that a portfolio of estates and offices, certainly by aristocratic families, was seen as a 'social resource' in support of the maintenance or further advance of their elevated – and therefore always dangerous – position in the higher echelons of society in which one could as easily fall to (great) depth as rise to great height. In short, many 'economic' transactions by members of the social elite should be seen as oil to grease the cogs of aristocratic networks; if markets were used, they had a supportive function.

The same conclusion emerges from the study of long-distance trade in the early Middle Ages, a subject of passionate debate for many decades, which keeps circling around a challenging theory put forward by the Belgian historian Henri Pirenne (1862–1935) in the 1920s and 1930s. The core of Pirenne's theory is that the Migration Period left the economic system of Late Antiquity, centred on the Mediterranean and linking southern Europe to the Middle East, largely unaffected. In Pirenne's view, the establishment of barbarian kingdoms did result in a certain amount of 'degeneration'; but the unity of the Mediterranean world would only be truly disrupted by the Arab conquests from the middle of the seventh century. From then on East and West drifted apart. It forced the Carolingian rulers in the West to create their own institutions, such as 'feudalism'. The importance of long-distance trade declined; its core came to lie in the North Sea basin, in particular in the region between the Seine and the Rhine, where the seed was planted for the budding of mercantile capitalism.

Over the years a number of objections to Pirenne's theory have been raised, the most valid being that the Mediterranean evidently continued to function as an important transit zone after the Arab conquests and that the Muslim world had a substantial share in the recovery of international trade in the eighth century. We would like to approach the Pirenne thesis from another angle. Pointers to the circulation of goods and coins need not necessarily be explained as trade, as transactions of a commercial nature. That is not true even for transports of bulk goods, especially grain, to provision the great cities. In the centuries following the Migration Period Rome's grain supply came from Sicily and present-day Tunisia where the popes had very extensive domains. Not unlike the Roman emperors of Antiquity, they gave most of it free to the non-aristocratic part of Rome's populace. So there is certainly no question here of commerce, or commodity exchange; it is the continuation of a system of patronage. Much of what we know as 'trade' in the early Middle Ages, when looked at more closely, seems to have fulfilled this support function. In general it only involved relationships within aristocratic networks. This also explains why 'trade' did not necessarily take place through towns and urban markets.

This interpretation of early medieval transactions of goods owes far more to an anthropological inspiration rather than an economic-historical one. Philip Grierson, the British numismatist, in a criticism of Pirenne's thesis, had already called for such an approach by the end of the 1950s. Grierson was himself inspired by two well-known anthropological studies about the meaning of gift-exchange in 'primitive', non-Western societies, produced respectively by Marcel Mauss and Bronislaw Malinowski in the 1920s. This anthropological view finds that trade should be seen first and foremost as a means of supplying the elite with highly valued, prestige goods which served as gifts, such as weapons, horses, gold and slaves. Unlike ordinary commodities gifts cannot simply be alienated by the recipient, because the relationship between giver and recipient, as opposed to that between buyer and seller, is not neutral, but constrained by a form of morally decided mutuality: the giving contains the expectancy of a gift in return.

This mutuality can have a like or unlike character. In exchanges based on like mutuality (between allies of equal status, for example) we can speak of reciprocity. In the case of unlike mutuality we speak of redistribution; in this connection it means the sharing out of wealth by a lord among his retainers but also among the members of his household, including servants and slaves. Here, not only were prestige goods involved, but also primary consumer goods and, at a later stage, land. Both types of non-commercial transaction are outlined in Figure 3.1.

We can refine Figure 3.1 by taking different contexts into account. It is obviously sensible to, once again, make a basic distinction between the Christian barbarian kingdoms on former Roman soil on the one hand, and, on the other, the still pagan world of northern and central Europe. In the first, the Church was part of the system of gift-exchange, kings enjoyed a relatively strong

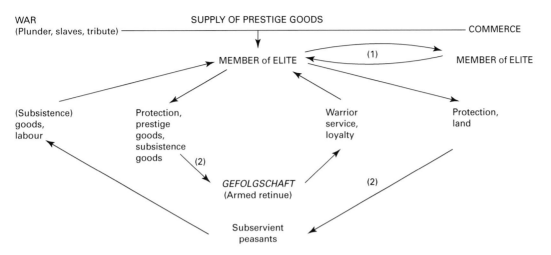

FIGURE 3.1 Non-commercial transactions in the early Middle Ages through reciprocity (1) and redistribution (2).

position and the aristocracy was much wealthier. All three factors had a profound influence on the extent and nature of non-commercial exchanges. Donating to monks and abbeys, in particular, linked tangible wealth to otherworldly motives of gift-giving, which in practical terms meant that the gift (whether movables or land) disappeared from economic circulation forever because the expected counter-gift was of a non-material, spiritual type.

The schematic representation of the relationships between lords and peasants in Figure 3.1 shows again that for the provision of the first necessities of life and the allocation of the two most important production factors, land and labour – so actually for the entire primary sector of the economy – there was hardly any question of market processes. On the other hand, the aristocracy did have to turn in part to real commerce through specialised middlemen (traders, merchants) for their supply of prestige goods and luxury articles: the spoils of war alone were not enough. This at once meant that such commerce was long-distance trade, because barbarian kings and warriors also valued the exotic products of the East which found their way to the few remaining large markets, such as those of Mainz and Verdun:

silks, costly perfumes, precious stones and ornaments, pepper and cloves. In addition to this there was a limited amount of trade in raw materials and non-luxury consumer items. It would include wool, cloth, leather, skins, earthenware, salt, honey and metal utensils, all of which came from more or less specialised production areas. This trade too was to a large extent fuelled by elite spending-power, because both lay aristocrats and large religious institutions needed considerable amounts of ordinary items for the running of their households, for the feeding and clothing of their staff and slaves, etc.

Such regional trade in small markets only picked up during the seventh century. Several Carolingian kings, including Charles the Bald, granted places market rights (mostly for weekly markets). They must have had a function in the exchange of bulk utilitarian goods. Although this type of trade remains almost invisible in our sources, it is assumed that fairly large amounts of grain and other necessaries, including salt, were yearly needed for the army and also for feeding the towns. Regional exchange linked up with the larger commerce through the first annual fairs that we know about. They were held close to important centres of agrarian surplus supply as well as elite consumption, such as the abbeys of Saint-Denis near Paris and of Saint-Vaast at Arras. The kings' courts, although still constantly on the move, were similar poles of attraction, where thousands of people (high-placed persons and their retinues) gathered for considerable periods of time to engage in what have been called 'tournaments of value'. These included, in addition to conspicuous consumption (showing off one's affluence), all kinds of symbolically charged acts of contract and transaction both between the king and his magnates, and between the terrestrial world of man and the spiritual world of God and his saints. There is no objection against calling such places towns as long as one keeps in mind that, as towns, they operated first and foremost as centres of power and consumption, not as centres of economic production and distribution. But one could of course lead to the other, and it has been argued that everywhere in early medieval Europe the presence of a resident bishop has been decisive for the survival chances of a place as a town.

But specialised long-distance trade gave rise to the emergence of a certain type of urban settlement as well. They are known as *porti*, *wiks* or *emporia*, and their primary function was to be a meeting-place of traders, active on the main axes of long-distance trade which linked Scandinavia, England, northern Gaul and the Rhineland with Lombardy and the Italian coasts of the Mediterranean. Long-distance trade was supported by a new means of payment, a silver coin minted in the Merovingian Empire from the end of the seventh century. This *denarius*, or penny, was worth one-twelfth of a *solidus*, the standard Roman gold coin. Its introduction was a great success. Within a short time imitations were being made in England and Frisia (they were known as *sceattas*), and altogether millions of pennies must have been struck during the eighth century. There was no lack of raw material, for the Franks had a rich silver-mine at Melle, in the vicinity of Poitiers. The introduction of silver money must be seen partly as a reaction to the continuous flow of gold to the East resulting from a struc-

turally negative balance of payments, which probably had swung round by the early years of Charlemagne's reign, when large quantities of Arab silver coins started to find their way to the West.

The new silver coinage also met the apparent need for a method of payment for small transactions. That the *denarius* stimulated a certain monetisation of the relationships between lords and peasants is evident from the primitive administration of large estates. As early as the ninth century, 47 holdings of an estate of the abbey of Saint-Bertin near Calais were held in exchange for a payment of money. But this was exceptional. The role of money in the demesnes of Saint-Germain-des-Prés was more limited at that time. Only a quarter of the obligations of the 'free' holdings (*mansi ingenuiles*) consisted of payments in cash, and these are data from one of the economically most progressive regions of early medieval Europe.

Traders, trade routes and trading posts

A growing share of the long-distance trade in luxury articles was directed towards Scandinavia and England. Important commercial contacts between the north and the Black Sea region, going via the Vistula–Dniester route, had existed until the beginning of the sixth century. When the Avars and their Slavic allies and subjects pushed their way into central Europe this route was closed, and Scandinavian trade moved to the relatively peaceful and powerful north of Gaul.

Initially, the Frisians played an important role as intermediaries in the commercial contacts between Scandinavia, England and the Frankish Empire. At that time their territory stretched from the Weser to the Flemish coast, so that they had control of certain vital traffic routes. With their centuries-old specialisation in cattle- and sheep-farming, imposed on them by their environment, the Frisians had a long tradition of sea and river trade. From the middle of the seventh century this was given a new impulse when Frankish power started to expand to the north. Frisian quarters developed in major trading stations in northern Europe, such as York and Birka (near modern Stockholm). It is also probable that it was the Frisians who were behind the development of the two most important types of ship of a later period: the *hulk*, whose round keel made it suitable for the North Sea trade, and the flat-bottomed *cog*, which was suited to the calmer waters of the Baltic.

The undisputed centre of Frisian commerce was Dorestad, a Frankish trading post that was established early in the seventh century in a bend in the Rhine just south of the old Roman garrison town of Traiectum (Utrecht). Afterwards, this area was reconquered by the Frisians, but Dorestad was at its largest and most prosperous when it finally

fell into Frankish hands in about 720. During the reign of Charlemagne the number of its inhabitants was estimated at a maximum of 2,500. To build its docking facilities and landing stages with a total length of over three kilometres, literally millions of trees must have been cut down in the surrounding woods.

The activities of the Scandinavian Vikings in the ninth and tenth centuries appeal even more to the imagination. Literally, 'Vikings' means something like 'men from the *viks* (bays, fjords) who do something'. That 'do something' is often translated succinctly as 'engage in trade' but 'go on a raid' is just as accurate. This is evident from the prose *Edda*, the Old Norse collection of myths whose oldest written version was produced in Iceland at the beginning of the thirteenth century. There, men who 'do something' do so either

BOX 3.2 LORDS OF RINGS

Rings were an important gift with which lords rewarded their warrior followers in the northern barbarian world. 'Ring-giver' (*beag-gyfa* or *beag-brytta*) was one of the epithets accorded to kings in the Anglo-Saxon epic poem *Beowulf*. In medieval Iceland, 'arm-ring' (*baugr*) was equivalent to money, hence *baugatal* ('list of rings') to indicate the various *wergeld* rates that had to be paid in compensation of manslaughter and other acts of violence. Numerous archaeological finds show that these rings took diverse forms, from thick rings for the finger to slender shoulder and neck rings made of gold or silver. Large quantities of them have often been found together. They were sometimes worn in combination with other jewellery made of precious metals. Typical of the period from the seventh to the eighth century was the use of bracteates, wafer-thin plates of gold, silver or bronze which were stamped on one side only. They were often worked together with rings to form one piece of jewellery, as can be seen clearly from this picture of a sixth-century necklace found at Hjørring in north Jutland. The effigy on these bracteates usually represented

the heathen god Wodan, whose head was sometimes modelled on that of the emperors on Byzantine coins. Opposite the head of the Wodan figure is another man waving a stick. The text of the runic characters on these Hjørring bracteates refers to the respect that the wearer of the ornament is keen to show to the (divine) protector portrayed. It was probably an amulet.

í vikingu or *í kaupferdum*. The latter means (going) 'on a trading voyage' so the former must be 'on a marauding raid'. To the Vikings, paradoxically, trading and raiding were part and parcel of each other. This may have something to do with the amoral ideas about the acquisition of wealth that were prevalent among the Scandinavian aristocracy. The accumulation of wealth was, as we have seen, indispensable in the barbarian world for obtaining the prestige essential for leaders to maintain their warrior retinues – and thus their position of power. How they acquired their wealth was unimportant.

Because of this ambiguous character of Viking activities it is difficult to appreciate their results in economic terms. It has been argued that the looting of rich estates and churches had a positive effect on liquidity, which was further enhanced by the fact that Viking war bands were often paid as mercenaries by Frankish and English rulers, but the same pattern is also recognisable much further to the east, where Danish and Swedish Vikings from the Baltic penetrated the river basins of the Volga and later, further westwards, of the Dniepr and the Don. They probably first went along this so-called northern arc soon after 850 as mercenaries in the service of warring Slav groups and steppe nomads, but immediately saw the commercial potential of trade with Byzantium and the Muslim world. They gained control over what has since then been called Russia. Although some modern-day Russian historians do not like it, the word 'Russian' comes through Finnish from the Old North German *rossmenn* or *rosskarlar*, meaning 'oarsmen' or 'seamen'. The oldest known princes of Novgorod and Kiev had pure Scandinavian names like Igor (from Ingvar) and Oleg (from Helgi). The success of the trade, or what passed for it, with the south is evident from the discovery of hundreds of thousands of *dirhams*, Arab and Persian silver coins, found in the soil of north-west Russia. Many of them would have changed hands in the great markets of Bulgar (near the confluence of the Volga and Kama rivers) and Itil (in the Volga delta on the Caspian

Sea) in the steppe empire of the Khazars. This eastern trade of the Russian Vikings dried up fairly suddenly after the middle of the tenth century, when the Khazar Empire collapsed and demand from the Middle East slackened due to a cooling of the climate with damaging effects on the production of such typical eastern crops as cotton, dates, figs and citrus fruits.

Despite the Vikings' unconcern towards the difference between trading and raiding there is no doubt that real trade formed an essential part of the proto-historic economy of south Scandinavia. This is evident from the large number of place-names ending in *-kaupang/-koebing/-køping* ('trading post') dating from this legendary period. Most of the coastal areas were unsuitable for arable farming but they had abundant water and rich pasture lands for animal grazing and stock rearing, an important source of wealth for the Scandinavian aristocracy. The vast inland forests provided a variety of products in demand in both the East and West, among them pelts, wax, honey and pitch produced from resin. The most important centres of Viking trade were Haithabu (Hedeby), strategically located on the shortcut through the Schleswig isthmus (by which merchants could save themselves the longer and more dangerous passage round Jutland), Ribe (in south Jutland), Kaupang (in the Oslo fjord), Birka (mentioned above) and the island of Gotland. From these centres, groups of Vikings sallied forth as traders, plunderers and finally, sometimes even as farmer-colonists over the whole of the then-known world.

The picture that emerges of trade in the early Middle Ages is one of a surprising dynamism in an overwhelmingly agrarian economy with a modest degree of commercialisation. In this connection the monetary historian Peter Spufford (1998) once called the enormous expansion of the minting of silver *denarii*, *sceattas* and *dirhams* in the decades round 800 'the false dawn of a money economy'. The ambivalent nature of the circulation of goods (gift-exchange or commercial transaction?) and of the use of coins (prestige object or method of payment?), and the indistinct purpose of 'journeys' (trade or plunder?) make it difficult to form a clear picture for the period before the seventh century. The same is essentially true for the phenomena of market and town in the early Middle Ages. Because of the direct and (almost) exclusive interest of the aristocracy in long-distance trade, such trade was directed more towards 'central persons' (who moved around a lot) than 'central places' as the British archaeologist, Richard Hodges, once put it. It also means that the few towns that survived were centres of power before anything else, 'public' places linked to the presence – permanent or frequent – of such important persons as kings, dukes, counts or bishops. Typical functions of later medieval towns such as concentrated craft production and regional provision were as yet underdeveloped. By that definition, the large trading posts of the period, such as Dorestad and Quentovic (near Montreuil), or Hamwic (near Southampton), may have been towns only to a limited extent. Their main function was to operate as gateway ports which ensured royal control over the international flows of high-value goods for either military use (weapons) or conspicuous consumption within aristocratic networks.

Early medieval politics

Frankish royal dynasties and the Carolingian century

The Merovingian dynasty, to which Clovis belonged, had monopolised Frankish kingship before the end of the fifth century. When Clovis died in 511 he left four sons from two marriages who all laid claim to the royal title. This led to the constitution of four separate Frankish kingdoms, composed of a more or less equal number of *civitates* (local districts) that did not necessarily have to form a continuous territory. The same situation occurred repeatedly afterwards – also because the Merovingian kings were polygamous

– but the frequent jockeying for power among sons who survived their father somehow never led to extreme territorial fragmentation. Weak candidates were relentlessly killed or, if they were lucky, coerced into becoming a monk. Between 575 and 585, when two of the four brother-kings at that time, Sigebert and Chilperic, had been murdered, probably by each other's servants, two parties formed among their supporters: those of Sigebert were called the Austrasians, meaning '[Franks] from the east', while their opponents came to be known as Neustrians, that is '[Franks] from the west'. After a savage civil war, in which the respective widows of Sigebert and Chilperic, Brunhild and Fredegund, played a major part (see Box 3.3), the ultimate winner, Fredegund's son Chlotar II, succeeded in 613 in re-uniting the Frankish kingdoms and reigned as a monarch. So did his son Dagobert (629–639). After Dagobert's death there were always either one or two Merovingian kingdoms; and when there were two, one was Austrasia, the other Neustria plus Burgundy. Adjacent territories such as Alemannia, Bavaria, Thuringia, but at a later stage also Aquitaine, had their own dukes, who were to a varying degree considered to be subordinate to Frankish hegemony.

From about the middle of the seventh century the highest officials of the Merovingian court – the *maiores domus* ('mayors of the palace') – made their presence increasingly felt. In Austrasia this office was virtually monopolised by members of the Pippinid family, so called after Pippin I of Landen. The basis of their power was formed by their extensive possessions in the Ardennes, a densely forested area where later they would found great abbeys such as Nivelles, Stavelot-Malmédy and Echternach. Shortly before 700 the Pippinids took over the office of mayor of the palace in Neustria as well. Even at that point, their position was far from unassailable, and in 714 after the death of Pippin II of Herstal, Pippinid power was almost broken. Only the vigorous action of Pippin's bastard son, Charles Martel ('the hammer'), prevented this from happening.

BOX 3.3 BRUNHILD

One of the rare women who came to great power in the early medieval world was Brunhild, daughter of the Visigothic king Athanagild and reputedly a girl of mesmerising beauty. In 566, she was married to the Merovingian king Sigebert I of Austrasia (561–575), who was murdered after he had invaded Neustria, the kingdom of his brother and rival, Chilperic. Soon afterwards, Brunhild was taken prisoner but then agreed to marry Merovech, Chilperic's son, without Chilperic knowing this. When Chilperic found out he flew into a rage, maybe out of jealousy, maybe because he saw this new liaison as an attempted coup. Brunhild was lucky to get away alive – after all, Chilperic had been married to her sister, whose throat had been slit after she had openly complained about Chilperic's relationship with his mistress, Fredegund. Now, Chilperic just forced the couple to divorce, and sent Brunhild back to Austrasia, where her strange move had raised deep suspicion among the leading aristocrats. For that reason, her son, the heir apparent Childebert, was taken away from her and brought up outside her influence. The tide for the queen-mother only turned in 584, when Childebert became fifteen years old and was declared of age. In the same year Chilperic I was murdered, 'the Nero and Herod of our time', according to the contemporary historian, Bishop Gregory of Tours. An attempt to make Childebert his successor to the kingdom of Neustria failed; instead the Neustrian aristocracy favoured Chilperic's son with Fredegund, Chlotar. However, in 592 Childebert did succeed in acquiring the kingdom of Burgundy, after his uncle Guntram's death. Now the time had come for Brunhild to avenge herself on all those in Austrasia and Burgundy who had previously stood in her way. Among them were an abbot, accused of treason, and Bishop Egidius of Rheims, who had conspired against her and her son, and was banished while the lay plotters were killed.

When Childebert died in 596 Brunhild once again held the powerful position of regent, now for her two grandsons, Theodebert II in Austrasia and Theoderic II in Burgundy. As regent, she corresponded with Pope Gregory the Great (590–604), who, among others, asked for her support for Augustine's mission to Kent. But when Theodebert II reached the age of fifteen, Brunhild's enemies among the Austrasian aristocracy succeeded in getting her expelled from court. Brunhild then found refuge with Theoderic of Burgundy, whom she set up against his elder brother. Also, with the help of local factions, Brunhild was able to dislodge Bishop Desiderius of Vienne, who had aroused her wrath with his criticism of the king's personal life, for which he paid with his life. Brunhild was able to procure the episcopal office for at least four of her supporters, among them Gregory of Tours, the famous chronicler, who never spoke ill of her.

In 612 she finally persuaded Theoderic to move against his brother. He invaded Austrasia and killed Theodebert and his son. Then, as if punished by God, Theoderic himself died shortly afterwards of dysentery. Once again Brunhild arranged the succession by helping her great-grandson, Sigebert II, to take the throne as the only successor to a re-united kingdom Burgundy-Austrasia. It turned out to be a deadly mistake, because this was not what most of the Austrasian aristocracy wanted. They took the royals prisoner and handed them over to King Chlotar of Neustria. Chlotar had young Sigebert and one of his brothers summarily executed. For his hated half-aunt, Brunhild, who must have been over 60 at the time, he had another fate in store. In a show trial he accused her of having killed ten kings – an exaggeration of her victims' rank, not their number – and then had her publicly humiliated and slowly tortured to death.

Charles eventually emerged as the winner out of this obscure period, and from him the dynasty took its new name of Carolingians. He held the office of mayor of the palace in both kingdoms and ruled without a king for the last few years of his mayoralty. He was a very successful war leader and did his utmost to expand Frankish rule to the north, south and east. Most memorable are Martel's campaigns in Aquitaine, which was under threat of Muslim invasions from Spain. In 733 the Frankish army halted a large invading force near Tours, an event that later was blown out of proportion – according to recent scholarship Christendom was not saved from extinction at Tours. More importantly, the Muslim raids gave Charles Martel the chance to strengthen his hold over Provence and Aquitaine.

These military successes naturally made a profound impression and brought him many loyal followers and supporters, who offered to enter his service no doubt in the hope of adventure, reward and booty. As victor, he could, moreover, demand tribute from the subjected regions and confiscate land with which to reward his bravest followers. Even Church possessions were not spared – which gave him a bad name among later ecclesiastical critics for stealing Church revenues.

The fact that, despite his military strength, Charles Martel did not put aside the Merovingian 'puppet kings' shows that kingship in the Frankish world was more than just the supremacy of physical force. Even though kings at this stage could be appointed and manipulated by the mayor of

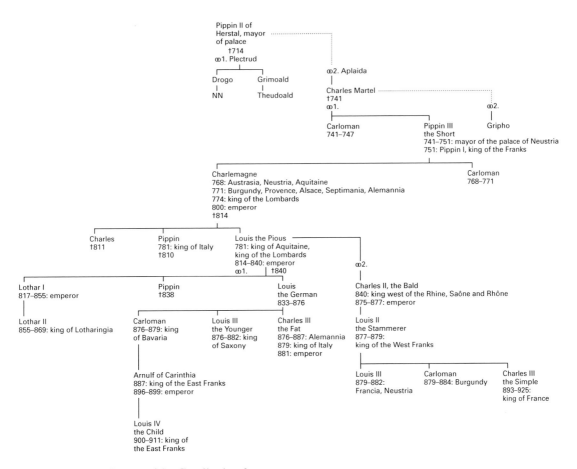

FIGURE 3.2 Family tree of the Carolingian dynasty

the palace, they retained a sacral legitimacy that was passed on through their lineage. But at King Theoderic IV's death in 737, Charles did not replace him and wilfully created an interregnum that would last until two years after Charles' own death in 741. Entirely in the style of a Frankish ruler, Charles Martel had divided his mayoralty between two of his sons, Carloman and Pippin III the Short. After several years of violence, Carloman heard the divine call and retired to the Italian monastery of Monte Cassino in 747, entrusting his share of the mayoralty, together with his son, to his brother, Pippin.

The combination of military success and powerful rule was probably behind Pippin's famous question to Pope Zachary in 749: 'whether it is good or not that the kings of the Franks should wield no power, as is the case now'. The pope, according to a Frankish version of events, agreed that the Franks were justified in deposing the Merovingian puppet king Childeric III and instead making Pippin king. In 754 Pope Zachary's successor, Stephen II, crossed the Alps and anointed Pippin, his wife Bertrada and their sons Charles – the later Charlemagne – and Carloman as the new ruling dynasty of the Franks. In return the pope received protection for the papal territories that formally still belonged to the Byzantine Empire, but which were systematically threatened by the Lombard kings in northern Italy. The theological estrangement between Rome and Byzantium, and the difficulties that the eastern Empire itself faced in defending its frontiers against the Muslims and the Avars, had already turned the protection given to the papal lands by the *basileus*, the Byzantine emperor, into being purely theoretical for some time.

At the anointing of Pippin the Short as king the Carolingians could present themselves as new and special protectors of the Church of Rome. Both were now dependent on each other in a special relationship of protection in exchange for legitimisation. This whole arrangement also enabled the Carolingians, finally, to elevate themselves above the numerous rival dukes and counts. They

would try to disguise the blemish of Martel's bastardy and the violent death of several heirs, as well as their coup d'état, by allowing their chroniclers to paint as negative a picture as possible of their Merovingian predecessors, and create a most positive image about their own family. This picture is still prevalent in modern historiography.

Military conquest and the Frankish armies

The reign of Pippin's son, Charles the Great or Charlemagne (768–814), deeply impressed his contemporaries and later generations. Court historians have certainly done much to idealise the life and deeds of their king and emperor, and this idealised representation of Charlemagne was often recalled in later centuries. Scores of European rulers had complicated genealogies constructed to 'demonstrate' their claims of descent from him. It cannot be denied that Charles' 46-year reign left a profound impact on the history of Europe. What most characterised the first 30 years of his rule was the aggressive, almost continuous-waging of war and conquest. He had inherited many challenges from his predecessors which he tackled with an intense determination. For a start, the popes made repeated calls for protection. In 774 Charlemagne attacked the king of the Lombards, urged on by Pope Hadrian I, who feared the Lombard rulers' threats and encroachment on the papal territories. Charlemagne succeeded in annexing the kingdom of the Lombards, with the exception of the southern dukedom of Beneventum, and installed Franks and Alamans as colonists and administrators. But the individual character of the region, with its rich, old culture, needed special consideration, and in 781 Charlemagne made it a semi-autonomous kingdom under his infant son, Pippin the Hunchback. In later years this Pippin conquered the Byzantine territories around Venice and in Istria, which brought him into conflict with the emperor in Constantinople.

As early as 772 a series of cruel wars with a clearly religious dimension was launched against the Saxons, which were to last until 804. Frankish victories were followed by Saxon rebellions, leading to bloody reprisals – such as the massacre of 4,500 prisoners at Verden (near Bremen) in 782. Ten years later a new revolt resulted in the massive deportation of Saxons to other parts of the Frankish kingdom, after which Frankish and Slav colonists settled in the area. In southern Germania one campaign was directed against the Ba[iu]varii (Bavarians), whose duke, Tassilo, was trying to expand to the south and east. After a rebellion in 757 King Pippin, who was Tassilo's uncle, had forced his nephew to 'swear numerous oaths to him', and to become his vassal and the vassal of his two sons, Carloman and Charles. In 788, Charles, then Charlemagne, punished his cousin's repeated breach of loyalty, and deposed him as a duke. Tassilo was forced into a monastery, and Bavaria was incorporated into the Frankish kingdom. From Bavaria, the Franks pushed on into Pannonia, modern lower Austria, where the Avars were settled. During successive campaigns in 791, 795 and 796 these people were terrorised and their fabulous treasure in the 'ring', the circular residence of the khan, was seized. Here the Franks established a border region, the Ostmark, the origins of the later dukedom of Austria.

In Gaul expeditions were undertaken into those peripheral regions that had never been completely subjected to the Franks: Brittany, Septimania (the area between Narbonne and the Pyrenees) and Aquitaine. In 781 Charlemagne accorded Aquitaine as a separate kingdom to his son Louis, just as he had given Italy to his oldest son Pippin previously. A first invasion over the Pyrenees led to the massacre of Charlemagne's rear guard by the Basques in the Pass of Roncesvalles in 778. This tragic event was mentioned briefly in ninth-century annals and transformed in the eleventh century into the epic *Chanson de Roland*. Further raids in and after 801 ended in the subjugation of the region around Barcelona and Tarragona as far as the Ebro, where the Spanish March was established.

Charlemagne was undoubtedly a vigorous leader who, like his forebears Charles Martel and Pippin the Short, was able to use his personal qualities to bring about the extraordinary expansion of his dynasty's power. There were no major advances in military technology behind their success, as has been argued. Such factors as improved armour and a more intensive tactical use of cavalry certainly had a part to play, but during the eighth century they did not cause any dramatic changes that might account for the success of the three great Carolingian rulers. By the same token, the disintegration of Charles' enormous empire during the ninth and tenth centuries cannot be explained by techno-military or organisational circumstances. So the personal factor must have been decisive: from 714 to 814 three exceptionally strong, charismatic, leaders succeeded each other, who were able to inspire great support and whose successes proved to have a great appeal to ambitious warriors.

Part of the lands with which the Carolingians rewarded these warriors came, more or less under pressure, from ecclesiastical resources. The decisions of the *Concilium Germanicum*, the Church council convened by Charles Martel's eldest son, Carloman, in 742 or 743, is the earliest text to show that the Carolingians and the Frankish Church had reached a *modus vivendi*, whereby the ruler could indeed request the Church to make land available to warriors, providing that the rights of the Church were recognised through monetary compensations. To this end, many Church institutions were entitled to a tithe from certain royal estates or other sources of royal income. This *decima regalis* (royal tithe) should not be confused with the ordinary ecclesiastical tithe (see Chapter 2). The land grants themselves were known as *precariae verbo regis* ('requests [for land] by the king's word'). The land was given as a **benefice**, that is, as a conditional tenure, and fell to those appointed by the king for services rendered.

MAP 3.1 Charlemagne's empire

With their constant wars of aggression and their regular successes Charles Martel, Pippin III and Charlemagne were able to grab so much land that they could mobilise exceptionally large armies. Until the beginning of the ninth century, the kings could use their authority to call up all adult free men for war. If they chose to do so, actual recruitment only took place on a regional basis because of the vast extent of the Empire and the slowness of communications. But shortly after 800, as we saw, Charlemagne reduced the military obligations of free men. Increasingly, Carolingian kings and their commanders relied on the heavily armed horsemen who made up the king's elite units and the large retinues of counts, bishops and abbots. Their equipment was perfected in the course of the eighth and ninth centuries with the stirrup, panelled saddle and coat of mail. The heavily armed cavalry would form the core of all western European armies until the fourteenth century, in contrast to the superiority of the infantry in Antiquity and its renewed importance after 1300. The military value of horsemen was not limited to armies, because in small formations they could show their superiority in speed, arms and strength against peasant folk or irregulars. In an agricultural economy with very low yields, which was characteristic of the early Middle Ages, equipping such warriors and providing for their big horses laid a heavy burden on the scarce resources available.

An incipient state

The French medievalist Georges Duby quipped in 1972 that Charlemagne's empire was 'a village chiefdom, stretched to the limits of the universe'. For our view of what further happened with this empire, and to what extent it could be called a 'state', much depends on our appreciation of the effectiveness of Carolingian royal administration, and in particular the ability of counts and dukes, appointed to represent royal authority in each and every corner of the vast territory which the Empire enclosed, to successfully act as public officials and to distinguish between 'public' and 'private' exercise of power. Ironically, one of Duby's major contributions to medieval history, the theory of the 'banal revolution', departs from a rather rosy picture of the Carolingian administrative machinery. We shall return to this point in Chapter 4.

However, nobody would deny that a certain amount of institutionalisation was necessary to consolidate the military successes. Charles surrounded himself with clerics who, despite his reportedly crude nature, introduced him to some of life's finer aspects. The most prominent of these clerics was the Anglo-Saxon scholar Alcuin of York, who had been called to Charlemagne's court to teach the king. Alcuin also was one of the advisers who elaborated ideas on Christian kingship and imperial rulership. These were partly based on classical Roman models and partly on the Old Testament. A Christian king was meant to be God's chosen protector of the faith, which allowed him to concern himself with the affairs of the Church and to carry out his own secular political activities under the sign of Christ. The idea of a reborn Roman-Christian empire was made clear to every subject through the new silver *denarii* that Charles had struck after his imperial coronation. On one side these pennies bore a cross in or on a classical temple, with the legend CHRISTIANA RELIGIO, and on the other the effigy of the emperor draped, just like his illustrious predecessors of Late Antiquity, in a toga and wearing a crown of laurels; the circumscription was KAROLUS IMPERATOR AUGUSTUS ('Charles, the august Emperor').

Charlemagne's imperial coronation was actually a repeat at a higher level of the events of 750–751, when Pippin had been anointed king. In 799 Pope Leo III came to Paderborn to ask for Charles's help against a faction of the Roman aristocracy, from whose intrigues he had narrowly escaped. This was Charlemagne's opportunity to invoke the principle that had been formulated back in 749: he who actually exercises the authority attached to a title deserves to bear that same title. Had Charlemagne not, like a true Roman emperor, established his authority over all – or at least many – of the lands of western Christendom? Was his might not indispensable as protector of the Church? When Charles left for Rome in the autumn of the year 800 to restore the pope to his authority, he displayed his effectiveness as protector of the Church, and in this quality proved himself to be superior to the Byzantine emperor. At the coronation ceremony in St Peter's church on Christmas Day, the pope ensured that he first 'created' the Emperor by crowning him, before the acclamation of the Roman people confirmed him in the dignity. By this act a precedent was created that would hold until the end of the Middle Ages.

There is no doubt that the Carolingians took good care of their own propaganda, which resulted in more and more interesting literary and artistic products being produced in their time than in the centuries before or after. These products still guide historians in their interpretations. Among them are the royal annals in which the most important events of each year were recorded, and especially Charlemagne's biography, written more than a decade after Charles's death by the erudite nobleman, Einhard, who had been a trusted adviser of the emperor. Following the model of Suetonius' *Lives* of the first twelve Roman emperors (*c.*125 CE), Einhard could affirm that 'during his whole reign Charles regarded nothing as more important than to restore . . . the ancient glory of the city of Rome'. The royal palace complex at Aachen was equipped with an impressive *aula* (hall) in Late Antique style, modelled after the great Constantinian basilica of Trier, and with baths (Aachen took its name from *Aquae*, that is to say '[thermal] waters'). The palace chapel with its octagonal plan was clearly inspired by a number of architectural models, not least the basilica of San Vitale in the former imperial city of Ravenna and the Lateran Palace in Rome. Marble pillars, capitals and mosaics were brought from Italy to Aachen to lend ancient lustre to the new church. From around 800 onward, Aachen would become the most important royal residence and the symbolic capital of the reborn empire, a rival – in reality, very small – to Rome. Richly illuminated manuscripts were produced at and for the court of Charlemagne and Louis the Pious. A clear and manageable new style of writing, the Carolingian minuscule, evolved from the Roman script system. With the encouragement of Alcuin and other scholars that he brought from Italy, Ireland, Francia, Saxony and Spain, Charlemagne stimulated the study of Latin. Ancient texts were copied and studied with the aim of achieving a more correct understanding of the Christian religion.

The king's palace included his household and some office-holders who were constantly on the move. Even Aachen never developed into the fixed capital of the Carolingian Empire – no more than did any of the later imperial residences. One of the reasons for this was that the king was always away on military expeditions during the months that were suitable for waging war. Another was that the presence of the king was essential in all corners of the Empire so that his authority would be respected. A third reason was purely practical: whenever possible, the king and his retinue stayed in one of the more than 200 palaces in order to make use of the revenues on the spot. In the manorial economy, where there was little traffic, it was simpler to allow large companies of demanding consumers to travel around than to attempt to centralise the harvest yields. The Latin word *palatium* has given us the word 'palace' and the German *Pfalz*, the central building on a royal domain that was the preferred stopping place of the itinerant king and his court.

Because of the Carolingian elite's Christian fundamentalism, court life at Aachen and Ingelheim was not all worldly pleasures. On the contrary, it had 'shades of monastic order', and under Louis the Pious, the royal court even turned into the centre of 'a penitential state' – two happy qualifications by Mayke de Jong (2009) which perfectly summarise the austere spirit and the highly moralistic overtone of Carolingian rule, especially under Charlemagne and his son. Both were deeply convinced that by divine order they had the task of morally purifying their people, and they did not shy away from the logical consequence that they themselves were sinners too who had to be corrected if need be. Both Louis the Pious and his sons disguised political purges as penance for sins committed against the Christian moral order. Louis did so immediately after his father's death when he purged the 'depraved court' at Aachen to put his own men in; his sons debased their father into a penitent during the revolt of 833 (see below). To the modern mind it is not easy to grasp how a deeply felt Christian faith made it possible for a man like Charlemagne to square the purposeful killing and maiming of thousands of 'pagan enemies' with small-minded moral crusades against the peccadillos of each and every one of his subjects. Significantly, Charlemagne launched his biggest moralising offensive, set down in the famous capitulary *Admonitio Generalis*, in 789, in the midst of his savage wars against the Saxons.

Apart from the king's itinerant household, the chancery, the administrative measures and legislation, the general assembly and the palace school took on early forms of centralised state institutions that were separate from the king's person. The Merovingian kings had the greater part of their paperwork carried out by a Church institution at hand, or by the person for whom the document was intended. A chancery of his own enabled the king to complete more written documents without external agency, and even to create an archive to give him closer control of his activities. The Merovingian kings had had a chancery with lay notaries, but later scribes were predominantly clerics, who were in the direct service of the king/emperor. A particularly important activity of the chancery was to issue numerous capitularies, royal or imperial decrees, split into separate chapters or sections, in which administrative and legislative regulations were promulgated. They often formed the written report of provisions orally agreed and proclaimed by the powerful men of the land at their annual general assembly (the so-called March Field or, after 755, May Field). In that context the spoken word had the power of law. The announcement in everyone's presence voiced the consensus, and at the same time laid the duty on all those present to abide by what had been agreed. It is, therefore, likely that the capitularies served in the first place as a sort of reminder for the chancery and for the *missi dominici*, the emissaries who were sent all over the Empire in the king's name to ensure that the rulings were obeyed.

Strenuous efforts to create a solid state institution in the Roman model were made when it came to the division of the territory in administrative districts, and the offices belonging to it. Because the Empire was so vast the king/emperor had to delegate his authority. We have already mentioned the foundation in 781 of the kingdoms of Lombardy and Aquitaine, which were held respectively by Pippin and Louis, Charlemagne's sons. One level lower were duchies – large territories that were supposed to be inhabited by distinct peoples, such as Bavaria and Saxony. Border regions with a strong military administration were called **marches**, such as the Spanish, the Breton or the Friulan marches; they were ruled by margraves. However, the standard administrative district was the **county**, of which there were about 600 in Charlemagne's time. The number of counts was considerably fewer, because quite often one count administered more than one county.

Counts were basically office-holders whose task it was to represent the king's authority in their district or county, to administer justice in his name there, to lead the general assembly, to summon to war and to ensure that the capitularies were observed. In return, a part of the royal domains in a county was placed at its count's disposal. The majority of counts were Franks, even in regions of a different ethnic composition, apparently because the common background fostered loyalty. The emissary counts and bishops sent in pairs as inspectors, *missi dominici*, were responsible for checking the counts' activities or related tasks. The offices of count, duke and *missus dominicus* were called *honores* ('honours') or, from the reign of Louis the Pious onward, *ministeria* ('ministries'), terms that combine highly moralistic ideas of an expected readiness of aristocrats to be at the (unpaid) service of the community of the realm and of great honour that such service brought to them.

The objectification evident in this organisation was no doubt a result of the efforts made – under the oft-repeated motto of *renovatio* – to restore the Roman imperium in a Christian form, based on the renewed study of Roman history, law and literature by the learned clerics of the court. In practice the ambitious project showed little sense of reality: the material circumstances of the eighth and ninth centuries simply made it impossible to achieve the results that had been possible in the fourth century. In this sense we must interpret the capitularies as ordinances through which the king/emperor *hoped to* change an unmanageable reality, but at the same time they were a reflection of that very reality. There are capitularies that decreed that counts could not go out hunting if they had to preside over a court session; must not be drunk while exercising their office; could not accept gifts from parties involved in court cases; or were not allowed to blackmail landowners with the threat of taxation or military service, etc.

Among the factors creating unity in the Carolingian Empire, we should again bear in mind the paramount importance of the interdependence with the Church. In Merovingian Gaul there had been *civitates* where bishops had the right to appoint counts, or to hold that office themselves. This was not without its dangers, because the bishops could easily find themselves embroiled in a merciless struggle for power. Under the Carolingians the autonomous position of the bishops was increasingly felt to be a problem, and in due course most of the episcopal lordships lost their immunity. But then again, the same Carolingian rulers had no difficulty in appointing bishops as *missi dominici*.

Whenever reference is made to a Carolingian state, kingdom or empire, such terms should not be understood anachronistically. In the everyday Germanic and Roman languages there was no word for an abstract concept such as the state. Power relations were linked to a person, concretely and directly. It was not until the reign of Louis the Pious that court scholars found a term that appealed to them in their Latin sources: *res publica* (literally, the public cause). But the concept scarcely filtered through to the reality of the structures of Carolingian government. An exception is provided by the frequent beheadings of counts accused of high treason, a typically Roman law concept introduced by the court scholars. Attempts made to establish public institutions were abandoned after a couple of generations. In many respects, the apparatus of state was limited to the court and a few hundred officials who struggled to impose laws in the enormous area stretching from the Ebro to the Elbe, and including large parts of Italy. In the absence of a developed tax system it was a hopeless task to impose a lasting administrative unit on the jumbled diversity of peoples belonging to different cultures and levels of development.

Creating loyalty: oaths of allegiance

One traditional means of exercising power was demanding an oath of allegiance. In the Carolingian Empire, this became obligatory between 786 and 792, after repeated uprisings, for all free male subjects above the age of twelve, also for clergy and monks, for the 'men' of bishops, abbots, counts and others, and for all sorts of bondmen 'who held fiefs (*beneficia*) or offices, or were vassals of lords and who could have horses, armour, a shield, a lance, a long sword or a short sword'. Moreover, all laymen who swore allegiance also had to be ready to join the royal host if commanded to do so, and otherwise maintain the peace in the place in which they lived. In 802 the emperor stipulated that allegiance should be sworn to him 'as a man should swear allegiance to his lord'. In 805 a more exclusive note was heard in the relationship of fidelity: besides swearing allegiance to the emperor, a free man would only be able to swear allegiance to his own lord. In short, oaths of allegiance were a typical means of exercising power in a society with a limited culture of writing; the bonds of fidelity were direct, personal and mostly unwritten. An oath was sworn with the hand on a holy object, such as a relic or the Scriptures. Breaking an oath provoked divine sanctions along with strong judicial punishment for perjury.

Creating loyalty: vassals and benefices

Furthermore, the Carolingian kings, in their relationship with their subjects, consciously intensified the use of vertical, non-familial bonds of loyalty and personal dependence. The foremost of these bonds was **vassalage**. Sources from the Merovingian era mention the term *vassus* (plural, *vassi*) in reference to lower, dependent members of the court. The term was used frequently from the end of the eighth century onwards. It did not have a clearly unambiguous meaning but always referred to free men who were in a relationship of service to a lord or *senior*. It was a relationship of mutual dependence: the vassal served and supported the lord, and the lord protected and maintained the vassal. Between 801 and 813 Charlemagne issued a capitulary (decree) referring to five cases in which a vassal might terminate the allegiance to his lord, from which it is clear that the relationship was tied to conditions for both parties, and that it could be broken. At that time the term *vassi dominici* or *vassi regis*, meaning the king's vassals, surfaced. It alluded to a somewhat lower placed category of *fideles*, i.e. men who were personally bound to the king by a special oath. All great magnates took this oath in a ceremony called *commendatio* ('recommendation of oneself')

or **homagium** ('homage', i.e. becoming another man's man). At a much later stage, *commendatio* or homage became a standard part of the ceremony in which a man became a vassal, symbolised by the ritual of 'joining hands' with the king (*immixtio manuum* in Latin).

The capitulary just mentioned puts it beyond doubt that the Carolingian kings had vassals, and there are a few other accounts, dating from the eighth and ninth centuries, which describe in detail the subjection of a royal vassal to his lord. Admittedly, all relate to strongly politically loaded situations where, after a rebellion, amidst great ceremony and before many witnesses, a humiliation was laid upon the subjected person who then had to swear a new oath of allegiance to the victor. This was how Pippin the Short treated his own nephew, the rebellious Duke Tassilo of Bavaria who offered himself to the king in *vassaticum* in 757. However, this is an untypical case that we only know from biased, pro-Carolingian sources and in practice there must have been a variety of forms, just as there was a variety of situations in which oaths of allegiance were sworn or conflicts resolved.

Even before the end of the eighth century, royal vassal (*vassus dominicus*) most certainly was not a degrading title. From the decisions of a Church council, held around 780, it appears that royal vassals were (also) substantial landowners who would normally own between 30 and 200 peasant holdings. One could even infer from this document that such men commonly held their possessions from the king 'in benefice', that is, in conditional tenure – in **fief**, as later sources would say. It indicates that the two institutions discussed in this section – vassalage and benefice/fief – came together, not yet structurally or in any systematic way, but off and on, when circumstances of which we do not always have knowledge made this suitable or dictated it. The first clear proof is the capitulary of Herstal of 779, which brackets together *vassi dominici* with counts. Apparently, the former could have benefices, just like counts, but not all of them did. That counts had benefices

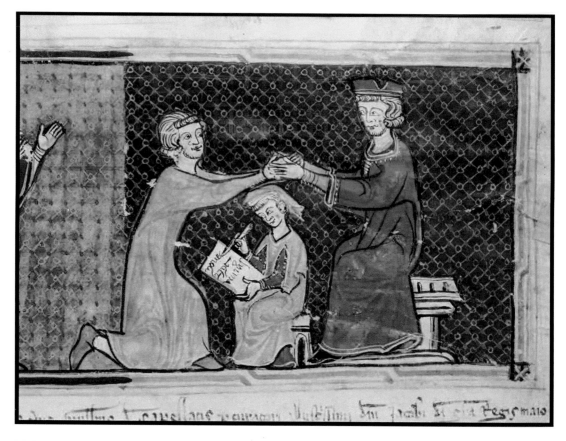

PLATE 3.1 Ritual of 'joining hands' with the king (*immixtio manuum* in Latin), the symbolic sealing of a contract with a vassal. The Royal Prosecutor, the Scribe and the Feudal Lord. *Capbreu de Clayra et de Millas*, 1292, Catalan School.

'ex officio' goes back to the Merovingian period, when it was not uncommon to grant the use of parts of royal estates to court officials and counts as a reward for the exercise of office. Under the Carolingians, this practice was continued, and connected with the concept of benefice. By the early ninth century Charlemagne, in one of his capitularies, was fulminating against counts 'and other men' (read: royal vassals?) who were trying to convert benefices into free property by devious means. Probably, this outburst was related to this use 'in benefice' of royal estates.

Feudal-vassalic relations and the issue of feudalism

The unmistakable acceleration in the deployment of **feudal-vassalic relations**, not only by the king, but at all levels of the Carolingian elite, raises three questions: at what point in time did benefices or fiefs become hereditary and/or could they be alienated by their holders? Could other things than land be the object of grants in benefice or fief? And did feudal-vassalic relations also take root outside the Carolingian Empire (and its successor states)? The answers to these questions are important in order to determine if it makes sense to speak of medieval states as feudal states or even of medieval society as a '**feudal society**'. Some historians abhor doing that, while others have no objection at all. One problem is that proponents do not always use the term feudalism in the same sense; another is that the earliest comprehensive treatments of the *ius feudale* ('feudal law'), which gives us an idea of what medieval legal experts thought of feudal-vassalic relations, are only from around 1200. Despite such objections, we are still in favour of using the f-word of medieval history, because it is an easy shorthand term to signify the most typical formal relationship, and to frame several key aspects of medieval governance, such as the 'outsourcing' of public authority and local lordship, the organisation of military service, but also the transmission of land among the social elite in a legal system that did not recognise the Roman law concept of exclusive property.

It is important to stress that in the Carolingian period only initial impetus has been given to the further development of feudal-vassalic relations in all these directions (see Chapter 4). The Carolingian Empire was in no way a feudal state. It would have been one if, for instance, such key public offices as counties had been systematically feudalised, that is to say, had become fiefs, and if all counts were royal vassals. That was certainly not yet the case.

The fiction of a united empire

In 806 Charlemagne made arrangements for his succession. In accordance with Frankish custom he divided the realm between his three sons. Two of them, however, predeceased their father so that the Empire would remain a monarchy. While Charlemagne was still alive, he made his only surviving son Louis 'partner in the imperial name', as say the Annals of the Frankish Realm. He was crowned by his father at Aachen in 813 – an event that might be interpreted as an insult to the pope. However, Pope Stephen came to Francia in 816 to anoint Louis at Rheims. During the early

years of his reign, Louis the Pious devoted himself to the protection of Church institutions, from the papacy to the local clergy, in the face of over-powerful secular lords. In 817 he, too, made arrangements for his succession, under which the Empire would again be divided between the three sons whom he then had. The emperorship was considered to be an indivisible unit. His eldest son, Lothar, was therefore proclaimed co-emperor and sole heir to the imperial dignity, and in 823 he was anointed and crowned by the pope. The other brothers were given the title of king: Pippin of Aquitaine and Louis of Bavaria – hence commonly called Louis the German – both territories with a strongly developed regional identity. This arrangement may have been intended as a compromise, but in reality the emperor had very little to say over the (sub-)kingdoms, each of which was allowed a vast degree of autonomy.

Things did not work out as planned in another respect. Within four fateful years, between 829, when Louis granted an inheritance to his six-year-old son, Charles (the Bald), with his second wife Judith, and 833, when the emperor was humiliated and taken prisoner by his elder sons on the Field of Lies near Colmar, the dream of a unified empire, meant to embrace and protect a united (Roman) Christendom, was shattered. And it did not stop when Louis the Pious died in 840. Lothar's demand for oaths of allegiance throughout the Empire, following his grandfather's example, stirred up bitter opposition from his surviving brothers, Charles and Louis the German. They defeated the new emperor after a violent struggle, and, at Strasbourg in 842, in the presence of their warriors, they swore solemn oaths of mutual assistance and promised that they would never treat separately with Lothar. These oaths are famous because both kings used the vernacular tongue of their opponents so that they would be understood by the other's followers: Louis swore in the Roman language (*Romana lingua*), Charles in German (*Theudisca lingua*). Then both groups declared, each in their own tongue, that they would not follow their king if he were to wage an unjustified war against his brother. The idea of this language switching was to reassure the lesser aristocratic warriors of both armies, who only understood their own language, of the sincere intentions of both leaders.

Under the threat of being deposed by a council of bishops and the pressure of his brothers' coalition, Lothar agreed to negotiations. They resulted in the partition of the Empire into three, laid down in the Treaty of Verdun in 843. The brothers divided the means of power as equally as possible between them. Charles the Bald received the territories west of the Schelde, Marne, Saône

and Rhône, and Louis the German all that lay east of the Rhine. Lothar, the emperor, kept Italy and the central territories, including both Aachen and Rome. The northern parts would later be called Lotharingia (*Lotharii regnum* or Lorraine) after Lothar's son and namesake, Lothar II, who received them as a separate kingdom after his father's death in 855. By the same partition Italy went to his eldest brother, while the younger one was made king of Provence.

After 843, Louis the German, who had been king of Bavaria since 817 and now became

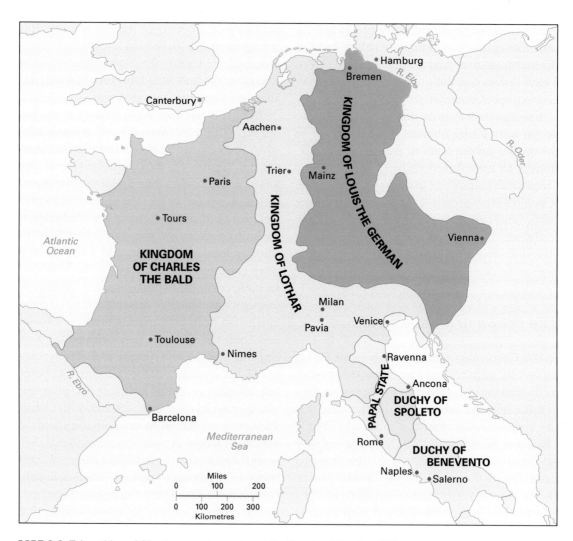

MAP 3.2 Tripartition of Charlemagne's empire at the Treaty of Verdun, 843

generally recognised as king of East Francia (843–876), proved himself to be a strong king. He consolidated the northern Elbe border against Danes and Slavs, and had them pay a yearly tribute in recognition of Frankish overlordship. The prince of Moravia, further to the south, was a tougher adversary, and Frankish control over lower Pannonia (present day lower Austria and western Hungary) was not reasserted until 865; further efforts to expand Frankish power into Moravia itself failed. Apart from that, Louis' mind kept being drawn to the west, and he repeatedly invaded Gaul. This western orientation would prove to be far-sighted, because bit by bit almost all of Lothar's central empire, including Italy, would fall into the hands of the East Frankish/German kings (Chapter 5). Louis the German was also an educated man, who surrounded himself with committed and learned churchmen, such as Hraban Maurus, abbot of Fulda and archbishop of Mainz.

Overall, the decades after Verdun were characterised by short reigns and a rapidly changing composition of territories as a result of repeated divisions of inheritances. In 875 the imperial title, already devalued under Lothar I, fell for just two years to the West Frankish king, Charles the Bald. In 881 negotiations with the pope resulted in the recognition of the king of East Francia, Charles the Fat, as emperor. The title would continue to exist in that part of the Empire, later known as Germania or Germany, with an interruption in the tenth century, until 1806. So, ironically, the fiction of upholding the Roman Empire came to rest upon rulers of a territory that once had been considered a land of wild and dangerous barbarians who were a threat to the *Pax Romana*.

Dynamic peripheries

The British Isles and Viking Scandinavia

In many respects the seven kingdoms of the Angles and Saxons followed an evolution that was not dissimilar to that of the Frankish Empire. Warrior retinues, some sort of a manorial economy and great social inequality could be found on both sides of the Channel. Now and then Anglo-Saxon kings, just like their Carolingian counterparts, would ask the Church if it could spare a piece of land for a well-loved warrior. One striking difference is that the *dooms*, the Anglo-Saxon laws, were written up in the vernacular, unlike the Frankish capitularies which were formulated exclusively in Latin. When the king of Wessex, Alfred the Great (871–899), followed Charlemagne's example and founded a court school, translations were made there from Latin into the vernacular. In the long term this brought about an indigenous legal tradition in the vernacular that was able to resist the introduction of Roman law, which took place on the continent from the twelfth century onward.

Another Carolingian imitation was tinging kingship with Judeo-Christian sacredness; the first Anglo-Saxon king to be anointed was Ecgfrith, son of Offa of Mercia, who became co-ruler alongside his father in 787. However, in precisely this period of time the Anglo-Saxon world was on the verge of rapid and irreversible change. Under the year 786 the Anglo-Saxon Chronicle records that three ships with 'Danish men' moored off the coast of Dorset, their crew killing the royal **sheriff** in a fight. It was the onset of a long episode of Scandinavian interference with the course of events in the British Isles, of Vikings operating not so much as traders but as conquerors and colonists. In the course of the ninth century Norwegian warlords and their followers took possession of the Shetland islands, Orkney and the Hebrides of northern Scotland, and the Isle of Man, putting pressure on the fragile united kingdom of the Scots that was taking shape around 850. Further west, they settled on the coast of Ireland, where they founded several towns, including Dublin in 917.

Meanwhile, war bands from Denmark concentrated their attacks on England, culminating in the invasion of the so-called 'great heathen army'

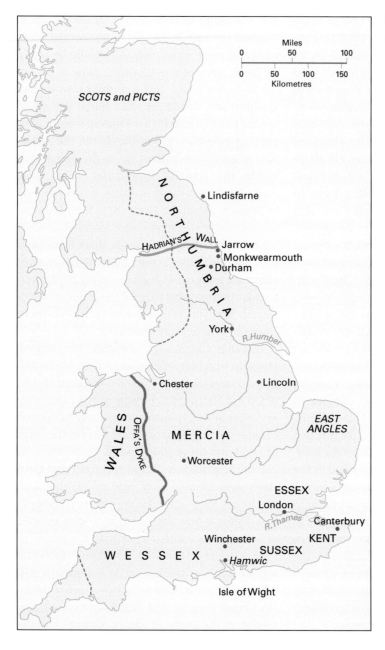

MAP 3.3 Anglo-Saxon England, c.800

in 865, which must have numbered between 2,000 and 3,000 men. It soon became clear that the Danes had no intention of leaving. The great army roamed England for more than ten years. In 876 it split up and while one half started to settle and 'to plough to support themselves' in Northumbria, the other part remained active as an army. In 878 it was decisively beaten at Edington by King Alfred of Wessex. It would be another decade before King Alfred could reach a settlement with the Viking 'king' Guthrum in which the old Roman road between London and Chester was established as a linear border between Wessex and the Viking territories. The remarkable density of place-names with a Scandinavian suffix north of this line, land thenceforwards known as the **Danelaw**, proves both that the agreed frontier was respected and that the invasion of the 'great army' was followed by massive immigration from Denmark.

King Alfred consolidated his military success by army reforms and by constructing some thirty *burhs*, fortified settlements in strategic locations, which more often than not grew into market towns. To pay for all his efforts, Alfred introduced the **Danegeld**, a land tax to be paid in silver coin, which was levied for the first time in Kent in 865 and maintained until 1162, long after the Norman Conquest. It enabled the English kings to collect immense quantities of silver: as much as 22 tons in the year 1018 alone, which would have represented about 42 per cent of the total supply of coins circulating in England at that time. Alfred himself had coins struck with the legend *rex Anglorum* ('King of [all] the English'), the title that in due time would be bestowed upon his successors.

The Scandinavians who had settled in the north-east of England were allowed so much freedom that they did not become a disruptive factor. While the Carolingian drive to conquer led to an imperial overstretch that shrank again as soon as the strong leaders were succeeded by weaker ones, the gradual merging of small kingdoms in England appeared to be permanent. The borders of the former kingdoms remained in the borders of the counties or **shires**, which in large part were created in the tenth century. At the level of the shires, and of the **hundreds** beneath them, courts of law were established where, under the guidance of royal judges, local notables passed sentence. So, in matters of administrative and legal organisation Anglo-Saxon England was quite similar to the Carolingian Empire.

Viking invasions in the western part of the Carolingian Empire had a slightly different pattern. Repeated, violent hit-and-run attacks around the middle of the ninth century led to the looting of major urban centres (Paris, Rouen, Nantes,

Bordeaux), emporia or gateway ports (Dorestad, Quentovic) and rich abbeys (Noirmoutiers). Although some of the expeditions seem to have been masterminded by the king of Denmark, there was never a 'great army' active on Carolingian territory for years at a stretch. However, the situation in Francia became more complicated than in England from the moment that Carolingian rulers started to hire Viking mercenaries to fight off either competing Viking war bands or rival brothers or sons with whom they were at odds. The former strategy ended up in the granting of coastal regions and river delta areas to Viking kings or chieftains to safeguard the interior. Among the earliest examples are the island of Walcheren near the mouth of the river Schelde, granted to the Danish prince Harald Klak in 841, and the Frisian coastal area, with Dorestad, that was given to two

PLATE 3.2 The hull of the burial ship found at Öseberg near Oslo, Norway, had ceremonial purposes, but is also a fine example of the large boats with which Vikings carried out their raids over the seas.

Danish chieftains, Rurik and Godfred, in 850. None of them succeeded in making their hold on these territories last for more than a few decades. The famous exception is Normandy, named after the Northmen under the leadership of a Dane called Rollo or Hrolf, who in 911 were allowed to settle in the lower Seine valley by the West Frankish king Charles the Simple. This agreement attracted new settlers from Denmark and Norway, and they stayed. The foundations were laid for the powerful duchy of Normandy.

The remarkable success of the Viking invasions can be attributed to the speed with which they made their attacks and then disappeared in their slender boats. The Frankish royal armies were not designed for surprise attacks of this sort. It took them a long time to mobilise and even then they often could do no more than watch from the riverbank or coast, while the Viking ships remained out of reach. Only when the Vikings started to spend the winter in sheltered places did they become vulnerable, particularly because their forces were small. Eventually it became clear that the Frankish kings were unable to protect their people, and it was the local lords who offered resistance by building forts along the rivers or fortified bridges. The bridge over the Seine at Pîtres in 864 was a late case in which Charles the Bald took the initiative in one of his domains. In this way the invasions helped to accelerate the process of decentralisation of power that had already begun.

On the other hand, the protracted Viking contacts in western Europe, though bringing destruction to the existing order, also brought expansion to the commercial activities of the region. Priests and monks must have found it terrible when their treasures were stolen, but from an economic point of view it meant that the precious metals that had long been hoarded were brought back into circulation as a means of payment in long-distance trade. The same goes for the English tax revenues in silver coin. A large part of this would have come from Frankish sources, through trade. By paying off the Vikings with Danegeld, this wealth (re-)entered circulation and supported the Vikings' brisk trade with the East. In this way Viking activities in western Europe stimulated the circulation of goods and capital there, and the entry of the region into an intercontinental trading system.

The activities of the Vikings in the British Isles and the West Frankish kingdom in the ninth and tenth centuries cannot be considered separately from what happened in Scandinavia during that same period. The formation of strong kingdoms and the fierce competition between powerful stakeholders and their warrior retinues that were part of this process led to the ruthless expulsion of losers or the voluntary departure of those who expected to find more luck elsewhere. It produced an endless stream of pretenders and exiles leaving their homeland in search of their own, new, territory. This explanation for Viking aggression had already been given in medieval Icelandic literature, but it has been confirmed by a plentiful amount of other data, and therefore must have been one of the driving forces behind the more sustained and large-scale Viking attacks on northwestern Europe.

Seen from a different angle, traditional 'Western' historiography has not been fair to the Scandinavians in its traditional description of this process. It has always followed contemporary lamentations in Frankish and Anglo-Saxon, mostly ecclesiastical, sources about the horror of Viking incursions in the west while not paying any attention to Frankish aggression against Denmark even before Viking attacks on the coasts of Frisia, Francia and England really started. Moreover, both Charlemagne and Louis the Pious intensively meddled in the violent struggles for succession to the Danish throne. Frankish aggression was the main reason behind the construction of a mighty defensive work on the Danish-Saxon border, known as the Danevirke. It consisted of three defensive lines, which were dug and laid out between 737 and around 970. The magnificent, circular royal fortresses whose remnants have been found further inland, such as Trelleborg on

Sjaelland, and Fyrkat and Aggersborg on Jutland, most probably were built to consolidate royal power in Denmark itself, and not, as has long been thought, as bases for large-scale attacks on England and the continent.

Much of Denmark had already been unified under one king before 800. His successors extended Danish power over southern Norway. The royal dynasty that emerged around the middle of the tenth century in the persons of King Gorm the Old, his son Harald Bluetooth and his grandson Svein Forkbeard was very successful. Svein invaded, and conquered, England in 1014. After his death he was succeeded by his son, Cnut the Great (1016–1035), who could style himself 'King of all England, of Denmark, of all the Norwegians, and of part of the Swedes'. Norway was first unified under one king, Harald Finehair, in the 880s. Only for Sweden does the picture remain rather obscure. In Charlemagne's time, a king of the Swedes was active in the Birka area, but the first to rule over the larger part of what we now know as Sweden is thought to have been Olof Skötkonung (c.995–1020).

Slav principalities

Other warrior societies of the barbarian north were also 'scaling-up' from chiefdom societies to early states in the course of tenth century, and it is no coincidence that this produced the first detailed written information. Obviously, the most successful of the many chiefdoms in this vast area now began to have sufficient size and political weight to seriously defy Frankish and/or Byzantine power. We first see this happen with the Frisian 'kings' or 'dukes' around 700, followed by Saxon and Slav 'dukes' by the end of the eighth century. Neither managed to stay outside the iron grip of Frankish power, but whereas the lands of the Frisians and Saxons were conquered by and incorporated into the Carolingian Empire, Slav warlords on the extended eastern border of the Empire managed to resist even if they often had

to accept Frankish dominance. This situation of supervised autonomy paved the way for the formation of larger principalities in the course of the ninth century, whose origins are rather hazy. In the Balkans these were the dukedoms of the Croats and the Serbs, whose leaders also had to deal with Bulgarian and Byzantine power in the south. Further north a Moravian principality took shape in the area of the present-day Czech Republic. In the second half of the ninth century its princes succeeded in more than doubling the territory over which they claimed overlordship; it stretched from the middle Elbe in the north-west to the Drava and Tisza rivers in the south-east. This 'Great Moravia' proved to be short-lived; it was destroyed by the Magyars in 906. By that time there were two other strong principalities with early state-like features and led by noble families with a long future ahead: the dukedoms of Bohemia (or of the Czechs) and Poland (or of the Polane). According to Ibrahim ibn Yaqub, an Arab traveller who visited Bohemia in the mid-960s, Poland was by far the largest, most powerful and best organised principality in the world east of Germany. Its duke, Mieszko of the Piast family, raised taxes in coin. From the revenues he paid his bodyguard of 3,000 elite warriors handsomely, including a child allowance.

Moorish Iberia

Almost immediately after the conquest of Egypt in 642–643 the Arab warriors turned their gaze further westwards. In a little over fifty years the whole of North Africa was under their control. When the Byzantines were finally expelled in 680, the native Berber tribes united in a confederation and offered fierce resistance to the Arab conquerors. Some of the Berbers had been Romanised and lived in towns along the coast, while others were still nomads. In 705 the whole of the Maghreb became the province of Ifriqiya, independent of Egypt. It is possible that reports of confusion in Visigothic Spain led to the crossing of the Straits of Gibraltar by Tariq's 7,000-strong army of Islamised Berbers in 711. The invaders had a rapid victory near Jerez de la Frontera, and then advanced on the royal capital at Toledo without meeting any opposition. With reinforcements of 18,000 men from the east, but also because they expanded their authority through treaties rather than by war, they reached the eastern Pyrenees within ten years. Only the small kingdom of Asturias, on the Cantabrian coast, and the adjacent territories of the Basques straddling the western Pyrenees, remained outside their reach. From that point, Muslim armies made raids over the mountains as far as the Rhône valley, but their fervour was broken when they suffered defeat at the hands of the Frankish leader, Charles Martel. In 751 they had to relinquish Narbonne. Three decades later the initiative was taken over by the Franks. Around 800, Charlemagne established the 'Spanish March', which extended Frankish power to Barcelona.

The core region of Muslim **al-Andalus** – the Arab name for the Iberian peninsula – was divided into provinces that stemmed from the dioceses of the late Roman and Visigothic period. From 716 Córdoba was the seat of the central government. Originally the administration was in the hands of governors serving under the authority of the governor in Kairouan and eventually under the caliph of Damascus. The fall of the Umayyad dynasty in 750 led to the de facto independence of small kingdoms in the Maghreb and Iberia. In 756 Abd ar-Rahman, a descendant of the Umayyads and a political exile, succeeded in having himself recognised as ruler in Córdoba with the title of emir. After he had suppressed the uprisings of new Muslims (see below) in the mountainous southern provinces, which had been going on for years, Abd ar-Rahman III proclaimed the orthodox caliphate of Córdoba in 929. With this he displayed his legitimacy as an Umayyad (although he was of mixed blood with blond hair and blue eyes)

PLATE 3.3 Moorish stronghold and city walls of Obidos, Portugal.

BOX 3.4 ST JAMES OF COMPOSTELA

According to twelfth-century sources, Charlemagne unsuccessfully besieged the Moors in Pamplona. But due to St James' intervention the walls collapsed, enabling the Christians to conquer the city. Charlemagne presented part of the plundered Saracen gold to the church of Santiago and to the foundation of other churches dedicated to St James. This reliquary from *c.*1200 depicts the saint's miraculous intervention.

Although Acts 12:2 tells us that the apostle James was buried outside the walls of Jerusalem in the time of King Herod, a Latin Breviarium of the Apostles dating from the late sixth century wrote that James had left the Holy Land to preach in Spain, where he died. This view fitted in perfectly with efforts of the Visigothic Christians to introduce their own liturgy. During the seventh century numerous altars and churches were dedicated to St James. In the late eighth century, after the Muslim conquest, Gallic clergy used his cult to give Spain's disorganised and oppressed Christians something to hold on to. In a liturgical hymn of 785 St James was presented as 'the shining golden head of Spain, our leader and patron saint'. Then, between 818 and 834, a tomb was discovered in Galicia, brightly lighted by a star (*stella*) that hung over the field (*campus*). It was taken as a sign from heaven that this was the burial place of St James (*San Iago* in Spanish). Since then Santiago de Compostela has been the patron saint of Christian Spaniards and supported them in their centuries-long Reconquest against the Muslims. Santiago quickly became the second most important place of pilgrimage in Christian Europe, after St Peter's in Rome.

distinct from the Abbasid caliphate in Baghdad and from the heterodoxy of the Fatimids who had established their own caliphate in Ifriqiya (present-day Tunisia) twenty years earlier.

Until the close of the tenth century, Umayyad rule was strong enough to prevent attempts at Christian reconquest making serious headway. Then the caliphs started to lose their hold on the extensive outlying areas or 'marches', which they controlled only for a short time or only in part. In particular the 'central march', with Toledo, and after 946 Medinaceli, as its capital, was from early on the scene of violent struggle against Christians from the north.

The first wave of conquerors of Iberia came from north Arabia early in the eighth century. They settled chiefly in the towns, and enjoyed a number of privileges which often led to uprisings by the Muslims who had arrived later, sometimes known as 'new Muslims'. These later arrivals from south Arabia, originally peasants, settled in the countryside. Among these 'Arabs' there undoubtedly would have been a large number of other people from the east who had joined the army and rapidly become Arabised. At intervals, large numbers of Berber immigrants from the mountains and deserts of North Africa ended up in central Spain, where they continued their traditional way of life as cattle herders. Their tribal links remained unchanged for at least three centuries. The region round Valencia and Murcia was farmed by coastal Berbers, using Roman irrigation methods and channels.

The native population of Iberia gradually became Islamised over the centuries. One-eighth were Muslim in the eighth century, a quarter in the ninth, and a third in the tenth. This also means that at no time did the Muslims form a numerical majority. Christians, like Jews, were treated with reasonable tolerance by the new rulers. They were allowed to hold religious services, their bishops were respected, they enjoyed a large degree of autonomy and justice was administered following their own customary law. They had to pay taxes, as *dhimmi* (non-Muslims),

in accordance with Islamic law. In the course of time many Christians adapted their way of life, their language and manner of dress – but not their religion – to the dominant Arabic culture: they were called *musta'rib* in Arabic, which is translated as '**Mozarab**'. Christians who did convert to Islam, *conversos*, were not treated as equals of the original Muslims, but they were able to climb the social ladder as clients. Jewish communities, which were particularly important in towns, welcomed the new Islamic authorities as liberators after the repression they had suffered under the Christian Visigoths.

Points to remember

- Economic and political conditions in the post-Migration Period favoured the expansion of land-based lordship in combination with the formation of a class of dependent peasants tied to the land, which also implied subjection to the authority of the landlord.
- This process was further reinforced when ordinary free men were relieved of their obligation to fulfil public duties such as attendance at public law courts and military service.
- In at least parts of the Frankish world, but also Anglo-Saxon England, large estates became organised as bipartite manors, the most innovative feature of which was that, in exchange for possessing their own farm, serf peasants were obliged to work the land which the manor lord had 'reserved' for direct exploitation.
- Outside the former frontiers of the Roman Empire the characteristics of a small-scale chiefdom society, centred around local warlords and their armed retinues, survived longer.
- In general, the early medieval world was a world in which towns and trade were only of secondary economic importance. The most conspicuous part of trade was international commerce in prestigious objects that was

closely linked to the extensive gift-exchange systems on which aristocratic society thrived.

- ■ Vikings were men from Scandinavia who were active outside Scandinavia as both traders and raiders. Larger-scale, aggressive Viking invasions led to permanent migration of large numbers of Scandinavian settlers to the British Isles, the Channel coast (Normandy) and Russia.

- ■ The most successful successor state to the Roman Empire in the West proved to be the Frankish kingdom or kingdoms, ruled by the Merovingian dynasty from the end of the fifth century until the middle of the eighth century.

- ■ The Carolingian Empire, constituted after a coup d'état by the mayor of the palace Pippin the Short in 749–754, reached its apogee under Charlemagne (768–814), who on Christmas Eve 800 was crowned as Roman emperor.

- ■ Whether one would call Charlemagne's empire a 'state' depends on one's appreciation of the effectiveness of its key state institutions, such as capitularies (royal decrees), public courts of law, the army, and the public offices of count, margrave, and *missus dominicus* (royal envoy).

- ■ In order to reinforce their personal bond with the aristocracy – probably first with young members of their elite guard – Carolingian rulers made extensive use of vassalage. However, this in no way made the Carolingian Empire a 'feudal state'.

- ■ A turning point in the history of England was the reign of King Alfred of Wessex (871–899), who brought the Viking advance in England to a halt, and prepared the way for a royal dynasty that could style itself 'kings of England'.

- ■ From the middle of the eighth century onwards, the larger part of the Iberian peninsula was consolidated into the Umayyad emirate of Córdoba, which prevented attempts at Christian reconquest from making headway until the close of the tenth century.

Suggestions for further reading

Barbero, Alessandro (2004), *Charlemagne: Father of a Continent* (Berkeley: University of California Press) (orig. Italian, 2000). Of the new historical biographies of Charlemagne that have appeared over the past two decades, Barbero's is certainly one of the most readable and accessible for non-specialist readers. It also deals with all important aspects of Charlemagne's reign.

Hodges, Richard (2000), *Towns and Trade in the Age of Charlemagne* (London: Duckworth). Brief, idiosyncratic, yet stimulating introduction to the archaeological and (but less) historical problematisation of urbanisation and long-distance trade in the early Middle Ages.

McCormick, Michael (2001), *Origins of the European Economy: Communications and Commerce*, AD *300–900* (Cambridge: CUP). Monumental reconstruction of early medieval commerce on the basis of exhaustive analysis of written, archaeological and numismatic evidence. Reconstructing roads, trade routes, traffic and travellers, McCormick's book makes the 'Dark Ages' look like an awfully busy place.

Smith, Julia M.H. (2005), *Europe after Rome: A New Cultural History 500–1000* (Oxford: OUP). Highly praised cultural history of early medieval Latin-Christian Europe. The book has a thematic approach, and deals in a modern, cultural-historical way with broad themes such as literacy, kinship, genderisation, ethnicity, gift-giving, social identity, honour, life and death and the ethics of (royal) rule.

Wickham, Chris (2005), *Framing the Early Middle Ages: Europe and the Mediterranean, 400–800* (Oxford: OUP). Awe-inspiring and extremely well-documented top-down description of the local societies that took shape in both the post-Roman world of the West and the neo-Roman world of the East, on both sides of the Mediterranean. A classical social-structuralist approach that is rare today.

Part II

The central Middle Ages, 1000–1300

4 Accelerated growth

The three centuries between about 950 and 1250 were a time of great change in many fields: economic, social, political, religious and cultural. This chapter will first concentrate on three aspects that are closely linked: population growth, increase in food production and concomitant changes in the relationship between lords and peasants. It will then concentrate on the rural segment of the medieval economy and society; the urbanisation process will be discussed in Chapter 9.

Population growth

The period between 950 and 1250 is usually depicted as one of relatively strong and sustained population growth. But was that really the case? Bold estimates for the whole of continental Europe (including Russia and the Balkans) place the number of inhabitants in the year 1000 at between 30 and 40 million, and by the beginning of the fourteenth century at 70–80 million. This means that the population of Europe more than doubled in the space of three centuries, an increase of 0.25 per cent per year. This figure was confirmed by recent estimates of the population

growth in England between 1086 and 1300, which are relatively well documented. In 1086, the year in which William the Conqueror ordered the compilation of the *Domesday Book*, the oldest European source in any way resembling a country-wide population statistic, England had between 2.5 and 2.75 million inhabitants: this number rose to between 4 and 6 million by 1300, pointing to a growth rate of 0.18–0.35 per cent per year.

Certainly, by present-day standards, population growth of this size can hardly be called spectacular and, besides, it probably would not have been much greater than in the preceding three centuries. As opposed to the model of an explosive growth between about 1000 and 1300, an argument can be made equally well for an alternative: a gradually built-up and frequently disrupted net population increase from the seventh century reached, between the eleventh and thirteenth centuries, the critical mass necessary to accelerate the processes of commercialisation, urbanisation and state formation that were so essential for socio-economic and political development.

Even then we should consider the fact that there were large regional differences. Looking at Europe as a whole, a dividing line can be drawn roughly between the south and the west, where the population grew considerably and was relatively densely populated by about 1300, and the north and the east (Scandinavia, Poland, the Baltic region and Russia), where growth lagged behind until the end of the Middle Ages. Demographically speaking, by 1200 the population density of western Europe was already greatly in excess of that of eastern Europe.

Volume and nature of agricultural production

However meagre the doubling of a population in the space of three centuries may seem to us, it would only have been possible if food production had also roughly doubled: roughly, because we do not know whether calorie intake remained the same, and we must also make allowances for increasing urbanisation. An increase in food production can be achieved in two ways: by a more intensive use of existing agricultural land and by expanding the acreage. The first option was feasible only to a limited extent. In other words, it would not have been possible to double land productivity (the physical yield per unit of surface area) in three centuries, even at the cost of falling labour productivity (the yield per worker deployed). Until long after the Middle Ages an increase of agricultural production primarily meant extending the acreage of arable land – either near existing settlements or by colonising areas far away, even on the frontiers of Latin-Christian Europe.

A formidable obstacle to the improvement of soil production was the low level of manuring, mainly due to the lack of integration between arable and pastoral farming. English manorial accounts dating from this period show no relation at all between harvest yields and the extent of livestock grazing. Opportunities to maintain manuring levels by using non-animal fertiliser were seldom taken, one of the exceptions being a wide swath through northern France where the land was regularly enriched with calcareous marl. A form of green manuring did take place, entirely unintentionally, through the regular but marginal cultivation of legumes (beans, peas); one characteristic of legumes is that they fix atmospheric nitrogen (the most important inorganic fertiliser) in the soil.

Nevertheless, three methods for achieving more intensive soil use are known from that period of expansion. The first and most obvious was to convert grasslands into arable land. The cultivation of grain that can be baked into bread provides between six and seventeen times more calories per unit of surface area than the grazing of cattle. Indeed, some historians believe that agricultural expansion in the high Middle Ages in the first place took the form of extending the cultivation of grain in existing settlements, a process known in German as *Vergetreidung* ('cerealisation').

A second possibility lay in pushing back the fallow. In traditional agriculture, peasants never used all their fields at the same time. Experience had taught them that after a few years the harvests became smaller, chiefly as a result of the land being overtaken by weeds. So a good part of the farmland was always left fallow. Cattle were then put to graze on this fallow land, in order to eat away the weeds and leave manure. The land was ploughed before it was seeded again. During the period of expansion peasants in different regions of northern Europe started, hesitantly, to experiment with various systems with restricted fallow. Best known is the so-called three-course system, in which only about one-third of the arable was left fallow; a winter cereal (rye or wheat) was grown on another third, and a summer cereal (barley or oats) or legumes on the remainder. Through annual rotation a different third of the land lay fallow every year. In reality, three-course systems were less common than is often thought. On English estates, for example, it was only one of seven cropping types that were commonly used.

Finally, the mouldboard-plough and horse traction combined two technical inventions

BOX 4.1 THE MEDIEVAL PLOUGH

Compared with the primitive, prehistoric ard, the mouldboard-plough, which was developed in Europe in the first millennium CE, demonstrated three major improvements in construction. First, whereas the ard had just one working part – a ploughshare made out of tempered wood – that could scratch the surface of a field, the mouldboard-plough had three: the coulter, a blade projecting vertically downwards from the plough-beam and whose height was adjustable; the ploughshare, which was attached asymmetrically at the end of the plough sole, the beam on which the plough rests; and the mouldboard, a wooden plate mounted diagonally on the plough sole. Second, two of the parts – coulter and share – were made of iron. Third, the plough-beam was no longer attached directly to the yoke of the draught animals, at least not on the slightly more developed types, but rested on either a sledge-shaped 'foot' or a two-wheeled fore-carriage. This meant that less traction was needed and that the depth of the furrow could be varied with a couple of small adjustments. A mouldboard-plough with a fore-carriage is usually called a wheel plough (Latin: *carruca*).

The mouldboard-plough was far more sophisticated than the ard: through a combination of a vertical (coulter) and horizontal (share) cut, the clods of soil were loosened; the mouldboard then turned the soil over. The turning of the soil uprooted the weeds, brought mineral nutrients from the subsoil to the surface, and helped to mix any added manure into the soil. The heavier construction and adjustable iron parts made it possible to till heavy or unstable soil at different depths. When the plough followed a certain set direction, it created a pattern of ridges and furrows that ensured good drainage, and thus facilitated the cultivation of winter crops, rye in particular. Finally, a more effective loosening of the soil made crosswise ploughing, which was essential when the ard was used, unnecessary. In this way one of the stages of ploughing was no longer really required. In fact, however, arables, at least in demesne, were usually ploughed more than once. Besides, mouldboard-ploughs required two persons to operate them: the *tentor* or ploughman, and the *fugator* or driver of the draught animals. Also, the ploughing gang was followed by another gang with a harrow to break up the loosened clods before sowing. Experienced ploughmen were highly esteemed in peasant communities and by estate managers. Paradoxically, therefore, ploughmen were often serfs or even slaves, because their lords or owners did not want them to leave their estates without express consent.

An early picture of a medieval wheel plough can be seen in the Bayeux Tapestry, the embroidery commissioned by Odo, bishop of Bayeux and half-brother of William the Conqueror, to commemorate the battle of Hastings. The plough has no mouldboard: this may be a mistake on the part of the embroiderer – after all, the peasant walking next to the plough lacks both legs – but coulter, share and fore-carriage are clearly recognisable. The same picture also shows the plough being drawn by a mule or a hinny, with a horse dragging a harrow in front.

which helped to intensify production as well as to extend acreage through land development, especially on the heavier soils of eastern and north-western Europe (see Box 4.1). The use of horses instead of oxen as draught animals has evident advantages in agriculture: horses are more manoeuvrable and quicker than oxen. They are also more powerful. However there are disadvantages too: oxen are less discriminating in what they eat and less susceptible to sickness, have more stamina, are easier to yoke to agricultural equipment and, when slaughtered, they provide more and tastier meat. The two major disadvantages would have been overcome during the medieval period of expansion: the problem of fodder through a strong expansion in the cultivation of oats (which besides being used for horse-feed was also an ingredient in beer); and the harnessing problem through the combined development of the horse collar (a padded leather collar), girth (belly-band), swingletree (a crossbar to which the traces are attached) and shafts. Through the improved method of harnessing the pressure point sat lower, while the padded collar prevented the draught animal from being choked. In this way the pulling power of horses could be used far more

efficiently, which in turn led to the use of heavier, cold-blood draught horses and heavier-built ploughs and other implements, but also of carts, equipped with a shaft.

Innovations of the sort described above never appear out of thin air, but often are the result of long, intermittent development and adaptation. The oldest archaeological traces of mouldboard-ploughs and harrows in central and western Europe date from the Migration Period, or even earlier. But the types with which we are familiar from the high Middle Ages only resembled their Roman and barbarian prototypes to a limited extent. We must also bear in mind that, as far as technical innovation in the pre-industrial period is concerned, there was often a considerable length of time between the first development and the widespread use of new implements or methods of working. There are two reasons for this. First, technical inventions cannot usually be utilised on their own. They must be applied in a particular technological environment or 'technological complex', as this is called. The success of the plough and harrow depended on the availability of two scarce and costly products: horses and iron. In the Carolingian period even large estates possessed only a few iron implements. The situation would have been even worse elsewhere, and probably the vast majority of peasants had only a spade or hoe to till their strips of land. Second, psychological and social factors play a role. Pre-industrial peasants were conservative; their principal survival strategy was the avoidance of risk, certainly in the absence of any market incentives to speak of. Besides, unless peasants were free landowners, they were not free to use expensive draught animals and farming equipment, even if it is not always clear whether dependent peasants worked their lord's lands (as well as their own holdings) with their own equipment and animals or with his. Both happened, but in neither case were such capital goods likely put to optimal use.

In north-west Europe the need for mouldboard-ploughs and horse power increased quickly after the tenth century when heavy, unstable clay and peat soils were rapidly reclaimed; before then such lands could only be used as hay meadows or summer pasture. The main reason behind these reclamations was the need for more arable land. By the tenth century, more intensive use of existing farmland was not enough to feed the net population increase, and most of the growth of agrarian production between the tenth and thirteenth centuries was reached by extension of the area of land used for agriculture at the expense of the vast expanses of woods and wetlands, moors and marshes that made up early medieval Europe's wilderness. The axe and the spade became the most useful tools of the central Middle Ages.

Reclamation of peat moors amounted to systematically draining the moors whose existence depended on being permanently saturated with water. At first arable farming was certainly possible on the drained peat bog if the land was high enough. After drainage the ground level subsided quickly as a result of the decreased volume and oxidation of the peat bog. This forced peat farmers in wetlands, such as the coastal regions of the modern-day Netherlands, to be ever-more ingenious in their water management, beginning with the digging of canals and the construction of embankments and sluices and ending with wind-driven watermills to expel the water from completely endyked peat polders into higher-lying channels. This stage was reached in the County of Holland soon after 1400, but the battle against the water was by no means won. The ground level had subsided to such an extent that the peat farmers were forced to give up arable farming and specialise in livestock, or make a living elsewhere. With their knowledge of drainage and dyke-building, peasants from Frisia, Holland and Flanders were welcomed as guest labourers (from the Latin *hospites*) when low-lying coastal marshes and peat bogs were being reclaimed in other parts of Europe. Right at the beginning of the twelfth century they were called in to help with the first phases of the **Ostkolonisation**, the German colonisation of the lands east of the Weser, the Elbe, the Oder-Neisse and later in Prussia east of the Vistula.

On the European scale, the reclamation of fens and marshes was insignificant when compared with forest clearance – the felling of tropical rain-forests in our own time is not an exaggerated comparison. Between one-quarter and one-third of all the land that was developed for cultivation between 950 and 1250 must once have been covered with woods and forest. In north-west Europe countless place-names ending in *-rode/-roth, -rade/-rath, rud* (see the German verb *roden* which means 'to clear') or *-sart* are reminders of this. Everything seems to indicate, too, that by about the year 1000 there were no longer any vast tracts of virgin forest in west or south Europe. Certainly there were still many woods, but with their numerous clearings of varying size they resembled a cheese with holes in it. Charcoal burners and woodcutters, miners and iron-workers, swineherds, pitch-makers and wax-makers, trappers, hermits and anybody who, for whatever reason, lived cut off from the civilised world shared a marginal and dangerous life there with bears, deer and wolves, animals that were increasingly forced to retreat. It was the peasant colonists who really accelerated the process of deforestation.

There is no indication at all of any ecological concerns. On the contrary, in literary and other texts the picture of the forest as a sinister, dangerous place that should really be eradicated continued to compete with the opposite view (at least as old) of the forest as an unspoiled Arcadia or a place of spiritual contemplation. The best-kept forests were those where kings or other territorial princes vigorously insisted on their royal right to wilderness – their claim to uncultivated land, particularly with an eye to hunting, a favourite pastime. That is why, in England, large forests survived the expansion phase, although in time it became necessary to enclose them as far as possible to keep the game in and the poachers out. This was not always easy, as we learn from the thirteenth-century folk songs about the legendary outlaw Robin Hood and his merry men who hid in Sherwood Forest, one of the large royal woods. Robin Hood is probably a product of the imagination, but the type certainly existed. In about 1280, for example, a search was made for one Geoffrey du Parc who prowled about Feckenham Forest in Worcestershire with a band of some hundred companions, including, sure enough, his own priest.

This feverish activity on the fringes between land that had long been settled and the wilderness outside created a typical frontier society – a world of busy peasant-colonists with a rolling, continuously moving frontier. Usually, a distinction is made between internal and external colonisation. In the former, expansion of agrarian land and peasant activity took place in waste lands adjacent to existing settlements and one could operate from a familiar institutional infrastructure (village communities, parishes, manors). In the latter, settlers were migrant colonists who reclaimed wilderness far away from their place of origins and often in remote areas. Here, frontiers were more challenging, whether because of the forbidding character of the surrounding nature, or because of the dangerous proximity of hostile neighbours,

who could be the subjects of native Christian princes but also outright pagans. Here too, frontier society took on a more violent, Wild West-like character which attracted not just peaceful peasant-colonists.

New types of local lordship

One of the logical consequences of the growing population density during the period of expansion was what the French historian Robert Fossier (1988) has called *encellulement* (meaning roughly 'compartmentalisation'). By this he meant that in this period land was more and more territorialised, that is to say, divided up into neatly defined units of political or ecclesiastical control where people were becoming more and more encased in a cascade of formalised local organisations, each with its own public rights and obligations. This process happened from below, for example, through the formation of village communities (more about this later), and from above, through the establishment of rural parishes and local lordships. It is this last phenomenon which we shall discuss first and most fully.

A banal revolution?

The repeated (sub)division of Charlemagne's empire after the death of Louis the Pious marked a crisis in royal power which seemed to lead unavoidably to the transformation of dukedoms, margravates and even counties into autonomous principalities. This tendency towards the creation of states within states will be further discussed in Chapter 5. The question to be dealt with at this point is what happened with 'public' (royal) governance further below, at the local level, in a situation, moreover, of expansion of settlement and slow population growth? If not the king or his officials, who then was exercising authority over increasing numbers of people? Since we characterised medieval society as an aristocratic society to the core, the obvious answer would be aristocrats, and nothing altered on that point. But the manner in which aristocrats took control over people underwent drastic, and according to many historians revolutionary, change. In the early medieval world aristocrats were first and foremost large landowners with natural rights of lordship over all common people who lived and were settled on their estates (Chapter 3). This is not to say that public authority was totally absent. In the Carolingian Empire, the king's *bannus* or supreme power of command and rule was exercised on the regional level by counts, who in their turn were represented by local officials bearing such titles as *vicarii* (vice-counts), *iudices* (judges) or *centenarii* (hundredmen). One may question the effectiveness or even reality of this three-layered hierarchy of public governance, but everybody agrees that no local officials in the Carolingian Empire ever called themselves 'lord of' a place or a territory that was not their estate. This was to change in the course of the tenth and eleventh centuries when the number of 'lords' of localities started to mushroom, as did the number of castles. Both are sure indications of the rapid diffusion of a radically new concept of local lordship, that is to say, lordship not based primarily on privately owned landed estates but on the exercise of some sort of public authority, derived from the royal *bannus* and operative within a circumscribed territory.

Most historians will agree nowadays that there are two scenarios for describing the origins of these new **banal lordships** or seigneuries, as they are called. According to the first the constitution of local lordships was guided from above, the result of a deliberate policy of counts to extend their reach and to strengthen their grip on villages and emerging towns through the appointment of local agents, now often called *ministeriales* (ministerials; knights of unfree origins) in Germany or *castellani* (castellans) in France, who remained accountable to them. This scenario was typical for strong principalities, such as the County of Flanders or duchy of Normandy in the West Frankish kingdom, but also, for example, for

the prince-archbishopric of Hamburg-Bremen in Germany, which, as we saw, facilitated large-scale reclamations of empty wilderness, which could then be provided in one stroke with a complete, pre-designed, public order.

The second scenario describes the same process in the opposite direction. In this scenario we can distinguish various tracks that all led to the establishment of banal lordships from the bottom up, aimed at fending off interference from above – and leading to 'absence of government' (Bisson 2009). Masters of landed estates could extend their authority over the peasants settled on them with 'banal' rights, such as monopolies on milling/grinding corn, pressing wine or baking bread. Aristocrats who acted as advocates of religious institutions that enjoyed immunity sometimes converted their position as protector into banal lordship. Local strongmen wealthy enough to build their own stronghold could try to impose their power on a village or small town while claiming to possess *bannus*. Finally, and actually midway between the two scenarios, local officials (*vicarii* or castellans), who on paper operated on behalf of counts, succeeded in detaching themselves from comital control. These diverse tracks betray a regional diversity in both scenario and chronology that has not yet been charted sufficiently well, but which no doubt was closely linked to differences in such basic structural features as the dominance of large landed estates versus the survival of small free peasant landownership, or the (f)actual power of dukes, margraves and counts in the post-Carolingian kingdoms.

The explosive proliferation of banal lordships or local seigneuries, from whatever direction, has been called the 'banal revolution', because it led to radical changes in the direct exploitation of people: no longer primarily through the lordship over peasants tied to privately owned land but through the high-handed exercise of public authority over all common people living within a well-defined local district.

Of what did this new type of local lordship consist? At its heart was the exercise of justice, including capital and corporal punishment – in other words the trying of serious crimes. This jurisdiction gave banal lords an excuse to confiscate goods and arrest people arbitrarily, and thus a means of forcing the small, free peasants off their property. In addition, it was possible to organise on a local scale what had been impossible to achieve at state level: the levying of general taxes, tallage – often referred to as *tallia* (*taille* in French) or *exactiones* in the sources – or the exacting of other general seigneurial rights that were not infrequently borrowed from the serf statute. Finally, banal lords managed to impose all sorts of labours and services on their subjects – such as compulsory work in and around their castles – and they exploited costly capital goods, like mills and bakers' ovens, as a monopoly, a practice that had earlier normally been restricted to great estates.

Taken together, these rights deriving from banal lordship were called *consuetudines* ('customs'), a euphemism that was sometimes qualified by the adjective *malae* ('bad'), not just because they were seen by local populations as undesirable infringements of their existing customary law but more because of their arbitrary character and the threat of violence that was always lurking behind their enforcement. Often enough, and certainly when local peasant communities were not protected any longer by the power of king or prince, banal lords made use of unrestrained, brute, force. Shortly after 1200 the noblemen of Catalonia even demanded from the king of Aragon the right to 'mal-treat' (*male tractare*) their peasant subjects. This opened the door to the development of new types of systematic exploitation of peasants, couched in the doublespeak term *remensa* ('redemption'). Banal

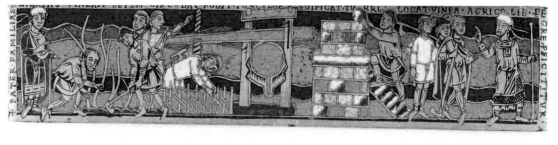

PLATE 4.1 Difficult relations between landlords and peasants are exemplified in the enamel decoration of a small portable altar in gilded copper created around 1160 in the middle Meuse region. The images are surrounded by quotes from Matthew 21:33–42, which are illustrated in four plaques 4.9 cm high, the larger ones 22 cm long, and two shorter ones 11.8 cm long. The iconography reveals inspiration from the tenth-century *Codex Aureus* from the abbey of Echternach (Luxemburg). The story tells of an absentee landowner who had a vineyard planted, and a winepress and a tower constructed. He leased his property to vinedressers. When he twice sent some of his servants and finally his son to collect the harvest, they were beaten, stoned and killed by the vinedressers, who saw an opportunity to seize the inheritance.

lords offered peasants the 'opportunity' to 'redeem' all kinds of arbitrary burdens that were first put upon them.

It is important to realise that, the whole of Europe considered, experiences of peasants in these centuries differed widely. Banal lordships were not set up everywhere, and where they were they were not necessarily of the malicious and violent kind. Now and then, ill-treated peasants received support from clerical circles, but there was always a touch of the hypocritical in that. Ecclesiastical lords and institutions complained, especially when the might of local lords was directed against Church possessions, while they often behaved with equal severity and violence against those under their own authority. The clergy never spoke out against the banal order as such.

It would have been less easy to establish exploitative lordships of such a potentially violent nature had not the seigneurs provided themselves with two powerful means of exerting their authority: a castle and a following of well-armed warriors. These castles were not the kind of great protective fortresses built throughout north-west Europe during the ninth and tenth centuries on the orders of kings and counts, near commercial centres such as Dorestad and Middelburg, to offer the people and their property some protection from the Vikings. In the context of banal lordship we are talking about more modest strongholds. They were not wholly unknown in the Carolingian era, but their number exploded to an estimated 2,000 in western Europe after the middle of the tenth century, quite a time after the last great invasions of Europe by barbarian groups (Vikings, Muslims, Magyars). The primary purpose in building these castles, therefore, could not have been to protect local populations against foreign invaders. Only Spain of the Reconquest, embroiled in a struggle to the death with the Moors, formed any sort of exception – both Castile and Catalonia mean 'land of castles'. Elsewhere the principal aim was more plain and simple. Where local lordships were created from

above – our first scenario – castles were erected by territorial princes to form the centre of a local district called *castellania*. Their main function was to support a smooth and efficient exercise of the *bannus* with the threat of terror. If castles were constructed at the private costs of local strongmen – our second scenario – they had the additional function of keeping rival lords out of the region and ambitious territorial princes at a distance.

This new type of castle consisted of little more than a motte, a natural or man-made mound, on which was built a wooden or stone tower, the keep (*donjon*), which was several storeys high and could only be entered by a staircase to the first floor. Some castles had a walled space next to the motte, where there was room for outbuildings, stables, etc. In urban settlements such castles were built within or close to the town itself. In the countryside, however, castles were more often situated in relative isolation, far from existing habitation. Only in Italy and southern France was this less often the case. Here, in this period, entirely fortified new settlements were built in many places, with a castle inside. The design of these *castra* or *castelli* included a concentration of habitation and not infrequently a reorganisation of the agrarian landscape adapted to it. The whole phenomenon is known in the literature as *incastellamento*.

All of these new types of castles had a permanent garrison of small contingents of professional soldiers who were in the service of the lord of the castle. The sources often refer to them as *milites castri* ('soldiers of the castle'), the *gregarii equites* ('ordinary horsemen') or *cavalcata* ('cavalry'). They were recruited from the young scions of lesser, local aristocratic families, but sometimes also from among free or even unfree peasants. They were well trained in mounted combat and were mobilised for the defence of the castle and for small-scale, often extremely violent operations in the surrounding area.

Regional differences and feudal-vassalic packaging

The whole idea of the banal revolution has been much disputed over the past three or four decades. One of the issues that has remained unresolved is whether banal local lordships also came into being in parts of Europe that had remained outside the Carolingian Empire, such as England and the Spanish kingdoms. A second complex question is how to fit banal lordships into the idea that kingdoms and comparable principalities at this stage were to some extent states that provided central government and had to guarantee some degree of public order. To what extent were banal lords accountable to a prince or a king for their unrestricted exercise of public authority?

Proponents of the idea that a restructuring and reinforcement of lordship on the local level also took place outside the Carolingian Empire underline similar demographic and economic conditions: population growth and condensing settlement offered opportunities for aristocratic enrichment and therefore asked, as it were, for localisation and territorialisation of lordship. In some respects English manor lords did indeed look like continental banal lords – for instance they enforced 'banalities' such as the use of their mills on their estates and exercised some form of jurisdiction over villein tenants in their manor courts – but they never succeeded in taking over public courts of justice on the local/regional level or in ruling out the authority of the king's sheriff. Only the so-called Marcher lordships on the Welsh frontier, where 'the king's writ did not run', came close to continental principalities; the Marcher lords even had the explicit right to exercise 'royal jurisdiction'. In the Christian kingdoms of Spain a strengthening of local lordship was stimulated by the extraordinary circumstances of the *Reconquista*, in particular during stages of intensified hostility between the kings of Castile and León on the one hand, and the caliph of Córdoba on the other, as in the last decades of the tenth century. In the County of Barcelona,

which would remain part of the kingdom of France until 1137, the evolution of banal lordships rather seems to have been the outcome of internal aristocratic uprisings, first, around the middle of the eleventh century, against the count of Barcelona, and later, during the last quarter of the twelfth century, against the king of Aragon.

As to the second issue it seems to be useful to connect the evolution of banal lordships to the deployment of feudal-vassalic relations. When doing that, one has to bear in mind that the weakening of royal authority through the simultaneous formation of quasi-autonomous principalities (counties, dukedoms, margravates) and banal lordships cannot be labelled simply as 'feudal anarchy', as has so often been done. The increasingly systematic use of feudal-vassalic relationships actually helped prevent long-term anarchy. At the intermediate level, counts, dukes and margraves were able to compel many banal lords into a feudal bond – or back into one – while at the local level many banal lords entered into feudal-vassalic relationships with their *milites*. The ramifications of this multi-layered network in about the middle of the twelfth century are evident in a survey that the count of Champagne had made in 1172 of all the vassals and their fiefs in his county, possibly with the intention of demanding *ligesse* (preferential fealty) from them all. This survey, known as the *Feoda Campanie*, contains the names of no fewer than 1,900 'lords' and 'knights'.

If feudal-vassalic relationships contributed to an early control over banal lordships, these lordships only really disappeared when central, territorial and quasi-sovereign authority was restored, either at the level of kingdoms – as in England and France after the middle of the twelfth century – or at the level of territorial princes – as in the **Holy Roman Empire** after the beginning of the thirteenth century. It meant that heads of state made strenuous efforts to monopolise and centralise those core responsibilities – administration of justice, use of force, public administration, legislation – which nowadays are recognised as state monopolies. The removal or subordination of autonomous seigneuries fitted into the framework of these efforts. When this could not be realised immediately, banal lords were at least forced into feudal relationships, had to cede part of their banal power or owed their **liege** 'open access' to their castles. How important – and articulated – feudal-vassalic relations could be to princes for controlling their territories through castles clearly appears from the feudal registers of the prince-archbishop of Trier in Germany during the first half of the fourteenth century. Of the 136 castles in his territory, 30 were managed by his own castellans, 65 were owned by liege vassals who owed open access to the archbishop, 4 by other vassals who owed open access, and 4 by liege vassals and 33 by other vassals who did not owe open access.

Was later medieval society a feudal society?

These examples point to a gradual expansion of feudal-vassalic ties as an essential – and increasingly 'juridicised' – template for structuring important political and economic relations in central medieval aristocratic society. In appreciating their value we should distinguish between levels of application (on what socio-political level were lord and vassal?) and objects (what was the object of **enfeoffment**?). It brings us to the following classification:

1. On the highest political level relations between a king and his major secular dignitaries could become feudalised. In this case all dukes, margraves and counts became vassals of the king, while their duchies, margravates and counties became fiefs of the crown. If this happened medieval monarchies turned into feudal states. By implication, a substantial part of royal or public government became **'mediatised'**, which means that the king had to leave the effective exercise of royal

authority in the larger part of his kingdom, that is to say, outside the royal domain, to crown vassals whose loyalty to and (military, political and financial) support of the head of state was conceived in a non-bureaucratic way and (therefore) could not be held accountable in a bureaucratic way. The ultimate, and absurd, consequence is that feudal monarchies tended to abolish themselves as states – which is what happened to the Holy Roman Empire in the course of the thirteenth century: the factual sovereignty of the principalities, free cities and other autonomous political units became so great that the emperor's suzerainty over them no longer justified him being called a sovereign head of state (see Chapter 5).

We will just mention in passing the political construction by which one monarch became the vassal of another. In such cases, feudal bonds expressed political dependency on an international level. Examples are the kingdoms of Sicily and England that at some point in time formally became fiefs held from the pope, while the kingdom of Scotland was considered to be a fief of the king of England. The political relationship between the 'dukes' of Poland and Bohemia and the German king was sometimes described in feudal terms, but after each of them had been recognised as a kingdom, one (Poland) became independent, while the other (Bohemia) turned into an imperial fief, which meant that from that moment on the kingdom was seen as part of the German Empire.

2. On the regional/local level this pattern could be reproduced in the relationship/connection between dukes, margraves and counts, on the one hand, and local lords, on the other, by the enfeoffment of local lordships, urban or rural, and with or without castles and other sources of income such as estates or tithes. This also led to mediatisation of public power, but now on the local level of public government over towns and villages.

3. On both levels land or, at a later stage, money rents could be enfeoffed by lords to vassals in return for military service as a **knight**.

4. Finally, in its most watered-down version, land could be enfeoffed without any military obligations. In this case fiefs were similar to hereditary leases, albeit leases not so much to land-users (farmers) as to landowners, and for no other fee than the 'relief' (*relevium*) that had to be paid to the lord each time the land changed hands. This type of fief became extremely widespread in later medieval Europe; if originally the vassals may have been chiefly aristocrats, soon we find many non-noblemen among them – townspeople but also common peasants. At the same time, this type of fief became commercialised, that is to say, they became objects that could be traded on the land market.

In any case, this whole range of feudal-vassalic options was only in place from the twelfth century onwards. Whether this whole development is enough to qualify later medieval society as a feudal society remains a matter of appreciation, also because of substantial regional differences. But in our opinion it would be unwise to just leave out any reference to feudalism in a textbook on medieval history; feudal bonds of all the kinds just mentioned were too meaningful for that.

Changes in the surplus extraction, adjustments in the demesne economy

The establishment of banal lordships led to considerable shifts in agrarian surplus extraction, that is the extent to which and the way in which income was transferred from peasants to lords. Before that time the transfer had been settled chiefly through obligatory services of labour and the payment of surpluses by serf peasants within the framework of landlordship. Banal lords, on the other hand, exploited people – whether as serfs or otherwise – in a well-defined territory on the basis of usurped public authority.

This is not to say that banal lords would have had no interest in owning land. On the contrary, many lordships had a hybrid character: their possessors were both large landowners and exercising banal power of command (see Box 4.2). The point is that many of them abandoned the direct exploitation of demesne land on bipartite estates. This shift was closely connected to the evolution of the manorial system which, during the period of expansion, fell into decline wherever it had been prevalent, except in England. There are a number of deeper-lying reasons for the decline. It is quite possible that financial problems of the aristocracy played a role. With the general increase in population, the aristocracy increased too, and that meant that the inheritances for succeeding generations gradually became smaller. In many regions the relative impoverishment was underlined by the often extravagantly large gifts of land and tithes made to Church institutions. These were probably intended as gifts with a proviso through which the donors retained certain rights, in particular rights of usufruct. However, in their attempts to reduce secular influences on the Church, and with the revival in canon law of ownership concepts borrowed from Roman law, abbeys and other ecclesiastical institutions began to look upon gifts as permanent transfers of property. In some areas, too, the ownership of many tithes, an important source of revenue for the aristocracy, was returned to the Church. Falling incomes contrasted with rising costs. These were caused in part by the increased costs of warfare, in part by the rising fiscal or other demands of kings or territorial princes of comparable standing, in part by the re-opening of trade with the Middle East which made countless desirable luxury goods (including spices, silk and ivory) available, so that the aristocratic way of life became more sophisticated but above all more expensive.

Moreover, the disappearance of the classical manorial system from many regions of Europe

BOX 4.2 THE LORDSHIP OF TALMONT IN THE COUNTY OF POITOU

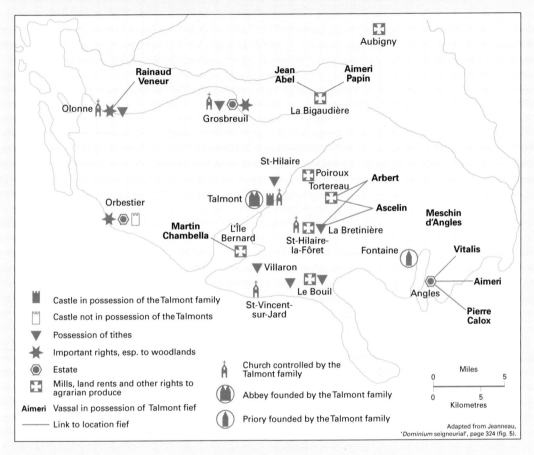

MAP 4.1 Possessions of the lordship of Talmont (Poitou)

A fine example of a succesful banal lordship is provided by the seigneurie of Talmont St Hilaire, situated near the Atlantic coast of the County of Poitou, which was part of the Angevin Empire between 1154 and 1242. At the heart of the lordship was the imposing castle of the Talmont family at Talmont, which was flanked by the abbey of Sainte-Croix, founded by the Talmonts. As well as Talmont itself, they held the lordship of two or three other villages in the neighbourhood (Olonne, Grosbreuil and Orbestier(?)). In those villages they also owned estates, tithes and the collation rights to the parish church, which they did in a number of other villages as well. In yet other villages they took rents from land and owned mills, baking ovens and wine presses for communal use. In sum, the lords of Talmont had three sources of income: private estates and rents from land; income following from the control of local churches and abbeys, in particular tithes; and all kinds of tax-like payments as well as the proceeds of the administration of justice (justicial fines, in particular) that followed from the exercise of banal lordship. Part of these possessions were enfeoffed to ten vassals. The lordship rights themselves were often divided between family members. This can also be observed elsewhere: rights to estates, banal lordships and even to castles could be subdivided, or exercised in common, between brothers or between brothers and sisters, or between families and third parties, such as religious institutions.

Source: Cédric Jeanneau, 'Le *dominium* seigneurial en question: exercice, territoire et adaptation aux marges du Comté Poitevin (1150–1250)', in Martin Aurell and Frédéric Boutoulle (eds), *Les seigneuries dans l'espace Plantagenêt (c.1150–c.1250)* (Bordeaux: Ausonius Éditions, 2009), pp. 309–334.

during the period of expansion can be explained more neutrally by two economic developments. First, rising urbanisation simultaneously created demand for agricultural products and offered employment outside agriculture. This partly offset the effects of the second development, namely the inversion of the land–labour ratio, the scarcity relationship between the production factors of land and labour. As a result of the growth in population, land became scarcer and more expensive, and labour more plentiful and cheaper. This stimulated the conversion of serf labour services into cash payments or deliveries in kind. Serf labour services in the manorial system were, after all, connected to the ownership of a farmstead, and were originally intended to ensure that labour, which was scarce, was kept on the manor. Large landowners, who had dispensed entirely with the labour services of serfs when it was no longer labour but land that was scarce, were now faced with a stark choice. They could completely abandon the direct exploitation of their demesnes, and then lease out the *indominicatum* (land held in demesne) in its entirety or in parts; or they could continue to keep the land in direct use, but now exploit it with the help of paid labourers. During the eleventh and twelfth centuries large landowners all over Europe chose primarily the second option, but in the longer term preference was given to the first alternative. The new monastic orders of Cistercians and Premonstratensians formed an exception, as did England. The former were able to continue with the direct exploitation of their land by bringing

in so-called *conversi*, simple lay brothers, who provided the order with cheap labour. In England, from the end of the twelfth century, many lords of manors (secular and ecclesiastical) resisted the switch from villein labour services in order to profit as much as possible from the high grain prices. That is why in various parts of England the manorial system was maintained in its classical, bipartite form until well into the fourteenth century.

Elsewhere not only did serf labour services tied to the direct exploitation of the manor disappear, but other servile obligations could also be gradually commuted into fixed money payments, like the lord's right to the best of the movable property in a serf's legacy or to compensation for serf daughters who wanted to marry someone from outside the manor. The entire development had three serious consequences. First, over time serfdom lost much of its real significance; in many areas this was translated into the disappearance of the legal status of serfs and the specific customary law attached to it (the whole complex of legal regulations to which serfs were subject). This led to greater social differentiation and geographic mobility in the countryside. Second, the fact that it was possible to commute serf labour and to buy off other servile obligations in regions where there were many manors meant a breakthrough in the commercialisation and monetisation of the rural economy. Peasants were now compelled to convert either their surpluses or their own labour into money. And third, the manor lords themselves suffered losses insofar as labour services or other servile obligations were converted into cash payments. Rents were fixed once and for all, while the thirteenth century was a century of rapid inflation. The real value of the periodic payments was soon eroded, to the advantage of the paying tenants. At a later stage manor lords tried to counteract this by letting out parts of the demesne over which they still had some control on a short-term lease for a limited number of years. An alternative was sharecropping or divided leasing (French *champart* is derived from the Latin *campi pars*, meaning 'part of the field'), which was most common in certain parts of France and Italy. In this system the owner received a fixed share, usually one-third or one-quarter – but in Italy later one-half also (*mezzadria*) – of the gross yields of the lands he had leased out.

Knights and peasants: image and reality

Horsemen become knights

The installation of local lordships can be seen as the tailpiece of an earlier-discussed, lengthy socio-historical process, that is to say, the gradual formation of a new style of warrior aristocracy which is commonly referred to as the **knighthood**. We have already touched upon two key factors in its formation: the growing military importance of heavily armed cavalry and, subsequently, the formation of mounted militias by banal lords. A third element should be seen in part as a clerical reaction to this, but at the same time it had deeper historical roots: the conscious policy of the clergy to represent the aristocracy as fighters in the service of the holy Church, with the king at the forefront, ready to take up arms to defend the Christian faith and the social order desired by God.

The first development led to a clear professionalisation of the mounted fighter, which was speeded up even further by progressive technological advances in weaponry and equipment: the perfecting of the chain-mail hauberk and of many types of weapons for striking and stabbing, horse armour, nailed horseshoes and the panelled war saddle with its high, wraparound cantle and pommel. In addition to great skill, the result of long training, the fighter on horseback needed a large fortune, and that was why armed horsemen – *milites* in the Latin of the time – were predominantly aristocrats. Already in Carolingian Francia, the recognition of an aristocratic youth as a *miles*, a true (mounted) warrior, by being ceremonially girded with a sword, was closely associated with the idea that it was this act which made men fit to exercise *honor*, public office, as well as to defend the holy Church against its enemies.

But professionalisation also implied that physical fitness, talent and assured loyalty all played a part alongside birth and wealth in the recruitment of mounted warriors, while specific historical

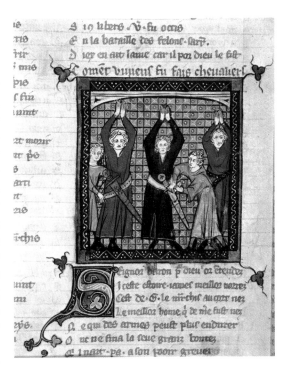

PLATE 4.2 Girding on a knight's sword. *Chansons de Guillaume d'Orange*, first half of the fourteenth century.

circumstances would also have an influence, of course. We have already seen that banal lordships were partly based on small private armies of horsemen who were equipped and maintained at the expense of the lords of the castles. The often denigrating references to these horsemen lead us to surmise that they were not always of noble origins. In the German Empire kings and holders of high office recruited their horsemen from the unfree estate of ministerials, especially in the decades around 1100. On the borders of the Reconquest in Castile and Catalonia there arose a class of peasant-horsemen, *caballeros villanos*. The cavalry of the communal armies of the free city-states of north and central Italy had from the beginning a mixed noble-bourgeois character. In England, the Norman Conquest of 1066 was of overwhelming importance: here *milites* referred to the ordinary mounted fighters in the army of William the Conqueror, often of noble French origin, who became 'tenants' of the 'tenants-in-chief', the barons and dignitaries of the Church who had a direct bond with the king. As we have already explained, in the first decades after 1066 the position of these *milites*-tenants and their enfeoffment with one or more estates (manors) was emphatically connected to their service as mounted fighters.

Through the growing degree of technical and tactical competence demanded of these mounted fighters, through the crucial role they played in the great military operations of the eleventh century, which at the time greatly fired the imagination, and through their increasingly expensive weapons and equipment, the prestige of the *milites* rose almost before their very eyes. What then happened is remarkable: *milites* of high aristocratic birth allowed themselves to be identified with horsemen of more humble origin. Even monarchs presented themselves as mounted warriors. William the Conqueror, for example, is depicted in the Bayeux Tapestry more often as a horseman among his *milites* than as a monarch on his throne. After Otto II of Germany, who was one of the first kings to have a seal made showing

him as a warrior on horseback, many rulers would follow this example. This fusion of high aristocratic, minor noble and non-noble, sometimes even unfree, elements into an elite military corps that in time became difficult to distinguish from the nobility, was coupled with the development of an *esprit de corps*, a new code of honour and behaviour with its own what we now might call sub-culture, while entry to the group was formalised in solemn ceremonial, such as being girded with the *cingulum militiae* ('the girdle of the militia'), and the bestowal of the sword – the *colée* or accolade only dates from the thirteenth century. From then on we no longer speak of horsemen but of knights, and we speak of the knighthood, of the social order of knights (*ordo militaris* in Latin), while **chivalry** is the word used to indicate the cultural and moral encasement of knighthood.

Within the knightly or chivalrous code of behaviour, traditional – many would say universal – values, such as courage, loyalty and fellowship, always remained important. But in addition to that, the construction of a knightly ethos received the support of the Church from the very beginning. For this purpose an old concept was unearthed: that of *miles Christi* or *miles Sancti Petri* ('soldier of Christ' or 'soldier of St Peter'). In early Christendom this title of honour was first given to clerics in general and martyrs in particular. In the fifth and sixth centuries it was passed on to the monks, the new body of the Christian elite. Then it was the turn of the bishops, as we can see from a pastoral letter sent by Pope Nicholas I to the bishops of the West Frankish Empire in 865. The pope forbade the bishops to take part in any more armed conflicts, for they were the *milites Christi* and, as such, should only fight battles of a spiritual nature and exclusively in the service of the pope.

Oddly enough, it was this concept of *miles Christi* that was regenerated in the circles around Pope Gregory VII soon after the middle of the eleventh century, in an attempt to harness the secular *milites* for the Church by propagating, in addition to bravery and fidelity, such Christian virtues as godliness, the defence of the helpless and peace (towards fellow Christians). The fight against non-Christians, the infidel enemies of the faith in Spain and the Holy Land, provided unprecedented new opportunities for cloaking the *milites* in Christian ideals. Conversely, efforts to make the clerical morality more military and heroic were much in evidence, as was clearly shown in the *Liber ad milites Templi de laude novae militiae* ('Book for the Knights of the Temple in Praise of the New Knighthood') written in about 1145 by that Cistercian pillar of the Christian Church, Bernard of Clairvaux. It is a eulogy of the new religious orders of knighthood, which came into being in the Holy Land to defend the conquered holy places and to protect, if necessary by force, the newly swelling stream of pilgrims.

The oldest of these unique orders was the Order of St John of Jerusalem, which dates back to 1048 when merchants from the Italian town of Amalfi were allowed by the Fatimid caliph of Egypt to start a hospital in Jerusalem for the medical care of Christian pilgrims. During the First Crusade the order became militarised, and it was recognised by the pope in 1113. In about the same period of time, a French crusader, Hugo de Payns, founded the 'brotherhood of the poor knights of Christ', which was recognised in 1128 as the Order of the Temple (the Knights **Templar**). The third great military order, the Order of the Hospital of St Mary of the Germans (the German or Teutonic Order) started in 1190 as an initiative of merchants from Lübeck and Bremen during the siege of Acre by the crusaders. Not much later, a whole series of smaller, less expansive orders were thrown up in the Baltic area and in Spain and Portugal, where they held huge estates until well into the early modern era. Both clerics and laypeople could join these orders but only the latter swore an oath of battle; as compensation, in some orders they were not bound to celibacy.

Bernard of Clairvaux found these new spiritual orders of knighthood the highest possible fulfilment of the new ideal of the *militia Christi*.

Ordinary knights – Bernard's *milites saeculi* – were not in the same league: in his view they renounced their original chivalric ideals by paying exaggerated attention to their appearance and their emphasis on outward show. By this outward show Bernard meant the sub-culture that was growing up around the knights and of which diverse matters such as heraldry, clothing, hair style and training formed a part. By the beginning of the twelfth century there was already much hostile criticism of knights' attire in clerical circles: knights looked like women, even on the field of battle where they were decked out in gold and silver jewels. Slightly later there were suspicions about the tournaments, with their *melées* (team fights) and jousts, which probably grew out of the knights' training in arms in about 1100 and rapidly developed into excessively popular spectacles. Because participants were frequently killed, the rules of the game were altered, partly under pressure from the Church which regularly prohibited tournaments, although never with lasting success.

Only the ritual of inauguration could count on the Church's unceasing approval. It was with this ceremony that the Church had the opportunity to immerse fully the candidate-knight, through rites and symbolic acts, in the Christian values which it saw as the foundations of chivalry. Those who aspired to knighthood also swore to protect the Church and clergy. Moreover, the whole ceremony usually took place in a church or chapel, unless a man was dubbed knight on the battlefield or at other events of mass knighting.

Chivalry and courtliness: new rules for moving in high circles

The new virtues of chivalry were imprinted during the inaugural ceremonial, by moral tracts and didactic poems aimed especially at the chivalric lifestyle, but also through completely new literary genres, which formed a part of the specific culture that took shape at the courts of monarchs and other great princes who set themselves up as the natural leaders of the new order of knights. That is why courtliness (*courtoisie* in French) became central to the knightly code of behaviour. Its hidden intentions were:

- to regulate tensions and avoid open aggression and feuds, especially between young men whose entire upbringing was focused on the use of force; and
- to achieve an important place at court through the acquisition of honour.

Such underlying thoughts were, to start with, translated into a programme of etiquette, aimed at civilising the knightly class. It was memorised in simple maxims such as the Middle German *Wirff nit nauch pürschem Sin//die Spaichel über den Tisch hin* ('Never expectorate over the table like a peasant'). Of a rather more elevated nature were the partly classical virtues which the ideal knight was expected to possess: loyalty, (moral) purity, moderation, steadfastness, sense of honour, generosity-largesse and readiness to help, coupled with physical strength and self-control, and a certain knowledge of the world. In this list honour – with its counterpart dishonour – was probably the most important. Honour adhered, as it were, to high social status, but could also be acquired by performing honourable deeds. Prowess, bravery in battle (*prouesse* in Old French), was of course essential for knights. But courtly culture required that a warlike spirit be directed to a more sublime goal. Gradually the idea developed that honour did not really count if it was not earned in the service of another person, preferably a lady or a great prince, or better still, the Christian faith. Only then did honour pave the way to high esteem, maybe personal salvation, but most importantly to 'courtly love'.

This 'courtly love' (*amour courtois* in French) is a concept created by literary historians in the nineteenth century – hence the inverted commas – to describe sublimated erotic feelings in courtly literature. Its two most important characteristics are the inversion of the traditional role pattern (in courtly love the man serves a lady, not vice versa) and the moral improvement to which such love can lead (courtly love makes the lovers, in particular the man, morally better people). For the improvement to be fully effected the lover should suffer the necessary privations and humiliations and perform deeds of self-sacrifice and valour for his loved one. But all is well that ends well, and he could then savour the true joys of love.

According to some of its literary expressions courtly love implied a sophisticated, and now and then perhaps mischievous, game with its own complicated set of rules. It was attended to in special parlour games, such as 'the law courts of love' and the *jeux partis* ('shared games'), where the various players took turns to defend another viewpoint over leading questions such as, 'If your lady makes the spending of a night of love with you depend on her toothless old husband, would you rather have your turn before or after?' Most historians would agree that such 'games' never took place in reality, but were fantasies enabling the authors to explore all the possibilities of a new literary style. Even so, their content must have reflected the mind-set of authors and their audiences.

Apart from the fact that such vulgar aspects of courtly love were completely at odds with Christian ethics on marriage and conjugal love, the whole complexity of ideas about courtliness and courtly love formed a 'social Utopia', in the words of Joachim Bumke, that bore little resemblance to the grim reality of everyday life in a medieval castle. This can be illustrated well by the way women were treated. If the idealised, courtly image of the woman was based on (in our eyes) toe-curling clichés such as 'external beauty is the reflection of a pure soul', it speaks volumes about the fundamentally ambivalent attitude towards women held by men from the higher classes in those days – women were by nature inferior but at the same time could be models of virtue. It is true that, incidentally, aristocratic women rose to great power, especially as queens or queens-regent over underage princes, but even in that latter situation there were almost always men pulling the strings. More generally, it has been said that, the more land and wealth a woman owned or could claim by right, 'the more likely she was to be controlled and manipulated by male relatives or lords' (Stafford 1989). Even if one is not inclined to follow such a cynical view of medieval society, one would have to admit that medieval women, certainly aristocratic women, did not enjoy anything like modern Western personal liberties. During their youth they were kept strictly secluded from men; many noble girls never married and disappeared into a convent; and those who did marry were married off and were then completely subject to the husband's authority. In terms of legal autonomy and freedom of action, the best position for women to have was that of a widow beyond the need or age of remarriage.

On top of ingrained convictions of male superiority and natural dominance over women, there was an unvarying double standard in cases of premarital or extramarital relations, and the whole concept of courtly love and the obsessive longing for unattainable women predominant in it has been interpreted as an outlet for the younger sons of noble families who often felt neglected in their inheritance and could never enjoy the prestige of their father or elder brother. They could do little more than hope for a good marriage or good fortune in battle. In anticipation of this they roamed from castle to castle, and from tournament to tournament, projecting their erotic feelings on the wife or daughter, for example, of the lord they served as *miles*. In the love of these young knights-errant for unattainable women, one variant sees a metaphor for the loyalty owed by vassals to their liege lord. Behind the (literary) expressions of courtly love, then, lay the hidden ambitions of the lower echelons of the nobility to win a place through their skill at arms at one of the larger or small courts scattered throughout feudal Europe. In both views courtly love still remained essentially a system men created with the dreams of men in mind.

Courtly culture and courtly love found a literary vehicle in three new genres which flourished in the twelfth and thirteenth centuries: the *chansons de geste*, the courtly lyric and the romances of chivalry. Of the *chansons de geste* (literally 'songs of exploits'), epic texts focusing on the deeds of one person, the subject matter of which is often borrowed from the time of Charlemagne, the oldest group is probably the most interesting from a socio-historical point of view. The texts belonging to this group, like *Raoul de Cambrai* (written in the last quarter of the twelfth century), paint a revealing picture of the feudal nobility of northern France as they liked to see themselves: extremely violent and preoccupied with problems of loyalty raised by the rapidly spreading feudal-vassalic networks. At the same time these texts betray the new sensitivity described above which at first sight belies the tough mentality of the knights. How could these bloodthirsty lovers of force ever be moved to tears by stories where ladies faint when they hear of the death of their beloved husbands? And yet this is the sort of sentiment sung in the oldest chanson we know, the *Chanson de Roland* ('Song of Roland', *c.*1120), which tells of the heroic death of one of Charlemagne's army leaders in a battle against the Basques.

The second literary genre that came into being at this time – the courtly lyric, sometimes called the poetry of the troubadours, and certainly meant to be sung – overflows with this new sentimentality. Its origins can in part be found in the Arabic and Mozarabic culture of Spain of the tenth and eleventh centuries. Not only the themes but also the rhyme schemes and music are of Arabic origin, as is the word 'troubadour' itself, which probably derives from the Arabic *tarraba*, 'to stir up emotions through song'. Other influences include the Christian religious genre of the Marian hymns and the revived intellectual interest in the love poetry of the Roman poet, Ovid. Out of this mixture there developed in Provence and the south of France a complex poetry with an exact form and a new worldview.

Although crude erotic verse also has a place in the genre, the woman is generally placed on a pedestal, and the love between a man and a woman is elevated to an ideal of moral self-fulfilment, often achieved only after intense inner conflict. During the thirteenth century the troubadours' poetry, which was composed in Occitan (the language spoken in the south of France at the time), became a symbol of the widespread resistance to the efforts of both the king of France who wanted to tighten his grip on the south, and the pope who wanted to stamp out Catharism, which had been condemned as a heresy. The poetry of the troubadours had a profound influence on the courtly lyrics of other regions, including Sicily (and through Sicily on the great Tuscan poets of the thirteenth and fourteenth centuries) and Germany, where in the thirteenth century Walter von der Vogelweide and Ulrich von Lichtenstein were considered the most accomplished *Minnesänger* ('love song singers').

Finally, the younger courtly epic, the real romances of chivalry, combined elements from the *chanson de geste* and the poetry of the troubadours. The works in this genre paint a strongly idealised picture of reality and are brimming with erotic and mystical religious symbolism. It is often difficult for today's reader to fathom the deeper meaning, and that makes it awkward to link the contents to the reality of those days. The pioneer in the field was Chrétien de Troyes, who in all likelihood was a cleric connected to the Angevin court. For his major works he drew from a new vein that had been opened in England in the twelfth century, the *matière de Bretagne* ('material from Brittany'), stories about another legendary figure of the early Middle Ages, King Arthur. In Chrétien's romances – written in French between about 1150 and 1180 – courtly and religious sentiments and ideals were woven together with a powerful imagination and a feeling for moral character development. The adventurous life of a knight was now presented as a spiritual quest in a dream landscape which can be interpreted at different levels – the quest for divine grace, the

search for his own identity or place in the aristocratic community, etc. Chrétien sees love as a magical power which can break all social conventions but also rise above them to a higher, transcendental level of experience. At the same time his views on love were not just romantic and mystic. In *Erec et Enide* Chrétien suggested to his aristocratic audience that only those who had a heart for the political community over which they were appointed, including the weak and the strong, were good enough to rule.

Chrétien's arrangement of the material from Brittany served as a model far beyond France and long after the Middle Ages, in both poetry and prose, but always in the vernacular. The German Arthurian romances of Wolfram von Eschenbach and Hartmann von Aue – both knights themselves – are considered among the most successful versions; the third great German composer of Arthurian romances in the Middle Ages, Gottfried von Strassburg, a cleric, used another French-language work as a model for his famous *Tristan*. The influence of courtly literature on Western literature has been enormous. It introduced the model of romantic love throughout Europe. What started as a stylised game for courtiers in real castles has been watered down over the centuries to become today's sentimental novel.

Tendencies towards classification and separateness

The time when Chrétien de Troyes was writing his great romances also marked the gradual conclusion of a process that had started two centuries earlier. In different parts of Europe this process took other forms and went at different speeds, but everywhere it comprised two tendencies: one towards separateness and distinction, the other towards internal ranking.

If around the year 1000 the word *miles* had been first and foremost a referent to a military man, two centuries later knighthood everywhere in Europe had become associated, if not identified, with nobility. Precisely in that period of time knighthood became hereditary everywhere. This meant that the initial criterion of achievement – a knight is an accomplished warrior on horseback – was gradually replaced by the criterion of birth and lineage – a knight is the son of a knight. Almost by implication, this double development/evolution asked for internal ranking. If all knights were now considered to be noblemen and most noblemen had no objection to being called a knight, not all noblemen were of the same level. Hence, texts from the eleventh century onwards started to distinguish between 'princes' (persons entitled king, duke, margrave, count, etc.) and ordinary 'knights'. In between were so-called barons or 'bannerets', that is powerful lords who led their own knight-vassals into battle under their own banner. Following the inheritability of the knightly status was the distinction between titled knights, who had received the accolade, and squires, who were aspirant knights. For financial reasons, many sons of knights remained squires until they were of advanced age, for the ceremony of **investiture** into the *ordo militaris* was extremely expensive. But the status of squire also required the maintenance of a knightly lifestyle which not every young man from a knightly family could afford and many of them had to give up, or lost, their privileged position. Others ended up as mounted assistants in the retinues of barons or princes.

In spite of this urge for distinction and internal ranking, in spite also of vehement criticism against parvenus – and even of legal attempts to block the entry to knighthood, such as the Imperial Land Peace of 1186, which laid down that children of priests, deacons and peasants could not become knights – nowhere in the late Middle Ages did knighthood become a fully closed estate, dictated by birth alone. Rich townspeople and even wealthy peasants always managed to find a way in. Everywhere, monarchs retained the right to elevate individuals to knights or noblemen, and they made use of that privilege often.

As always, there were considerable regional differences in the extent and speed with which

knighthood and nobility – or aristocracy – merged. The assimilation went furthest in France and Aragon, while in Germany the association of knight with nobleman was hampered for a long time by the fact that originally many *milites* had been *ministeriales*, unfree servants of powerful lords, which imprinted on German knighthood a stain of servility. In the city-states of north and central Italy it was the other way around, because old noble families usually had urban residences and so they mixed with the wealthiest and most powerful non-noble, bourgeois, families. Therefore, Italian knighthood from early on formed an amalgam of noble and non-noble elements with one aristocratic lifestyle. Problems only arose with the admission of knights from the affluent urban middle classes, the **Popolo**, that in many places gained access to city-state governments – or even took these over. That is why cavalries of mighty Italian city-states such as Florence had two divisions: that of the *milites de granditia* or *milites nobiles* ('noble knights') and that of the *milites de popolo* or *milites popolani* ('knights from the Popolo').

Finally, in England soon after the Norman Conquest, the *milites* or knights formed a fairly sizeable group of between 4,000 and 5,000 men, which was to swell during the twelfth century. Their position was then still chiefly defined in feudal-military terms: they were liegemen of crown tenants who had to follow their lords as fully armed horsemen in times of war. This was the basic agreement of their fief, known as the 'knight's fee' ('fee' is derived from *feodum*, a fief). The social status of this group was not particularly high, and the knights of this time were not generally counted as nobility. This changed in the thirteenth century when their numbers began to dwindle, to about 3,000. By that time compulsory attendance had long become commutable, for a sum of money known as scutage (from *scutagium*, literally meaning 'shield money'). From that time, too, the *knightly class* should be seen as strictly separate from the *knighthood*. The former included all families who carried the title of knight; the latter included only those who could, or wished to, afford the lifestyle of a knight and who had themselves formally been admitted to the *ordo militaris*. While members of the high nobility (barons or peers) entered this *ordo* at will, not all members of the old knightly class could afford to do so. In 1200 the English knighthood would have had about 1,500 members. From the thirteenth century on, the knightly class began to be identified with the lower nobility, in later sources usually referred to as the gentry. The gentry would gradually acquire a permanent role in local government and be looked upon as the natural representative of the English countryside, and also as a section in parliament's House of Commons.

Peasants

Around the year 1000, the workers (*laboratores*) of the tripartite scheme of estates were predominantly peasants. The literate, clerical elite viewed them with mixed feelings. In one passage of the *Carmen ad Rothbertum regem*, Adalbero of Laon speaks compassionately of the harsh fate of the serfs; in another, of the 'lazy, misshapen and in every respect contemptible rustic' (*rusticus piger, deformis et undique turpis*). Adalbero's views on this matter were not very original either. From the Carolingian period many small, free peasants, with their essentially public tasks (attendance in the army and courts of law), lost not only their standing but also, as we have seen, their personal freedom. The rise of knighthood and the growth of towns then led to an increasingly negative stereotyping of peasants, which was completely at odds with the vital social function that was invariably allocated to them in the organic view of society, with the Christian ideal of poverty that they represented and with the concern for the violent circumstances in which they were obliged to live. Attitudes towards particular social groups are often ambivalent. They express a mixture of contempt, compassion and fear, and perhaps, too,

an unconscious need to rationalise and justify clear social inequalities.

At the centre of this negative stereotype was a sort of bestialisation, the identification of peasants with beasts, which in some respects can be compared to the ancient and early medieval view of barbarians, infidels (Muslims, Jews) and slaves. A wide range of harmful and harmless vices was then given to that beast image, from wild savagery to madness, stupidity and 'an extraordinary proclivity for flatulence' (Freedman 1999). They are referred to in a wide variety of works. Learned political tracts from clerical circles spread the notion that peasants were boorish 'barbarians' or an 'asinine race'; 'half-savages who cannot govern themselves and are therefore doomed to serfdom' found Aegidius Romanus in *De potestate ecclesiastica* ('On the Power of the Church') in 1301. Deadly serious historical works thought that peasants were not able to make love, because one could hardly call their animal urge to copulate by such a name (*Li histoire de Julius César*). Peasants were – even then – the butt of countless crude jokes (*fabliaux, Schwanken*) in which their ignorance, filth and violence formed an easy target for merciless ridicule. Legal texts such as the *Usatges de Barcelona* ('Customs of Barcelona') defined peasants as 'beings that possessed no other value than that of being Christian' – and even that was openly doubted sometimes. And in the standard work on courtly love, *De amore* (1185), the author, André the Chaplain, bluntly suggests that the courtly gallantries to which (noble) ladies were entitled were wasted on peasant girls. André advised his (noble, male) readers to mount them without ceremony, a counsel that was repeated in countless variations in another popular and most appropriate literary genre of the later Middle Ages: the pastourelle or shepherd's song. Both in courtly literary works in the proper sense, and even more so in parodies, such as Neidhart's poetical praises of country girls (*c.*1225), courtliness was willingly contrasted with *rusticitas*, lumpish rusticity. Peasant behaviour was non-courtly in every respect, and contrary to everything a knight stood for: honour, skill at love, courage, moderation. Peasants were just cowardly and lecherous yokels with no sense of decorum.

Should peasants now be considered the underdogs of the medieval world only on the basis of their negative treatment in literary and legal works? There are three reasons for a more balanced view. First, there is the impression that the burden of surplus extraction (see page 140 above) slowly diminished during the period of expansion. The deeper background to this is that by medieval standards even peasants were not without rights. Local customary law remained strong in rural areas throughout the Middle Ages, and in the long term the strength of certain customs turned out favourably for the peasants as a class – among them was the serfs' right to transmit their farm and their land to their children, and the custom that once dues had been set they could not be changed. Second, the increasingly open nature of the agricultural economy during the period of expansion offered peasants opportunities to operate on different product and factor markets, although the risks attached were very real. Third, the social position for negotiation and political involvement of peasants was improved considerably by the development of village communities. In the early Middle Ages the inhabitants of country settlements certainly built up collective activities. These activities were expanded and accentuated with the growth of settlements and housing density and the disappearance of the manorial system. We have already pointed to collective decisions inherent in open-field farming and the use of extensive waste lands surrounding rural settlements. In low-lying fen and clay areas, permanent settlement depended on the good organisation of drainage and dyke-maintenance. Then the expansion and density of the network of country parishes brought a collective concern for the building and maintenance of parish churches (for which the parishioners were themselves responsible), and coupled to this was the organisation of the local poor relief.

All this led to the establishment of a great variety of local institutions, such as neighbourhoods, marks (local organisations for the management of common pasture and woodlands), water boards and foundations for the maintenance of the parish church and poor relief respectively; they all came together in what was called the village community or 'community of the vill' (communitas villae in Latin). The term is also found in older sources but it acquired a new connotation in the twelfth and thirteenth centuries. Not only were these village communities based on collective oaths and had a de facto legal personality, which gave them the competence to act on behalf of the local community, they also started to exercise local public government within the latitude offered them by local lords: they issued local regulations or bylaws, they administered common land and common infrastructure, and they imposed fines on offenders. A bench of jurati ('sworn men', jurors) or scabini (aldermen) was often elected to exercise these powers, which were not as yet separate; it consisted of resident peasants, and its composition changed periodically. Sometimes there was no bench and it was the assembly of all the villagers together that governed and administered justice. In this case local officials were appointed simply to carry out the tasks. The competence of village communities in the administration of justice was often (but not in principle) limited to judging disputes and infringements of local regulations. Here, serious crimes, for which corporal or capital punishment was laid down, had to be brought before a higher court of law. Just like the towns, villages could also acquire privileges granted by charter, so that they became 'liberties'. We know these existed in central Italy, the north of France and the duchy of Brabant. The propagation of liberty in this type of charter was sometimes coupled with a rather ridiculous appeal to ancient Roman or biblical-Christian traditions, as if villages became republics freed from tyranny overnight, or, like the Jewish people, had left the slavery of Egypt and crossed the Red Sea in search of the Promised Land. In practice, the granted liberty meant little more than that all the villagers were personally free (the denial of serfdom) or that the *malae consuetudines* were eased, and that the local authority could apply its own law and generally had slightly wider powers than ordinary village communities.

This development of village communities with statutory powers did not take place in Scandinavia or England. Sweden was simply too thinly populated. There the *hundare* or *härad* remained the lowest unit of local government, districts that usually comprised a number of villages or parishes and held jointly a law court or *ting*. In England there were indeed communities of the vill, but they were of little significance because of the continued existence of the manor, the English version of the continental *curtis* or *villa*, which was the most important framework of local organisation in rural areas; local government and justice was dealt with in the manor court, the law court of the lord of the manor, and by present-day standards was not of a public nature.

Finally, in emergencies, medieval peasants did not shrink from organising armed resistance to oppressive lords, thus showing themselves to be far less helpless than clerical and courtly literature was eager to depict. From the thirteenth century there are examples of knightly armies being cut to pieces by peasants' militias: in 1227 near the village of Ane in the northern Low Countries, in about 1230 during the so-called revolt of the Stedingers on the lower Weser, and in 1315 at the pass near Morgarten in the Swiss Alps. But, as we see from the countless individual and collective lawsuits which they fought in higher courts of law against noble or clerical landowners and which often dealt with everyday matters, such as the use of woods and peat lands, even if there was no physical combat involved, medieval peasants were able to hold their own.

Points to remember

■ Net population growth and urbanisation in the central Middle Ages were matched by an increase in food production that was attained far more by an expansion of land for cultivation through reclamation than by a more intensive use of existing farmland.

■ Both the weakening of royal power and the tremendous expansion of human settlement elicited the creation of a new type of local lordship, whose base was the unauthorised and unaccounted exercise of public power by local strongmen.

■ Both in the construction and reinforcement of local lordships, and in the attempts of kings and princes to bring them under control, feudal-vassalic relations were abundantly used.

■ Both the proliferation of local lordships and the increasing importance of (expensive) warfare on horseback contributed to the origins of a new class in the medieval aristocracy: the knights.

■ Religious sanctioning of knightly violence, bound to certain basic rules, the desire of the highest aristocrats (including kings and princes) to identify with knights, and the development of a refined court culture (including a prolific literature) all contributed to both the 'courtly' sophistication of knighthood into chivalry and to the 'nobilisation' of knighthood.

■ Peasants, although belittled and ridiculed in courtly culture as a matter of course, were well able to defend their customary rights.

■ The basis of peasant strength was the village community which developed into a body of public government and acted not just as a continuation but also as a counterweight to local lords. Basically, the chartered liberties of village communities were not different from those of towns (cf. Chapter 9).

Suggestions for further reading

Bagge, Sverre, Michael H. Gelting and Thomas Lindkvist (eds) (2011), *Feudalism: New Landscapes of Debate* (Turnhout: Brepols). One of the latest updates on the charged debate on fiefs and vassals in medieval history, covering all corners of medieval Europe. With contributions from key discussants such as Susan Reynolds and Dominique Barthélemy.

Bartlett, Robert (1993), *The Making of Europe: Conquest, Colonization and Cultural Change 950–1350* (London: Allen Lane). Daring attempt to describe the 'making' of Europe in terms of the export of certain key institutions (and their related value systems) from core areas to peripheries during a long-drawn phase of conquest and colonisation between the tenth and the fourteenth century. Works well for northern Europe, less so for the Mediterranean world.

Bumke, Joachim (1991), *Courtly Culture: Literature and Society in the High Middle Ages* (Berkeley/Los Angeles/ Oxford: University of California Press) (orig. German, 1986). Classical treatment of the core concept of central medieval elite culture by a leading literary historian; still unsurpassed in its scope, its thematic richness, and its submersion in primary source texts, and therefore rightly translated into English just five years after its first appearance in German in 1986.

Crouch, David (2005), *The Birth of Nobility: Constructing Aristocracy in England and France, 900–1300* (Harlow: Pearson). Very systematic, debate-driven study that 'stands like a border post looking out on an uncertain country', as its author says about another book on more or less the same subject. A must for anyone who wants to begin to grasp the intricacies of medieval nobility, knighthood and aristocracy (e.g. the possible differences between these three terms), and all that has been said about them over the past century or so.

Freedman, Paul (1999), *Images of the Medieval Peasant* (Stanford/Cambridge: Stanford University Press). Startling view, not so much of the 'real life' of medieval peasants, but of their representation in various contemporary social discourses and their concomitant imagery.

5 Early kingdoms and principalities

Charlemagne's legacy

The East Frankish and West Frankish kingdoms

The unified structure that Charlemagne's rapid conquests had imposed on the vast reaches of his empire eventually seemed to penetrate far less deep into society than he must have hoped. Of the three kingdoms that sprang from the Treaty of Verdun (Chapter 3) only Lothar's Middle Kingdom was subjected to further subdivision; in the end, its three main parts – all three kingdoms – were successively added to the East Frankish kingdom: Lorraine in 925, Lombardy/Italy in 951 and finally Burgundy/Provence in 1034. After the last annexation the western border of the Empire came to lie along the line of the Rhône, Saône, Meuse and Schelde. In the east, the frontier, stretching from the Baltic to the Mediterranean and along the Danube, had since Carolingian times consisted of reinforced and colonised 'marches' (border territories) – the Elbe Marches, the Eastern March, Styria, Carinthia, Krajina and the Marches of Verona and Friuli – intended to hold back the Magyars and Slavs, and also to contain the outposts of Byzantium. This did not in any way impede cultural integration of Western Slavic and German populations. The German Empire, certainly after its extension with the kingdoms of Italy and Burgundy, had a richly diverse population including Germanic-, Romance- and Slavonic-speaking peoples covering a wide variety of regional identities.

Although the West Frankish and East Frankish kingdoms themselves, which from this point on we shall call 'France' and 'Germany' respectively for convenience's sake, were never subdivided again after 843, it is difficult to say what kept them together. In both, a clear tendency towards the transformation of what originally had been the districts of royal office-holders into autonomous and hereditary principalities can be observed from the late ninth century onwards. In Germany this happened at the level of dukedoms, of which there were five (Saxony, Franconia, Swabia, Bavaria and, from 925 on, Lorraine), and in France at that of both duchies and counties, of which there were about twenty that counted (e.g. Flanders, Normandy, Aquitaine, Toulouse, Burgundy). But what exactly the relationship between kings and princes turned out to be, and what exactly determined the latter's loyalty to the former, is difficult to fathom. For instance, in the famous description of the election of Hugh Capet to the kingdom of France in 987 by the monk Richer of Rheims, no reference at all is made to the nature of the bond that existed between the king and the princes – called *principes Galliarum*, i.e. 'the princes of the Gauls' (*sic*). For Richer it was more important to stress that Hugh, after his coronation at Noyon, became the king of many peoples. Even when Hugh's great-grandson, Louis VI, was crowned king in 1108, some of the major princes of France – the dukes of Normandy, Aquitaine and Burgundy – when explicitly asked, refused to do homage to the king; they promised to be his *fideles* ('loyal supporters'), and that was it. Only gradually in the course of the twelfth century did feudal-vassalic ties between the king and the princes became normal; in this case the princes became the king's 'barons', their principalities fiefs held from the crown. From that point on we may call the kingdom of France a 'feudal state' because what held the kingdom together was not something like a national identity shared by all subjects of the French king, but the feudal-vassalic ties between the king and the French 'princes'.

In Germany, a similar move towards the formation of territorial principalities was initially slowed down by the imperial ambitions of the German kings as well as the creation of the imperial Church (see below). But after that the territorial princes (dukes and margraves) in Germany, just as in France, accepted that they formally 'held' their principalities from the king, in other words that their principalities were fiefs of the German crown – the Concordat of Worms of 1122, which ended the Investiture Controversy (see Chapter 6, p. 159), may have been instrumental in this 'mental change'. In the further course of the twelfth century direct enfeoffment

by the king even became a marker of political exclusivity: it separated the most elevated layer of princes from the common counts. In that sense the German Empire had also become a feudal state.

However, from this point on the agreement between what happened in France and Germany ended, and their further political fates started to diverge dramatically: while France developed in the direction of a centralised monarchy, Germany was soon to turn into a federation of myriad state-like principalities, held together by an emperor whose power was largely symbolic. This story of one of the most fateful developments in European political history will gradually unfold in this and later chapters.

The establishment of the German Empire

After the Carolingian dynasty died out in 911, Henry, duke of the Saxons, nicknamed 'the Fowler', was elected king in 919 because of his successful struggles against the Norsemen, Slavs and Magyars. But for the time being, a further increase in royal power was impeded by the German dukes who on several occasions formed coalitions to thwart the king. Thanks to his military superiority, Henry's son and successor, Otto I, was able to escape from these perilous situations: he forced rebellious princes into humiliating submission, and then either banished them or gave them positions elsewhere. In addition, the Saxon kings tried to guarantee the continuity of their dynasty by following the standard recipe under such circumstances: to appoint a son as successor and have him elected and crowned during the ruling king's lifetime. In Germany, this practice soon eroded the tradition of royal election to a point that it became little more than a ritual preceded by painstaking negotiation and horse-trading.

Only when there was no son as heir did other contenders have any chance. This was the case

MAP 5.1 The German Empire, 1030

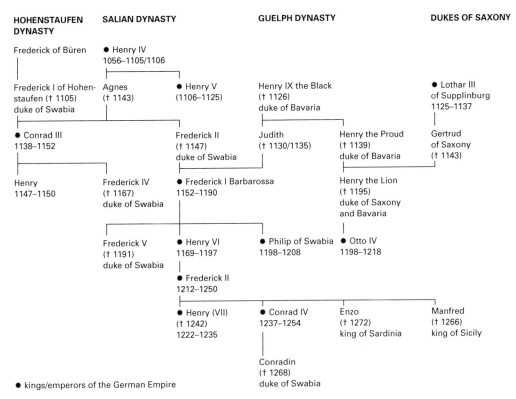

FIGURE 5.1 Family tree of the emperors and kings of the German Empire, showing changes in dynasties during the twelfth and thirteenth centuries.

when Henry II (1002–1024) died childless and the House of Saxony then died out. Under the decisive influence of the archbishop of Mainz, the smooth transfer of power to the Salian dynasty showed, with the election of the duke of Swabia as Conrad II (1024–1039), that by this time the German kingship was firmly anchored. Family ties were an essential instrument in consolidating royal power as well as enhancing its splendour, even though they frequently concealed seeds of jealousy, between brothers and half-brothers first, and later, wives. Otto I himself was the brother-in-law of King Louis IV of West Francia and the uncle of the latter's rival and eventual successor, Hugh Capet. For Otto, his son from his second marriage, he procured a Byzantine princess. Furthermore he made his eldest son, Liudolf, duke of Swabia and his son-in-law, Conrad, duke of Lorraine; another son became archbishop of

Mainz. His elder brother Henry was elevated to duke of Bavaria, and his younger brother Bruno to the combined dignities of archbishop of Cologne and duke of Lorraine. The two archbishops in the family played a key role in the political construction of the Empire. In spite of this openly preferential treatment of family members by placing them in key positions, there was much discontent, and dissatisfied sons, cousins or nephews regularly rebelled.

This proves that, as important as dynastic interests may have been, they were not enough to guarantee successful kingship. In this period, kings still had to prove themselves as successful warlords, and in Otto's case success in war very much depended on his ability and power to overcome regional-ethnic differences. Otto I clearly possessed all these qualities. His stunning victory over the Magyars at the Lechfeld near Augsburg in 955 was the result of the joint efforts of Saxons, Franks, Alamans, Swabians, Bavarians, Lotharingians and Bohemians, who shortly before this challenge were fully occupied in fighting among themselves. Augsburg also secured German interventions over the Alps that had started a few years before and which ended in the realisation of Otto's imperial dreams.

The imperial dream and the restoration of the Roman emperorship

The intervention of Otto I in conflicts in Italy caused a crucial twist in the relationship between Empire and Church. Otto was married to Adelheid, the widow of a claimant to the Italian crown, but naturally he also appealed to the Carolingian inheritance, of which the Lombard kingdom of Italy was a part. Encouraged by local rivalries, Otto led a great army over the Alps in 951. After a successful siege of the old capital of Pavia he had himself elected 'king of the Franks and Lombards', the title Charlemagne had assumed nearly two centuries earlier. The long struggle between the old noble Roman families of the Crescentii and Tusculani led the threatened pope, John XII, who had been 'called' to the highest office at the age of seventeen, to turn to Otto for protection and to offer him the imperial crown in exchange, exactly as had happened in 800. At Candlemas (2 February) 962 the victorious Otto – whose appearance with his armies was enough to put his enemies to flight – together with the pope made a triumphant entry into the holy city. The latter anointed the king and his consort, and crowned him emperor 'amidst the applause of the people of Rome'. In agreement with Carolingian tradition the Romans then pledged him their allegiance. But Otto's ambitions did not stop in Rome; he sent his armies to southern Italy, where he received homage in Capua, Beneventum and Salerno, and further campaigns in Apulia and Calabria brought him into the

centuries-old Byzantine sphere of influence. It resulted in the marriage in 972 of his heir and successor, Otto (II), to the Byzantine princess, Theophanu.

For the German kingship, this renewed link to both the Carolingian and the Byzantine imperial traditions meant that the position of hegemony it had won in Europe was underpinned by a prestigious ideology of supremacy. This was most gloriously expressed under Otto III, who had his former tutor, the learned Gerbert of Aurillac, elected to the *cathedra Petri* (999–1003). Gerbert chose the significant name of Silvester (II), as a token of his affinity with Silvester I (314–335), the bishop of Rome at the time of Emperor Constantine. In the short term, this new close link between pope and emperor confirmed the latter's hold on the Church. In the long term, the reassessment of the papacy held the seeds of inevitable conflict over areas of competences. Moreover, the orientation towards Italy, in addition to German expansion eastwards, demanded considerable military efforts which in time placed an enormous burden on the Empire's resources without producing lasting results. Otto I stayed in Italy from 966 to 972. In the north his position was never really in danger, thanks to capable and trustworthy deputies. The risk for his successors would be greater: after suffering a humiliating defeat at the hands of the Saracens in south Italy in 982, Otto II was immediately faced with grave problems in Germany. It is no exaggeration to say that from the middle of the tenth to the middle of the thirteenth century, that is from Otto I to Frederick II, the German kings' fascination with the imperial crown weakened their position of power in both Germany and Italy because in the end they lacked the means to give substance and meaning to the emperorship and were not able to stop the disintegrating tendencies it aroused everywhere.

Still, almost all the German kings from Otto I to Frederick II made the journey south across the Alps at some point in their reign to have themselves invested and crowned as 'Roman emperor' by the pope in the basilica of St Peter in Rome. With the act of anointing, the highest religious authority in the West bestowed a sacral legitimacy on the emperor's authority. In reality, the *imperium*, the imperial power, comprised the royal crowns of Germany, Lombardy and Burgundy (still an autonomous kingdom at that moment). In addition, the emperors considered themselves to be the highest (suzerain) lords over the kingdoms of Hungary and Poland, and over the former Langobard principalities of Capua, Salerno and Beneventum in southern Italy. Finally, they laid claim to the title *patricius Romanorum* ('protector of the Romans'), which in 751 had been granted by the pope to the Carolingian rulers to give them the right to intervene whenever they liked in the turmoil of local faction strife in Rome. The inspired young emperor Otto III took his Roman protectorate so seriously that he had a residence built on the Palatine, the hill in Rome where the ruins of ancient imperial palaces could be found.

Yet the German hegemony over Italy was never very significant in practice. After infrequent imperial visits, local and regional powers were always able to regain the upper hand. Resistance was often very real. In 1037 Conrad II stood powerless before the closed gates of Milan, while ten years later Henry III in vain laid siege to Beneventum. In the city of Rome, the emperors were usually represented by an imperial governor, but the northerners never became popular. The first German pope, Gregory V (996–999), who had been elected on Otto III's instigation, was expelled by an anti-pope as soon as Otto had left Rome after his coronation. When the emperor returned in the winter of 997 he had to use force to retake the city and to restore order. Small wonder that Otto and his (second) pope, Silvester II, were driven out of the eternal city in 1002. Both died soon afterwards in miserable circumstances.

The imperial Church and the contest for supreme power

One essential factor that explains the ascendancy of the German Empire in Europe lies in the fact that the kings called in the resources of the Church to support royal government. For that reason, we can speak of the '**imperial Church**' (*Reichskirche* in German). To start with, bishops and abbots had the duty to support the king in times of war by equipping heavily armed cavalrymen (*loricati*), paid for from the revenues of their extensive possessions. A recruitment list of 982 shows that the prelates were responsible for the costs of between two-thirds and three-quarters of the *loricati* in the imperial army. Second, at court, the kings surrounded themselves with highly educated clerics who were entrusted with the most important office of **chancellor** and other central positions. Then, at the king's instigation, they were invested with ecclesiastical dignities such as that of archbishop, bishop or abbot so that they could fulfil their duties to the Empire at the expense of the Church patrimony, and contribute to its supra-regional integration. Under Henry III (1039–1056) more than half the German bishops were drawn from the royal court chapel. The chapters attached to cathedrals also started to function as locations for an extensive network of educated confidants and relations of the king, who himself held the dignity of canon. But royal interference with the deployment of clergy to further the interests of the Empire did not stop here. From the reign of Otto I the kings once in a while invested archbishops and bishops with secular power by appointing them to counties or even duchies as a counterpoise to the intransigence of dukes or other secular office-holders. Because of priestly celibacy, bishops could not pass secular offices to heirs. From the beginning of the twelfth century onwards, such appointments became normal policy, a systematic and crucial part of the imperial Church. Henceforth, many German archbishops and bishops, in addition to their spiritual authority, also exercised secular power – in districts that did not always overlap. Nowhere else in Latin-Christian Europe were ecclesiastical prelates so involved in matters of the world than in Germany.

It will become clear that the imperial Church could only function well if the German king/emperor had the authority to select and appoint (arch)bishops and abbots of major monasteries. And this exactly was what put a time bomb under papal–imperial relations. Until well into the eleventh century everything was still working well, if only because popes in this period usually were appointed by the king or through his intercession. Moreover the Saxon kings/emperors turned into Christendom's greatest protectors and they actively supported the spread of Christianity. The archepiscopal see of Magdeburg, established in 967 on the initiative of Otto I, served as an advance German mission station against the Slavic pagans. With lavish gifts, Otto showed his fondness for the church of Magdeburg. More generally, the construction of monumental cathedrals flourished as a result of direct royal initiative. Henry II built the cathedral in Bamberg, where the chapter school developed into an important intellectual centre with a valuable library. Conrad II of the Salian dynasty built the imposing cathedral at Speyer, in whose crypt many members of the royal dynasty were buried.

But things started to change under Bishop Bruno of Toul, who became Pope Leo IX (1048–1054). He, too, was appointed by the emperor, but he belonged to the Burgundian-Lotharingian movement for Church reform that strongly resisted secular influences in the Church (see Chapter 6). In the mind of the deeply religious Henry III, who was strongly committed to the reform movement, there was no discrepancy between the fact that he appointed popes (just like he appointed other bishops) and the need to purify the Church of secular influence. Did he not consider his own office to be sacred? But for the leaders of the reform movement their spiritual ideals were irreconcilable with the imperial Church as it had been set up around the middle of the eleventh century.

During a whole century, from 1024 to 1125, four successive German kings belonged to the Salian dynasty, who, as dukes of Swabia, had their home base in south-west Germany. Like their Saxon predecessors, the Salians had to defend their kingship against the regional aristocracy, for whom any sign of royal weakness triggered opposition or even open revolt. Conrad II strove to improve his position by concentrating and expanding the royal domains, the administration of which he entrusted to a class of knights of unfree origin, the so-called ministerials. Henry III subdued the Slavonic dukedom of Bohemia in 1040 and strengthened the south-eastern border by the creation of the imperial borough of Nuremberg as the centre of a belt of fortified margravates. He died at the age of 39, leaving his son of 6, already crowned as Henry IV, under the protection of the pope.

The reign of Henry IV was certainly one of the most dramatic of the Middle Ages. During the nine years of his minority, secular and ecclesiastical princes mainly took care of their own territorial interests. Saxony grew into a permanent hotbed of opposition against the young king's rule. The Saxon magnates reacted against the construction of fortresses in the eastern parts of the duchy, where ministerials instead of their own kinsmen had been appointed as wardens. They would continue to provide the core of aristocratic resistance against the king at any moment of royal weakness. And they did not have to wait long. When in 1075 Henry appointed the archbishop of Milan, the most important city of imperial Italy, and the bishops of two towns within the papal sphere of influence, Spoleto and Fermo, this provoked a fierce reaction from the dogmatic Pope Gregory VII. Henry was not only excommunicated but also deposed as king. Almost automatically, Henry's political opponents took this as a legitimate opportunity to rise against the fallen king.

These disgraceful events were the prelude to one of the showpieces of medieval history. Henry realised that the only way to turn the tables was to gain papal absolution after doing public penance in order to re-legitimise his position as king. So he decided to take action and his action was as quick as it was daring. In the beginning of 1077, in the depths of winter, he crossed the 2,000 metre (6,500 feet) Alpine pass of Mont Cenis to elude his enemies before reaching the pope. At the time Gregory was staying in Canossa, a stronghold south of Parma of his faithful ally Mathilda, margravine of Tuscany. It was before the walls of Canossa that Henry had to put on the penitential sackcloth and stand in the snow until the pope deigned to receive him. Whether or not the gesture was sincere, Gregory could not refuse forgiveness, and so there was no war against Henry. It reduced his opponents to a small minority of bishops and princes. They elected three successive anti-kings but their influence remained marginal, the pope's open support notwithstanding.

The further conflicts between Henry and a number of successive popes feature other dramatic episodes, due to the protagonists' obstinate characters. In 1080, Gregory VII excommunicated and deposed Henry once again, this time accompanied by a prophecy of the king's imminent death. However, not Henry, but the anti-king Rudolph of Swabia died on the battlefield. Henry retaliated with a synod which deposed Gregory along the rules of canon law, and elected his own pope. In 1081–1084 Henry felt strong enough to make a journey through Italy, where he took Rome, drove Gregory into exile and had himself crowned emperor in St Peter's basilica by the anti-pope. Three years later he achieved the election and coronation of his eldest son Conrad as king of Germany. Henry also presided over a synod that proclaimed a *Pax Dei* ('**God's peace**') over the entire Empire; by doing this, he had adopted an ecclesiastical instrument to consolidate his secular power. Remarkably, in 1103 he issued a comparable general territorial peace (*Reichslandfriede*) but now as a secular measure. It would last for four years and explicitly included the Jews, who had been victims of horrible pogroms in several imperial cities under the pressure of years of food scarcity and the chaotic start of the First Crusade.

In Italy, Henry's conflict with the papacy was exacerbated by the struggle for power over central Italy, where the popes had territorial interests. Pope Urban II (1088–1099) tried to undermine imperial ambitions by supporting an anti-imperial party. In 1089, he arranged the marriage of Mathilda of Tuscany, who had been a widow for a long time, with the much younger heir of the influential oppositional Guelph family. They even lured Henry's eldest son Conrad into their camp, and had him crowned as king of Italy in Milan in 1093. In the same period the first urban league against the emperor was created, including the Lombard towns of Milan, Cremona, Piacenza and Lodi. In reaction, Henry deposed Conrad and had his younger son, Henry, elected king and crowned in 1099. But within a few years, young Henry, supported by the pope and many bishops and princes, rose against his father as well. Old Henry was taken prisoner and died in captivity.

Henry V (1105–1125) still had to face the same problems as his father: opposition of the Saxon aristocracy, rivalry with the pope over Tuscany, the contest over the imperial Church, **excommunication** and deposition. However, the ecclesiastical sanctions had lost much of their impact. In 1121, after years of struggle, a peace committee of 24 princes, 12 from each side, forced emperor and pope to come to terms with regard to the issue of lay investiture. Its result was the Concordat of Worms of 1122 (Chapter 6).

The Mediterranean ambitions of the Hohenstaufen

With the election of Conrad III of Hohenstaufen, duke of Franconia, in 1138, another dynasty from south-west Germany came to power. In 1152, Conrad was succeeded by his nephew, Frederick Barbarossa; it marked the dawn of a century in which two impressive emperors of the Hohenstaufen dynasty, Barbarossa himself

(1152–1190), and his grandson Frederick II (1212–1250), dazzled Europe. They took part in crusades and maintained close, although often tense, relations with the Byzantine emperors and the kings of Castile, France and England. The universal scale of their ambitions and the further consolidation of kingdoms in the West led to a period of genuine European diplomacy. In addition to consequently styling himself as 'king of the Romans' (*rex Romanorum*), a title frequently used by German kings since the end of the tenth century to express their exclusive claim on the Roman emperorship, Frederick I, after his coronation as emperor, was the first to upgrade his imperial authority to 'sacred' (*sacrum imperium*).

To ensure his election and then to stabilise his position Frederick Barbarossa had to make far-reaching concessions as soon as he assumed power. Most important was his policy towards his one great rival in Germany, Henry the Lion, duke of Saxony and Bavaria, and head of the Guelph dynasty. Although in 1180, after a deep conflict, Barbarossa deprived him of his ducal dignities, this did not break Guelph's power, because Henry remained in possession of his family's rich estates and lordships in the Harz mountains and around Brunswick. Bavaria was reduced in size by the separation of the margravate of Austria, which in its turn was elevated to the status of dukedom, to be ruled by the Babenberg dynasty. At the same time, Barbarossa did all that he could to strengthen the *Hausmacht* of the Hohenstaufen, which was concentrated of old in the duchy of Swabia. Through marriage, Barbarossa sought to extend his power over the so-called Free County of Burgundy (Franche-Comté in French), so that the influence of the Hohenstaufen now stretched over the entire south-west of the Empire. More revealing, however, was the emperor's failure to add the duchies of Saxony and Bavaria to the crown domains after the downfall of Henry the Lion. This was in sharp contrast to how things were going in France during this period (see below). If Barbarossa had accomplished this feat,

German history might have taken a completely different course.

However, the Hohenstaufen also had to deal with Italy. Their Italian aspirations brought them repeatedly into conflict with the papacy and the powerful city-states of northern and central Italy. Frederick Barbarossa led no fewer than six expeditions into Italy, but none of these lasted longer than three years. At first he succeeded in subduing the Lombard cities and, in a **diet** held at Roncaglia in 1158, he issued a manifesto in which the king's traditional prerogatives or **regalia** were defined, and permanent royal officials appointed to supervise their full enforcement. He had the assistance of lawyers from Italian towns, in particular from Bologna, by then already a renowned centre for the study of Roman and canon law. They provided Barbarossa's legislative activity with a Roman varnish; in reality regalia had little, if anything, to do with Roman law.

Apart from that, Milan, the major Lombard city, did not give in so easily. It assumed the leadership of broadly based resistance against the emperor. Barbarossa's terrible destruction of Milan in 1162 could not prevent the formation of a new Lombard League, which in 1167 comprised 26 cities in Lombardy and Emilia. The League held 'parliaments' to organise military cooperation. In 1183, Frederick was forced to grant Milan and the other members of the League substantial jurisdictional autonomy plus far-reaching control over their surrounding rural areas or *contadi* (sing. *contado*, derived from the Latin *comitatus*, 'county'). The antagonism had sharpened the cities' awareness of their constitutional singularity vis-à-vis all external powers, including feudal lords in their vicinity.

In 1184, Frederick made a seemingly brilliant move when he betrothed his eldest son, Henry VI, already crowned king of the Romans, to Costanza, heiress to the kingdom of Sicily, which comprised all of southern Italy. By the time Henry was crowned emperor in 1191 he could claim to rule a territory that stretched from Sicily in the south to the Danish border in the north and was interrupted only by the Papal State. After Henry's premature death in 1197, the struggle between the Hohenstaufens and Guelphs flared up again during the minority of his three-year-old son, Frederick II. It would last from 1197 to 1212, during which time Pope Innocent III in his capacity of liege lord of Sicily acted as guardian of the young Frederick. Meanwhile, both sides had their own candidate crowned king of the Romans: the Hohenstaufen, backed by the French king, chose young Frederick's uncle, Duke Philip of Swabia; the Guelphs, supported by Richard the Lionheart of England, Henry the Lion's son Otto of Brunswick. When Otto – who had succeeded Philip on his death in 1208 as Otto IV – began to reinforce his authority over Italy, he was excommunicated by Innocent III. It was the beginning of a complex international tug of war which increasingly came to be seen as an extension of the bitter Anglo-French conflict at the time and which only ended in 1214 on the battlefield of Bouvines (see below). Once again, the Hohenstaufen prevailed, and Frederick II was generally recognised as king of Germany, Italy and Sicily; in 1220 he was crowned emperor.

The ambition of ruling all three kingdoms proved to be simply unrealistic, and Frederick had to make concessions somewhere. Because of his affinity with the Mediterranean world, he allowed Germany to be ruled by regents, often archbishops. The subsequent regency of Henry VII, Frederick's eldest son, did not meet with much success either; Frederick even had his son imprisoned for treason. Wherever he went, the emperor behaved like an exotic foreigner, and of course his contemporaries noticed this. 'Many camels and dromedaries, Saracens and Ethiopians who could perform diverse tricks, with apes and leopards' were found in his retinue. His efforts to modernise justice and administration along the lines of the professional and centralised Sicilian model with which he was very familiar failed in Germany, simply because the necessary resources were not available and local customary law would not allow them.

Finally, in 1220 Frederick II yielded to the demands of those bishops, archbishops and abbots who had been invested with secular powers, for an extension of their autonomy and for the permanent transfer of such regalia as mintage and toll collection. Eleven years later, in 1231, in the *Statutum in favorem principum* ('Statute in Favour of the Princes') by and large the same freedom from royal interference was granted to all secular office-holders, who at that time were involved in a fight with the countless towns that in their turn attempted to gain administrative autonomy. From that moment on we can rightly term the dukes, margraves, counts and prince-bishops of Germany 'territorial princes'. It was the fateful result of the emperor's unwillingness to leave Italy and be more forcefully involved in German policy.

Emperor and pope, again

But neither did things always run smoothly in Italy. In 1226, the Lombard League revived as a strong anti-imperial alliance of 17 cities, including Milan and Bologna. In 1238 Frederick went to war with Milan, which was as usual supported by the pope, while the emperor had the help of a number of other towns in the Po valley. His army contained thousands of Saracens whom he had settled at Lucera in Apulia. Again the emperor had the victory, but no definitive result. While the war was raging, the pope excommunicated Frederick on two occasions, and both protagonists organised a vigorous propaganda campaign to win sympathy and support. One of the sixteen complaints made against the emperor was an accusation of heresy:

> The emperor has described as idiots everyone who believed that God could be born of a virgin, because nobody can see the light of day unless he was conceived in the union of a man and woman. According to him man should not believe anything that he cannot prove through the power of his intellect and nature.

At first, the excommunication of the emperor had few consequences. Even in 1245, when Pope Innocent IV (1243–1254), who had fled from Rome to Lyons, had a synod depose Frederick, the kings of England and France remained neutral. Not many German bishops put in an appearance at Lyons, but the three Rhine archbishops (Cologne, Trier and Mainz) now switched allegiance to appoint rival kings, among them Count William II of Holland (1247–1256). His authority did not extend beyond the lower Rhine region.

Innocent IV went to extreme lengths, instructing the clergy, the mendicant friars in particular, to preach a crusade against the emperor rather than against Palestine. In response, Frederick's criticisms of the clergy echoed the widespread anti-clericalism of his day, which sometimes bordered on heresy:

In truth, the enormous incomes with which they enrich themselves through their exploitation of many kingdoms, make them mad . . . It is therefore necessary to return the

PLATE 5.1 Silvester, bishop of Rome from 314 to 331 and as such the first pope, baptizes Emperor Constantine. This is one of eleven scenes of mural paintings dated 1248 in the church of the Quattro Santi Coronati (Four Crowned Saints) in Rome. They illustrate the legend by which Emperor Constantine was healed of leprosy thanks to Silvester's invocation of Saints Peter and Paul and his baptism. This iconographic programme fitted into Pope Innocent IV's propaganda against Emperor Frederick II, claiming the superiority of the Church.

clergy of all ranks, especially the highest, to the condition of the original Church, imitating the humility of the Lord in apostolic conduct. . . . Therefore you and all princes must direct all your efforts, together with us, to ensure that they lay aside all excesses and, content with moderate possessions, serve God.

The sudden death of Frederick II in 1250, followed four years later by that of his son, Conrad IV, who had made a heroic effort to keep his inheritance together, plunged the Empire into a deep crisis that was to last for almost two decades. In Italy, the cause of the Hohenstaufen was lost in 1268 after its last defenders, Frederick's bastard son Manfred and grandson Conradin, had been killed by the agency of the new master of Sicily and southern Italy, Charles of Anjou, brother of the French king, Louis IX. In Germany, there would be no king who was generally recognised until 1273, when Rudolf, count of Habsburg was elected. Consequently, the autonomy of territorial princes and free cities would only increase further during this period.

The Italian communes

In Lombardy, as we have seen, the emperors had been faced with rapidly growing towns. Cities of some importance were seats of a bishop or archbishop who had effectively taken over many of the public functions of the counts and margraves from the Carolingian period. The bishops' secular rule over a city and diocese was also based on their rural lordships and their connections with the high nobility who were their vassals. As the urban population grew from the tenth century, citizens strove to emancipate themselves from both imperial and episcopal authority in much the same vein as citizens of towns north of the Alps demanded autonomy from their lords (see Chapter 9). To press their claims home they organised in (sworn) **communes**, which then took over local government. By 1085 Pisa had consuls, appointed by the commune, and we know of at least twelve other cities that appointed consuls in the following decades.

The factual stalemate between Frederick I and the Lombard League paved the way for a further, remarkable extension of the autonomy of the towns of north and central Italy that now grew into real city-states, often of considerable size. Gradually, year by year, and partly through negotiation, partly through sheer conquest, the major cities of Lombardy, Tuscany and the Romagna succeeded in subjecting villages and smaller towns in their surroundings (*contado*). In this way they extended their territories to areas of between 2,000 and 4,000 square kilometres.

In the twelfth century, most of these city-states were ruled by small councils in which both the old landed nobilities and the wealthy merchant families were represented. Increasingly, they were torn apart by party strife between adherents and adversaries of either emperor or pope. The imperial party became generally known as the Ghibellines, a corruption of Waiblingen, an important stronghold of the Hohenstaufen in Swabia. Their opponents rallied under the name of Guelphs, corrupted from Welfen, the Hohenstaufen's most obstinate enemies in Germany. From the rule of Frederick II onwards, the Guelphs became the rallying point for anti-imperial sentiments, usually in favour of the pope. The conquest of the kingdom of Sicily by Charles of Anjou in 1266 made him the leader of the Guelph-papist party, which perpetuated the antagonism for several decades to come.

In the same, dramatic phase of Italian history, another phenomenon announced itself, that is the taking over of city-states by military strongmen, usually from powerful noble families, who monopolised key functions in a city-state's government, and from that position established autocratic rule known as *signoria* (Italian for 'lordship'). The first such *signori* were successful generals from the wars between Frederick II and the northern city-states in the 1230s and 1240s, such as Ezzelino da Romano, from the imperial-Ghibelline side, who became the undisputed lord of, among others, Verona, Vicenza and Padua, or Azzo d'Este, a Guelph general who became the first *signore* of Ferrara. In the fourteenth century the establishment of *signorie* became the order of the day in north and central Italy; it put an end to republican aspirations almost everywhere (see Chapter 11).

Vassal states in central Europe?

Seen from the double perspective of Christianisation and pacification it is understandable that the Empire and the papacy worked hard to establish Christian kingdoms on the exposed eastern flank of Christendom. In Charlemagne's time the eastern border of the Frankish world had already functioned much like the frontier of the late Roman Empire: on the – Slav – outside it fostered the concentration and consolidation of power in the hands of the strongest and cleverest local and regional leaders. In the ninth century the first powerful early Slav state had emerged in the area that is now within the Czech Republic: the kingdom of Moravia. It reached its zenith and greatest extension in the 870s, but was destroyed by the Magyars in 906. Soon it would dawn upon the Slav world that the East Franks or Germans, and not the Magyars, would be the adversary to reckon with. East of the Oder since 960 a strong alliance had formed under the leadership of Prince Mieszko, in reaction to the growing pressure of the German margraves. Mieszko was obliged to recognise the hegemony of the German Empire and pay tribute. However, when he was baptised in 966, the German aggressors lost the excuse that they supported the conversion of pagans. The development of a native Polish monarchy was accepted, and Mieszko was recognised as an ally. In 992 he sought the more detached protection of Rome by 'offering Poland to St Peter'. The foundation of the archbishopric of Gniezno in the year 1000 was a joint initiative

of Emperor Otto III and Pope Silvester II. Mieszko's successor, Boleslaw, was able to maintain his position so successfully that he had himself crowned king in 1025 without any German intervention. But soon the Polish king's power started to weaken. In the twelfth century the German emperors forced Polish dukes to become their vassals.

In Bohemia, the Germans found greater internal cohesion. As early as the beginning of the tenth century, the House of Przemyslid gained control. In 1085, while tensions were mounting between emperor and pope, Henry IV granted the status of kingdom to Bohemia, but the Przemyslid kings became imperial vassals.

The fateful implication of all this was that vast areas of Slav land – and large Slavonic-speaking populations – were taken into the German Empire as feudal principalities: in addition to Przemyslid Bohemia, which by this time included Moravia, these were the former Polish duchies of Pomerania (Pommern in German) and Silesia.

After Otto the Great's victory over the Magyars, Magyar Hungary began to become a German vassal state as well, and initially Magyar leaders were fairly dependent on German support. This was certainly the case with Prince Vajk of the Árpád clan, who came to power with German aid – after all Vajk was the brother-in-law of the later Emperor Henry II. In the year 1000 or 1001, Pope Silvester II, with the consent of Emperor Otto III, crowned Vajk as King Stephen – the Christian name he had chosen at his baptism. But in the 1030s Stephen started to shake off Hungarian dependence on the Empire. He also challenged the still-active pagan opposition and kept the Magyars under control in the vast lowland plain that was protected on the north and east by the Carpathians. From there Transylvania was annexed in 1003 and Croatia in about 1100, while between 1120 and 1150 Bosnia became a Hungarian protectorate. The incorporation of Croatia gave Hungary access to the Adriatic Sea, to which it would cling for centuries. Further south, Serbia struggled out of the Byzantines' grasp in the second half of the twelfth century. It was recognised as an independent kingdom in 1217, and over the course of the thirteenth century would expand remarkably in the direction of both Macedonia and Bosnia.

The emergence, with German support, of three Christian kingdoms in the border zone between the Slavonic and German-speaking worlds – Poland, Bohemia and Hungary – was without doubt of enormous significance for the future. The names and status of those kingdoms have remained a reference point for the political activities of their modern successor states throughout all the uncertainties of history, right up to the present day.

France: the concentric model

With the accession of Count Hugh Capet as king of France in 987, after a carefully staged election, the French kingship had to be built up from scratch. For almost two centuries to come, Hugh and his successors had to share effective sovereignty over France with about two dozen dukes, counts and margraves over whom the Capetians had little or any control. Some of them were princes of European stature and grandeur, such as Duke William of Normandy (1035–1087), who conquered England in 1066, or Count Philip of Flanders (1157–1191), who took part in the Second and Third Crusades and was on equal footing with Emperor Frederick Barbarossa and Kings Richard of England and Philip II Augustus of France. During all that time the royal domain, that is the territory in which the Capetians could exercise direct government and mobilise their own army, was limited to the Île-de-France, the area around Paris, with narrow extensions to Compiègne in the north and the Loire valley to the east of Orléans in the south. Even within that area they sometimes had to tolerate the high-handed authority of local lords.

Only from the late twelfth century onwards was the Capetian dynasty in a position to slowly expand the royal domain and direct royal gov-

ernment in a concentric movement. The turning point is a typical case of small events having significant consequences. In 1152, after fifteen years of marriage, which produced two daughters, King Louis VII (1137–1180) reached the conclusion that his wife, Eleanor of Aquitaine (1122–1204), was too closely related to him to continue living with him in accordance with the rules of the Church. The real reason, of course, was the lack of a son, and French law stated that the French crown could only be inherited through the male line. But women were not excluded as heiresses to principalities, and because Eleanor was the only surviving child of the duke of Aquitaine, in area the largest of all French principalities, the marriage of Louis and Eleanor had brought about a promising beginning to the union of northern and southern France. Now this promising prospect was shattered at once by the royal divorce. It is true that Louis soon remarried another important heiress – to the County of Champagne – who after another ten tantalising years finally bore him a son, the future King Philip II, but the joy and satisfaction of all this were subdued by the actions of his ex-wife and their startling consequences.

Within a month of her divorce Eleanor had married the king's arch-rival, Henry Plantagenet, count of Anjou, and at that moment the most important contender for the English crown, which indeed fell to him in 1154, when he was recognised as King Henry II (1154–1189). Since Henry's titles, besides that of king of England, included duke of Normandy and count of Anjou, Maine and Touraine, while Eleanor retained the County of Poitou and the duchy of Aquitaine (which at that time included all of Auvergne), the new royal couple ruled over close to half the total territory of the kingdom of France. This power complex, usually called the Angevin Empire ('empire of Anjou'), was also many times larger than the French royal domain. Besides, Eleanor of Aquitaine was perfecctly capable of having sons: she bore her second husband no fewer than eight children, four of whom were sons.

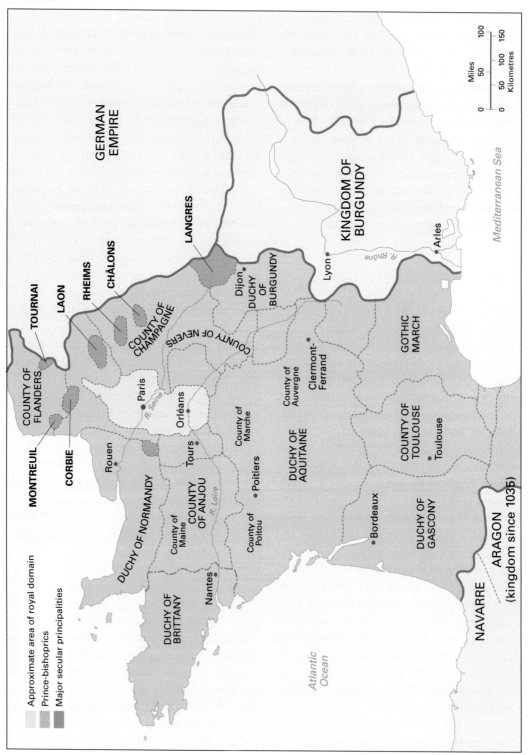

MAP 5.2 The kingdom of France in the year 1000

Approximate area of royal domain

Prince-bishoprics

Major secular principalities

GERMAN EMPIRE

KINGDOM OF BURGUNDY

Mediterranean Sea

Atlantic Ocean

TOURNAI

LAON

RHEIMS

CHÂLONS

LANGRES

MONTREUIL

COUNTY OF FLANDERS

CORBIE

Paris
R. Seine

Orléans

Rouen

Tours
R. Loire

Poitiers

Nantes

DUCHY OF NORMANDY

County of Maine

COUNTY OF ANJOU

County of Poitou

DUCHY OF BRITTANY

COUNTY OF CHAMPAGNE

COUNTY OF NEVERS

Dijon

DUCHY OF BURGUNDY

County of Marche

County of Auvergne

Clermont-Ferrand

DUCHY OF AQUITAINE

Lyon
R. Rhône

Arles

GOTHIC MARCH

COUNTY OF TOULOUSE

Toulouse

Bordeaux

DUCHY OF GASCONY

NAVARRE

ARAGON
(kingdom since 1035)

Miles
Kilometres
0 50 100
0 50 100 150

BOX 5.1 POPULAR SOVEREIGNTY IN FLANDERS IN THE YEAR 1128

In medieval Europe, recognition of a monarch or a prince of similar rank by the most prominent among his subjects was required, but at the same time conditional: representatives were invited to swear an oath of loyalty as vassals or pseudo-vassals (e.g. towns). This implied that the assent could be withheld or revoked, just as in a feudal contract. An early example of such an action is described in contemporary chronicles in Flanders from [?]1128. After the murder of Count Charles the Good, William Clito of Normandy, a grandson of William the Conqueror, had been inaugurated as the new count in 1127 under condition that he showed respect for the privileges of the land and particularly for those of the rapidly growing cities. Within a year he had violated so many stipulations that citizens rebelled in Saint-Omer and Lille and a broad movement of opposition arose. In Ghent, the citizens had the following request addressed in their name to the count by a sympathetic nobleman, in the wording of the count's chancery clerk Galbert of Bruges:

> Lord count, if you had wished to deal justly with our citizens, your burghers, and with us as their friends, you would not have imposed evil exactions upon us and acted with hostility toward us but, on the contrary, you would have defended us from our enemies and treated us honourably. But now you have acted contrary to law and in your own person you have broken the oaths that we swore in your name concerning the remission of the toll, the maintenance of peace and the other rights which the men of this land obtained from the counts of the land, your good predecessors . . . and from yourself; you have violated your faith and done injury to ours since we took the oath to this effect together with you. . . . Let your court, if you please, be summoned at Ypres, which is located in the middle of your land, and let the barons from both sides, and our peers and all the responsible [*sapientiores*] men among the clergy and people, come together in peace and without arms, and let them judge, quietly and after due consideration, without guile or evil intent. If in their opinion you can keep the countship in the future without violating the honour of the land, I agree that you should keep it. But if, in fact, you are unworthy of keeping it, that is, lawless and faithless, a deceiver and perjurer, give up the countship, relinquish it to us so that we can entrust it to someone suitable and with rightful claims to it. For we are the mediators between the king of France and you to guarantee that you undertake nothing important in the county without regard for the honour of the land and our counsel.

This remarkably clear and early pronouncement of the principles of constitutional government under the control of the representatives of the three estates emanates from the feudal notions of contract: a vassal had the right of resistance if he was wrongly treated. The argument introduced the widening of this concept to all citizens; it was grounded on their mutually sworn fealty on the basis of law. The count, however, refused the proposal, rejected the homage previously done to him by the spokesman and challenged him to combat. His reaction refuted the notion of the countship as a public office subject to judgement by the 'wisest' representatives from the three estates, united in his council. The proposed meeting of the enlarged *curia*, the count's court, was never held, and arms finally decided in favour of the citizens. During the remainder of the twelfth century, successive counts did not repeat the same mistakes but granted new privileges to the cities; no mention is to be found of any effective assembly of the kind announced in 1128.

Source: excerpt taken from *Galbert of Bruges: The Murder of Charles the Good, Count of Flanders*, ed. J.B. Ross (New York/London: Harper Torchbooks, 1967), ch. 95.

Kings of France from the House of Capet (until 1285):

- Hugh Capet (987–996)
- Robert II (996–1031)
- Henry I (1031–1060)
- Philip I (1060–1108)
- Louis VI (1108–1137)
- Louis VII (1137–1180)
- Philip II Augustus (1180–1223)
- Louis VIII (1223–1226)
- Louis IX (Saint Louis) (1226–1270)
- Philip III (1270–1285)

FIGURE 5.2 Kings of France, 987–1285

Not surprisingly, the Angevin Empire posed a tremendous challenge – if not outright threat – to the Capetian monarchy, and it was King Philip II 'Augustus' (1180–1223) who would take up this challenge with overwhelming success, which makes him the most important king of medieval France, and one of the great heroes of French history. First, in 1185, after a military confrontation with Count Philip of Flanders, he succeeded in taking over the entire south of Flanders, which came to form the County of Artois. In addition, he acquired Picardy (the area around the town of Amiens) and the County of Vermandois (the area around Péronne). Consequently, the income of the French crown increased by 46 per cent during the first twenty years of King Philip's reign.

But this was just the beginning. The next target was to link Paris with the North Sea, which in fact meant control of Normandy, the prize possession of the Plantagenet kings of England. After incessant intrigues aimed at stirring discontent within the Plantagenet family, Philip Augustus used the violations of feudal law made by Henry II's youngest son and new king of England, John Lackland (1199–1216), as an excuse to censure him as his vassal. After a month-long siege of the stronghold of Château-Gaillard, strategically built on a rocky promontory by the Seine at the entrance of Normandy, French troops seized Normandy and the lands along the Loire in 1204. After Normandy the other Plantagenet territories north of the Vienne river followed one by one. John's efforts to break the power of the French by forming a coalition with Flanders and the Guelph emperor, Otto IV, failed dismally at the great battle of Bouvines (1214). For the time being, Aquitaine remained English, soon to be reduced to Gascony, the coastal stretch from Bordeaux to the Pyrenees. Aquitaine or Gascony: each remained a fief from the French crown, and for that reason inevitably turned into a new bone of contention.

The tide had now definitely turned in favour of Philip Augustus. For the first time a French king had a marked preponderance over all crown vassals, in both military and financial terms. Crown income had easily doubled between 1180 and 1220, and whereas King Philip at the end of his reign could boast of receiving over 130,000 pounds a year, his wealthiest vassals, the count of Flanders and the duke of Burgundy, had to be satisfied with about 30,000 pounds.

And that was not all. In the preceding years, King Philip had also profited from Innocent III's witch-hunt against the Cathars in southern France and Aragon, who had been accused of heresy. In 1208, the pope proclaimed a crusade against the heretics. From the beginning, this crusade, known as the Albigensian Crusade (after the town of Albi, supposedly the main centre of Cathar heresy), was derailed because the entire population of Languedoc was too easily identified with a minority of Cathars, and in bloody events such as the capture of the city of Béziers, thousands of people were indiscriminately massacred. Attempts by regional princes, Count Raymond of Toulouse and his brother-in-law, King Peter II of Aragon, to start with, to limit the damage and prevent the crusaders, most of them barons from the north led by the ambitious baron Simon de

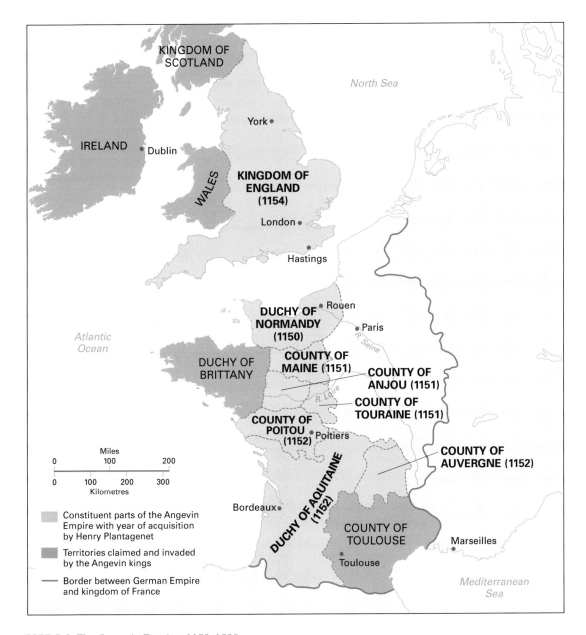

MAP 5.3 The Angevin Empire, 1150–1200

Montfort, from conquering the area were shattered in the battle of Muret (1213). For a while, the County of Toulouse was held by Simon de Montfort. In 1229, Raymond's son, another Raymond, was forced to surrender part of his county to the French crown, while his daughter and heiress was given in marriage to a younger son of King Louis VIII (1223–1226). This assured that the County of Toulouse would eventually fall into Capetian hands, and the kingdom of Aragon had no further role to play north of the Pyrenees.

Fifty years after 1180 the area under the direct control of the French crown had been quadrupled in the north, west and south. Only after the Hundred Years War (1337–1453), and especially in the period 1463–1532, would the French monarchy continue to expand its territory in every direction through the systematic annexation of previously autonomous principalities, such as Brittany, Burgundy, and the Dauphiné and Provence, east of the Saône–Rhône line, which for centuries had formed the frontier between France and the German Empire.

A parallel development to this territorial expansion of French royal power, which would not stop until well into the eighteenth century, was the centralisation of government. In this respect the reign of Philip II Augustus was also a turning point. In domestic government, he systematically replaced the great vassals in his council with members of more modest origins but with greater technical expertise. He brought in the Order of the Templars to take care of his treasury and also to finance the annexation of Normandy. His most drastic innovation, however, was the introduction after 1190 of regional officials, known as **baillis** in the north and **sénéchaux** in the south, an innovation which we shall discuss further below. The steady strengthening of royal power in France was quite unique in Europe, and may well be connected with the exceptional continuity of the Capetian dynasty, which reigned from 987 to 1328 and succeeded in gradually expanding its direct rule, starting from a solid domanial core. This evolution was diametrically opposite to the 'imperial overstretch' which led to strong regional powers in Germany and Italy.

Alternative modes of early state formation

The making of England

Shortly after the year 1000 the House of Alfred of Wessex, which had ruled over England for more than a century, had to make way for the Danish king, Svein Forkbeard, who in 1013 invaded and conquered the country with a large expeditionary force. His son, King Cnut the Great (1014–1035),

PLATE 5.2 Harold, earl of Wessex, swears his oath on holy relics as the successor to King Edward the Confessor, 1066. The tapestry preserved in Bayeux, Normandy, is a uniquely realistic depiction in fifty scenes of the power struggle ending in the battle of Hastings. The embroidery on cloth is nearly 70 metres (230 feet) long. It was made shortly after the events and the colours are wonderfully preserved. The central scene has titles in Latin, and strips at the top and bottom show animals and drolleries as well as highly precise images such as the oldest representation of the mouldboard-plough.

then ruled over Denmark and Norway as well as England. He based his strong position of authority on his recognition by the thegns, the local Anglo-Saxon aristocrats. Cnut was succeeded by his son, but in 1042 the Danish intermezzo came to an end, and with the accession of Edward the Confessor, the House of Alfred the Great was again on the throne. Through Edward's mother Emma, daughter of the duke of Normandy, many noblemen from her native Normandy gained influence in England. A number of earls, the Anglo-Saxon equivalent of counts on the continent, were opposed to this. They found a leader in Harold, the earl of Wessex, who was proclaimed king when Edward died. He had to defend his position against his own brother who sought help from Harald Hardråde, the king of Norway. Their great invasion force was routed near York in September 1066. In the meantime, William, the duke of Normandy, had crossed the English Channel with a large crowd of warriors eager for booty, estimated at a minimum of 5,000 men to fight for his claims. In the famous battle of Hastings on 14 October 1066 William's mounted knights defeated the English thegns and house-carls (the king's personal guard), and Harold was killed.

Hastings and its aftermath mark a turning point in English history, because at a stroke England's ruling elite was gone, its power taken over by another, of French-speaking foreigners. These most dramatic events also set in motion a revolutionary changing of landowners, which was unparalleled in the Middle Ages. The new king departed from the legal fiction that, as the conqueror of England, he could dispose of *all* its land. In the years following Hastings the native Anglo-Scandinavian aristocracy was virtually wiped out and replaced by a Norman landed elite that received about 80 per cent of the land from the king – the remaining 20 per cent the king kept for himself as royal domain. All landholders who received land from the king directly, whether Norman warriors or ecclesiastical institutions (abbeys and bishoprics), were called **tenants-in-**

Kings of England:

House of Normandy:

- William I the Conqueror (1066–1087)
- William II Rufus (1087–1100)
- Henry I Beauclerc (1100–1135)
- [Mathilda (1135–1154)]*

House of Blois:

- Stephen of Blois (1135–1154)

House of Plantagenet (Anjou) (until 1272):

- Henry II (1154–1189)
- Richard I the Lionheart (1189–1199)
- John Lackland (1199–1216)
- Henry III (1216–1272)

*claimed throne; not generally recognised

FIGURE 5.3 Kings of England, 1066–1272

chief ('main [land]holders'). What tenants-in-chief actually received were not specified quantities of land but estates called manors, after the Norman word 'manoir' (although the economic format already existed in pre-Conquest, Anglo-Saxon England). Usually, manors were organised as bipartite estates (Chapter 3) whose demesnes (parts 'reserved' by the manor lord for direct exploitation) were worked by serf peasants or villeins. The number of manors received by the most important tenants-in-chief was impressive (e.g. 793 by the Conqueror's half-brother, Robert of Mortain). Understandably, these so-called barons, but also lesser tenants-in-chief, gave a large part of their estates to subtenants, common aristocrats both of native, Anglo-Scandinavian extraction (the minority) and Norman newcomers (the majority), who in return had to follow them into war. An estate held in return for military service was called a 'knight's fee' (*feudum unius militis*, in Latin). Soon, military service could be redeemed with a tax called *scutage* ('shield money'), and in particular, land held directly from the king came to be burdened with other tax-like payments that were often reminiscent of feudal obligations, such as 'aid' and 'relief'.

In accordance with aristocratic landownership of this period elsewhere in Europe, landowning by tenants-in-chief and their subtenants was connected to lordship over the peasant families that were settled on their estates and worked the land. In England these rather imprecise judicial franchises enjoyed by lords were expressed in the term 'sake and soke'. It remains clear, however, that jurisdictional rights of landlords – even barons – were always limited by the rights of the king and of royal officials such as sheriffs, in particular with respect to the prosecution of crimes that could result in capital punishment.

So, if the Norman Conquest had been absolutely revolutionary with respect to the ethnic composition of the social and political elite, it did not produce a type of feudal state such as the kingdom of France – the Normans' home base – was at the time. If there is no objection against calling the Anglo-Norman tenants-in-chief royal vassals or vassals to the crown, it must be clear that their fiefs comprised land, estates, not the classical public offices of early medieval continental kingdoms such as counties, margravates or duchies. It is true that the Norman kings maintained the old Anglo-Saxon title of earl, later to be followed by the continental title of duke, but these were honorary titles, to be extended to princes of the royal family and very distinguished aristocrats. Their conferment did not involve the grant of any public authority. As foreign conquerors the Normans were in a vulnerable position and therefore they had to build a strong system of government. They used the Anglo-Saxon tradition as a solid basis. The shires, or counties, which still exist today within practically the same boundaries, date from that time, as do the local districts called hundreds into which they were divided. The king appointed a sheriff to each shire, most of them Normans, who had fiscal, military and judicial responsibilities. The office of sheriff never became hereditary; it was never granted as a fee (in fief), and from early on sheriffs were literally held accountable for their action, that is to say, they had to submit yearly accounts of receipts and expenses.

In sum, one could argue that Anglo-Norman England was both the most and the least 'feudalised' kingdom of later medieval Europe: the most because *all* the land of the kingdom, with the exception of the royal domains, was enfeoffed; the least because public offices were never the object of enfeoffment, which means that in England much less of what we nowadays consider to fall under the category of public authority was 'mediatised' (Chapter 4) than in the feudal states on the continent. Therefore, there was no move towards the formation of autonomous principalities in England, with the exception maybe of the Welsh frontier. The Anglo-Norman barons who acquired land and castles there, the so-called Marcher lords, were granted a larger amount of autonomy from royal interference, for strategic reasons, than normal tenants-in-chief had.

When the Conqueror died in 1087, the 'restyling' of the governance of England as just outlined was still very much in the making. Its outlines clearly appear in the *Domesday Book*, the famous 'description of all England' that William ordered to be made in 1086. It is a survey that for each shire describes how many royal estates there were and which tenants-in-chief held manors, or (parts of) boroughs, followed by a close description for each and every manor of all the means of production present: the number of peasants (free and villein), of livestock, capital goods (ploughs, mills etc.), rounded off with an estimated (yearly) value of its proceeds. In this way, the king obtained a better view of the assets of his kingdom and their distribution among the aristocracy and the Church.

After the Conqueror's death, his work was vigorously pursued by his sons William II Rufus and Henry I. The latter, whose sobriquet 'Beauclerc' refers to the general idea that he was 'well served by his clercs', is seen as an astute, even if inflexible and cruel, statesman, who determined the direction in which key administrative institutions were going to move (to be discussed in more detail below). However, much of Henry's work was undone when he died in 1135 with only a daughter alive, the empress-widow Mathilda ('Maud') who claimed the throne, promised to her by her father, against the opposition of a Norman party, led by a grandson of the Conqueror in the female line, Stephen, the count of Blois. England was now plunged into a civil war, the Anarchy, which lasted for fourteen years (1139–1153) and ended in Stephen's recognition of Mathilda's son by her second marriage, Henry Plantagenet, count of Anjou, as sole rightful heir to the English throne.

As a king, Henry II, whose marriage to Eleanor of Aquitaine and subsequent formation of the Angevin Empire have already been discussed, made a profound impression. Henry was a forceful personality, an indefatigable traveller through his own realm, who must be given credit for reversing some of the de-centralising tendencies that were set in motion during the Anarchy, in particular the development of hereditary offices and autonomous local lordships. Even Henry II could not prevent baronies, earldoms and knight's fees from becoming hereditary, but he succeeded with respect to the key royal offices of sheriff and justiciar. However, Henry's long reign was tainted by two other long-standing issues: the repeated rebellions of his sons and the conflict with the archbishop of Canterbury, Thomas Becket. The reasons behind the former were partly purely coincidental: Henry just happened to have a number of capable sons who all grew up to maturity and then asked their father for a stake in the wielding of power. Henry met these demands by having his oldest son crowned king, while the second one was appointed duke of Aquitaine and the third one married to the heiress of Brittany. The lack of land of his youngest son (the late arrival John) was compensated with the promise of the kingdom of Ireland, yet to be conquered – a first attack was launched in 1171–1172, with little success. But Henry was not disposed to give any one of his sons a real say in any matter that would diminish his own authority. Feelings of discontent, even hatred, about this were stirred up by other players in the field, like their mother, Queen Eleanor, or the cunning King Philip of France. The Becket affair only added to the troubles.

Even if England had no 'imperial Church' in the way the German Empire had, the English king always claimed a say in the appointment of at least the primate of the Church in England, the archbishop of Canterbury. So, there was nothing unusual about Henry's engineering of the appointment of his chancellor, Thomas Becket, to the see of Canterbury in 1162. Becket was of modest origins, although by no means poor – his father was a London merchant of Norman descent – and he had studied for short periods of time in Paris, Bologna and Auxerre. He successively became clerk to the archbishop of Canterbury and archdeacon of Canterbury cathedral. In December 1154, the then archbishop, impressed by Becket's personal qualities, recommended him to the newly crowned king for the post of chancellor. Becket would have been at least thirty-five at the time, Henry just twenty-one.

The king and his chancellor became firm friends. Thomas was a meticulous and loyal servant to the king, even when his master's claims conflicted with the English bishops' efforts to fend off secular influence over the monasteries. The chancellor made himself particularly unpopular with the bishops and abbots by his relentless demand for scutage for the royal campaigns. At the same time he readily accepted the rewards of *custodia*, the interim supervision of vacant bishoprics, and the incomes tied to them. With his newly acquired wealth the chancellor enjoyed an exuberant lifestyle which attracted the attention of his contemporaries. In addition, the enthusiasm with which he headed the king's military operations in France astonished many people.

With his encouragement of Thomas's appointment as primate of England, Henry must have expected that the energy and decisiveness of his faithful servant would help him to solve certain tricky questions in his relationships with the Church. In particular, the king was annoyed with the ecclesiastical courts' claims to exclusive jurisdiction over all clergy and all Church lands, even when criminal matters were involved. But just as Thomas had served his new master unswervingly when he had been made chancellor, in his position as archbishop he would devote himself wholeheartedly to the defence of the liberties of the Church. In the spirit of Church reform, he now tried to resist secular influences, although he was hindered in this by his status as tenant-in-chief for the Canterbury Church lands.

According to one of his modern biographers, Frank Barlow (1986), Thomas behaved like a 'typical parvenu' in this matter, trying to make the very most of the independent and powerful position that he had acquired. He prosecuted important noblemen in the king's service for their moral failings. He resisted secular judgements on the clergy. As archbishop he opposed a royal land tax which he had defended as chancellor. He demanded total obedience from other bishops. Since some of them were better theologians than he was, and his greed made him generally unpopular, within a few months Thomas found himself in conflict with both the English Church and the king.

The king put Thomas on the spot during a meeting of the magnates of the kingdom – the high clergy, barons and holders of royal office – at Clarendon in January 1164. He made Thomas, and after him the other bishops, swear in good faith to observe the laws and customs of the realm. Once these had been put down in writing in the Constitutions of Clarendon, they proved to be formulated entirely to suit the king, and Thomas immediately revoked them. He appealed to the pope, which of course took a long time. In November of that year he felt that he had so little support from his bishops and was so threatened by the king and his entourage that he had no other course than to flee to the continent.

Six years of exile in French monasteries followed. In the abbey church of Vézelay, where St Bernard had called for the Second Crusade, Thomas pronounced a ban against the Constitutions of Clarendon, in particular against the articles attacking the rights of the Church. He excommunicated eight people for furthering 'royal tyranny' and appropriating property belonging to the church of Canterbury. Pope Alexander III gradually put more pressure on Henry and his supporters among the English prelates to effect a reconciliation with Becket. This made it possible for Becket to return at last to England, in December 1170, but his tactless actions soon brought matters to a head. His intransigence roused opposition everywhere and once again Henry's wrath was enflamed.

Four of Henry's knights took matters into their own hands and rode to Canterbury, on 29 December, where they murdered the archbishop after an argument in the cathedral. Soon the dead archbishop was revered as a martyr. Miracles were attributed to him; pilgrims flocked to his grave. In 1172 he was canonised. Under threat of a papal interdict Henry was forced to admit that he was the cause of Thomas's cruel death and to retract the laws that were so disadvantageous to the

PLATE 5.3 The murder of Thomas Becket.

Church. He also promised to go on a crusade for three years. This, of course, he did not do, but in 1174 he did do penance at Thomas's grave in Canterbury, where the prelates and monks gave him hundreds of strokes with a whip.

The conflict between Henry and Thomas typifies the tensions between the Church that was reforming itself and the growing power of the state. The character of the individuals also influenced the course of events. With a little more flexibility and tact, the pope and king reached a compromise, in 1176, on the same issues on which Thomas Becket had refused to give way.

Like the Conqueror before him, Henry II was succeeded by two of his sons: first Richard I the Lionheart, then John Lackland. At first sight there are similarities. For instance, it is tempting to pair Richard with Rufus and John with Henry I: the first two both dashing knights, the second two both calculating schemers. At a closer look all four of them – not just Beauclerc – were 'well served' by bureaucratic counsellors, capable of taking care of all kinds of problems of government and finance that dashing chivalry and dark plotting created. These new bureaucrats were often men of obscure origins, who were 'raised from the dust'

to the pinnacle of power, particularly in the holding of the office of chief justiciar, which, from the reign of Henry I onward, became the most important position in the royal bureaucracy.

It is also thanks to them that the monarchy survived profound political and financial crises, such as the capture and ransoming of the Lionheart in 1192–1194, the loss of Normandy in 1204, and the interdict placed on England in 1208. In the end, only King John had any limitations imposed on his powers by his barons. Years of war with France over his overseas possessions made him increase his demands on the feudal obligations of the royal tenants and other subjects. Not only did he by far exceed what was commonly felt as fair and in accordance with the law and custom, he moreover lost his battles, and gave up ancestral territory – Normandy – in which many English barons owned large estates. John's utter failure to turn the tide against Philip of France while putting the screws on his barons finally led to open rebellion in the spring of 1215. To save his kingdom, the king had to give in, and he did so in a remarkable document: the Magna Carta.

BOX 5.2 'NO TAXATION WITHOUT CONSENT' IN THE *MAGNA CARTA*, 1215

The stretching to the limit of feudal obligation included longer service further from home, greater levies on fiefs and unlawful appropriation by the crown. These were the abuses formulated by the barons over the years and issued in 1215 by the royal chancery as a charter – known as the Magna Carta – containing no fewer than 63 articles. Although this document certainly did not emanate from a representative assembly since the barons could speak only in their own name as the king's tenants, many of its articles were nevertheless referred to later as a constitutional act announcing essential principles to be kept in respect for many centuries.

[12.] No scutage or aid is to be levied in our realm except by the common counsel of our realm, unless it is for the ransom of our person, the knighting of our eldest son or the first marriage of our eldest daughter; and for these only a reasonable aid is to be levied. Aids from the city of London are to be treated likewise.

[14] To obtain the common counsel of the realm about the assessing of an aid (except in the three cases aforesaid) or of a scutage, we [King John] will cause to be summoned the archbishops, bishops, abbots, earls and greater barons individually by our letters; and we shall also have summoned generally through our sheriffs and bailiffs all those who hold of us in chief, for a fixed date, namely after the expiry of at least forty days and to a fixed place; and in all letters of such summons we will specify the reason for the summons. . . .

[15] We will not in future grant any one the right to take an aid from his free men, except for ransoming his person, for making his eldest son a knight and for once marrying his eldest daughter, and for these only a reasonable aid shall be levied.

[16] No one shall be compelled to do greater service for a knight's fee or for any other free holding than is due from it.

The separate mention of the city of London in article 12 can only be understood as referring to an independent status on a par with the tenants-in-chief, not as the representation of the commune. Notwithstanding Pope Innocent's – who was John's nominal liege – declaration of the Magna Carta to be null and void, Henry III reissued an abbreviated version on his accession to the throne in 1216. Certain legal principles as embodied in some of the articles of the Magna Carta, such as the ban on arresting, holding, dispossessing or outlawing any free person 'save by the lawful judgement of his peers or by the law of the land', are held of value until the present day.

Source: excerpt taken from H. Rothwell (ed.), *English Historical Documents, Vol. III (1189–1327)* (London: Eyre & Spottiswoode, 1975)

Iberia

Among the oldest of Europe's expansive kingdoms were those on the Iberian peninsula. In the tenth century the emirate of Córdoba – in 929 elevated to caliphate – had emerged as a major power in southern Europe. Its economic and cultural development was far ahead of that of Catholic Europe. In the irrigated regions of Andalusia, and along the east coast of Spain, there was widespread market gardening and agriculture, with a great variety of products: cane sugar, various spices, cotton, linen, grain, rice, wine, dates and even some semi-tropical fruits were exported. State revenue rose from 600,000 gold dinars in around 800 to 6,250,000 dinars in around 950. In the tenth century Córdoba grew into a metropolis of several hundred thousand

inhabitants, 3,000 mosques and 300 bath-houses. Only Constantinople and Baghdad – and a century later, Cairo – were of a similar size. Elsewhere in Europe, the thinly spread towns of the time had just a few hundred, certainly no more than a few thousand, inhabitants. The enormous size of the Mediterranean towns was only made possible through the intensive agriculture and extensive trade in the region. Commercial relations with the Byzantine Empire were generally good, and contacts – varying from plunder to trade – were also maintained with the Latin-Christian regions around the Mediterranean Sea. The Islamic world provided a vast market stretching from Persia to Portugal. Trade brought products like silk and spices from the Far East to Arab markets. These products formed the basis of advances in pharmacology in which Arab doctors, building on the knowledge of their Greek predecessors, invented preparations containing gum, sugar, musk, nutmeg, cloves and so forth, which were combined in syrups and elixirs (both words come from Arabic).

There was a constant supply of gold and slaves from inland Africa to the Islamic regions. Trade and plunder also brought slaves from Europe. In the eighth century Arab traders used techniques that were to be taken over by the Latin-Christian world only centuries later: association, credit, money transfers and payment by cheque (from the Persian word *sakh*), and capital reinvestment. In the towns of al-Andalus – the Arabic name for Islamic Spain – the different ethnic and religious communities lived in separate neighbourhoods but had close contact with each other. Craftsmen of luxury goods specialised in leather-working, arms-making, the production of glass, paper and ceramics, and silk-, textile- and carpet-weaving.

The court (*alcázar*) at Córdoba was a prominent centre of culture. Caliph al-Hakam II (961–967) collected a library of 400,000 manuscripts. Even if that number is exaggerated it stood in marked contrast with the largest libraries in western Christendom, those of the popes in Avignon and the Sorbonne library in the fourteenth century, neither of which contained more than 2,000 volumes. Caliph al-Hakam also enlarged the Mezquita, the great mosque of Córdoba, and placed magnificent Byzantine mosaics in its *mihrab*, the prayer wall facing Mecca.

Over the course of the eighth century the Arab language and Islam – the latter used the former exclusively – came to dominate in the conquered areas. Through them the diversity of peoples and political regimes jelled, without really eliminating the disparities between the different population groups. In the tenth and eleventh centuries, the growing homogenisation of Arabic culture in al-Andalus led to an exodus of Mozarabs (Arabised Christians) to the Christian kingdoms in the north, which began to adopt a more aggressive attitude. Military expeditions caused the two cultures to grow apart, both stressing their indi-

vidual character more strongly. Homogenisation and integration exacerbated the polarisation on either side of the border zone. Yet, during the eleventh and twelfth centuries, in the towns and at the courts of al-Andalus, cultural activity flourished, becoming highly refined and many-sided. It included sophisticated architecture, various branches of science – astronomy, medicine, pharmacology, botany (botanical gardens were established in Córdoba and Toledo) – jurisprudence, theology and philosophy. The royal courts vied with each other in cultural matters: troubadours' poetry sprang up, emotional, profane – even libertine – and dealing with the liberated position of women. Love, battle and nostalgia were themes later to be adopted by the courtly lyrics of western Europe. The puritanical regimes of the Almoravids and Almohads were a reaction to this.

At the beginning of the eleventh century, the caliphate of Córdoba lapsed into anarchy as a result of crises in the succession, and in 1031, some years after a Berber army had taken its capital, it was even formally abolished. It crumbled into more than twenty small kingdoms grouped according to ethnic origins and known as *taifas* (from the Arabic *muluk al-tawa'if*, meaning 'faction kings'). The rivalry between the regional Islamic rulers played into the hands of the Christians. King Alfonso VI of León and Castile (1065–1109) succeeded in advancing deep into the south and laying a heavy tribute on Muslim territory. After the fall of Toledo, in 1085, the Muslim princes of Seville, Badajoz and Malaga asked for the help of Yusuf ibn Tashufin, the leader of the Berber tribes from Mauretania that had united under strictly puritanical, Islamic principles. They called themselves *al-murabitun*, 'warriors living together in a ribat (house)', the origin of the word 'Almoravid'. In the preceding years, they had united large parts of Morocco, founded Marrakesh in 1070 and, moving northwards, taken Tlemcen, Oran, Algiers and Ceuta. Between 1086 and 1114 Yusuf and his son and heir, Ali, eliminated all the *taifa* rulers and then marched north towards Zaragoza and Barcelona. The Muslims of al-Andalus were again united under one power, the heart of which lay in the western Maghreb.

In 1098 the caliph of Baghdad recognised Yusuf as emir. A new ruler, Yusuf needed religious legitimacy – which he only received because he seemed to be able to guarantee the defence of Islam. The Almoravid government was originally based on strict moral principles, which were at odds with the Hispano-Arabic tradition. This worsened the relationship with the Christians who became more militant, and, in 1125–1126, Alfonso I of Aragon led a Christian army as far south as Malaga. Despite the struggles, cultural adaptations and interchange took place on a large scale – an example of this can be seen in the architecture of North Africa.

Almoravid rule in Morocco and al-Andalus came to an end in the years around 1145 after rival groups of Berber tribes had united in a religious programme that embraced *jihad*, holy war, first of all against the Almoravids. They were known as *al-muwahhidun*, Almohads ('those who profess the oneness of Allah'). This did not deter them from creating thousands of victims among those who did not share their beliefs. Their leader, Abd al-Mumin, called himself caliph. His first operation in al-Andalus, in 1147, was particularly brutal, yet part of the population recognised him. In 1172, al-Mumin's successor, Abu Yaqub Yusuf, added all of al-Andalus to the Almohad caliphate.

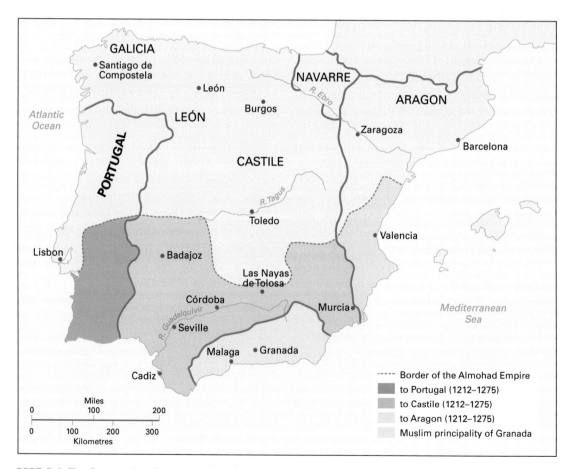

MAP 5.4 The *Reconquista* (Reconquest) in the thirteenth century

PLATE 5.4 The castle of Montsó, constructed by the Muslim rulers, conquered by the count of Barcelona in the middle of the twelfth century, was strategically located on the border between Catalonia and Aragon. The Military Order of the Temple exploited it as one of its principal 'commanderies'.

A vast Christian coalition that Pope Innocent III pronounced to be a crusade finished off this regime in 1212, in a battle near Las Navas de Tolosa, on the southern slopes of the Sierra Morena. This was a turning point for Islam in the Iberian peninsula: the Muslims managed to survive only in the south. Protected by its mountain ranges the kingdom of Granada attracted large numbers of the Islamic population, so that it became very densely populated. Granada held its own against the Christians – who now in their turn were divided among themselves – but was forced to pay tribute to Castile. The clement natural environment made al-Andalus very prosperous, and a lively trade with North Africa and Italy ensued.

In spite of the territorial losses suffered by the Muslims during the twelfth century, in the following centuries their region still continued to be a cradle for the transfer of culture for which Christian Europe is deeply indebted. Europeans, unfortunately, have tended to see things from another viewpoint and to look upon every small parcel of land regained from Islam as progress. From that point of view, southward expansion of the Christian kingdoms, on the pretext of crusades called for by the popes since 1063, took place along three parallel axes from north to south. After military victories, the count of Portugal proclaimed himself king in 1137, a title later confirmed by the popes in recognition of the region's role in the **Reconquest**. In 1147 Lisbon fell into Christian hands. The rest of the conquest took place in fits and starts; crusaders from north-west Europe, and from Provence in particular, sometimes sent reinforcements. The lands of the Alentejo and Algarve were for the most part taken over by the military orders which ensured both the conquest and the exploitation that followed. Faro was reached in 1249.

In the central kingdoms of León and Castile, which were united under a personal union in 1230, the Christian advance similarly took place in phases. Toledo was taken in 1085, but it was not until 1236 that Córdoba fell, and Seville in 1247; then there was stagnation for another two centuries. On the east coast the centuries-long struggle against the Muslims brought about the dynastic union of the individual regions: the March or County of Barcelona, the kingdoms of Aragon, Mallorca, Valencia, Murcia and various overseas settlements of merchants from Barcelona. The integration of Christian Iberia thus took place from north to south, but it enabled the kingdoms of Portugal, Castile-León and Aragon to advance separately. This can be seen in the linguistic boundaries that came into being in parallel with the three axes of expansion right across the area of the Reconquest: Portuguese, Castilian and Catalan.

One problem of the southward expansion resulted from the shortage of peasants to work the conquered land. The land retaken by the Christians was so thinly populated that the Muslims who lived there, now usually called *mudéjares* ('those who have submitted'), were treated tolerantly in order to keep agriculture going. They were allowed to keep their land, have local self-rule and practise their own religion. In the valley of the Ebro and the kingdom of Valencia, *mudéjares* still formed a majority of the population. This made it necessary to give attractive privileges to the Christian communities in towns and villages, which in the long term seriously limited the authority of the kings, especially in rural areas. In the division of

lands that followed the conquest, the monarchy rewarded the nobility for its participation by granting it important concessions of land and jurisdiction. The principal Castilian cities were governed by a knightly class (*caballeros villanos*) who were assigned control over the surrounding countryside in return for their unconditional support to the crown.

The institutionalisation of the state

Kingship becomes an office

The preceding sections attempted to show the circumstances in which the new European monarchies emerged. It was noticeable that from the tenth to the thirteenth century the foundations were laid for a whole series of monarchies that still exist today within essentially the same territories and with more or less the same names. The first great kingdoms largely determined the future destiny of Europe, because they were important units that combined forces and fought out conflicts. Some of the kingdoms considered above were much later absorbed by force or marriage into larger political units – think, for example, of the royal wedding that united the kingdoms of Castile-León and Aragon or of England's union with Wales, Scotland and Northern Ireland. On the other hand, some larger entities fell apart into a myriad of smaller states, as happened to the medieval Holy Roman Empire.

Medieval kings and emperors had every reason to add lustre and persuasiveness to their position by assuring themselves of the support of the clergy. Making their function sacred helped to prop up their often shaky position. The clergy in turn not only provided kingship with its ideological justification, they also put strong emphasis on propagating the Christian faith in secular government. Laboriously and gradually, from the late tenth century, the clergy managed to impose with more success than before Christian values on the conduct of kings and princes. This was expressed in the following prayer at the coronation ceremony of Otto I in 962 in Mainz:

> Lord . . . enrich the king who stands here with his army with your abundant blessings, make him strong and stable on his royal throne. Appear to him as you did to Moses in the burning bush, to Joshua in battle, to Gideon in his camp, and to Samuel in the temple: fill him with the constellation of your blessing, replenish him with the dew of your wisdom which was given to the blessed David in his psalms, and which his son Solomon received from heaven through your goodness. Be his armour against his enemies, his helmet against disaster, his restraint in the days of prosperity, his eternal shield of protection: make his peoples remain faithful to him, and the mighty keep the peace; may they reject greed in neighbourly love, proclaim justice and defend the truth. May all of the people be filled with your eternal blessing so that they will be joyous in victory and in peace.

God was thus very directly involved in maintaining Otto's supremacy, which in the eyes of his contemporaries must have given him an exalted and powerful position. After the dual process of election as German king and papal approval of his elevation as emperor, and the anointing belonging to the rites of both coronations (respectively by the archbishop of Mainz in Charlemagne's church in Aachen and by the pope at St Peter's in Rome) the imperial function acquired a sacral character. Its visible emblems, the royal and imperial insignia, specifically the sacred lance, were viewed as venerable relics. From the second half of the eleventh century, when energetic and scholarly popes led the Church, they therefore tried to restrict the emperor's position, especially when it interfered in Church matters.

During the eleventh century great kings of recently Christianised nations, such as Olaf of Norway (d. 1030), Stephen of Hungary (d. 1038) and Cnut IV of Denmark (d. 1086), were looked upon as saints because of the miracles they performed in person. They asserted that they had been given their authority by the grace of God, so that no one could tamper with it without incurring God's wrath. The Church supported the sacralisation of princes in the hope of their help and protection. It could also discredit a ruler by denying or depriving him of that blessing. The Church's movement for peace was imitated by rulers who saw it as a means of curbing turbulent lords who constantly undermined their authority. God's peace thus became the peace of kings and comparable princes. On several occasions in 1043, the German king, Henry III (1039–1056), called upon his subjects from the pulpit to put an end to the feuding of the nobility, to forgive each other and to keep the peace. His successors repeatedly proclaimed territorial and imperial peace treaties. In the German Empire, the land peaces imposed and guaranteed by the territorial princes within their own jurisdictions gradually became more effective than any royal proclamation. In their turn, they could control the lesser lords. Once again the example of the Church had worked in the secular structures.

Making kingship into an office, rather than a charismatic dignity, was of course not brought about solely by the views expressed by the clergy. Their ideas did no more than substantiate an evolution that, from a purely organisational point of view, must have been inevitable. Through the extension of their lands, the most successful contenders in the power struggle to stabilise the territorial gains were forced to create a structure of government. Pacification was their first concern, above all the suppression of potential internal resistance from rivals or other subjects. In this way they could also assume the aura of someone serving not merely a private interest but the public good, in the knowledge that the Church would support them. The spiritual counsellors and court officials close to them would have encouraged them in this, just as those who shared the renewed interest in Roman law had done since the twelfth century.

BOX 5.3 A CATHEDRAL FOR A ROYAL SAINT

In 1152/1153 Cardinal Nicholas Brekespear, who was born in England and would become Pope Hadrian IV in 1154, travelled as papal legate to Scandinavia, to reform the regional Church. He made the long journey to a town halfway up the coast of Norway called Nidaros, which meant the mouth of the river Nid. Nowadays, the city is called Trondheim. There he elevated the bishopric to an archbishopric which would encompass the huge distances of all present-day Norway, Iceland, Greenland and the groups of Atlantic islands, the Faeroes, Orkney's and Shetland. Situated between the 63rd and 64th parallels, this is the northernmost medieval cathedral, after that of Skálaholt in Iceland. Its location was the burial place of King Olaf (995–1030) who had been active in imposing Christianity, destroyed heathen temples and tried to impose some central government. An uprising of clans supported by Cnut, the king of Denmark and England, forced him into exile in 1028, and it was in trying to restore his power that he was killed in battle. He soon was hailed as a saint and his body brought to Nidaros.

Around 1150 the construction of a cathedral in Anglo-Norman style began, and Olaf's grave under the high altar became the centre of a very popular pilgrimage. The shrine was placed in an octogonal choir at the eastern edge of the church. It was carried out in annual processions on St Olaf's Day and other important celebrations. All new kings of Norway swore their inaugural oath on the shrine, before the popular assembly. The political situation remained highly unstable in Norway until c.1240. Out of fear of King Sverre, Archbishop Øystein Erlendsson went into exile in 1180–1183. He spent part of this time in the abbey of Bury St Edmunds, where the royal cult may have inspired him. He must also have been impressed by the vivid memories of the conflict between Archbishop Thomas Becket and King Henry II, just a decade earlier. He may have

Death and enshrinement of St Olaf, king of Norway. Altar frontal c.1300. Trondheim, Nidaros cathedral.

observed the spectacular cult of St Thomas in Canterbury, and he may have seen the Romanesque polygonal eastern church. Anyhow, shortly after his return in 1183, works started to restyle the Romanesque cathedral at Nidaros with its remarkable octagon, which shows clear similarities with English models in York, Canterbury and Lincoln. In the thirteenth century, a nave in the Gothic style was added at the west side, and the old Romanesque church was enlarged and newly decorated. The screen front with two towers to the west was finished by 1300. With its rows of sculptures, it followed the model of Lincoln cathedral and Westminster abbey. The porches on the south and north were decorated with figural sculptures which demonstrated a clear programme. They illustrated the ambitions of the reform movement, highlighted in the Fourth Lateran Council in 1215 in which Archbishop Guttorm had participated. On the north side, facing the town, themes of the battle between Good and Evil were to be seen by all who entered the consecrated space. On the south side, facing the archbishop's palace, the judgement and penance of man, including the heads of a king and a queen, affirmed the authority of ecclesiastical jurisdiction. In the octagon, conspicuous crocket pillars added to the lustre of St Olaf's cult.

In 1537, the Lutheran Reformation led to the plundering of the cathedral's treasures. The nave and the west front fell into decay, precipitated by the disintegration of the soapstone. The coronation of the new king of Norway and Sweden (from the French House of Bernadotte) in 1818 took place in a cathedral whose nave was a roofless ruin with walls reduced to their lowest layer. Patriotic rhetoric led to an ideologically driven restoration programme, which was started in 1869. The nave was entirely restored in 1930, and the rebuilding of the west front was completed in 1969. The last statue was placed as late as 1983. The future king of Norway will be crowned in a dignified cathedral.

Source: M. Syrstad Andås et al. (eds), The Medieval Cathedral of Trondheim: Architectural and Ritual Constructions in their European Context (Turnhout: Brepols, 2007).

Servants of the state

Until the late Middle Ages the government of the German Empire was based above all on personal relationships, which from the twelfth century were increasingly formalised in feudal ties. Germany has been described as an 'aristocracy with a monarch at the top', while in northern and central Italy, as we have seen, monarchic power became altogether rather theoretical from the late twelfth century onwards.

In Germany, the ministerials (literally 'men in service') formed an estate of unfree men who could own fiefs but could not pass them on as a hereditary right. From the middle of the twelfth century, the German kings burdened them with specific functions and offices for which they received a living in the form of an estate from the king's domain. These tasks often included the guardianship of a castle, but increasingly also other positions in the king's service, at court, in the imperial army and as legal officials in the imperial towns. At the intermediary level, (prince-)bishops and princes started to appoint ministerials too. In the thick of the Investiture Contest, when his vassals had deserted him, Henry IV found significant support for his army among the ministerials of the Empire. They might have grown into an estate of civil servants which could have strengthened the administrative centre of the Empire as happened in France. However, the discontinuity and gradual weakening of the kingship brought any such development to a standstill. The ministerials, of course, were focused on rising in society; in the German context this was easier to achieve as lesser nobles in the feudal framework than as government pen-pushers. When Frederick II introduced a civil servant class in his modern kingdom of Sicily, therefore, he did not choose Germans – like so many popes and bishops who had been appointed by earlier emperors in Italy – but well-educated Sicilians.

There is a marked contrast between developments in the German Empire and those in France and England. England was tightly organised before the Norman Conquest, but the new rulers strengthened the system of government even further with the aim of enabling the foreign minority to keep control by the introduction of a system of quasi-feudal landholding tied to military service, which has already been discussed. Just as happened elsewhere, central institutions in Anglo-Norman England were created from the royal court council (*curia regis*) through the increasing reach of their competences, specialisation and then division into independent organs. Everywhere, this sort of functional differentiation first took place in the technical field, in matters of jurisprudence and finances. It is possible that, in late Anglo-Saxon times, there was already a central accounting office before which the royal receivers were held accountable. In the twelfth century it evolved into a real financial department, called the **Exchequer**. The office of sheriff ('shire reeve') was certainly of Anglo-Saxon origin; the sheriff acted as the king's representative at the level of shires, the English equivalent to continental counties. The Normans strengthened this office and turned sheriffs into almost modern civil servants, in the sense that they carried out a reversible mandate that was not hereditary and for which they were held accountable. The only modern element lacking was a salary.

But the most far-reaching extension of royal control was in the field of law and justice. Over the course of the twelfth century there came into existence, by fits and starts, a 'common law', which can best be equated to 'the king's law'. It was dispensed by the sheriffs but also by key itinerant royal justices, who heard all kinds of pleas, both criminal and civil, but also handled all other royal business in their 'eyre' or circuit. Royal interference went furthest in the field of criminal law, because, from the start, the Norman kings quite understandably were devoted to the general maintenance of 'the king's peace', and keen on prosecuting all breaches of it. In the trying of criminal offences the royal justices were initially led either by private accusations or by ex officio pleas of royal prosecutors. From the time of Henry I onwards criminal pleas were more and more dependent on the sworn declarations of 'juries of presentment', local jurors who gave testimony over felonies or statements about the reputation of notorious suspects. In this way, the English kings succeeded at a relatively early date in monopolising to a large extent the prosecution of crime – at least of all serious crime. In the sphere of civil law, because of the nature of cases – largely questions of right and possession – royal, 'common' justice was only available for free men, who are estimated to have constituted no more than one-third of the population at the time. In civil lawsuits – usually called 'common pleas' – the accession to royal courts of justice was assured by the use of royal writs or written commands ordering that pleas be heard before a royal official; the use of sworn local informants as 'juries' was introduced in this sphere as well. By the end of the twelfth century a central court for civil lawsuits was instituted: the Bench or Court of Common Pleas, residing at Westminster.

By feeding an 'ideology of royal-dominated justice' (Hudson 1996) the English common law indeed became gradually 'common', that is to say, applicable to all the king's subjects. This process came at the expense of enormous diversity of local customary law, which would remain so characteristic for other parts of medieval and early modern Europe.

Obviously modernisation of officialdom was only possible in those areas where the economy was sufficiently monetised. The first really modern-type officials were probably appointed in Flanders, by Count Philip of Alsace, who in 1170 started to appoint *baljuws* (*baillis* in French), who were salaried and dismissable at will. Their main tasks were to maintain the count's prerogatives, organise the administration of justice following the principles of objective examination of the facts, and collect the revenues for the count. At the same time the count ordered the rationalisation of criminal law in all the large towns. The count's liege, King Philip Augustus of France, followed the example; the earliest known royal *baillis* are from around 1190. Their position was somewhere between that of the receivers on the desmesnes (*prévôts*) and the royal council (*curia*), so that a clear hierarchy was established. Unlike the *prévôts*, they would no longer lease their office or hold it in fief, but they received a salary out of the revenues it was their task to collect and were bound to the king through an oath of office (itself a relic of the oral feudal tradition). It was their task to accept homage of royal vassals in the king's name, watch over the administration of the king's justice and tax collection, and on the king's orders summon the crown vassals for military service.

Philip Augustus's grandson, Louis IX (1226–1270), put an end to the itinerant character of the *baillis'* service. In 1254 he created officially demarcated districts, called *baillages*. From that moment on a great deal of money was spent on fortifying castles, where the *baillis* lived, and on strategically situated towns within their jurisdiction. King Louis also appointed the first *baillis* in the south of the kingdom, where they were called *sénéschaux*; their districts *sénéchaussées*.

Points to remember

- The typical states of the central Middle Ages were monarchies, that is to say, either kingdoms or principalities (counties, dukedoms, etc.) of comparable stature. Relatively rare were autonomous, republican city-states, best known from northern and central Italy.

- The successor states to the former East Frankish and West Frankish kingdoms – the kingdoms of Germany and France, respectively – underwent a political development during the second half of the Middle Ages that was diametrically opposed: whereas Germany disintegrated bit by bit into a myriad of autonomous polities, France experienced increasing monarchical centralisation.

- The imperial title imposed upon the East Frankish and German kings a sense of superiority and ambition that was out of proportion to their means of power. This imperial ambition was a major cause of the fact that in Germany and Italy, until the middle of the nineteenth century, a centralised monarchical state never got off the ground.

- The contest for supreme authority between popes and emperors followed logically from the coincidence with Church reform, aimed at pushing back lay influence, with the growth of secular state power.

- In the central medieval period, the political fates of England and France became closely entangled as a consequence of the Norman Conquest after 1066 and the formation of the so-called Angevin Empire after 1154. These events turned the king of England into the most powerful vassal of the kings of France, which created a political powder keg that would not be completely deactivated until the end of the Hundred Years War in 1453.

- On the Iberian peninsula, the balance of power between Muslim rulers and Christian kings shifted definitely towards the latter after the beginning of the thirteenth century.

- The process of state formation in the central Middle Ages was characterised by a further sacralisation of kingship, the introduction of new types of civil servants and specialised government departments – such as the Exchequer in England – and attempts at extending royal justice.

Suggestions for further reading

Bartlett, Robert (2000), *England under the Norman and Angevin Kings, 1075–1225* (Oxford: OUP) (The New Oxford History of England). Masterful survey that in no way resembles the good old diachronic histories of events. Clever reconstruction of English society and polity within all-important thematic fields (lordship and government, warfare, town and country, Church and religion, daily life, worldview), full of well-chosen references to primary source texts.

Brink, Stefan, and Neil Price (eds) (2011), *The Viking World* (London/New York: Routledge). Encyclopedic, multi-authored volume that brings together the latest on the Viking history of Scandinavia from all possible scholarly angles, including archaeology, numismatics and comparative anthropology and religion.

Curta, Florin (2006), *Southeastern Europe in the Middle Ages, 500–1250* (Cambridge: CUP). Welcome and well-documented survey of the history of the Balkans in the early and central medieval periods, unfamiliar to students in the west. The author stresses the relationships between the early Bulgarian, Bosnian and Croatian states with their neighbouring 'superpowers': the Byzantine Empire and the kingdom of Hungary.

Dunbabin, Jean (2000, 2nd edn), *France in the Making, 843–1180* (Oxford: OUP). Anyone who is really interested in French medieval history should consult the five superb volumes covering the medieval period in the new Belin *Histoire de France* edited by Joël Cornette. Dunbabin's work remains a fine, insightful, one-volume survey of early French history in English, even if it is limited to high politics and the upper echelons of society. The three sections on formative trends are especially worth reading.

Fuhrmann, Horst (1986), *Germany in the High Middle Ages, c.1050–1200* (Cambridge: CUP). Classic political history of the German Empire in the central Middle Ages by a leading German medieval historian. This remains to date one of the few adequate, single-authored general introductions for laypeople in the field available in English.

6 Religious reform and renewal

The Western Church of the early Middle Ages in many ways gave the appearance of a house under construction, for which architects with differing ideas had drawn up the plans. On the one hand, the monks' ascetic ideology, aimed at renouncing the world, had set a standard for moral values and spiritual ideals that was beyond the reach of ordinary laypeople. Only by association with these model Christians through the donation of gifts could they hope to secure salvation in the next world. This subtle form of indoctrination ensured a phenomenal growth in the wealth of the abbeys. On the other hand, all aspects of the affairs of both Church and clergy were intertwined with secular interests. Countless churches and monasteries belonged to laymen, who were involved in the appointments of bishops and abbots; once they had been appointed, these bishops and abbots were directly involved in the affairs of secular government in all manner of ways.

The Church was to undergo radical change on all these points in the course of the eleventh and twelfth centuries: the monks' moral grip on the Church and society would weaken and be challenged by an alternative spiritual ideal; the worlds of the cleric and layman would diverge far more than in the early Middle Ages; the interference of secular aristocrats, the masters of the world, in ecclesiastical business would be drastically reduced; the power and ambition of the pope would reach a record height; the ordinary faithful would be addressed in the vernacular languages by fervent preachers and manifest themselves in large numbers and prominently in the Church, as bearers of both old Christian traditions and new religious sentiments. This programme was launched under the motto *libertas Ecclesiae*, liberty of the Church, that is to say, freedom from lay interference. At the same time, ordinary believers developed all kinds of initiatives to give expression to new forms of devotion.

Aspirations to reform

Throughout its long existence the Catholic Church has always shown a considerable capacity to purge itself. Long before the Reformation frequent demands for reform had been heard. We must not confuse attempts at reformation with the desire for innovation. Church reform was always aimed at the restoration of old values and relationships, which, in the eyes of those in favour of reform, had been lost or were in danger of being lost. But the attempts at reformation that became apparent in the tenth and eleventh centuries differed in one essential respect from earlier offensives, such as those made under Charlemagne and Louis the Pious. They had always been aimed at improving the morals of individuals: of the monks and lay clergy, to begin with, and then of ordinary laypeople too. The reformers of the tenth and eleventh centuries still considered this an important aim, but in addition they proposed drastic alterations to 'the mystical body of Christ', the Church as an institute. The first step necessary to do this was to purge the Church of worldly pollution by curbing the profound secular influence in the Church on all fronts. One of the reformers' constant objectives was to enhance the clergy's observance of moral purity, and at the Second Lateran Council of 1139 it was decreed that all clergymen of the four higher orders (subdeacon, deacon, priest and bishop) should live in celibacy and 'separate themselves from the women with whom they dared to copulate trespassing the holy commands'. Only that would provide them with the authority to prescribe moral restraint to lay society. The imposition of strict rules for marriage, now defined as a sacrament, provided the clergy with the means to control legitimate descent, i.e. the continuity of aristocratic property and power. As one can imagine, the reformers met fierce resistance, not least from higher clerics themselves, who would not give up the comfort of concubinage.

Pope versus emperor: the Investiture Controversy

The reformers' first target was lay investiture, the early medieval practice whereby clerical digni-taries – bishops and abbots – after their election by 'clergy and people' and before their consecration by archbishop (or pope), were invested by the king or his representative with the supreme signs of spiritual dignity, a staff and a ring. The king thus had de facto control of the appointment of bishops and abbots, because they could not exercise their office without the investiture. That was why it was also customary for the king to give his approval to the election.

For those in the Church who were in favour of reform, this practice was a thorn in their side because it created the opportunity for the buying and selling of clerical offices, also known as the sin of **simony** after a certain Simon who had admitted to it according to the Acts of the Apostles. The conflict over lay investiture was exacerbated in the German Empire by two developments. First, German kings since Otto I – or since the recovery of their control of north Italy and their claims to the imperial dignity – had frequently intervened in the selection of the pope. Second, the policy of the German kings was to involve bishops in state government. Of course this was not entirely new. We have seen that it was common enough for bishops to represent the secular authority in their dioceses during the early Middle Ages. The Carolingians often brought in bishops and abbots as royal emissaries. However, as we saw in Chapter 5, the German kings went a step further: initially just on occasion, but then systematically under the Salian dynasty (1024–1125), bishops were invested with the title of count or duke, which gave them important secular authority in addition to their spiritual authority. As part of a system of royal government, this arrangement could only work if the German kings had the right to appoint bishops and abbots.

In England after 1066 bishops and abbots of great monasteries became tenants-in-chief of the crown, and received estates and the rights attached to them as fiefs, but they were never appointed as government officials. In France the problem of lay investiture did not become as pressing for yet another reason. In some areas, bishops were frequently invested with the rank of count. And in various important northern French cathedral cities such as Rheims and Laon, on the basis of their rights as count, they acted as lord of the town and its surroundings. However, in the eleventh century, the position of the king remained simply too weak to make the bishops' activities in secular government a cornerstone of royal policies; the king even lacked the right to appoint (arch)bishops and abbots in many (arch)bishoprics. This precluded the French version of the Investiture Controversy from becoming an exclusive struggle between king and pope.

The reform programme

Ironically enough, the popes' great offensive against secular investiture in Germany was set in motion by the king. It was Henry III (1039–1056) who shortly before 1050 put an end to the abuses to which the Holy See in Rome had fallen victim and who had had his cousin, Bruno of Egisheim, bishop of Toul, elected pope as Leo IX (1049–1054). Leo IX turned out to be the first in a line of competent German popes under whom papal authority was undoubtedly strengthened. He still respected the sacred character of kingship and even recognised the king's right to make clerical appointments; however, he pleaded against the practice whereby lay rulers bestowed religious symbols on churchmen. He received strong support from reform-minded elements in the Curia, the papal court. Their two most radical representatives were Humbert, a scholarly monk from the Burgundian abbey of Cluny, whom Leo IX elevated to be cardinal-bishop of Silva Candida, and Hildebrand of Soana, who was also a monk, native of Rome. From 1059 onward, Hildebrand was responsible for controlling the papal finances.

The reformers' first success, in 1059, was to revise the procedure for the election of the pope. Humbert of Silva Candida is generally seen as the genius behind this ruling. Until then, the popes,

just like ordinary bishops, had been chosen by their diocese's 'clergy and people'. In practice this meant that the quarrelsome Roman aristocracy determined who became pope. The ruling of 1059 placed the choice of pope in the hands of the 'college of **cardinals**', the collective name for the most important clergy in Rome. Among their number were the bishops in the immediate vicinity of Rome who had performed liturgical tasks in the basilica of the papal residence, the Lateran, since the eighth century (cardinal-bishops), and the priests and deacons attached to the most important churches in Rome (cardinal-priests and cardinal-deacons). All together, there were about 50 cardinals in 1100; later there would be many more of them. In 1179 it was decided that all the cardinals were equal, and that for the election of a new pope, a two-thirds majority of the votes would be required. However, this did not mean that the selection of the pope was safe from secular interference, for many of the cardinals were scions of Rome's noble families. Moreover, as long as the elections were held in public, there remained a danger of outside interference. The year 1216 saw the first conclave, the election in strict seclusion, which is still the custom today. It did not meet with immediate success: the cardinals were shut up for days in a room which was too small and lacked adequate sanitary facilities, an indescribable situation. This unfortunate start meant that the conclave did not become the rule until 1274.

It was Hildebrand of Soana who would make the Church's supreme authority a cornerstone of papal policy when he himself was elected pope. He radically opposed lay investiture of the clergy and private churches. His fierce attitude provoked strong reactions from the emperors in particular because of their specific role in the protection of the Catholic Church and their involvement in Italian politics. As Gregory VII (1073–1085), he ensured from the very beginning that there would be no mistaking his intentions. We are familiar with them through a curious document, *Dictatus Papae* (Papal Statements) of 1075, drawn up by the new pope soon after he took office. At first glance the *Dictatus* is reminiscent of a megalomaniac's wish list. Twenty-seven short, staccato sentences sum up whence the power of the pope should come:

> [The pope] alone may have control over the imperial insignia. That he may remove emperors. That he may be the only one whose feet must be kissed by all rulers. That he cannot be judged by anybody. That the bishop of Rome [i.e. the pope], if consecrated according to canon law, is undoubtedly sacrosanct through the merits of St Peter.

In fact what we have here is an extreme re-interpretation of the doctrine of the two swords – the spiritual and the secular – through which the highest authority in the world was granted to the pope without the batting of an eye. What was new was how unambiguously Pope Gregory made explicit old radical claims which had always remained more or less veiled, and presented them as the official papal standpoint. The *Dictatus Papae* should then be seen as the blueprint for a new hierocratic world order which was to replace the old imperial/papal order, in which kings considered themselves as head of the Church in their own kingdoms. The successors of Gregory VII propagated this view with considerable vigour. The change in the procedure for the imperial coronation introduced by Pope Innocent III (1198–1216) was particularly significant in this respect. Until then, when the new emperor had been girded with the sword, the next words in the ceremony stated that the emperor had received the sword 'from God' in order to protect the Church. Innocent changed this to 'from the pope'! This made it perfectly clear that the pope had both swords at his disposal. This was not entirely original. The same idea had already been hinted at in the *Donatio Constantini* ('Donation of Constantine', see Box 6.1). The fact that this new order was never actually realised in no way lessens the tremendous impact that the papacy, but-

tressed by this new ideology, had on the twelfth and thirteenth centuries – but on that period only.

It became increasingly obvious that a conflict between the pope and the German king could not be avoided. The struggle came to a head in 1075 when Henry IV (1056–1106) installed his chaplain Tedald as archbishop of Milan, after a canonical election had already taken place and the candidate-elect had received papal approval. This was the first step towards one of the most memorable events in medieval history. First of all Gregory not only excommunicated the emperor, but also removed him from office. The first had happened before, but never the second. Now it was clear how great the power of the pope had become, even though he did not have a king's army; there was turmoil in the German Empire and Henry's position was seriously threatened. Henry made the best of a bad job by, literally, going to Canossa to ask the pope for forgiveness, which Gregory could not refuse (Chapter 5). Yet Henry had to pay a high price for this tactical victory: a German king had implicitly recognised that the pope had control over his kingship, and this set a dangerous precedent.

As for the pope, events at Canossa allowed him to formulate his ideas concerning the relationship between kings and popes more broadly and more rigidly. In short, they asserted that the king should be obedient (*obediens*), useful (*utilis*) and suitable (*idoneus*), respectively to the pope, for the pope and in the eyes of the pope. In addition, the German king should no longer have the exclusive right to the emperorship in the West. The stage was set for the struggle between the German king/emperor and the pope, each supported by a part of the German and Italian episcopacy. The nadir was reached in the half century between 1076 and 1122. With daggers drawn, emperor and pope used every means available to harm and humiliate the adversary: from appointing or supporting anti-kings or anti-popes to denouncing or demonising the opponent. Gregory VII, himself called 'the holy devil', regularly identified Henry with Satan and even developed the idea, for that

BOX 6.1 THE *DONATIO CONSTANTINI*

One of the most famous documents in medieval history is the so-called *Donatio Constantini* (Donation of Constantine). This document is in the form of a solemn deed of a gift, in which, shortly before his definitive departure for Byzantium Constantinople, Emperor Constantine not only confirmed the primacy of power of the pope in Rome over the Christian Church, but also transferred to Pope Silvester I his palace in Rome, all his imperial insignia and all his authority over the western part of the Roman Empire, including the city of Rome and all Italy and the islands of the West. Constantine further confirmed that he had placed the imperial crown on Silvester's head himself, and on that occasion 'as a mark of respect to St Peter' had held the reins of the pope's horse and helped him to dismount, as if he were Silvester's squire.

It is perfectly obvious that Constantine never issued this document; in this sense it is spurious, but the question is whether it is also a *falsum*, a purposeful falsification, because it is not at all clear who (or what group) would have wanted to make it appear real, and above all why. It has often been suggested that there was a connection with the well-known reversal of 754, when Pope Stephen II, under pressure from the Lombard threat, turned away from the emperor of Byzantium and found a new protector in Pippin the Short, ruler of the Franks. This is understandable, because it is generally agreed that the first version of the *Donatio Constantini* must date from the third quarter of the eighth century. Yet none of the sources point to Pippin or any of his successors being familiar with the text of the *Donatio*. Nor is there any indication that its contents played any part in the ideological basis of papal policies in that turbulent time. What is certain is that the *Donatio* was created in clerical circles close to the pope. There are three theories concerning its purpose. One suggests that the text is no more than a frivolous practice-exercise in rhetoric, in which case the *Donatio* is indeed spurious, but not falsified. The second theory argues that the production of the text served a purely local Roman aim: its authors wanted to stress the importance of the great basilica near the papal residence of the Lateran in a period when the Vatican and the basilica of St Peter threatened to overshadow the Lateran. The supporters of the third theory take an even broader view: the *Donatio* would have been used against the new Frankish allies to support the claim that the popes had secular supremacy over extensive parts of central Italy – a claim that would appear to be successful. With the last aim the text – in a splendid new transcript that was meant to pass for the so-called fourth-century original – was in any case deployed in the diplomatic game for the 'restitution' of Church areas to Pope John XII (955–964) at the time of the arrival of the German King Otto I in Italy.

With the reform movement from the middle of the eleventh century the *Donatio Constantini* became a real ideological pillar in the defence of papal claims to the highest authority in the Christian world, despite the repeated oaths of the pope's opponents that the document was 'false'. Even the scientific unmasking of the *Donatio* by the humanists Nicholas of Cusa and Lorenzo Valla, who between 1430 and 1440 used other arguments to prove irrefutably that it could not possibly be dated to the beginning of the fourth century, did not prevent various Renaissance popes from appealing to the Donation of Constantine. It is famously referred to in the Treaty of Tordesillas in 1494, where Pope Alexander VI as alleged lord of the western hemisphere divided the New World into a Portuguese and a Castilian sphere of influence.

Sources: H. Fuhrmann, lemma 'Konstantinische Schenkung', in *Lexikon des Mittelalters V* (Munich/Zurich: Artemis Verlag, 1991), cols 1385–1386; Hartmut Hoffmann, 'Ottonische Fragen', *Deutsches Archiv für Erforschung des Mittelalters* 51 (1995), pp. 53–82.

time bizarre, if not heretical, that all secular authority originated with the devil. Henry's son and successor, Henry V (1106–1125), was not unfavourable to the moral aims of the papal reform movement, but he would not yield an inch on the question of the bishops' investiture, which he considered to be indissolubly linked with his *ius regni* ('right of kingship'). So the battle continued. A compromise was eventually reached at the Concordat of Worms in 1122. The king gave up the investiture insofar as it related to the confirmation of the spiritual office. He was also obliged to guarantee the 'free' election of bishops, meaning that elections would be safeguarded from interference by laypeople. It meant that thenceforth bishops were elected by the most important priests in the bishopric, usually the canons of the cathedral chapter. The king was allowed to retain the right to investiture with the symbols of any secular authority that might be granted to bishops.

The popes attached great importance to the Concordat of Worms, and the full text of the agreement was put on the walls of the great receiving hall of the Lateran Palace, visible to one and all. Of course Worms, and similar arrangements with other monarchs, did not provide a true solution to the problem of lay intervention in Church affairs. As long as the offices of bishops and abbots remained profitable and their holders belonged to the literate elite and had some secular authority or extensive worldly possessions, then princes and the aristocracy would continue to interfere in elections, only no longer overtly and directly.

The half-hearted ruling for secular investiture and the appointment procedures to high ecclesiastical office were the most radical aspects of the papal reformers' more general efforts to stem lay influence in the Church. Another path was to limit the proprietary church system. This was successful particularly when new churches (often parish churches) were established, and very gradually through the revision of the status of existing churches. The right of appointing a person as the local priest still often lay in the hands of noble lords, but sometimes in those of local communities too, as was the case in the mountain villages of the Alps and Pyrenees and in several places in Italy. Parishioners everywhere now had a say in looking after the church building and related matters such as church properties and local poor relief.

The impulse for the Crusades

Lacking adequate military, and often also political, weapons, the popes had to resort to canonical sanctions, diplomatic bravura and ideological propaganda to realise their hierocratic claims. Undoubtedly, the single most formidable as well as ambitious expression of this was the general exhortation to wage holy war against all enemies of the Christian faith in defence of the Church. The first instance was Pope Urban II's famous call for a crusade to free the Holy Sepulchre issued at a council at Clermont in 1095. The response was unbelievable: an estimated 150,000 people vowed to take the cross and set out for Jerusalem. About a quarter of them may really have done so, most of them commoners, including quite a few women. In several waves this people's crusade moved over land to Constantinople, fired up by fanatic preachers such as Peter the Hermit. Their fate was to perish when crossing enemy territory in Anatolia or to be sold off as slaves. Only the main body, consisting of several thousand trained knights, who marched in four separate armies to Constantinople to join forces there, reached Jerusalem, three years after the first had departed from their homes.

The overwhelming response showed that the Roman popes had the authority to use the new dynamic of the western aristocracy to achieve the Church's objectives. Many more appeals for crusades would follow (Chapter 7) – until long after the Middle Ages – directed not only against the Muslim masters of Palestine, but soon also in conjunction with the *Reconquista* of Muslim Spain, with the conversion of the still pagan Baltic area, with the extermination of heresy in the Latin-Christian heartland and, finally, with combating the pope's political enemies in Italy.

It was above all bishops and archbishops from France and Spain who took part in the council gathered at Clermont on 24 November 1095. On the agenda was the matter of the excommunication of Philip I, the king of France, who had repudiated his queen and refused to end his affair with the wife of one of his barons. Pope Urban II also inveighed strongly against the lay investiture of bishops and the acts of violence and injustice committed by knights contrary to the Peace of God alliances supported by the Church. It is in this light that his call for a crusade – addressed to the knights at the end of the council – should be seen. Several chronicles report that the pope urged them to devote their forces instead to the defence of their brothers in faith in the East, who had become the victims of the infidels' violence. The canons of the council record that those warriors of the faith who went to Jerusalem without thought of vain glory or material gain, but only with the intention of visiting the Holy Sepulchre, would be granted plenary indulgence, that is to say a full remission of punishment in **Purgatory** for sins committed in life.

In addition to the sincere wish to promote the Christian faith and the purity of the Church, the pope would also have had political considerations in mind. The request for military support from the Byzantine emperor offered the Western Church the chance to strengthen its position there, as it had already done in Sicily and Iberia. The aim of the expedition was certainly not the defence of the Byzantine Empire – the crusaders travelled straight through. The Turkic Seljuks were put to flight, but not eliminated. A papal vassal state in Palestine, on the Sicilian model, however, would have been an excellent result from the opportunities offered. Seen in this light, it can be understood why the pope tied the Church hierarchy in the newly conquered regions to Rome and not to the patriarch of Constantinople.

The western invasions in the Middle East that followed Urban II's proclamation were accompanied by an intensive propaganda campaign for the greater glory of the Catholic Church and the nobles who took the cross. Practically all the surviving sources in the West relating to the Crusades breathe a virulent partisanship and portray a clichéd image of the enemy, which fitted in logically with the Church's campaign to crusade. The opening verses of Psalm 79 were frequently quoted to vindicate what was to be seen as a war of liberation of the Holy Sepulchre: 'O God, the heathen are come into thine inheritance; thy holy temple have they defiled.' On earlier occasions, when Jerusalem was taken by the Muslims in the seventh century or at the destruction of the Holy Sepulchre by Caliph al-Hakim at the beginning of the eleventh century, the Catholic Church had not yet attained the moral and organisational strength it acquired in the second half of the eleventh century. The great Church Reform, the Peace of God movement, the Investiture Controversy and the encouragement of the Iberian *Reconquista* were all expressions of this newly acquired self-confidence.

Neither is there any need to doubt the deeply religious motives of most crusaders. Chroniclers called the men (and some women too) who took the cross pilgrims, or even martyrs or new apostles, and the expeditions themselves pilgrimages – all terms that underlined their elevated religious status and their willingness to make great sacrifices in the eyes of contemporaries. Abbot Guibert de Nogent, one of the non-participating historians of the First Crusade who finished his 'God's Deeds through the Franks' in 1108, and who had been in personal contact with crusaders, connected the various ideological elements that, together, constituted the Christian concept of holy war against the infidels – knightly virtue, earthly salvation, God's grace and religious vocation. Crusades were never 'simply military campaigns' but always and primarily 'acts of devotion and a means of salvation' (Madden 1999). Crusaders were unlikely to be driven by love of gain alone: they wanted to cleanse their sins and save their souls. To that end they and their families had to make huge financial sacrifices, and they often had to face appalling hardships on their journey. Most of them eventually returned to their homeland, which also indicates that the acquisition of new land was never their prime motive.

On the other hand, the behaviour of the crusaders in the Holy Land was quite another matter. The cruelty of their actions, in particular the plundering and wholesale murder for which they were responsible, for instance, during the First Crusade, in Ma'arrat al-No'man and Jerusalem, filled the local population with revulsion, and exposed the desire of many 'Franks' to take as much booty as quickly as possible.

Papal claims to the highest authority in the world

The other two most important weapons in the papal arsenal were excommunication and **interdict**. By excommunication we mean the exclusion of individual disobedient believers from the Christian community; by interdict we mean the suspension of Church services within a certain area. An even heavier penalty was to accuse a person of heresy, which meant that secular rulers could be asked for military support. So it was that, in 1074, Gregory VII asked King Sven Estridsson of Denmark to come and drive the 'heretical' Normans out of south Italy. A similar appeal was made to Count Robert II of Flanders in 1102, this time aimed against Emperor Henry IV. In such cases heresy should, of course, be seen not as a deviation from the Church's doctrine, but as a serious disturbance of the world peace that was guaranteed by the Church. In such circumstances it was the popes' sacred duty to take action.

Bravura formed the basis of papal claims to territorial authority over large areas of Europe. On the basis of the island clause in the *Donatio Constantini*, just before 1100 Urban II laid claim to Corsica, and soon after 1150 Callistus III bestowed Ireland on the English king, Henry II. Then the popes looked for allies prepared to recognise them as liege lord. That was not always successful. The oldest case is also the best known: the remarkable alliance that Gregory VII made with the Norman lords of southern Italy in 1080, during the second phase of his trial of strength with Henry IV, took the form of a feudal-vassalic bond. Other princely vassals of the pope included the count of Barcelona and the duke of Dalmatia and Croatia. The latter promoted himself to king in 1076 with Gregory's acquiescence. The kings of Aragon and Navarre and the dukes, later kings, of Portugal maintained a peculiar relationship with the pope that was called *patrocinium*, a kind of patronage. Nor did Gregory hesitate to ask William the Conqueror to become his *fidelis* (vassal) in return for the political and spiritual support he had received from the papacy in 1066. Nowadays it is generally believed that William did not fall for this, just as Frederick Barbarossa would not be misled by a sly diplomatic attempt to present him as the pope's vassal in 1157. More than fifty years later, England's King John could not avoid it: he became the vassal of Innocent III in 1213, and acknowledged that he held England and Ireland in fief from him. In exchange, the pope took John's side in the struggle against the defiant barons, and lifted the interdict which had been placed on England in 1208. In the same period the pope also established his formal lordship over the kingdom of Sicily.

It goes without saying that the popes' efforts to secure their authority above that of kings and emperors did not remain unopposed. Of all the German kings and emperors most affected by the question, it was Frederick Barbarossa (1152–1190) who took up arms against the pope over this and other matters. He was the first emperor to refer consistently to his authority and his empire as the *Holy* Roman Empire (*sacrum imperium (Romanorum)*), something just as holy and God-given as the Holy Church. Moreover, not all clerical circles shared the extreme interpretation of the doctrine of the two swords which had been current since Gregory VII. The moderate or dualist view – that the two powers in the world are more or less equal – was laid down in the *Decretum Gratiani* (*c.*1140), the most authoritative compilation of canon law in the Middle Ages.

The papal monarchy

The struggles of the popes with kings and emperors about supremacy in the world should not be seen separately from the gradual strengthening of the papal hold on the Church itself. It was coupled with the expansion of central administrative organs in Rome. The College of Cardinals, known as the Sacred College (*Sacrum Collegium*), developed in the twelfth century into the popes' most important advisory and administrative body. The popes sent the cardinals everywhere as their personal, authorised envoys (*legati a latere*), ensuring that their authority was felt in every corner of Christendom. The actual administration was based on the papal Curia. From the second half of the twelfth century, departments began to specialise and become separate; jurisdiction and finance were the first.

The popes had, of course, always had some form of supreme judicial authority in the Latin Church, but it was not institutionalised until the twelfth century. The popes began to take on more jurisdiction, while papal judgements were increasingly sought. At first the pope and cardinals dealt with everything themselves in the consistory, as the regular meetings of the pope and Sacred College were called. One official, the chancellor (*cancellarius*), had a key role in these meetings. He heard cases together with the pope and later presented a verdict in accordance with the judgement that had been formulated in the consistory. The Curia tried to channel the enormous increase in papal jurisdiction through the formation of specialised law courts: the *Poenitentiaria* to try moral questions, and the *Audientia* for other matters. Native clergy, schooled in canon law and

with a special mandate, were appointed for cases wherever they occurred.

The twelfth century also showed a considerable growth in the income of the Church in Rome. There were two separate funds for administration: the *Camera Apostolica* – the Apostle's Office – for the papal share and the Office for the cardinals' share, which after 1289 was as large as that of the pope. The *Camera Apostolica* came under the supervision of the papal treasurer (*camerarius*). In this period the papal domains and the sums irregularly received from secular princes, to finance crusades, amongst other things, still provided the major part of papal revenues. This second source was less dependable, because the pope had few sanctions to extract payment from an unwilling prince. In time other, regular sources of income would become more important. Under Innocent III the first attempt was made to tax the clergy by means of a three-yearly levy on their income. Further experiments were made along these lines, much to the dismay of some rulers who viewed in horror the flow of clerical income out of their kingdoms.

The easing of the financial situation and the improvements in financial management then contributed to a strengthening of the pope's hold on what, for the sake of simplicity, we earlier called the Papal State (Chapter 2). The whole complexity of properties and vaguely defined seigneurial rights that made up the Papal State was considerably extended in 1102 with a large number of possessions in Tuscany, Emilia and Lombardy belonging to the estate of the reform-minded margravine Matilda of Tuscany, who died childless in that year, bequeathing all her worldly goods to the Church of Rome. From about the middle of the twelfth century the step-by-step consolidation and territorialisation of the worldly power of the popes in central Italy can be traced.

The twelfth and thirteenth centuries were also the era of a new series of ecumenical councils rather different in nature from the papal synods of the early Middle Ages. The conventional idea that questions of doctrine could only be decided by a general Church council still existed, but there had not been many of these meetings since the seventh century. This was chiefly due to another tradition, that ecumenical councils should be chaired by the emperor, and there had not been one for a long time, at least not in the West. Leo IX was the first pope to summon an assembly of bishops from different parts of Latin Christendom, and to preside at it without the emperor being present. In 1049 he had the relics of Saint Remigius, who had baptised Clovis, placed upon the altar of the cathedral of Rheims and urged all the prelates to declare that they had not paid for their appointment (the sin of simony). Three were deposed, two of whom were immediately reinstated by the pope, and one was excommunicated. This gathering was a prelude to a new series of ecumenical councils in the West which were held regularly from the beginning of the twelfth century, and which marked the transition to a more offensive strategy of the popes. They also started to use councils as a magnificent stage to exhibit their doctrinal power and display the unity of the Church. The legislative role of those attending the councils was soon limited to hearing what decrees had been prepared by the pope and his legal experts before giving them their loud and undivided assent: *fiat!, fiat!* ('Let it be! Let it be!').

From 1123 the scene of these new-style Church assemblies was normally the papal residence in Rome, the Lateran, with its great basilica and adjoining palace. The Third and Fourth Lateran Councils, held in 1179 and 1215 and summoned by Alexander III (1159–1181) and Innocent III (1198–1216) respectively, were the high points of these new ecumenical councils. Both produced comprehensive regulations in many areas: the Third in relation to the election of the pope, but also in the field of marriage and kinship. The Fourth Council approved 71 decrees dealing with a variety of matters: how often a good Christian should make his confession, the morals of the clergy, the prohibition on the clergy against taking part in trials by ordeal, the recognition of certain religious groups and the condemnation of others as heretics, and the injunction that Jews should thenceforth wear a yellow badge on their clothes. The Fourth Council also broke new ground in that it was the first council to which not only bishops but also other clerical and secular dignitaries were invited. This was a sign of self-confidence bordering on arrogance and belief in their own supremacy that had been built up by the popes since Gregory VII, for the invitation was certainly not based on any intention to give the Christian community a say in Church affairs through its 'natural' representatives. The rulers were not asked to take part in the decisions, only to join in the deliberations and chiefly to witness an event that concerned all Christendom. That does not mean that the sessions were all sweetness and light. When the question of whether or not Frederick II should be recognised as emperor was being dealt with, supporters and opponents alike created pandemonium, and the pope himself joined in vehemently.

The pontificate of Innocent III is traditionally considered to be the climax of papal power in the Middle Ages, but in recent years the reasons for this view have changed. Previously, Innocent was admired as an administrator and politician, for his impressive legislative and managerial activities, his strenuous efforts to consolidate further the Papal State in the making, his successful mobilisation of crusader armies and his skilful manoeuvres in international politics. More recently, Innocent has been seen above all as the embodiment of the exalted aspirations and ideals of a new papacy that was aimed at the spiritual and eventually political leadership of all Christendom. An important means to achieve that aim was the development of the concept of *plenitudo potestatis* (the fullness of power) which had already appeared in the works of Pope Leo the Great (440–461). Innocent's predecessor, Alexander III, had reintroduced the term to indicate what he saw as the unrestricted and exclusive judicial and administrative power of the pope within the

Church. Innocent III went a step further. By linking *plenitudo potestatis* with the well-known passage in Matthew's Gospel on St Peter's power of the keys (Chapter 2) he could substantiate the pretension that the authority of the pope was superior to any other worldly power.

Reformation and renewal in monastic life

Cluny and the Ecclesia Cluniacensis

The cradle of most of the Church reforms just discussed was Cluny, in the West Frankish duchy of Burgundy. William the Pious, duke of Aquitaine, founded an abbey there in 910, which within two

PLATE 6.1 The imposing buildings of the abbey of Cluny, destroyed during the French Revolution, after a lithograph by Émile Sagot, after 1798.

centuries would become one of the richest ecclesiastical institutions in the West. As early as the second abbot, Odo (927–942), reforms aimed at restoring the Rule of Benedict were carried out, especially in connection with the command to pray. A lengthy liturgy took shape, and Cluny was the first abbey in which praying for the salvation of the dead – not just dead monks and their relations, but also outsiders – became a serious occupation. With this particular aim Odilo (998–1049), Cluny's fifth abbot, introduced a new Church feast, All Souls' Day, celebrated on 2 November. The idea that the souls of the individual dead were painfully cleansed of their earthly sins before the Last Judgement, or were even punished in hell, gathered weight in about 1000. In their cosmic struggle with the forces of the devil, on All Souls' Day the Cluniac monks gathered together in a dazzling ceremony of singing psalms and chorals. A vast cemetery was laid out next to the abbey for those members of the faithful who wished to be buried within striking distance of holy Cluny. The Burgundian abbey prospered from it as gifts flowed in. Liturgical garments in silk, gold and silver showed off the abbey's extraordinary wealth. By about 1150 Cluny, with 300 monks in residence, most of them priests, was far and away the largest monastery in Latin Christendom. The private donations led to an overflow of masses and litanies naming the pious donors in the numerous memorial services. Every day more than two hundred psalms were recited, and hundreds of poor people crowded through the abbey gates in the hope of receiving food. Altogether this must have formed an agglomeration comparable, for that time, to a large town.

Cluny owed its special place in the religious landscape of the dynamic tenth century to four other factors: first, the success with which it conveyed its efforts at reformation to numerous other monastic communities, both new and already established. Eventually, at the beginning of the twelfth century, the Cluny circle, *Ecclesia Cluniacensis*, numbered more than one thousand houses which depended on the mother abbey in various ways. Existing abbeys (possibly with their daughter houses or offshoots) kept their own abbot, while new foundations were guided by a lower-ranking prior appointed by the abbot of Cluny. Through a system of visitations or inspections from Cluny itself, the mother abbey's hold on the associated monasteries was fairly strong.

Second, from the end of the tenth century, Cluny enjoyed an unusual form of Church exemption. The abbey was exempted from local episcopal supervision and every form of secular authority. It is true that other great medieval cloisters, Bobbio, Saint-Denis and Fulda among them, had enjoyed this exemption before Cluny, but the granting of it to the Burgundian abbey had even more far-reaching consequences when it was extended to all its houses in 1024: it made Cluny almost a kingdom within a kingdom, and a powerful bulwark in the emancipatory struggle to free ecclesiastical institutions from secular control.

The third factor was that Cluny had a special relationship not only with the pope but also with the principal apostles, Peter and Paul. This came about in 981 through the ceremonial transfer of relics of Peter and Paul from Rome to Burgundy. For pilgrims from the north the road to Cluny could thus be seen as a sort of second-best pilgrimage to Rome. Gifts of land made to Cluny were expressed as gifts to St Peter, so that the (aristocratic) landowners could imagine themselves to be the 'neighbour of St Peter' (Rosenwein 1989). Could there be a more powerful protector?

Fourth, Cluny soon developed into a centre of learning and intellectual training. The abbots enjoyed an impressive reputation throughout Christendom. Their advice was highly valued by kings and popes and they were much in evidence at all great festivities, such as the Peace of God gatherings where lay and ecclesiastical lords promised to collaborate in keeping the peace and to prevent violence.

Despite its exceptional allure, Cluny was not an isolated phenomenon. The Burgundian and German kingdoms had their own centres of monastic reform, which had no connection with Cluny, such as the abbey of Saint-Victor at Marseilles and the abbey of Gorze in Lotharingia. In the core regions of the German Empire the efforts at reformation were concentrated on the richest and best-known Carolingian abbeys: Corvey, Lorsch, Fulda, Prüm, Echternach, Reichenau, Sankt Gallen, and so on. Other great Benedictine abbeys, notably Monte Cassino, the mother of them all, which enjoyed a flourishing period in the eleventh century, managed to avoid all attempts at reform.

The new orders

Soon, however, serious criticism was levelled at Cluny from within monastic circles. It was directed at the splendour of its festivities, the relative luxury in which the monks lived and the intensive involvement of many of Cluny's abbots with secular politics, none of which was compatible with the original monastic ideals of renouncing the world, contemplation and an ascetic lifestyle. The protest led to the establishment of two new monastic communities, both of which stood for a rigorous observance of the Benedictine Rule: La Grande Chartreuse, in the mountains above Grenoble (1084), and Cîteaux, north of Cluny (1098). They were the mother houses of the first two well-organised monastic orders, the Carthusians and the Cistercians. The Cistercians were especially successful. The number of Cistercian houses grew to around 350 in 1150, and by 1250 to around 650 for men and around 900 for women, in the furthest corners of Latin Europe. The order had a congregational structure of mother and daughter houses linked to each other. The highest administrative body was the chapter-general; it consisted of the abbots of all the houses and met once every three years. The abbots were chosen by the monks, to whom they were accountable.

As an expression of the Cistercians' return to the roots of monasticism, they chose isolated

PLATE 6.2 The abbey of Fontenay in north Burgundy is a fine example of Cistercian principles: located at the fringes of civilisation, it was built in a sober style, contrasting with the luxury of the older Benedictine abbeys, and there was a clear involvement in agricultural and technical innovations. The location was chosen in 1118 by Bernard of Clairvaux in a valley amply provided with running water, which was used to supply energy to watermills which powered bellows and hammers in the forge. In this 53-metre long twelfth-century building, iron-ore mined nearby was worked into metal tools.

locations at the fringe of civilisation, as in the original 'desert' of early Christianity, an attempt to live in strict seclusion from the world. They rejected the domain exploitation of land, including serfdom, unfree labour and surplus extraction in kind, in rents or tithes, and coupled with feudal forms of power. They restored the original sober Benedictine liturgy and lifestyle, rejected ornaments in their churches and they returned to the order to work. As the Cistercians wanted to live on the products of their own work, they organised their rural estates into large compact units of exploitation, outlying farms known as *grangie*, supervised by a monk living on the farm itself. These exploitations often applied innovative methods in agriculture, artisanal techniques and administration. In the abbey of Fontenay, founded in 1118 by Bernard of Clairvaux (1090–1153) in a marshy valley in northern Burgundy, a metallurgical factory had hammers and bellows powered by watermills. Surpluses could be sold on the emerging urban markets. The manual work was mostly carried out by *conversi*, monks of simple birth who had taken monastic vows but had few liturgical duties because they were illiterate. They were also known as lay brothers because they had not been ordained and were not tonsured. In addition, wage labourers were hired to work in the *grangie*.

The explosive increase of Cistercian monasteries in the early stages was chiefly due to the inspirational activities of Bernard of Clairvaux, named after Cîteaux's third sister monastery which he had founded to the east of Troyes: 'Clear Valley'. Even though he was the leading figure in a rapidly growing order that considered seclusion from the world and strict asceticism of paramount importance, Bernard himself behaved more like a Cluniac abbot seeking constant involvement in what was happening in the world outside. Spirited and committed as he was, and being a brilliant preacher and orator, he gave synods, councils, popes, kings, fellow abbots and intellectuals the benefit of his advice and admonitions, whether they asked for it or not. A fervent champion of a hard, and if necessary armed, fight against non-believers, heretics and other dissidents, in which he included all supporters of the new rationalistic approach to theological questions, Bernard was one of the driving forces behind the Church's growing militancy.

From their side, the popes liked to deploy Cistercians as 'missionary storm-troops' (Sayers 1994). They took part in crusades and everywhere established themselves on the borders of the non-Christian world, such as the Slavic regions east of the Elbe. Their example inspired the foundation in Spain of the military orders of the Knights of Calatrava and Alcántara, which followed the Cistercian rule and maintained links with the order of Cîteaux. And it was the Cistercians whom the pope charged with the (non-military) suppression of the 'heretical' Cathars in Languedoc soon after 1200. Their organisational model was soon followed by the other new orders, the Carthusians, Premonstratensians and the Mendicants.

The Carthusian order, founded around 1100 by Bruno of Cologne, a close adviser to Pope Urban II, sprang from the heremitic tradition inside Christian monasticism which underwent a spectacular resurgence in the eleventh and twelfth centuries: witness the enthusiastic veneration of the two prototypical hermits who had played such an important part in the life of Jesus himself: St John the Baptist and St Mary Magdalen. In their version of the hermitage, Carthusians lived a community life, but the monks spent the greater part of their time in strict segregation, each in his own cell in the closed precincts of the monastery.

Equally successful was the initiative of Norbert of Gennep (1092–1134) who became the founder of the order of the Premonstratensians. Dissatisfied with his comfortable life as a canon of the chapter of Xanten in the duchy of Cleves, Norbert retired into the wilderness. His reputation as a preacher of repentance brought him many followers and resulted in the formation of a religious commune in the woods of Coucy, near Prémontré. Norbert ended his life as archbishop of Magdeburg on the German-Slav border, several years after the pope had recognised the Premonstratensians as a new monastic order. Strictly speaking, Premonstratensians are not monks but canons, higher, ordained clergy who live in accordance with a monastic rule, in this case a rule attributed to St Augustine. This happened quite often in those days. All over Europe communities of Augustinian or 'Austin' canons sprang up like mushrooms. This created a difference between regular canons and secular canons. The former were clergy living together in a monastery, who held to monastic rule and were not allowed personal possessions; the latter did not live together and were allowed personal possessions.

The attraction and rapid growth of the new monastic orders responded to the need for authentic spirituality, which had been lost in many of the old Benedictine abbeys and even in the tremendously successful Cluny movement. In a way, as a consequence of their own impact, over the course of the centuries these institutions became so wealthy that they deviated from their original goals and thereby lost credibility. It was certainly a sign of the Church's remarkable vitality that it showed the capacity to time and again adapt the institutional model to new challenges. The choice made by many thousands of men and women to take the vows, and for innumerable others to facilitate them with their lavish donations, is a clear demonstration of the strong spiritual movement in these centuries.

In conjunction with spiritual needs, the huge increase of monastic houses certainly also reflects the profound expansion of western society as a whole, which supported this growth both in demographic and in economic terms.

Vita apostolica *and the new spirituality*

In addition to varied attempts at reform in the eleventh century a new religious sensitivity with two main features presented itself. One was the idea that good Christians must live following the example of Christ and his apostles in the New Testament. This effort towards *nudus nudum Christum sequi* (literally meaning 'to follow naked the naked Christ') – to lead a morally pure and evangelical or 'apostolic' life (*vita apostolica*) stripped of material excesses – linked itself quite naturally with the second feature, spirituality, the search for a personal, intimate relationship of the mind with God, fed by prayer and meditation. The manifestation of the divine with which clergy, monks and ordinary laypeople now identified themselves more than ever before was God the Son, Jesus Christ – and his mother, Mary. Of vital importance in this was that in sculptures and paintings both were given an emotional, human image. Christ changed from a distant, sovereign conqueror of death into a helpless Saviour suffering unimaginably – but not beyond human empathy – before death; Mary, from a majestic queen of heaven into a caring and grieving mother, whose sorrow was so much aggravated because she had foreknowledge of her son's human fate. Both turned into objects not only of awe and devotion but even more so of compassion and passionate love, becoming, therefore, the path to true inner conversion.

The new religious fervour found its most radical form of expression in groups that wanted to give more than a spiritual and internal moral meaning to the ideal of the apostolic life. They also wanted to live as Christ and his apostles had lived – according to the Gospels, in poverty – and passionately to proclaim the word of God. With their critical attitude towards laxity and 'depravity' inside the Church, these new secular movements balanced constantly on the edge of being condemned for heresy. The earliest of these radical apostolic movements came entirely from lay initiatives in the rapidly growing towns of Lombardy, the Rhine valley and the southern Low Countries, where concentrations of wealth paradoxically inspired a fascination with absolute poverty. In Lyons it was a cloth merchant, Waldo (*c.*1140–*c.*1218), who gave up all his possessions to go and preach in Languedoc and beyond the Pyrenees and the Alps. He invested all his money in the translation of the Bible into Provençal, with which he hoped to be able to reach his audience better. The Waldenses (the followers of Waldo) were themselves declared to be heretics in 1184 because of their particular interpretation of the Bible. They shared that fate with the Humiliati (who were later rehabilitated), the collective name for small communities of pious laypeople in various towns throughout northern Italy. They lived a celibate and sober life, doing their normal work and preaching in their free time.

The Beguine movement, which began in the bishopric of Liège in the same period, was of a rather different nature. Beguines were pious women who lived together in casual communities and supported themselves with their own handiwork. Thanks to the intervention of highly placed admirers of their movement, they were absolved of any suspicion of heresy and received papal recognition, on condition that they held to a cloister rule. The great spread of Beguine communities apparently answered unmarried women's needs to lead a spiritual life in a protected environment in the heart of the cities.

The mendicant orders

Just like the Waldenses, the Friars Preachers, or Dominicans, aimed at challenging the Cathars of southern France by advocating the ideal of evangelical poverty. After his order received papal sanction in 1216, Dominic Guzman (1170–1221), the Spanish canon who was their founder, preferred another option: to preach to the ordinary faithful in the vernacular. This meant that the Dominicans had to know their theology and thus had to be well educated. The Dominicans therefore established their own educational system that would allow the best pupils preliminary training followed by top-quality academic theology studies. In large towns the order set up advanced schools for the study of the arts and theology, an initiative that was rapidly copied by other orders, including the Franciscans.

In other respects, too, the Dominican order was excellently organised. The principal house was in Bologna, and the order's general chapter or assembly often gathered there. The basis of the order was formed by the houses or priories, of which *c.*1350 there were nearly 650, usually set up in the poorer quarters of towns and headed by a prior and his *socius* (assessor) – the mendicant orders rejected the lofty position of the abbot of the old Benedictine tradition. The provinces were one level above the local foundations and were governed by provincial chapters, which in turn sent representatives to the general chapter.

In comparison with the threat of persecution of new lay movements insisting on poverty, the enormous success of the movement of Francis of Assisi (1181–1226) is particularly remarkable. Neither in his background (he was the son of a cloth merchant from the town of Assisi in Umbria) nor in his activities was Francis very different from someone like Waldo. Francis was a layperson, unschooled in the new scholastic tradition, with little Latin, and not very interested in allegorical interpretations of the Bible: he wanted to take the text literally, especially that of the New Testament, and immerse himself in it. For Francis, the ideal of the apostolic life meant above all the *imitatio Christi*, the empathic reliving of Christ's life. Francis went far in this, for shortly before his death his hands and feet bore the

PLATE 6.3 St Francis supports the Church, which has collapsed. Allegorical fresco by Giotto (c.1267–1337) in the upper church of the basilica of St Francis at Assisi.

stigmata, the wounds of the crucified Christ. In addition, Francis wanted to embrace life as God had created it in all His infinite goodness, both the breathtaking beauty of nature (Francis and his followers were the first to have an eye for natural beauty and respect for flora and fauna) as well as the horrors of sickness and death. Francis also advocated possessing absolutely nothing; he even spoke out against owning a book. Whoever wanted to follow him had to wander with him and beg for food and shelter. Francis himself struggled between the sacred duty to preach the Gospel to the world and a personal inclination towards contemplation and ascetic isolation.

Francis was on good terms with Ugolino, cardinal-bishop of Ostia and subsequently Pope Gregory IX (1227–1241). This was an important connection for the transformation of his movement into a religious order as it assured him of permanent support in the Curia. It led, amongst other things, to a fairly problem-free recognition of the Order of the Friars Minor, as the Franciscans soon came to be called. Francis' early disciple Clare, a noblewoman of Assisi, founded a female community nearby, which she intended to follow the rule and lifestyle of the Franciscans. In 1228 at least 24 female communities in northern Italy followed Francis' model, but it was inconceivable for the Church hierarchy to approve women to go out and preach. When the Order of St Clare was finally recognised in 1263 as the Second Franciscan Order, the sisters had to accept remaining within their **convents'** walls under the traditional Benedictine Rule. The participation of laypeople was arranged in special statutes for a Third Order (tertiaries), intended for sympathisers who wanted to commit themselves to a life spent in the spirit of the Gospel but who lived a normal married life and continued to work as usual.

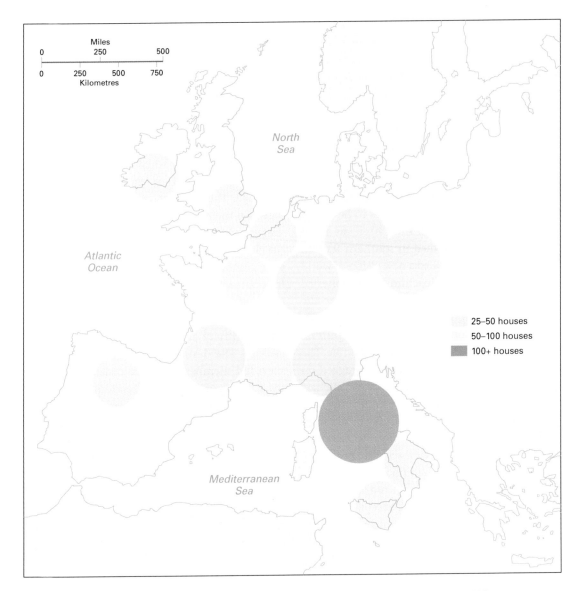

MAP 6.1 Density of houses of mendicant orders (Franciscans and Dominicans) in about 1300

During the fourteenth century the tertiaries, with increasing frequency, would take monastic vows and live in a closed community. Even before Francis died, the Order of the Friars Minor had spread far beyond Italy, and its phenomenal success continued after his death. By the middle of the fourteenth century the order had some 1,400 houses.

These houses were of course contrary to the founder's aim to have no possessions at all. It is a question that divided minds for a very long time, and proved almost fatal for the survival of the order. It demanded what C.H. Lawrence (1994) has called 'heroic gymnastics of conscience' to reconcile the ideal of absolute poverty with the needs of a successful movement eager to spread its message across the world. Two schools of thought were soon evident. The realists, or conventuals, realised that the order needed property and income in order to perform its tasks properly. The other school, the principled or spirituals, wanted to hold on to Francis' ideals. Moreover, they allowed themselves to be led by the unusual philosophy of the Cistercian abbot Joachim of Fiore, who died in southern Italy in 1202, and who had distilled a new vision of world history from the Bible. Joachim had prophesied that a new era of spiritual purity under the aegis of the Holy Ghost would dawn before Christ's Second Coming, in which the spiritual Franciscans foresaw their own important role. The differences between the two schools dragged on until, in 1318, the General of the order, Michael of Cesena, laid the matter before Pope John XXII for a definitive ruling. To the dismay of the spirituals the pope issued the bull *Cum inter nonnullos* in 1323, arguing that the view according to which Christ and the apostles had no possessions was heresy. Though this may seem outrageous, the pope no doubt realised that the acceptance of the dogma of apostolic poverty would put a bomb under the Church of Rome in its historically evolved structure.

The importance of the four major mendicant orders – besides the Friars Preachers (Dominicans) and the Friars Minor (Franciscans), there were the Carmelites and the Augustinian hermits – can hardly be overestimated. They were the first orders to settle in the cities and go out of their convents to care for souls on the basis of a solid theological training. The principle of humility and poverty made them opt for the construction of relatively sober buildings without high towers. In contrast to the Benedictine tradition, the communities' heads were not called abbots but priors. The friars had to live without personal property and were supposed to go out on quests for alms – hence, 'mendicants'.

The mendicants' first generations inspired their flocks by their true enthusiasm. Their phenomenal success rested on the revolution in the Church's communicative strategy: from the splendid isolation of the rural abbeys into the urban communities and even their poorer outskirts; from a mainly ritual and magic liturgy in Latin to an approach of the believer in his own language, the content of their preaching was based on the monks' superior learning, dwarfing that of the traditional parish priests, as well as on the choice of popular themes. This brought about an enormous increase in the religious and moral indoctrination of the laity, the cognitive and emotional internalisation of the belief. It also enabled the Church to respond to the new spiritual sensitivity among the most fervent of the faithful. The desire to spread the word of God soon led members of these orders far beyond the borders of Latin Christendom. Among the Franciscans were such famous travellers to Asia as John of Pian del Carpine, William of Rubroek and John of Monte Corvino, who visited Mongolia and China in the thirteenth century and left detailed reports about their observations. The downside was that it encouraged intolerance of everyone who did not believe in Christ in accordance with the orthodox views of the Catholic Church.

The faithful become visible

God's peace and God's truce

In 1033 it was one thousand years since Christ had died on the cross and to commemorate the event – so wrote the Burgundian monk Rudolph Glaber (Rudolf the Bald) in his chronicle – large gatherings were organised at various places in Aquitaine where, to the great enthusiasm of the crowds, relics were shown, sermons were preached and truces were concluded with local lords. These events, which in reality had begun during the last two decades of the tenth century, were so popular that they were soon copied in the furthest corners of France and Burgundy. Everywhere the entire populace turned out to listen to their shepherds, miraculous healings took place and invariably there were shouts for 'Peace, peace' – a reference to the movement for 'God's peace'. This came into existence as a result of the unfettered violence that accompanied the establishment of banal lordships in France. Some bishops and abbots, sometimes in cooperation with counts or dukes, then convened synods to establish rules to limit violence. Local lords and their knights were invited from far and wide to swear a solemn oath to observe these rules. Originally the rules were aimed at protecting social groups that were helpless in the face of violence, beginning with the clergy and later extended to include (unmarried) women and children, pilgrims, merchants and other travellers, and finally even peasants, who were only once called upon to end their own (counter)violence. We know of some twenty-five of these peace occasions dating from the first half of the eleventh century. A second, more radical phase forbade acts of violence on specific days and later during longer periods of the year, indicated by the Church calendar. This was the 'God's truce', the oldest of which dates from soon after 1020. In 1038, the archbishop of Bourges encouraged the peasants to attack the castles of lords who refused to comply. By 1050, the aristocracy and the high clergy rallied to protect their privileges against

popular uprisings; as a result, lords and princes preferred to take the lead themselves in territorial peace movements in which they also swore to protect Church property.

With this movement the Church leaders were in fact trying to fulfil one of the primary tasks of secular rulers, namely to protect their subjects. Adalbero of Laon, a fervently royalist bishop, recognised this and fiercely reviled the pretensions of the abbots of Cluny in particular for their take-over of the king's most essential task – maintaining the peace in his kingdom. Adalbero believed that monks should remain inside their cloister walls and lead a life of contemplation. Kings and other secular princes responded by explicitly proclaiming their own peaces, which in the Empire even took on a territorial character (the so-called *Landfrieden,* territorial peaces). The ecclesiastical peace concept may further have influenced the idea of a normative peace within town walls or in relation to particularly vital objects of public interest such as markets and dykes.

The formation of a persecuting society

In the eleventh century heretical groups, in the sense of a religious community that set itself apart from the Church, sprang up in many places, first in Champagne, and very soon thereafter throughout the Rhineland, France and England. It is difficult to see any connection between the various dissident groups at this period. The point upon which they were probably most in agreement was their sharp criticism of the corruption and secularisation inside the Church, focusing on the secular clergy and their far from apostolic way of life. In that respect the creation of heretical sects and new monastic orders can be seen as two sides of the same coin. There was a fine line between canonisation and being burnt at the stake so to speak, and for modern observers it is still not clear why some groups (the Franciscans, for example, and later the Humiliati) were recognised and accepted by the Church, while others, notably the Waldenses, were denounced as heretics.

Cathars, *kathari* (from the Greek, 'the pure'), believed that the material world was not created by God but by Satan. Satan was the lord of Genesis; the good God did not reveal Himself until the New Testament, and the physical existence of Christ was only a sham, to mislead Satan. In order to approach the good God, all material things had to be radically foresworn; one had to be cleansed of matter by regular fasting, by not eating meat and by complete sexual abstinence. Because this was too difficult to achieve for ordinary people, the Cathars – just like the Manichaeans at the time of Augustine – had two levels of believers: the ordinary *credentes* (believers), who did not follow the strict moral commandments to the letter, and a select elite of *perfecti* (perfect), who did and thus acquired an almost saintly status. Most *credentes* did not become *perfecti* until their deathbed. This was brought about by the administration of the 'sacrament of consolation' (*consolamentum*). The *perfecti* read the Scriptures intensively, and they circulated translations in the vernacular. The Church firmly opposed this practice out of fear of unorthodox interpretations that were not guided by the designated spiritual leaders.

Whether or not in any organised way – a contested issue – Catharism spread over Languedoc, Provence, Lombardy and Tuscany during the twelfth century. There was at that point no question of systematic persecution by Church or civil authorities. This situation changed dramatically at the end of the twelfth century, with the emergence of what the British historian R.I. Moore (2012) has called 'the persecuting society'. By this he meant that both the Church and the now budding states of the great European kingdoms and principalities were beginning to define their own aims and ideologies so precisely that they could identify any conflicting groups or interests much better than before. The content of the Catholic religion had become established through the development of dogmatic theology, the systematisation of canon law and the growing number of rules issued. Once it had been determined what was soundly orthodox, and what was not, dissidence could no longer be tolerated; whoever had once been seen as 'erring' was now a 'traitor' or an 'enemy of the faith'. The turning point was reached in about the middle of the twelfth century. The Church no longer acted reactively, but began an active search for the truth by developing inquisitorial procedures. The pope himself continued to play a steering and controlling role in the whole process, by sending legates, mobilising the new religious orders (first the Cistercians, later the Dominicans), involving secular military power, issuing anti-heretical decrees and council decisions and, finally, by establishing – under Gregory IX – a special, mobile papal tribunal, the **Inquisition**, which was intended to counterbalance the laxity of many bishops in persecuting alleged heretics.

The Cathars of southern France were the first to feel the full weight of this coercive machinery during the Albigensian Crusade (Chapter 5). Systematic persecution of the Jews had been preceded by the appalling pogroms that took place during the build-up to the First Crusade. The connection is obvious: who else but the Jews were responsible for the crucifixion of Christ in the holiest of places that now had to be liberated from the infidel? At a deeper mental level this traditional and essentially theological conviction now became broadened into the idea that the Christian community, as the unsullied bearer of Christ's legacy, had to guard its purity and destroy every stain with fire and sword. With every new crusade to the Holy Land and with every Christian advance made in the Reconquest of Spain and Portugal, the persecutions flared up again. Other factors exacerbated them, such as the growing resentment at the Jews' dominant position in the exchange and credit business, also in connection with the levying of direct taxes by spendthrift kings. Jews could fill this economic niche because in their business dealings with Christians they were not hindered by the Church's prohibition on requiring interest on loans.

There are many other indications from the eleventh and twelfth centuries that a centuries-long latent anti-Semitism had become virulent: Jews were driven off their land or forced to live together in certain areas of towns. The earliest accusations of infanticide and cannibalism surfaced more or less simultaneously with the theory of an international Jewish conspiracy. Jews would have talked Caliph al-Hakim into destroying the Holy Sepulchre in 1009, and Jews would have smuggled weapons to the Mongols who attacked Poland and Hungary in the 1240s. For the first time we hear of anti-Jewish purification rituals, such as stoning Jewish quarters or beating Jews at Passover. Jews were forced to wear distinctive clothing. They were exposed to new, massive pogroms and slaughters in the German Empire and in France in the first half of the fourteenth century, and especially in the years of the Black Death.

Whereas expulsions of the Jews by public authorities – town governments and states – had been rare and temporary in the early and central Middle Ages, these became ever more frequent and radical in the late Middle Ages. The king of England set the example in 1290, followed by the king of France in 1306 and again in 1322, followed by the Catholic kings of Spain in 1492, who proclaimed that the Jews were 'a damage to the realm' and 'an offence to the Christian religion'. The fact that occasionally expulsions were followed by recalls, as in France in 1315 and 1359, made the behaviour of kings 'unpredictable' (Stow 1992). For the Jews, this was more dangerous because in the course of the twelfth century their direct dependency on secular rulers had been increased by a change in their legal status. From being a special ethnic group falling under the tuition of the king, just like any other foreign group (Chapter 2), Jews now became *servi camerae*, 'serfs of the [royal] chamber', a unique status which further enhanced their social isolation. In practice it meant that their freedom of movement

was limited, that they had to plead their cases before royal courts (which was not always a disadvantage) and that the king could take his share of Jewish credits, or tax the Jews arbitrarily.

All this is evidence that the attitude of negative tolerance, formulated in the days of Augustine, was turning into open discrimination, stigmatisation and chronically active persecution. This change in the treatment of the Jews reveals more painfully than anything else that economic expansion, consolidation of the faith, the ideal of service to and the fight for God – in short, everything that was so characteristic of the great period of expansion in medieval history – had a darker side.

Among the believers

Rudolph Glaber's chronicle and other texts about the movements for God's peace are actually the first historical documents in which attention is paid to the common faithful. The common people had also figured in Carolingian writings, but then only in a non-specific background role. In the eleventh century they made themselves heard, loudly and in an active role. It proves that local communities had become self-conscious entities with the rural parishes as their core. Not only written texts but other, material, sources too, such as buildings, bear witness to the active involvement of growing numbers of believers. The first really monumental stone churches, catering for a stream of many hundreds if not thousands of faithful, date from the eleventh century. It is no coincidence that the largest lay on the increasingly busy pilgrim routes: Saint-Sernin in Toulouse and the Burgundian showpiece, Sainte-Madeleine in Vézelay, on the main routes to Santiago de Compostela (which had its own impressive church); and in other busy places of pilgrimage: Sainte-Foy in Conques, for example, or Durham cathedral, built over the grave of St Cuthbert, or in populous and economically successful towns such as Pisa.

The eleventh-century texts reveal strongly divergent aspects of the commitment of the laity. On the one hand, they create the impression that the religious enthusiasm of the masses was to a high degree directed, and possibly also abused, by Church authorities. This happened, for example, through adjustments in the liturgy relating to the most important sacramental activities in the Church: the consecration of bread and wine during mass. The lifting of the host and chalice high in the air after consecration so that the congregation could see, answered the wishes of the laity to be directly involved in one of the great mysteries of the faith: the dogma of the real presence of Christ in the Eucharist. Sometimes holders of high Church office who also had secular powers were able to exploit the military potential of their faithful. After the proclamation of a 'God's peace' they would, as we saw, mobilise religiously inspired people's militias and use their help to break down the power of the banal lords in their territory who were too independent, giving no quarter and, if necessary, using brute force. There are also repeated accounts from this time of the lynching of Jews and heretics.

On the other hand, sources dealing with the traditional elements of the perception of the Christian faith, such as the worship of relics, increasingly reveal manifestations of genuine popular faith. Relic-worship has a magical background: in relics the believer experiences the saint's physical presence and his or her miraculous power. This double experience is felt more intensely the closer the believer comes to the relic. Naturally, this is best achieved when relics are worn on the body, a practice that already existed in the eleventh century. Not everyone could afford to purchase personal relics, however, and certainly not the physical remains of important saints. Most believers had to resort to visiting the places where saints were buried or their relics preserved. To achieve optimal physical contact between pilgrims and saints, the tombs and reliquaries, which in pilgrimage churches were usually placed directly behind the main altar,

were made easily accessible so that pilgrims could even clamber over and under them. Some of the faithful were also happy to spend the night close to the reliquary hoping for a dream in which the saint would appear to them and perform a miracle, a form of superstition from as far back as Greek Antiquity. Physical contact with relics or reliquaries was not an essential condition to being able to profit from the miraculous power of the saints. People who were in trouble, wherever they were, could just call upon their favourite saints in a short prayer, and that frequently produced the desired effect – if we may believe the countless stories of miracles that were in circulation.

The sorry state of medical knowledge makes it easy to understand why the faithful looked to the saints to heal their physical or mental ills. It soon led to specialisations, traces of which are still visible today, such as St Dympna of Geel in Brabant, a saintly princess of Irish origin who, soon after her grave had been found during reclamation work, enjoyed the reputation of helping in a variety of mental illnesses. This later led to the foundation of madhouses in Geel, the forerunners of the much talked-about open psychiatric institute that is still located in the village.

Even then, miraculous cures were carefully scrutinised. Official recognition was only given after extensive questioning of both the patient (who might also be put to a test) and witnesses. If a believer was certain that his or her prayer had been heard by a saint, then the rules of reciprocal exchange came into action, and something had to be done in return to reward the saint and to convince the believer of the miraculous powers of the saint. This quid pro quo came in different forms. It could be a replica of the healed body-part, life-size or smaller, and made of wax, silver or gold; or the object that had caused the ill (the pitchfork on to which someone had fallen, the pin that had been swallowed); the aids that the healed person no longer needed (crutches, bandages); or gifts of thanks in cash or in kind (often a quantity of wax or candles), entirely unconnected with the miracle. The most extreme gift was the dedication of the whole person, who then became the servant or maidservant of the saint. They could always be called upon, in the name of the saint, by the church with which the saint was connected.

Pastoral care

Demographic growth required the Church to adapt its structures in order to bring the flock under its control. Pastoral care had not always been the clergy's priority, as, until around 1200, monasticism had prevailed. It was assumed that the ascetic and spiritual lifestyle would please God and incite his benevolence for the society as a whole. Care for individual souls mostly remained limited to the aristocracy patronising the monasteries. At best, they would act as role models of good Christian behaviour. In the twelfth century, however, apostolic action was required more than mere contemplation in order to keep up with the newly founded rural and urban communes. That meant a strong effort to create new parishes, building new and larger churches, providing them with priests to deliver the sacraments, and with sources of income for the charitable works. The number of parishes in England, for example, estimated at about two thousand at the end of the eleventh century, would quadruple over the next two centuries.

Most parish priests were still illiterate, unable to read the Bible. Equally, most of them must have been unable to access the manuals for confessors, which produced list of sins likely to be brought up during confession, with the corresponding penitence to be imposed. Because confession, before 1300, was not yet a generally embedded and regular practice, this exceptionally interesting type of document would have circulated among the higher levels of the clergy rather than that of the ordinary parish priests. External practices had to be imposed in the first place: rest on Sundays and attendance at mass,

penitence at least once a year before Easter, participation in the Eucharist. Furthermore, there were the rites of passage: baptism, burial and increasingly also the benediction of marriage. Even a thousand years after the introduction of Christianity, it proved difficult to turn pagan beliefs and practices into Christian orthodoxy. Synods repeatedly had to forbid, for example, dancing rites in cemeteries, intended to chase the deceased into the realm of the dead. Dragons belonged to popular beliefs, as representations of uncontrollable damaging forces which were to be pacified by processions.

In his *Dialogue about Miracles*, written between 1219 and 1223, the Cistercian monk and master of the novices Caesarius of Heisterbach (see Box 6.2) mentions a number of ignorant priests (*sacerdotes idiotae*) who have doubts about the dogma of the transubstantiation during the Eucharist, who spoil the host, who celebrate mass in an unworthy manner, and then provoke Christ's image to weep or turn its head, who are insecure about how to deal with the secret of the confession, who have a concubine and children, and who commit fornication.

What then did ordinary Christian people believe? The belief in some kind of an after-world where good behaviour would be rewarded was surely quite general. Notions of good and evil were widespread, as were perceptions of the signs of heavenly wrath. Fear of damnation was associated with the devil, while God was seen as immanent justice. As people were scared of death, it was a matter of great concern to die a 'good death', which the clergy sought to channel through confession and extreme unction, wherever possible accompanied with pious donations to the Church and the poor. Magical thinking was directed to the miracles performed by saints and their relics.

The Church inculcated by all means the fear of eternal damnation for evildoers, such as robber knights and usurers. Threats of the most extreme and everlasting torments were thought to curb even the worst individuals and encourage desired behaviour. Visual representations of the Last Judgement showed in detail a wide open lion's mouth, all kinds of monsters, devils torturing the souls of the damned with hooks, and the pains of hell's fire. Preachers constantly referred to the implications of a sinful life. In the twelfth century, theologians further developed the concept of Purgatory, a transitional stage between death and the deceased person's ultimate destination: hell or heaven. The length of stay was thought to be proportional to the required penitence before becoming eligible for heaven. This implied that human beings were now thought to be able to influence their after-life by pious and charitable conduct, including donations to the Church, and, above all, sincere confession. Moreover, the survivors might help to shorten their beloved's stay in Purgatory by praying and having a substantial amount of masses read or sung in favour of the tormented soul-in-suspense. This practice of memorial services, many of which were endowed to be performed in perpetuity, became very popular in the late Middle Ages and thereafter. Apart from the immense transfer of capital to the Church it provoked, these services strengthened considerably the intermediary role of the clergy between the believers and the after-world.

BOX 6.2 HUNDREDS OF EXEMPLARY STORIES

Miracles, including re-appearances of deceased persons and visions of the future, were thought to be signs of God's absolute power, able to intervene in a way that could not be explained by natural laws. Such magic thinking is widespread in all cultures. The Catholic Church defined lots of natural phenomena as signs of God's will and connected unexpected events, such as natural disasters, sudden illness, physical impediment or death, with heavenly punishment for sin. A blasphemous knight would be struck by deadly lightning; a blasphemous baker saw her bread transformed into dung. Miracles also occurred in a positive way: a wife was told she would survive only by consuming the host; the host remained intact after a church burnt down; flat beer was transformed into wine; inexplicable healings rewarded the pious believers.

One of the most influential collections of miracle and visionary stories is that composed between 1219 and 1223 by Caesarius, monk and master of novices in the Cistercian abbey of Heisterbach, south of Bonn. During his travels as a companion to his abbot on visits to dependent abbeys, he heard lots of these stories, many of which had been told during general chapters of the order. He found other stories in the existing literature. His compilation consists of 746 stories, thematically structured in 12 'distinctions' which deal with the sacraments, miracles, visions, Mary, Christ's body, demons, temptation, death and remuneration of the deceased. Caesarius presents his stories in the context of dialogues between a monk and a novice. His style is captivating, partly because of the use of quotations. He is fairly precise about his sources and the identification of the narrated events, in as far as privacy allowed. His aim was obviously to provide a solid instruction for young Cistercians monks, many of whom would become priests.

In a number of chapters, Caesarius explains how proportionality of punishment functioned in Purgatory. No authority was immune from God's sanctions. A Cistercian abbot who had performed his task perfectly, except for the fact that he did not fulfil his share of the manual labour with the brothers, appeared thirty days after his death to his fellow-brother who was praying for his soul. His legs were black as coal and full of ulcers, causing him 'pains too great for words'. His brother's prayers liberated him from his pains. A certain prior of Clairvaux appeared in a poor condition before a praying nun, and explained that he suffered immense torments, but that, thanks to the strong support of a brother, he expected to be liberated by the next Feast of Our Lord. She said: 'But we held you for a most holy man', upon which he answered: 'God punishes me because I was focusing too much on the extension of the abbey's property. Under the appearance of virtue, I have been misled by the evil of avarice.'

The wife of a usurer in Liège protested against the bishop's refusal to bury him in the churchyard. She appealed to the pope, quoting 1 Corinthians 7:14: 'For the unbelieving husband is sanctified by the wife', declaring that she was prepared to expiate his sins by living as a recluse giving alms, fasting and keeping vigil. After seven years, her husband appeared to her in a dark habit, and said: 'Thanks to your labours I escaped the depth of Hell (*de profundo inferni*) and the worst penances. If you can continue these benefices during seven more years, I will be entirely liberated.' Which she did, and he re-appeared in a white cloth, because he had confessed.

Lots of the stories deal with the weaknesses of the flesh: priests, monks and *conversis* sleeping during the choral prayers, a nun impregnated by a cleric in a *grangia*, or a nun who had aborted a child, become ill and died without confessing: she had to walk continuously with the glowing child amidst scorching fire. Satan harassed a young recluse and nun with strong carnal lust (*gravissime per stimulum carnis colaphizavit*). A helpful angel liberated her from this torment after citing psalms. However: 'What a wonderful thing! As soon as the spirit of fornication was chased, immediately appeared the spirit of blasphemy, which tempted her even stronger and more perniciously.' In the end, the nun resigned herself to suffering the temptation of the flesh. A confessor committed sin with an adolescent and confessed to his abbot before dying, but without naming his companion. He re-appears to his fellow, saying: 'I am suffering the worst pains because of my sin committed with you. I have a burning chain around my genitals, on which I am hanged and tormented.' The adolescent is too ashamed to confess, until the abbot calls together all members of the community, upon which the adolescent confesses and accepts the penance which will liberate his partner.

As it appears from these kinds of stories, Cistercian novices would be well prepared for their tasks as pastors.

Source: Caesarius von Heisterbach, *Dialogus Miraculorum. Dialog über die Wunder*, edited and translated by Horst Schneider and Nikolaus Nösges, 5 vols (Turnhout: Brepols, 2009).

Churches as the visualisation of Christian knowledge

The era of the great religious reforms in the eleventh and twelfth centuries was also the period of Romanesque and Gothic art. The first of these terms was proposed by modern art and architectural historians; it does not go back to any such contemporary expression. The name Gothic was first used in sixteenth-century Italy to designate the northern origin of a certain 'barbarian' style of painting, sculpting and building. The characteristics attributed to both styles are identified primarily from church architecture and religious sculpture, and even then we have to consider the regional diversity that is so characteristic of political and socio-economic life in the central Middle Ages.

An important starting point is the maxim of Nikolaus Pevsner, the famous architectural historian, that 'technical innovations never make a new style'. By this he meant that we can only speak of a new style if we can discern a specific total concept that is fundamentally different from the prevailing one. Most distinctive for Romanesque church architecture, from that perspective, is the emphatic articulation of the interior and the embellishment of the exterior: before, only the inside was considered important, but now the outside of churches was given a majestic religious character. The development of this new concept in all its component parts was closely connected to the new and varied functions that churches began to take on from the end of the tenth century. There was a boom in the worship of relics, meaning that costly reliquaries were given a central, easily accessible place in churches which had to provide room for a massive stream of pilgrims. At the same time the offering of prayers for an increasing number of souls required more altars, so that mass could be said by more priests in the same church at the same time. In monastery churches this was necessary as more and more monks were ordained priests, who had to be in a position to celebrate mass frequently. In cathedral churches, and possibly in other parish churches in the growing towns, the increasing number of canons and other priests attached to one church kept pace with the growth of the parishes and increased spiritual care, but it was also connected to the religious activities of specific groups of laypeople with their own patron saints, such as fraternities. All this meant that there was a greater need for internal spaces that were clearly divided up, and within which there was room for different chapels with their own altars. The exterior provided the opportunity for visual support to sermons, which often were preached in the open air, in front of the church's main entrance.

At first sight, Romanesque churches may look very different. Some are built to a central plan, and have domes. The Saint-Front in Périgueux is a fine example. The west fronts of many Italian churches have retained the pure form of the Late Antique basilica, with its high nave and low side aisles. The facade does not then have the flanking towers, but there is generally a tall bell tower that is free-standing, or gives the impression of being so. The early Romanesque churches in the German Empire catch the eye with their massive, closed west fronts, sometimes built out further to a second, west transept with its own apse. They are flanked by rather slender, often round, towers. They often have four or five towers, two flanking the west front, two at the ends of or above the transept and one heavy crossing tower. The so-called imperial domes were built to celebrate the successive dynasties, including their mausoleums. The domes of Mayence, Worms and Speyer along the Rhine, and Bamberg along the Danube, were founded in the early eleventh century by emperors, and used for their coronation ceremonies. Their symmetry represented the two powers: the east side with the altar, oriented towards the Holy Land, was the space of the spiritual power, while the west side contained above the entrance hall a throne for the secular power which, in a way, overlooked the whole. Many western French and Norman churches have a more 'open' main facade, and the flanking towers rise higher.

Cathedrals heralding a completely new architectural concept were built in a series of cities all over the French crown domains in the Paris basin during what looks like an astonishing competition for the most daring novelty, which took place between 1130–1140 and about 1270. From there, Gothic, as the dominating architectural style, but, again, with a large regional variety, spread all over Europe until well into the sixteenth century, from Norwegian Trondheim in the far north to Sicily in the deep south. It all started in the 1120s, when Abbot Suger of the abbey church of Saint-Denis north of Paris, where the French kings were buried and valuable relics were kept, was irritated by the continual jostling of the faithful. He believed that an abundance of light was necessary to honour God fittingly. Wasn't light the primordial manifestation of God? In order to give the faithful the chance to get near the relics he designed a passage round the main altar, around which a series of chapels in a half-circle enabled many priests to read the mass. This ambulatory was consecrated in 1144. It gave extraordinary lustre to the French monarchy that at that time was engaged in enlarging its power over the territorial princes.

The new concept was introduced into cathedrals built in the wide vicinity of Paris. Their walls were thinner and yet higher than the thick walls of Romanesque churches, and, to let more light in, much larger windows were left both in the aisles and in the facade, where the window took the form of a rose. In order to support the exterior walls, buttresses and flying buttresses were constructed. The weight of the roof was spread geometrically over a large number of abutments through the construction of pointed arches, which in addition stressed the height of the interior. In short, Gothic was characterised by an upward thrust, soaring towards God. In the second half of the twelfth century, a period of feverish building, there was intense competition to create ever more spectacular projects. The roofs became higher and higher: the central nave of Notre Dame de Paris, started in 1163, was 32.8 metres high; thirty years later, in 1194, Chartres reached 36.55 metres; Rheims measured 37.95 metres in 1212 and Amiens 42.30 in 1221. The record was achieved in Beauvais, where building began in 1247 and 48 metres was reached. This proved however to be beyond the limit of technical ingenuity and the roof collapsed in 1284.

Many a Romanesque church was reconstructed in the Gothic style, in its entirety or in part. Meanwhile the glories of Gothic had spread to neighbouring countries, each of which had its own variant on the basic concept. In English Gothic the vaulting was flatter and lower but with more ribs in it; in the coastal areas of the Low Countries, and later in the regions round the Baltic Sea, the style was adapted using bricks. In time the decorative elements became very profuse, and the term flamboyant Gothic was used. Milan, extravagantly decorated, considerably wider and proportionally lower than the French models, is one of the rare examples of an entirely Gothic cathedral in Italy. Nevertheless, Gothic stylistic elements were very popular even there.

How could this new concept come into being in the Paris basin, and spread so widely and so rapidly? As far as the architects were concerned, it must be remembered that from the eleventh century education in cathedral schools – those of Chartres, Paris and Rheims, for example – was increasingly associated with the knowledge of mathematics and geometry borrowed from the Arabs. It was this knowledge, added to their own empirical findings, that enabled architects to make accurate studies of the distribution of weight in their plans. A collection of precise drawings with designs for sections of buildings, dating from *c.*1235 and made by the French architect Villard de Honnecourt, has been preserved, as have the very accurate plans of the west front of Strasbourg cathedral, drawn on parchment and dating from 1275. The famous art historian Erwin Panofsky pointed out that the first flourishing of the Gothic style coincided in time and space with the heyday of Scholasticism. Both reflect the same mind-set of striving after transparent encompassing structures with elegant divisions, subdivisions and membrifications. In Panofsky's view, a Gothic cathedral was like a summa of Christian knowledge in stone.

The fact that the Gothic building style could spread so successfully owes much to the prestige that the French kings, who were so eager to expand, lent to cathedral building in the twelfth and thirteenth centuries. And not only kings: without the strong financial support of the citizens in the rapidly growing towns the immense building projects would never have been realised. There was competition between the towns for the finest and most daring project. In a technical sense the style was spread through the mobility of the master builders, who were organised into lodges and moved from one building yard to another. There was competition among them, too, and pupils sometimes developed their masters' designs further in other places. The demonstrative example of the kings caught on: citizens saw it as a means of expressing the worth of their town, and other leaders did not lag behind. The rivalry was now centred on the height of the towers: the dukes of Austria wanted to see the Stephen's church in Vienna elevated to a cathedral and commissioned the highest spire of Christendom, which was effectively achieved in 1436 with 136 metres. Alas, Strasbourg broke the record soon after in 1439 with its 142 metres. In both cases, the planned second tower was never completed, nor were several other ambitious projects. Some of them, such as the cathedrals of Cologne and Ulm, were not finished until the late nineteenth century.

The cathedral's primary function was to make divine worship as glorious and effective as possible. Other functions came later: the prestige of a monarchy, a region and a city. With that in view the same style was adapted for palaces and purely civic buildings such as town halls, market halls, guild halls and private residences. The generalisation of the most typical artistic expression of Christianity shows the impressive progress the Church had made by the late thirteenth century in the dissemination of its values. They now penetrated all segments of European society.

Points to remember

- The higher clergy's intellectual standards and growing self-awareness of their role led them to claim the liberty of the Church from lay interference on all levels.
- The clergy's strict observance of its own rules and purity (chastity of all priests) strengthened their role as mediators between the sinful common believers and God. This motivated ever more donations to the exemplary religious institutions.
- From the end of the tenth century, the clergy became more assertive in imposing their norms on lay society, in the first place on the powerful aristocracy. They curbed the use of violence against unarmed people, and

re-oriented it towards the expansion of Christianity.

- At the highest level, the papal claim to universal authority as the ultimate judge on earth of the behaviour of laypeople unavoidably led to conflicts with kings and emperors. This had the most far-reaching consequences in the Empire.
- The consolidation of the Church's internal structures underpinned its high ambitions; at the same time, it proved sufficiently flexible to adapt constantly to new spiritual and social needs – with the exception of those of women. It included the foundation of great numbers of new parishes, in line with demographic growth.
- The creation and rapid dissemination of the successive new types of monastic orders expressed and channelled the remarkable spiritual vitality of this period.
- Thanks to the greater effectiveness of preaching and spiritual care, the ordinary faithful became more actively and emotionally involved, which led to mass movements such as pilgrimages, crusades and the cult of relics. In the thirteenth century, the Church fought to keep control of its self-declared orthodoxy.

Suggestions for further reading

Blumenthal, Uta-Renate (1988), *The Investiture Controversy: Church and Monarchy from the Ninth to the Twelfth Century* (Philadelphia: University of Pennsylvania Press; orig. German, 1982). In the confrontation between Church and monarchy known as the investiture struggle or Gregorian reform, ideas cannot be divorced from reality. The official thought is therefore presented in its contemporary political, social and cultural context.

Constable, Giles (1998), *The Reformation of the Twelfth Century*, 2nd edn (Cambridge: CUP). This is a 'reexamination of what it meant to be a Christian' in a world where traditional social ties and structures were changing, which led to a tension between a contemplative life – previously thought to be the highest form of religious life – and an active life within the world, engaged with society. The author takes into consideration hermits, recluses, wandering preachers, crusaders, penitents and other less organised forms of religious life. In particular he studies the variety of reform movements, the relation of the reformers to each other and the outside world, and their spirituality and motivation as reflected in their writings and activities.

France, John (2005), *The Crusades and the Expansion of Catholic Christendom, 1000–1714* (London/New York: Routledge). A detailed examination of the First Crusade, the expansion and climax of crusading during the twelfth and thirteenth centuries and the failure and fragmentation of such practices in the fourteenth and fifteenth centuries. The author considers the motivation behind the Crusades and examines chronologically the whole crusading movement, from the development of a 'crusading impulse' in the eleventh century through to the imperialist imperatives of the early modern period.

Lawrence, C.H. (1994), *The Friars: The Impact of the Early Mendicant Movement on Western Society* (London/New York: Longman). The preaching orders that arose in the early thirteenth century around the charismatic figures of St Francis and St Dominic were the most effective instrument for the Church to switch from the primarily ritual liturgy in Latin to a persuasive strategy through the spoken word in vernacular languages. So, the Church could confront the challenge of an increasingly confident, secular and independent-minded age. The author shows how papal patronage turned unruly beggars into a disciplined force for orthodoxy, and he analyses the extraordinary impact they had on western society in their first hundred years of existence.

Moore, R.I. (2012) *The War on Heresy* (Cambridge MA: The Belknap Press of Harvard University Press). By the end of the eleventh century, a more defined version of 'orthodoxy' was created which, for political and theological reasons, excluded many people for the first time. What were the beliefs and practices the persecutors defined as heretical? And why were they such a threat? The traditional 'exuberant variety of religious belief and practice' became a problem only whenever it seemed to be (or led to) a questioning of authority. Fears of heresy inspired passions that moulded European society for the rest of the Middle Ages and resulted in a series of persecutions that left an indelible mark on its history and culture.

Part III

Expansion and maturation, 1000–1500

cooperation to collect the taxes in their areas, in exchange for a part which they kept for themselves. Other elements of state power also fell into their hands, including the administration of justice, maintaining order, the conscription and command of troops. The landowners thus became real warlords who tried to make their position hereditary. Independent peasants were forced out of the market by the heavy tax burden, which they could only escape by seeking the protection of the warlords – on whom they then became directly dependent and to whom they had to make payments. Imperial power was thus gradually eroded. The highly developed bureaucracy proved to be no match for the warlords, who were of course indispensable for warding off the constant attacks from nomadic peoples. The use of mercenaries (usually 'Franks', by which western Europeans were meant, sometimes Turks too) did not bring long-term solace to the emperors, because a lot of money was needed to pay them and the forces often proved untrustworthy. Like so many other imperia the Byzantine Empire collapsed under a combination of internal erosion and external pressure.

The other major power in the eastern Mediterranean was the Fatimid Empire in Egypt, which within a short time of its establishment in 969 had emerged as the dynamic centre of the Muslim world. Already in 909, when still only ruling over what is now Algeria, the Fatimids had declared themselves caliphs. The move of the caliphate to Egypt meant humiliation to both Baghdad and Córdoba. The new capital, Cairo, just a few kilometres south of the older capital Fustat, grew into one of the most important markets in the Near East, attracting cotton from Nubia, slaves from sub-Saharan Africa and wood from Calabria, Kabylia, Lebanon (its famous cedars) and the Taurus mountains. Caravans of thousands of camels brought supplies to Cairo from sub-Saharan Africa, which was forced by military action to pay tribute in the form of slaves. This flow of humanity to the Mediterranean region has been estimated at 20,000 people per

year – men for the army and heavy labour, women for household tasks. This slave trade continued from the ninth to the twentieth century and most certainly contributed to the demographic stagnation and the dislocation of social ties in central Africa. In the Near East wood, needed particularly for shipbuilding and as fuel, was the most strategically scarce raw material. The major powers fought each other continually for control of wooded regions. High-quality, traditionally made products fed a rich export trade. The prominent Jewish community in Cairo was specialised in glass-making and in dyeing fine linens and cottons. They formed an important link in these industries, which according to surviving letters and bills must have included 265 different crafts.

Besides military power and economic prosperity the Fatimid Empire radiated a high degree of cultural activity. This was reflected in its own architectural style for mosques and palaces, decorated with coloured enamel tiles. The caliph's palace contained a library of 18,000 volumes, including 1,200 copies of the *Universal History* of al-Tabarî (d. 923). Caliph al-Hakim (996–1021) founded a great Shi'ite school near the al-Azhar mosque, with the purpose of spreading the moral principles of the Qur'an. His religious fanaticism led to new tensions and divisions, and it was under his rule that the Holy Sepulchre in Jerusalem was destroyed.

Largely responsible for the shifting balance of power in the Near East during the eleventh century were the Oghuz or Turkmen, a nomadic Turkic people recently converted to Islam. They underwent a period of tremendous expansion. Their leaders, the Seljuks, made a pact with the Iranian aristocracy who were anxious to restore political unity and religious orthodoxy. From 1038 they took over effective power in Baghdad, and in 1055 the caliph made their leader sultan and 'king of the East and the West'. Hence the caliphate of Baghdad was more properly called the 'Empire of the Great Seljuks'. Syria and Palestine also fell into their hands, with only the ports

Part III

Expansion and maturation, 1000–1500

7 The beginnings of European expansion

The West becomes more aggressive

From the eleventh century a general expansionary movement manifested itself in the West in diverse regions and in various forms. The basis for this movement must be sought in the stabilisation which the West achieved from the middle of the tenth century, when the devastating invasions from Hungary and Scandinavia finally came to an end. Agricultural production and population grew steadily, so that after a few generations the existing social ties came under pressure. In western Europe from the eleventh century a start was made to reclaim peat and marshlands, clear woods and cultivate the land. The most visible expression of this was the search for new areas of settlement, both in the direct vicinity of the old western European centres of habitation and further away.

The conquests that most appeal to our imagination were certainly those of the Normans, themselves descendants of Viking settlers. Some decades before the conquest of England, enterprising knights who had not achieved the success

they had dreamt of in Normandy set out for south Italy where the first lordships were in Norman hands by 1029. The sons of Tancred of Hauteville were the boldest of these knights. One of them, Robert Guiscard, defeated the forces of Pope Leo IX in 1053, and even took the pope prisoner. Six years later the same pope, who needed Robert's support in his confrontation with Emperor Henry IV, recognised him as duke of Apulia and Calabria. In 1084 Robert rescued Pope Gregory VII from Castel Sant' Angelo in Rome, where he was besieged by the emperor (see Chapter 5). His expeditions took him as far as Serbia, whence in 1081 he intervened in the contest for the imperial crown of Byzantium. His youngest brother, Roger, took Sicily from the Moors in the years between 1061 and 1091. The pope gave his blessing to this offensive against Islam and even appointed Roger as his legate, a position normally filled by a prelate. This was an important precedent for the Crusades in Palestine. By 1130 the newly created kingdom of Sicily included all of south Italy as well as the isle of Sicily, and later even some of the coastal regions of Tunisia. It was based on the institutions founded by Byzantine and Arab rulers. It lasted for centuries in this formation. Roger II (1130–1154) recognised the pope as his overlord and paid him an annuity, in return for which he could do as he pleased. His position was of great strategic importance for Rome, against the Muslims and Byzantium, and also as backing against the German emperors.

A part of the growing population of western Europe sought new means of existence to the east in the thinly populated German Empire and in the Slavic regions beyond. It is striking that from the middle of the thirteenth century this eastward mass migration, which in fact was nothing less than the occupation of land, was presented as a crusade against the heathen Slavs and Balts. By then, Christian enterprises in Palestine had come to a standstill and part of the West's drive for expansion was directed at the European frontiers of Christianity in Iberia, central Europe and the Celtic periphery of the British Isles.

The active resumption of trading relationships from the West was another form of the same expansionary movement. By the ninth and tenth centuries, when there were still frequent Arab raids along the coasts of the western Mediterranean, Amalfi and neighbouring villages, well protected on the steep and rugged coast of the peninsula of Sorrento, could develop a mighty fleet and become the great entrepôt in the West for trade with the surrounding Muslim regions. The Amalfitans stood under the purely nominal rule of the Byzantine Empire and possessed wharves and warehouses in Constantinople, but they developed close ties with Egypt as well. In the tenth century, a colony of merchants from Amalfi was established in Fustat. Up to 160 of them were killed in a riot in neighbouring Cairo, in 996. Disregarding papal interdictions, the Amalfitans nevertheless continued to conduct trade with Jews and Muslims. They supplied wood and iron for shipbuilding, and bought as many as possible of the luxury goods that the highly developed Arab market economy had to offer. In the middle of the eleventh century a Persian traveller observed Christian ships in the Syrian

port of Tripoli whence they set sail to other Islamic harbours. Muslims who wanted to go from the Maghreb (the western lands of Islam) to the Levant (Syria and Palestine) travelled on Christian ships from that time on.

Venice was another centre for the expansion of commercial links between Italy and the eastern Mediterranean Sea. Located on a series of islands far north in the Adriatic, it was fairly invulnerable to Muslim raids. The city still formally recognised the supremacy of Byzantium, which in 1082 as a reaction to the Norman advance into Serbia had given Venice exclusive free-trade privileges without any levies or duties. There was a lively slave trade in people who had been captured during raids in the Slav regions of central Europe and the Balkans. This trade decreased as those areas became converted to Christianity, and it was replaced and diversified by trade in other products. For Byzantium, threatened as it was on every side, the support of the Venetian fleet was of strategic importance. For their part, the Venetians profited from the vast material and cultural riches that Byzantium could still provide.

It is very likely that Sicily's trade with Egypt and Syria continued under Norman rule. In the western Mediterranean the ports of Pisa and Genoa carried out a successful naval attack on what they saw as a pirates' nest at Mahdiya in Tunisia in 1088. The pope gave his blessing in retrospect to this undertaking, which was motivated in the first place by economic reasons but was included into the increasingly aggressive attitude of the Catholic Church towards the Muslims. It is striking that in all these regions the Westerners took the initiative in the contacts with the far earlier-developed eastern and southern Mediterranean coasts, and this in the period preceding the Crusades. Religious differences were no barrier at all to close commercial ties.

Everything indicates that it was this very intensification of the contacts with the higher developed regions in the Near East that offered the West additional opportunities for growth, based on the adoption of more valuable and varied products, technology and other cultural features. Through their commercial activities the Italians in particular learnt to deal with other cultures, new products and the advanced trading methods that were commonplace in Constantinople, Tripoli, Alexandria and Cairo. Indirectly they gained entry to large and distant markets which in turn gave them a head start on other western Europeans. They were able to set themselves up as the great intermediaries between East and West, a position they would hold until the sixteenth century. The expansionary Westerners showed greater dynamism and drive, and they were more open to innovation, all of which enabled them to overtake their stronger rivals in the long run.

Shifting centres of gravity

The period from the ninth to the eleventh century formed the apex of political, economic and cultural developments in the Byzantine Empire and in the various Muslim kingdoms. After the death of Basil II in 1025, the Byzantine Empire was plagued for more than half a century by the misgovernment of a series of weak emperors, at the very time when strong new adversaries appeared on its borders. The Byzantines managed to check the Turkish Pechenegs, yet another nomadic people who had entered the region of the lower Danube, but they were powerless against the threat from the Normans in south Italy and the Seljuk Turks in Asia Minor. The greater part of all the regions they had conquered with their blood, sweat and tears during the tenth century was lost in the course of just a few years. The disastrous year of 1071 was symbolic of the course of events: this was the year of Manzikert (see below), the year, too, when the Normans took Bari in the west. The two events marked the loss of Byzantine power in south Italy and the largest part of Asia Minor.

The strong emperors of the Comnenus dynasty, which came to power in Constantinople in 1081, could not rectify this loss of territory, but they did succeed in preventing further erosion of Byzantine possessions in Asia Minor. Alexius I Comnenus (1081–1118) made clever use of the long-term presence of the first western crusade army in the region. It led to the Byzantines again having all the coastal regions of Asia Minor firmly under their control.

As a result of these developments the Byzantine Empire underwent a power-shifting process from the centre to local potentates from the eleventh century onwards. Great landowners ruled over several village communities and thousands of slaves. The emperors had to rely on their

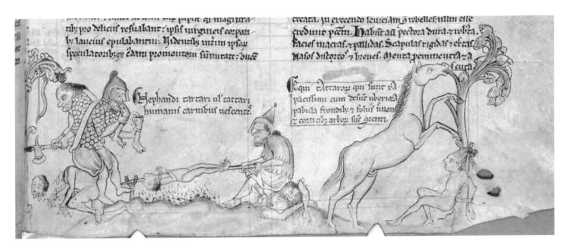

PLATE 7.1 Depiction of the cruel habits of Tartars in a western chronicle.

cooperation to collect the taxes in their areas, in exchange for a part which they kept for themselves. Other elements of state power also fell into their hands, including the administration of justice, maintaining order, the conscription and command of troops. The landowners thus became real warlords who tried to make their position hereditary. Independent peasants were forced out of the market by the heavy tax burden, which they could only escape by seeking the protection of the warlords – on whom they then became directly dependent and to whom they had to make payments. Imperial power was thus gradually eroded. The highly developed bureaucracy proved to be no match for the warlords, who were of course indispensable for warding off the constant attacks from nomadic peoples. The use of mercenaries (usually 'Franks', by which western Europeans were meant, sometimes Turks too) did not bring long-term solace to the emperors, because a lot of money was needed to pay them and the forces often proved untrustworthy. Like so many other imperia the Byzantine Empire collapsed under a combination of internal erosion and external pressure.

The other major power in the eastern Mediterranean was the Fatimid Empire in Egypt, which within a short time of its establishment in 969 had emerged as the dynamic centre of the Muslim world. Already in 909, when still only ruling over what is now Algeria, the Fatimids had declared themselves caliphs. The move of the caliphate to Egypt meant humiliation to both Baghdad and Córdoba. The new capital, Cairo, just a few kilometres south of the older capital Fustat, grew into one of the most important markets in the Near East, attracting cotton from Nubia, slaves from sub-Saharan Africa and wood from Calabria, Kabylia, Lebanon (its famous cedars) and the Taurus mountains. Caravans of thousands of camels brought supplies to Cairo from sub-Saharan Africa, which was forced by military action to pay tribute in the form of slaves. This flow of humanity to the Mediterranean region has been estimated at 20,000 people per

year – men for the army and heavy labour, women for household tasks. This slave trade continued from the ninth to the twentieth century and most certainly contributed to the demographic stagnation and the dislocation of social ties in central Africa. In the Near East wood, needed particularly for shipbuilding and as fuel, was the most strategically scarce raw material. The major powers fought each other continually for control of wooded regions. High-quality, traditionally made products fed a rich export trade. The prominent Jewish community in Cairo was specialised in glass-making and in dyeing fine linens and cottons. They formed an important link in these industries, which according to surviving letters and bills must have included 265 different crafts.

Besides military power and economic prosperity the Fatimid Empire radiated a high degree of cultural activity. This was reflected in its own architectural style for mosques and palaces, decorated with coloured enamel tiles. The caliph's palace contained a library of 18,000 volumes, including 1,200 copies of the *Universal History* of al-Tabarî (d. 923). Caliph al-Hakim (996–1021) founded a great Shi'ite school near the al-Azhar mosque, with the purpose of spreading the moral principles of the Qur'an. His religious fanaticism led to new tensions and divisions, and it was under his rule that the Holy Sepulchre in Jerusalem was destroyed.

Largely responsible for the shifting balance of power in the Near East during the eleventh century were the Oghuz or Turkmen, a nomadic Turkic people recently converted to Islam. They underwent a period of tremendous expansion. Their leaders, the Seljuks, made a pact with the Iranian aristocracy who were anxious to restore political unity and religious orthodoxy. From 1038 they took over effective power in Baghdad, and in 1055 the caliph made their leader sultan and 'king of the East and the West'. Hence the caliphate of Baghdad was more properly called the 'Empire of the Great Seljuks'. Syria and Palestine also fell into their hands, with only the ports

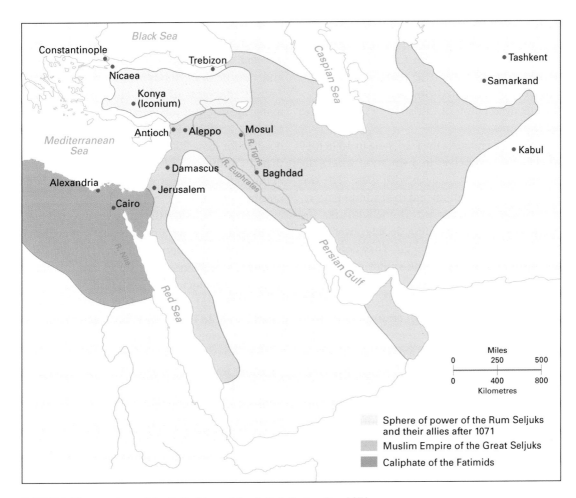

MAP 7.1 The empires of the Fatimids and the Seljuk Turks after 1071

remaining under Fatimid rule. In about the same period another group of Seljuks started to raid the upland plains of eastern Anatolia, to the detriment of the Armenians and Byzantines. In 1071 they so thoroughly destroyed the imperial army at Manzikert that all Asia Minor except the coasts came under Seljuk control, after which it was known as the Empire of the Rum Seljuks (Rum meaning 'Roman').

The Seljuks encouraged religious orthodoxy in the areas they conquered. Between 1071 and 1092 their rule was characterised by laborious efforts to establish some degree of state authority, not an easy undertaking for a nomadic people unfamiliar with abstract power constructions of this sort. On the Catholic side the ferocity of the Seljuk conquests was given as a decisive reason for launching the Crusades. Yet it must be remembered that Christians were by no means the only victims of the admittedly violent Turkmen. More intolerance was directed against radical Shi'ites than against Christians. Among the Christians it was the representatives of the Byzantine Orthodox Church rather than other Christians who were unacceptable to the new rulers. With a few exceptions, all the Christian monasteries were allowed to remain. Even the Greek patriarch kept his position in Jerusalem. Evidence from different sources shows that pilgrims from the West were also allowed to visit Palestine under the Turkish rule. St John's hospital and two monasteries near the Holy Sepulchre, founded for pilgrims by merchants from Amalfi in 1080, continued to function as usual. The sources contain no evidence of Christians being persecuted or of systematic desecration of Christianity's holy places by the Turks.

When the crusaders invaded Syria in 1096 they thus found themselves in a situation where the opposition was not on a par with them. The two great powers, Byzantium and the Fatimid Empire, were weakened and divided. The Seljuk Turks, the conquerors of the preceding decades, were now entangled in a dynastic struggle. They dominated Bagdad and, after 1071, the sultan of the Rum Seljuks installed a permanent residence in Nicaea, and later in Konya/Ikonion. Others hired their military might for their own strategic purposes. The Near East, already extremely complex and rarely stable, found itself in a new, very unsettled constellation as a result of the western intervention. During the first half of the twelfth century this brought about a weakening of the Muslim empires which was to the advantage of the Byzantine Empire and the Latin crusader states in Syria.

The multicultural Near East

It is important to remember that in origin Islam did not aim at being a religion essentially different from Judaism or Christianity. In theory the Muslims recognised the beliefs of the two other 'peoples of the Book', on the understanding that these did not claim to possess the undistorted, definitive version of the message. This makes it easier for us to understand the Muslim attitude towards peoples of other faiths in the lands over which they ruled. In principle they allowed everyone to choose between Islam and their own faith (provided this was Christianity or Judaism): should they choose the latter, then they were expected to recognise the political supremacy of Islam and not to dispute it. On payment of a special tax, *jizya*, non-Muslims could enjoy the traditional Arabic contractual hospitality, *dhimma*, which guaranteed their personal safety and that of their goods and religious services. Even if adherents of other faiths were discriminated against, this was certainly an exceptionally tolerant attitude for the time. That made it possible for some 200,000 Arabs to rule over more than 10 million people of different cultures and, in the course of time, to gradually assimilate large numbers of them.

In the region where the crusaders directed their attacks there was certainly no clear-cut evidence for a religious situation of dominant Muslims and subjected Christians. No less important than the religious differences between Muslims, Jews and Christians, and within Islam itself, between Sunnis and Shi'ites, were ethnic, linguistic and cultural differences. The general picture is one of a great variety of peoples led through clans whose authority was based partly on a specific religious conviction.

In Syria (in which the Muslims also included Palestine) the crusaders encountered mostly Shi'ites in the north and Sunnis in the south, each with their own rulers. There were diverse other cultures, too, such as the Druses who recognised the Fatimid caliphate. Another Shi'ite sect with the ominous name of *hashîshiyûn*, or hashish-drinkers, lived in the north of Iran and Syria. Because murder was their most important method of fighting the Sunni Turks, the name of these *hashîshiyûn* became 'assassins' in the French of crusaders.

Among the Christian communities in the East, in addition to ethnic and linguistic differences, there was a diversity of religious currents from the early centuries that had been pronounced heterodox in the West, but which had survived in a fossilised form in the East under Islamic rule. They included the Nestorians, Maronites stemming from the Monothelite tradition, and three Monophysitic Churches: the Armenian, the Jacobite (with a liturgy in Syrian) and the Egyptian-Coptic; there were also orthodoxies following the patriarchate of Constantinople or of Antioch, Jerusalem or Alexandria (see Chapter 2). It must be obvious that in this region of very divergent communities the Catholic Church in Rome had no authority at all.

The Jews lived in small scattered communities, especially in towns. They looked upon the Islamic rulers as their liberators from the heavy-handed Byzantine or (in Iberia) Visigothic rulers. This view was also shared by many Christian communities who had welcomed the Muslims as their liberators from an exacting imperium. There was no segregation or ghetto-forming. On the contrary, from the ninth to the eleventh century the Jews flourished economically and culturally throughout the Arab world.

There is thus every reason to look for the motives for the Crusades not in the East but in the West, as expounded in Chapter 6. Moreover, so far as we can tell from surviving texts, any knowledge of Islam and the situation in Palestine was demonstrably lacking in the West. The Crusades, then, can be interpreted as a form of western expansionism on both religious and political grounds. Thanks to the unbroken tradition of pilgrimages to Jerusalem, and the economic relationships between Italy and the Near East which had been in existence long before, it was possible to consolidate the effects of this expansion.

Crusades, crusader states and western colonies in the East

The proclamation of Urban II was followed by the fervent preaching of Peter the Hermit, who won over great numbers of supporters among ordinary people. This still unstructured movement in all its enthusiasm proceeded to pogroms against the Jews in the towns along the Rhine but was entirely wiped out in its first encounter with the Turkmen. The real crusades would be led by the experienced warrior class of knights and princes. However, there was no logistic provisioning for the hordes of many thousands of fighters and followers.

Most of those who took part in the First Crusade came from the north of France, where Urban II himself was born. His relationship with Emperor Henry IV was very tense, because the latter still stood by the anti-pope he had appointed. Very little cooperation could thus be expected from the German Empire, even though Godfrey of Bouillon, of the powerful House of Boulogne and the most famous leader of the First Crusade, was, as titular duke of lower Lorraine, technically a German lord. An important force came from Norman Sicily under the leadership of Bohemond of Taranto, elder son of Robert Guiscard, who had lost most of the territories he was meant to inherit to the Byzantines. Of all the city-ports of northern Italy only Genoa came into action immediately; its ships would ensure that the 'Franks' were provisioned. Genoese carpenters built the equipment needed for the siege of Antioch, and, together with English vessels, supplied the wood for the construction of siege towers and catapults just in time for the decisive attack on Jerusalem. In 1104 they provided valuable assistance at the capture of Acre. The Genoese, and subsequently also the Pisans, accepted rich remuneration for their services to the crusaders, above all in the shape of extensive commercial privileges and allocations of property in the conquered regions. Venetian involvement was more limited; the Venetians were mostly interested in keeping their rivals out of the region where they had obtained a monopoly from the Byzantine emperor. In Constantinople itself they were the only foreigners who had been assigned their own quarter.

The success of the First Crusade is indeed almost a miracle. Having been ferried piecemeal over the Bosphorus in the spring of 1097, the crusader army immediately gained an important victory by defeating Kilij Arslan, sultan of the Rum Seljuks, under the walls of Nicaea. Shortly afterwards it embarked on a summer-long, disastrous crossing of hot and dry Anatolia. Then, in the autumn, the tide turned again. The crusaders took Edessa and Antioch, which became the centres of the first two crusader territories or states in the

Near East: the County of Edessa, which would last until 1144, and the principality of Antioch, which managed to survive until 1268 and whose first lord would be Bohemond of Taranto.

Jerusalem was taken on 15 July 1099, after a siege lasting less than five weeks. Godfrey of Bouillon had himself proclaimed 'defender of the Church and the Holy Sepulchre', bringing him much personal renown. No doubt it was good for the salvation of his soul, and he died just one year later. His brother Baldwin succeeded him and took the title 'king of Jerusalem', thus relegating his dependence on the pope into the background. The crusader-kings of Jerusalem did not enjoy any supremacy over the other Latin rulers in the region. A fourth state, the County of Tripoli, was formed by Raymond of Toulouse and was a magnet for Italian traders. In 1187 it became part of the principality of Antioch. For the first twenty years the 'Franks' fought fiercely to win the cities along the coast. The support and provisioning from Italian fleets was essential for this. Acre fell to them in 1104, Sidon and Beirut in 1110 and Tyre in 1124.

Relationships between the Byzantines and Latin Christians were fraught with difficulty, despite the originally undoubtedly good intentions of emperor and pope. Moreover, it was hard to discern any feelings of mutual solidarity between the Latin rulers. After the great conquests perhaps a few hundred 'Frankish' knights and some thousands of footsoldiers remained in the conquered regions, but in the tangle of coalitions they made to survive and prosper they did not form a homogeneous block that could challenge the Muslims or Byzantines. Every sort of combination was made, cutting straight across religious borders. From 1128 there was close cooperation between the Muslims of northern Syria and Iraq, in which the latter took over control of Aleppo and pushed back the Latin states of Antioch and Edessa. In southern Syria a form of peaceful co-existence grew up with impregnable Damascus.

The Latin colonisation was generally limited to the towns because the Westerners were relatively few in number and therefore needed the cover of robust walls to ensure their safety. They settled only sporadically in villages, under the protection of castles. The strongholds, known as *kraks*, were situated in high places and could stand firm against Muslim sieges. Later it was mainly the military orders that formed domains where vineyards were planted and sugar cane, indigo and grain cultivated. The 'Franks' of Syria and Palestine did not create an extensive feudal system based on the holding of land, such as existed

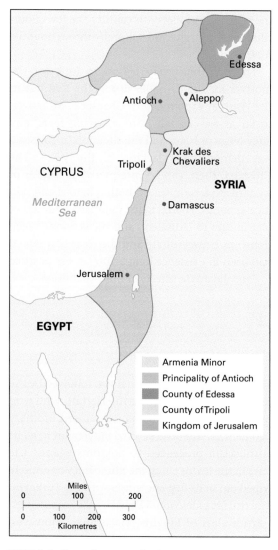

MAP 7.2 Crusader states in about 1150

PLATE 7.2 The crusaders' fortress Krak des Chevaliers was raised in the County of Tripoli, Syria, after the First Crusade. It could house 2,000 soldiers.

in their land of origin. The shortage of men compelled them to make very flexible rules of succession in favour of younger sons and daughters, making it difficult to accumulate property, while the continual struggle made everything uncertain. Knights were tied to more powerful lords by 'bezant feoffs', rents paid in cash; the 'bezant' was a Byzantine gold coin that was imitated locally. In this way the greater degree of monetisation in the East compensated for the lesser degree of control over the land by western standards.

Besides the knights, the military orders (Chapter 4) helped to consolidate the Latin presence in the Holy Land. The number of knights offering their services to these new orders grew quickly, and pious gifts began flowing in. All sorts of banking practices developed to transfer these riches from the West to the East. Pilgrims leaving for the Holy Land could 'buy' a credit in one of the western houses of these orders, in Paris or

London for example, which they could cash in the local currency once they had arrived safely in Jerusalem – a sort of early traveller's cheque.

The military orders formed the largest concentrations of Latin power in the Levant. They accumulated enormous estates and fortunes, in the West as well as in the East. By the end of the twelfth century the Templars owned some 20 strongholds north of Tripoli, one of which housed 1,700 fighting men. Besides their own heavily armed and solidly trained knights they also took Islamic mercenaries into their service. For the latter, money apparently prevailed over faith.

The third category of Latin colonists in the East, after the knights and the military orders, was formed by Italian traders. They benefited from the military protection offered by the Latin strongholds and accepted substantial rewards for their services. An excellent example is the agreement the doge of Venice made with representatives of the king of Jerusalem in 1123. With an eye to the conquest of the port of Tyre, which was still in Islamic hands, the Venetians insisted on being given a legally autonomous commercial quarter in every town in the kingdom, and fiscal advantages, in return for their fleet's support. Should Tyre and Ascalon be taken, one-third of those towns would come to them in free and permanent possession.

The privileges that the Italians acquired from the conquerors were probably more attractive on paper than in reality. The endless years of war would have thoroughly disrupted commercial relationships with the Near East. During the first half of the twelfth century Egypt continued to be the most important connection, and the commercial significance of the new Latin settlements in the Levant in that period should therefore not be assessed too highly. Surviving documents relating to overseas commercial transactions show how important the trading monopoly in Byzantium was to the Venetians, while Genoa concentrated more on Egypt. The Genoese also maintained intensive commercial relations with Sicily where, among other things, they bought grain and sold cloth from Flanders, and further round the western Mediterranean with Marseilles, Sardinia, Almeira, Ceuta, Bougie and Tunis. For both Venice and Genoa the contact with the ports of the Latin East was sound but in no way dominant.

Antioch, Tyre, Acre, Cyprus and Armenia Minor were among the sites of the substantial trading posts now built by the Italian cities; they demanded exclusive jurisdiction over the posts and sent their own representatives as administrators (consuls or *bayles*). On the pattern of the *funduq* in Islamic areas these trading posts were blocks of houses or entire quarters of a town where the foreign traders stored their goods in warehouses, lived, had their churches, bathhouses, ovens, administrative and court buildings, and often even a watchtower and fence. They enjoyed full administrative and judicial autonomy and could enjoy their own culture in their own circle. In Acre, which became the capital of the kingdom after the loss of Jerusalem in 1187, economic life was completely dominated by the three Italian *fondachi* (the Italian corruption of *funduq*), where caravans arrived from the interior, ships moored and craftsmen and money-changers set up their establishments.

This colonisation formed the steady undercurrent of western expansion, while the Crusades were its spectacular but not very effective phases of concentration. Although commercial relations before 1096 should not be underestimated, and those of the first decades of the twelfth century were not focused primarily on the Latin East, it cannot be denied that the Crusades gave a new impulse to the commercial expansion of the West. Italian shipping was given new functions in the logistical support of militant and peaceful pilgrims overseas, and Italian traders had fantastic opportunities to explore new markets. They had no difficulty, then, in adding eastern products to their supplies when Egypt closed its doors to them. The advancing Westerners were an irritant, especially to the Byzantines, who had expected that the Crusades would restore their own empire and certainly not establish Latin competition in their backyard. The Pisans and Genoese had followed the Venetians and acquired trading rights in Constantinople. In 1182 a wave of disaffection broke out against them and they were completely annihilated.

The later Crusades

The rise to power of the dynasty of Zengi, the Turkish ruler of Mosul in northern Iraq, provoked the Second Crusade (1146–1148) after Zengi invaded the Christian County of Edessa, and conquered its capital. The Crusade, now headed by the kings of Germany and France, was aimed at recapturing Edessa and attacking Damascus, but it was a failure in all possible respects – the County of Edessa was lost for good. A new threat to the remaining crusader states appeared when Zengi's

BOX 7.1 LEGAL PROTECTION OF FOREIGN TRADERS

Letter from Al-Abbas, vizier of the Fatimid Caliph Al-Zafir, to the archbishop and commune of Pisa, 17 February 1154:

. . . Your ambassador Raynerio Botaccio has come to us with letters from Archbishop Villano and from the consul and notables of the city of Pisa. In them you tell us that traders from your town, your brothers and relations, whom you sent to us as a son to his father, were last year arrested and deprived of much of their merchandise, which is not fitting for such a large kingdom, far greater than any on earth. Therefore we have sent you this embassy with a splendour that you only use for the greatest occasions, with a galleon where an ordinary ship is usual, in order to arrange everything in accordance with his judgement. . . .

We have explained to your ambassador that his complaint is not based on the truth. We have been informed that our traders in Alexandria, who embarked in good faith on the same ship as your traders, were killed most treacherously. They had been told that Frankish pirates had been sighted, and therefore descended into the hull, whence one by one they were thrown into the sea. Your men then took their wives and children and property for themselves. The law and the trading agreement between us provide for the imprisonment of the guilty people and their accomplices, and that we hold your traders who are staying in our land until you have delivered the culprits to us with compensation for the families of the victims. . . . Your ambassador also complained that many of your compatriots are in our prisons. To this we have replied that we captured those Pisans while they were making war against us with the Franks, to whom they gave help and supplies. According to the treaty between us, Pisans who are found on the same ship as the Franks are treated in the same way as the Franks. . . .

After long negotiations with us and with his companions, your ambassador has promised to remain completely loyal to us and not to threaten our subjects in any way at all. They will not enter into any agreement with the Franks, nor with any of our possible enemies, on land, at sea, or in our harbours. They will not undertake any enemy action against our army, either on their own or together with others. None of your traders will bring a Frank from Syria here, disguised as a trader. . . .

Now we extend you the privilege of coming to Alexandria for gold, silver and all your business affairs and allow you to live there in your *funduq*. You may transport everything that you have for sale to all places in our empire, after payment of 12 per cent customs duty, and also take them back with you, with the exception of wood, iron and pitch which our customs purchase at the market price. . . . We hereby confirm all the privileges that were previously granted by us, and in addition grant you a *funduq* in Cairo and exemption from the duty on silver.

Source: C. Cahen, *Orient et Occident au temps des Croisades* (Paris: Montaigne, 1983), pp. 228–230.

son, Nur ed-Din, conquered Fatimid Egypt in 1171, thus uniting Syria and Egypt. When Nur ed-Din died three years later, his Kurdish vizier (governor) of Egypt, Saladin, staged a successful coup d'état and was recognised as the new ruler of Egypt and Syria. Subsequently, he turned a fierce power struggle over the throne of Jerusalem between several noble 'Frankish' families and their supporters to his own advantage. In 1187 Saladin crushed a crusader army on the Horns of Hattin, a dry plateau above Lake Tiberias, and shortly afterwards captured Jerusalem and most of Palestine. Saladin's empire would stay in the hands of his dynasty, known as the Ayyubids, for more than fifty years, without ever achieving a high degree of centralisation.

News of Saladin's conquest of Jerusalem is said to have caused the death of Pope Urban III. It provoked his successor into calling upon all Catholic princes to take the cross. He allowed them to collect one-tenth of the Church revenues within their realms to support their endeavour. In May 1189 Emperor Frederick Barbarossa, by then aged 66, took command of a huge army in Regensburg. The kings of France and England, Philip II Augustus and Richard the Lionheart, needed two more years to set aside their rivalry before joining the advance on Palestine. Some narrative sources tell of 100,000 participants, which is of course a gross exaggeration, but even 15,000 would have been a large number, and would have created enormous logistical problems. Frederick's threat to conquer the Byzantine Empire if it did not support the crusaders resulted in more than just the immediate acquiescence of the Byzantine emperor. Frederick faced the greatest difficulties in taking his army through Byzantine territory. German troops laid waste to Thessaloniki and Adrianople. Shortly afterwards, Frederick drowned while crossing a torrential river in Asia Minor. The remnants of his army joined the French and English troops that retook Acre in July 1191, after the English had conquered the isle of Cyprus from the Byzantines. Also King Richard twice came close to the walls of Jerusalem, but on both occasions decided to retreat because he judged an attack to be unwise under the circumstances. All things considered, the Third Crusade was not a great success, even if the recapture of the coastal towns of Palestine and the conquest of Cyprus assured the 'Frankish' presence in the Near East for another century.

The Fourth Crusade (1201–1204) highlighted the lack of a coordinated western policy with regard to Palestine. The emperor of Byzantium seemed to have become the prime enemy. After his experiences with Barbarossa's army in 1190 he refused to allow the crusaders to cross through his territory. Now that the crusaders were forced to go by sea, Venice had a golden opportunity to make its mark on events. The target now became engineering a change of power in Constantinople. Before the crusaders had embarked, the Venetians decided that they would have the right to three-quarters of the booty, three-eighths of the territorial conquests and one-half of the committee to select the new emperor of Constantinople. In 1204 the crusaders took the proud capital and established their Latin Empire there, which extended over most of Greece and lasted until 1261.

The distraction of the Fourth Crusade from its real goal persuaded Pope Innocent III to suggest at the Fourth Lateran Council of 1215 that a new crusade be preached as soon as possible. The date of departure was set for 1 June 1217. The massive mobilisation had a modest success with the capture of the fortress on Mount Tabor, so that Acre was no longer under threat. The goal then shifted to Egypt since that was the stronghold of Muslim power in the Near East. In February 1218 the 'Franks' laid siege to the port of Damietta at the mouth of the Nile. The town was taken after 22 months, its garrison exhausted and its people starved, but in 1221 the 'Franks' had to give it up again.

The West cherished great hopes that Emperor Frederick II would join the Crusade, as he had vowed to do at his coronation. Differing views on relationships with the Arab and Greek world, and tension between him and the popes, however, made him hold back. In 1228 his fleet finally put to sea. Frederick was accompanied by just a few hundred knights; using his knowledge of the Arabic language and culture he made a peace treaty with the sultan, under the terms of which the Christian king of Jerusalem would again have authority over the city and a few places on the road to the coast. Jerusalem was again under Christian rule, with the exception of the holy places of Islam on the Temple Mount. Christian pilgrims were allowed to visit the Holy Sepulchre if they behaved with respect and discretion. The Muslims would be allowed to keep their own law. This ten-year peace was respected on both sides, but the haggling over the most holy city in Christendom and one of the most sacred places of Islam was seen as a despicable act of treason by most Christians and Muslims alike. Frederick had himself crowned king of Jerusalem in the chapel of the Holy Sepulchre, demonstrating his direct link to God. This was exactly what the pope had feared and why two years earlier he had excommunicated the emperor.

Soon after the ten-year peace came to an end a Sixth Crusade took place, from 1239 to 1240. Because of the refusal of the emperor to take part, the Crusade was led by Thibaut IV of Champagne, king of Navarre and Richard of Cornwall, count of Poitou. Once again their military successes were little more than the retaking of former positions. The role of diplomacy increasingly supplemented that of force. The Christians held their ground by allying themselves to one of the rival Muslim princes, in particular trying to play Syria and Egypt against each other. Their game was completely disrupted in 1243 when a huge army of the expelled Ayyubid ruler of Syria, as-Salih, and his allies from northern Iran advanced through the Bekaa valley into Jerusalem, murdering even in the church of the Holy Sepulchre. In October 1244 the Christian army lost many thousands of men. The Latin positions had received a blow from which they never recovered.

BOX 7.2 CULTURAL EXCHANGES

Most Muslim sources dealing with the Crusades present the Westerners under the common name of 'Franks', without any distinction by region of origin or language. Generally, authors described the invaders as rude, violent and courageous in fighting, but stupid, unlettered, disrespectful for social order except for knights, and as showing laxity towards women and in morality.

Over the course of time, contacts between 'Franks' and indigenous people became more frequent, through raids and skirmishes, but also through market exchanges, diplomatic contacts, alliances, personal friendships and even participation in religious ceremonies. One of the best informants about the Muslim perception of the Franks is the knight, diplomat, courtier (both in Damascus and in Cairo), poet and chronicler Usama ibn Munqidh (1095–1188). At the end of his long life, he described everyday events he witnessed and heard of in his broad experience. He belonged to the family of the lords of Shayzar in northern Syria, living in a castle on a high rock promontory surrounded on three sides by the Orontes river. The lords had become tributaries to Tancred, the Christian prince of Antioch, and his successors. The Munqidh clan had to face attacks from the four consolidating crusader states, but they also encountered many Muslim foes in the principalities of Hama and Aleppo, and scores of neighbouring local lords. The political and religious geography was extremely scattered, and the great powers in Damascus, Cairo and Byzantium made themselves felt everywhere. In all that turmoil, friendly relations nevertheless occurred.

Usama described all kinds of strange habits he observed among the Franks, by which it is apparent that they mixed in marketplaces, in public baths, in private houses and even in churches. He named some of them as his 'friends'.

So, some of Usama's 'friends' among the Templars had allowed him to pray in the al-Aqsa mosque, then converted into a Christian church. A Frankish newcomer seeing him praying towards Mecca grabbed him and turned him to the east, saying:

> 'This is the way you should pray!' The Templars came in to him and expelled him. They apologized to me, saying: 'This is a stranger who has only recently arrived from the land of the Franks and he has never before seen anyone praying except eastward.' Everyone who is a fresh emigrant from the Frankish lands is ruder in character than those who have become acclimatized and have held long association with the Muslims.

As an example of acculturation, Usama tells the story of one of his men who had been invited to the home of a retired Frankish knight in Antioch who came with the early expeditions.

> The knight presented an excellent table with food extraordinarily clean and delicious. Seeing me abstaining from food, he said: 'Eat, be of good cheer! I never eat Frankish dishes, but have Egyptian woman cooks and never eat except their cooking. Besides, pork never enters my home.'

On the other hand, Usama recounts the anecdote of a bath-master, in which the encounter confirms his wish that God may curse and confound the Franks. The bath-master is the story-teller, Usama adds his moral comment.

> Mostly Franks scorn loincloths. One knight came to me and tore off mine and threw it away. When he saw that I had my pubic hair shaved, he said: 'Very well, by the truth of my belief! Shave me in the same way.' He laid himself on his back. He had there so much hair that it looked like a beard. After I had shaved him, he stroked the spot with his hand. Feeling how smooth it was, he said: 'By the truth of your belief, do the same with Ad-dama!' He thus meant his own wife, and ordered one of his slaves to go and call her to come . . . She similarly laid down on her back, and the knight repeated: 'Do with her as you did with me!' So I shaved her, while her husband was sitting at my side and looking on. Then he thanked me and paid me for my services.
>
> Look at this great contrast! They don't know envy nor honour.

Source: *Die Erlebnisse des syrischen Ritters Usama ibn Munqid*, edited and translated by H. Preissler (Munich: C.H. Beck, 1985), pp. 151–153, 157–168; P.M. Cobb, *Usama ibn Munqidh, Warrior Poet of the Age of Crusades* (Oxford: Oneworld Publications, 2005).

Louis IX of France now took control, embarking for Cyprus in 1248. The scale of the investment is indicated by the fact that the king had built for this purpose the first Mediterranean harbour of the French kingdom directly on the Mediterranean: Aigues-Mortes. By May 1249 Louis had assembled an international crusader army of more than 2,500 knights, 5,000 archers and 15,000 other troops. Once again their target was the Nile delta. Damietta fell into their hands quickly, but then the crusader army was decimated by scurvy and hunger. To make matters worse the king was captured, together with thousands of his men, after which they were all ransomed. Louis' Second Crusade was even more disastrous, ending with his death in Tunis in 1270 where he had sought an operational base for his army, which had been weakened through sickness. King Edward I of England carried on to Acre. The idea of the crusade had not yet disappeared, but when in 1291 the Christians were forced to evacuate Acre, the last Latin city held, there was no longer any effective reaction from the West.

The spread of faith and colonisation

For two centuries the West had sent relatively large streams of people, services and capital eastwards. It is not difficult to imagine that without this outlet the West would have suffered far greater internal tensions. The Latin Empire established in 1204 made it possible for the Venetians to build up their network of trading posts in the Aegean Sea and the Peloponnese. After 1212 Venetians went on to found a colony on Crete. The island was divided into six, on the model of the 'six parts' in their own city, and a Latin Church hierarchy was established. Sugar plantations were established (the name of the capital, Candia, became a generic name for sugar candy) and later, other islands in the Aegean Sea, such as Euboia, were colonised and provided with a plantation economy and slave labour. Long before 1300 the trading cities of the Mediterranean had ventured upon such a colonisation movement which continued without any serious interruption until after the fifteenth century along the coast of Africa and then across the oceans. Two forms of colonisation developed: networks of

trading posts along distant overseas routes and settlement colonies where slaves worked on plantations. The former were the links in the chain between regional commercial circuits offering goods of different kinds.

The Byzantine Empire was split into a number of small principalities along the south coast of the Black Sea and the Aegean coast as far as Smyrna. In the tradition of the great rivalry with Venice the Genoese supported these rulers, which enabled them to set up trading posts with monopoly rights along the Black Sea in Trebizond, in Tana on the mouth of the river Don and, above all, in Caffa in the Crimea, where they installed a consul in 1281. Through these places they could stock up on slaves and exploit the overland routes to the Mongol khanates and China, whence they brought back silk and spices. Because of the support they gave to the Greek emperors who regained control in Constantinople, the Genoese were allotted an important settlement in Pera on the Golden Horn, just opposite Constantinople, as well as the island of Chios. This was an enormous breakthrough for the West: in economic terms, they were now masters of all the Mediterranean and a large part of the Black Sea. The Italians had eliminated the Muslims as middlemen in the trade with the Far East. In the western Mediterranean the Genoese, Pisans and Barcelonans similarly created the link with the caravan routes bringing gold from Senegal, across the Sahara.

Italian and Catalan merchants had no objection to employing and trading slaves whom they bought initially at their trading posts on the north shores of the Black Sea. On the boundaries of the western steppes, Christians, Muslims and heathens raided and enslaved each other intermittently. In 1421, the doge of Venice, Tommaso Mocenigo, estimated a minimal yearly import of a thousand slaves. The western Balkans was another recruitment region, with Ragusa (Dubrovnik) and Zadar as the main markets on the Dalmatian coast. After the Reconquest of the kingdom of Valencia in 1239, the Christians felt entitled to enslave the Muslim population and to employ them on rural estates and in their households. Although in the late Middle Ages it could no longer be generally assumed that slaves were heathens, Christian merchants nevertheless regularly bought and sold them at public markets. The Ottoman conquest of Constantinople in 1453 and of Caffa in 1455 cut off the Westerners from that traditional trading circuit, and made them search more actively at the Dalmatian markets and in North Africa. Frequent Ottoman raids impoverished and depopulated the Balkans in the second half of the fifteenth century, and they implied massive deportation of people and cattle. In Bosnia and Albania, the most destitute even sold their children in order to survive themselves. These slaves were employed in the Ottoman economy, households and army, as well as being sold to Italian and Catalan merchants. In Castile, slaves were regularly employed in all sectors of the economy, for domestic and artisanal work, and as labourers on the haciendas. From the middle of the fifteenth century, Portuguese fleets had brought black slaves from West Africa to the markets in Lisbon, Seville, Granada and Valencia. Fragmentary sources provide some minimal figures for the period around 1490: they reveal that up to 500 slaves per year were registered in Lisbon, and up to 300 in Valencia. From there, Genoese traders are recorded as regular providers of the Florentine market, via the port of Livorno. Slave trade by Christians was thus a continuous tradition from Byzantium to the Italian and Iberian markets, which adapted rapidly to changing conditions, to the massive transatlantic transports of the early modern period. Faith did not prevail in this trade, and even if authorities occasionally signalled a bad conscience, the trade was officially tolerated.

Events in the Islamic world during the thirteenth century were influenced less by the Crusades than they were by Mongol invasions. First, Chinggis Khan (*c*.1167–1227) annihilated the Iranian Empire of the Khwarazm shahs in 1220. Then, in 1253 Chinggis's grandson Hülegü

invaded Iran, Iraq and Syria with a huge army. Five years later he conquered Baghdad, where he caused a horrifying bloodbath in which the last caliph of the Abbasid line was one of the thousands of victims. Aleppo and Damascus followed soon after, but in 1260 the Mongols were defeated at Ayn Jalut by the army of the sultan of Egypt. Hülegü's Mongol dominion, the so-called Il-Khanate, was centred on Iran. The Mongols would never rule over Palestine, but their failed attempt at taking it also heralded the end of the last crusader states. The Christians' original hope of consolidating their crumbling positions with the help of the Mongols evaporated. The impressive Mongol conquests in central Asia and the Middle East caused terrible losses of human life and the devastation of irrigated agriculture and of old cultural centres such as Samarkand, Bukhara and Baghdad. It is estimated that the population of Iran was reduced by a half in the course of Mongol occupation. It has to be added that a substantial part of these losses was caused by an outbreak of the plague from the late 1330s onwards. Recent epidemiological research proves that the pathogen of the Black Death had its origins in Mongolia, and must have spread from there to China, to central Asia and eventually to Europe.

The region's new rulers were the Mamluks, horsemen of generally Turkish origin who played a key role in Egyptian warfare. In 1250 a Mamluk coup had ended Ayyubid rule. Egypt, Syria and Palestine came under the rule of Mamluk generals, who, just like the Ayyubids, took the title of sultan. Between 1516 and 1520 their sultanate was absorbed into the Ottoman Empire.

East meets West

Although in Latin-Christian Europe fear of the Mongols was great, only the eastern part of the continent – the Pontic steppe and the Russian principalities north of it – really came to suffer the burden of Mongol dominion. This was effectively established in 1237–1242, when a large Mongol army, led by Chinggis Khan's grandson Batu, took hold of the Pontic steppe, then inhabited by Kipchak Turks, and attacked Russia. After having taken Kiev, the Mongols rampaged through Poland and Hungary, but without any intention of conquering these Christian kingdoms. The Mongol khanate of the western steppes, on the other hand, would remain for centuries a great challenge and contributed indirectly to the formation of the Russian Tsarist Empire (see Chapter 11).

If the Mongols did not show much interest in western Europe, various western travellers made the long journey to the Mongol rulers in Mongolia and, later, China and reported the presence of highly developed cultures, states and economies about which hardly any reliable knowledge had existed in Europe until then. The Franciscan friar Giovanni da Pian del Carpino was sent in 1245 by Pope Innocent IV to Khan Batu. He met him at the lower Volga and the Great Khan Guyuk in the Mongol capital Karakorum. The negotiation did not lead to direct effect as Batu first wanted the pope's submission before agreeing on an alliance against the Arabs. In 1253

King Louis IX sponsored the journey of the Flemish friar William of Rubroeck. In the detailed account of his journey, he contrasted his own observations with the traditional geographical insights which were still based on Isidore of Seville and his sources from Antiquity. Their accurate observations on regions and peoples that had been unknown to Europeans did not lead to an immediate adaptation of the western worldview. Not one of the world maps produced in the second half of the thirteenth century actually mentions the Mongols.

The different Mongol empires, kingdoms and coalitions, stretching from China to the Sea of Azov, brought relative stability during more than a century, which stimulated contacts between East and West over the land routes that bordered the Eurasian steppes and which are commonly known as the Silk Road. The Western Khanate of the Golden Horde, with its centre at the lower Volga and its harbours on the Black Sea coast, favoured close exchanges with the Italian maritime powers. Venetians and Genoese bought huge amounts of grain, slaves, horses, wine, furs, leather and wax, and sold mainly textiles. They used their trading posts, respectively in Tana and Caffa, to connect

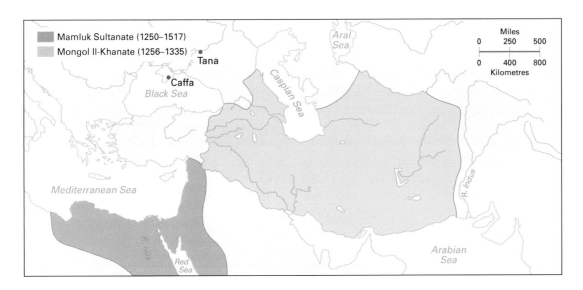

MAP 7.3 The Mamluk Sultanate 1250–1517, and the Mongol Il-Khanate 1256–1335

PLATE 7.3 The silk routes connecting China with the western trading posts in the Near East passed through the south Asian deserts where only camels could endure the hard conditions. During the Tang dynasty (618–907), trading relations intensified. Earthenware from that period represents various types of travellers.

with the overland routes to China. However, rivalries and outright wars between the various Mongol khanates frequently impeded such collaboration and at times even blocked the overland routes between Persia and China. The most famous of the explorers, the Venetian merchants Maffeo and Niccolò Polo, and the latter's 17-year-old son Marco, who set off to visit Kublai Khan in 1271, didn't trust the maritime connection from Cape Hormuz in the Persian Gulf and preferred the caravan route, which took them nearly four years. Some twenty years later, their return journey was made on Chinese junks to Sumatra, and then further by various, probably Arab, ships via Sri Lanka and the west coast of India, back to Hormuz and from there back to the Mediterranean harbours. The Chinese Empire's economic core was located at the mouth of the Yangzi river. Arab and Persian merchants could establish themselves in the harbours of southern China. As a matter of fact, sea routes have always been more important and more secure than the caravan routes; ships can carry much heavier loads than pack-animals. An Arab ship dating from the ninth century, found sunk off the Indonesian coast, was fully loaded with thousands of bowls and dishes in Chinese earthenware.

When in around 1340 the Florentine merchant Francesco Balducci Pegolotti wrote down the knowledge he had acquired about business practices in the course of a life-long experience (see Box 7.3), he described in detail the overland journey from the Venetian trading post Tana eastward to China. He never performed this journey himself, but obtained his information from various colleagues. Overall, about eight months were required to cross the chain of mountains and vast barren deserts on one of the various routes. They had been used since Antiquity, and in the early Middle Ages, Sogdian merchants controlled most of the route. Very few travellers completed the whole journey of some 3,000 kilometres, as specific groups controlled particular sectors and assured the transport of high-value products. At some stages, wagons could be used, drawn by oxen or camels, and further on camels and asses had to be packed. Camels were particularly adapted to the harsh conditions of the desert. They can carry up to 450 kilos during a journey of 50 kilometres per day, and they are able to go several days without any food or water. This long, complicated and risky journey was only profitable for products of high value and relatively low weight such as Chinese silk and spices. The Chinese were keen buyers of horses, camels, glass, jewellery, jade and slaves. The Tang dynasty (618–907) favoured trading connections with the Turkish and Persian realms, permitting the settlements of Sogdian merchants from central Asia in their northern capitals Chang'an and Luoyang; Sogdian temples even emerged near market squares. They also established themselves in minor towns in the valley downstream of the Yellow River, where they could deal directly with the silk producers. In Pegolotti's days, transit was relatively safe and crucial for the transfer of techniques from the highly developed Asian cultures to the West.

Colonising central and eastern Europe

The stagnation of the colonisation of the Holy Land after the thirteenth century gave a new impulse to the movements of colonisation of the continental peripheries of Europe itself. This link is clearly visible among the citizens of Bremen and Lübeck who, first in Jerusalem and later in Acre, maintained a hospital for their pilgrims. In Acre they were even allocated their own quarter. There they founded a religious order of knights whose rules were approved by Pope Innocent III in 1199. This German (or Teutonic) Order first acquired considerable property in both the East and West. After 1211 its primary focus was on the protection of Christianity on its European eastern frontier. In the meantime, in 1197, the bishop of Riga had founded another order of knights, with the telling name of 'Brethren of the Sword', specifically to suppress the heathen Latvians and Livonians. From 1230 German bishops proclaimed a permanent crusade against the Baltic and Slavic peoples. Both military orders were given considerable political, legal and material rights to spread Christianity by force of arms through the sparsely populated regions of central and eastern Europe, and to deprive the few inhabitants of their land and liberty.

The Teutonic Order took the land on the fertile plains of the lower reaches of the Vistula and established a series of towns there between 1231 and 1237. These towns were laid out in a chequerboard pattern, and were populated with Christians from the lower German linguistic area in the west. The native Prussian inhabitants of the region were forced to pay rents in kind to the order. Others were set to work as serfs on the great estates where grain was cultivated in vast quantities. In the fifteenth century this grain would occasionally help to reduce the food shortage in western Europe in years of bad harvests. From the sixteenth century, exports of rye rapidly increased to a huge and continuous stream. This was a typical export economy, in the hands of a foreign upper class. The knights were generally recruited from among the lower, partly unfree German nobility of service (ministerials) who could thus achieve the ideal of acquiring large estates. Thousands of villages were founded in this way by groups of migrants from the west, whose own Flemish, Dutch, Brabantine or west German customary law was often recognised; their language and culture, and most noticeably such place-names as 'Flamen', 'Fleming' and 'Holland', also left permanent traces in the regions they settled. There were analogous expansion movements elsewhere, in Iberia with the Christian Reconquest, and under the Anglo-Norman kings the English pushed deep into the border regions of the British Isles.

In these waves of conquest and colonisation, religion played a mobilising role. Yet the religious factor should not be seen as decisive in each and every respect. On both the Islamic and Christian sides there was a clear lack of solidarity. The caliphs in Baghdad did not do much for their fellow believers in Syria; their main interest was to maintain or restore their own authority. The Almohads in Iberia showed no interest in the struggle in the Levant. On the Christian side the increasingly serious clashes are particularly noticeable; they led to a full-blown war between Latins and Greeks, and eventually to the decline of the Byzantine Empire. Latin princes and Latin trading cities were so busy quarrelling with each other that they missed opportunities and even brought harm upon themselves. Yet was it not these typically western divisions of power – Church, princes, traders and multiples of the last two – that had produced a more dynamic, flexible and therefore more durable system than the Greek-Byzantine dominions of Christianity or Islam? In the long run it is the western system of autonomous spheres of power for religion, state government and market economy, including its two forms of colonisation – plantation colonies and trading posts – that has become dominant in the world. Its origins lay in the events just discussed.

Take-off to a commercial revolution

From the tenth to the nineteenth century, north-west Europe established its economic superiority in the world, after having lagged behind the other continents until then. The relative autonomy of the towns with respect to ecclesiastical, feudal and monarchic authorities was a basic condition for this 'European miracle'. Nowhere in the earlier developed urbanised societies in India, China or in the Near East had a comparable level of autonomy been established by citizens. Because of the relative freedom, which the multitude of separate jurisdictions helped to bring about, it was possible for a social pattern with its own norms and values to develop in the towns. It arose from the citizens' need to associate in order to protect their common interests against the feudal world around them, which was pursuing fundamentally different aims. Part of it was a rational, boundless pursuit of material riches through the accumulation and reinvestment of profits from trade.

R.S. Lopez (1976), the Italian-American economic historian, has characterised this swing as the 'commercial revolution', a breakthrough whose effects were similar to those of the Industrial Revolution. Beginning with Italy during

the tenth century, he saw how trade took an ever-stronger hold on the production process and on mentality and way of life in general. Far-reaching innovations in traffic and transport, commercial practices and institutions and available products were introduced in Europe. Italian shippers and merchants adopted many of them from their experience in the Muslim world, and these are still in existence: accounting systems, credit notes, maritime insurance, bills of exchange, banking, share companies, the capitalist mentality. In this, Italy played the role in the commercial revolution that England was to perform later in the Industrial Revolution.

The causes of these innovations were complex and reinforced each other. Just as demographic growth was the fundamental motor for agricultural progress, agriculture in turn formed the essential basis for the commercial revolution. The steady growth of agricultural production was certainly a precondition of commercialisation, since it resulted in surpluses which could be put into circulation. In those regions that were by nature particularly suited for this, specialised products like wool, salt, minerals or wine were involved; elsewhere, ordinary foodstuffs. Specialisation took shape, and in itself contributed to trade. This interaction between agriculture and trade certainly benefited from the growing political stability at the local level. Italy played a pioneering role in this because it was supported by its contacts with those Mediterranean shores that were in the lead. Its shortage of raw materials forced Italy to explore overseas possibilities as its population increased. The cultural and material heritage of Roman Antiquity, the links with Byzantium and its central geographical location contributed to Italy's initiating role. Internal growth and external events, economy and politics thus seem to be closely linked in the search for an explanation for the *take-off* of the western European economy.

In addition to the internal causes of commercialisation, there were external causes. In the first section we referred to the reversal in the power relationships between western Europe and surrounding cultures. There should be no doubt about the considerable extent to which this part of the continent lagged behind the Mediterranean area. In about the year 1000 the leading zones lay clearly in Byzantium and the Muslim areas. In northern Europe, southern Scandinavia – which was also in contact with Byzantium and Persia, through overland routes straight across Russia – functioned as a centre of development, although on a far more primitive level. Trade with the less developed regions provided the core areas with raw materials, primarily wood, which was always extremely scarce in the Muslim world, but also with weapons and slaves. In the periphery this trade set its own dynamics in motion. Southern Italy and Venice profited most from it. Merchants from Amalfi settled in their own district in Constantinople even before 944, and there must have been several hundred of them in Cairo. Around 1070 they built two monasteries and a guesthouse for pilgrims in Jerusalem. Three years later the Normans would conquer Amalfi, cutting short its commercial growth, but not the relations of Sicily and southern Italy with the East. Above all, Genoa and Pisa needed to secure their transit route via Messina to the eastern Mediterranean. Sicily became their main resource for grain, leather, sheep cheese and even silk, the production of which imitated Persian models. Venice owed its ascendancy to its close ties with Byzantium, its unique geographical location, salt-winning and the glass industry.

In about 1000, fleets from Pisa and Genoa cleared the Tyrrhenian Sea area of Islamic pirates and raiders. In 1016 Pisa conquered first Sardinia, then Corsica. Sardinia would become their first colonial experience. In particular the Genoese exploited the island's pastoral economy before Sicily became an even better provider. At the time of the Reconquest of Iberia, and sometimes in coordinated actions, the Pisans and Genoese frequently captured Muslims off the east coast, but this seemed to make no difference to regular trade. In 1087, Pisans and Genoese attacked the stronghold of Mahdia on the Tunisian coast, where the trans-Saharan caravans fed the gold from the Niger into the Mediterranean trade circuit. One century later, the Genoese had found more sustainable ways of dealing with north-west Africa: they obtained concessions for commercial settlements, *funduqs*, in Tunis, Bougie, Mahdia and other harbours, which together represented 37 per cent of their trade in 1182. Fine ceramics, grain, leather and, above all, gold were the main export products.

The fleets of the north Italian cities played a key role in transporting large armies to Palestine and Syria and in providing the warriors with logistic support, which testifies to the level of their development. In 1097, Genoa sent out twelve galleys with a crew of about 1,200 men, which was essential in the occupation of Antioch one year later. These combative seafarers took advantage of the situation by accepting substantial rewards for their services and then followed the crusaders and gained a firm foothold in the seaports of the Levant. In Antioch, the Genoese obtained a warehouse, a church and thirty houses, the start of a trading post. In 1100, twenty-six Genoese galleys and four supply ships carried about 3,000 men who captured and looted the coastal city of Caesarea and the main port of Acre. Between 1098 and 1110 the Genoese obtained concessions in Antioch, Caesarea, Arsuf, Acre, Beirut, Gibelet and Laodicea. In 1099 Pisans also won trading rights in Antioch and Laodicea. Venice already had a firm footing in the Golden Horn and the Byzantine Empire, where its merchants had been exempt from all taxes and customs duties since 1082. The Republic was slow in supporting the crusaders as they didn't want to jeopardise their positions, including that in Alexandria. By 1124 Venice nevertheless also established another solid bridgehead in Tyre.

If we were to look at all these facts through the eyes of the people who lived in the eastern Mediterranean around the year 1100, there would be no reason to attach special significance to them. After all, the highest level of development in the world had been concentrated in that region for 8,000 years, and it was still by far the richest in every respect. Shifts of core locations and territorial authority, and even the temporary supremacy of the Roman Empire, had not essentially affected the situation. That handful of barbarian 'Franks' in Palestine could never hold out against the superior strength of the enormous armies of Islam. The Westerners' heavy armour did give them some advantage but was not suitable for use on the Arab horses. Although this analysis is not wrong in itself, it does not take into account the growth effects that the intensification of commercial relationships in Italy, Provence and Catalonia, and also in the hinterland of north-western Europe, would produce.

However, external factors effectively led to a stagnation of the brilliant Arabic culture in the Near East from the thirteenth century onwards. First, the Abbasid Empire, with the caliphate of Baghdad, lost momentum to the Fatimids and to their Ayyubid successors. In the eleventh century Seljuks seized power and drove Byzantium into a defensive position. Moreover, until the 1230s, northern Iran and Baghdad had suffered unusually cold winter temperatures, which turned into a continuous pattern accompanied by drought. The persistent cold winters were affected by the Siberian high wind system and severely damaged the cotton plantations as well as various other crops such as dates, figs and citrus trees. As a consequence of these climatic changes, Baghdad was depopulated well before the Mongols' conquest, and Egypt took over as the main supplier of cotton and flax for Europe. Second, the Mongol invasions deeply ravaged and disrupted west Asia, which led to a shift of the trade routes to India away from Persia to Egypt, via Alexandria, Cairo and the Red Sea. Third, the aggressive enterprises of the Christian fleets in the end drove the Muslim seafarers out of the Mediterranean, and made them turn towards the Red Sea, Yemen and the Indian Ocean. So, Egypt secured the main linkage between the Mediterranean trade networks and those around India, bringing to Europe

spices, precious stones, perfumes, but also more common indigenous products such as alum and paper. The weft of linen warp and cotton weft, fustian, which was very popular and imitated in Europe for centuries, was named after the capital of Old Cairo, Fustat.

Characteristic of the commercial development in the tenth to thirteenth centuries was that, in comparison with the early Middle Ages, it was no longer limited to very scarce or unique commodities, in small quantities and with a very high value. Merchants no longer came only from distant leading regions such as Syria. From the thirteenth century commerce became more wholesale and increasingly included everyday consumer articles such as grain, wine and a wide variety of cloth, which for many centuries was the source of the wealth of northern France and Flanders and an exchange value for Italians in the Near East. This was only possible through the increase in demand and purchasing power and because the evolution of methods of transport could carry the growth.

The transport revolution

The Roman network of roads was built primarily to enable the state to fulfil its administrative and military functions. In later centuries no political unit was able to build roads on a similar scale and with the same technical standards as the Romans. Although it was no longer maintained by a powerful authority, and surely deteriorated over the centuries, much of the system continued to be used. However, a good deal of the new urban growth from the tenth century onwards occurred in locations other than the former Roman cities, and was more closely connected to rivers. These new locations grew along a waterfront, while Roman cities outside Italy had as their centre a *forum*, the square on the crossroads. Most bulk goods had to be carried by boat, which was much cheaper than overland transport. The modernisation of country roads was limited to the small territories of trading towns. Medieval towns grew up at traffic junctions with watercourses, and in the first instance these were then extended, connected and adapted. During the first half of the thirteenth century great efforts were made to regulate the water level in the Po valley and to link all the towns by canals. In Flanders, in the second half of that same century, Ghent, Bruges and Ypres dug canals in order to improve communications with each other, with peat production areas (relevant as peat was the main fuel) and, above all, with the sea. Florence, situated on the Arno, with its extremely fluctuating water levels, elaborated a transport system to ensure its grain provision and the supply of other bulk goods. It took three days with seaworthy barges 10 metres long and 3 metres broad, and on the way a transfer to smaller boats, to travel from Porto Pisano upstream to Signa, 14 kilometres from Florence. In Signa the city built warehouses and a paved road to carry the goods to their destination on four-wheeled wagons. The costs of this transport meant that in 1284 salt was 28 per cent more expensive in Florence than in Pisa.

At the end of the fourteenth century a fruitless attempt was made to cut through the 60-kilometre-wide neck of land between Lübeck and Hamburg, in the hope of cutting out the sea journey round Jutland. Traffic over the Alps was made easier by constructing new roads over passes and improving existing ones – the St Gothard in 1237, and the Great St Bernard even earlier. The enormous investments required for such undertakings could only be recovered through the levy of tolls on the vastly increased flow of traffic.

The market price was under heavy pressure from the manifold transaction costs of goods on their way from producer to consumer. Merchants therefore sought their competitive advantage largely in the reduction of these transaction costs. Shipping overseas traditionally took place along the coast. The Chinese already had a primitive ship's compass, which consisted of a magnetic needle floating in a wind rose in a bowl of water. During the twelfth century this instrument became known to Christian seamen through their contacts with Muslims. It was not perfected until the fourteenth century, when it was mounted on an axis. The Islamic knowledge of geography was similarly far more advanced than that of the Christian world. In the thirteenth century, through their mutual contacts, and building on their own experience, the Italians and Catalans learned to draw charts showing the navigational routes from harbour to harbour along visually recognisable coastlines; these were known as portolan charts.

An even more important discovery was the rudder, attached to the stern-post and turning on a beam, first introduced along the coast of the North Sea from which it spread to the south. The most important type of ship in the north was the cog, a fairly high, single-mast ship with a rounded bow, 30 metres long, 7 metres broad with a draught of 3 metres, able to carry a cargo in excess of 200 tons. In the Mediterranean the ancient tradition of the flat-bottomed galley was continued, each propelled by 100–200 oarsmen. Although it was suited to the windless and mainly calm inland seas, the galley did not have much cargo space, and was expensive because slaves or convicts were needed to row: this made it ideal for transporting luxury goods. To transport goods in bulk, the Italians began using the *nave* during the thirteenth century; this was rather similar to the cog, but had two masts and triangular sails. In the fourteenth century the Italians designed the *coca*, a vessel which, with its fixed rudder and square sails, bore even more resemblance to the cog. In about 1470 the Genoese were the first to reduce manpower and yet enlarge the cargo space to 450 tons. Thanks to this technical advantage, they were also the first to sail round Gibraltar to the North Sea and the ports of Sluis/Bruges and Southampton. The oldest reference to this is found in a notarial contract of 1277, and in the early fourteenth century the connection became a fairly regular service, which Venetian ships joined. Although the distance of the maritime route was three times that of the one overland, the greater cargo capacity, better security and lower transaction costs made it the best response to the increased volume of trade between the Mediterranean and the North Sea area. In addition, Venice also maintained its connection with south Germany and central Europe via the Brenner Pass, as did Milan via the Gotthard.

Progress in organisation

ASSOCIATION A merchant's major concern was to reduce the risks to which he and his wares were exposed. As long as merchants accompanied their wares they sought protection by travelling in groups that were linked by reciprocal oaths of solidarity and support. Some of these organisations were called guilds, others **hanse**. This Germanic word means 'contribution', the membership fee which was a substantial sum for new members, intended to guarantee their loyalty. Merchant guilds and hanses basically met the need for safety. As collectives they tried to obtain guarantees of legal protection and exemption from tolls for their members from the local governments in the relevant areas. Traders from different regions organised themselves for their own protection on certain routes. Specific associations were formed during the twelfth and thirteenth centuries for the Anglo-Flemish trade, for example, and for the trade from Flanders, Artois and Brabant to the annual fairs in Champagne. These were private organisations, formed to provide mutual assistance, which were granted privileges by the regional rulers. The best-known of them is the German Hanse, in the thirteenth century a league of older, regional merchants' associations from the regions around Lübeck and Westphalia, Saxony and Prussia. In 1358 the German Hanse transformed itself into an alliance of towns. At its peak it had some 200 member towns, from Novgorod via the Scandinavian coast to the Low Countries. It functioned until 1669 on an interregional scale to promote the trading interests of the citizens of its member towns and acted externally as a collective, public body.

In theory, privileges for foreign merchants meant that they enjoyed the protection of the authorities. This implied that they could apply their own jurisdiction to settle disputes among themselves, and disputes with the local people would be resolved in accordance with the customs of international mercantile law. If that did not succeed, then reprisals were generally used as a means of applying pressure: a fellow-townsman or fellow-countryman of the debtor would be arrested, or his property confiscated, in the hope that his local authority would put pressure on him to settle the matter. Measures of this sort were liable to escalate quickly, so the solution to trading disputes was sometimes very complicated and could drag on for years.

TRADING POSTS This system of protection applied both to merchants who went abroad for just a few weeks and to those who were settled in trading posts of the *funduq* type on a semi-permanent basis. In their contracts for the year 1197, Genoese notaries recorded 5,261 sales of cloth, for which Flemings were present as sellers in 2,046 cases, northern Frenchmen in 1,942 and Englishmen in 258. These foreigners must have been well organised to have travelled so far with their products. Some decades later, 198 foreign merchants were recorded as living in Genoa, of whom 95 were Flemish and 51 French. For their own mutual protection, and so that local authorities could keep a check on them, foreign merchants lived close to each other in a particular building, or in a designated street or quarter. In 1228 the Venetians housed the south German merchants in the *fondaco dei Tedeschi*, near the Rialto bridge. In Bougie and Tunis, in 1261, the Barcelonans enjoyed the jurisdiction of their own consuls and had at their disposal a notary, their own shops, a bakery, an inn and a chapel.

The establishment of trading settlements demanded enduring relationships, based on trust and mutual interests on the part of hosts and foreigners alike. A permanent settlement overseas was only worthwhile when there was a considerable volume of profitable trade. Different routes would meet there, such as the caravans from China and Persia, which the Christians met in the ports of Syria and Palestine, or in Caffa or Tana. Here, the Genoese and the Venetians encountered transports from south Russia, Bulgaria and modern-day Romania.

The Italian system of trading settlements was by far the largest in Europe during the Middle Ages. From the twelfth century a similar system of trading settlements was developed by the north Germans in Scandinavia and the Baltic coast, although on a more modest scale. The most important centre was the island of Gotland, off the east coast of Sweden, where Danes and north Germans from Lübeck, and later also from Westphalia, came into contact with local traders and from there engaged in trade with Novgorod – where the Germans had a settlement by about 1190 – England and Flanders. Merchants of the German Hanse in London stayed in the Steelyard, close to the Thames, and in Bergen, in Norway, they stayed in the *Tyske brygge*, literally 'the German harbour'. Together with Novgorod, and also Bruges, these four cities hosted the so-called *Kontors*, the main privileged locations of the Hanse outside the German Empire.

FAIRS   Local and territorial authorities understood that there were advantages in protecting foreign merchants from being indiscriminately plundered by robber barons. It was better to protect them: after all, their well-regulated activities stimulated the local economy and helped increase the revenues from tolls, mintage and the administration of justice. Not only did they bring incentives to the local economy, they could also be helpful as money-lenders, informants and messengers. Influential abbeys, towns or large landowners could try to further trading activities within the areas under their jurisdiction by guaranteeing protection on the road to an annual fair, where they proclaimed the market peace,

vouched for the safe conduct of the visitors and levied low tolls. Differences could be settled on the spot in a special court of justice, while notaries, clerks or a local magistrate were on hand to record agreements in writing. The important abbey of Saint-Denis, a few kilometres north of Paris, protected the Lendit fair in this way. In theory, the local saint's feast-day was the occasion for holding a fair lasting several weeks. Merchants poured in from far and wide with everything they had to offer, but farmers and craftsmen from the region, on payment of a small levy, could also do business safely and freely with a large and varied buying public. The main advantage of fairs was the concentration of a global supply and a broad demand. The proximity to Paris obviously contributed to the success of the Lendit fair.

The location of fairs was decided by their proximity to a large town, or their situation on an important trading route or in a production area. The English wool trade was concentrated in a few places in south-east England, which certainly formed a network by 1180. Individual markets, some of which were founded by an abbey or a large cattle-farmer, were associated under a joint royal privilege that assured visiting merchants of justice throughout England. The dates of the fairs in all these places were fixed so that they followed each other in a yearly cycle. In this way, merchants were able to travel from one market to another. The English cycle commenced at Stamford in Lent, then around Easter it was the turn of St Ives, then Boston in July, King's Lynn at the end of July, Winchester in September, Westminster in October, Northampton in November and Bury St Edmunds in December. Another fair that was coupled to a particular product was Schonen (Skanör), on the south-western cape of Sweden. Spurred on by the merchants of Lübeck, fairs flourished in Schonen during the fourteenth century, centred round the sale of the enormous herring harvest in the Kattegat. Lübeck supplied salt for the brine from the mines in Lüneburg and was the largest customer for the herrings which were gutted and

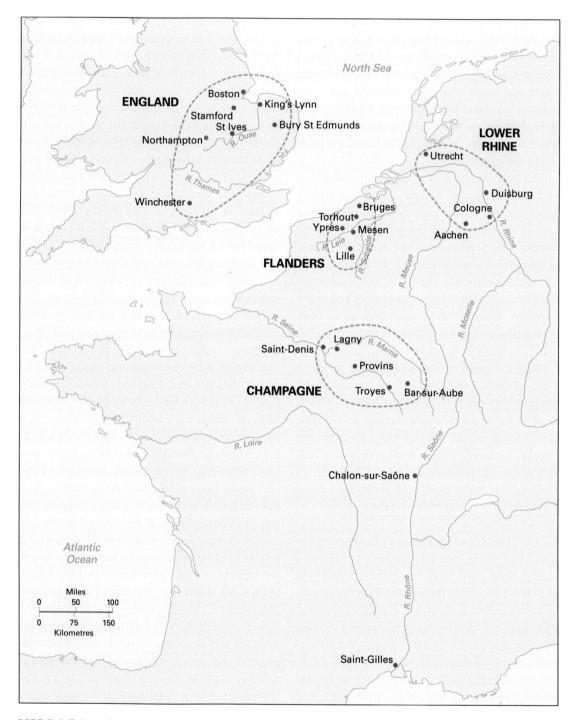

MAP 7.4 Fair cycles in north-western Europe in the twelfth and thirteenth centuries

packed in barrels, primarily for resale. These fairs lost their importance when the herring catch declined sharply around 1400.

The other important fair cycles were those in Flanders (Lille, Ypres, Mesen, Torhout and Bruges) and especially in the County of Champagne (Lagny, Bar-sur-Aube, Provins and Troyes; the last two held a market twice a year). The Champagne region was fairly central on the overland route between England and Italy, and was thus an excellent place for merchants from all over Europe, in particular from the southern Low Countries and Lombardy. In the lower Rhine region, a cycle was formed round the markets of Cologne, Aachen, Duisburg and Utrecht at the end of the twelfth century.

All these fair cycles allowed travelling merchants to journey in safety and do business with each other on a regular basis. Mutual trust grew out of this regularity, and credit transactions from one market to another became common. The sanction on *mala fide* practices consisted of defamation and exclusion, which implied that merchant's ruin.

In general, fairs served distant trade and regional and local trade at the same time. For the two latter functions there were smaller fairs in several places, some of which specialised in a particular product, such as horses or linen. The locations, which owed their importance mainly to their situation as staging points on a route, fell into obscurity as a result of shifts in macroeconomic and political circumstances. So it was that the fairs of Champagne lost their role as west European meeting places in about 1300, chiefly as a result of the further growth in the volume of trade. The shipping links along the Atlantic coast then became more efficient than the land route, and trading houses began to work through permanent representatives. On top of this, political vicissitudes around 1300 disrupted the peace of northern France, while the taxes levied by the king, who in the meantime had inherited the County of Champagne, soared sky-high. Other fairs came in their place: the duke of Burgundy

promoted the fair of Chalon-sur-Saône, the duke of Savoy that of Geneva, and in 1460 the king of France lent his support to the Lyons fair in a sort of economic war. During the late medieval period of contraction (see Chapter 10) fairs would enjoy a new lease of life. In Brabant the cycle of Antwerp and Bergen-op-Zoom prepared the role that Antwerp, on the Schelde, would assume in the sixteenth century as a western metropolis. The Deventer fairs linked the Rhineland with the Hanse and a growing Amsterdam; Frankfurt, besides being the gateway to the overland routes to central Europe, was linked to this cycle as well as to that of Brabant.

Although the fairs in Frankfurt, Leipzig and some other towns still take place every year, their function as a central location for all products and payments has disappeared. There is a simple reason for this: with the further growth of commercial traffic the short-term meetings no longer sufficed and there was a growing need for permanent markets. This is why international fairs only survived in the fifteenth and sixteenth centuries in large towns where local production and sales already formed a solid basis. Elsewhere, more modern forms of organisation took over their functions. The density of the northern Italian network of towns explains why fairs never played such an important role there as in the north: the urban facilities provided a constant and comprehensive supply and demand.

COMPANIES   As early as the twelfth century companies (derived from the Latin *cum pane*, 'eating bread together') were forming in the towns of Lombardy and Tuscany, whose family core enlarged its capital by issuing shares that yielded a proportional share of the profits. All the partners, together with their fortunes, had an unlimited liability for the company, which naturally presupposes a strong bond. Companies from Piacenza, Lucca, Siena, Florence and Pistoia operated collectively at the fairs in the north. Moreover, their business with the pope was a gold mine, as they channelled papal revenues from all over Christendom to the Apostolic Chamber. It suited both parties that the Italian partnerships in the north could accept Church monies and transfer them to Rome. It enabled the merchants to buy wool in England, cloth, linen or furs in Flanders and Champagne, and give the pope what they owed him – after the deduction of certain expenses, of course – from the sales of those goods in Italy, without having to move or invest one single penny themselves. It was indeed the Church pennies that gave Italian merchants a good deal of their working capital.

Italy, thanks to the volume of its trade, which was considerably larger, more valuable and more varied than in the north, made further steps in commercial organisation. The general tendency was towards a division of labour between the merchant and the transporter, towards an increase in the scale of commercial enterprises and the formation of networks of permanent representatives. Family concerns sent their younger offspring for a number of years to the *funduqs* overseas to learn the business. They corresponded regularly with the home office. For the spreading of risks, overseas trade required forms of cooperation between a partner on land and a captain at sea. The financial risk was assigned to the 'sleeping partner' at home. Later, people no longer invested in an entire cargo: to spread the risk of loss, parts or shares were bought in the cargo of a ship, and then in several ships or cargoes at the same time. In Genoa forms of marine insurance came into use during the thirteenth century through notarial contracts. According to various sources and depending on the circumstances, this cost between 7 and 15 per cent of the value of the cargo on the route of a Genoese *nave* from London or Southampton to Porto Pisano (at the mouth of the Arno). For journeys on the safer Mediterranean, a rate of 4 per cent was normal. In Venice, where the great merchant families exercised their authority over the city in relative harmony, the state took upon itself the collective protection of the merchant fleets, by having them sail in convoys, escorted if necessary by armed galleys of the state. This reduced the cost of insurance to 1 or 1.5 per cent for journeys by galley to Alexandria.

The activities of a company had to be put down in writing so that the trading operations, as they became more complex, could be run more efficiently. Shareholders wanted to have some insight into the trading results in order to calculate their profits. Commercial correspondence between partners was another symptom of this. From 1260 couriers travelled regularly between Tuscany and Champagne. A century later 17 Florentine companies together set up the *scarsella*, a private courier service linking the major trading towns of western Europe. These couriers travelled between 50 and 60 kilometres per day, depending on the state of the roads. Rapid reporting of the situation of the markets enabled the headquarters of the medieval multinationals to make the best deals. Trade representatives, known as factors or agents, kept their principals informed about exchange rates, the prices of products and political situations that might have repercussions on trade. They also advised them by letter of the contents of the cargoes they shipped, so that verification was possible on arrival or in the case of loss. In its heyday in the fourteenth century the Florentine company Bardi had 120 factors in its service who supplied the headquarters with a mass of information about hundreds of products in more than twenty places. The entire archive of one trading house – that of Francesco Datini from Prato, who was active between 1380 and 1410 – is still in existence, and contains many thousands of letters that his correspondents in Barcelona, Paris, Avignon, Bruges and London sent him almost every week. Datini was certainly not one of the biggest merchants of his time, but his business produced a mountain of paperwork – nearly 500 account books, 300 contracts of partnership, 400 insurance policies, thousands of invoices, bills of exchange and cheques, and about 150,000 letters. The greatest businesses, such as that of the Medici family, were split into different companies for production (silk and cloth), commerce and banking. Towards the end of the fifteenth century all the branches were given an independent status so that if business was going badly in one division it would not necessarily bring the concern as a whole into difficulties.

BILL OF EXCHANGE   The practice of the bill of exchange for the transfer of money emerged at the end of the thirteenth century. In place of the older declarations of debt, drawn up by a notary or town clerk, the Italian firms introduced this completely informal method of payment. There were four parties in two places, linked to each other through their regular trading relationships. The drawer gave a bill to the deliverer; this was addressed to the drawer's trading agent in another place. This drawee was invited to pay a sum of money to the party accredited, the payee, who was a partner of the deliverer. The bill was of no use to any highwayman emptying an agent's bag of letters, because he was not a partner in the money transfer. Like the bonds arranged at the annual fairs this was a combined operation: the loan of a short-term commercial credit, the exchange of currency and the transfer of money from one place to another with no coins involved. Some weeks would elapse before the drawee received the letter and could look for the person whom he must reimburse in another currency for the goods bought by his partner in another place. A price to cover the service and the use of a few weeks' credit were included in the calculation of the exchange rate.

This system could only function if a number of transactions could be arranged at the same time in the framework of an extended network of enduring partnerships. The more frequent the operations and the closer the contact between representatives, the easier it became to commission an associate or partner elsewhere to settle a debt with one of the creditor's partners. In Bruges and Barcelona, a bourse, or exchange, was held every day at a set time and a set place to fix the rates of exchange. There, anyone who had a bill of exchange to redeem or pay out could decide if the time was suitable to do so. At the exchange it was easy to find the necessary partners with whom the bills could be traded. In Bruges the exchange was in the middle of the merchants' quarter where the 'nations' of the Genoese and Florentine merchants had their houses, and which was also the site of the famous inn belonging to the Van der Beurse family. The great advantage for the users was that they could settle their business without a gold or silver coin changing hands, avoiding the risk of debased currencies, and thus avoiding loss. At a time when precious metals were scarce this method of transferring money allowed an unlimited expansion of the money supply. The bill of exchange considerably simplified international payments, as long as one had sufficient reliable contacts. The northern border of this critical mass, necessary for the use of bills of exchange, was formed by the line London–Bruges–Cologne, then due south to Frankfurt and Geneva.

Paper currency existed in imperial China, and Marco Polo was amazed that the Chinese attached value to this stamped paper. When the Polos were in China, the Mongol Yuan dynasty issued money with texts in both Chinese and Mongolian. The difference with Europe was of course the unity of authority. Europe found its integration through the market: Italian gold florins and ducats were eagerly accepted as a means of payment everywhere. Moreover, commercial networks created their own paper money, the fiduciary currency circulating among the merchants in the form of bonds, cheques and bills of exchange. In addition transferable money became popular: deposits with a money-changer or banker could be used as a current account from which money could be transferred by *giro* (Italian for 'by return') to a different account with the same or another banker. Whereas in China it was the imperial bureaucracy that determined the value of the paper money, which would hold for a considerable period of time, none of the monarchs in Europe were in a position to control effectively the value of their own currency, as trade transgressed all borders. All of them tried to prescribe by ordinances the value of foreign coins or even forbid some to circulate, but it was practically impossible to control the circulation of coins, and even harder to effectively impose exchange rates on the market. These fluctuated constantly, as they do today, on the basis of the factors perceived as positive or negative by the major financial agents. No monarch could avoid allowing the circulation of the three dominant currencies – the Genoese *genovino*, the Florentine florin and the Venetian ducat – within his realm and merchants would always assess all other money against that standard, a trinity which remained unalterable thanks to the solidity of their dominant economic basis and to the mutual competition between the three city-states. None of them would take the risk of a depreciation, the infamous practice launched by King Philip IV of France, *le roi faux-monnayeur* ('the counterfeiting king'), and his numerous profit-seeking followers. In the same way, the market determined the exchange rates applied for the fiduciary money circulating in the form of credit notes and bills of exchange. This paper money was created by merchants and bankers, and uniquely controlled by them, without any possibility for a ruler to exert authority over that financial market. At the moment of contracting a debt, both parties were free to decide about the currency in which, and the place where, the reimbursement would have to be made. They chose on the basis of the market situation, calculating their best profit opportunities. The financial market was not bound to a territory and thereby beyond the reach of political and ecclesiastical powers. Moreover, both belonged to their best clients. The financial system developed in Europe around 1300 is not so different from that of today.

ACCOUNTANCY The system of book-keeping had to be improved so that the complex relations and data could be scrutinised and the chances of profit assessed. The double-entry system of book-keeping was devised in Venice in the fourteenth century. The principle behind it was that separate accounts were kept per partner, client, associate, etc., per product and per type of transaction. Every account showed the debit, what the person owed, on the left-hand page, and the credit, what the person had, on the right-hand page. Every transaction was noted twice: once as a transfer in the liquid assets of the firm, and once as a transfer in its relationship with a partner. In this way the manager was able to make up the accounts of a particular partner, a product or the balance at any given moment.

Merchants had to be very well trained in arithmetic, knowledge of commodities and commercial skills. By the twelfth century, schools in the towns had already broken the Church's monopoly on education as the merchants demanded practical knowledge. As in the crafts, boys were given a practical training at the side of experienced family members. Moreover, in Italy there were textbooks containing information about a number of different places: how best to travel there, what products could be found there and their quality, what measures, weights and coins were in use and which local customs should be respected (such as the payment of bribes to customs officers). The fourteenth-century merchant revealed a mentality that clearly saw the rational pursuit of the maximum possible profit as an aim in itself; he was inclined to reinvest a goodly portion of that profit in his business so that it would surpass that of rival firms and thus make an even greater profit. Such an attitude is called a capitalist mentality.

This actual development of commercial capitalism was in sharp contrast with the teaching of the Church, which still strongly condemned the unrestrained pursuit of material gain and usury. Some theologians certainly looked for conditions which would justify the application of a moderate interest to a loan, such as the risk of damage. The theory of the 'fair price' challenged exaggerated profits, but accepted nonetheless the principle of profit in return for services rendered. Yet the preachers of the mendicant orders, in particular, gave many a merchant an uneasy conscience, leading to the introduction of God as a creditor in merchants' accounts and to many account books opening with a short prayer to God 'and the profit He may give us'. And, of course, the drawing up of a will gave usurers another opportunity to make restitution.

The evolution of the instruments of payment reflects the powerful growth of the movement of goods and services, at least until the middle of the fourteenth century. Italian financial specialists were welcomed by north-west European princes as their councillors, treasurers and mint-masters. Bankers from Piedmont settled their family-based companies all over Europe under the generic name of Lombards. Unhindered by ecclesiastical prohibitions on usury, they lent huge sums to princes, bishops and aristocrats, as well as to ordinary people. Gradually, local financial experts and capitalists adopted their techniques, but the Italians operated on a scale unparalleled by others in the amount of capital, the geographical extent of their transactions and the sophistication of their organisation. Lending huge amounts of money to princes was always tricky, as their incapacity to reimburse and arbitrary sanctions always loomed large. The Florentine banking companies of the Peruzzi and Bardi families went bankrupt in 1342 and 1346 respectively, as a consequence of their unwarranted loans to King Edward III in the early years of the Hundred Years War.

A negative balance of payments

The fact that the Italians controlled the contacts with the Levant meant that they were the sole distributors of Mediterranean and eastern products throughout the rest of Europe. South Germans collected the products themselves directly from Venice or Milan. Italians took them to the fairs in Champagne, and from the last quarter of the thirteenth century shipped them to Bruges, where the spice trade was one of the most important

activities, just as it was in the fairs of Antwerp. What could they offer their trading partners in the East in exchange? For many centuries far less than they bought, and this led to a continuous outflow of precious metals. The economic historian Eliyahu Ashtor calculated that the balance of payments between the Levant and the West showed a deficit of 56 per cent in the fifteenth century. Expressed in pure gold, this was an annual outflow of 1,317 kilos. The West imported goods from the East to a total value of 630,000 ducats, and could barely sell 260,000 ducats worth of their own products, mostly woollen goods, linen, weapons and wood. The difference (370,000 ducats) had to be made up in liquid assets.

Through their commercial ties with the Maghreb, Iberian and Italian merchants were able to obtain gold dust from West Africa, which reached the ports by caravan. In exchange, the Christians offered textiles, copper objects, foodstuffs and general cargo trade along the north coast of Africa. In 1231, this enabled the Emperor Frederick II in Sicily to mint the first western gold coins since the seventh century, the *augustales*, which bore a portrait of him, strikingly modelled on those of the Roman emperors. Since 650 only Byzantine and Arabian gold coins had been in circulation in the Christian world. When the Mongol conquests in central Asia put an end to the supply of dinars (Arabian gold coins) in 1252 the great commercial centres of Genoa and Florence turned to issuing coins of pure gold with a weight of 3.54 grams. Venice followed in 1284. These three coins, the *genovino*, florin and ducat, became the gold coins in standard use throughout Europe for centuries. Their stability rested on the economic domination of the three cities that issued them. The fact that they were of equal weight and value was a matter of economic insight.

The West always had to compensate the heavy negative balance of payment with the East. This was only made possible through a whole chain of relationships reaching all the way back to the gold

BOX 7.3 A FLORENTINE MERCHANT'S MANUAL

Francesco Balducci Pegolotti became a representative of the Florentine trading house of Bardi in 1310. In that capacity he reached an agreement with the duke of Brabant at Antwerp in 1315 that the same favourable excise duties that the Germans, English and Genoese already enjoyed would apply to the merchants of Florence. From 1317 to 1321 he acted for his firm in London, to collect the papal revenues in England and transfer them to Avignon. In 1324 he obtained from the king of Cyprus the same excise privileges for the Florentines as the Pisans. In the years following he guaranteed the collection of the papal revenues in Cyprus and their transfer to Avignon. During the long years of his stay in Famagusta in Cyprus he carried out detailed research into the quality of local syrups and sugar, their pure weight and their packaging. While he was there he also collected precise information about products and routes in the Levant, Constantinople and Alexandria. After 1329 he held various positions in the ruling council of Florence. As one of its most prominent members, in 1347 he was involved in the liquidation of the Bardi firm, which in the meantime had been declared bankrupt.

During his journeys Pegolotti must have made notes on the quality of products, popular sizes, weights, coins, excise duties and commercial practices in sundry locations, which would have been useful to a merchant. Between 1338 and 1342 he compiled these into a voluminous book that he called the 'Book about the differences between countries, trading sizes, and other pieces of information for merchants from diverse parts of the world etc.'

He gives detailed conversion tables of weights and currency, and information about the differences in the quality of goods available and about commercial practices in the major trading towns round the Mediterranean and the Black Sea and in France, Flanders and England. More of these practical handbooks for merchants were in circulation in north Italy, all written in Italian, but Pegolotti's is one of the oldest and certainly the most comprehensive. The modern printed edition has 383 pages. It contains numerous tables and sketches.

An example of the long survey of weight conversions from Famagusta follows:

> With Bruges in Flanders.
> One Cyprus *cantaro* makes 518 pounds in Bruges.
> 80 *Ruotoli* alum in Cyprus makes a cartload or 400 pounds in Bruges.
> 40 *Cafissi* grain in Cyprus makes 1 *hoet* in Bruges.
> One mark of silver in Bruges, or 6 ounces, makes 6 ounces and 13 sterling in Cyprus.

In his survey of the levies on trade in Constantinople Pegolotti notes:

> Remember well that if you show respect to customs officials, their clerks and 'turkmen' [sergeants], and slip them a little something or some money, they will also behave very courteously and will tax the goods that you later bring by them lower than their real value.

Source: Francesco Balducci Pegolotti, *La Pratica della Mercatura*, ed. A. Evans (Cambridge, MA: The Medieval Academy of America, 1936), pp. xvii–xxvi, 42, 100.

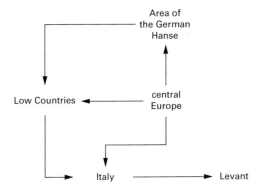

FIGURE 7.1 Deficits on the balance of payments between European regions in the fourteenth century (after Spufford 2002)

the repayment was made in another currency; it could also be used to complete other transactions for the creditor. Naturally, substantial rates of interest were charged for this, although they were generally not specifically recorded. A rate of 10 to 15 per cent was held as entirely reasonable for short-term commercial credit; an interest rate of up to almost 45 per cent was considered acceptable for risky loans. Only when higher rates were asked did it become a question of usury, for which Church prescribed severe punishments.

Italian merchants tried to reduce their dependence on eastern suppliers by starting to produce themselves what had not been produced before in

and silver mines in Saxony, Bohemia, Slovakia and Hungary. Production flowed from those lands to Italy and the Low Countries where high-quality articles and exotic goods were bought. The Low Countries, and, indirectly, England as well, were thus able to bring their negative balance of payment with Italy into equilibrium. The Hanse, too, brought silver to the Low Countries because it imported many finished products and luxury goods from there, including large quantities of textiles, French and Mediterranean wine, arts and crafts, while its own exports consisted mainly of cheap bulk goods (beer, iron, wood, hides, amber, wax and, increasingly, grain).

The Italians needed to use their positive balance of payments – the unit value of their supply was higher than that of the northerners – productively. They invested the hard cash surplus, preferring to make more profit than run the risk of losing it on the journey home. For this reason they extended relatively cheap credit to their customers, further strengthening their dominant position as wholesale merchants. They rapidly emerged as financiers who provided credit for nobles and princes. They had this sort of transaction recorded briefly but objectively in written bonds, payable at a particular fair in another place, sometimes to associates or business partners of the creditors. The credit transaction was thus coupled to a money exchange transaction, since

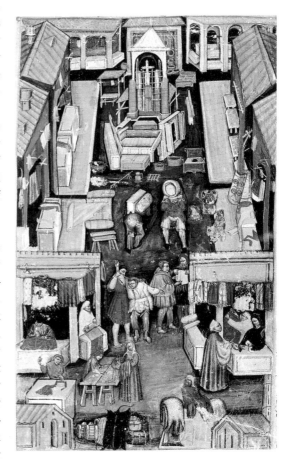

PLATE 7.4 The drapery market at Bologna in the fifteenth century, as represented in the drapers' guild register.

western Europe – they introduced the cultivation of rice, cotton, sugar cane, saffron and the silk worm, for example. In warmer climates silk was not only a luxury, it was also much more pleasant to wear than wool or linen. The large demand for silk stimulated production under their own control and this substituted some of the imports. The same applied to cotton and cane sugar, which were cultivated in certain Venetian colonies and also, at the end of the fifteenth century, on islands in the Atlantic, such as Madeira. Paper – which from the thirteenth century had supplemented and largely replaced parchment which became much too expensive as literacy increased – was an eastern product that the Europeans copied so as not to have to import it any longer. The toughest relationships ruled in the areas round the Black Sea, from where slaves, hides, grain and wood were imported. Genoa in particular, which was built right up against the mountains and did not have a natural hinterland, had to rely on massive imports of grain, first from Sardinia and Sicily, but if that was not sufficient, then from Thrace and the Crimea.

The commercialisation of the countryside

During the twelfth and thirteenth centuries the supra-local consumptive demand was increasingly focused on bulk goods. The growth of the towns created consumptive demand from a professional and specialised workforce. This was one way in which the use of money penetrated the rural economy. Another was by means of dues in cash owed by peasants to their lords. And, finally, in the countryside too, an increasing number of people could no longer live exclusively on the proceeds of their small plots of land, and looked for a supplementary cash income as manual workers or labourers. In correlation with these three developments, and stimulated by the consolidation of territorial principalities, trade and transport improved in various ways so that transport and transaction costs were lowered.

In England the earliest phases of the process of commercialisation in the countryside to which we refer are relatively easy to follow, thanks to excellent sources. Even before the Norman Conquest of 1066, Anglo-Saxon England had a network of more than 150 places in which regularly held markets provided their lords with income – and that number does not include the probably large number of places where merchants met informally. The penetration of money into England's rural economy is also fairly well documented. So we know exactly how much money the tenants-in-chief, the Anglo-Norman crown vassals after 1066, received from their estates (most of it paid by the peasants living on them). Scattered information from the eleventh and twelfth centuries likewise indicates the broad distribution of coins among ordinary people: the oldest demesne accounts of Church estates already contain many cash payments by villeins; royal courts of justice collected fines in cash from all sorts of people; pilgrims from all over England who visited the tombs of national saints, such as that of St Cuthbert in Durham, filled the offertory boxes with coins.

The commercialisation of the rural economy in England really gained momentum between about 1180 and 1330. In that period, as grain prices were beginning to rise, many large landowners preferred to exploit the demesne lands on their estates commercially with the help of hired labour. This meant that many labour services of villeins were transformed into money payments. When land was developed outside existing settlements the exploitation was no longer organised through the manorial system; dues from peasants to their lords were predominantly in the form of money payments right from the beginning. In the countryside there was a steady growth in the number of people who could no longer supply their own food needs and were dependent on the market. They constituted as much as 45 per cent of the rural population by about 1300.

The proportion of England's urban population increased between the end of the eleventh century and the beginning of the fourteenth from about 10 per cent to 15 or 20 per cent. London, England's largest city, had grown into a metropolis with 60,000 to 80,000 inhabitants by the beginning of the fourteenth century. Such a sizeable concentration of people needed a strongly commercialised agriculture in a wide surrounding area. Regional specialisations were also strengthened, partly in response to the growing foreign demand for raw materials such as wool and tin. Tin ore had been mined in Cornwall since prehistoric times, but its extraction was expanded considerably between the twelfth and the fourteenth century; by 1300 it provided work for more than 2,000 people. In other remote and thinly populated areas, the Lake District for example, the growing use of water-driven fulling mills similarly led to specialised industrial activity outside the urban sphere in the same period.

All in all, a substantial part of England's agricultural production – according to estimates, at least 25 per cent of the yields from arable production and considerably more from cattle farming – was intended for the market at the beginning of the fourteenth century. This strong commercialisation of the rural economy went hand in hand with a broadening of the supply of agricultural products and an increase in and sophistication of trading networks, with marketplaces as logical nodes. The number of markets increased considerably during the twelfth and thirteenth centuries and a certain hierarchy became evident. The 'intermediary markets' were of the greatest significance in the commercialisation of the agrarian economy; every county had a couple of intermediary markets that formed vital links between the direct agricultural producers and the more than fifty larger regional trading centres found in England around 1300, which in turn were linked to interregional and sometimes even international trade.

The transport of bulk goods of low value (such as grain) over large distances was not profitable at normal market prices, because of the high costs of transport and transaction. The transportation of grain by cart in England in the thirteenth century cost 0.4 per cent of the grain's value per mile; so transport over 10 miles (more than 16 kilometres) increased the costs by 4 per cent, and transport over 100 miles by 40 per cent. This did not include the cost of the many tolls on the journey, which would easily have been a couple of per cent of the value of the cargo.

Still, in the most densely populated regions of Europe, regular interregional trade in grain appeared to be worthwhile. The fertile loam soil and intensive methods of agriculture made very high yields possible for the wheat harvest in Artois, even before 1300. The south–north flow of the rivers enabled the enormous surpluses – an average of 1.5 million hectolitres per annum, enough to feed 400,000 people – to be shipped down river to the towns of Brabant and Flanders, which could never have become so densely populated without such a fertile agricultural hinterland so near by. During periods of grain shortages in the fifteenth century Flanders imported massive quantities of rye from Prussia, because the trebling of the market price more than made up for the transport costs.

Raw wool was a different story altogether. By the first half of the fourteenth century the wool from nine million sheep was exported from England to the continent. Some of this eventually returned in the form of fashionable felt hats and trousers cut to the latest style in Bruges. At the height of the trade, between 1350 and 1360, England exported 30,000 sacks of wool per year. After 1450 that number varied between 2,000 and 11,000, when protectionism stimulated the domestic production of cloth. The export of finished cloth from England rose from 10,000–20,000 pieces between 1355 and 1360 to 60,000 in 1480–1500. When the war taxes levied by the kings made English wool too expensive, merchants from the Low Countries began to look for other sources of supply. At the end of the fifteenth century Castile sent the wool from nine million merino sheep to Bruges, where it was transformed into richly coloured tapestries, and also into cheap clothing that was shipped to Prussia in exchange for grain. This proves that the European market was already well integrated during the fourteenth and fifteenth centuries, and that the effects of commercialisation in advanced areas could be strongly felt in the periphery.

Points to remember

- The Byzantine Empire lost most of Asia Minor to the Seljuks in 1071, and conceded strategic commercial privileges to Venice in 1082.

- Demographic growth triggered west European expansion in the form of the Christian advance in Iberia, the western Mediterranean and eastern Europe.

- The new self-confident spirit in the Catholic Church exacerbated the Schism with the Orthodox Church and motivated the successive mass mobilisations of the Crusades.

- Crusader states and commercial settlements in the ports were the first west European large-scale overseas colonial experiences. They established dominance over the eastern Mediterranean and the Black Sea.

- The devastation caused by Mongol raids, climatic change in Iran and western aggression led to the re-orientation of Islamic trade networks to the Indian Ocean.

- The significant growth of cities in northern Italy was boosted by their intermediary position between Byzantium, the Maghreb, the Near East and Egypt on the one hand, and western and central Europe on the other.

- Northern Italy became the core economic region in Europe, initiating new techniques of commercial organisation, new products and maritime transport with bulk cargoes along the Mediterranean and European coasts.

Suggestions for further reading

Britnell, R.H. (1993), *The Commercialisation of English Society 1000–1500* (Cambridge: CUP). Exemplary analysis based on uniquely preserved quantitative data of the deep impact on the English economy and society of market-oriented production.

Hunt, Edwin S. and James M. Murray (1999), *A History of Business in Medieval Europe, 1200–1550* (Cambridge: CUP). The authors explain the forces that shaped the organisation of the various sectors of expanding economic life. They deal with the responses of businessmen to manifold risks and opposing forces. The success in coping with this hostile environment was 'a harvest of adversity' that prepared the way for the economic expansion of the sixteenth century.

Jacoby, David (2005), *Commercial Exchange across the Mediterranean: Byzantium, the Crusader Levant, Egypt and Italy* (Aldershot: Ashgate) (Variorum Collected Studies). A volume of essential articles on the intercultural exchanges leading to the Italian breakthrough. They underscore the economic vitality of the countries bordering the eastern Mediterranean, their industrial capacity, the importance of exchanges between them and the contribution of the merchants based in that region to trans-Mediterranean trade.

Lopez, Roberto S. (1976), *The Commercial Revolution of the Middle Ages, 950–1350* (Cambridge: CUP). A classic essay on the structural changes in the orientations and organisation of trade during decisive centuries. How did an underdeveloped economic system give birth to the commercial revolution which shaped Europe? How was commercialisation diffused, and how did it relate to agricultural dynamics?

Spufford, Peter (2002), *Power and Profit: The Merchant in Medieval Europe* (London: Thames & Hudson). A very accessible, well-informed and thoughtful overview of the role of commerce in the Middle Ages, with a particular interest in monetary issues. Scores of documented actual situations illustrate vividly how the European economy functioned in daily practice.

8 Thinking about man and the world

The medieval view of the world and mankind

When an educated observer around 1300 went outside on a cloudless night and peered into the sky, he may have marvelled at the vast expanse of the star-spangled firmament, and, awestruck, praised the Lord as the creator of the universe. But he would not have been confused. What he saw was not bewildering chaos, but order that made sense. First of all, he would have thought of himself as being in the middle of things. The earth on which he lived was the immovable centre of the universe; around it there moved in concentric order ten transparent convex spaces or spheres, beginning with those of the seven known planets, in which the Sun and the Moon were included. Beyond the sphere of the last planet, Saturn, began that of the fixed stars (*stellatum*). Then came the vaguer circles of 'the crystalline', presented as a thin fluid mass encircling the entire firmament, and that of the *primum mobile*, the first of the spheres to show movement and to pass that movement on to the lower spheres. Beyond the *primum mobile* extended the immovable *empyreum*, where heaven was located. While earth then formed the centre of the universe, it was nevertheless fully understood that it was insignificant on the cosmic scale. One estimate showed that a complete revolution of the stellar sphere round the earth took 36,000 years. An English chap-book (popular book) from the fourteenth century calculated that a journey from the earth to the *stellatum* would take 8,000 years, at an average travelling speed of 40 miles per day. This is nothing compared with the actual 40 trillion kilometres (a 40 with 12 zeros) which separates our sun from the nearest sun in our galaxy, Proxima Centauri, but was still a vast distance to imagine for our medieval observer.

It was presumed that the stars, the planets and the earth, just like the spaces which moved them around, were spherical in shape – the idea of a flat earth never found favour in intellectual circles. Planets were seen as animate, often even as intelligent bodies which influenced life on earth. It was the task of astrology to discover and determine that influence. Astrology in the Middle Ages, just as in Antiquity, was accepted as a source of rational knowledge, although those elements that were clearly contrary to Christian orthodoxy were forbidden by the Church, among them 'reading the future' from the stars and the worship of heavenly bodies. It was seriously believed that the planets had an influence on the formation of metals and on people's physical and mental state, to give just two examples. Doctors and apothecaries in particular made frequent use of astrological knowledge, but kings and princes of the Church had their court and personal astrologers too.

Our observer may have had a rough idea of earthly geography if he had seen one of those marvellous *mappae mundi* or world maps, either a small one inserted in a history book or an encyclopaedia or a big one, painted on animal skin or embroidered on linen and suspended from a wall in a cathedral or a great hall. Some of these pictured the earth as composed of five ring-shaped zones, three of which – two at the poles and one

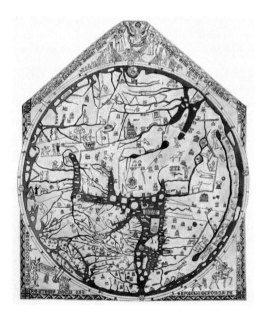

PLATE 8.1 Hereford *mappa mundi*, depicting the three inhabited continents, with Jerusalem in the centre, directly below the Tower of Babel and the Garden of Eden.

wide band on either side of the Equator – were uninhabitable because of either extreme cold or extreme heat. Only the two temperate zones – one in the northern, the other in the southern hemisphere – were inhabited. The antipodes dwelt in the southern hemisphere, but they could never meet the inhabitants of the northern hemisphere as it was impossible to penetrate the hot intermediate zone. Some Christian writers found this difficult to believe because the Bible stated that all the people who lived on earth after the flood were descendants of Noah, and all the peoples of the earth should sooner or later be able to receive the word of God. A second dominant image was a representation of just the northern land mass divided into three continents, Europe, Africa and Asia (with Asia on top), separated from each other by a T-shape of three broad stretches of water: the Mediterranean Sea (Europe–Africa), the Don and the Black Sea (Europe–Asia) and the Nile (Asia–Africa). Its geometric centre was Jerusalem, the sacred stage where the New Covenant had started and where human history would end. The continents' periphery was rimmed on all sides by almost uninhabitable areas, where strange, monstrous creatures lurked, and no one could really say whether they were human or animal.

It goes without saying that such *mappae mundi* were not made for travelling; they were intentionally symbolical representations not just of earthly geography but also of those essential historical events, such as the exodus of the Jewish people out of Egypt, that marked humankind's destiny on earth which was the fulfilment of God's Salvation Plan. We can see all this on the largest extant map of this kind, which can be admired in Hereford cathedral (see Plate 8.1). It has a Final Judgement scene painted on top of the image of the world, which itself is encased between four capital letters: M.O.R.S. – Death, a clear reference to the (preliminary) destiny that awaits all living creatures on earth.

Geographically more accurate maps of the known world became a possibility once Ptolemy's standard geographical work, the *Geography*, was recovered by a Greek monk in around 1300 and translated into Latin a century later. This work propagated and indicated the use of degrees of latitude and longitude, showing how the curved surface of the earth should be reproduced in a flat depiction. Even before 1300, and just at the period in which some of the finest specimens of traditional *mappae mundi* were made, the technical improvement of the compass – a Chinese invention of the eleventh century – led to the drawing of quite detailed and precise maps of Europe's coastlines that were meant as an aid for mariners.

From the universe to the human individual was but a small step to medieval man. A human being was seen as a microcosmic reflection of the macrocosmos: the unity of the universe caused celestial bodies and human beings to be connected, and therefore it was thought that planets and stars had a direct influence on the well-being of the human body and mind – a strange idea that still exists among those of us who believe in casting a horoscope.

In a material sense, the human body was composed of the same four elements – fire, air, earth and water – that were detectable via the four primary or sensible qualities of which everything on earth (or according to some even everything in the universe) was made: hot, cold, dry and wet. Just as four different combinations of the four primary qualities formed the four elements of matter, so on the scale of the human body they formed the four humours, or bodily fluids: hot and wet made blood, hot and dry made yellow bile or choler (*cholera* in Greek), cold and wet made phlegm (*flegma* in Greek), cold and dry made black bile or melancholy (Greek *melancholia*). All individuals had their own mixture of four fluids, which determined their **complexio** or temperament. In addition to more or less 'melancholic' and 'choleric' types, there were also 'phlegmatic' and 'sanguine' ones. Temperament not only had a particular exterior and a particular physical state, it also generated specific character traits. To complicate matters even further, it was believed that other factors, preferably divisible by four, could influence the *complexio* and thus the state of health of an individual; these factors included the four divisions of the day, the four seasons, the four points of the compass and the four gustatory qualities (salty, sour, bitter, sweet). Should a person fall ill, physically or mentally, then the foremost task of the attending physician was to diagnose how the patient's specific mixture of humours had been disturbed by studying the colour of his/her urine or by feeling his/her pulse; the treatment could then be adapted accordingly, aimed at restoring the bodily fluids' balance, either by putting the patient on a diet, by prescribing physical exercise, by giving him drugs, or by abstracting excess fluids by purgation or bloodletting. When deciding on the type or form of treatment, the physician had to take into account all kinds of external circumstances, ranging from the patient's sex or age to the part of the day or the season in which he administered his medicine.

According to medieval people, the human body was not just a bag of bones and intestines, spiced with a temperament of bodily fluids, and provided with a network of veins, arteries and nerves for the transport of all vital physical and mental functions to all parts of the body in the form of volatiles called *spiritus* (± 'spirits'). It was also the seat of an immaterial, immortal component, the soul (Latin *anima*) which, for humans, harboured three essential abilities: the ability to feed the body, sensory perception and the unique quality in which humans were different from other living beings, animals and plants: the capacity of reason, activated through divine enlightenment – or put more simply, through the intervention of the Holy Ghost. Thoughts about what happened to the immortal soul after the body died were highly speculative. Where did the soul remain until it was reunited with the resurrected body on the eve of the Last Judgement – a central tenet of Christian eschatology? Did souls have to roam the air as floating spirits – good and evil – or was there some fixed place for them to stay and wait? And what did this place look like? Was it indeed a locus of 'refreshment' or an oven-like place of purification that would prepare the soul for entrance into paradise as was the orthodox position from around 1200?

Moreover, human souls were not the only immortal and immaterial intelligences in the universe. There also were angelic beings (Latin *genii*, cf. Arabic *djini*), who dwelt in the air above the earth. The invisible good spirit who, in the ancient view, guided every individual and was 'witness and keeper' of a person's life, in the New Testament took on a Christian shape as the 'guardian angel', who protected every human being day and night from the tricks and guiles of devils. The latter in turn had emerged from the evil spirits of Antiquity. Many other angels dwelt, hierarchically ordered into nine 'choirs', in the planetary spheres and in heaven; they were purely ethereal beings.

Greek origins

This is in a nutshell how more or less educated people viewed the world and themselves; what ordinary people thought is less easy to find out, and if we could we should immediately have to differentiate in time and space. Much depended on where one lived and how much access one had to people who were educated – members of the clergy and the aristocracy, first of all, but also, and increasingly, members of the upper middle classes, and once in a while men from humbler origins, whom the Church or a lord had offered the chance to enter a school.

The worldview just outlined is the simplified version, already tailored to a wider audience, of a more sophisticated, scientific paradigm that was studied within a small intellectual elite of highly educated scholars, and that we are now going to discuss. To start with, there was nothing originally medieval to this paradigm. It was almost entirely Greek in its origins. More precisely, it can be traced back to the great Greek philosophers of the fourth century BCE, Plato (427–347) and Aristotle (384–322), the Alexandrian mathematician Euclid (323–283), and two Hellenist scholars who both lived in the second century CE: the astronomer and geographer Ptolemy of Alexandria and the physician Galen of Pergamum.

Of these 'big five', Plato and Aristotle were deemed by far the greatest. It is fair to say, however, that medieval scholars were acquainted with only scraps of Plato's oeuvre. Plato's immense influence on the philosophical shape of Christian theology was indirect, via Plotinus, an Egyptian Greek who set up a successful school of Platonic thought in Rome around the middle of the third century. The later neo-Platonic works of Plotinus have been instrumental in providing philosophical support for the Christian belief in God as the sole, transcendent, eternal and perfectly good creator of the universe, as well as in the immortality of the human soul. Aristotle stood at the basis of two other, more earthly, scholarly traditions in the Middle Ages: the study of formal logic (or dialectic, the art of correct argumentation) and the study of nature on a firmly empirical basis, that is to say, starting from observation, and aimed at rational understanding of the fundamental laws of nature – the natural causes of things, as Aristotle would put it.

Athens and Jerusalem

Of course we should ask ourselves why were Greek philosophers accepted in medieval Christendom as the wisest men who had ever lived, when they were all pagans? As to this paganism, many medieval philosophers felt that wise men like Plato were monotheists, or even proto-Christians, in disguise long before the Incarnation. But this was an idea that only arose later in time. In the early Christian communities of the later Roman Empire there had been heated discussion on the question of how to deal with pagan philosophy. Some, like Tertullian at the end of the second century CE, rejected every approach. 'What has

BOX 8.1 ADVANCES IN MEDICINE? HUMAN DISSECTION AND SURGERY IN THE MIDDLE AGES

During the Middle Ages the practice of the medical and paramedical professions was as many-hued as it was obscure. At one extreme were the better-educated doctors, who were university-trained from the thirteenth century onward. At the other extreme was 'folk medicine', based entirely on experience, which was handed down and practised by a disordered army of amateurs and charlatans who promised to cure their needy patients with magic spells, numerical formulas, little prayers, tarot cards or their own home-made potions, prescriptions and pills. Between the two extremes, there was a growing army of surgeons, apothecaries and herbalists (*herbarii*), especially in towns, all organised into recognised guilds; in their wake came yet other artisans and tradesmen who were involved with medical treatments on the side, such as the barbers who let blood, pulled teeth and performed minor operations – 'prodding' a cataract, for example – bath-house managers and masseurs, who specialised in setting broken limbs, and midwives who, in an emergency, carried out life-threatening caesarean sections.

The fact that university-educated doctors were not visibly more successful in their treatment of patients explains why they never managed to gain a far-reaching monopoly over medical practice or to control it by other means. This again was due to the lack of progress in medical study in the medieval universities. Just as nowadays, the study consisted of a theoretical and a practical part. Pathology, governed as it was by the ancient Greek theory of humours, was central to the theoretical part. The tripartite division of the practical part into dietetics, pharmacy and surgery was borrowed from the same tradition. The increasing emphasis on the theoretical aspects of the study of medicine, influenced by the great success of Aristotelian natural philosophy in the thirteenth century, was crippling for the advance of practical surgery and, moreover, heightened tensions between university-educated doctors (often called *fysici*, later *doctores medicinae*), and traditionally trained surgeons, apothecaries and herbalists. Physicians believed that the latter did not have the theoretical knowledge to make accurate diagnoses.

Real progress in one branch of medicine, surgery, seemed to become possible when dissection of the human corpse, which had met much resistance and aversion in both ancient Greco-Roman and Arab-Islamic medical science, became tolerated in the Latin-Christian West. Certainly, surgery was a type of medical treatment that was generally avoided, both because of the dangers for the patient's life and the traumatic experience inherent to cutting into a body without anaesthetic: 'if there was anything obviously heroic about medieval surgery, it was the patient' (Lindberg 2007). Apart from this aspect, the Arabic world initially had a significant lead on the West. Most works of the vast Galenic corpus were translated into Arabic long before they were available in Latin, and it may not come as a surprise that, after this finally had happened, Arab commentaries and textbooks by al-Razi (Rhases), 'Ali ibn Abbas al-Majusi (Haly Abbas) and Ibn Sina (Avicenna) became set literature in the medical faculties of universities in the medieval West.

The earliest reports of anatomical dissection in the West are related to the medical school at Salerno and date from the first half of the twelfth century. The subjects were pigs because it was assumed that a pig's anatomy was more or less the same as a human's. The first reported human dissections are only from the late thirteenth century; they took place in north Italian universities like Bologna. Despite regular protests from the Church, secular authorities did allow dissection from that time onward. Yet this did not immediately deepen the knowledge of human anatomy and physiology. Again the main reason for this seems to be the authoritative way of thinking: when dissecting corpses, academically educated doctors were in fact only looking for confirmation of what they believed they knew already from the textbooks of Galen and Avicenna. There was nothing resembling systematic anatomical and physiological research, and the gradual advances in surgery seem to have been made outside the remit of academic medicine.

Research in Italy has shown that the dissection of human corpses took place within four different contexts. First, in surgery practicals used in medical training at universities. From the end of the thirteenth century new manuals were written specially for this purpose by famous academic surgeons from Italy and France, such as Lanfranc of Milan, Henri de Mondeville and Guy de Chauliac. Second, in the exercise of their profession, physicians who were curious and wanted to know what their patients had died from opened up their bodies. This could be called real autopsy. It sometimes happened at the express wish of the patients themselves, or their relatives, who hoped thus to avoid dying from the same sickness; in other cases, family members were opposed to any such post-mortem examination. Third, in the context of forensic autopsy: dissection could take place at the request of a court of law which wanted to establish the cause of a victim's death, hoping for clues about the perpetrator and the weapon used. The fourth context was that of the disposal of the dead. In the Middle Ages, bodies of important people were embalmed in a number of ways; the brains and internal organs were removed as a first step in the procedure. In the case of saints, it was hoped that dissection would reveal external signs of their saintliness, like the form of a cross that was clearly visible on the heart of St Clara of Montefalco (d.1308), cut open by her sister nuns. In addition, if people had died far from home but their relatives wanted to bury them nearby, it was easier to transport mere bones than complete bodies. To this end a body would be cut up and boiled. Occasionally, the heart would be kept separate.

The bodies of executed criminals were normally made available for scientific dissection, not so much to make the sentence tougher, but because the criminals often were estranged from their families and there was therefore little danger of hurting their bereaved relatives. By the end of the fifteenth century, for the same reason the bodies of people who had died in hospitals without any family were increasingly used for dissection. At that time there was an enormous increase in the demand for corpses because of the sudden broadening of surgical education. It was only then that the study of human anatomy reached a higher level. This is evident from the new generation of high-quality surgical manuals appearing rapidly one after the other from about the middle of the sixteenth century – among them those of Jacopo Berengario da Carpi, Niccolò Massa and especially that of Andreas Vesalius of Brabant who taught in Padua. Painters and sculptors were often present at dissections in Italian universities; their efforts to emulate Antiquity's great works of art made them particularly interested in human anatomy. The brilliant sketchbooks of Leonardo da Vinci reveal how this custom bore fruit.

It seemed that nothing could quench the passion of university teachers, students and visual artists for anatomical and physiological research. The great Vesalius was famed for the enthusiasm with which he seized upon bodies, sometimes, it was said, of people who were not yet truly dead.

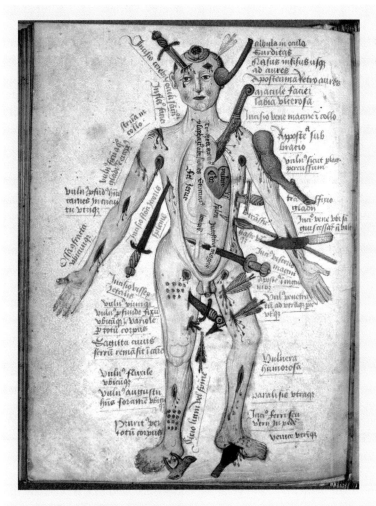

'Man with wounds', from the manual *Surgical Treatment for Blows, Stab and Gunshot Wounds.*

Cases are known from Italy in which the courts handed over criminals, sentenced to death, directly to surgeons, who could then kill them before making a start on dissection. Occasionally dissection devotees went too far in the eyes of their contemporaries. In his *Lives of the Artists,* Giorgio Vasari (1511–1574) recounts a story of the sculptor Silvio Cosini from Fiesole, rather reminiscent of the movie *Silence of the Lambs*; after a dissection he had the complete skin of a criminal made into a coat, convinced that if he wore it the dead bandit's physical strength would be transferred to him. This sort of story, whether true or not, led to a growing opposition to human dissection in the middle of the sixteenth century.

Sources: Heinrich Schipperges, *Der Garten der Gesundheit, Medizin im Mittelalter* (Munich: Artemis Verlag, 1987); Nancy G. Siraisi, *Medieval and Early Renaissance Medicine: An Introduction to Knowledge and Practice* (Chicago/London: Chicago UP, 1990); Luis García-Ballester *et al.* (eds), *Practical Medicine from Salerno to the Black Death* (Cambridge: CUP 1994); Katherine Park, 'The criminal and the saintly body: autopsy and dissection in Renaissance Italy', *Renaissance Quarterly* 47 (1994), pp. 1–33; Peter E. Pormann and Emilie Savage Smith, *Medieval Islamic Medicine* (Washington DC: Georgetown UP, 2007). Illustration: Schipperges, p. 115.

Athens to do with Jerusalem? What pagans with Christians? Now that we believe we do not want anything else but our faith!' Others had been prepared to accommodate, and rather spoke in biblical terms of taking the spoils of a conquered enemy. Why leave the opulent intellectual resources of the pagans untouched? One should take from them what could be of value to enrich the Christian faith. Subsequently, this latter point of view was mixed up with the conviction that every scientific and scholarly endeavour should always be subservient to the effort of better understanding God and his message to human-kind as it was laid down in Holy Scripture. This was the basis of the so-called handmaiden comparison, which was first formulated by St Augustine and then repeated over and over again: secular philosophy – which was mainly Greek philosophy – should be the handmaiden of 'mistress' theology.

The heavy burden of auctoritas

The handmaiden formula implied that the authority of the Bible as the fountain of divine revelation was absolute. Holy Scripture was the unavoidable point of reference for every form of intellectual effort. Its main task was to disclose the irrefutable truth that lay hidden in the Bible. If this fact alone hampered the freedom of scientific research to a degree that would be unacceptable in the modern world, at the same time it extended the room to manoeuvre with respect to other authoritative texts. The Fathers of the Church and the Greek philosophers did deserve respect. However, their textual authority was not unassail-able. The leading Dominican natural philosopher Albert the Great (Albertus Magnus, c.1200–1280) opened his commentary on the Physics of Aristotle by stating that he had written his book to enable his readers (first of all, his fellow Dominicans) 'to understand correctly the books of Aristotle'. But Albert did not follow his intellec-tual master slavishly. If need be, he supplemented his ideas, or corrected those that he thought of as

false. Even the greatest Fathers of the Church did not go without criticism. Not all the works of St Augustine, for example, carried the weight of *auctoritas*. It was also realised, especially after the twelfth century, that the authority attached to any text other than the Bible was not absolute, but depended, among other things, on the quality of textual tradition and the reader's interpretation of the text. And interpretations did vary. 'An authority has a wax nose; it can be turned in different directions (*in diversum sensum*),' wrote Alan of Lille at the end of the twelfth century with a sense of humour, for the Latin word *sensus* means both 'direction' and 'meaning'.

This turned scientific research into a cumu-lative learning process on the basis of a critical reading of authoritative texts. Its result has been worded in a chiselled phrase by the renowned master, Bernard of Chartres:

> We are like dwarves on the shoulders of giants, so that we can see more than they can, and at a greater distance, not by virtue of any sharpness of sight on our part, or any physical distinction, but because we are carried high and raised up by their giant size.

Such a metaphor testifies to both profound respect and great self-confidence, and that is precisely the feeling that must have been in the air c.1100 when Bernard made his statement. The reverse of the image is also true. When Bernard was alive, most of the giants had been dead for a thousand years or more, but the weight of their authority continued to press no less heavily upon intellectual enquiry. From that perspective, it was the dwarves who dragged the giants as a heavy burden behind them. As we shall see, this is exactly what happened with the works of Aristotle in the schools and univer-sities of later medieval Europe. They were admired, and adapted, criticised, and at times even rejected, but in the end they remained unsurpassed. In 1500 the Aristotelian worldview seemed unshakeable as never before, and it took great effort to make it falter in the half century that followed.

It was no different in the Muslim world, where the Qur'an and hadith were unassailable, but other authoritative texts could be freely criticised. In Arab scientific writing of the ninth and tenth centuries a whole new genre of scientific 'publication', called *shukuk*, thrived. Its literal meaning was 'doubts', and its main intention was to politely criticise the old Greek masters. A fine example from the beginning of the eleventh century is the *shukuk* that Ibn al-Haitham – in the West known as Alhazen – wrote on Ptolemy's works on astronomy. Alhazen wiped the floor with the inventive but questionable stereometrics and the absurd physics which the great Alexandrian polymath had developed to turn the summary Aristotelian model of the universe into a consistent description of the courses of sun, moon and planets which adequately predicted their continuously shifting positions in the sky. In order to make the universe work predictably one had to assume that planets took eccentric courses around the earth, made loops while doing that, accelerated and slowed down, or came to a halt and turned around. Astronomers like Alhazen found this hard to believe, but neither he nor any other astronomer in the Islamic or Christian world found a real solution to the Greek problems, which in the end went back to the refusal to see that the earth turned around its own axis, that the moon was no planet and that the planets – including the earth – orbited the sun. We had to wait for Nikolaus Copernicus (1473–1543) before the penny dropped, and even Copernicus was troubled by doubts and fears for years before he dared to have his revolutionary ideas printed – after which he immediately became the object of accusation and derision (see Box 8.2). His case shows how limited the room to manoeuvre really was for medieval intellectuals and how dependent on authority they remained.

BOX 8.2 THE HEAVY WEIGHT OF *AUCTORITAS*

On several occasions, medieval scientists seem to have been on the verge of revolutionary discoveries that, if they had actually been achieved and published, would have run ahead of the early modern scientific revolution by several centuries. However, in the end, there was always a reluctance to accept what had been found, a self-imposed limitation which must have been the consequence of either ingrained conservatism or serious fear of sanctions by religious authorities. We shall give two examples, one from the Islamic world, the other from Latin Christendom.

At the end of the thirteenth century a Syrian physician by the name of Ibn al-Nafis al-Qurashi (d. 1288), who worked at the public hospitals of Damascus and Cairo in the Mamluk Empire, gave the first correct and accurate description of the so-called pulmonary transit of the bloodstream – that blood in the right cavity of the heart is pumped to the left cavity indirectly, via the lung. It is difficult to imagine that al-Nafis could have made his discovery without dissection and close study of a human body. Also, from that point on, it would have been logical for al-Nafis to chart complete blood circulation. But this did not happen. Instead, al-Nafis, in his report, repeatedly stressed that he had not broken *shari'a* and that he respected the integrity of the human body; there had been no dissection; he had based his conclusions on rational inference from the works of pagan predecessors, in particular 'the excellent Galen'. In this way, al-Nafis disappeared into obscurity and the medical world had to wait another three centuries before, around the middle of the seventeenth century, Harvey and Malpighi correctly described the complete venous and arterial circuits, and the capillary system that connected them.

Not long after al-Nafis, John Buridan (*c.*1300–*c.*1361), a professor of the arts faculty at the University of Paris, and his most gifted pupil, Nicholas Oresme (*c.*1325–1382), argued that a lot of things in cosmology were easier to explain when one accepted that the earth turned around its own axis rather than believing that the whole universe made a daily orbit around a stationary earth. However, Oresme ended his cogent plea with the mysterious comment 'that which I have said by way of diversion . . . can be valuable to refute and check those who would impugn our faith by argument'. So, his whole theory was just a gimmick that could be used as a whip to beat sense into those who wanted to surmount faith with reason! Many historians of science cannot believe that Oresme's closing words were serious; they must have been meant in an ironic way. Or was Oresme just afraid of what really conservative minds could do to radicals? Something of this fear may still have been present in the Polish canon and polymath Nikolaus Copernicus, who defended the real, physical, existence of a rotating earth as a planet in a heliocentric cosmos by testing the calculations of Ptolemy and a number of late medieval Islamic astronomers against his own observations. Copernicus first sketched the outlines of this grand new scheme in 1514, in a notebook he never published. Almost twenty years later, in 1533, a papal secretary who corresponded with Copernicus gave an exposition of the latter's ideas to the pope and two of his cardinals, who all seem to have been fascinated. But another decade would pass by before Copernicus, pressed by close friends, finally had his revolutionary theory printed – the story goes that he died, at the age of 70, with the first printed copy in his hands. Why this endless delay, which is so unmodern? Was Copernicus just insecure about his own calculations, or was he afraid of what the publication of views that were irreconcilably inconsistent with the Bible would do to him? The latter concern was not overestimated. Despite earlier sympathy from the pope, criticism after publication of *De revolutionibus orbium coelestium* ('On the Rotations of Celestial Bodies') was devastating, and it came both from Rome, and from Wittenberg and Geneva. In 1547, four years after it had appeared, Martin Luther's close collaborator Philip Melanchthon summarised the three main reasons why the abominable ideas of Copernicus should be rejected. They ran counter to observation, to scientific consensus and to the authority of the Bible. Science was back to square one.

Sources: Toby E. Huff, *The Rise of Early Modern Science: Islam, China, and the West* (Cambridge: CUP, 2003, 2nd edn), pp. 167–171; Edward Grant, *The Foundations of Modern Science in the Middle Ages: Their Religious, Institutional, and Intellectual Contexts* (Cambridge: CUP, 1996); Thomas S. Kuhn, *The Copernican Revolution: Planetary Astronomy in the Development of Western Thought* (Cambridge, MA: Harvard UP, 1985, 2nd edn); Peter E. Pormann and Emilie Savage-Smith, *Medieval Islamic Medicine* (Washington DC: Georgetown UP, 2007), pp. 45–48; George Saliba, *Islamic Science and the Making of the European Renaissance* (Cambridge, MA: MIT Press, 2007), chapter 6.

The higher education programme of Late Antiquity and its survival in the early Middle Ages

It must be clear that access to ancient wisdom, whether biblical, patristic or pagan, required a formal education that went quite a bit further than learning how to read and write. It had to be aimed at the practice of *scientia* or *philosophia*, as science was called in medieval Latin. In the early Middle Ages, the heart of such a programme of higher education was still the Roman study of the **artes liberales** ('free arts' or 'free skills'), a broad spectrum of disciplines standardised by

Marcus Terentius Varro (116–27 BCE). Varro distinguished nine of them: grammar, dialectics or logic, rhetoric, geometry, arithmetic, astronomy, harmonics (music), medicine and architecture. Over the centuries medicine and architecture were reclassified as 'mechanical' arts. This separation between liberal and mechanical arts, whereby 'liberal' (free) referred to the fact that their practice was free from manual labour, may be the most tragic mistake of classical and medieval learning. It impeded the development of a mechanical infrastructure that would have enabled medieval scientists to systematically experiment under controlled conditions and with the aid of more advanced instruments. Systematic experiments certainly took place now and then, and sophisticated measuring instruments were developed here and there, but systematic and controlled experimentation never developed into a *standard* procedure of scientific research. To do science was largely a combination of reflection on authoritative texts, empirical observation and logical inference, with a dash of mathematics.

From the Carolingian period the seven liberal arts that had remained were usually divided into two groups, the *trivium*, the collective name for the linguistic arts, those connected with the spoken and written word, and the *quadrivium*, the collective name for the four mathematical disciplines. During the early Middle Ages education in the seven 'liberal arts' was supplemented by training in the *ethica*, ethics or moral philosophy.

For all these subjects, there were of course textbooks. For the liberal arts by far the most popular was the encyclopaedia of Martianus Capella, a contemporary and compatriot of Augustine, although some objected to the fact that Martianus had been pagan. Bishop Isidore of Seville (*c.*570–636) borrowed from Martianus in his own treatment of the liberal arts in the beginning of his *Etymologiae*, an encyclopaedic text in twenty books that, with the help of word definitions, attempted to give a systematic overview of all the knowledge available at the time, reaching from grammar in chapter 1 to 'cooking, kitchen

utensils, wagons and harness' in chapter 20. For the whole of the Middle Ages, the *Etymologiae* enjoyed an enormous popularity, apparent from the more than one thousand manuscripts of this vast work still in existence.

Even though the Roman study of the arts remained at the heart of all higher education in the Middle Ages, it served a different purpose from that in Antiquity: to provide the resources and develop the intellectual skills necessary for the 'real work' towards which every intellectual effort should be directed: the study of the Bible, of the great Fathers of the Church and of other important canonical texts such as the creeds and confessions of faith established in Church councils. For therein was every truth worth knowing. Much of the meaning lay hidden, however, and could only be exposed with support from the liberal arts. This was why Augustine cherished the pious hope that every Christian would receive at least an elementary education.

In reality, the number of young people who had access to any form of intellectual education was drastically reduced in the early Middle Ages. Education was only available for a small circle of young people destined for a life as a monk or as a priest. Hence, there were two sorts of places where an education could be acquired: in the schools attached to cathedrals and in monasteries, although it is unlikely that each and every cathedral and abbey had its own school. Moreover, the repeated calls to improve education heard at councils until the twelfth and thirteenth centuries strongly suggest that in many schools little more than elementary grammar and Bible studies were taught; there was certainly no question of generally available full education in the liberal arts. The few schools that did flourish in the early Middle Ages often existed in perhaps unlikely places, such as Anglo-Saxon England. These produced a number of the most prominent intellectuals of the early Middle Ages, the greatest of whom was the Venerable Bede (673–735). Bede spent most of his life in the abbeys of Wearmouth and Jarrow on the east coast of the kingdom of

Northumbria. Among his principal works are a history of Anglo-Saxon England (*Historia ecclesiastica gentis Anglorum*, 'Ecclesiastical History of the English People'), written in classical style, and a survey of the natural sciences (*De natura rerum*, 'On the Nature of Things'), which was partly based on Isidore, but which also betrayed direct knowledge of the most comprehensive encyclopaedia of natural science from Roman Antiquity, the *Historia Naturalis* ('Natural History') by Pliny the Elder (d. 79). Bede's compatriot Alcuin (735–804), who was equally famed as a scholar and who in his later life became a close adviser of Charlemagne, was the product of a cathedral school, that of York.

The Carolingian Renaissance

In addition, wealthy aristocratic households appointed private tutors to cram some of their children for high secular or ecclesiastical offices. The pinnacles of such private schooling facilities were the court schools of kings. Best known is Charlemagne's court school, the most prominent pupil of which was Charlemagne himself, 'an admirer and great collector of wisdom', according to his late ninth-century biographer Notker the Stammerer. Another, earlier, biographer, Einhard, tells us that Charlemagne was instructed by Alcuin in the arts of writing (*sic*), rhetoric, logic calculus, and in particular astronomy. How intensive this study programme was, and to what extent it paid off, is difficult to say. The only proof of intellectual abilities that Charlemagne has left us is his handmade monogram, an ingenious configuration of all letters of the Latin name 'Karolus', which he used as a signature. However, Charlemagne's ambitions extended much further; he may have even been the first king in history who officially promulgated that free elementary education should be accessible to all young people – well, to all young males – 'not only children of unfree status, but also the sons of freeborn men', as the strange formulation in the capitulary

Admonitio Generalis ('General [Public] Order') of 789 ran. This literacy offensive was meant to function as the flywheel of a comprehensive moral-religious revival. Texts from the time referred to the *emendatio populi christiani*, 'the improvement of the Christian people'. This revival, and the reforms of churches and monasteries connected with it, transformed the worldly ruler – entirely in the Roman-Byzantine and also the Arab-Islamic tradition – into the principal guardian of the religious community. Among his primary tasks was that of furthering *pietas* ('piety'), a life which was acceptable to God and which would lead his subjects along the narrow path to salvation.

There was, of course, a wide gulf between such lofty ideals and their realisation. The adornment of the Carolingian court with the flower of international scholarship, and the subsequent appointment of many of these erudite men as bishops and abbots of important monasteries, cannot shroud the fact that the intellectual elite remained tiny. Monasteries were hesitant to open their doors for laymen, even the young and ambitious. More generally, there was a lack of teachers. For that reason there has been some debate over the question of whether it is justified to speak of a 'Carolingian Renaissance', as older textbooks do. If we understand 'Renaissance' as a period in which the continuous effort of humanist scholars and craftsmen to recover, copy and study the largely secular intellectual and artistic heritage of the ancient Greeks and Romans reached an extraordinary intensity, there is something to say in favour of maintaining the concept of Carolingian Renaissance. The really energetic collecting and copying of manuscripts of ancient texts during the Carolingian period, which in part logically followed from Charlemagne's conquest of Italy, was of exceptional significance for western culture. The oldest surviving version of most ancient literary texts dating from the Roman period can be found in Carolingian manuscripts. Without them knowledge of the famous works of Cicero, Virgil, Ovid, Julius Caesar, Tacitus, Seneca and countless others would have been lost forever.

Despite these undisputed achievements, the Carolingian Renaissance did not introduce any changes to the educational curriculum, nor did it bring about the paradigmatic shifts in scientific orientation that were sometimes floating in the air. One example is the encyclopaedic didactic poem of Lucretius, *De natura rerum* (before 55 BCE), which was copied and studied in the Carolingian age, but then forgotten until it was rediscovered in the fifteenth century. If Lucretius's work had become the measure of scientific research in the ninth century, medieval **natural philosophy** might have taken a different course or even brought a scientific revolution closer, because *De natura rerum*, besides a materialist concept of the soul difficult to accept for Christian dogmatic, advocates atomist-mechanical physics that anticipates seventeenth-century developments in natural philosophy. Another example is provided by one of the rare ninth-century experts in the field of physics, John Scotus Eriugena ('John, the Irish-born Scot') (*c.*810–877), court scholar and close friend of Charles the Bald. John was one of the few western scholars who still knew Greek in his time. He translated several works by the neo-Platonist author Pseudo-Dionysius the Areopagite from Greek, which became very popular for the precise description of the celestial hierarchy and the harmonious singing of the angels that could be heard in outer space. But he also, and more sensibly, proposed that not only Venus and Mercury orbited the sun that circled around the stationary earth (a common thought, found in Martianus Capella), but also Mars and Jupiter. This so-called geo-heliocentric theory would soon be forgotten. Instead, Eriugena himself was said to have become a star that roamed the firmament after he died. Clearly, the time was not yet ripe for a Copernican revolution.

But soon after things started to shift and the herald of change was a man of simple origins called Gerbert of Aurillac. As a boy, Gerbert had received an education in the liberal arts in a monastery in the Spanish March, where thanks to Arab influences, a far greater importance was attached to the mathematical subjects of the *quadrivium* than elsewhere in the West. Later, as a teacher in the cathedral school at Rheims, Gerbert created a sensation by using scale models, Arabic numerals and figures that were displayed in the front of the class on large pieces of parchment sewn together – the earliest known use of a flipchart. His familiarity with instruments like the abacus and the astrolabe gave him the mystique of a wizard, while to his enemies he was a 'servant of Satan'. In reality, he became the spiritual adviser of the German king/emperor Otto III (983–1002) and architect of his policy for the 'renewal of the Roman Empire'. Otto appointed him archbishop of Ravenna and later pope (Silvester II, 999–1003).

The rationalist turn and the twelfth-century Renaissance

Gerbert of Aurillac was a harbinger of change, who announced what has been called 'the rationalist turn' in the history of learning and science (Lindberg 2007). This term refers to the sustained and heroic attempts, made by scholars in the eleventh and twelfth centuries, to replace irrational and magical explanations of natural phenomena with explanations based on rational demonstration supported by logical argumentation. Wasn't God's greatest gift to human beings the power of reason, so why not use this power to penetrate and expose the miracle of divine creation?

This new, optimistic attitude fits into a broader cultural revolution that is generally called 'the Renaissance of the twelfth century', after the eponymous book by the American medievalist Charles Homer Haskins, published in 1927. Contradicting the title of his own book, Haskins painted the elite culture of the twelfth century not so much as a rebirth of Antiquity, but as a magnificent revival of literary and intellectual life, the result of a 'general quickening of the spirit'. Many attempts have since been made to give a more exact explanation of the concept 'twelfth-century Renaissance'. Some have seen it as a sort of Italian Renaissance, taking place three centuries earlier, whose glorious epicentre was France, not Italy, but which otherwise shared the same main features: a flowering of humanism and a clear recognition of human individuality. Others have given the twelfth-century Renaissance a character of its own by embedding it in the exceptional dynamics of the years between about 1000 and 1200. Sustained population growth and rapid urbanisation, increasing geographical and social mobility, the hesitant start of state government and public administration, the growth of international trade, the colonisation movements and the Crusades formed the background to a new spiritual hunger, to a new openness of mind and self-awareness, to a drive for intellectual renewal and superiority; even to a real belief in progress.

Two aspects of this cultural-intellectual revolution that are of particular relevance here were the growing importance of urban schools (cathedral schools or schools attached to urban monasteries and chapters) as centres of learning, and the hunt for new translations of Greek and Arab texts to satisfy the intellectual appetite. Some of the oldest schools for higher education in the Mediterranean – notably the medical school of Salerno, first mentioned in the middle of the ninth century – may have had a continuous existence since Late Antiquity, and profited from their commercial relations with Egypt (see Chapter 7). But the obvious new loci for higher education were the thriving commercial centres of northern France and northern and central Italy. The Carolingian kings of Italy were active in establishing new schools in Lombard towns, as were the popes in central Italy; by the first half of the eleventh century Roman law was studied in Bologna. But 'public schools' are also mentioned in sources from the same period, related to English and Flemish towns; they would have been instituted by the enlightened Danish king Cnut the Great, and the local merchants' guilds respectively. These (urban) *scholae* ('schools'), the

forerunners of the universities, were at the very centre of the new humanistic ideas and methods. This close link was aptly expressed in the term **scholasticism**, which broadly refers to the education in the *scholae*. In addition, scholasticism has acquired a narrower, technical meaning in the sense of a particular analytic method based on Aristotelian logic, which was adopted in every subject in schools and universities from the twelfth century onwards, both in teaching and in the production of textbooks.

By the beginning of the twelfth century, the Greco-Roman legacy was as yet not fully exploited, certainly not in the natural sciences, mathematics and logic. We have already mentioned one important reason for this: most elementary texts in these fields were written in Greek, which, with a few exceptions, was no longer known by western intellectuals in the early Middle Ages. Renewed acquaintance with ancient Greek learning depended, therefore, on an increase in translating. At the end of the eleventh century, there were two major channels, the Byzantine world and the Islamic world. The great conquests of the first century following the establishment of Islam in the Middle East and North Africa had brought the Arabs into contact with the achievements of ancient Greek philosophy. These were avidly absorbed, and then expanded in different fields. Far earlier than in the West, the Arabic world showed a serious interest in sciences such as mathematics, astronomy, optics and medicine.

During the eleventh century, Spain and Sicily served as conduits for Arabic knowledge to the West. The conquest in 1085 of Toledo, the centre of Moorish culture, and the establishment of Norman power in Sicily at about the same time, were strong stimuli to the intellectual encounter between East and West. The Christian elite's hunger for new knowledge overcame its aversion to Islam, and some openly admired the scientific achievements of the infidel. One of them, the Englishman Adelard of Bath (*c.*1070–1150), scoured the Mediterranean in his search for Arabic knowledge which he equated with independent and critical rational thought and considered far superior to slavishly following '*auctoritas*'. He was the first to translate the complete text of two elementary mathematical treatises, Euclid's *Elements* and the *Algebra* of al-Khwarizmi (d. *c*.850), the bane of every schoolchild even today. It is thanks to al-Khwarizmi that we use 'Arabic' numerals for counting, although we should not forget that the Arabs brought this notation from Hindu India.

The most productive of the translators was an Italian, Gerard of Cremona, who in the middle of the twelfth century spent some time in Toledo translating between 70 and 100 Greek and Arab treatises from Arabic into Latin. In addition to *Analytica Posteriora*, a cornerstone of Aristotle's philosophy of science, these included *Technè*, Galen's principal medical work, and Ptolemy's astronomical compilation, *The Great Treatise*, better known under its Arabic name, *Almagest*, works which were of the greatest importance for the further support and refinement of the western view of man and the world.

Translations made directly from Greek became available not much later, thanks to the efforts of Italians from cities with commercial interests in the eastern Mediterranean, such as Venice and Pisa. Even before the middle of the twelfth century James of Venice had translated most of Aristotle's logical treatises from the Greek. These direct translations were important because Arabic – a non-Indo-European 'intermediate language' – often corrupted the quality of the original Greek versions. The Fourth Crusade and the establishment of the Latin Empire (1204–1261) gave a further powerful spur to the translation and collection of Greek texts, because during that period Greece was under western rule and western scholars had unfettered access to the treasures of Greek libraries. The Flemish Dominican William of Moerbeke (*c*.1215–1286) was one of those who took advantage of the situation. After he had been appointed bishop of Corinth, he found the time and opportunity to translate some fifty

works from Greek into Latin, including almost all the works of Aristotle and Archimedes. In the same period, Michael Scot (*c*.1175–*c*.1232), a Scotsman who earned himself a reputation as Emperor Frederick II's court astrologer, alchemist and personal physician in Sicily, provided translations, all from Arabic, of Aristotle's *Metaphysics*. Several major commentaries on Aristotle were translated by the Andalusian philosopher Ibn Rushd (1126–1198), generally known in the West as Averroës.

Making sense of the world in new ways

The two main products of early scholastic scholarship were Platonic naturalism and Aristotelian logic. Both of these fields of enquiry were, each on its own terms, telling symptoms of a burning intellectual desire to make sense of the world in a new way.

Platonic naturalism, as an attempt to understand the evolution of the natural order of the universe, was quite fashionable among a group of scholars in the first half of the twelfth century, many of whom seem to have been connected in one way or another to the cathedral school of Chartres. Central to their ideas was a conception of the creation of the universe that was taken from *Timaios*, the only one of Plato's 36 dialogues that at this point in time was within reach of scholars in the Latin West, thanks to a Latin translation, provided with an ample commentary, made by the Roman philosopher Calcidius, who lived at the time of Emperor Constantine. There were two reasons why Platonist naturalism did not really catch on. First, doing physics on the basis of *Timaios* as a scientific alternative to Genesis did not enlarge insight into the laws of nature very much. Plato's dialogue (like Genesis!) was too poetical, too symbolist, too imprecise on which to build a programme of scientific research. To get any further, the knowledge base had to be extended. Second, attempts to accommodate

PLATE 8.2 The 'three philosophies' (natural, rational, moral) reign as a three-headed queen over the seven liberal arts. Gregor Reisch, *Margarita Philosophica* (Freiburg 1508).

Timaios as an acceptable authoritative text were doomed to founder in the end on insuperable dogmatic problems. *Timaios* presents the creator as a divine master craftsman who after a Big Bang-like creative act at the beginning stays outside, or rather functions as cosmic background radiation – radiating perfection. He does not interfere with humanity's fate. In Plato's view, the actual ruling of the universe was left to a force called the 'World Soul', which was not meant as a metaphor. This imagery proved impossible to fit into Christian orthodoxy, despite all kinds of attempts in that direction by William of Conches and other naturalist philosophers amongst others, by identifying this World Soul with the Holy Spirit of the Christian Trinity, or with divine Providence. So, in the end, William of Conches was prepared to

hang his head if his admired Greek master proved to be wrong, and to openly declare: 'I am a Christian and not a member of Plato's Academy.' William's soulmate Thierry of Chartres went even further: after his heroic but vain attempt to solve the mystery of the divine Trinity with Platonic mathematics, he voluntarily left the cathedral school of Chartres, dropped his title of doctor and retired in a convent.

Nevertheless, William, Thierry and their intellectual partners signalled something that could not be missed, namely that separating the realms of science (which was about nature) and religion (which was about God, who stood above, that is, outside, nature) was worth considering. This signal receded into the background for a while, but, as we shall see, it made a deafening comeback in the second half of the thirteenth century.

It was Gerbert of Aurillac who, around the turn of the first millennium, had struck a new course in higher education by introducing certain novelties in his classroom that improved the quality of the liberal arts curriculum. Apart from the flip-chart and the scale model already mentioned, he introduced the *disputatio* or oral debate as a didactic art in his teaching of rhetoric. In addition, he made more room in the curriculum for lessons in logic, or dialectics, in order to improve his pupils' debating skills. The field of logic or dialectic was first developed by Aristotle, and the Aristotelian basics of logic had not been entirely lost during the early Middle Ages, mainly thanks to Anicius Boethius (c.480–524), a statesman and philosopher in Ostrogothic Italy. Boethius translated Aristotle's elementary treatises on logic, together with an introduction by the neo-Platonist Porphyrius (end of the third century CE), into Latin, and added his own commentaries about the theory of argumentation. However, very little of this had permeated the teaching of logic in the arts curriculum until Gerbert made the case for the reintroduction of what later came to be known as 'old logic'. From the beginning of the twelfth century Aristotle's more advanced treatises on dialectics were rescued from oblivion, constituting what we refer to as the 'new logic'. Only one work was still missing, the *Analytica Posteriora*, which was eventually translated first from the Arabic and soon afterwards (*c*.1150) from the Greek. Aristotle's complete works on logic, sometimes called *Organon* or 'Instrument', were available to the West once again.

The enormous importance of the revival of dialectics/logic as a fully developed academic discipline must not be underestimated. In a world with very little insight into the workings of natural phenomena, at least, not at the level of physical laws and chemical processes, and in which there were few impulses to expand that insight, dialectics – the art of logical reasoning – provided the best possible intellectual anchor to bring order into what must have seemed infinitely varied and complex. In this light the scientific work of the first generation of intellectuals, who combined their extraordinary knowledge of authoritative Christian texts with a sound training in the 'new' Aristotelian logic, radiated an almost shameless optimism and self-confidence. They thought that all of life could be understood by using logic to make a systematic record of the relationships between man and nature and, above all, between humankind and God. The real motive was the growing realisation that the traditional authorities (the Bible and Church Fathers) were in themselves too often contradictory. Many scholars were convinced that inconsistencies could be confronted and then eradicated only by careful and logical analysis of texts. This presented them for the first time with the fundamental epistemological question: to what extent does language, processed into written texts, represent perceptual, 'objective' reality?

From the polemic between Master Berengar of Tours and Abbot Lanfranc of Le Bec about the essence of the Eucharist (see Box 8.3), it appears that Aristotelian logic was given an entirely new dimension when it was applied to matters of Christian dogma. The value of this application was contentious from the outset. Its supporters believed that God and the divine became more approachable through a process of rational thought. Opponents such as Peter Damian (1007–1072), one of the leaders of the Gregorian reform movement, were equally firm in their conviction that the possibilities of reason were limited in that respect, that the dogmas of the Holy Church were threatened by rationalism or that God could only be found by a mystic path, that of non-rational contemplation. In the middle of the twelfth century, these contrasting views were personified in the Cistercian Bernard of Clairvaux, 'the most vigilant watchdog western Christendom had ever had' (Southern 2001), and his opposite, the famous logician and theologian, Peter Abelard. To Abelard's maxim, 'we can only come to [rational] inquiry through doubt and only through inquiry can we reach the truth', Bernard's blistering response was:

> Be done! Away with the mere thought that the Christian faith knows any of the limits suggested by those academics who doubt everything and know nothing. I am certain of one sentence of Paul, 'For I know him whom I have believed' (II Tim. 1:12). And I know for certain that I cannot be brought into confusion.

But there was no stopping the advance of the new approach. The ultimate confidence in what human reason could achieve stemmed from the rational proofs of God's existence dating from this time, such as those made by Anselm of Aosta (1033–1109), who followed Lanfranc first as abbot of Le Bec and later as archbishop of Canterbury. In the end, however, Anselm had to admit that human reason was not sufficiently adequate to fully understand God and that his drive to prove that God existed was prompted by his unshakeable *a priori* conviction that God did exist! One of Anselm's maxims, taken from the Old Testament book of Isaiah, was *credo ut intelligam*, 'I believe in order that I may understand.' However powerful an instrument human reason might be, Anselm found that deeper insight was not possible

BOX 8.3 'THIS IS MY BODY': LEARNED DISCUSSION ABOUT TRANSUBSTANTIATION IN THE EUCHARIST

One of the most renowned debates of early scholasticism concerned the real meaning of the sacrament of the Eucharist. It brought Berengar, a teacher at the cathedral school of Tours, into conflict with Lanfranc of Pavia, abbot of the Norman monastery of Le Bec and, from 1066 until his death in 1089, archbishop of Canterbury. The question was what exactly took place during mass in the ritual commemoration of the Last Supper, when the priest, while breaking bread and drinking wine, speaks the words, 'This is my body' and 'This is my blood'. Nobody could contend that the host had outwardly changed from bread into human flesh or the wine into human blood, yet nobody dared to deny that Christ was literally present after the consecration of the bread and wine. Both Berengar and Lanfranc, therefore, saw the sacrament of the Eucharist as a *figura* or *similitudo*, a symbolically charged metaphor. But in Lanfranc's interpretation the metaphor contained a mysterious manifestation of the 'naked truth', and pointed directly to a higher spiritual reality. Bread and wine do not turn into actual flesh and blood, but are experienced as such through the consecration. Berengar found this absurd: for him, the words spoken at the consecration were a linguistic designation (*significatio*) of the living body of Christ. Only through linguistic and dialectical study of that application of meaning (*significare*) would it perhaps be possible to reveal the deeper truth of the Eucharist.

What is interesting is that both opponents used two fundamental concepts of Aristotelian logic, *substantia* and *accidentia*. Aristotle had introduced these concepts in order to be able to make a distinction between what we would now call the essential, tangible substrate of an object (*substantia*) and its inessential, external features or characteristics (*accidentia*). Lanfranc's contention was that the change of bread and wine was indeed essential (of substance) but not outwardly visible (accidental) – hence his solution has been called 'transubstantiation'. According to the physics of Aristotle, such transformation of substance without the *accidentia* changing also was impossible. Hence it could take place only because God had intervened miraculously during the consecration of the host and sacramental wine, briefly suspending the laws of nature. Berengar refuted this interpretation on logical grounds, and also produced the linguistic argument that in the formula 'This is my body', 'this' could only refer to the host which at that selfsame moment was raised on high by the celebrant. Clever as it was, Berengar's interpretation did not survive because at the Fourth Lateran Council (1215) the doctrine of transubstantiation became official dogma.

without first believing. His other famous dictum, *fides quaerens intellectum*, 'faith seeking support in reason', stresses the crucial importance of faith. The difference in nuance between these two maxims expresses perfectly the contradictory feelings of devout men like Anselm who struggled with the relationship between faith and reason, which for Anselm coincided with the mysterious, yet emotionally tangible, and therefore knowable, connection between self and God.

Long after Anselm, theologians who were trained not only in Aristotelian logic but also in Aristotelian physics (which Anselm was not) made new attempts to prove God's existence by combining reason (logic) with empirical evidence. The most famous of these was Thomas Aquinas (see below), who construed a number of arguments for the existence of God *a posteriori*, which means that they all led from creation (the product) back to the creator (the producer). According to modern logic and science they are all flawed by either the refusal to consider the possibility of infinite regress or of the eternity of the universe (like most Greek philosophers had been prepared to do), or the assumption that a first and final cause of everything cannot be other than (the Christian) God.

The man who finally made Aristotelian logic a cornerstone of scholastic rationalism was the Breton Peter Abelard (1079–1142). As a young man he acquired a great reputation in Paris, first as a freely established teacher of dialectics, and later as a teacher of theology at the cathedral school of Notre Dame. His treatise *Sic et non* (literally 'Yes and No', meaning 'Pro and Con') shows his approach as a logician and is particularly interesting from a methodological point of view. For the first time the scholastic method of working can be seen in action. The text consists of 158 theological topics, **quaestiones**; each one opens with a question, after which the pros and cons of the possible answers are weighed up systematically and using the technique of logical analysis, before drawing a balanced conclusion. This treatment of *quaestiones* became an increasingly fixed component of higher education in the course of the twelfth century.

Nowadays we do not find this very surprising, but we should not forget that, until then, intellectuals were much burdened with *auctoritas* and by modern standards did not have a very critical approach to their source texts. Numerous errors and contradictions in the body of authoritative texts came to light through Abelard's methodical approach. His aim was most certainly not to cast doubt upon the deeper truth of the texts that were so authoritative for Christian faith, but to critically examine the versions of the text in which they survived. Known by friend and foe alike as 'our Aristotle' and as *peripateticus palatinus* (literally, 'Aristotle's pupil from Le Pallet [Abelard's birthplace]', but also meaning 'the paladin of Aristotle' or 'the vagrant from Le Pallet'), the Breton scholar even surpassed his Greek master; witness, for instance, his treatment of so-called universals (see Box 8.4).

BOX 8.4 MAKING SENSE OF THE WORLD THROUGH CONCEPTS: LOGIC, METAPHYSICS AND THE STATUS OF UNIVERSALS

Two ways to gain a firmer grip on reality are the study of physics (which is aimed at establishing the laws of nature, and understand their working) and the study of language (which is aimed at understanding how we process cognitive information from the world around us into a system of arbitrary signals directed towards communication). In the development of both fields giant strides were made by the Greek philosopher Aristotle.

Let us have a closer look at the language part. If we want to confront reality with language it makes sense to distinguish between 'words' and 'thoughts', between words for concrete things and abstract concepts, and between 'propositions' (assertive statements) that are valid and those that are not. This is the task of logic.

Aristotelian logic divides all that can be into four classes: there are particular things of two kinds and there are universal things (or concepts) of two kinds; particulars are either non-accidental (like 'this horse') or accidental (like '[this horse's] whiteness'), whereas universals are either essential (like 'horse' [as a species]) or accidental (like 'whiteness' [in general]). Now according to Aristotle, who contradicted Plato on this point, only particulars exist in physical reality – we can see 'this horse' walking around, and admire its (particular) whiteness, but not 'whiteness' in general, nor the species 'horse'.

Most of us will probably agree with Aristotle on this point. Still, Aristotle's point of view may raise problems of internal contradiction, and some of these have been tackled – and solved – by the two most brilliant logicians of the European Middle Ages, the Breton Peter Abelard and the English Franciscan, William of Ockham.

Consider for instance the sentence 'Fido is a dog', in which 'dog' is an essential universal because 'is a dog' means 'belongs to the species dog'. Consequently, the rule 'only particulars exist' seems to be false, because if Fido really exists, so does his dog-ness. Abelard argued however that the universal 'dog' is connected to the existing Fido only by 'signification', that is to say by attaching meaning to Fido in two different ways: by nomination (by calling Fido 'dog'), and by mental imaging (by intentional thinking of Fido as a specimen of the species 'dog'). This makes it possible for us to accept that there are universals without attributing to them any real existence or 'ontological status' as philosophers would say.

For this reason, Abelard is sometimes numbered among the 'ontological reductionists', philosophers who wanted to reduce the categories of being(s) that according to them really existed. Foremost among them was William of Ockham who went much further than Aristotle and Abelard by stating that of all particulars only non-accidental ones ('this horse') had real existence, plus only one of the nine categories that Aristotle distinguished among the accidental particulars, namely those of quality (such as '[this horse's] whiteness'). His slogan for 'ontological parsimony', known as 'Ockham's razor', is famous: *entia non sunt multiplicanda preter necessitatem* ('plurality is not to be posited without necessity').

One of the paths Ockham followed to implement his reductionist programme in formal logic was the development of his theory of *intentiones animae* (literally 'intentions of the soul'), meaning the 'inner words' that (according to medieval philosophers) we use to silently denominate our mental images. Ockham believed that *both* such 'mental/inner words' *and* spoken/uttered words referred directly to objects/things in the extra-mental world. He also believed that there were two types of *intentiones animae*: 'primary' ones to signify existing particulars (such as 'this horse'), and 'secondary' ones to refer to universals that did not really exist (such as 'horse' [as a species]). In a similar manner he distinguished between 'terms of first imposition' to indicate spoken words referring to things/particulars and 'terms of second imposition' to indicate spoken words referring to concepts/universals.

In an even more subtler and more sophisticated way than Abelard's theory of mental imaging, Ockham's theory of *intentiones animae* enables us to refer in different ways to universals or general concepts, without having to accept that they really exist.

Sources: *The Stanford Encyclopedia of Philosophy*, s.v. 'Aristotle's Categories'; John Marenbon, *Medieval Philosophy* (New York: Routledge, 2006), pp. 139–143, 297–300.

In addition to being a competent logician, Abelard was, to say the least, a colourful figure, as brilliant as he was arrogant, a man who 'made enemies with the dedication of a stamp-collector' (Brooke 1989). 'Truly, the man takes pleasure in disputing everything, be it matters of faith or matters of the world', sighed one of his many critics with a mixture of dislike and admiration. It comes as no surprise, therefore, that Abelard's views were twice condemned by the Church, first in 1121, and then again in 1140 (in the presence of the pope), in both cases after he had burnt his fingers, with logical bravura, of course, on the treacherous doctrine of the Holy Trinity. On the second occasion, Abelard was declared a heretic and sentenced to eternal silence. It was Bernard of Clairvaux who voiced the accusations, closing his speech with the words, 'Peter Abelard, from now on stick to your schoolboys and your young ladies.' The latter was a malicious reference to the event which brought Abelard more fame during his lifetime than his philosophical works – the turbulent relationship he had earlier with Heloise, niece of a canon of the Notre Dame in Paris. When she became pregnant he married her in secret and was castrated by Heloise's enraged relatives after they found out. Both Heloise and Abelard then retired to a convent. We know of this from Abelard's frank autobiography, *Historia calamitatum* ('The Story of my Calamities') and from the passionate, but above all devout, letters that the now separated couple wrote to each other. Although their authenticity sometimes has been questioned, these documents are proof of the existence of a great sensitivity that was directed not only towards God and the saints but also towards personal introspection and interpersonal relationships.

In this connection, another tract by Abelard, *Scito te ipsum* ('Know Thyself', a reference to a saying from a Greek oracle and also the motto of the Roman emperor-philosopher, Marcus Aurelius) is considered a milestone. For the first time in western Christian thought it is clearly contended that in judging sins (or crimes), the intention of the sinner (or criminal) – or more specifically, the conscious decision of a person to commit a sin (or a crime) – should weigh as heavily as the sin/crime itself (whether or not it was committed in the end). For Abelard, morality was thus always internal and personal. External penance without internal repentance and recovery of one's own moral integrity was completely meaningless. These ideas resonated with contemporary spirituality (Chapter 6), with the revival of theological interest in the matter of predestination and with the greater emphasis put on admission of sin and repentance in the confessional. At the same time, they reveal the existence of a realisation that human individuals are complex, self-conscious and responsible personalities who have interior lives and who are equipped with diverse and unique characteristics.

The formation of universities

We have seen that the only avenues of intellectual advancement during the early Middle Ages were the schools attached to cathedrals and monasteries. Considered in this light, the formation of the universities can be seen as a liberation movement, gradually detaching higher education from the monopoly of monks and bishops. This happened against a background of three very different situations. First, there was a tendency in the great *scholae* for teachers or students, or both together, to organise themselves into corporations in order to look after their own interests. The common medieval Latin term for this type of corporation was **universitas**, which could very well be translated as 'guild'. Second, the growing demand for higher learning led to a broadening of the supply of education. Outside the scope of the liberal arts, specialised schools began to appear for the study of medicine and written law, that is Roman Justinian law or Church canonical law. The special teaching of the Bible and Church Fathers, which traditionally had crowned the study of the liberal arts, gradually developed into a separate theological discipline, whose aim was not, as it had been before, to investigate the nature of God, but in addition, more generally, to study the Church and its doctrine. In those towns where there was more than one *schola*, this diversification in higher education led quite naturally to their working together, so that the first large schools with a number of faculties or branches came into being. Larger schools, which attracted students from far and wide, now started to call themselves *studium generale* ('principal centre of study') to distinguish themselves from the small ones. Third, following the resolution of the Third Lateran Council in 1179, the Church relinquished its monopoly on education when it compelled the bishops to yield their exclusive rights to issue 'licences to teach everywhere' (*licentiae ubique docendi*) to recognised schools in their dioceses.

The teaching establishment that we now know as a university evolved gradually from all these developments, although it is difficult to say exactly when this happened. Nor did the liberation of higher education sketched above take place without a struggle. From the beginning, the schools were assured of the not insignificant support of the popes and of many rulers who made higher education the spearhead of their policy to improve the quality of government and the officials involved in it. There was fierce opposition, however, from bishops, chapters and the monastic world. In Paris, for example, the chancellor or bishop's secretary disputed the infringement of his unique authority to grant the *licentia docendi* which he would never give up. That the share of the monastic schools in higher education decreased was partly the fault of the monks themselves, for they had been severely critical of the direction in which higher education was moving. We already mentioned how Bernard of Clairvaux, the eloquent and intimidating leader of the new monastic order of the Cistercians, hurled abuse at Abelard, calling him a danger to society and a heathen and a monster. But eight years later, in 1148, Bernard himself was

discredited after he had attacked another master logician, Gilbert of Poitiers, because Bernard had never been properly trained in the schools and therefore did not grasp the intricacies of the new dialectics. This was exactly the problem. Since canon law forbade the Cistercians and other monks to attend a school outside the monastery, they ran the risk of becoming intellectually isolated by not responding to the new directions that the study of the arts was taking. The mendicant orders, especially the Dominicans, recognised this problem and solved it by founding their own schools in large towns like Paris and Cologne, which, strictly speaking, remained outside the universities. They had their own teachers but in this way they could still keep in touch with what was happening on the frontier of science. These schools were intended primarily for members of their orders, but very soon opened their door to other interested students. The example set by the mendicant orders was copied in time by other religious orders, including the Cistercians. It would soon turn out to be a recipe for a new round of conflicts with the secular scholars.

The process of trial and error, of support and opposition in the realm of administration and organisation can be best explained in the light of developments in the two most important centres of learning in western Europe, Paris and Bologna. In twelfth-century Paris there were, next to the old cathedral school of Notre Dame, two other schools on the left bank of the Seine which attracted crowds of students: that of Saint-Victor (a convent of regular canons) and the public school that was connected to the Benedictine abbey of Mont Sainte Geneviève. In addition, a number of small schools appeared, many of them no more than a gathering of students with one teacher. Even before 1150, Paris was a mecca for young people from all over Europe; by 1200 it had between 3,000 and 4,000 students, perhaps 10 per cent of the town's population. There were nearly 150 *magistri* teaching there, more than 100 in the arts, 20 each in medicine and law, and 8 in theology – these fields of study were called 'faculties' for the first time in 1220. All masters, whether teaching in one of the schools or practising privately – which was perfectly allowed provided one had a *licentia docendi* – had joined together to form a guild of teachers, first referred to in 1208. It may have been created to guard over professional standards and professorial behaviour, but doubtless also to form a united front against possible interference by the bishop of Paris and his chancellor. Moreover, the influx of students caused all sorts of problems, varying from the organisation of teaching programmes and the form that lectures and exams should take to strained relationships between town and gown (including soaring room prices and regular street fights between students and shopkeepers). All parties concerned (bishop and secular authorities, townspeople, teachers and students) realised that matters concerning education in the schools required better regulation. This did actually happen in around 1200, for in that year 'the commonality of the masters and students' received a number of royal privileges, which were somewhat toned down ten years later. Two provisions were of immense significance. First, the *scolares* ('scholars', being masters and students) were placed under special royal protection from physical violence and damage to property. Second, they were placed under Church law: only the trial of very serious crimes would be heard in the royal court of law. This in fact put the *scolares* legally on an equal footing with 'real' clergy, of which by now there were large numbers. This measure was to have far-reaching consequences, for it became the norm for all recognised universities of Europe when the pope confirmed the Paris privilege in 1231 in the bull *Parens scientiarum*. It meant that members of university communities everywhere stood outside the episcopal as well as the secular system of justice, and enjoyed clerical status.

The oldest known statute of the Paris university, issued in 1215 by the papal legate and master of theology Robert of Courçon, despite its messy make-up, regulated a number of things that were vital to the university's functioning, such as minimum qualifications for teachers; the minimum number of terms a teacher had to stay; the composition of curricula; rules of good behaviour; the submission of students to teachers; and, last but not least, the funerals of masters who had passed away. In addition to bringing clarity to what may have been unclear for too long, these rules also stressed the new institution's corporate identity by articulating some of its 'common values, objectives, and ideals' (Ferruolo 1985).

As to its internal organisation, the University of Paris basically developed into a federation of four faculties, of which the arts faculty was by far the largest. Before the middle of the fourteenth century the number of its masters had risen to over 500, at least five times the total number of masters connected to the other three higher faculties (theology, law and medicine) together. This explains why the arts faculty alone was led by a rector (and not by a dean), while its thousands of students were subdivided into four 'nations' (the Gallican, English, Picardian and Norman nations), each with its own procurator or proctor, and beadle, who was responsible for the day-to-day running of teaching activities. All things concerning curricula, syllabi, examinations and degrees were organised at the faculty level. The university as a whole was governed by a board, led by the rector of the arts faculty; its other members were the three deans of the other faculties and the proctors of the four 'nations' of the arts faculty. Since the bishop of Paris had always refused to cede his power to confer degrees (the *licentia docendi*), the chancellor of the cathedral chapter remained vital to the ratification of degrees; the actual work, that is, the conferring of degrees, was traditionally left to the chancellor of St Geneviève who also acted as the university board's financial expert.

In these early days, the University of Paris did not yet have its own buildings, let alone a university 'campus'. Teaching space was always a problem. Teachers did their lectures and disputations at home, in halls or churches, or in empty rooms that were rented in convents or private houses. Often only the teacher had a chair; the students would sit on straw on the floor. The first piece of real estate the University of Paris acquired was a meadow, to be used for recreation!

The background to the University of Bologna's foundation was very different and had its origins in the training of lawyers unrelated to the Church. The Roman custom of recording business transactions between private individuals in writing had never disappeared in Italy. It was done by professional scribes, *notai* (Latin *notarii*, whence 'notary'), who were trained in the use of correct, legally valid notation. The revival of the study of Roman Justinian law in the second half of the eleventh century gave a powerful stimulus to notarial training (which was initially part of the *trivium* curriculum). Since Roman law was imperial law, the development of these notarial schools into a university was closely connected to imperial intervention, evident in the events of the Diet of Roncaglia in 1158, for which the emperor, Frederick Barbarossa, had received support from lawyers from Bologna (Chapter 5). Shortly afterwards, and in appreciation, the emperor put all students of law in the Empire under his special legal protection.

Unlike the University of Paris, which formally started as a guild of teachers, Bologna was a typical students' university, because student unions, usually called nations, had a firmer grip on the local law schools than the teachers' guild had. By 1200 the number of student nations was restricted to two, one for Italians and one for non-Italians. They rapidly grew into powerful organisations which, if necessary, would enforce demands made on the teachers or Bologna's commune government by shutting everything down through strikes or threatening to leave the town and continue their studies elsewhere. Two of these threats were actually carried out and the academic exodus led to the foundation of the universities of Vicenza in 1204 (which was not a success) and Padua in 1222 (which would become one of the most reputable universities of Italy). However, this did not break the reputation of the legal schools

of Bologna that were tacitly recognised as a university at about the same time. A law school existed in Montpellier as early as 1160, allegedly founded by experts who had come from Bologna. At that time, a medical school was already functioning in Montpellier; it was first mentioned in 1137. That may have been influenced by the advanced knowledge in Islamic Spain.

Besides the great universities of Paris and Bologna, the thirteenth and fourteenth centuries saw the origins of dozens of other universities. One would expect them to have originated in large towns or densely urbanised regions, but this was only partly so. The two oldest universities in England, for example, those of Oxford and Cambridge, were established in relatively small, albeit old, towns that had no bishops (and therefore no cathedral schools), and not in urban centres of more importance like London, Winchester, York or even Canterbury. The University of Cambridge was founded in 1209 after a secession of masters and students from Oxford, following a violent riot which had ended in the execution of a number of students. The German Empire, by no means a backward region in the twelfth and thirteenth centuries, was devoid of a university for a long time. The oldest was at Prague, in Bohemia (1348), followed in the second half of the fourteenth century by Vienna, Erfurt, Heidelberg and Cologne, although Cologne already had two illustrious *studia* for higher learning long before – the cathedral school and the already mentioned school of the Dominican Order, founded in 1248. The relatively densely populated Low Countries did not have a university until 1425. It was established not in Flanders but at Louvain, in Brabant. Of a special type were universities that were created 'out of nothing', which means that they were founded on royal initiative and always with royal or papal approval. The oldest were the universities of Salamanca in Castile (1218) and Naples (1224).

All in all, between 1200 and 1500, around 75 universities were set up all over Europe. Some were small and specialised (such as the medical

MAP 8.1 European universities in the late Middle Ages

school at Salerno and the legal school in Orléans), others large and offering a broader range of subjects (Paris and Oxford). It is estimated that between 1350 and 1500 a total of 750,000 students registered at universities – all male; women were not allowed. Then, as now, many students did not stay at one place, but took courses in several centres of learning, following specialisations or going to teachers of renown. This gave rise to the image of wandering students or *vagantes*; they were sung of in bawdy songs.

Many peripheral phenomena that are still characteristic of student life date back to this formative period, like the positive relation between numbers of students and numbers of pubs, rituals of ragging, student housing problems and the tricky

business of private visits by members of the opposite sex. By the beginning of the fourteenth century the small university town of Oxford had over 200 ale houses, while in 1340 firm measures against excesses committed at the ragging of freshmen were taken by the University of Paris. In the same city, members of the Sorbonne college – admittedly, all of them theologians – who received ladies in their private room were fined sixpence. In fifteenth-century Heidelberg teachers or students who were caught in a brothel were not just fined but also blacklisted.

In agreement with their formally clerical status students were required to be tonsured and dress uniformly, in clerical style. Of course, this precept was interpreted most liberally; in Cambridge, students were soon accused of sporting long hair and long beards, of dressing in fur and wearing chequered pointed shoes (that incomprehensible whim of late medieval fashion), of adorning themselves with rings and other jewellery, and of wasting precious time at the tennis court. In general, medieval student life was far more violent than it is nowadays, probably because many medieval students had a noble background, and were used to thrashing things out when their privileges were infringed or, worse, when they felt their honour was offended, certainly by ordinary townspeople. Sometimes, innocent brawls or verbal disputes ended in real street battles, in which people were killed, as in Paris in 1200 and in Oxford in 1306.

Up to a point, and also quite recognisable for those of us who have witnessed the explosion of university education over the past half century, universities were prepared to answer the enormous influx of students with an easing of study programmes. And then as now this touched on a sore spot with conservatives. A revealing testimony can be found in the works of John of Salisbury (*c.* 1115–1180), a man of humble origins who in one way or another had managed to become a student in the schools of Paris and then started a successful career as a secretary and diplomat. In one of his books, called *Metalogicon* ('In Defense of the Artes Logicales') John, despite being himself a shining example of upward social mobility through intellectual study, deplored the consequences of the broadening appeal of higher education that was taking shape during his lifetime: the lack of motivation and the laziness of many students, the appointment of mediocre teachers and their ever narrower specialisation, the inevitable relaxation of the reading list that followed. The study of the arts, and especially the *trivium* part, threatened to be downgraded to a 'frying pan of verbiage' (*sartago loquendi*).

Although quite a lot of students may have been aristocrats, there were few obstacles for inquisitive young men of modest means to enter university. Of course they had to be able to read and write, and to understand Latin (all courses were taught in Latin), but entrance fees in both grammar schools and universities were low, and from early on there were scholarships for poor students. Universities could even have a graduated system of (yearly) entrance fees; in Valence this ran from nothing at all for poor students to three florins for wealthy students of noble birth. An alternative way for poor young men to get educated was to enter a religious order; the mendicant orders especially were easily accessible. The reverse side of this relative accessibility was that universities tended to be poorly equipped and that teachers were not normally salaried. Secular masters often lived from (multiple) prebends, but they also accepted fees from their students. Only in Italy did university professors receive salaries, at least in the late Middle Ages. These could vary widely (depending on the master's reputation and experience) and were paid by the communal governments, who contracted masters for periods of four to five years (but these terms could be renewed). If lectures were missed or attracted less than a minimum of students, this was deducted from the master's salary.

In the north, the foundation of so-called colleges must be seen as an answer to several of these problems: the housing shortage, the lack of esprit de corps, the large differences in earnings of teachers and in the income of students. This also means that the objectives of colleges were quite different, even if they all were charitable institutions in the sense that they were founded by private benefactors. In Paris, colleges were originally student hostels that offered free board and lodging to poor students; the oldest one was the Collège des Dix-Huit ('College of the 18'), founded in 1180 by a wealthy Londoner, Josse, whose example would be followed by dozens of others. However, the famous Collège de Sorbonne, founded in 1255, was built as a communal residence for *teachers* in theology. It would become the model for colleges at English universities, the oldest of which was Merton College in Oxford (founded in 1274). They were communities of 'fellows', university teachers from various faculties who were incorporated as members for life and hence were assured of board and income.

University scholarship in action: grades, curriculum, teaching methods

University studies in the Middle Ages took a long time. A minimum of seven years was originally prescribed for a full education in the liberal arts: two years for undergraduate courses, three to four years for the baccalaureate (bachelor; BA) and then another two to three years to obtain the title of *magister artium* (master of (liberal) arts, MA) with the teaching qualification, *licentia docendi*, attached to it. Higher studies were equally long – certainly theology, which normally took at least ten years. Since most students, at least until the fourteenth century, studied the arts before embarking upon advanced study, those who stayed spent a considerable part of their lives at university. They probably formed a fairly small group, however, as most students dropped out after a couple of years or else settled for a notarial diploma or the baccalaureate. Twelfth-century satirical texts may tell a different tale, but for a long time even a baccalaureate would have offered considerable prospects for a good position in society. There was a growing demand for academically educated clergymen, physicians and lawyers. The University of Naples was established with the explicit purpose of satisfying that demand.

On the reading list of the arts curriculum, Aristotle's preponderance was not limited to his works on logic. The great Greek philosopher had also written extensively on natural phenomena, metaphysics and ethics. This entire corpus was translated into Latin between about 1150 and 1250. It comprised, first, the *libri naturales* or 'books on nature', a series of treatises on physics, cosmology, meteorology, zoology and on sleep, dreams and memory. Of no less importance was *Metaphysics*. The term 'metaphysics', which literally means 'what comes beyond physics', refers to Aristotle's treatment of what he himself had called 'being as being'. Metaphysics is the philosophical search for the foundations of 'being', separate from sensory experience. It deals, for instance, with the status of universals (general concepts) and the difference between substance and particular, with the nature of the universe, and with epistemology (the study of the nature of knowledge, and the accepted methods of acquiring knowledge). Some commentators on Aristotle argued for a close connection between metaphysics and theology, others for the very opposite – in any case, *Metaphysics* is the only book of Aristotle that speaks of God as 'first principle'.

Aristotle's contribution to ethics includes a broad moral guideline, known as the *Ethica Nicomachaea*, presumed to have been written for his son, Nicomachos. It stood as a model for the second and most elaborate part of the *Summa Theologiae* of Thomas Aquinas. The last important work of Aristotle that was received in the West was *Politics*, translated by William of Moerbeke around 1260. It has been described as the pinnacle of naturalist thinking in the sense that it propagated the idea that the secular state was not instituted by God, but was a logical product of man being a *zoon politikon*, a creature that by its nature lives in a political community. The exegesis of *Politics* helped to sharpen the distinction between Church and state in the fourteenth century, without solving it (see Chapter 12).

The towering authority of Aristotle led to radical changes in the liberal arts curriculum of the universities. They took the form of superimposing the three so-called philosophies on the traditional teaching of the seven subjects of *trivium* and *quadrivium*: natural philosophy (around Aristotle's *libri naturales*), metaphysics (around Aristotle's *Metaphysics*), and moral philosophy (supplementing existing ethics with Aristotle). Of these three, natural philosophy needs some further explanation, because rendering it as 'physics' could easily create wrong associations with modern physics. (Aristotelian) natural philosophy was aimed at the rational investigation of the four ways or modalities by which physical objects, both 'natural bodies' and artefacts, can change in conjunction with the four basic 'causes' or principles of movement or change in the universe: the form (external appearance) of a thing, the matter of which it is made, the agency by which it changes and the end to which change occurs. As such, the study of natural philosophy comprised the entire fields of cosmology and astronomy, as well as physics, biology and psychology.

While Aristotle dominated the liberal arts curriculum – his works made accessible for students in innumerable manuals and commentaries – in the theological training everything revolved round the study of the Bible and Church Fathers. For the first time, useful aids to Bible study were produced, facilitating systematic access to the text, such as a standard division into chapters and verses, subject indexes and concordances. In the intellectual tradition of the early Middle Ages the Bible had of course been annotated countless times in the form of extensive treatises and commentaries and short marginal notes or glosses. Collections of these glosses had been made, but their quality was improved with the compilation of the *Glossa Ordinaria* ('Standard Gloss'), for a long time attributed to Walafrid Strabo, but actually only begun in 1100 by Anselm of Laon and completed some years later by Gilbert of Poitiers and Peter Lombard. In about the middle of the twelfth century the latter produced an extensive collection of the teachings of the Roman Church concerning Christian dogmas, all treated in accordance with the new format of logical argumentation. This compendium, based on about 5,000 extracts from the Church Fathers, major councils and papal letters, was called the *Quattuor libri sententiarum* ('Four Books of Sentences') after its four sections, dedicated to the nature of God, the creation, the Incarnation and the holy sacraments, respectively. It rapidly achieved the status of the standard university textbook for theology. As an aid to the study of the Bible in about the same period a new

handbook of biblical history (a summary of the supposedly historical books of the Bible) came into use. It was the *Historia Scholastica* by Peter Comestor ('Peter the Eater'), a compatriot of Peter Lombard and, like him, a prominent member of the clerical elite of Paris.

The bibles for the study of law were the Justinian *Corpus Iuris Civilis* for Roman-secular law, and the greatly enlarged and complex corpus of canonical texts, such as council decisions and papal decrees, for canon law. In the 1140s the Italian monk, Gratian, brought some order to the chaos in canon law with the publication of his *Concordantia discordantium canonum* ('The Harmonisation of Contradictory Laws'), which soon became known as the *Decretum Gratiani*. It dominated the study of Church law to such an extent that graduates often were referred to as 'decretists'. The most important medieval addition to this corpus, the *Liber Extra*, was completed in 1234. To simplify the study of Roman law, Accursius, a leading Bolognese jurist, in the middle of the thirteenth century compiled a *glossa ordinaria* ('standard gloss'), a systematic overview of nearly 100,000 glosses to Justinian's *Corpus Iuris Civilis* produced over the years in the law schools of Bologna. And, finally, the works of Hippocrates, Galen and their two most important medieval epigones, the Muslim convert Constantine the African (c.1010–1087) and the Persian physician and philosopher Avicenna (Ibn Sina, 980–1039), dominated the study of medicine.

The course of an academic career in the early days of the medieval university is well illustrated by the life of the great theologian Thomas Aquinas (1224–1274). He was a descendant of a high noble family near Monte Cassino, where he was sent at an early age to prepare for a career in the Church. Between 1239 and 1244 he studied the arts at the recently founded University of Naples and then, very much against the will of his family, he entered the Dominican Order. There, his intellectual gifts were immediately recognised and he was sent to Paris and Cologne. Thomas immersed himself in the works of Aristotle and studied theology under the first Latin-Christian intellectual in the Middle Ages who fully mastered all aspects of Aristotelian philosophy, Albertus Magnus (c.1200–1280). As an advanced student in Cologne, Thomas held the function of *cursor biblicus*, which meant that he had to teach elementary Bible studies to beginning theological students. At the age of 27 he became a *baccalaureus* in theology. Now he was allowed to give instruction in Peter Lombard's *Sententiae* and to assist the *magister residens* (professor with a tenured chair) in holding disputes. Finally, in 1255, Thomas himself became a *magister in Sacra Pagina*, professor of biblical studies (i.e. theology).

The main teaching tasks of a *magister* consisted of giving lectures (*lectiones*), which could have two formats: the *recitatio-cum-expositio* and the *quaestio*. In the former, the master read out an authoritative text – say a treatise by Aristotle – while offering a commentary, passage by passage. The latter, as we have seen, required the systematic treatment of a topic (*quaestio*) in accordance with the dialectical method. A distinction was made here between ordinary *quaestiones*, *quaestiones disputatae* ('disputed topics' or disputations) and *quaestiones quodlibetales* ('arbitrary topics'). Ordinary *quaestiones* were completely dealt with by the master himself. During disputations two students, or a student and a bachelor or a fresh master, were asked to present the objections and responses to the *quaestio* under discussion, after which the lecturing master 'determined' the dispute. Since about the middle of the thirteenth century, every *baccalaureus* or 'bachelor' had to determine a dispute as part of the final examination for the bachelor's degree. While ordinary *quaestiones* and disputations treated more or less set subjects, for lectures on so-called *quaestiones quodlibetales* students suggested topics, which could be as unusual as 'Whether it is better for a crusader to die on his outward journey than on the journey home' – one gets the impression that such sessions were primarily meant to give students the opportunity to put their masters' logical abilities to the test.

To underpin his lectures, Aquinas, just like many other masters, wrote a number of treatises in *quaestio* form, one of which was the *Summa Theologiae*, intended for those embarking on theology. He also put down in writing the 253 *quaestiones disputatae* which he had conducted, and for which there was great demand amongst his audience. At the beginning of the fourteenth century this collection, in 46 loose quires, could be rented for copying at the price of four silver coins. Understandably, in the pre-printing age, books were extremely expensive. It has been calculated that purchasing a book of 200 folios (400 pages) took half the yearly salary of an Oxford fellow. It was not uncommon to lay down the acquisition of a book in a written deed. The high prices of books must have made a university study for many students prohibitive, unless they could earn their own books by doing copying work for others. It is also true that the number of set texts mandatory for exams was very limited.

The 'war between science and religion'

When, despite his young age, Thomas Aquinas received his master's degree, his order appointed him to one of the two chairs of theology held by the Dominicans at the University of Paris. Even then the number of chairs per faculty was limited. In 1255, the faculty of theology had 12 chairs, half of which were allocated to the secular clergy, two to the Dominicans, one to the Franciscans, and the remaining three to the regular canons of the Paris cathedral chapter. This division was the result of heated discussions on the place of the new mendicant orders that would remain dominant in theology in the long term. Of the close to 200 teaching licences in theology that were granted by the University of Paris in the last quarter of the fourteenth century, about half went to friars against a quarter to secular clergy.

Related to the controversy between secular masters and mendicants was a deeper-seated conflict that has sometimes been labelled as a 'war between science and religion'. It all started when in 1210 Aristotle's freshly translated 'books on nature' were banned for teaching natural philosophy in the arts curriculum at the University of Paris, because their contents were irreconcilable with the Catholic faith. The prohibition was reissued several times, and maintained until around 1255. It meant that students who wanted to hear the latest in the field of science had to go elsewhere, to Oxford or Bologna, for instance, or become a Dominican and go to Cologne, or stay in Paris and follow clandestine lectures on physics. Meanwhile, a papal initiative to find a solution by purging the *libri naturales* of undesirable content failed, but this created new problems as soon as the ban was lifted. From that point on, conservative theologians started to act as watchdogs over the masters from the arts department as well as over their own more progressive colleagues in theology, and to denounce each and every suspect teaching. Theologians were well equipped to do so, because at this period a study of theology was only initiated after the completion of a Master's in the arts, so they knew perfectly well what science was all about.

Tensions increased in the 1260s and 1270s, and they came to a head in 1270 and 1277, when the bishop of Paris, Stephen Tempier, published lists of short propositions that the Roman Church forbade the teaching of. The list of 1270 numbered only 13 items, but that of 1277 numbered no fewer than 219, and whereas in 1270 the word buzzing around was 'error', in 1277 this had been changed to 'heresy'. Without really mentioning their names some of the most popular secular masters of the Paris arts faculty were targeted, two of them in particular: Siger of Brabant and Boetius of Dacia (= Denmark). Some months before the publication of the list of 1277, Siger and two associates had been summoned to appear before an inquisition. Wisely, they failed to turn up and fled to Italy.

To make matters worse, the two Parisian lists did not stand alone. Several influential masters of theology from the mendicant orders – the Augustinian Egidio Colonna of Rome and the head of the Franciscan Order, Giovanni Fidanza, better known as Bonaventura – supported the lists by producing treatises that specified these heretical 'errors'. Bonaventura (1221–1274) did not reject the work of Aristotle on principle. On the contrary, he happily used it in his own writings, but he was opposed to its excessive use in theological education, realising that Aristotle only offered limited possibilities to reach a deeper knowledge of God. According to Bonaventura, this knowledge could only be reached by a mystical path and necessitated a burning desire for God and a blind faith in divine grace that would rise above every call upon reason.

Bonaventura had a point. It was immediately clear that many items on the lists could be traced back to Aristotle's 'books on nature' and *Metaphysics*, or to their most prominent commentator, Averroës. There were three of Aristotle's ideas in particular that could not be squared with Christian dogmatic: the eternity of the world, the idea that God's power had limitations (for instance, by the exclusion of internal contradiction) and the immortality of the individual soul. These were all long known, and until then no master teaching Aristotle had made an insurmountable obstacle of them, as none of them intended to do now. The defensive line they took up was a sensible one. They argued that doing physics in the arts department was a completely different ball game from doing theology in the theology department. They adapted Tertullian's slogan, as it were, to their own profit: what had Athens (here: Aristotle) to do with Jerusalem (here: Catholic orthodoxy), what reason with faith? Were these not separate avenues of enquiry into separate truths – meaning that what held true in natural philosophy was on principle open to doubt or contradiction, and did not need to be true according to the Catholic faith? So what? Of course, they were immediately prepared to duly recognise that, in the end, faith always is superior to reason; they were even prepared to swear an oath that they would never consider any theological questions – which was what the Parisian masters of the arts faculty actually did in 1272.

This idea of a 'double truth' fostered an attitude among natural philosophers that bordered on 'intellectual schizophrenia' (Pedersen 1997). Witness the famous master of arts John Buridan who, when wanting to investigate the possibility of a vacuum in nature (impossible according to Aristotle), had to state beforehand that to his regret he had to consider the vacuum phenomenon from two different starting points, one of which was the possibility that God created a vacuum supernaturally. Similarly, Buridan argued that there was no evidence in the Bible for the assumptions that Greek philosophers had made about the movement of celestial bodies, or that those bodies were animated beings. In such cases, one might argue, the Church's prohibition to follow the ancient Greeks may have encouraged a reorientation of scientific research in the right direction. If Aristotle had declared a lot of phenomena 'impossible' according to his conception of the laws of nature, conservative theologians argued: God can do or make anything he wants; so anything is imaginable and, more importantly, should be the object of scientific investigation, except for God himself and the mysteries of the Christian faith. This was more or less the position of the famous Franciscan logician and theologian, William of Ockham (before 1287–1348).

For Ockham, theology was not a science, based on rational proofs supported by logic or by natural philosophy; nor did it allow him any certain statements about God. The only thing that he knew with any certainty was that God was perfectly transcendent and autonomous. God was powerful in the sense that no power could compel him. His freedom of action was circumscribed only by the requirements of internal consistency and order: even God could not do anything that lacked order or that at the same time was the opposite of what was happening. The creation was no more and no less than the contingent product of a choice made by God out of an infinite number of options, but within the two limitations he had set for himself.

In Ockham's eyes, only faith could lead to insight into the sort of higher truths that were indispensable for achieving eternal salvation, not because such truths were possibly irrational, but because human reason was restricted. Faith could not be achieved solely by study, theological or otherwise; an essential part of it was instilled (*infusa* in Latin) as it were through the grace-giving sacrament of Holy Baptism. With this proposition, Ockham openly stood against the rationalists, such as Aquinas. Reason and faith should be separate on principle, as should science and theology. Science should be directed towards reason and the 'natural' forms of proof that reason could reach, while theology should be directed towards faith, and faith towards divine revelation.

Ockham's impact on higher education in the late Middle Ages must not be underestimated. Based on his innovative approach, schools were formed soon after his death, which caused a true divide in the arts faculties of late medieval universities. On the one hand, there was 'the new way' (*via moderna*), also called the Ockhamist school (*doctrina* or *scientia okamica*), because it followed Ockham's proposal to strictly separate natural philosophy from a more spiritualised-mystic theology. The 'old way' (*via antica*), on the other hand, was associated with the writings of Aquinas, and offered more room for interference between natural philosophy and theology. The difference between these two schools of thought, which also revealed an intellectual rift between the Franciscans and the Dominicans, dominated the university arts curriculum well into the sixteenth century. Universities made it quite clear whether they followed the *via moderna* or the *via antica*, or both, but obviously a lot depended on the personal preferences of individual masters. The University of Erfurt in Germany, for example, traditionally followed the *via antica*, but by the time young Martin Luther studied the arts there, the resident professor, Jodocus Trutfetter, had switched to the *via moderna*.

Historians of science such as Edward Grant are convinced that the relative separation of science and religion that started to take hold in the 1270s worked: certainly in the *via moderna*, natural philosophy was left on its own. This meant that science was no longer drenched in theological or dogmatic issues; natural philosophers always had the excuse that what they argued was done by 'speaking in terms of natural philosophy' (*loqui naturaliter*). But there was another benefit: by stressing the dogma of God's omnipotence science was also freed, as it were, from Aristotle's burden. This led on the one hand to a new wave of openly criticising Aristotle, and on the other hand to some extremely interesting speculations on problems of infinity and infinite regression among such brilliant natural philosophers as Gregory of Rimini (*c.*1300–1358), whose work approached present-day mathematics of infinite sets. But in the end, no final leap into modern science was made, because medieval natural philosophers were like steeplechase horses refusing to jump over an obstacle. In the end, they always respectfully (but also sincerely?) deferred to the authority of the Church – and also, although to a lesser degree, to that of Aristotle.

So, if it is true, as Grant argues, that late medieval theology was far more indebted to natural philosophy than vice versa, the reverse side was that science could not shake off religion. Many theologians seem just to have used theological questions – even essential articles of the faith – as an excuse to plunge into exercises on natural philosophy, mathematics and logic, whereas the other way around, natural philosophers were not equipped, and were not allowed, to venture into theological problems. John Buridan, the secular arts master already mentioned, ended a *quaestio* on infinite magnitude that touched upon the nature of God with the humble admission that 'with regard to all the things that I say in this question, I yield the determination of them to the lord theologians.' This forced marriage between science and religion caused theology to remain analytic, inquisitive and rational rather than spiritual and emotional but at the same time it prevented science from leaping over God's shadow. It slowed down the development of natural philosophy towards a natural science focused less on metaphysical and theological problems and more on observation, experimentation and measurements related to purely physical phenomena.

There always are rare birds, like, in this case, the works on optics and refraction of light by the Englishmen Robert Grosseteste (*c.*1170–1253), and his eccentric pupil, the Franciscan Roger Bacon. Grosseteste, who first taught arts and then theology at Oxford University from about 1220, later becoming bishop of Lincoln, could read Greek and was influenced by both Plato, the neo-Platonists and Aristotle. In studying a wide range of scientific phenomena he developed his own research methods, including the formulation of model-like hypotheses for which he used mathematical descriptions – Grosseteste is perhaps the spiritual father of the scientific hypothesis. He also did more or less controlled experiments. He applied these methods in a ground-breaking study of the refraction of light in rainbows that would later be refined by Bacon and the German Dominican Dietrich of Freiburg. It is true that the theory does not correspond on all points with current theory, but Grosseteste and his followers proved that in barely fifty years it was possible to make great advances in the physical sciences with the help of experiments and mathematics.

But Grosseteste and Bacon were the exceptions to the general rule of academic conventionality. Only such a mental disposition may help to explain why the unique breeding ground that was established with the foundation of universities for a fairly autonomous scholarship in the European Middle Ages did not lead to a scientific revolution until the seventeenth century. Before that time, the Greek model of the universe, which had reigned supreme for almost 2,000 years, was challenged far less from the bulwarks of science than from the adventurous world beyond. Two of the most important discoveries of the thirteenth century, the mechanical clock and spectacles, were developed, as far as we know, outside the universities. And it was merchants and navigators – helped by such practical inventions as the astrolabe (probably of Hellenistic origin, but vastly improved in the eleventh century), the magnetic compass, the double compasses and the calculation of coordinates – who made it clear that many Aristotelian laws were simply incorrect. It explains the joke circulating in the middle of the sixteenth century that you could learn more from the Portuguese in one day than from the Greeks and Romans in a hundred years.

The humanism of the late Middle Ages

Studia humanitatis *and the new humanism in Italy*

While scholasticism was reaching its zenith in the course of the fourteenth century, an entirely new educational ideal was being propagated in Italy. Contemporaries spoke of the *studia humanitatis*. Instead of the strong accent the scholastic liberal arts course put on technical logic, natural philosophy and metaphysics in the Aristotelian tradition, the *studia humanitatis* programme was constructed around five disciplines – grammar, rhetoric, history (not then a separate discipline), knowledge of poetry and moral philosophy (meaning philosophy focused on ethical, non-metaphysical or theological questions). The basic texts for the subjects were by classical, primarily non-Christian, Roman writers, in due course followed by the Greek giants Homer, Hesiod and Sophocles. Favourite genres became discursive dialogues and speeches.

The new programme certainly did not take the world of higher learning by storm. Quite the contrary, it only very slowly gained a firm foothold in the grammar and rhetoric departments of the arts curriculum. Initially, prominent humanists thought little of teaching in a university; the honour was small and the pay was poor. Only in the latter part of the fifteenth century did several universities – those of Florence, Bologna, Rome and Ferrara, in particular – succeed in hiring famous humanists as professors of grammar, rhetoric and literature/poetry, either full-time, against often princely salaries, or part-time when teaching duties were combined with functions in chanceries or as private tutors at courts. Lectures by renowned humanists were very popular, and attracted large audiences, from among not only students but also local civic elites.

Although in the long term, the *studia humanitatis* would not triumph in the university syllabus, they were successful at a lower level, that is, in the Latin schools founded in large towns all over late medieval Europe to educate children from the upper echelons of the bourgeoisie, but not necessarily to prepare them for a university education.

At first sight the demand for the *studia humanitatis* appears to have been a plea for a reactionary, not revolutionary, shift of emphasis in intellectual formation, a return to the arts programmes from before the Aristotelian revival. In reality, a substantial change in mentality lay behind it. The new humanists wanted above all to expand the practical value of higher education that they felt was lacking in scholastic learning. In addition to a direct focus on the human condition, the revolt against scholasticism therefore reflects a new sort of 'utilitarian thinking' that was emerging among the urban elites and higher middle classes. In contrast to our own times, this way of thinking did not aim to extend individual material well-being but to develop those character traits which enabled individuals to make sensible moral, business and, above all, political decisions in a pragmatic way. In the communes of northern and central Italy, where the new mentality first took root, both the degree of civic participation and the amount of informal association were far greater than in western society today. For that reason, we ought to be wary of putting too much stress on the individualistic and secularising trends in the new humanism, as was done particularly by nineteenth-century historians like Jakob Burckhardt. On the contrary, direct involvement of the better-off in local political life furthered a feeling of collective responsibility and a natural readiness to do one's best for the public good. Neither was this endeavour seen as primarily secular, as opposed to Christian piety; rather, it was regarded as its complement.

Cicero replaced Aristotle as the great classical example for the new humanists. No other figure in the ancient world so effectively combined high public morality with unrestrained political activity as he did. Cicero's writings also taught that eloquent expression or rhetoric was an important skill through which to achieve moral wisdom, because only clarity of expression in the written and spoken word could lead to the correct formulation of that wisdom.

The renewed interest in Antiquity's literary treasures led to important methodological innovations in textual criticism. For the first time the authenticity of a text was questioned through a systematic study of such characteristics as the writer's style and vocabulary, supplemented by a number of exterior features. In addition, context-bound interpretation was given a wider range than had been common since Abelard's time. It was realised that what a writer intended to say at a certain place in the text could not be determined solely by a semantic analysis of the vocabulary. In a philological study, the complete text had to be used as well as its author's other works or works by others writing at the same time, or other possibly relevant historical information. The new philological criticism, the prelude to modern scientific philology, was thus both comparative and historicist in nature. It achieved resounding results, including the definitive exposure of the *Donatio Constantini* as a forgery by the papal secretary, Lorenzo Valla, the German humanist and cardinal, Nicholas of Kues, and the controversial English bishop and royal councillor,

Reginald Pecock, who came to the same conclusion independently. It helped the new humanists to reject the medieval Christian idea that their own time was the depressing lowest point, the very nadir of world history. Without breaking with the inevitable scheme of Christian salvation history they began to take more heed of history's vagaries – which true leaders should try to surmount or bend to their will. But the new, historical textual criticism had much wider advantages, for even if the Greek model of the universe did not give way as yet, the conditions for its undermining were enhanced by the availability of more and better versions of the original texts in which the model was couched.

It is impossible to imagine the flowering and enormous growth of the humanistic education programme without a new stress on the study of Latin. The new humanists were convinced that classical Latin was the only vehicle worthy of expounding their ideals. They were horrified by the 'barbaric' Latin of the scholastics, which admittedly was contorted by the need to give modern Latin equivalents to the very complex and often obscure terminology of Aristotle's Greek and which often resulted in rather ugly neologisms. It was a source of pride for the new humanists to master Latin so perfectly that it was indistinguishable from the best literary Latin from classical Antiquity. The choice of material or genres was also based on classical models, not always to the satisfaction of the modern reader, who can perhaps recognise the ingenuity but not the pleasure of interminable imitations of the great epic poems of Virgil or Lucan, of incomprehensible mythological imagery in rigid metric verse, or of bombastic letters and speeches inspired by Cicero or Seneca. No wonder then that of the works of the most illustrious of the early humanists, Petrarch and Boccaccio, only those written in Italian (which were also very much appreciated in their own time) are read nowadays, whereas their far more numerous and extensive works in classical Latin have been all but forgotten.

Petrarch (Francesco Petrarca) (1304–1374) was surely the more remarkable of the two. He was the son of a lawyer from the neighbourhood of Arezzo, who settled in Avignon where the papal court was in residence and where he made influential friends who helped him obtain his first position in the household of the renowned Colonna family. As a cleric in the lower orders he enjoyed income from various ecclesiastical benefices in Tuscany and Lombardy which he fulfilled nominally. Petrarch soon became known as an orator and poet and was perhaps the first writer since classical Antiquity to achieve celebrity status. The high-point of his career undoubtedly occurred in 1341, on the Campidoglio (the Capitoline Hill of ancient Rome), where, after his poetic abilities were tested by King Robert of Naples, he was crowned with the laurel wreath, the symbol of the writer's glory. Thereafter Petrarch became the eloquent advocate of the popes' return to Rome and lent his half-hearted support to the 'revolution' of Cola di Rienzo, the parvenu tradesman who seized power in Rome in 1347 in the belief that he could restore the eternal city to its former glory. Meanwhile, Petrarch journeyed from one princely court to another in an Italy torn by political strife, trying to put his talents as an orator and diplomat to use. He died in the summer of 1374 at his house in the hills above Padua, while reading a book – the most beautiful death a poet and a scholar can imagine. The *Canzoniere*, a collection of 366 poems in Italian, is considered to be his most important literary legacy.

Petrarch's friend and kindred spirit, the Florentine Giovanni Boccaccio (1313–1375), died not long afterwards. He is best known as the author of the *Decameron*, a collection of short stories written in the vernacular, but like Petrarch he was a passionate Latinist, philologist and collector of manuscripts of classical literature. The two shared a profound admiration for the works of Dante Alighieri (1265–1321), who in no way can be considered a humanist; he was much more an exponent of the scholastic tradition. The Florentine magistrates gave Boccaccio the first teaching commission to lecture in public on Dante's masterpiece, the *Divina Commedia*. Even more important, however, was that he made Florence the heart of the new humanistic movement. It is telling that the two most prominent spiritual heirs of Petrarch and Boccaccio, Coluccio Salutati and Leonardo Bruni of Arezzo, were both chancellor or town secretary in Florence. Salutati was the first humanist to use the *studia humanitatis* for political gain, for he employed his rhetorical gifts as a mighty weapon in Florence's struggle with Milan in 1401–1402. His reflective prose works show strong secular leanings and a genuine dislike of ivory-tower intellectuals and religious contemplation. 'Must I call someone learned', he wrote in a letter, 'who knows everything the human intellect can grasp about heavenly and divine matters but who never looks at himself? Who has never done anything useful for his friends, his family, his parents or his town?' This sophisticated attitude was not immediately representative of the intellectual climate in which the new humanism took root. Petrarch, for example, favoured a withdrawn, contemplative existence, a sort of Christian version of the Roman ideal of *otium*, and he looked to Augustine as his spiritual guide even more than to Seneca and Cicero – a preference shared by many later humanists.

Intellectual life in Florence during the fifteenth century, then, was not dominated entirely by the moral humanism strongly oriented towards public service that Salutati and Bruni propagated. No less popular among the elite in the second half of the fifteenth century was the so-called 'Florentine Platonism', an esoteric brew of original ideas of Plato, widely known since by then his works finally had been translated from Greek, mixed with a dash of neo-Platonism and a good measure of magical and occult humbug taken from the Jewish Kabbala and the Hellenist cult of Hermes Trismegistos. The result resembled some of today's New Age philosophies, for Florentine Platonism, sponsored by the Medici family, had a strongly egocentric and apolitical slant. A typical product of this thinking was the work on the dignity of man by Giovanni Pico della Mirandola (1463–1494), published posthumously. It defends the extremely voluntaristic view that the human individual, with no limitations to his own free will, creates his own personality. Visual pointers to the ideas of this philosophical current can be seen in the early paintings of Sandro Botticelli (1444–1510).

The work of Niccolò Machiavelli (1469–1527) was less high-brow and more akin to the early political-moral humanism of around 1400, but it lacked the optimistic view of human nature and human potentialities that was so characteristic of early moral humanism and Florentine Platonism. One of the aphorisms of Machiavelli, also a chancellor of Florence but thrown out of office in 1512 after the political comeback of the Medici, is that 'People only do good when they are compelled to.' Humans were by nature evil and their actions were determined by self-interest, by a desire for gain and glory, by opportunism and hypocrisy. To be sure, human nature could not be changed; what could be manipulated and reformed, though, was 'character', constituting that part of man's disposition that was dependent on circumstances and free will. People did indeed have free will, but they could only determine half their fate, the other half being in the hands of fortune. A good ruler was one who succeeded best in adapting to historical circumstances either by trying to master fortune or by presenting the state's interest as the self-interest of (the majority of) its subjects or by bending their characters to serve the common good of the state rather than his will. Machiavelli was rather ambiguous about the best possible type of government; while in one of his principal works, *The Prince* (*Il Principe*), he argues in favour of monarchy, in the other, *Discourses on Livy*, he seems to prefer a republic with a mixed, aristocratic-popular regime.

Machiavelli's ideas about the limits of force that a state may use are best known from *The Prince*, a mirror of princes tinged with Aristotelian ideas on psychological motivation of human action. It evokes two kinds of comments. First, a good prince is never a tyrant, but on the other hand allows himself to be guided by his subjects' preferences only if expedient. When necessary – that is to say, when laws do not work properly – he should be prepared to take an uncompromising and unambiguous stand, combining the strength of a lion with the cunning of a fox. The man whom Machiavelli believed to possess all the desired qualities, and who was held up as an example to the reader of *Il Principe*, was Cesare Borgia. The son of Pope Alexander VI, Cesare was an unscrupulous scoundrel but also a gifted strategist. Nonetheless, in Machiavelli's eyes, he was the embodiment of the right character of a forceful 'prince', being a combination of *virtù* (personal ability), *ingegno* (innate talent or 'genius') and *fantasia* (power of imagination) – all three keywords of the Italian Renaissance to describe the individual.

Second, if in *The Prince* the idea of an amoral *raison d'état* in which the actors are allowed almost unlimited latitude and freedom of action is expounded for the first time, it must be made clear that Machiavelli only approved of amoral actions (which could also imply immoral actions) if they served the public interest of the state. Good Christian that he was, Machiavelli strongly condemned immoral actions motivated by self-interest.

We will only briefly discuss the relationship between Italian humanism and the visual art of the Italian Renaissance, which nonetheless played an important role in the debate about the unique nature of this period of Italian history. At a cursory glance the link with humanism is plain and uncomplicated. Just as in the study of letters, so too in the language of forms, geometrical proportions, and the solving of problems of perspective in architecture, sculpture and painting there was a conscious and direct return to the models of Antiquity. The watershed between 'old' and 'new' art came in the 1420s, when Filippo Brunelleschi completed the dome of the cathedral church in Florence, Donatello made his first free-standing sculptures of human figures in a natural pose (known as the *contrapposto*) and the painter Masaccio applied the technique of vanishing-point or optical perspective and made considerable efforts to ensure that his figures were anatomically correct. As the technical mastery of Renaissance artists grew, so did their social ambitions. They were no longer content with being seen as craftsmen, practitioners of the *artes mechanicae*; they wanted to be considered as scholars, practitioners of the *artes liberales*. The techniques and constructs applied and the elab-

oration of subjects and motifs surely demanded more than just a superficial knowledge of different disciplines of the *trivium* and *quadrivium*. This claim was honoured only in part. On the one hand, leading artists like Leonardo da Vinci (1452–1519) and Michelangelo Buonarotti (1475–1564) were considered 'universal', even divinely inspired geniuses (and this was reflected in the level of their fees); on the other hand, Leonardo was frustrated throughout his life that he was never accepted by the learned humanists as one of their own.

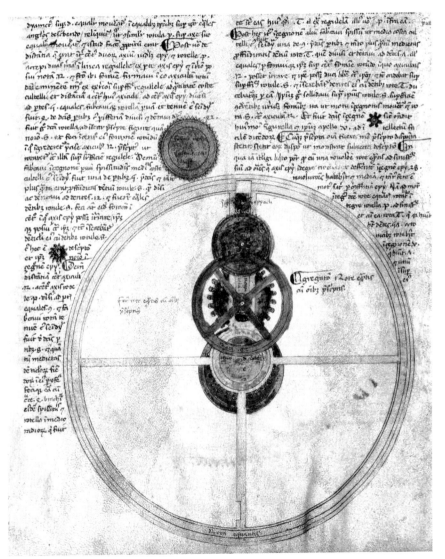

PLATE 8.3

Astronomical clock originally constructed in 1344 by Jacopo Dondi in Padua.

Unlike the new humanism, the new Italian visual arts were not received north of the Alps until relatively late, with a few exceptions such as Albrecht Dürer (1471–1528), the south German graphic artist and painter. A unique and distinctive realistic style of painting and sculpture developed in north-western Europe during the fifteenth century, finding its most sublime expression in the works of the Flemish painters Jan van Eyck and Rogier van der Weyden. Their works were highly appreciated and bought throughout Europe, including Italy.

The new humanism outside Italy

From Italy, the new humanism gradually spread over the Alps, where it was linked more closely to the intellectual debate about reforms in the Catholic Church than in Italy. The influence of northern humanism was originally found in comparable, densely urbanised regions such as southern Germany and the Low Countries, but it has now become clear that the intellectual elite elsewhere – England, France, Spain and Poland – also came into contact with the programme of the *studia humanitatis* at an early stage. The networks which existed between universities and the personal connections between intellectuals, kept up by travels to Italy (the *iter Italicum* as part of the intellectual formation of artists and aristocrats), by correspondence, by employment and by diplomatic missions, apparently were far more important than strictly socio-geographical structures. Peter Luder (1415–1472), the German humanist who as a young man travelled to Italy several times to study, is a good example. He discovered the *studia humanitatis* and transferred his enthusiasm to his students and colleagues in the many universities of the German Empire at which he taught. The most important northern humanist was undoubtedly Rudolf Agricola (1444–1485), who studied in Pavia and Ferrara for more than ten years before taking an official position in Groningen in the northern Low Countries, from where he originated. Among his writings is a textbook inspired by humanistic thought, *De inventione dialectica*, which was widely used for teaching philosophy in the sixteenth century. Agricola argued that the humanistic ideal of a pragmatic search for plausible solutions to everyday questions was worth more than all the speculation about things that could not be experienced to which scholastic dialectics was devoted.

Through men like Luder and Agricola the new humanism permeated the circles of higher education and the governments of towns and principalities outside Italy, though it also encountered objections. The propagation of ancient 'pagan' virtues aroused particular suspicion in conservative clerical circles, and for this reason the humanists failed to get university curricula adapted to their educational ideals, even though they certainly tried often enough in the German Empire during the second half of the fifteenth century. From time to time their efforts procured the appointment of a humanistic teacher to lecture in rhetoric or classical poetry. Martin Luther was closely connected to one of the attempts at reform which bore some fruit. Luther was not a humanist in the strict sense – he was not interested in pre-Christian Latin or Greek literature – but he had an intense dislike for the scholastic teaching of philosophy and theology. In his view, the teaching of theology should be based solely on the Bible, and good teaching of the Bible benefited from humanism's new historical-philological methods.

Other northern humanists shared Luther's attempts to use the *studia humanitatis* to implement necessary reforms in the Church, and they, too, saw the establishment of a historically and philologically sound new text of the Bible as the first desideratum. The most famous of them was Desiderius Erasmus of Rotterdam (c.1467–1536). His religious ideals, which he referred to as the 'philosophy of Christ', were greatly influenced by his upbringing in the spirit of the *Devotio Moderna* (see Chapter 12). Erasmus found that the basis of faith could never be learned theology; it was a personal and unbounded trust in God, driven by internal experience and complemented by a morally pure life. He found the Church's outward show of minor importance, and in *Praise of Folly*, a work still popular today, he used his most feared weapon, satire, to poke fun at the carnivalesque features of Catholic religious life of the time and at the greed and tyranny of prelates and monks. Yet Erasmus never wanted to break with the Church of Rome. He was more in favour of a rebirth than a reformation of Christianity, and that was precisely where he differed from Luther, from whom he openly distanced himself in 1520.

Education was at the heart of the rebirth of faith envisaged by Erasmus, education aimed at the moral improvement of individual believers in the spirit of early Christianity, and not at rejecting the Church's doctrines and institutions. Erasmus wrote a sort of moral guideline especially for the purpose entitled *Enchiridion militis Christi* ('Handbook of a Christian Knight'), advocating knowledge and prayer as weapons to be used in the fight against vice and sin.

Erasmus and Luther belonged to the earliest generation of intellectuals who were able to disseminate their views through a revolutionary new medium, the printing press. Erasmus was the very first to recognise its enormous potential: twenty-three editions of his *Enchiridion* appeared between 1515 and 1521. He could often be found in the offices and workshops of the Swiss and Italian printers who published his works, and, without ever having held a public office of any significance, Erasmus achieved the status of a best-selling writer and cultural megastar. At the height of his fame, around 1515, his name was on the lips of every intellectual of importance in Europe.

Points to remember

■ The medieval worldview, at least for educated people, was basically ancient Greek. The reception of ancient pagan knowledge was secured in Late Antiquity through the development of the 'handmaiden' doctrine.

■ Nevertheless, the Bible and the great Church Fathers of Late Antiquity were the unquestionable bench-marks of all medieval science and scholarship.

■ The basis of any programme of higher education in the Middle Ages consisted of the study of the seven *artes liberales* ('free/intellectual skills'). These could be studied in two types of schools that were connected to monasteries and cathedrals, respectively.

■ The quality of higher education and scholarship changed dramatically with the 'rationalist turn' that was taken in the eleventh and twelfth centuries. Its core was a growing trust in the power of human reason. Its first two 'products' were the reintroduction of (neo-) Platonic cosmology and Aristotelian logic.

■ A further boost to higher education came from the formation of universities from the end of the twelfth century onwards. These developed from professional organisations for teachers and/or students into full-blown educational institutes with fixed curricula, teaching and examination requirements, and grades.

■ In universities, the study of the *artes liberales* would remain by far the most popular discipline, but its programme was fundamentally altered by the addition of the 'three philosophies' (physics, metaphysics, ethics), which were all three dominated by textbooks of Aristotle.

■ Tensions between certain religious authorities and theologians on the one hand, and secular masters of the arts faculties on the other, ended with a more or less implied agreement to separate the domains of reason/science and belief/religion.

■ In the fourteenth and fifteenth centuries a new wave of humanist scholarship washed over Italy. The Italian humanists propagated a new educational ideal, sold as *studia humanitatis* ('study of the humanities'), that was far removed from scholastic university learning by its far more secular and social-activist orientation.

■ In the fifteenth and early sixteenth centuries, Italian humanism spread over the Alps, where it took on a more concentrated form, often with a narrow focus on biblical study and Christian ethics.

Suggestions for further reading

Grant, Edward (2004), *Science and Religion, 400 BC to AD 1550: From Aristotle to Copernicus* (Baltimore: the Johns Hopkins UP). Expert survey of the history of science that is also comprehensible for non-scientists (which most historians are), with a focus on the fateful relationship between medieval science, which remained deeply rooted in non-Christian traditions, and the Christian faith and its Church that dictated a worldview that could not always be reconciled with science.

Jaeger, C. Stephen (2000), *The Envy of Angels: Cathedral Schools and Social Ideals in Medieval Europe, 950–1200* (Philadelphia PA: University of Pennsylvania Press). Eye-opening monograph on the awakening of scholastic science and scholarship in the cathedral schools of Germany and France, with a focus on schools and their teachers, on the new humanism and its spiritual opposing force, and on the link between scholarship and court culture.

Nauert, Charles (2006, 2nd edn), *Humanism and the Culture of Renaissance Europe* (Cambridge: CUP). Updated edition of exemplary, succinct treatment of the concept of civic humanism and its dissemination outside its Italian city-state cradle.

Pedersen, Olaf (1997), *The First Universities:* Studium Generale *and the Origins of University Education in Europe* (Cambridge: CUP). This engaging history of the early universities and their predecessors, besides discussing intellectual climate, curricula and degrees, is concerned with all kinds of institutional aspects, including housing and financial structure. It also pays ample attention to student life.

Siraisi, Nancy G. (1990), *Medieval and Early Renaissance Medicine: An Introduction to Knowledge and Practice* (Chicago IL: University of Chicago Press). Lucid account that addresses all subjects of any importance in this specialist field: medical knowledge and education, afflictions and therapies, magical versus rational diagnostics. The book's argument goes up and down the intersection of academic learning and medical practice. It fully recognises western indebtedness, first to the great physicians of Greek Antiquity, and especially Galen, and then to medieval Arab and Persian medicine.

9 Towns and the urbanisation of medieval society

The phenomenon of the pre-industrial town

The scale of towns and of urbanisation

No other phenomenon in European history before industrialisation has had such a profound influence as the process of the growth of towns that started during the tenth century. Like most features of development undergone by Europe over the centuries, this transformation appeared earlier and was more intensive in the southern and western regions of the continent than in the north and east.

By urbanisation in this context we mean three different things. First, the growth of the number of settlements that could be called towns – places characterised by the spatial concentration and relative density of habitation, by the predominantly non-agrarian nature of economic activities and by the exercise of all kinds of centralised functions, ranging from economic and political to cultural. Second, the expansion in size of existing towns. Third, the increase in the proportion of the total population living in towns (the so-called urbanisation rate), which was only possible if food production rose in equal measure. For lack of data, none of these three developments can be captured in exact figures, let alone specified in time and space. However, the tendencies are undisputed.

Also undisputed is that in Europe between roughly 1000 and 1300 all three tendencies coincided; after that, the size of most towns stagnated, or even fell. While this ties in with general population decline in the late Middle Ages (see Table 9.1), quite remarkably the share of the urban population on the whole kept increasing, judging by the growth of the number of small and medium-sized towns during that same period (see Table 9.2). Moreover, regions where urbanisation had been weak before 1300, such as the northern Low Countries, central and northern Europe, now experienced a modest increase.

TABLE 9.1 Estimated population of Europe, in millions

Year	Population
1000	38
1300	75
1450	50
1500	61

By 1500, some 10 per cent of Europeans lived in towns with a population of at least 5,000. In Iberia and Italy this share was clearly above the average, namely 14 per cent – and in Italy it had been much higher two centuries earlier. The scale of medieval towns remained relatively modest: in 1300 only Venice, Florence, Milan and Paris had (slightly) more than 100,000 inhabitants. By 1500, Florence was reduced to 40,000 inhabitants, and only around 150 towns had above 10,000. The population of the great majority – about 3,500 of the 4,000 places which enjoyed town rights – varied from a few hundred to a few thousand. The numerous small towns were mostly situated in the land mass of the continent, while the larger towns developed mainly along coasts and major rivers. The reason for this was that for the supply of bulk goods such as grain, building materials and raw materials for other industries, accessibility by ship was of overriding importance. Transport by ship was many times cheaper per unit of weight than transport by land. All the big towns in Europe were of necessity ports, therefore. Only massive surplus extraction through coercion

by a strong centralised state could overcome this rule, as in some Chinese and Islamic capital cities. In 1500 the really large towns were still around the Mediterranean Sea, where during Antiquity, Rome probably had a population of one million, and, in the early Middle Ages, Constantinople and Córdoba grew to half a million.

What was the reason for the existence of towns of such exceptional size in the Mediterranean region? The explanation must be sought in the productivity of agriculture in the region, accessibility for large ships, availability of raw materials for a large-scale export industry, and the attraction or pressure that a major town could exert on an extensive hinterland. In Europe north of the Alps and Pyrenees only one or two metropolises had as many as 100,000 inhabitants until the sixteenth century. Antwerp, then the heart of the economic world system, was one of them by 1560. The other one was Paris, the capital city of a large kingdom, which attracted the population surplus from a wide countryside where there were no other important cities. A century later Amsterdam reached a new threshold – 200,000 – which was easily surpassed by London in the eighteenth century. These were the unique centres of the world economy in their time; they could only grow to such a size because they formed the core of an ever-expanding economic system.

Not all towns had commerce as their primary function: a number of them came into being or were founded to provide services to a cathe-

TABLE 9.2 Urban population by size of towns

Population	Number of towns		Urban population (thousands)	
	in 1300	in 1500	in 1300	in 1500
>100,000	4	4	(400)	450
40,000–99,000	15	14	(750)	704
20,000–39,000	33	37	(890)	981
10,000–19,000	73	99	(950)	1,306
5,000–9,000	?	363	?	2,468
Totals	?	517	?	5,909

Note: parentheses denote estimated figures.

dral or some other administrative centre. The capitals of reasonably centralised states, such as Constantinople, Paris and London, had a special attraction because central administrative organs could concentrate their resources there. On a far more modest scale episcopal towns and the administrative centres of territorial princes served as concentration points for the consumer expenditure of the elites and their clients. The taxes centralised there on the spot created a separate market for specific goods and services. Iberian towns derived their great freedoms from the Reconquest, led by the kings, and thus functioned as bases of conquest and occupation. During the Middle Ages, towns with such one-sided functions were usually relatively small, like the archepiscopal seats of Canterbury, Sens and Esztergom.

We can conclude that a town could never be considered without its hinterland. A town population was formed in the first instance by migration from the countryside; we know from later centuries that pre-industrial towns always had a mortality surplus, so that a town's population could only remain static or increase through immigration. The primary explanation for the growth of the towns must always be sought in the countryside or in smaller towns, through chain migration.

From an economic perspective, every town was both a market and a production centre for industries and services. In the first place, the town's inhabitants could eat only if there were sufficient food surpluses in the surrounding countryside to be sold in the town. As the town grew, food had to be brought from a wider hinterland, and the market took on interregional dimensions. Townspeople had to be productive themselves, of course, in order to buy their food and raw materials. In this way, every town was entirely dependent on its supply lines and potential markets for its own products. Hence, the more a town grew, the more its control over longer trading routes through an extensive hinterland became necessary.

Conversely, the presence of an urban market stimulated the rural economy: the demand encouraged market-oriented production, in the sense of both enlargement and diversification of the supply. Purchasing power was concentrated in the town for a variety of foodstuffs, such as meat and dairy products, as well as for the raw materials from the countryside needed for industry – brewing grains, flax, wool, leather, building materials, fuel, dyes and more. The townspeople themselves contributed directly to diversification in rural production by buying up land as a safe investment, in order to make certain of their own supply by buying rents in grain and keeping livestock, and by becoming owners of peat-lands, lime kilns, stone quarries or vineyards.

Some scarce goods, such as wine, certain sorts of wood, metal and stone, could be brought from much further afield. Urban demand had a profound effect on its immediate surroundings, but for specific products the effects were felt at a distance too. Sheep-farming in rural England, for example, was greatly stimulated by the demand for wool from the cloth industry in northern France and the Low Countries from the eleventh century onwards, and later also in Italy. Alum (used for fixing colours in textiles) was mined in Asia Minor, amber collected on Prussian beaches, and pitch and tar gathered in Poland's forests to be worked in industries in the West. This created a need for long-distance transport. In this way relatively few urban merchants and entrepreneurs brought about the transformation of a considerable part of the economy's primary sector.

The interlinking of town and hinterland can be seen in the correlation between the degree of urbanisation and the population density of a specific region. Where there were relatively high numbers of townspeople, the density of population in the hinterland was also proportionately high. This is logical because only an overpopulated rural area could afford to lose people to the town, but also because the proximity of the town, with its demand and investment capital, led to an intensification of agriculture.

The American historian Jan de Vries (1984) has devised a sophisticated method to express in one single standard the growth of the towns in pre-industrial Europe (omitting the Balkans for source-technical reasons). It is based on three factors: 1) the absolute population numbers of towns with more than 10,000 inhabitants; 2) the distances between these towns; 3) the geographical location, expressed in a quotient. For each one of the 154 towns with at least 10,000 inhabitants in about 1500 he calculated what he called an 'urban potential' at different moments in the three centuries between 1500 and 1800. By charting the measured ratings it was possible to reconstruct a geography of town growth moving through time, one which was not determined or defined by continually changing and often random political units but by the socio-geographical reality.

In 1500 Venice scored the highest absolute rating. This is not surprising: with possibly 120,000 inhabitants it was the biggest town of its time; there were several other large towns nearby, and it was a port. Three regions stand out with the highest relative ratings, namely 80 per cent of that of Venice: the Po valley including Milan and Genoa, the southern Low Countries and the Gulf of Naples. These three regions formed a large area of high consumption, emphasising even more the enormous predominance of the northern Italian belt of towns.

After these three peaks the ratings drop quickly to just above 50 per cent around Paris and 50 per cent in the great region between London, the Loire and the area of the lower Rhine; the Rhône valley and the coastline of the Ligurian Sea also appear to have had a fairly high urban growth. Very low ratings applied in the Iberian peninsula, with the exception of the north-east and Andalusia, central and north Europe and the Celtic periphery of the British Isles. In northern Italy and the coastal and river regions of the Low Countries one in three inhabitants lived in a large town. In central Europe this was less than one in ten. This is a significantly marked contrast, revealing clearly the enormous regional diversity within Europe.

Of course there are some drawbacks to the method used by de Vries. In particular, his decision to consider only settlements with a minimum of 10,000 inhabitants as towns means that, for the Middle Ages, too many smaller places which actually functioned as towns are ignored. De Vries made his choice in order to be able to maintain an equal measurement gauge in his long-term perspective until 1800. In the period before 1750 the thousands of towns with just a few thousand, or even just a few hundred, inhabitants formed points of reference in their area for economic and administrative activity. Some had a special significance for a particular branch of industry, as a fishing port or a market for an important agricultural hinterland, for example. The role of small towns was particularly important in areas with very low levels of urbanisation.

The morphology of the medieval town

Contemporaries of the medieval towns were clearly aware of their distinctive character, and in many cases archaeological remains still bear witness to their typical manifestations. Town walls, ramparts and gates marked the separation between the urban space and the surrounding country. The urban community shut itself off from its environs both literally and metaphorically. Its walls protected it from attacks and invaders. The model of a town's defences was actually an enlargement of a castle's defences: walls one could walk around, battlements, watchtowers, fortified gates and drawbridges. The urban community came into being in a world dominated by feudal warriors, like a foreign body that had to use the same means to defend itself.

In the early Middle Ages the old provincial capitals, *civitates* within the former Roman Empire, still retained some administrative functions as episcopal seats and thereby some urban characteristics of a town, albeit greatly reduced in comparison with the situation in the third century. Rheims, the metropolis of the province of Belgica Secunda, spread over some 30 hectares;

Cologne, the capital of Germania Secunda, enclosed more than 96 hectares within its ancient walls. Many of these ancient towns were at the heart of the medieval expansion.

The oldest town communities that were formed spontaneously grew up in new locations with features very different from those of the Roman towns. Many Roman towns had been planned within a centralised empire with a substantial network of roads. Most medieval towns were unplanned but developed, so to speak, organically, and their location was primarily determined by navigable waterways. Favourable locations were river confluences (Ghent, Mainz, Coblenz, Dordrecht), river mouths (Pisa, Marseilles, Hamburg, Danzig), small islands which made a crossing easier (Paris, Strasbourg, Lille, Leiden), natural harbours (Southampton, Venice, Genoa, Rouen, Antwerp), fords (Bruges, Utrecht) and junctions of rivers and roads (Frankfurt, Maastricht).

The earliest urban settlements were populated mainly by merchants and artisans. They often settled in the vicinity of an older centre of authority, such as the seat of a bishop, an abbey or a fortress, as well as in geographically favourable locations. The demarcation of the spheres of influence of the established lords might involve much negotiation and not infrequent struggles, but, in the event of a threat, an existing fortification could always offer protection. As towns continued to grow, they had to provide their own security: originally an earthen wall with a palisade and a moat, later on a stone wall. In Cologne a wall was built round a suburb, the *Rheinvorstadt*, in 948: the name recalls that this was a settlement on the Rhine outside the walls of the ancient town. Verdun, on the Meuse, an important centre of the slave trade in the early Middle Ages, seems to have had a fortified commercial settlement before 985.

The chronology of the growth in size of the towns can be seen in the succession of walls, still often recognisable as concentric circles in the ground-plans of city centres. The city wall of Paris,

dating from the beginning of the thirteenth century, was 2.8 kilometres long on the right bank of the Seine, 2.5 kilometres on the left bank, and encompassed 253 hectares. When these fortifications were extended at the beginning of the fourteenth century, the town covered 439 hectares. In Flanders, towns were fairly spread out, less densely built and, above all, buildings were not as tall as in the south. Ghent was the most spacious, with around 1300 a surface area of 644 hectares, and walls of almost 13 kilometres in circumference.

Two things stand out at this point: urban communities made very considerable investments in these fortifications, for which they must have collected financial resources. The first public works, with their own book-keeping, were thus created in the name and under the control of the community. On the other hand, the increased size of the towns made it more difficult to lay siege to them during wars.

In general, the morphology of the medieval town was the result of a natural process of growth that, according to the condition of the terrain, expanded concentrically out from one or more cores in all possible directions. This made the ground-plans of medieval towns irregular, but either semi-circular or circular (on one or both banks of a river) in form, bisected by axes running from the central marketplace to the gates. Only those towns founded and built at the same time revealed the chessboard pattern of Roman towns: in the Low Countries examples of these were the harbour towns of Nieuwpoort, Damme and Gravelines, founded by Philip, count of Flanders in the 1160s, while King Alfonse VIII of León founded a series of harbour towns on the Cantabrian coast, such as Santander (1187) and Laredo (1200) with the aim of linking the Castilian economy to Atlantic trade. The duke of lower Austria built Wiener Neustadt in 1194 as a bulwark against the Hungarians, financing it with the ransom that shortly before had been paid for Richard the Lionheart (see Chapter 7). As part of the eastward expansion, German colonists shortly after 1200 settled in a series of towns along the south coast of the Baltic Sea, among them Stralsund, Greifswald, Rostock, Danzig and Riga. Some of these had older Slavic roots, which led to the juxtaposition of urban settlements by the different ethnic groups separately. Colony towns, newly founded by the Teutonic Order in Prussia (Torun/Thorn and Elblag/Elbing on the Vistula) had a more geometrical ground-plan.

If the general tendency was towards unplanned, spontaneous development, old rich towns sometimes spent large amounts of money on carefully planned embellishment of public spaces. A famous example is the Tuscan town of Siena, whose council, the College of Nine, at the end of the thirteenth century decided to completely redesign and rebuild the city centre. It would take about half a century and the spending of tens of thousands of lira of public money before the entire project was completed. Special commissioners were appointed to watch over the aesthetics of the reconstruction works, whose main aim was to add to 'the beauty of the city for the delight of both citizens and foreigners'. To this end, houses in the city centre had to be aligned and the design of the facades of buildings along the main streets strictly controlled. The results leave visitors dumbfounded even today when their eyes travel from the majestic Palazzo Comunale to the magnificent, shell-shaped square that stretches out in front of it, neatly divided into nine equal wedges, representing the city magistrates who point their fingers – and bend their minds – in harmony to the city hall.

The beginnings of urban society

Merchant guilds and urban patriciates

During the early stages of urban growth, merchant guilds, also named *hanses* and confraternities, were closely interwoven with the government of towns. The guild hall was the seat of public authority, and eligibility for office depended on membership of the trustworthy guilds. Economic and public power were thus vested in the same class. In the oldest surviving statutes of such merchant associations – such as that of the confraternity of Valenciennes, dating from between 1051 and 1070 – membership was still completely open, and most attention was given to religious ceremonies, and to mutual assistance on the journeys undertaken in armed groups to distant markets. Solidarity was a bare necessity, especially for the travelling merchants who were exposed to robbery and arbitrary treatment by foreign authorities. It also helped to pacify disorderly behaviour and fights that might occur during drinking bouts, aimed at strengthening social ties. In contemporary regulations of the merchant guilds of Saint-Omer and Arras in northern France, particular attention was given to maintaining order and setting standards of behaviour during the meetings and binges. Charitable gifts of wine were also prescribed for the clergy, the poor and the lepers of the town. Community spirit had to be strengthened by the oath compulsory on joining the sworn alliance of burghers.

As towns grew rapidly due to immigration of new inhabitants who had various social and geographical, and sometimes also different ethnic backgrounds, the primary concern was to establish law and order within the expanding community. A core group of propertied free citizens involved in trade tried to create trust networks in order to protect themselves and their fellow members against outside risks, and to reduce transaction costs. Trust could be built upon acquaintance, rooted in family ties and secured by a guarantee of solvency, the high membership fee for newcomers.

It is clear that, over several generations, a mixture of merchants and local noble families were able to emerge as a new social elite, labelled in scholarly literature as **patriciate**, after the urban elite in Roman Antiquity. Its superiority was no longer based on physical force or other people's lack of legal freedoms. It was founded on profits earned in long-distance trade and on the economic dependence of artisans from merchants. The merchant guilds were in control of production in various English towns by the beginning of the twelfth century, and in Cambridge for example as early as the eleventh. It was the merchants who as entrepreneurs coordinated the production process and delivered the semi-finished articles to the various specialised artisans for completion. And, finally, it was these same merchant-entrepreneurs who were responsible for exporting the finished products. In this way, all the artisans in their workshops were dependent on the orders and price-fixing of the merchants.

In every town, the urban patriciate had its own name. In Paris the elite organised itself into a guild of merchants who controlled the river trade; they elected the merchants' provost and four aldermen who, in addition to holding certain powers in the city, issued economic regulations and administered justice. In Ghent the members were *viri hereditarii*, hereditary men, meaning that they owned land in the town. In Bruges, the London Hanse, the association of merchants engaging in trade with England, formed the heart of the town's government; in Florence and Louvain, meanwhile, it was important to be a member of one of the guilds of cloth merchants. An extreme example of this was the Council of Venice in 1297: the names of a thousand notable families were entered in a Golden Book; over the centuries many families died out and fewer and fewer survived, but no new ones were admitted until the end of the Republic, conquered by the French in 1796.

The new elite had enough capital at its disposal to buy up freehold land in the town. The phenomenal rise in the value of such land resulting from urban development formed a new source of wealth, and possibly also of prestige, for whoever could build a big stone house with towers, battlements and embrasures in the heart of the old town was indeed a real **seigneur**. Such a lord looked beyond the town walls for even greater status by copying the lifestyle of the nobility. He travelled on horseback, so that he was literally higher than the ordinary people, and surrounded himself with a retinue of squires and servants decked out in the colourful livery of his family. He bought property, if possible a feudal benefice with seigneurial rights and the prestigious obligation to serve the prince in his wars, on horseback and with a number of followers. He used a personal seal, assumed a coat of arms, and even dreamed of a noble title, or at least of marrying his children to aristocratic heirs. The noble lifestyle, which actually dated back to the stylised forms of medieval chivalry, continued to exercise a great attraction for socially climbing burghers until the nineteenth century. In northern and central Italy, the integration between the merchant elite and the old landed nobility took place much earlier and more quickly than it did further north, because in Italy noble families traditionally had urban residences and were not loath to involve themselves financially in commerce.

The rise of the urban middle classes

Merchant guilds gradually acquired an exclusive character whereby the less wealthy, perhaps also the less well-behaved, and certainly the less powerful townspeople were excluded from what would thenceforth be a club for the elite. The explanation for this process of closure and exclusion is two-fold: it was about numbers – solidarity does not work above a critical limit – and about saturation. After the initial, immense possibilities for growth, as competition became fiercer the longer-established burghers tried to keep the privileges they had won for themselves and their children.

This strategy would not remain uncontested. During the second half of the thirteenth century there were uprisings in several towns, caused by popular anger at a falling economy and new taxes. It was not the worst-off who stood to benefit from these revolts, however, but the newly rich and the higher middle classes. Until then, they had been excluded from power, but, by placing themselves at the head of a popular movement, they were able to force a breakthrough. In north and central Italy the middle classes organised into the so-called Popolo, which in many city-states succeeded in grabbing power from around the middle of the thirteenth century. Often, like in Florence, Popolo regimes were closely connected to the major merchant and craft guilds. In Flanders the liberation movement against the French occupation broke the patrician monopoly in 1302. In the German Empire the 'council families', as they were called, meaning the old patriciate, generally retained their authority or even their monopoly. In Nuremberg, Zürich and Strasbourg, their position was not threatened until the nineteenth century, and in Lübeck revolts at the beginning of the fifteenth century were crushed. The extent to which town authorities could be forced open to allow in new generations of merchants and artisans depended on the relationships of numbers and power inside a town and on the opportunities to form a coalition. As was the case with the acquisition of town privileges, the result varied considerably from region to region and often also from town to town. As social movements occurred mainly on a local scale, law and governance largely remained specific for individual towns.

Autonomy and liberty

Medieval towns are often thought of as islands of liberty and peace amidst oceans of lordly violence and suppression. This image needs correction in at least four respects. First, medieval towns were rarely places without lords. On the contrary, towns were favourite places for lords to control because towns, as concentrations of people doing business, were generators of wealth to a much larger degree than villages or rural estates could be. By implication, the rise and growth of towns

has been a less spontaneous process than is often suggested. It is better to think in terms of 'controlled development' (Lilley 2002). What really mattered was the *degree* of autonomy, which depended on the relative power as expressed by the size of the population and their capital accumulation. German 'free imperial cities', especially those in the north, hardly felt any interference from the emperor and the larger ones were well positioned to keep off the local and territorial lords, at least until the middle of the fifteenth century. Also, urban liberty was not so much liberty *to do* whatever citizens would have liked to do with their place as it was liberty *from* too much interference by any lord or bishop. The autonomy that towns pursued in the eleventh and twelfth centuries was precisely the aspiration to govern themselves without the direct interference of their lord.

Even this limited idea of liberty should not be confused with any ideal of equality, let alone democracy. Certainly in the early stages of urban development, inhabitants were not all legally free by definition (town dwellers could be serfs or slaves of some native landlord or, in the Mediterranean area, slaves from non-Christian origins bought on the slave market), and neither were all inhabitants treated as equals. Ethnic groups were openly discriminated against or privileged. More generally, as far as we can see, towns had oligarchic governments (see below), and the large majority of inhabitants, starting with the female population, were kept from exercising full rights to participate in government either actively or passively. In most cases full citizenship was only obtained (if not by inheritance) by being officially registered; and newcomers could only register against payment of a substantial entrance fee. Finally, in considering all these basic characteristics of medieval towns it is worth realising that the differences with villages were graded and relative, not essential and absolute. For instance, as we saw in Chapter 4, in their (often successful) aspiration to establish autonomous local government, that is to say, government without direct

PLATE 9.1 Ypres was a large centre of textile production and one of the cities where international fairs had been held since well before their first mention in 1127. At the height of its development, the local government decided to construct a worthy drapers' hall to facilitate the trade. Works started in 1260 and in 1304 the largest civic building of the Middle Ages was finished. Its façade was 133 metres long and its surfaces totalled 5,000 square metres. The heavy belfry tower was 70 metres high. Originally, a belfry was a symbol of seigneurial power, but the cities of Flanders and Hainaut adopted this model as a watchtower where bells signalled alarm as well as working hours. The building was nearly destroyed by the bombardment in November 1914, but entirely reconstructed after the war.

interference of the local lord, villages were not unlike towns. Like towns, villages could also be chartered, or walled, for that matter.

Urban law and privileges

The physical demarcation of urban space by walls was a symbol of the separate legal status of the town community. One of the characteristics of the pre-industrial town in Europe was that it enjoyed its own set of customs and laws, specifically tailored to each urban society in particular.

The origin of this can be found in the sworn pact that the earliest townspeople made with each other for their mutual protection. They swore to help each other should they be attacked in the town or on a journey, and they arranged a peaceful coexistence. These *coniurationes*, literally meaning 'swearing together' or 'sworn societies', put into practice a very old legal remedy, typical of most illiterate societies and groups of people who react against the dominant order, namely the collective oath, sworn on holy objects so that the threat of divine retribution as well as human punishment hung over the violator of the oath.

Such *coniurationes* are also known from rural communities, but the threat they posed to the authority of lords was many times bigger when towns and wealthy merchants were involved. The close community spirit of the early townspeople is understandable, although for different reasons in northern and southern Europe. In the north, most towns were new; their first inhabitants had come together from near and far. Many of them had escaped from dependent relationships of serfdom, and forced return to their (former) lords was still a possibility. The 'statute' of Valenciennes, originally referred to as a 'peace', came to be called a 'community' or *'commune'* in later charters, meaning the community of sworn

burghers who enjoyed the full privileges of the town. These citizens were legally free, without any of the limitations attached to the status of serfs on a demesne: no labour tasks, no servile dues in cash or kind, no restrictions on their freedom of movement or choice of marriage partner. For this reason, the urban area was also known as the 'freedom' of the town. Town privileges were personal: they did not apply per se to all inhabitants of the town area but to all its registered, honourable burghers, wherever they might be, inside the town or elsewhere.

On the other hand, in the south, and especially in Italy, most medieval towns were continuations of Late Antique cities, under the nominal lordship

BOX 9.1   THE 'PEACE' OF VALENCIENNES

An early example of a comprehensive town statute is the so-called 'peace' of Valenciennes, which was granted by the count of Hainaut in 1114. The grant followed a whole series of enactments of town privileges in what is now northern France: Cambrai in 1077, Saint-Quentin in 1080, Beauvais in around 1099, Noyon in 1108 and Laon in about 1109. These first written documents generally mean no more than the recognition by the lord or bishop of an already existing situation, where a 'community' or 'commune' with its own (customary) law had been formed on the basis of a sworn association. The designation 'peace' indicates the primary concern of the citizenry: protection from the violence of the world of the knights. The peace movement that had been set in motion by the bishops and abbots of southern France shortly before 1000 had paved the way for the foundation of more specific territorial jurisdictions where peace could be established in accordance with their own, non-feudal law. Towns were thus islands of peace in the midst of a world where legal uncertainty and lack of safety reigned.

On reaching the age of sixteen, every burgher of Valenciennes had to swear faithfully to observe the 'peace'. Should he refuse to do so, even after a day's grace to reconsider the matter if necessary, he was required to leave the town immediately and his house was pulled down. The community was based on compulsory mutual support and solidarity, inside the walls and outside. The 'peace' formulated punishments typical for the towns, in which private revenge was replaced as far as possible by officially imposed fines. Exclusion from the 'community', later systematically worked out as banishment, was one form of punishment. Corporal punishment was imposed exclusively on strangers – described as those who did not belong to the circle of 'men of the peace'. The 'peace' aimed to replace irrational proof (trial by ordeal and the judicial duel) whenever possible by the testimony of at least two 'men of the peace' or fellow burghers. This is one of the oldest non-ecclesiastical texts where such a procedure is provided for. The articles below (there were 57 articles in the oldest version) shed a clear light on the burghers' concerns.

1. It is solemnly observed and agreed in peace that every merchant who comes to the market in Valenciennes or goes from it may be secure at all times, himself and his wares, the only exception being the burghers of Douai. Whoever contravenes this, even if he is a knight, and is caught in the act or charged through the evidence of two men from the peace of Valenciennes, shall firstly be required to make good the damage that he has done to the merchant and further pay a fine of 60 shillings, of which the merchant shall receive 20 and the chancellor of the peace 40. . . .

2. Any person, be he knight or not, who takes commodities or other goods, movable or not, from men of the peace of the town of Valenciennes on their way to the market at Valenciennes or elsewhere, and who is caught in the act or charged through the evidence of two men of the mentioned peace, must make amends as laid down above. . . .

3. If a person from the surrounding countryside comes to and departs from the market of Valenciennes between sunrise on a Thursday and sunrise on a Monday, his lord may not arrest him unless it is to bring him to the count's law court. . . . Should the governor or the lord maltreat the man it shall be considered a violation of the peace for which there is a fine of 60 shillings for the count and his chancellor. . . .

4. Should a person who is a member of the town peace be accosted or molested at a market elsewhere because of the administration of justice of the town or for another cause, then shall his accuser be charged with violation of the peace as if it had happened in our own town.

Source: P. Godding and J. Pycke, 'La paix de Valenciennes de 1114. Commentaire et édition critique', *Bulletin de la Commission royale pour la publication des anciennes lois et ordonnances de Belgique XXIX* (1981).

of the local bishop. Of old the regional nobility had (fortified) houses in major towns, which made their presence very much felt. So, when the urban upper classes of noble families and rich merchants in Italy started to aspire to liberty and administrative autonomy, this emancipatory movement was completely different from the struggle for urban liberties in the north. Both struggles took place in the eleventh and twelfth centuries and were often violent, because after all this was a world dominated by knights and private warfare. The trial of strength between Emperor Frederick Barbarossa, also king of Italy, and the towns of Lombardy which, as communes under the leadership of their own elected consuls had won their freedom from the territorial power of the bishops in about 1100, is well known. Despite his military victory over Milan, Barbarossa could not hold on to his power in the face of the league of Lombard towns, and in 1183 he was forced to recognise their factual autonomy. In the twelfth century the German kings also recognised the rights to freedom of the inhabitants of the old episcopal towns along the Rhine, but here there was no question of real autonomy for a long time. In about the same period the kings of France granted rights with local autonomy to several towns in the north of their kingdom, partly with an eye to strengthening the monarchy against the great feudal lords who until then held these territories in their grasp. King Louis IX explained this in so many words in the *Enseignements* ('Instructions') to his son: 'I well recollect that Paris and the good towns of my kingdom helped me against the barons when I was newly crowned.'

Bishops who had been lord and master in their episcopal seats since the establishment of the bishoprics were the least inclined to give up any of their rights to the urban community. The struggle was primarily about the personal freedom of all the residents of a town, a recognition that they were no longer tied to the duties and restrictions resting on them as serfs. Agreement was reached that the inhabitants of that town would acquire their freedom under law after living in a town for a period of a year and a day.

An important step in the movement towards the emancipation of the towns consisted of their claim to have the right to formulate their own customs and laws and regulations for their own community, and to exercise jurisdiction over it. This meant that the lord of the district in which the town originated had to relinquish his direct authority over the area. Most lords set a price for this, receiving compensation in the form of perpetual rents or levies and a share in the growing yields from taxes and administration of the law. The results of these struggles varied from place to place, depending on the proximity and power of the town's lord and how far the size and wealth of the town commune could tip the balance. Similarly, the privileges of a town were continually subject to revision and adaptation, prompted by the evolution of society and changing power relations.

Hence the customs and law of a town consisted of an odd mixture of privileges granted in writing by various authorities over centuries, and their interpretation and extensions in daily practice. In tangible form, it could be seen as a heavy chest full of solemnly sealed documents and deeds from diverse authorities – from popes, emperors and kings to local lords. Everyone had his say on specific matters and sometimes the ruler granted extensive statutes dealing primarily with criminal justice and economic rights. There did not seem to be much system to it. Because many statutes stated that the magistracy had the right to interpret the statute and to alter it if necessary, unwritten customary laws grew up alongside the written laws. This was a sort of jurisprudence based on the force of precedent. Customary law could be reconstructed only from the records of a town's juridical actions, or by appealing to the

memory of old officials. This gave rise to frequent disputes between rulers and town councils or among local officials. The situation changed only very slowly from the fourteenth century onwards with the development of a judicial hierarchy, whereby the rulers' central courts were allowed to review the verdicts of local courts of justice.

The personality of the law was nevertheless maintained on the continent until the French Revolution and its dissemination; it meant that a person fell under a specific judicial system either because he belonged to a privileged estate (clergy, noble, royal official) or was a burgher of a particular town or village with privileges. Law that was applied strictly territorially was extremely rare. Indeed, the stronger the economic and demographic weight of a town, the better its chance of safeguarding its juridical autonomy. Town law was therefore both territorial, or rather, local, in that it applied in principle to everyone inside the walls and in the surrounding **banlieu** of a few miles which fell under the town's jurisdiction, and personal, in that citizens of towns often appealed to their own law when they were summoned to law courts outside their town. The geographical extension of the law to state territory did not occur until after the French Revolution. It is interesting to note that the terms 'burgher', 'bourgeois', 'citizen', all of which nowadays indicate state citizenship, came from the environment in which the concept of public law was reinvented in Europe: the town.

In the urban environment, the idea of *res publica*, in its narrow sense of republican state, acquired a very real and original meaning for the first time since the Roman era. In fact the medieval concept of a commune referred to the community that formed a collective identity and organised its affairs in a public context, in far more concrete terms than the *res publica* borrowed by scholars from the language of Antiquity. In this respect, the towns went much further than monarchies, which found it difficult to make the distinction between the public domain and the ruler's private patrimony. Yet the fundamental constraint of the town's concept of public government was its particularism; every town enjoyed its own laws and no more wished to have them meddled with than it wished to share them. This desire to be separate and to remain so became characteristic of urban societies all over pre-industrial Europe. If they occasionally did reach some form of mutual cooperation, then it usually happened either on a very unstable basis, or through the subordination of smaller towns to larger ones – such as in the Italian regional states dominated by metropolises like Florence, Milan and Venice and in the colonies controlled by Genoa and Venice. Citizens focused on their own immediate interests and were unwilling to share their privileges with others. Even within the towns themselves, fierce conflicts broke out between clans, classes and occupational groups. Corporative egoism was thus the outcome of the townspeople's originally egalitarian concept of community.

Urban government and public order

As a result of the successful struggle for autonomy with city lords – whether they were kings or other princes – the government of a town from the late eleventh century onwards was always vested in the community of burghers, which initially coincided with its patriciate or local elite of wealthy merchants and noblemen. Later on, as we saw, the well-to-do middle class succeeded to a limited degree in gaining access to city councils, but urban government in the Middle Ages was almost by definition oligarchic. However, in two important respects, the situation in the north differed greatly from that in the cities of north and central Italy. First, in the north, town councils commonly consisted of a president or bailiff and a fixed number of aldermen (*scabini*), but in the cities of north and central Italy they consisted of boards of consuls or, later, priors. All such councillors were usually appointed for a maximum of one year. The difference is in the figure of the bailiff (or sheriff in the north) who was an official appointed and salaried by the town's lord, who in this way kept a say in urban government. Second, whereas in the north city councils exercised undivided legislative and executive as well as judicial power, in Italy the three powers were actually divided from the end of the twelfth century onwards, when everywhere judiciary power – including elementary police functions – was separated from the legislative and executive authority of town governors, and consigned to a special magistrate, called *podestà*. To safeguard neutrality and independence, these *podestàs* were always noblemen who came from elsewhere and who brought their own staff of trained judges, lawyers, bailiffs, policemen and servants with them – the costs were met by their employers, of course. By the thirteenth century the authority of the *podestà* was undermined to some extent in cities where the Popolo succeeded in dominating government. One of its predictable demands was always to appoint its leader, called *capitano del Popolo*, both as a member of the city council and as commander in chief of the dominant city's army, a task that until then was often assigned to the *podestà*. From the fourteenth century onwards, the role of the *podestà* was further weakened by bureaucratisation or by the establishment of 'tyrannical' regimes (*signorie*), such as that of the Visconti family in Milan, and that of the Scaligeri in Verona. In 1313, Dante complained in his *Purgatory* (VI, 124–125) 'the towns of Italy are full of tyrants'.

In the larger towns, councils of limited size as just mentioned were flanked by political advisory boards. These were often manned by ex-magistrates and could have a permanent or an ad hoc character. Finally, most towns had so-called 'General' or 'Great Councils', that originally may have consisted of all (male, adult, registered) citizens, but which for practical reasons, at least in large cities, were reduced to still large, round, numbers of several hundred or sometimes even several thousand. They met occasionally, at the

PLATE 9.2 Republican theories of power emanating from the citizenry were formulated in Tuscany both in treatises and in monuments. In the town hall of the autonomous city of Siena, with its impressive 120-metre high tower, the meeting room of the Council of Nine Governors (*Signori*), elected from the merchants' oligarchy, was decorated with frescoes by Ambrogio Lorenzetti, painted between 1337 and 1340. They illustrate the city's good government, based on the constitution and the commune's desire for peace, concord and justice. This idealistic view of a city shows various artisans at work in their shops, in construction and transport.

sounding of the city bells, to approve major decisions or measures taken by the city government, and often they had a role in the election of new magistrates.

In town law, which was valid within a town itself and its banlieu or surrounding area, the rule of peace, at least in theory, prevailed. It meant that all kinds of legal measures were taken to contain the pernicious practice of feuding. In medieval society, feuding could refer to two different phenomena that were loosely related: first, to taking blood revenge after somebody had been killed or gravely injured. This right was strictly reserved for the victim's recognised kin group. In addition, feuding had a second meaning: making private war on someone after a formal declaration of enmity for reasons of grave injustice or heavy insult. Feuding in this second sense, which may have originated as an unwritten right of the nobility, but ended up being practised more widely (by townsmen, but by ordinary peasants as well), did not necessarily imply the families of both sides, if only because legal persons, like towns, could be involved. Neither did such private 'wars' have to end in people being killed or wounded, which would have given cause to feuding in the first sense. Besides, feuding in the first sense – taking blood revenge – was more often than not prevented from being executed by an old judicial procedure aimed at reconciling both sides involved and centred on an appropriate financial and moral compensation of the victim and his/

her kin to be paid by the perpetrator and his/her kin. On the continent, this procedure was generally applied in all kinds of secular courts of justice; it was certainly no urban invention or especially developed for urban law courts. However, city governments may have added to the rigidity of this procedure by forcing both sides involved in such 'cases of vengeance' to accept a 'peace' – actually more a truce – that was imposed on all parties involved in violent rows and fights in public spaces and places. The larger towns in the Low Countries had special officials appointed, called 'peacemakers', to patrol the streets and shout something like *oyés, faites pais* ('listen, make peace!') – as they did in Douai – if a fight had broken out and blood been drawn. This 'peace' or truce was meant to hold for a set number of days – often 40 or a quarantine – in which period it was strictly forbidden to retaliate; on the contrary it was meant to be used by victims and perpetrators to negotiate a satisfying settlement that could lead to reconciliation.

The juxtaposition of reconciliation procedures, in which town magistrates acted mainly as intermediaries and observers of negotiated settlements in cases of homicide and the infliction of heavy physical injury, and the active, public prosecution of crimes *ex officio* disappeared entirely from western Europe between the fourteenth and sixteenth centuries. This presupposed, however, that peace, still an exceptional circumstance in the eleventh and twelfth centuries, would thenceforth

PLATE 9.3 The relatively small Tuscan town of San Gimignano still features a number of impressive medieval towers belonging to the fortified houses of the patrician families. Originally, they expressed the pride of the dominant families, and in times of conflict, they served a military purpose. Most of these towers here and in other towns collapsed over the centuries or were torn down by order of the local authorities.

be considered the normal situation. It could only be maintained effectively if a government had sufficient superior strength, based on the recognition of its use of force as the only legitimate option. The criminal ordinances issued by Emperor Charles V in 1530–1532 in the German Empire and the Low Countries formally ended toleration of the right of retaliation. In regions where government authority was weak, the Tyrol, south Italy, Sicily and Corsica, for example, blood vengeance remained common practice for several centuries.

Feuds in the sense of acts of private warfare were far more difficult to curb. They tended to become entangled with larger political issues, such as the party strife between the Ghibellines and Guelphs in Italy (originally the adherents and opponents of the House of Hohenstaufen, whose major stronghold near Stuttgart was called Waiblingen, hence Ghibellines), and most likely very powerful persons or families were implicated. This type of violence was far more of a nuisance in the city-states of Italy, where noble families traditionally lived in towns, than in the north, where this was less often the case. These noble families were organised as clans, with a strict hierarchy of descent through the male line and surrounded by other kin, associates and livery servants who were often armed. We are strongly reminded of the knightly culture when we consider such clans in the towns of Italy and Flanders, decked out in the heraldic colours of the family, exhibiting reckless group virility as a means of affirming their honour and status and, if necessary, of showing their superior strength. The magnificent stone-built houses of these clans dominated the townscape. With their obvious ability to withstand a siege their solid construction, battlements and towers radiated strength to one and all. In the towns of northern and central Italy, with San Gimignano still a good example, all the great aristocratic houses had tall towers, which had both a military and a symbolic function. However, most of them were destroyed when Popolo regimes came to power from the second half of the thirteenth century onwards.

They took severe action against those noble families who refused to submit to the public authority of the city council and who were denounced as magnates. Eventually, magnate families in such cities as Florence were excluded from political power altogether and expelled from the city at the slightest provocation.

Common good and public domain

Faced with such challenges, town authorities all over Europe strengthened their legitimacy by taking on an intermediary role and presenting themselves as defenders, not of private interest, but of the common good. A number of terms were used to express the abstract ideal, linking it to the principles of Roman law: *bonum commune, utilitas publica, quod interest civitati*: in short, the common good, in the public interest. This may sound like an abstract term but actually it did imply a programme of action which made it clear that city councils claimed a monopoly on the use of violence, and that those who defied the council's authority could expect to be severely punished, irrespective of their social background.

As city governments could better appeal to such general principles in individual decisions, their actions acquired greater authority while the cohesion of the elite and the town was also enhanced. The support given to city councils by professional lawyers helped the former to rise, as an institution, above parties. Their role as judge was decisive, because it demonstrated the effectiveness and credibility of the establishment and maintenance of public order. Criminal proceedings brought by the officer of justice *ex officio* on the grounds of offences against the common good, such as breaches of the peace, placed greater demands on the ability of city governments to trace offenders and build up a legitimate case against them.

In less politically sensitive areas, city governments were able to create public functions much more quickly. In the north, the city magistrate usually carried out tasks which in Italy and France were vested in notaries in the Roman tradition, in particular the registration of private agreements and testaments. Another case in point is the construction of town walls, which obviously required enormous investments in both money and time. A system of taxation had to be created for the purpose, raised mainly by levies on consumer goods. The burghers knew, therefore, that they were making efforts for their own community, just as they had done for the raising of taxes or ransoms for their lords. By the late thirteenth century, management of collective resources was already a bone of contention between the established oligarchy and the artisans, who were beginning to organise themselves into guilds and demanding accountability for how the tax money was spent. After revolts by the craft guilds in 1279–1280, Count Guy of Flanders forced the magistrates of his major towns to keep accounts of public income and expenditure, and thus to be accountable for their policies.

In addition to walls, towns erected stone buildings with a public function: the town hall, of course, but also often free-standing bell towers, the *belforts*, belfries of France and Flanders. They served diverse purposes: that of watchtower, tolling the bells to mark public events, mobilisation of the militia, and the start and finish of the day's work; they bore sundials or mechanical clocks; the chest containing the town's charter was kept there under lock and key. In time, the impressive tower became a symbol of the town itself. Other building works with a public function included trade halls, halls for the sale of foodstuffs, warehouses, harbours, canals, locks, bridges, roads, cranes, weigh-houses, water conduits and fountains. Moreover the town created public spaces: in the first place the markets, the primary function of the town, but also streets and squares which were the stage for public demonstrations or everyday urban life. Churches similarly served as public buildings; they were often largely financed by monies from the town

community, although they were managed by the clergy and local Church councils made up of laypeople. As an orderly architectural entity, the town formed a framework for the way of life which gave tangible and visible shape to the concept of community.

It is interesting to consider the extent of the public domain in the towns. Social care was originally in Church hands, but through foundations by citizens it came increasingly under the control of representatives of the town authorities. They supervised the financial management and also laid down regulations; their three-way relationship with private donors and religious charitable care was much respected. This was also true of hospitals, whose management was left to the religious orders, and of poor relief which rested mainly with the parishes. The care of old people, widows and orphans, in so far as it was not covered by these two categories, was in the hands of guilds and confraternities. The numerous unskilled workers who were not eligible for guild membership depended in times of hardship on alms-giving by parishes, convents, hospitals, almshouses and individuals, although this support was not sufficient during economic crises and in cases of sickness and old age.

In short, life in a town was an all-inclusive, cradle-to-grave arrangement, at least for its 'full' citizens. The levels of personal involvement, and of political and social participation that were required, were far higher than in any modern city. We saw that in Flanders, parts of Germany and Italy hundreds of citizens were members of the Great Councils. More generally, town dwellers were incorporated into all sorts of local and sublocal associations that were organised at the neighbourhood level. Most people worked at home or on building sites or in workshops close by. All went to church in their neighbourhood that often coincided with a parish and was the abode of other religious houses (chapels, convents) that offered specific forms of spiritual wellbeing and social welfare. This is where people were baptised and morally educated, this is where their relatives who had passed away were buried and commemorated in prayer, this is where holy days were celebrated. All sorts of entertainment were organised at the neighbourhood level, ranging from church processions and fairs to ritualised street fights and games, including horse races, of which the famous *palio* of Siena is a spectacular relic that has survived to this day. In larger towns, districts or neighbourhoods also provided the basis for the recruitment and training of the city militia. Young men had to be prepared to fight and to die for their city, and many did so, but they could be assured that until their last breath they would be in the company of friends, mustered behind their guild's or neighbourhood's banner. City militias gave a very forceful expression to the self-awareness of the burghers.

In most of these social arrangements and types of association, the town authorities only exercised a supervisory function, which was sometimes formalised. In many towns, governors appointed by the city council supervised the guardianship of orphans. This was done to keep check on any quarrels between and within families with an inheritance at stake and a feud as a likely outcome. The guardianship of the mentally ill was seen as a public-order problem which, like the prison, was looked after by the town. In the fifteenth century, towns sometimes employed doctors and midwives to provide help in cases of public disasters such as famines and epidemics. In the early decades of the sixteenth century town authorities throughout Europe started to interfere more emphatically with such sublocal, neighbourhood organisations as just mentioned, especially with a view to coordinate the diverse forms of social care and to impose controls on it. With the new increase in population there was a keenly felt need for rationalisation. In the fourteenth century a number of towns had already set up one or more schools, a clear break with the traditional monopoly of the Church. The spread of the Reformation accelerated this, because now all denominations rushed to win the soul of a child.

Urban networks and hierarchies

The largest commercial metropolises enjoyed a wide degree of autonomy with respect to their surrounding states until well into the eighteenth century. They were often situated in small states where they exerted considerable influence on government. They were able to expand this position of relative autonomy if their own development took place before royal power had been consolidated, particularly in coastal areas. Moreover, metropolises were concerned primarily with matters that were not of interest to rulers, such as the safety of traffic routes, the protection of travelling merchants, negotiating business agreements with diverse partners and providing efficient regulations for conciliation and jurisdiction. Neither the feudal lords nor their ecclesiastical advisers knew much about such matters, so that it was merchants directly involved who developed the relevant institutional rules and even put them into effect, in some cases with the formal seal of a neighbouring prince.

Good examples are Pisa, Genoa, Barcelona and Valencia which developed their maritime network from the eleventh century, chiefly in the western Mediterranean, with settlements in the Balearics, Sardinia and Sicily and consulates in the main harbours on the North African coast. Their primary aim was to organise markets and ensure the safety of trading routes and the protection of their own citizens abroad. For this purpose, concessions were made with local rulers, including those in Islamic areas. Practical experience of shippers and merchants became formalised in codes of maritime law applied by the local specialised judges. The king of Aragon left his metropolises entirely free to handle their business, as long as he shared in the profits.

Groups of towns employed a variety of means to arrange their own protection in a world that, with the fragmentation of effective authority, had become extremely unsafe for travellers. Because good traffic links with their hinterland and other markets were essential for these towns, the safety of the roads was a continual concern. Small feudal lords found it very tempting to exploit their control over a particular area through which a strategic route passed by threatening travelling merchants with robbery and violence if they refused to pay the toll demanded. At best, tolls were the going price for what in a positive sense was called protection: if the toll was paid then the merchant could be certain of safe passage. The amount of the toll was often a subject of controversy, for it was difficult to rule out arbitrariness on the part of either the ruler or his toll collector.

A vital traffic axis such as the Rhine was strewn with local rulers who profited from the busy river traffic. From the thirteenth to the fifteenth century it was common for towns in this region

and in Alsace and Swabia to join together to seek protection from assaults on their safety or that of their citizens and their commercial traffic. In a number of cases they were even able to involve some feudal lords in their alliance or, in exchange for financial support, were given guarantees or rights from the German king or emperor. The first major alliance of the Rhine towns dated from 1254, when the Interregnum (the period between 1254 and 1273 when there was no king generally recognised in Germany) created problems in the field of public order. By forming a sworn alliance which placed them directly under the protection of Christ, the allied towns tried above all to maintain peace, to resolve conflicts by legal means or by arbitration, to organise the joint prosecution

PLATE 9.4 Venice was the largest and wealthiest medieval metropolis, heading a huge maritime empire. The cathedral, the bell tower and the palace of the doge are in the centre of the image; the arsenal and shipyard is a walled area with docks on the extreme right.

of peace-breakers and to limit the tolls on rivers and roads. These agenda points were clearly in conflict with the activities of noblemen, yet the movement did succeed in persuading a number of territorial rulers in the region, archbishops and bishops, the count palatine of the Rhine and a few counts and lords to join the alliance. Just as the Peace of God movement had done earlier, the alliance thus took upon itself a task that was in essence the province of the king, namely maintaining peace and justice in the public interest and stopping the nobility from feuding and taking the law into their own hands. Such alliances between towns did not last long, however, and their rare joint military actions met with only limited success. The great exception was the German Hanse, which up to 1358 was primarily an organisation of regional merchant guilds, only later becoming a league of cities which survived until the seventeenth century (see Chapter 7). What did unite towns were their trade interests. But towns also had to support and safeguard a flow of people and goods to and from the surrounding rural areas to provide for their livelihood.

Relationships between the towns were even less idyllic and were strictly defined by their mutual dependency in a hierarchy of markets. Every town made efforts to protect its own production by prohibiting similar activities in its vicinity. Larger towns exercised as stifling a hegemony over smaller ones as they did over the rural areas. The larger towns also fulfilled specialised functions in a particular region. As we have seen above in the case of Florence, these were only profitable in large centres where they could attract enough customers from a wide hinterland. The region that relied on this sort of specialised function of a town is called its service area. Towns and villages fulfilled central functions for their own service areas at different levels, depending on their size and the diversification of specialised productions and services. A hierarchy of markets to three or four levels was a common phenomenon. This insight helps us to understand the diverse forms of interdependence that existed between town and country and between towns of differing size within the same system.

The most sharply crystallised relationships were found in the most urbanised region, that of northern and central Italy. In the fourteenth century, the largest cities entered a fierce competition for the domination of a wider hinterland, the *contadi* or city-states. The conquest and subjection of Pisa by Florence, in 1406, meant that Florence finally gained control over a harbour. Its *contado* gradually expanded to a territory of about 12,000 square kilometres. Between 1404 and 1428, Venice captured a huge area in the Po valley, measuring some 30,000 square kilometres and reaching as close as 20 kilometres to Milan. The subordinate towns came under an administration appointed by the capital, but local law and government were largely left intact. The capital's law courts enjoyed precedence throughout the entire countryside, the *contado*; in legal matters townspeople received preferential treatment over country dwellers; rural goods were taxed more heavily than those from the town; town guilds enjoyed more privileges than the country artisans; and urban landownership penetrated deeply into the country. In this way political hegemony numbed market relationships which still offered more scope to the larger centres than to the small.

In those parts of Europe where the formation of feudal and monarchic power did not take place early and did not penetrate deeply, towns thus developed their own political and social structures in order to look after their vital common interests. Using the maintenance of the peace as a pretext, they arranged to protect their trade independently, locally and along the routes linking them. Where they enjoyed superiority, they formed hegemonic market systems of colonial dimensions. Outside Italy, the relationships of power were less emphatically to the advantage of (large) towns, and other configurations were formed, in which kingdoms and comparable principalities would prevail. As these expanded their territory and power, they naturally came into contact with the power systems that urban networks had already built up in some areas. Conflicts of compe-tence and open power struggles arose between them, yet various forms of cooperation also proved to be possible. What is clear is that the urban communities gave the history of Europe a unique character, thanks to their relative auton-omy and their corporative organisation.

Urban society and urban economy in the later Middle Ages

A burgher worldview

The concentration of thousands, or even tens of thousands, of inhabitants within a town's walls made life there extremely difficult, a consequence of the often unhygienic living conditions. The spread of leprosy during the twelfth and thir-teenth centuries was certainly connected to this. Moreover, the supply of food, grain in particular, was precarious. There were famines throughout western Europe in 1125 and again in 1195–1196. In both cases, chronicles describe how people's stomachs were swollen from undernourishment, how bread prices increased tenfold or even twentyfold in a short time, and the mass of starving people dying on the streets in search of food and alms. The large concentrations of people dependent on grain supplies from the hinterland heightened the vulnerability of the towns to natural fluctuations in harvest yields resulting from changing weather conditions. While farmers could attribute the failure of a harvest to the will of God, town-dwellers saw that the price of bread in times of scarcity rose more sharply than seemed to be justified by the dwindling supply. They also saw, or suspected, that large religious institutions, grain dealers and comfortably-off burghers had well-filled grain lofts that they kept for their own use, or that they sent only small quantities of grain to the market in order to fetch the highest prices. Human actions were visible in the events which threatened the existence of poor townspeople.

The artisans were also affected by changing situations in the international markets for their raw materials and finished products. It was not difficult to realise that the middlemen made more profit from their labour than they themselves did, and that interruptions in trade as a result of wars or boycotts were the work of humans. Unlike the farming communities, a more rational and secularised insight into the causes of life's uncer-tainties developed in the towns where there was direct evidence of human behaviour. So a specifically burgher mentality grew up, different from that of clergymen, noblemen and peasants. The French medievalist, Jacques Le Goff (1980), has strikingly illustrated the pragmatic mentality of the medieval town by pointing to the change in the awareness of time. In the country, nature, with its cycle of seasons and the unequal division of light and darkness, determined the rhythm of life. The farmer arranged his daily activities according to the position of the sun and moon, and the seasons. There was the church, whose bells tolled in the rhythm of the services and feast-days. In the towns nature and Church had far less influence on the rhythm of life. The town bell towered above the churches, and rang out the working day. Mechanical clocks appeared in the late thirteenth century. They divided the day into hours of equal length, determined by the people themselves. Time was no longer in God's hands.

This more businesslike worldview fostered the idea that the reality was not a God-given order that could not or should not be challenged, as the theologians had maintained. If society was the work of humans then it could also be changed by humans. A challenge to the established social order was no longer blasphemous. It can even be assumed that the fervent preaching of the mendi-cant orders, in particular the Franciscans, against amassing worldly wealth and supporting the ideal of poverty in imitation of Christ, had contributed to the fact that the urban proletariat now became more articulate, condemned exploitation by 'the rich' and started to make demands (see also Chapter 12).

Professional structures

The question of how an urban society was structured can be approached from both a legal and a socio-economic point of view. Legally speaking, there were a number of categories of townspeople, each of which fell under its own statutory laws. Many of them were unable to fulfil the financial conditions for citizenship, but remained in the town to carry out low-paid work. Because chances of surviving extreme poverty were greater in towns than in the countryside (as were, paradoxically, chances of dying as a consequence of all kinds of contagion), medieval towns, and certainly large towns, always had many marginal inhabitants who could not afford to register – think of armies of day labourers, beggars, criminal gangs, pimps and prostitutes – and therefore were seen and treated as second-rate citizens. This group formed a mobile mass that could react quickly to fluctuations in the economy and moved to where the opportunities seemed most favourable.

There were also diverse categories which were not, or not fully, subjected to the civic authorities because they had a different legal status; they included members of a prince's court, members of the clergy, nobles with their retinue, foreigners, Jews and Muslims. In those parts of the Iberian peninsula that had been recovered by Christians, there were countless Muslims and people of a mixed religious background who would be systematically persecuted under Philip II and in 1609 were deported en masse to North Africa. They worked mainly on the land and were unflatteringly known as *mudéjares*, 'tamed animals' in Arabic. There were large numbers of Jews, too, particularly in Mediterranean towns. The 25,000 Jews of Catalonia represented almost a seventh of the urban population there. In Carpentras it was one-tenth. Among them were not only merchants and money-lenders but also doctors and scholars. They lived in their own neighbourhoods, known as *juiveria*, *juderie* or *calls*, depending on the local language. Legally they enjoyed the protection of the king or prince; in return for payment of a sum

of money to him, they were his 'servants'. In the north-west, Jewish presence was much smaller because of an early lack of tolerance. In England, the relatively small numbers of Jews who had entered the land in the wake of the Norman Conquest were kicked out under Edward I in 1290, while the French king Philip IV promulgated a law aimed at the expulsion of all Jews in 1306. In the first years of the Black Death, 1348–1349, massive pogroms nearly halved the Jewish population in many west European towns.

In the cities of central Europe, such as Prague and Cracow, diverse ethnic, religious or social categories lived inside the same agglomeration in separate, adjacent townships, with their own institutions and often also their own walls, town hall, market square and more. There was greater integration in the West. In Italy and Iberia, slavery continued to exist throughout the Middle Ages, particularly for members of the household staff. Slaves were also used to a limited extent on the Italian sugar plantations in Cyprus and Crete and for salt production on Ibiza. The slave markets were most lively round the Black Sea, where Tartars (people of Mongol descent), Circassians and Abkhazians (people from the Caucasus), Russians and Bulgarians were bought and sold; in Andalusia, the trade was in black Africans from Guinea and Muslims from the reconquered parts of Mallorca and Valencia.

From a socio-economic viewpoint, the populations of the towns could be distinguished in economic sections, categories of well-being, and so forth. Some insight is possible through statistical data, thanks to the rich documentation of the towns of Tuscany (see Table 9.3). The social structure according to occupation was more varied in large towns than in small ones. In other words, there were more different and more specialised occupations in a town like Florence than in the small towns of the region. The larger the town, the smaller the proportion of people there who made a living from agriculture, and the larger the proportion who made a living from the service sector. Craft specialisation in one sector was only

TABLE 9.3 Division of occupations in Florence, Pisa and the small towns of Tuscany

	Florence (%)	Pisa (%)	Small towns (%)
Agriculture	0.3	6.0	32.7
Selling of food	4.7	5.9	1.9
Cloth	16.3	7.0	2.1
Other textiles	4.7	3.4	0.5
Paper	0.1	0.2	0.2
Leather, skins	5.7	9.3	2.6
Spices	1.2	2.0	0.7
Metalworking	2.8	3.2	1.9
Wood, masonry, etc.	4.0	5.0	1.1
Service industries	16.3	13.5	7.1
Unknown	43.9	44.6	49.3
Total number of households	9,722	1,714	6,262

Source: D. Herlihy and C. Klapisch-Zuber, *Tuscans and their Families* (New Haven and London, 1985), p. 127.

profitable on a large scale: in Florence, with a total population of 44,000 in 1427, the textile sector represented at least 21 per cent of the workforce (but the real percentage was probably considerably higher); in Ghent around 1356 as much as 63 per cent of a total population of 64,000; in Pisa, only 10.4 per cent and in small Tuscan towns barely 2.6 per cent.

The capital resources of the members of diverse occupational groups varied greatly: the wealth of the Florentine bankers was on average 83 times larger than that of a transport worker, that of a wool merchant about 31 times greater, and of a spice merchant 10 times. Among the artisans themselves, there was a considerable difference in status between specialised occupations which required a certain amount of capital and skill, ordinary skilled trades and the jobs which required no skills at all. The greatest differences were found at the top of the social pyramid. The thousands of small towns of late medieval Europe still had a much more agrarian character. One can understand why Louis IX instructed the city council of Bourges in 1262 to 'drive all the roaming pigs out of the town because they are completely ruining it'. On the other hand, certain commercial activities were responsible for a large share of the employment opportunities, particularly in towns with more than 10,000 inhabitants.

Craft guilds and guild regimes

In the larger towns, artisans were organised into occupational groups from the thirteenth century onwards. For some specialised workers, such as goldsmiths, basket weavers or leather workers, this involved living in the same street. For expensive products, the central location was critical because of the basic price and the proximity of customers. In Florence, the street of the tapestry weavers, the *arazzieri*, is just one block away from the Medici palace, and two from the Duomo. As is well known, goldsmiths were concentrated on the old bridge, close to the palaces of the nobles. For other, sometimes polluting, activities the availability of sufficient flowing water and the actual distance from the town centre to limit environmental damage were deciding factors. This applied to tanners in particular, while fullers and brewers were dependent on clean water. For reasons of hygiene and also to facilitate quality control, town authorities concentrated the vendors of fresh foodstuffs in one street or market hall. There is still a very large meat hall in Ghent dating from the early fifteenth century, Brussels has its Butchers' Street, and vegetable, fish and cattle markets are familiar everywhere.

In the earliest stages, in Milan before 1068 and in Florence, the members of the local aristocracy and the merchants seem to have taken the initiative to organise the artisans, in order to have a better grip on them. In time, town militias would be formed on the same basis. In a number of French towns, Toulouse for example, some craft guilds were already recognised by the authorities in the twelfth century; notably these were in the sectors for food and leather-working, most sensitive to deterioration and environmental pollution. The members of these craft guilds were obliged to take an oath promising to obey the regulations. During the thirteenth century artisans formed religious and charitable fraternities in Catalonia and Flanders, as the first urban merchants had done two centuries earlier. The aim was mutual assistance and religious services, with a view to counteracting the uncertainties of life such as disablement, unemployment and widowhood. During the fourteenth and fifteenth centuries large fraternities and craft guilds founded homes for their aged and needy members. For those working in industries dependent on long-distance trade for their raw materials and the export of finished products, the hazards of international relations and business cycles could suddenly deprive them of their income for protracted periods of time. Under such circumstances, up to half the population of an industrial town could drop into poverty from one year to the next.

CORPORATIVE ORGANISATION   Control of production and of the artisans themselves was a strong motive for the town authorities to prescribe a certain organisational form to corporations. Price controls and the hallmark of product quality were in the interest of traders and consumers alike. Even in the period of exclusive patrician rule, therefore, craft guilds received legal recognition as monopolistic occupational groups: only members of the guilds were allowed to practise a particular craft, and training was arranged by the artisans themselves.

Town authorities laid down regulations for working hours and technical matters to guarantee standards of quality and to combat unfair competition between fellow artisans. For a prescribed number of years (often two to four, eight to ten in many cases in Paris in 1268, sometimes as many as twelve) an apprentice lived and worked with a recognised master artisan, and so learned his trade in practice. In that sense, workshops had a decidedly family character, contributing to the close ties which existed between master artisans and the lower ranks. When the apprenticeship was completed, the apprentice became a journeyman, a skilled worker in the employ of a master. In some cases, recorded from the thirteenth century onwards, the journeyman could then qualify as a master after submitting a 'masterpiece' to the guild masters as proof of his professional skill. To be recognised as a master artisan a man was required to be a burgher of the town, to pay an entrance fee, to provide a banquet and to have his own workshop and tools. Here, there was a class distinction between master and journeyman, because a master owned his own production means. Just as in the thirteenth century the merchant guilds became more exclusive as the competition became stiffer, so in a period of a stagnant or contracted market the legal and material requirements to become a master worked as a barrier which the established masters could use to protect their own positions against newcomers. This happened particularly during the demographic decline of the fourteenth century. The right of entry was made considerably more expensive for members from outside the town or from the country and cheaper for the sons of existing masters. There was thus a tendency for a craft to become hereditary, especially in those sectors where the potential markets decreased. In the German Empire, where most towns were relatively small and the chivalric ethic still largely determined the pattern of values, many craft guilds set the requirement of 'honourable' conduct as a condition of entry: 'honour' there was concerned with the exclusion of unmarried cohabitants or people of Slavic origin. Among those professions considered lacking honour, and thus not permitted to form guilds, were those of executioner, grave-digger, barber and bath-house master.

CLASS CONFLICT   Under the rule of the patricians, the merchants-entrepreneurs-administrators exerted close control over the craft guilds. They had an interest in social and economic regulations and tolerated the charitable and religious activities of guilds. For entrepreneurs, these had the useful effect that the artisans held themselves in reserve when there was not much work. In large towns with a dominant textile industry, there were many thousands of workers in the same objective circumstances. The masters in the sector could hardly act as small independent entrepreneurs because the raw materials remained the property of the merchant-entrepreneurs during the production process. Even though their primary aims may have been charitable and religious, and even though they were strictly controlled by the patricians, the existence of craft organisations nevertheless provided a framework within which artisans could share experiences and invent alternatives. This explains the fact that in the typical textile towns of Douai, Ypres and Ghent, the earliest collective actions of workers organised into guilds took place in periods of recession or other encroachments on their standard of living. In 1274, the weavers and fullers of Ghent deserted their town in protest against bad working conditions. The entrepreneurs reacted to this by making an agreement with employers in other towns not to employ strikers, an early form of lock-out. In 1302, another strike broke out in Ghent among all the *artes mechanicae*, the artisans who worked with equipment, in reaction to a tax increase imposed by the patrician authorities. By 1300, the social contrasts had become sharpened in all the large towns partly because the economic downturn interrupted the powerful growth of the preceding centuries, making incomes insecure, while entrepreneurs tried as far as they could to shift their risks on to the artisans.

POLITICAL PARTICIPATION   In some towns, upheavals resulted in some artisans winning a certain degree of autonomy and a political voice. Control of a craft guild was then no longer in the hands of patricians but of members elected from their own circle. The guilds themselves had gained the right to exercise authority over their members, impose and collect fines and issue regulations. In Florence the twenty-one main guilds were permanently represented in the town government from 1293 on. Whoever was then finally allowed to converse with the old aristocracy in the *Palazzo del Comune*, the City Hall, belonged to what we would call the labour aristocracy: small, independent entrepreneurs and merchants who were only too keen to forget their modest origins and, like the old patricians, enjoy the respect accorded to the seniors. The breakthrough of the artisans in Flanders was more radical and more general than elsewhere because, in 1302, their militias had played a decisive part in reversing the French occupation of the county at the battle of the Golden Spurs at Courtrai. This was the first time that an army of urban footsoldiers, mustered for the occasion, defeated a mighty king's army of knights. Even though the townsfolk may have been helped by the marshy terrain, their victory made a great impression on their contemporaries, and they capitalised on it by appropriating political and social rights for themselves. In some textile guilds not only masters but journeymen as well could be elected to be governor of their guild, or their voice was heard indirectly. This revolution in Flanders was imitated in neighbouring regions, so that artisans in Liège, Middelburg, Dordrecht and Utrecht won a considerable share of political power and were able to hold on to it for centuries. In Ghent by 1360, the majority of the seats in the city council were awarded to the artisans: as many as twenty out of twenty-six. In the Empire, only in Cologne and a few other towns along the upper reaches of the Rhine (Worms, Speyer, Freiburg, Basel) did the artisans triumph.

CORPORATIVE PROTECTIONISM What could artisans do with the political and social power they had won in this fashion? In the first place, they could defend their standard of living when their purchasing power was eroded as a result of the steady devaluation of gold and silver coin during the fourteenth century. They placed restrictions on the combination of wholesale trade and entrepreneurship. This enabled the weavers, who technically controlled the entire production process in the textile sector and formed by far the largest occupational group in towns like Ghent and Leiden, to work their way up to become small entrepreneurs (drapers) and employ other specialised workers, such as dyers, fullers and shearers, on a piece-work basis. From that moment, however, like all free entrepreneurs, they were faced with a recession all over Europe, so that the margins to improve the lot of their workers became narrowed. In villages and those areas where there were no craft guilds or where the craft guilds had little power, wages remained low. This made them attractive to entrepreneurs. It was easy for them to shift their activities to the countryside because in the common putting out system, the burden of the costs of the means of production, workplaces and tools in particular, was largely shouldered by the artisans themselves. Under this system, an entrepreneur brought the raw materials or semi-finished articles to the cheapest workers, in the country. The de-industrialisation of the once-leading areas and the industrialisation of low-wage areas took place on a large scale during the fourteenth century. The rural areas of Flanders and England and the towns of Brabant and Holland, where the corporations were weaker, eagerly took over a large share of the cloth-production that had become too expensive in the old Flemish centres.

The response of the craft guilds worsened the situation: they sought salvation in a restrictive protectionism and the exclusion of newcomers. In this way, the established workers used legal and economic discrimination and even force to try to hold on to their share of the market. They took prohibitive measures against imitations and imports in the vain hope of salvaging their own position. In those crafts for which the markets became increasingly weak due to the dramatic population losses during the fourteenth century, the hereditary position of master was even laid down in statutes. In the long run, market forces proved stronger than regulations, and the old textile centres could only survive in a slimmed-down form by focusing on refined, high-quality and fashionable products, of which the famed Flemish tapestries were the glorious masterpieces. In the new production centres, whether rural areas or small towns, which were aiming for the production of cheaper textiles, the small scale made it impossible to impose the divisions of labour and specialisation that was normal in the large towns and, partly as a result of this, to achieve a similar quality.

During the Middle Ages there were no craft guilds specifically for women, yet many women followed a skilled occupation and even took the lead in some occupations, such as spinning and selling foodstuffs in the marketplace. In general women were under someone's guardianship: of their father, uncle or brother as long as they were unmarried, of their husband, or of a priest (male, of course) if they were in a convent. Only widow-hood could emancipate them. An artisan's widow, who had been accustomed to work with her husband in his workplace or shop, could carry on the business as an equal and, in that capacity, could enjoy all the rights of a guild member. As long as they did not remarry, widows in 's-Hertogenbosch could acquire the title of master in the dyers' guild and in Breda in the victuallers' or grocers' guild. Around 1470, there was even some rivalry among the fullers of Leiden between women and the apprentices who found that the women were taking the bread out of their mouths. There were also, however, specifically female occupations, that of midwife being the most obvious. To become a recognised midwife, one had to follow a practical training under an established midwife, after which a skills test gave entry to the profession and membership of the guild, often the guild of surgeons.

As entry to the craft guilds became more difficult for newcomers, the journeymen began to look for alternatives. In some towns they organised themselves in separate journeymen's associations (*compagnonnages*), which in time also received recognition. Furthermore, countless unskilled workers remained outside the organisational framework of the craft guilds. Employment for them was often as uncertain as it was flexible: if there was a large construction project somewhere, a dyke to be reinforced or a military expedition undertaken, then hundreds of labourers were required. Farmers needed temporary workers at harvest time. Out of sheer necessity unskilled labourers moved around to wherever they could earn a living. As they had to be very mobile and could not organise themselves in any town, their position remained weak.

The system of guilds, or corporatism, was an original form of social organisation endowed with varied powers and rights which would continue to exist in France until 1792 and elsewhere until the nineteenth century. In general it can still be seen that the organisation by occupational group of apprentices, journeymen and masters had far-reaching consequences for the nature of social differences in the late Middle Ages. Craft guilds formed the framework for their members' way of life, within which they saw the expression of their social, political and economic rights and responsibilities, and through which they also took part in town festivities or organised their own church celebrations or secular rites. Furthermore, they could count on support in times of need. The craft guilds built imposing guild halls in which they held their meetings and stored the banners that the members carried in processions and battles. Artisans thus identified themselves very closely with their guilds. Inside this framework they focused their hopes of social promotion, of becoming masters and ultimately of achieving positions of authority in the guild or even in the town itself. Such vertical organisation within

occupational groups meant that social conflicts were defined not in terms of class distinctions (capital versus labour) but rather according to rivalries between the sectors. This fact, as well as the entire working of craft guilds, leads us to the conclusion that this form of organisation, in spite of all the conflicts that it brought, contributed in the long term to the social stability of the larger towns of pre-industrial Europe.

Points to remember

- Until 1300, towns grew substantially and many new ones were founded, as a consequence of the general growth of the European population.
- Urbanisation levels differed substantially across Europe, with the highest density in north and central Italy and the Low Countries.
- Urban communities fought successfully against the aristocratic powers for their autonomy and self-government.
- Merchant elites formed supra-local organisations to protect their trading interests in their immediate hinterland as well as over long distances and overseas, in conjunction with but fairly independent from monarchical powers.
- Class conflicts between the governing merchant elites and the artisanal masses resulted in the creation of craft guilds which obtained forms of political participation in the largest industrial cities.
- The corporative organisations defended social security for their members but tended to become highly protectionist for their own craft and town.

Suggestions for further reading

Frugoni, Chiara and Arsenio Frugoni (2005), *A Day in a Medieval City* (Chicago: University of Chicago

Press) (orig. Italian, 1997). A vivid and captivating description of all aspects of daily life in a late medieval city.

Jones, Philip (1997), *The Italian City-State: From Commune to Signoria* (Oxford: Clarendon). The fundamental book on the evolution of the Italian cities (*civitates*) since the sixth century, via the self-governing communes to the *signorie* (princely rule) expanding over considerable territories and smaller towns.

Lynch, Katherine A. (2003), *Individuals, Families, and Communities in Europe, 1200–1800: The Urban Foundations of Western Society* (Cambridge: CUP). Examining the family at the centre of the life of 'civil society', on the boundary between public and private life, the author traces a pattern which emerged in the late medieval period through to the nineteenth century. Women and men created voluntary associations outside the family – communities, broadly defined – to complement or even substitute for solidarities based on kinship.

Ogilvie, Sheilagh (2011), *Institutions and European Trade: Merchant Guilds, 1000–1800* (Cambridge: CUP). A highly systematic and very broadly source-based analysis, inspired by the 'new institutional economics' theory, of the economic 'efficiency' of a wide range of organisations. Were these institutions beneficial to the *whole economy*? Or did they simply offer an effective way for the rich and powerful, the established and the insiders, to increase their wealth, at the expense of outsiders, customers and society as a whole? Why do institutions exist, which types of institution made trade grow, and how are corporate privileges affecting economic efficiency and human well-being?

Pounds, Norman (2005), *The Medieval City* (Westport, CT: Greenwood Press). An introduction to the life of towns and cities since the Roman Empire's urban legacy. Deals with advantages and hazards of urban life, planning or lack thereof, and the various aspects of the urban way of life, including sketches of street life and descriptions of fairs and markets.

Part IV

The late Middle Ages, 1300–1500

10 Between crisis and contraction: population, economy and society

War, famine and pestilence

In the fifth chapter of the last book of the Bible, the enigmatic Revelation of John of Patmos, there is a reference to a scroll 'written within and on the back, sealed with seven seals'. The scroll is held in the right hand of God who is sitting on his throne in heaven. It announces the seven disasters that the Lord has in store for mankind at the end of the world. An angel speaks with a great voice saying, 'Who is worthy to open the book, and to loose the seals thereof?' Only one creature felt the call to do this, a lamb with seven horns and seven eyes – a mystical symbol for Christ himself, who had been crucified (slaughtered like a lamb) and risen from the dead. The lamb broke open the first four seals and each time a horse and rider appeared. When the fourth seal was opened the horse was a 'pale horse' and the name of its rider was Death, and a crowd of dead people from the abode of the dead followed him. And they 'were given authority over the fourth part of the earth, to kill with sword, and with famine, and with death, and by the wild beasts of the earth'. This image of apocalyptic terror, of an army of skeletons sowing death and destruction through war, famine and pestilence (*bellum, fames et pestis*), was often found in the literature and visual arts of the late Middle Ages. It is not difficult to understand the reason for this: between the beginning of the fourteenth and the middle of the fifteenth century, Europe, with terrifying frequency, was struck by the disasters foretold in the fourth seal (only the wild beasts were lacking).

Famines and subsistence crises

In the pre-industrial period, food shortages were a regularly recurring nightmare for large groups of people. Even the failure of just one harvest was enough to cause serious problems, making the formation of reserve supplies uncertain. This happened about once every ten years in pre-industrial agriculture with its low yields and absence of any effective defence against vermin and diseased crops. Such disruption is generally referred to by modern scholars as a subsistence crisis, a term which is usually related to the disastrous effects of harvest failures on market prices. The English statistician Gregory King (1648–1712) described the effect whereby differences in the size of the harvest were magnified in the market. This was due to three mechanisms. First, even in the late Middle Ages only a small part of the grain harvest was intended for the market, with the result that there was much greater fluctuation in the annual market supply than in the size of the annual harvest. Second, large price fluctuations attracted shifts in consumer preferences that were contrary to economic laws. Normally, in pre-industrial Europe, a typical artisan family with four to five members spent 44 per cent of its income on bread. If grain suddenly rose in price then such consumers needed to spend even more of their income on grain, in order to have the largest quantity of calories at the lowest price. Calories in grain were always cheaper than those in vegetables, fish, meat or dairy products because these had a heavier footprint on the ecological system. This further increased the demand for grain and the price rose even higher, while demand for other foodstuffs, artisanal products and services fell. Through this mechanism every major increase in the price of grain resulted in a general depression as one branch after another was dragged into an avalanche of declines in spending. Third, market prices – at least in the spring – were partly determined by the expectations of the forthcoming harvest. Grain dealers speculated on these foresights, for example by cheaply buying large quantities in spring while the grain was still in the field, and then raising prices by bringing the harvest on to the market in small portions. If the crops in the field looked bad, and shortages could thus be expected on the market, then grain prices started to climb even before the harvest.

No wonder that the popular culture of the late Middle Ages fantasised over a land of plenty,

Cockaigne, an 'extraordinary out-door restaurant with unusually good service', as Mullett (1987) described it, where roast chickens flew through the air and a dessert of ice-cooled strawberries made daydreamers' mouths water. In many cases, the first action of rebellious peasants was to plunder the storerooms and wine cellars of rich aristocrats and abbeys.

Unlike nowadays, trade was barely able to compensate for shortages in one region by large-scale imports from another. Because of highly imperfect roads, means of transport and trading networks, especially for bulk cargoes, there were significant regional differences in the price of grain. Nevertheless, in the late Middle Ages, price fluctuations throughout north-western Europe were more or less equal as a result of increasing commercialisation of agriculture and growing market integration. In other words, if grain was expensive in Paris, it was also expensive in Cologne. This did not mean, however, that the price in Paris was the same as in Cologne. The price could vary considerably, depending on how far the large towns were from the production areas supplying them and the actual volume of the supplies. Market integration could only help to remove extreme imbalances in supply, because the volume of the international grain trade was still far too small to remove them entirely. The shipping of grain required large ships and was profitable only when the price difference largely made up for the transport cost. Such services functioned effectively between Genoa and the grain-producing areas in Sicily and the Crimea. Regular exports of large quantities of rye from Prussia to north-western Europe became increasingly important from the 1480s onwards.

Yet real famines, with widespread mortality as a direct result of undernourishment, occurred relatively seldom during the late Middle Ages. The greatest killer was without any doubt the notorious famine of 1315–1317, caused by a series of serious harvest failures in three successive harvest seasons in north-western Europe due to exceptionally abundant and continuous rainfall. To be able to appreciate the magnitude of the disaster, we must remember that the low average yields of medieval agriculture meant that the grain harvested was consumed in the year following the harvest: storage for a longer period was out of the question. Overall, the yields in 1315 and 1316 were about 40 per cent below the long-term average for 1270–1429. The harvest failed again in 1321, at 33 per cent below that average.

The consequences of the situation are easy to surmise. Worst hit were the urban populations that were entirely dependent on the market for their food supply. Grain prices soared to unprecedented heights – in Hainaut at the height of the famine wheat was between 25 and 30 times more expensive than during normal years. Moderate wage increases could not keep up with such rising prices. But there were shortages in the countryside too, and even peasants went hungry. After a while, many of them could no longer pay their rents and were obliged to sell their land and their farms for next to nothing, or to borrow money at an exorbitant rate. Even the great landowners suffered. They were able to ask high prices for any grain they could still bring to the market, but the quantities available were far lower and – especially in the case of ecclesiastical landowners – falling incomes contrasted sharply with rising expenses necessitated by the enormous increase in the demand for charity.

Government intervention in removing the negative effects of grain shortages was characteristic of the strong ruling authority developing in the states at this time. In England the king and diverse town governments took steps to control prices and prosecute hoarders and speculators. Great effort was made to import as much grain as possible from English possessions in south-western France, which had been spared the poor harvests. But powerful government also showed its darker side in these circumstances. During those calamitous years, King Edward II continued to raise taxes for the war against the Scots. His French counterpart used hunger as a weapon in the struggle against the rebellious Flemish,

hindering the export of grain to Flanders in all manner of ways. The authorities of Bruges reacted by purchasing as much grain as possible from Italian, Catalan and Scottish merchants. By selling these extra supplies to local bakers at regular intervals and at fixed prices, price speculation could be avoided. However, this kind of intervention was only possible in an international seaport town. In France and the Holy Roman Empire food riots were suppressed by force.

Chronicles and other written sources dating from the time show how the protracted grain shortage of 1315–1317 threatened the lives of large groups of people. The symptoms of serious undernourishment were clearly described. Horrifying stories circulated of emaciated people, their stomachs swollen from hunger oedema, grazing like cows or resorting to cannibalism. Eating unusual or rotten foods led to epidemics of diarrhoea or ergotism. Ergotism, which was known during the Middle Ages as St Anthony's Fire, was caused by eating rye poisoned by fungi. Precisely how many people died during the Great Famine is not known, but the best estimates suggest an *extra* mortality of about 70 per thousand (7 per cent) in the stricken regions for 1316 alone, which is about twice the normal rate in late medieval populations. And the Great Famine, although exceptional in its ferocity, did not stand alone. The dreadful situation of general harvest failure in successive years occurred again in the north-west in 1437–1438, 1481–1483 and 1527–1534. In many regions, military conflicts worsened its effects. War implied economic blockades and disrupted normal supply routes. And movements of troops could accelerate the dissemination of contagious diseases. Southern Europe, too, had its catastrophic years. There was famine in Catalonia, for example, in 1333–1334, in Navarre and Tuscany in 1346–1347, the years immediately preceding the Black Death.

The long-term consequences of famines are difficult to guess. On the one hand, famines have very little effect on female fertility. On the other hand, epidemiologists have established that

BOX 10.1 THE TRIUMPH OF DEATH

One of the most remarkable architectural spaces created in the Middle Ages was the 'square' or 'field of miracles' (*Piazza* or *Prato dei Miracoli*) in the centre of Pisa in Tuscany. Three separate buildings were constructed there during the eleventh and twelfth centuries, all in pure white stone: the cathedral church, the round baptistery (*baptisterium*) and the bell tower (*campanile*), the world-famous 'leaning tower of Pisa'. A grave-yard was laid out on the north side of the square at an early date and incorporated sometime after 1278 into a monumental new building called the *camposanto* (literally 'holy field'). This was a square
construction which looked from the inside like a cloister around a central open space, the original burial ground, containing earth brought from Golgotha, the hill outside Jerusalem upon which Christ died on the cross. At some date after 1330 the inside walls of the ambulatory were decorated with frescos painted by the first of the Tuscan artists, including Benozzo Gozzoli. One of the frescos was known as 'The Triumph of Death'. The theme of the fresco was a traditional story – three young men, in the prime of life and enjoying the pleasures of the hunt, were suddenly confronted with three corpses in various states of decomposition in which they recognised themselves. The death theme was enlivened by the young men's female companions, a hermit who displayed a biblical text about the futility of worldly pleasures, a skeleton flying overhead and an aerial battle between angels and devils fighting for the souls of the dead.

For a long time it was believed that 'The Triumph of Death' was painted soon after 1348, when Pisa was stricken by the Black Death. Today an earlier date, about 1330, has been assumed and the painting has been connected with either the visit to Pisa of Emperor Louis in 1328 or the preaching activities of the Dominicans in Pisa; the scene on the fresco was apparently borrowed from a passage in the collection of saints' lives by the Pisan friar, Domenico Cavalca. There is also disagreement about the artist. It used to be thought that the Pisan Francesco Traini was the painter, but a more detailed study has suggested other possible artists, in particular the Florentine Buffalmacco.

Many of the frescos were severely damaged during the twentieth century, by local youths playing football in the *camposanto* and by the American bombardment of German positions during the Second World War. Fortunately the frescos were known in detail from old engravings and photographs which were used in the recent, successful restoration.

Sources: *The Dictionary of Art*, 34 vols (Oxford: OUP, 2003), SVV 'Pisa' and 'Masters, anonymous. 1. Master of the Triumph of the Death'. *Camposanto monumentale di Pisa. Affreschi e sinopie.* Guiseppe Ramalli (pres.) (Pisa: Opera della Primaziale, 1960). Joseph Polzer, 'Aspects of the fourteenth-century iconography of death and the plague', in *The Black Death: The Impact of the Fourteenth-Century Plague* edited by Daniel Williman (Binghampton: Center for Medical and Early Renaissance Studies, 1982, pp. 107–130).

children who have been seriously undernourished for a long period of time run a high risk of incurring infectious diseases like lung infections, tuberculosis, diarrhoea and malaria.

The problems of grain shortages in these disastrous years were aggravated by another catastrophic effect of the heavy rains: they soaked the meadows and caused shortages of hay and fodder for the cattle. The accounts of English demesnes show that one in five animals died during the famine. Moreover, in 1316, a highly contagious epizootic mortality broke out in central Europe and spread across famine-struck northern Europe, to England and Ireland. Between 1319 and 1321, half to two-thirds of the cattle, sheep and pigs on English demesnes died. Since adequate restocking took a number of years, the resulting 'protein famine', due to a substantially reduced intake of dairy products and meat, is estimated to have lasted for over a decade.

It is not easy to calculate the multiplier effects of the epizootic. The production of leather and wool must have diminished dramatically for years. Far fewer oxen were available as draught animals and less manure could be spread on the fields, which would logically have a negative effect on the agricultural production. As the surviving cows were weakened and gave less milk, dairy products became scarce and expensive, just like meat. This implies that the human generation after the famine remained undernourished in qualitative, and at occasions also in quantitative, terms, while they were already vulnerable to infections. It is shocking to realise that King Edward III decided under these circumstances to launch a major war against France.

The Black Death and its echo epidemics

The Black Death is the name traditionally given to the great epidemic that raged throughout Europe between 1347 and 1353 and which, according to a cautious estimate, cost the lives of more than one-third of the total population of about 75 million in 1300. In England, where the best quantitative sources have been preserved, the losses are now estimated at 40 per cent of the total population at least. Losses in the same order of magnitude were suffered in China and the Islamic Middle East. This earned the Black Death the reputation of being one of the most fatal disasters ever to affect mankind. The Black Death is usually thought to have been the plague, a contagious disease that is caused by the bacterial strain *Yersinia pestis*, named after the Swiss physician Alexandre Yersin, a student of Louis Pasteur. Yersin was the first to identify the bacterium during a plague outbreak in Hong Kong in 1894, and correctly described how it does its deadly job: the bacterium lodges in fleas that when they die infect their carriers – animals (usually rodents) or humans. Yersin immediately claimed that he had discovered the evil culprit behind the medieval pandemics of the sixth and fourteenth centuries, but until recently no epidemiological proof existed for that. Moreover, there are many inconsistencies in contemporary descriptions of the Black Death and its dissemination. However, in 2010, an interdisciplinary team led by Barbara Bramanti undisputedly identified traces of *Yersinia pestis* in DNA material of Black Death victims buried in medieval cemeteries in Hereford, Bergen-op-Zoom (a harbour on the Schelde river in the duchy of Brabant) and Saint-Laurent de la Cabrerisse in southern France. A decade before, similar observations had already been made in Montpellier. The inconsistencies in medieval descriptions are then to be ascribed to possible mutations in the bacterium over the centuries and to differences in ecological and climatological conditions at the time.

The origins of the infection can be traced to the territories of the Mongol Golden Horde on the Caspian steppe, where plague was endemic among rodents such as rats. The Black Death was brought to Europe from the Crimea to the Mediterranean region at the end of 1347. From that moment, its triumphant progress through

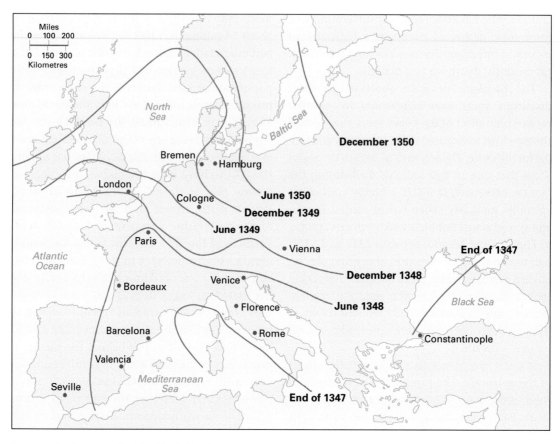

MAP 10.1 The spread of the Black Death

Europe can be closely followed, from Messina northwards to the harbours along the Italian west coast, to Marseille and further on. It spread from the harbours to other trading cities inland, and from there to the countryside. The extraordinary travelling speed of the Black Death, 3.2 km per day or 1,170 km per year, points to dissemination through direct contacts between humans. The human flea, *Pulex irritans*, is therefore the obvious carrier. From Italy the disease reached Paris, the heart of medieval Europe, in the summer of 1348; southern England followed shortly afterwards. From there it spread further northward through the British Isles and Scandinavia, and eastward to the Low Countries, the Empire and eastern Europe. By the end of 1350 the Black Death reached Russia after a long roundabout journey.

Thinly populated regions like Norway and remote island groups such as the Faroes, Shetlands, Orkneys and Hebrides were hit as hard as the densely populated metropolises of Constantinople, Cairo and Florence. The fact that the plague spread into northern regions, while its outbreak normally depended on a warm climate, and that it even reached Iceland (in 1402–1404) where no rats were living, shows again that its pandemic dissemination had passed from an infection through rats to one between humans.

On the other hand, entire regions, such as Bohemia, and a number of major towns are known to have suffered relatively little. As far as the former are concerned, there must have been an ecological reason (Bohemia, for instance, did not have the conditions suitable for foreign rat populations). The towns that were spared owed this above all to sensible government. Although medieval doctors had not the slightest idea about the bacterial origins of diseases, or of how they spread, people did realise that they could be highly contagious and therefore, that it was best to keep the disease at a distance. This could be done in two ways: a town could be isolated from the outside world by strictly controlling the traffic entering, and within the town itself, houses, streets or certain quarters where disease had broken out could be completely closed off. These methods were applied successfully in Milan, a city with a population of 100,000, which the Visconti family ruled with an iron hand. It is estimated that no more than 15 per cent of the population of Milan died during the epidemic. The magistracy of Nuremberg went a step further, for Nuremberg experienced virtually no extra mortality because of its hygienic regulations, which seem almost modern and which were not introduced specifically in connection with the epidemic. The roads were paved and the streets were swept; the inhabitants were expected to dispose of their own household refuse; the town had fourteen public bath-houses which were carefully supervised and were frequented by local civil servants who received a salary bonus in the form of bath money. In later outbreaks other towns introduced similar policies. Dalmatian Ragusa (modern Dubrovnik) was the first town to experiment with a system of quarantine in 1377. It was soon followed by Venice, where quarantine became compulsory during the fifteenth century. This meant that everyone who wanted to visit the city during periods of contagious disease had first to stay on an island in the lagoon for forty days (quarantine means 'a period of forty days'); whoever was alive and well after this term was allowed to enter Venice.

Despite quarantines and hygienic regulations, the Black Death struck mercilessly and repeatedly, in 1361–1362, 1369, 1375, 1382–1384 and 1400–1402 and on other occasions in the following centuries. Between 10 and 20 per cent of the population of Europe succumbed in every epidemic. After 1402 the length of time between epidemics increased, and they were less widespread. Nevertheless, the frequency with which the sickness reared its head continued to hinder demographic recovery, the more so because it sometimes appeared along with other apocalyptic horrors. This was the case, for example, in 1437–1438, when war, famine and disease stalked the land together, in that precise order, and, at least in part, in that order of causation. In Normandy, where the effects of the Hundred Years War were felt most harshly, the population decreased by one-third at that time. Nor should we forget that various diseases could take on epidemic forms in more or less the same period. Although the vague descriptions found in sources do not always permit a proper medical diagnosis, we do know that, besides plague, various forms of typhus, diphtheria, dysentery, malaria and occasionally influenza proved fatal to many of their victims.

We already mentioned that it is still debated whether the mortality of the Black Death was so extremely high because the plague hit a population weakened by malnutrition as a consequence of the famines and livestock diseases which had infested large parts of western Europe during the preceding thirty years. Although this seems rather obvious, it would imply that the Black Death had fewer victims in southern Europe (which was not stricken by the famine of 1315–1317, although it did experience famine in 1346) than in the north, or significantly fewer victims among the rich than among the poor, or skipped sparsely populated areas altogether. Neither was demonstrably the case.

The damage and suffering of war

It is difficult to calculate the demographic effects of wars on the late Middle Ages. Compared with wars in our own time even protracted conflicts such as the Hundred Years War did not directly cause many civilian casualties, until the French

PLATE 10.1 From cardinal to minstrel, everybody is dragged into death by skeletons. The theme of the *danse macabre* became popular after the recurrent outbreaks of the plague. Early fifteenth-century mural painting in the church of La Ferté-Loupière (France, Dep. Yonne).

king, Charles VIII, set a depressing new standard during his invasion of Italy in 1494. Actual hostilities were limited to a number of years, armies were relatively small when compared with those in later centuries, and the theatre of war changed constantly. It is true that large battles did claim the lives of thousands of soldiers, a relatively high number. For this reason there was a high mortality rate among the nobles who took an active part in war during the late Middle Ages. For common people, however, the consequences were more local, depending on the movements of armies and war bands; many only felt the effects of war indirectly and in the long term.

A common tactic was to lay siege to a city, and thus to starve its inhabitants. In addition, it was usual to make raids into the enemy's territory, to pillage and ravage whatever the soldiers could reach. In the countryside, they would steal cattle, plunder granaries and burn farms, which implies the destruction of essential means of production. Troops on campaign or people escaping from the violence of war increased the risk of contagious diseases spreading. In those areas through which armies crossed or where mercenaries remained once the campaign was over in the hope of finding new employment, there was no end to the misery, for all was pillaged and ravaged relentlessly. This would have affected the fertility rate more than mortality. Yet the war-stricken population of France recovered from the economic depression of the late Middle Ages sooner than that of England, which was spared the violence of war – civil war – until 1455.

Theories on demographic decline and economic development

There is not the slightest doubt that the size of the population during the fourteenth century decreased markedly all over Europe. It is generally assumed that the population of Europe around 1450 was approximately two-thirds of what it had been in 1300. It then made a hesitant recovery, with considerable regional differences. In 1520 England still only had about half the estimated number of inhabitants it had had at the end of the thirteenth century; that number was not reached until about 1600. Demographic recovery started earlier in France, and the population size of about 1300 would again have been reached by 1550. In certain strongly urbanised regions, such as Flanders and Holland, the population level of 1300 was probably reached even before the end of the fifteenth century; but others, among them Tuscany, would only approach the estimated population density of the thirteenth century in the course of the nineteenth century.

This difference in the phases of demographic recovery cannot be ascribed to large regional discrepancies in the mortality rate. There must have been other factors at work, for instance, differences in labour relations related to marital fertility, and cultural differences. For England it has been demonstrated that after the Black Death young women often took jobs for a while, which had a negative influence on fertility. Cultural factors may well have played a role in Tuscany, where it was no longer customary for young widows to remarry. That, too, helped keep the fertility rate low in a period of high mortality.

The relation between demographic decline and economic development is more complicated. Between the 1930s and 1970s prominent economic historians, such as Wilhelm Abel and Michael Postan, saw pre-industrial society as being governed by a cyclical alternation of so-called secular trends, in other words, of protracted, sluggish phases of expansion and contraction. This view is usually termed neo-Malthusian, because it falls back on the ideas of Reverend Thomas Robert Malthus (1766–1834), a famous British political economist and demographer.

In his influential *Essay on the Principle of Population* of 1798, Malthus put forward the theory that each population tends to grow more quickly than does the amount of food that it can itself produce. Sooner or later, population growth is thus restructured to remove the tensions between population pressure and food production. This can happen favourably, by means of what Malthus called preventive checks, or unfavourably through positive checks: favourably, by limiting the number of children, that is the number of births (a fall in the birth rate), which in pre-industrial Europe implied lowering marital fertility; and unfavourably, as a consequence of disease, famine and violence in an over-full world (increased mortality).

David Ricardo, a contemporary of Malthus, provided an explanation for Malthus's position by formulating two economic laws. The first, known as the law of diminishing returns, predicts that the addition of increasing amounts of labour to a constant area of land will very soon lead to a drop in labour productivity (yield per worker deployed). Expansion of agricultural production through the cultivation of new land does not help either when there is continuing population growth because, according to Ricardo's ground rent theory, the best land will be the first to be cultivated. As population pressure makes it necessary to exploit less suitable land so land productivity (yield per unit of area) decreases as well. Ricardo realised that technological developments could counteract a reduction in productivity, but he believed that the chances of that happening were limited, and that over time technology would always be outdone by nature.

According to modern development economists, such as Esther Boserup, this is the weak spot in Ricardian theory. She argued that when a population comes under sufficient demographic pressure, food production will be expanded almost automatically through increasing labour intensity and technological innovation: 'Necessity is the mother of innovation'. Others have added that under such circumstances commercialisation helps peasant producers in underdeveloped societies to give up their subsistence strategy, which is aimed at self-sufficiency and generates poverty. Left-wing critics of this positive thinking, such as the American historian Robert Brenner, have countered that in medieval agriculture insufficient investment in technological development was caused not by the unwillingness of primitive peasants, caught in tradition, but by the weight and compulsive, non-economic nature of surplus extraction by lords, who over-burdened dependent peasants with all kinds of arbitrary charges. That may also explain why regional variations in surplus extraction caused population growth to lead to tensions in one region earlier than in another.

Europe 1300: a society under pressure?

Despite critical objections and qualifications and despite the greatly increased availability of statistically valuable information on prices, wages and weather conditions in later medieval Europe, the neo-Malthusian view of demographic developments during the first half of the fourteenth century is still generally accepted. There appear to be enough indications of growing demographic pressure towards the end of the thirteenth century. Regulated agriculture had penetrated agro-ecological marginal regions, such as the Alps and the Scottish Highlands. In more densely populated areas the pieces of land owned by peasants were radically split up, the communal use of pasture, wood and waste land came under

pressure, and the rate of urbanisation flagged. Colonisation and land reclamation came to a standstill. Each of these indications on its own does not say much, but together they support the picture of a relatively overpopulated Europe. It is impossible to say whether the tensions between population growth and means of subsistence would ever have resulted in a Malthusian discharge, for the Black Death intervened as an exogenous factor in its origin, not a positive check in the Malthusian sense raised by internal circumstances. The same is only partly true of the Great Famine of 1315–1317. The exceptionally bad weather conditions were its primary cause, but its severity depended on human factors, namely the high urbanisation with questionable hygienic provisions, and the limited transport facilities.

From that perspective, the population in some parts of Europe may indeed have reached a threshold level around 1300. Moreover, from recent historical climate research we know with certainty that the extremely bad weather in 1315–1317 and 1348–1351, measurable in frequent years of low grain yields, fitted into a century-long phase of global cooling. During the twenty-five years after the Black Death, cooler, wetter and stormy conditions persisted and had a negative impact on agricultural production, tree growth and salt evaporation (which is an indication of lower solar radiation). Massive environmental dislocations worsened the nutritional conditions of entire generations which may have enhanced the impact of infectious diseases, whose quick dissemination was promoted by frequent wars. Again, human activities worsened the effects of the natural disasters that struck humankind during the fourteenth century.

The agrarian crisis of the late Middle Ages

This brings us to the next component of the neo-Malthusian view of the economic history of the late Middle Ages that raises questions. It rests on two suppositions. First, that the demographic devastation caused by the Black Death and its recurring epidemics set in motion a deflationary economic spiral which struck the agricultural sector in particular extremely hard. Second, that this economic crisis was an impediment to rapid population recovery because of its negative effects on marriage patterns and marriage fertility, and thus on the birth rate. Also in this respect, more recent research by, amongst others, John Hatcher

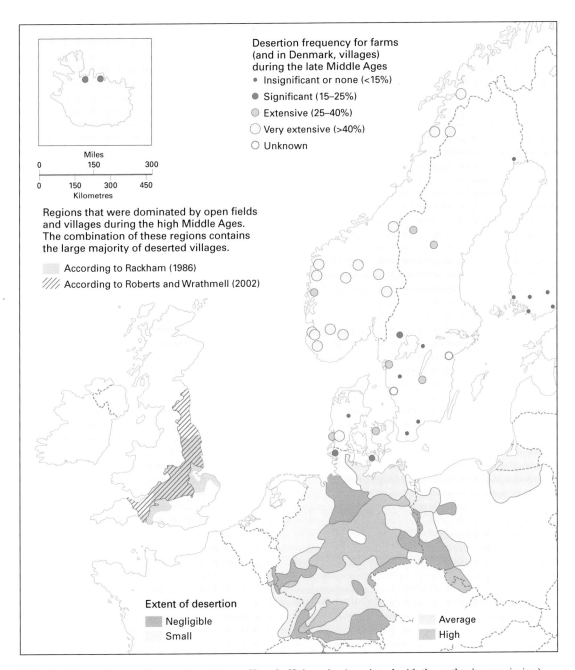

MAP 10.2 Lost villages. Map by Hans Renes, Utrecht University (reprinted with the author's permission)

and Mark Bailey (2001), Bruce Campbell (1991) and John Munro (1992) has refined our current interpretation.

SYMPTOMS   The drastic reduction in population numbers after 1350 had far-reaching consequences for economic developments in the late medieval countryside. In the first place, there was a change in the land/labour ratio, the relationship between the acreage available for cultivation and the number of people working on that land. This led to agricultural land being used more extensively, or even being entirely neglected, if the land was in an unfavourable location or of poor quality. A typical late medieval phenomenon was that of deserted land, which often resulted in entire villages being abandoned. In the German Empire 40,000 out of a total of 170,000 settlements, almost a quarter, were lost. Certainly there may have been other reasons behind the loss of these villages, administrative or military, for example, but there is no doubt at all that the need for farming land decreased. It led everywhere to a radical fall in the rents and sale-prices of farmland.

A second consequence was linked directly to the first. The severe decline in the size of the population pushed down the price of grain, the basic foodstuff, after a while. This seems logical because the falling size of the population made it possible to concentrate grain production on the most suitable land so that the average yields per unit of area rose. Now, perhaps the first of these things did happen, but the second one certainly did not, because the fields were worked less intensively than previously as a result of the shortage of labour. Moreover, at least in some parts of Europe the number of people living in towns increased, which means that more people had to buy food in the market.

Why then did market prices of grain tend to go down in the long term? There are two main reasons. First, because land was cheap, many smallholders or even landless workers managed to acquire enough land to avoid being dependent on

the market for buying grain. Second, the shortage of labour caused wages to rise. This favourable development in wages in relation to prices led to an improvement in the standard of living of those groups who were largely or entirely dependent on wage income. The improvement was reflected in greater consumption, not of bread but of more expensive foodstuffs. This structural change in consumer preferences can partially explain the tendency towards low grain prices. But it was only a tendency. We have seen that the market prices of grain could fluctuate under the influence of great variations in the size of the harvests from one year to another and that crises of subsistence occurred just as often in the late Middle Ages as in the periods before or after.

SOLUTIONS   The new scarcity and price relations that came into existence after the Black Death did not have the same effect on every social group involved in agricultural production. Those hardest hit were the traditional large landowners, the nobility and the monasteries in particular. Falling incomes, either from surpluses which they brought to the market or from rents or leases in cash or kind, contrasted with soaring wage costs and the rising expenses of non-agricultural goods. In sum, this group found itself trapped in a price-cost squeeze. In such circumstances many landowners felt forced to capitalise on parts of their land. Others, private individuals rather than (ecclesiastical) institutions, tried either to 'marry money' or find an alternative source of income in the growing official, diplomatic or military apparatuses of kings and princes.

Less drastic solutions allowed large landowners to keep their position intact and sometimes even to strengthen it. One such way included every attempt to counter market forces by keeping wages low, obstructing the free movement of labour or increasing all sorts of traditional payments in spite of their inalterable character. Such solutions were applied under pressure in Catalonia, but not often in north-western Europe where lords attempted to placate peasants by offering them favourable levies and leases or dangling the prospect of improvements in their legal status before them. In England, the two reactions followed each other: landlords first used legal means to compel people to work and to fix a maximum wage. This solution was probably initiated by the Commons in parliament, the representatives of the lower nobility and the prosperous middle class, both groups which could not compete with the wealthy higher nobility and ecclesiastical landowners who simply used force if they found it necessary. The earliest of these legal measures was the Ordinance of Labourers issued by Edward III on 18 June 1349 when the Black Death caused havoc in England. Special judges, the justices of labourers, were appointed to enforce the ordinance. Less than two years later, a more systematic law dealing with the same issue was introduced, the Statute of Labourers. Several stricter measures followed, among them the petition 'against rebellious peasants', passed by the Commons in 1377. England was not alone in taking such steps. Similar measures were taken elsewhere in the same period, including France (for the Paris region), Castile and Austria.

When the passage of laws to ensure that agricultural labour remained affordable proved ineffective, many English landlords abandoned the direct exploitation of their estates. It often meant that they leased out the demesne parts or *réserves* (the parts of manors reserved for the lord) and made written contracts, known as **copyholds**, with their bondsmen for the possession of their holdings in a form of hereditary lease. This in fact finally brought an end to serfdom in England. The Catalan peasants were equally successful in their resistance to the reactionary attitude of their landlords, albeit over a longer period.

Those landlords who continued to exploit their land and turned to the market had to make sure that they profited from altered price relations. Not all agricultural products showed the same tendency to drop in price. As a result of the changes in consumer preferences and the expansion of urban industries, the prices of animal products

(wool, beef, leather and butter in particular), luxury foods (wine, vegetables and fruit) and any variety of crops that could be used as raw materials in urban industries (flax, hemp, barley and hops for brewing, vegetable dyes and flavourings) were generally far more stable than the price of grain. Because the cultivation and processing of cash crops was particularly labour-intensive, this provided a solution for smaller peasants who did not have the means to hire labourers.

Large landowners profited more by specialising in extensive forms of pastoral farming, which required plenty of land but not much labour. There was a phenomenal growth in sheep farming during the Middle Ages, especially in the more sparsely populated regions of England and Castile. It has been said that sheep changed from being a peasant's animal to a lord's animal, even if this had been the case in the coastal regions of Flanders for many centuries. By the beginning of the fourteenth century, England had already exported the wool of an estimated eight million sheep. A further expansion of sheep flocks was prevented for the time being as a consequence of the draconian increases in the export taxes on wool. Large landowners had to wait until the second half of the fifteenth century, when the boom in domestic cloth production began, before it became profitable to switch to sheep farming. Then, English landlords soon found themselves clashing with peasants, who traditionally had grazing rights allowing sheep to use the vast tracts of waste land. This heralded the break-through of the enclosure movement, whereby the landlords enclosed grazing lands and shut them off to common use. In the kingdoms of Naples and Castile, the growing number of sheep led to increased transhumance, the seasonal migration of livestock between the higher-lying summer pastures and the plains and valleys. This, too, caused all sorts of problems. In an effort to deal with them, sheepowners sometimes organised themselves into associations, the best known of which is the *Mesta* in Castile. Dominated from the beginning by noble landowners and knightly orders, this brotherhood by 1360 exploited a total of one million sheep; by the middle of the fifteenth century that number had increased to three million, and by 1500 to five million.

In addition to more extensive land use, the application of labour-saving techniques sometimes brought relief because they kept wages down while the capital investment needed was not exceptionally large. Two of these innovations were developed in Flanders: the light plough, which needed fewer horses and labourers, and the reaping hook, or short scythe, which replaced the sickle for harvesting. It was possible to work far more quickly with the reaping hook and also to harvest more straw, used as a roofing material and in the preparation of manure.

And what of the peasants themselves, the direct agricultural producers? In order to assess what happened to them it is best to divide them into three groups: a middle class, which had just enough land to support itself; above that, a (small) group of peasants with substantial holdings who regularly produced surpluses for the market and who employed labourers; and, at the bottom, a broad underlayer of smallholders and people without any land at all, dependent more or less entirely on irregular or seasonal wages. As wages were relatively high at the time, the late Middle Ages was generally a favourable period for this last group. They often had to find extra income from non-agricultural or para-agricultural sources. Urban traders and entrepreneurs found it attractive to move some aspects of cloth production, such as spinning and weaving, to the countryside where the wages were lower than in the towns with their guilds and collective protests against excessive exploitation. In some parts of fifteenth-century Flanders and England, completely new centres for the production of cheap woollen cloth emerged, such as Hondschoote and Poperinge in West Flanders or Castle Combe in Wiltshire. In the vicinity of Ghent, large numbers of smallholders specialised in the labour-intensive cultivation of flax. After the harvest, they added extra income by combing, retting and spinning the raw flax

themselves. Only then was the flax thread sent to the linen-weavers as a semi-manufactured product.

The integration of non-agrarian activities into the rural economy is not necessarily limited to the textile industry only. In the County of Holland, small-scale farming was combined with a medley of non-agricultural activities: shipbuilding, shipping and fishery, peat and salt extraction, reed cutting and brick-making. There was also always a great demand for wage work in the construction and maintenance of dykes, ditches and sluices. As a result, by 1500 more than half the rural population of Holland had become heavily dependent on wage earnings for its income. The same proportion has been mentioned in connection with East Anglia, where wages were usually earned by labour on large farms in the region. In those parts of England rich in minerals (coal, tin, copper, lead), such as Durham, Devon and Cornwall, the exploitation of smallholdings was often combined with work in the mines.

The middle group of peasants, in possession of its own land, always remained vulnerable, because it had difficulty in building up financial reserves. These peasants were not only unable to profit from the low price of land, but if they were particularly vulnerable to damage from war or natural disasters such as failed harvests, storms and floods for they had no resources on which to fall back, then they were also easy prey for large farmers and landowners. Their pitiful situation worsened in many parts of western Europe when their tax burden increased rapidly after the fifteenth century.

The prospects for the third group, that of large farmers, were better in this respect. They were able to create a financial buffer and, through diversification, could gear production to market demand better than those peasants whose primary occupation was simply to subsist. Certainly some peasants ended up in the grip of the negative price scissor, but not to such an extent as the great landowners. The peasants had a far more modest pattern of consumption and they could keep the costs of hired labour to a minimum by getting members of their family to help or by taking in farmhands and helpers as boarders or paying them in kind. In this way, many better-off peasants managed to enlarge their fortunes and invest their savings in cheap land. The trend continued during the period of renewed expansion, starting in around 1450. A class of prosperous large farmers then emerged in England, the yeomen, whose social status was just below that of the lower nobility or gentry.

Economic crisis or contraction?

Many authors who have studied the economic history of the late Middle Ages use the terms crisis and contraction rather indiscriminately, which we think is wrong. We have preferred to typify the period as a whole as a phase of contraction, and not as a crisis. Demographic shrinkage is not disputed, nor is the resulting fall in the total production of goods. To what extent and why this situation was detrimental for certain forms of income has been discussed above. It became clear that not all social groups who could lay claim to income from agriculture found themselves in a crisis situation.

Approaching the question from other angles, we can put the alleged late medieval crisis even further into perspective. Wage-earners – first and foremost urban groups – saw a considerable increase in their real earnings, and thus in their standard of living. Not without reason, the fifteenth century has often been referred to as the golden age of the labourer, and the improvement, in addition to free time, would have been reflected in the purchase of more expensive foodstuffs and products of industry. This development stimulated the production of and trade in goods of mass consumption for the first time in medieval history. There are clear indications that, by and large and despite the horrors of chronic crises of existence, late medieval people were better fed,

better clothed and better housed than their forefathers. This can be deduced from certain economic-institutional developments as well as from an archaeological and art-historical study of the material culture.

During the late Middle Ages, economic institutions such as markets were increasingly given a primarily regional function. Hundreds of new fairs were introduced, for example. The largest and most important – at Antwerp and Bergen-op-Zoom each twice per year, Lyons, Frankfurt-am-Main, Geneva, Vienna, Nuremberg, Cracow – became part of dynamic new cycles of annual fairs with an international character. They were just the tip of the iceberg, however, showing that more and more small places were linked up with trading networks into the continent, enabling people of modest means to buy simple goods from other places. By the same token, these same people could try to find bigger or more distant markets for their local produce. Information from Flanders shows how well they succeeded in this: cheap woollen materials produced in the new rural textile centres found their way to Russia as early as the fifteenth century. It is therefore generally accepted that the total volume of trade was far larger in 1500 than it had been at the end of the period of expansion two centuries earlier. Even in this optimistic scenario, however, cyclical movements and regional differences in tempo must still be taken into consideration. Regions that did well at a relatively early date, such as Castile and southern Germany, formed a contrast with those that only got under way later, such as Normandy and England.

Characteristics of late medieval society

Openness and closure

With its frequent epidemics, the late Middle Ages was a period of intermittent dynamism. Apart from the social and psychological disruptions, which at times must have been unimaginably hard, the lottery of death – it was impossible to predict who would die or who would survive – led to radical rearrangements of capital. No wonder that the ancient theme of vicissitudes of fortune enjoyed such popularity. That was true of another new motif as well, the dance of death, the procession of rich and poor, young and old, man and wife, led by death (often depicted as a skeleton holding a scythe), which was intended to make all mortals realise that death was no respecter of persons and could carry anyone off, at any time.

If the mortality crises furthered geographical and social mobility, paradoxically enough they also advanced the tendency to social closure. The paradox is admirably illustrated by the development of the late medieval English nobility. Under the influence of the Hundred Years War in particular, the nobility was considerably enlarged through the recognition of two additional noble ranks, those of (e)squire and gentleman. The number of nobles tripled. This new nobility then became increasingly exclusive. Taxation was the background to this development: when the crown taxed the nobility it had to be clear who belonged to the group.

Even after enlargement, therefore, the English nobility remained a select group, comprising no more than 1.6 per cent of the taxable population by the middle of the fifteenth century. Table 10.1, with an overview of the English nobility in 1436,

clearly shows the enormous differences in income within the nobility, especially within the highest category of nobles, the peers. The richest peer in England in that year was Richard, duke of York, who had a taxable income of £3,230. This was more than fifty times greater than the £60 listed for Lord Clinton, the least well-off peer in the tax records. Further, the records also show that Clinton's income was only twelve times the minimum annual income of £5 necessary to be counted a gentleman.

The nobility was never hermetically sealed off, however – had that happened it would have soon died out everywhere! One road open to it was to embrace people who were closest to the nobility in wealth and lifestyle: in England the ownership of extensive property largely determined entry, whereas in the Low Countries it was often the possession of seigneurial rights. On the other hand, nobility and knighthood excluded members who were no longer able to maintain their position, whatever the reason. More or less fixed mechanisms were in place to regulate this: one important criterion to exclude an individual was whether he himself performed farm work or other forms of manual labour.

A similar paradox applies to urban settings. On the one hand, urbanisation increased rather than decreased during the late Middle Ages. Moreover, life expectancy was shorter in towns than in the countryside. For both reasons, there always was a

TABLE 10.1 Stratification of the nobility in England according to income tax demands in 1436. The total number of tax payers was about 450,000.

Category	No.	Range	
		Taxable annual income (£)	Average annual income (£)
Peers	50	60–3,230	865
Knights (knightly class)	933	40–600	88
Esquires	1,200	20–39	24
(Larger) freeholders	1,600	10–19	[14.5]
(Ordinary) gentlemen	c.3,400	5–10	[7.5]

Source: Calculated from S.H. Rigby, *English Society in the Later Middle Ages: Class, Status and Gender* (Basingstoke and London: Macmillan, 1995), p. 190.

steady flow of migrants into the towns resulting in greater flexibility and mobility of labour, which in large and medium-sized towns led to the formation of a highly mobile, almost floating, underclass of people who did not have the formal status of burgher, were employed on a daily basis or not at all and who thus lived from hand to mouth. On the one hand, the increasing organisation and regulation of labour and production in crafts, the retail trade and services reinforced the tendency to exclusion. This was particularly the case in sectors which suffered from the decrease in demand for their standard products, such as butchers and traditional urban weavers. They tried to uphold their market share by protectionism and the exclusion of newcomers. On the other hand, some sectors proved able to adapt to the shifts in demand, discover new markets and develop new products such as cheap woollen cloth in England, Holland and south-west Flanders, and linen and fustian in Swabia. In regions with a booming trade, such as Holland, the region of Antwerp, south-west Flanders and Swabia, more liberal regulations and openness to newcomers were required to meet the demand for labour.

This entire development fits in with the more general tendency in western European society during the later Middle Ages and the early modern period towards social compartmentalisation and the formation of what Max Weber called status groups. By this he meant groups which were clearly separate from each other socially and sometimes even legally, and reinforced that separation by their way of life and their own codes of behaviour. The origin of this tendency to classification must be sought in the twelfth century, when all sorts of new urban groups and associations had to find their places in the social order which, according to medieval social ideology (cf. Chapter 4), had to be firmly and hierarchically constructed and able to function organically; as society became increasingly complex, however, the social order showed symptoms of emancipation and mobility that were difficult to reconcile

with this ideology. The listings and plans of social groups from that time betray the need felt for an appointed place; all segments of society had to be absolutely certain of what was expected of them, by which external signs they could be recognised, the sort of behaviour fitting for their members, and so on. All sorts of social categories were even provided with 'typical' virtues and vices. Moral group assessments of this sort were imprinted through the so-called *sermones ad status*, literally meaning 'sermons addressed to the [social] orders'. The tendency was articulated even further during the late Middle Ages. One famous literary witness of the set mentality of this period was Geoffrey Chaucer's verse narrative, the *Canterbury Tales*; this story of a company of pilgrims on their way to the shrine of Thomas Becket at Canterbury formed a perfect frame for an ironic parade of pilgrims, each of whom represented a recognisable social type.

The position of women

What influence did the socio-economic climate of the late Middle Ages have on the position of women in society? The answer to this question must begin with the observation that virtually no one during the period ever got beyond the essentially ambiguous attitude that has in fact been characteristic of the entire history of Christian European culture, from ancient times right up to the present time. The misogynous undercurrent within it went far back in time, to Greek philosophers like Aristotle, and was reinforced in Late Antique Christian theology. Along the way the negative image of women became firmly embedded in medical, theological and legal views. According to those views, not only were women inferior to men in a physical respect, they were also less intelligent and less inhibited emotionally. Nevertheless, Christianity set a positive countercurrent in motion by admitting women from the outset to the heart of the gallery of Christian saints, beginning with the Virgin Mary, mother of

Christ. This counter-current was reinforced under the influence of the new religious and courtly sentiments that came to the fore from the eleventh century onwards and by changes in the Church's ideas on marriage. A Christian marriage could only be founded on the agreement of both marriage partners, and mutual affection between spouses became the basis of a good marriage.

But all this brought little change in the prevailing negative attitude towards women in medieval society. Through their assumed lesser nature, women had an essentially different function from that of men. They always needed the protection of a guardian who had authority over them, protected and represented them in law: the father, brother, uncle, husband, priest and confessor. As a rule, women had no place in public life and no business there. Outside the private sphere, women had only limited rights. They could not hold public office, except for that of abbess or the temporal ruling positions such as queen, duchess, countess or dame of a lordship, often connected with considerable genuine power. Ordinary women, on the other hand, could act independently on their own behalf or on behalf of another, without the aid of a male guardian, or appear before ecclesiastical or secular courts only in very precisely described, exceptional cases such as expert witness or as a midwife. Full emancipation was acknowledged only for widows who were entitled to inherit and continue their late husband's business.

From a socio-economic point of view, there was less inequality between men and women in the lower classes than in the upper classes. In the lower classes, a woman was normally actively involved in income earning, there was little property or capital for men to manage and men had few or no public (administrative or judicial) responsibilities which gave them a sense of superiority. The relative degree of autonomy allowed to women who were active in trade or retail business in towns was particularly remarkable. In Flanders and Cologne, every generally recognised *coopvrouw*, female merchant, was allowed to carry on business on her own account and at her own risk, whatever her civil status. We have seen something of the position of women in craft guilds in Chapter 9. A noticeable exception was midwives, whose professional training was regulated by municipal authorities and who could become members of craft guilds and enjoy the status of master/mistress. Most working women, however, were employed on the fringes of the economy and not in association with guilds. They often performed undervalued tasks in the textile trade, such as spinning, combing, knotting and knitting, or they peddled foodstuffs on the street, sold cheap cloth or ran a junk shop. Many women worked as domestic servants while others cared for the sick, clearly risky but therefore better paid.

From a purely legal viewpoint, widows were the best off. As long as they did not remarry, widows had far more control over their own affairs than did married women. For economic reasons, however, many women could not afford to permanently escape 'a man's rod', in the words of the Antwerp poetess Anna Bijns (1493–1575), and thus they remarried unless there were strong cultural prejudices against remarriage, as was the case in the Mediterranean area. Not without reason widows were placed under the special protection of the Church as *personae miserabiles* even into the fourteenth century. Only the well-off widow, with sufficient means to carry on or possibly rent out the business of her deceased husband, could gain recognition as a full master (or mistress) within a craft guild. It is also noticeable how many widows were among the creditors mentioned in countless loan letters dating from the late Middle Ages.

Whether the position of women improved or worsened during the late Middle Ages is a much discussed matter. One theory broadly suggests that women's chances in life were much improved in the late Middle Ages in comparison with the early period. Their negotiating position on the marriage market had weakened, however, because they had become far less scarce. Such demographic reasoning may appear rather far-fetched,

BOX 10.2 A WOMAN FIGHTS BACK WITH THE PEN: THE LIFE AND WORKS OF CHRISTINE DE PIZAN (1364–*c.*1430)

Perhaps the most remarkable example of a successful widow in the late Middle Ages was Christine de Pizan (1364–*c.*1430), daughter of the Venetian court astrologer to the French king, Charles V. After the death of her husband, the royal secretary, Étienne de Castel, Christine became a public figure with an extensive literary oeuvre consisting of poems in the lyrical, courtly style, biographies and didactic works. The *Livre de la cité des dames* ('Book of the City of Ladies') and *Epistres sur le Rommant de la Rose* ('Letters about the *Roman de la Rose*') are considered her most important works. The first, completed in 1405, was a very free translation into French of *De claris mulieribus* ('Concerning Famous Women'), a poetical work written in Latin by Giovanni Boccaccio. While Boccaccio had included only the biographies of exemplary women from pagan Antiquity, not considering it fitting to describe the saintly lives of Christian women in the same context, Christine had no hesitation in doing

Christine de Pizan writing in her study. She presented her writings, *Oeuvres*, to Isabeau, queen of France, in 1407.

just that. And after a comparative enumeration of virtues that were mirrored in the lives of those famous women from the past, she proffered a philosophical defence against the misogynous mainstream of medieval intellectual thought. The city of ladies was built under the supervision of Reason, Rectitude and Justice; its citizens had proved that they contributed at least as much as men did to the formation of an ordered Christian society. Women were different from men, but it was not possible that they were less perfect creations of God, and for that reason their natural weaknesses were amply compensated for by positive characteristics. In Christine's view, the withholding of a proper education from women was the main reason for their seeming inferiority.

The same themes were dealt with in the *Epistres*, though in a less veiled way, for in this polemic Christine took the side of female honour and honesty against the uncomplimentary treatment of women in the immensely popular *Roman de la Rose*. The interminable *Roman* was an allegorical treatment of courtly love. It was begun around 1240 by the northern French knight, William de Loris, and continued in a much more satirical, and anti-female, vein by John of Meung, a poet of bourgeois origins, a quarter of a century later. Christine's criticism provoked heated public discussions about the value of the *Roman*, in which she could count on the support of the famous preacher and chancellor of the University of Paris, Jean Gerson, who called Christine 'a woman like a man' (*femina ista virilis*).

On her own, Christine de Pizan was of course no more a proof of the existence of wide support for the emancipation of women than was Joan of Arc, the Maid of Orléans whom Christine praised in one of her poems. Moreover, Christine's works were traditional in form and, above all, encouraged conventional marital virtues and female codes of conduct. Nonetheless, they had an emancipatory tenor, especially because they propagated the idea, previously defended only by Abelard, that women too may have *auctoritas*, and that they deserved a full and valued place within the community. In this connection Christine also urged that elementary education be made available to women.

Sources: Maureen Quilligan, *The Allegory of Female Authority: Christine de Pizan's 'Cité des dames'* (Ithaca: Cornell UP, New York, 1991); Liliane Dulac and Bernard Ribémont (eds), *Une femme de lettres au Moyen Age: Etudes autour de Christine de Pizan* (Orléans: Paradigme, 1995); Alcuin Blamires, *The Case for Women in Medieval Culture* (Oxford: Clarendon Press, 1997).

but the idea of a relative surplus of women in the late Middle Ages is by no means absurd, so long as it is applied only to towns. Comparatively large numbers of women lived in towns. Wealthier households generally had many live-in female servants. Older widows from the countryside often moved within the protection of the town walls if they could afford to do so. For similar reasons the towns housed many women's convents and, especially in the Low Countries and Germany, beguinages (see Chapter 12). This form of open cohabitation of single laywomen in individual houses protected by a wall and a gate met in some way the desire for emancipation from patriarchy.

Towns then were places where there were concentrations of women without them necessarily forming an economic or social problem for urban society, a perspective suggested in German historiography in particular. The supposed excess of unmarried women, all of whom secretly desired a husband, was often ridiculed in the satirical literature of the time. It also provided a fertile breeding-ground for another, by no means harmless, phenomenon: the demonisation of single, elderly women. The stereotype of the ill-tempered old woman who used magic spells to cause harm had been around for much longer – there was a continued demand for practitioners of magic throughout the entire Middle Ages – but now a new element was added, one which was particularly dangerous for those concerned: that malicious people could make a pact with the devil. This demonisation of women who were wrongly suspected of practising magic had a variety of backgrounds. The ubiquitous presence of death and decay certainly contributed to it, as did the fixation on determined (social) categories discussed above and the growing moralism in public life through which more and more emphasis was laid on the moral reputation of individuals – and the reputation of a single women was easily besmirched. And, finally, the gradual professionalisation of medical and pharmaceutical care and the rise of a professional care sector (again, mainly in the towns) would have played a part as they tried to submerge all forms of popular medicine and magic, which came to be seen in an increasingly bad light. In short, by the end of the Middle Ages, there were clear signs of a religious-psychological climate of fear and rejection that would end in the great witch-hunts of the early modern period.

Social contrasts and social conflicts

Town and country

In addition to the old antithesis between peasants and aristocratic lords, the rise of the towns created a new contrast, one between town and country, between farmers and townspeople, between a rustic and a civic culture. It seemed to be a logical consequence of the tendency of the towns to dominate the surrounding countryside judicially, economically, politically and militarily. That tendency was reinforced in the late Middle Ages in those parts of Europe with an increased degree of urbanisation.

Late medieval urban imperialism caused the distinct, multidimensional interrelation between town and country to widen rather than to narrow the social and cultural gulf between country people and town-dwellers. In 1525, Wolfgang Königstein, a canon of Frankfurt, could refer to the Peasants' War which had just broken out as an *uffruer von ein folk, genannt die bauern* ('a revolt of a people, known as the peasants'), as if he were talking about the Huns or the Mongols. A revealing remark. The urban elite had a profound dislike of everything rustic, and this dislike was translated into stereotypes which sometimes merely repeated the old aristocratic prejudices against peasants and sometimes reflected new ones. Peasants were seen as clumsy, churlish, dirty and stupid, lacking any sense of proportion or self-control either in eating and drinking or in dealing with conflicts. An Italian proverb summed it up: *la città buon' huomeni de' fare, la villa buone bestie*: 'the task of the town is to make good people, and of the village to make good beasts'. In the eyes of literary historians the 'burgher culture' was rooted in the positive view that contrasted with the negative characteristics of rustic life. If we are to use the term burgher culture, we must remember that it refers exclusively to the culture of the urban elite. It was a reaction against both peasant rudeness and the aristocratic culture of violence and disdain for manual work. There was continual social interaction between the nobility and the patriciate in the towns, which not only led to marriages and political or economical unions but also brought about a cultural blending.

Peasants' revolts

Throughout the Middle Ages internal peace and order was cruelly broken from time to time by the violent discharges of social tensions that were hidden behind the ideal of harmony in an organically functioning society professed by the clerical elite. The late Middle Ages were no exception in this respect: there were a number of large uprisings in both the country and the urban sphere. It appears that three factors seem to promote rebellion. First, the structural shortage of labour was the cause of tensions between serfs and lords, landowners and leaseholders, and between employers and employees. Sometimes these tensions revolved around the claim to abolish unfree personal status and the limits to mobility, sometimes around wage levels or political representation. Second, there was a rapid growth in fiscal demands imposed by rulers upon their subjects at this time. This teething trouble of the early modern state was without doubt one of the major reasons for revolt. Finally, the call for Church reformation, and especially the aversion to the papal appointments of foreign prelates in the Empire, punctuated with widespread anti-clerical feeling linked with a desire for far-reaching social change fuelled some major revolts, such as that of the Hussites in Bohemia in the 1420s and the Peasants' War in Germany in 1525–1526. So, what we see as the basis of revolts is a mixture of grievances against landlords and more or less ideologically driven resistance to rising demands of the state and abuses in the Church. The latter two seem to have been conditional to scaling-up local struggle to something bigger, something that could set alight entire regions, districts or

Abb. 112. Aufständische Bauern mit der Bundschuhfahne umzingeln einen Ritter. Holzschnitt aus: Petrarca's Trostspiegel. Augsburg, Steyner, 1539.

PLATE 10.2 Rebel peasants, carrying their union's standard, arrest a knight. Woodcut, 1539.

principalities. It explains why there were far more large-scale popular revolts from the fourteenth century onwards than there had been before.

Large-scale revolts of peasants, which also linked up with some urban movements, stood out as a strikingly new phenomenon in the late Middle Ages. The Flemish Peasant Revolt of 1323–1328, the French Jacquerie in 1358, the English Peasants' Revolt in 1381, the German Peasants' War in 1525–1526 and the Catalan *remensas* movement – which was not limited to just one year (and for that reason alone was rather different) – are all classic examples of peasant uprisings in the late Middle Ages. Most of the late medieval social revolts underlined the differences between town and country, for a real coalition between peasant rebels and urban rebels occurred only occasionally, although at times there was a feeling of mutual sympathy or inspiration. In Germany,

for example, there were riots in several towns in 1525, clearly inspired by the peasants' rebellion. Yet none of them led to joint action, or even to a joint programme of action. The Flemish revolt of 1323–1328 was the only exception. The basis for the revolt was the extremely high land rents and the serious complaints made by the well-organised peasant communities in the district round Bruges about the unfairness, abuse of power and corruption of the country nobility and village notables when taxes were levied. When the count, Louis of Nevers, imposed a heavy fine on the rebels, the peasants' hatred was directed at the lords in general, including the great abbeys with their large estates and revenues from tithes. The aristocrats reacted as they usually did, answering violence with more violence. Meanwhile, the third and politically most important social party – the major towns – was split by internal rivalries:

Bruges joined the rebels, while Ghent remained loyal.

At first the revolt was successful. Supported where necessary by Bruges militias, the peasant armies had a number of impressive military victories in what is now West Flanders. In Courtrai and Ypres, the peasants could count on massive help from the local people at the crucial moment. They even captured the count and held him hostage for six months. In the meantime, alternative administrative structures were put in place, and they managed remarkably well to keep customary law and order on the basis of a representative government. Parish priests no longer obeyed the interdict, imposed in 1325 on the whole region by the bishops, which had exacerbated anti-clerical feeling. But without the cooperation of Ghent, and with the eventual intervention of King Philip VI of France, who according to feudal law was obliged to come to the help of his vassal, the insurgents stood no chance. When the uprising threatened to radicalise again, the king mustered a formidable army of knights on the Flemish border in the summer of 1328, which crushed the peasants. From the confiscations of property recorded from almost 3,200 of them who were killed in battle one can infer that the rebels came from every layer of society.

The Jacquerie – the name is derived from the traditional nickname for a French peasant, Jacques Bonhomme (Jack Goodfellow) – was first and foremost an outpouring of anger at the nobility, who were considered responsible for the depression in the countryside resulting from low grain prices, the growing tax burden and a wage freeze. To make matters worse, the countryside was being ravaged by disbanded mercenaries of the French army which had suffered a humiliating defeat by the English at Poitiers in 1356 – yet another reason for bitterness. The ferocious insurrection, in which the peasants raved like mad dogs, according to the anti-peasant chronicler Jean Froissart, was crushed swiftly and bloodily.

The immediate cause of the great Peasants' Revolt of 1381 was what many peasants believed to be an unreasonable increase in the poll tax, a tax introduced a few years earlier and levied on every individual. Rebellious peasants from Kent and Essex marched on London where the governing council around the young king, Richard II (1377–1399), deferred military action. Led by Wat Tyler, the peasants forced their way into the city and razed the Savoy, the palace belonging to the duke of Lancaster, the unpopular regent and uncle to the king. At Mile End, not far outside the city walls, the rebels handed their demands over to the king in person. Although the king appeared willing to make concessions, the peasants stormed the Tower of London, the royal fortress. At a second meeting outside the city walls, this time at Smithfield, the mayor of London struck Wat Tyler dead after Tyler, in the king's face, rinsed his mouth out with water and then ordered a mug of beer. The king succeeded in regaining control over London and severe repressions followed. The petitions of Mile End and Smithfield give a good idea of what the rebels actually wanted and why, especially outside London, the great abbeys formed the target of the peasants' aggression. The most important demands were the definitive abolition of serfdom to which many peasants in south-east England were still subject, the repeal of the labour laws limiting wage increases passed after the Black Death, participation of common people in the government of the country and the dismantling of the worldly riches of the Church in England. The last point was less radical than it may appear, in view of John Wycliff's ideas on Church reformation that were circulating at the time – and to which the hated duke of Lancaster was reputed to be sympathetic.

The Catalan *remensas* movement, which began during the third quarter of the fourteenth century, evolved from persistent protests by the peasantry against the policy of the spiritual and temporal lords to end the popular practice of allowing peasants to buy off all seigneurial obligations (the sources speak of *payese de remensa*, literally peasants of redemption, hence *remensa*). In addition to this, the resettlement policy of the owners of large estates who took on migrants from beyond the Pyrenees met with widespread resistance. Curiously enough the Catalan peasants were supported in their fight by lawyers who believed that, in the case of the *remensas*, the lords were acting contrary to natural law – peasants, too, were by nature free! Even the king of Aragon shared this view. In spite of such powerful allies, however, the peasants had to wait until 1486 for satisfaction when after a long struggle, most of their demands were acceded to in the Compromise of Guadalupe.

There were several causes for the great Peasants' War that blazed through southern and central Germany (including parts of present-day Austria and Switzerland) in 1525. Many peasants in the area were still serfs, weighed down by the heavy burdens attached to their personal status. Moreover, everyone, free or unfree, was faced with the spread of local lordships, for these areas were swarming with the so-called *Reichsunmittelbare*, minor lords holding the title of count, abbot or knight. Subject only to the purely nominal authority of the German king/emperor, these lords had autonomous rule over territories the size of a few villages where they were often important landowners or landlords as well. It was this combination of lordships that caused such antagonism.

The rebellion of the south German peasantry was remarkable in that it involved not only public violence but also a propaganda offensive of an almost apologetic nature. The hotbed of the revolt was upper Swabia where the peasant communities printed their tersely formulated demands and spread them as a manifesto. The so-called 'Twelve Articles of Memmingen' were so well known that they served as a model for countless other 'article letters'. The demands were concrete and succinct, varying from a village's right to choose its own pastor to the abolition of serf taxes, curtailment of the tithe levy, the autonomous right to decide over the use of common woods, meadows and waters, and the guarantee that justice in local courts would be administered in accordance with local customs and not following the statutes

mixed with Roman law that many lords had prescribed for their subjects on their own authority.

The new medium of the printing press in particular ensured that the uprising spread like wildfire. Some historians, Peter Blickle (1998) among them, believe that it took on the characteristics of a revolution solely because of this medium, for it was only in this way that the radical ideas about social renewal hinted at in the 'article letters' could be so widely disseminated and discussed. This social renewal had two aspects. On the one hand, the insurgents demanded a voice for the common people, *gemeine Mann*. By this they did not mean every Tom, Dick and Harry, but the more substantial peasants and craftsmen who owned their farmhouse or workplace, the rural equivalent of the citizens in Marsilius of Padua's *Defensor Pacis* ('The Defender of Peace') (Chapter 12). In this respect the peasant revolt was more conservative than revolutionary. On the other hand, there was a revolutionary zeal, grafted on to the ideals of the Reformation. What the peasants envisaged was a drastically improved society in which the common good would be defined in evangelical terms and no longer derive from the interests of the lords; a society, too, in which divine justice and not the arbitrary rulings of the lords would be the guiding principle of regulation and justice.

The leaders of the Reformation did not always welcome the socio-religious ideals of the discontented peasants. After initial hesitation, Luther decidedly rejected the 'rebels'. Yet others, such as Thomas Müntzer in Thuringia and Michael Gaismair in Tyrol, sided wholeheartedly with the peasants. Gaismair, a 'tireless advocate of the Christianisation of the state and society' in Blickle's words, wanted to turn Tyrol into a radically egalitarian society modelled on the Old Testament. Müntzer, a frustrated disciple of Luther, was a substitute pastor in a village in Saxony with no hope of a glittering career in the Catholic Church. His theological views were influenced by mysticism, but he was increasingly prone to apocalyptic delusions to which he bore witness in a violent vocabulary where the keywords were purification and destruction. The end of the world was at hand, but a thousand-year reign of evangelical purity before the Last Judgement was in the offing. It would emerge after a terrible struggle in which countless true believers would die a martyr's death. On the battlefield of Frankenhausen it became clear whom Müntzer had preordained for that martyrdom: the 8,000 Thuringian peasants who, singing psalms and brandishing cudgels and pitchforks, were sent to face the trained lancers of the Landgrave of Hessen.

At Frankenhausen the German princes sent out a horrifying signal of what was in store for the subjects who failed to obey them. Nearly 100,000 peasants perished on the battlegrounds and execution sites of Thuringia, Hessen, Franconia and Swabia in 1525–1526. Many German historians consider the failure of the Peasants' War a decisive moment in German history. The development towards autonomous territorial principalities which had begun under the Hohenstaufen was from now on irreversible. The noble and ecclesiastical owners of local lordships were the great losers, not the peasants. Further on, it was out of the question that central and southern Germany would switch to the Reformation.

A new culture of revolt?

In a recent survey, the British art historian Samuel Cohn (2006) counted no fewer than 1,112 social revolts in Europe between 1200 and 1425, and the latter date marked in no way an end to the phenomenon. Among these, urban uprisings were by far the most frequent, and it cannot be accidental that they occurred most often and most violently in highly urbanised regions and in the largest cities. So northern and central Italy, the Low Countries, the Rhineland and the north German Hanse cities stand out as the most virulent places of recurrent revolt. The pre-eminent example of urban rebellion took place in Florence

in the summer of 1378. The so-called revolt of the *ciompi* ('fullers') was in fact the outburst of the disaffection that had smouldered for a long time among the lower craftsmen and workers (*sottoposti* in Italian, meaning 'the lowly placed') in the textile industry, an estimated 13,000 people, most of them without their own means of production. These true proletarians were named after the largest group among them, the *ciompi*. The *sottoposti* were not organised into guilds and thus had no political influence because members of the town council were chosen from among the merchants and craft guilds. The *sottoposti* were powerless against the arbitrary decisions of officials when it came to taxation and against every form of exploitation by the great entrepreneurs. The fiasco of an expensive war against the pope was the last straw. The *ciompi* took to the streets and forced three new craft guilds to be established. The place given to the three new guilds in the various organs of public administration was negligible, however, and their leaders, one of whom was the wool-carder Michele di Lando, were hedged in and rapidly neutralised. The *ciompi* felt betrayed by their comrades, and the result was a revolt-within-a-revolt, the revolt of the *popolo di Dio* (God's people). Michele di Lando refused to back down and led the bloody reprisals in person. The *ciompi* revolt lost its momentum soon afterwards, although relationships in the governing council of Florence did not return to normal until 1382.

In recent years there has been a tendency to see the great social upheavals of the late Middle Ages as the resistance of peasants and craftsmen to either landlords and capitalist employers or to ever more exacting states. Yet, without wishing to detract from the importance of the socio-economic and fiscal motives that were undoubtedly very real, we do not want to use the term 'class struggle' in the classic Marxist sense. First of all, most rebellions showed remarkably little social homogeneity – this was equally true of the peasants' movements and of the *ciompi* revolt in Florence. There always seem to have been considerable differences in the economic position, well-being and goals of the insurgents. Class ties were mixed with other binding social relations of a more vertical nature, which cut across classes. In this context we can consider factions or parties, clientage-like networks, professional, neighbourhood or religious groupings. This also means that there was no consistent revolutionary ideology reflecting class consciousness, an essential ingredient of class struggle in the Marxist sense. Most of the late medieval uprisings did not seem to have been aimed at overthrowing the existing social order. The only serious exceptions were the rising of the Hussites, the German Peasants' War and episodes in the Flemish Peasant Revolt. In these cases, the rebels pressed for a new, biblically inspired society of autonomous peasant communities and urban republics.

Contrary to what one might think, peasant uprisings were generally better organised than urban revolts. This proves how strong and self-assured village communities had become by then. The peasants of the Jacquerie in the Île-de-France were probably the only ones not to operate out of their own village communities, hence their rapid defeat. The Flemish, English, Catalan and German peasants in the other uprisings mentioned here were most emphatically based in village communities. It also meant that rebellious peasants were not just desperados, driven by hunger and poverty; on the contrary, many of them, starting with their leaders, belonged to such village elites as well-to-do peasants, smiths, innkeepers and local bailiffs or judges.

A world of ubiquitous poverty

Because of technological and economic underdevelopment and the regular occurrence of subsistence crises allied to it, as well as the lack of anything at all approaching our modern system of social security, the medieval world was one filled with undisguised, grinding poverty. Poverty is never a clear and unequivocal concept. Even if we were to start from the seemingly simple definition that the poor are in every case people who cannot or can only barely obtain the minimum biological necessities of life, it would still be impossible to gain a true impression of the extent of poverty in the Middle Ages from the sources available. In those sources roughly three sorts of poor appear, which only partly overlapped:

1. The fiscally poor, meaning permanent residents of villages and towns whose capital resources were too small to have to pay taxes. Taxation records from various parts of the Low Countries in the fourteenth and fifteenth centuries show that they would have formed between 20 and 30 per cent of the total population.

2. People who could be considered eligible for poor relief, meaning occasional support from charitable institutions. Such support was usually in the form of food rations, sometimes accompanied by other basic necessities, such as shoes, clothing and fuel.

3. Marginal people who did not have any resources of their own and lived on the fringes of society. They would include unskilled labourers, vagrants, beggars and prostitutes with no fixed place of residence and no fixed income.

Institutionalised care for the poor as it existed in the late Middle Ages first started at the end of the twelfth century. Before then it had been a matter for the parish churches, convents and bishops who at specified times doled out food and clothing to paupers waiting at the gates. New religious sentiments ensured that laypeople became increasingly involved in poor relief, resulting in the creation of various types of facility. The first of these consisted of hospitals and hospices. Hospitals were originally institutions for the care of the sick, aged, pilgrims, travellers on a journey and the poor. In large towns the care became more specialised in the thirteenth century, but the sick and the poor were often housed in the same institution. The oldest urban hospitals were staffed by religious orders specially trained for this purpose, such as the brothers of the Holy Ghost and the Trinitarians. Many hospitals were partly financed though legacies and gifts – often with the condition that the donor or legator would enjoy a pension for life.

The second type of facility was local parish funds for poor relief called Tables of the Holy Ghost, that were supported by the local community and intended for the needy of the particular parish only. These were mostly the housebound poor, people who were either structurally poor, such as elderly widows, or people who had only occasional or insufficient work – people who could not find work in the winter, for example. Research into care for the urban poor in the Low Countries in the fifteenth century shows that relief was very meagre and, even more alarming, tended to shrink just when demand was greatest. The main reasons for this were the lack of funds and too many religiously motivated overhead costs. The situation was especially disastrous when the economy remained weak for a prolonged period of time. Poor tables then had less chance to replenish their coffers from legacies, gifts and suchlike while the number of the poor could rise alarmingly and with frightening speed. Those afflicted could only hope that emergency measures set in place by religious institutions or rich individuals would offer some help, or they would leave the place, searching for a better life elsewhere.

Through their presence, the poor offered to everyone who could not live an authentically destitute life in direct imitation of Christ and his apostles the opportunity to relieve the troubled soul by means of 'good works' (alms-giving) and thus to shorten the length of time spent in Purgatory. On the other hand, the commercialisation of the economy and the rise of commercial capitalism, aimed at financial gain, gradually created a mentality in which (manual) labour was regarded in an extremely positive light and poverty was seen as the direct consequence of an unwillingness to work, thus as something for which many indigents had only themselves to blame.

PLATE 10.3 Distribution of bread to the poor, one of the panels representing the Seven Works of Charity commissioned in 1504 by the confraternity of the Holy Ghost in Alkmaar (North Holland). Various religious institutions distributed food and other necessities to poor people, whose numbers might grow in years of bad harvests to one-quarter of the population.

During the late Middle Ages these contradictory views became sharper for several reasons. The demographic contraction caused a structural shortage of labour, which easily gave the impression that there was work for everyone who could and would work. By contrast, among the increasingly widespread and louder calls for reformation in the Church there were bitter complaints that too many Christians, above all the Catholic clergy, allowed themselves to be governed by the sin of greed (*avaritia*) and showed no interest in the Christian duty of charity. In this 'clash of two value systems' (Mullett 1987) poverty was defended loudly and publicly by socially conscious preachers from the mendicant orders. They appear in the sources as champions of a truly moral revolution, by which the old aristocratic gift-exchange economy with its conditional grants would have to make way for a real alms economy, based on voluntary and unconditional giving, which in fact was no more than restitution by the rich of what belonged to the poor. The observant Franciscan St Bernardine of Siena (1380–1444) did not shrink from using apocalyptic threats against the rich in his sermons, which also were interspersed with communist ideas even before the concept existed:

> The poor call for alms and only the dogs react . . . You, rich people, who have so much wheat lying in your warehouses that you cannot even keep it clean so that the stuff rots and is eaten by worms and starlings, while the poor suffer the pangs of hunger – what do you think God will do with you? I tell you that your surpluses belong not to you but to your poor neighbours.

His no less celebrated compatriot, the Dominican Girolamo Savonarola (1452–1498), aired similar ideas by pleading for economic and political rights for the poor. Not only did he preach, he also took action. After the expulsion of the Medici from Florence in 1494, under the pressure of the French royal army, Savonarola led a popular movement to establish a republic. A new constitution enfranchised the artisans, opened minor civic offices to selection by lot and granted every citizen in good standing the right to a vote in a new Great Council. He breathed new life into the *monti di pietà* ('mountains of charity'), the credit banks where the needy could borrow money at a low rate of interest. He also agitated for a tax on the extravagance and luxury in which rich Florentines lived at the time of the Renaissance; if the Dominican had had his way, the famous museums of Florence would not now be stuffed full of the works of art which we so admire today. With the demagogic arsenal of a modern American televangelist, he brought his audience of believers to deeds of collective self-mortification bordering on mass hysteria. In one solemn public meeting his wealthy followers went so far as to throw their sumptuous luxuries – from jewels and cosmetics to playing cards and perfumes – on to a great bonfire of vanities while Savonarola did his utmost to give the whole show a feeling of mutual solidarity and social harmony. Not long afterwards, during the traditional carnival, he persuaded well-to-do young men to dress in rags and go begging for the poor. Finally Savonarola's activities sowed more hatred than harmony, even resulting in the formation of anti-Savonarola groups in Florence. Savonarola himself ended his life on the gallows.

The opposed value system found eloquent supporters in humanistic circles. Poggio Bracciolini (1380–1459), for many years attached to the papal Curia as a secretary and thereafter chancellor of Florence, was the first to publicly put the sin of avarice into perspective, even though he was himself a cleric. He considered the desire to acquire more and more as something productive. 'Money', wrote Poggio, 'is a necessary good for the state, and for that reason people who love money are the foundation of the state.' Several great humanists from the beginning of the sixteenth century, men like Erasmus, Juan Luis Vives and Thomas More, spoke disapprovingly of begging and believed that everyone who was able to work had a moral duty to do so. These sentiments, inspired by classical texts, echoed the ideas behind acts of legislation in the years following the Black Death and were repeated numerous times in the century thereafter.

Poverty, unemployment and vagrancy were always consciously put in the same category. The poor were all idlers and layabouts, lazy scum who needed a heavy hand to make them improve their ways. This view gradually became more firmly fixed in the mentality of the upper levels of society as the early modern period advanced, and the poor were increasingly stigmatised. Poor relief was seen more and more as a minimum provision, to be used solely to lighten the needs of the poor in their own community who really could not be blamed for their situations. In that light, one can understand that, in the period of long-term rising grain prices and occasional shortages between 1522 and 1541, the authorities in no fewer than sixty European cities reorganised their poor relief system through centralisation, stricter control on morals and incentives to seek employment.

Points to remember

- A series of disasters in the form of famines, livestock diseases, plague epidemics, wars and revolts reduced the European population by one-third to a half in the course of the four-teenth century. The frequent recurrence of the plague prevented a quick recovery of popu-lation sizes to pre-Black Death levels.

- Famine and plagues of livestock and humans have their origins in climatic and biological circumstances, exogenous to human societies. Their impact and dissemination, however, are related to human factors such as mobility and concentration of populations.

- The huge population losses led to a structural labour shortage and, in the longer term, improvement in the standard of living of labourers and artisans, as well as greater per-sonal freedom and mobility.

- Peasants and landowners with the most land felt the need to reduce their labour cost by switching to leaseholding and more extensive cattle raising.

- Middle-sized peasants could profit from new types of consumer demand by turning to diversified, market-oriented and partly non-agrarian production.

- Rural and urban revolts were often triggered by fiscal pressure by landlords and growing states. Insurgents demanded better living conditions, personal freedom and in some cases they were motivated by anti-clerical and national feelings.

- The recurrent hazards of life made one-quarter to half of the population vulnerable to extreme deprivation. Institutional poor relief could only marginally help as their resources shrank when the need was highest.

Suggestions for further reading

Benedictow, Ole J. (2004), *The Black Death 1346–1353: The Complete History* (Woodbridge/Rochester NY: Boydell & Brewer). The most recent and well-documented overview.

Dyer, Christopher (1998), *Standards of Living in the Later Middle Ages: Social Change in England, c.1200–1520*, 2nd edn (Cambridge: CUP). A detailed analysis of the incomes and spending of the various social classes, and the differentiated effects of inflation in the thirteenth, crises in the fourteenth and apparent depression in the fifteenth century.

Hatcher, John and Mark Bailey (2001), *Modelling the Middle Ages: The History and Theory of England's Economic Development* (Oxford: OUP). An accessible introduction to medieval economic history, an up-to-date critique of established models, and a succinct treatise on historiographical method, written by eminent specialists well-founded in empirical studies. The most powerful of these guiding inter-pretations are derived from theories formulated in the eighteenth and nineteenth centuries by Adam Smith, Thomas Malthus, David Ricardo, and Karl Marx. Historians moulded these ideas into three grand explanatory models which focus on 'com-mercialisation', 'population and resources', or 'class power and property relations' as the prime movers of historical change. The authors provide not only detailed reconstructions of the economic history of England in the Middle Ages, but also discussions of the philosophy and methods of history and the social sciences.

Jordan, William Chester (1996), *The Great Famine: Northern Europe in the Early Fourteenth Century* (Princeton: Princeton University Press). A detailed account of the cause and effects of the famine, and the reactions to it.

Shahar, Shulamith (2003), *The Fourth Estate: A History of Women in the Middle Ages*, 2nd edn (London/New York: Routledge). Study of the varying attitudes to women and their legal and social status in western Europe between the twelfth and the fifteenth century, as religious persons, married or noble, and in urban or rural settings.

11 The consolidation of states

Types of state: sovereignty versus suzerainty

If a state is generally defined as an autonomous polity with a relatively centralised administrative organisation, claiming to control a specific territory, and having at its disposal superior means of physical force, then few would deny that the kingdoms of the early and central Middle Ages, as described in chapters 3 and 5, were states of some immature sort. However, during the late Middle Ages, European states underwent a rapid and fundamental process of change, which we prefer to describe as a transition from feudal states to 'modern' states. In our view, this transition coincided with a decreasing importance of suzerainty versus an increasing importance of sovereignty. Before explaining these two key terms more precisely, we will start by pointing out that in the course of the late Middle Ages, that is between 1300 and 1550, the polities in Europe that claimed some kind of what we would now call (sovereign) public authority, and could for that reason be described as states, showed great diversity in size, form of government and internal structure. They are listed here in ascending order of extent:

- free peasant communities joined in a loose federation (East Friesland, Graubünden);
- autonomous towns with a more or less extensive agrarian hinterland (German free imperial cities such as Nuremberg and Hamburg; Genoa, Novgorod, Ragusa/Dubrovnik);
- local lordships which may at some point have been elevated to a higher status such as a duchy or principality (Mechelen, Salins, Liechtenstein, Monaco, San Marino, Andorra);
- federations of autonomous towns and rural communities (Swiss Confederation, Friesland);
- regional states dominated by one large city which subordinated other towns, lordships and rural communities to it (Venice, Florence, Milan);
- ecclesiastical principalities: the Papal State in central Italy, the states of the German Order in Prussia and the states of the Order of St John, later the Maltese Order, prince-bishoprics (Cologne, Münster, Utrecht, Liège);

■ effectively autonomous (secular) territorial principalities (the duchies of Brittany, Saxony and Ferrara, and the County of Toulouse before 1271);

■ personal unions of territorial principalities in which each of the constituent entities kept its own institutions, but where the prince determined a common policy (Hainaut, Holland and Zeeland under the houses of Hainaut and Bavaria; the Low Countries under the houses of Burgundy and Habsburg; Jülich, Marck and Berg);

■ kingdoms (England, France, Portugal, Scotland, Sweden);

■ personal unions of one or more kingdoms and/or territorial principalities (Poland-Lithuania; Bohemia-Moravia-Lausitz; the Crown of Aragon, comprising Aragon-Catalonia-Mallorca-Valencia (1412), since 1442 Sicily and the kingdom of Naples, and Sardinia, all united by marriage with the Crown of León-Castile in 1469; Denmark-Sweden-Norway in the Union of Kalmar (1397–1523);

■ empires (Byzantine Empire, Holy Roman Empire, Ottoman Empire).

By definition, sovereignty implies an indirect and impersonal relation between a ruler and all his subjects. A **sovereign** also claims a monopoly (in reality rather the supremacy) on such basic components of public government as legislation, taxation, the use of physical violence, the administration of justice and public administration. **Suzerainty**, by contrast, defines a (monarchical) state in feudal terms, that is, as a personal and direct relationship between the ruler as a feudal overlord and his vassals, with mutual obligations: the king had to protect and provide for his men, the vassals had to serve their lord loyally, which meant that they had to support him in governing his land, go to war with him and give him counsel. In many kingdoms that took shape in central medieval Europe this added up to suzerain kings ceding the full exercise of public authority

over parts of their kingdom's territory to aristocratic vassals with a princely status. In technical terms this was a form of mediatisation of public authority.

As we have seen in Chapter 5, this process most clearly occurred in the successor kingdoms of Charlemagne's empire, because public offices became hereditary and royal power was too weak to oppose this tendency. Even before the year 1000 counts and dukes in both the East and West Frankish kingdom had turned into factually autonomous rulers. For instance, the duke of Bavaria and the count of Toulouse did recognise, respectively, the German king and the king of France as their **liege**, but ruled over Bavaria and Toulouse as if they were kings themselves. One could say that in this situation *both* the kingdoms of Germany and France, *and* the duchies and counties that made part of them had characteristics of a primitive state. Attempts by the German kings, in particular, at forcing back this tendency by appointing bishops and archbishops as counts or as dukes were to little avail. In the thirteenth century the kings formally accepted that the Holy Roman Empire was in fact a confederacy of territorial states; from that point on, the German kingship meant little more than the theoretical supreme authority enjoyed by the office-holder; the king's real power rested on the resources which he had at his disposal as a territorial prince of his own, his *Hausmacht* or princely domain (for instance, the County of Luxemburg and the kingdom of Bohemia for the German kings from the House of Luxemburg). Meanwhile, the counts, dukes, margraves and prince-bishops in the Empire faced the same problem as their king/emperor. Because their principalities were first and foremost feudal states, they left a substantial part of their public authority on the local level to be mediatised by their own (aristocratic) vassals.

More successful in counteracting this tendency was the policy of the French kings from the second half of the twelfth century to enlarge their royal domain (that is, the area over which they themselves could exercise full public authority) by marriage, inheritance or sheer conquest at the expense of the territorial princes in France. Still, the French royal domain did not yet cover more than about half the territory of the kingdom by the beginning of the fourteenth century. Of the principalities that formed the other half, two, the duchy of Guyenne in the south and the County of Ponthieu in the north, were possessions of the king of England. The French king's aggressive attempts to end this situation and make his suzerainty, if not his sovereignty, felt there were the major cause of the Hundred Years War (see below). New problems arose when this successful domain policy was thwarted by the granting of principalities to younger sons or brothers of the ruling king. These were called *apanages* if certain conditions were stipulated for their return. But occasionally grants of full possession were made as well. Most consequential from hindsight was the enfeoffment of Philip the Bold, a younger son of King John the Good, with the duchy of Burgundy in 1363. His subsequent marriage to Margaret of Male, daughter of, and heiress to, the count of Flanders, brought him the County of Artois in France, and the so-called Free County of Burgundy (or Franche Comté) in the Holy Roman Empire, followed after the death of his father-in-law, by the counties of Flanders, Nevers and Rethel. This was the beginning of the Burgundian composite state that would expand further, especially under Philip's clever grandson, Philip the Good (1419–1467), who took over a number of principalities in the north-western part of the Empire (on a disputed legal basis), later known as the Low Countries, and started to transform them into a centralised federate state. At that point, the power of the dukes of Burgundy, in coalition with the king of England, became a threat to the continued existence of France itself.

Outside the former Carolingian Empire the development of suzerainty in feudal kingdoms took different directions, because royal vassals never received public offices in fief, but only in land. This was, for instance, the case in Norman England and Castile. In England, after 1066, the Norman and Angevin kings succeeded in further extending the reach of royal, 'common' law and royal justice, which made even less room for royal vassals to exercise public authority (Chapter 5). In the kingdom of Castile, just like in England, public offices were never enfeoffed; only land was, but large landowners in Castile (be they aristocrats, religious institutions, military orders or even cities) often acquired such far-reaching public authority over the people living on their land that they were territorial princes in all but name. As a result, the Castilian crown exercised direct jurisdiction over no more than 55 per cent of the Castilian population by the beginning of the fourteenth century. This had been the direct outcome of the extraordinary circumstances created by the Reconquest, which forced the crown to be generous with privileges, not only towards the warrior aristocracy but also towards towns (whose governments generally consisted of *hidalgos*, knights). Towns in the reconquered territories acquired extensive freedoms with the aim of attracting Christian immigrants to replace the Muslims who had fled. Besides, some towns were given extensive tracts of land. Seville is an extreme case: this large, wealthy city was conquered in 1248 and its new Christian government received 9,000 square kilometres of land. Quite logically, therefore, Castile developed relatively early representative assemblies – called *cortes* (courts) – in which municipal councils (*concejos*) played a forceful part when the king needed their support.

In sum, in all four feudal kingdoms just discussed the ruler's suzerainty remained undisputed, but at the same time his claim to sovereignty was undermined by various forms and degrees of mediatisation of public authority. Around 1300, neither of the essentials of sovereignty just mentioned was anywhere near being fully completed, but, as we shall see, substantial efforts in that direction were in the making everywhere. In late medieval Europe the word sovereignty danced in the air, and the concept of sovereignty was redeveloped in political theory from the end of the twelfth century onwards. Its aim was partly to get rid of the feudal hierarchy in monarchical positions that had always been silently accepted in medieval Europe (the Roman emperor at the top, then kings, dukes, counts, etc.), and partly to bolster up the supreme power of all types of kings and princes within their own polities. This meant that the first-rank position of the Holy Roman Emperor no longer went unquestioned. Shortly before 1200 lawyers in the service of kings started to use the formula *rex imperator in regno suo* (the king is emperor in his own kingdom) to define the (theoretically) sovereign power of kings. In the early fourteenth century this was analogously extended over territorial princes (prince-bishops, dukes, counts), and city-state governments within the Holy Roman Empire.

The course of events

State-making and nation-building through warfare: English and French kingship united?

When one thinks of late medieval political history, the first event that springs to mind is the Hundred Years War. The causes of this titanic struggle between the two most powerful kingdoms of the time, France and England, were twofold. First, there was the matter of Guyenne, the new name for the quite reduced, coastal part of the old duchy of Aquitaine that was still held by the English crown as the last continental remnant of the once glorious Angevin Empire. The fact that the king of England held Guyenne in fief from the king of France became a matter of discord between the two monarchies; sooner or later it was bound to lead to war. Second, the king of England, Edward III (1327–1377), attempted to claim the French throne after the House of Capet died out in the direct male line in 1328. His claim was based on descent through the female line (King Philip IV, the Fair, of France was his

maternal grandfather). However, the **pairs de France**, the twelve peers (equals), the six highest prelates and six dukes in the realm, rejected the idea of the dynastic union of France and England, raising the argument, based on Salic law, that the French monarchy could only be inherited through the male line. They chose the side of Philip, a son of Charles of Valois (a brother of Philip the Fair), who was crowned Philip VI (1328–1350). In 1337, both issues came together, when Philip seized Guyenne, whereupon Edward pressed ahead with his title, proclaiming himself king of France.

The first stage of the ensuing Hundred Years War (1337–1453) was convincingly to the advantage of the English. The French army of knights suffered dramatic defeats at Crécy in 1346 and ten years later at Poitiers. Here, the Black Prince, the heir to the English throne, captured the French king, John the Good, for whom an enormous ransom had to be paid. In 1358 the craftsmen of Paris rose in revolt against the pressure of high taxation and the economic slump resulting from the war. In this disastrous period the Estates General were summoned to approve emergency

House of Capet (from 1285) (direct line)

- Philip IV the Fair (1285–1314)
- Louis X (1314–1316)
- Philip V (1317–1322)
- Charles IV (1322–1328)

House of Capet (Valois branch)

- Philip VI (1328–1350)
- John II the Good (1350–1364)
- Charles V the Wise (1364–1380)
- Charles VI (1380–1422)
- [Henry VI, king of England (1422–1453)]
- Charles VII (1422–1461)
- Louis XI (1461–1483)
- Charles VIII (1483–1498)

House of Capet (Orléans branch)

- Louis XII (1498–1515)
- Francis I (1515–1547)

FIGURE 11.1 Kings of France, 1285–1547

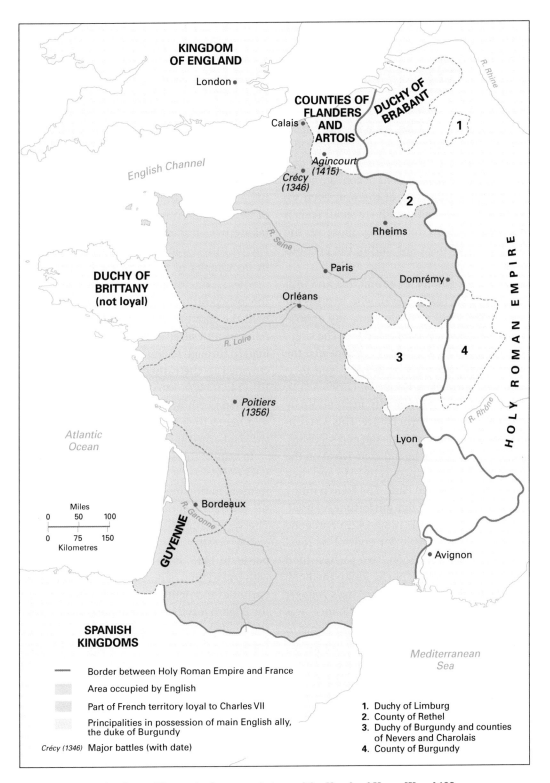

MAP 11.1 The kingdom of France in the second stage of the Hundred Years War, 1428

taxes. The peace of 1360 consolidated a considerable expansion of the English possessions in central France, which now became sovereign, in exchange for the renunciation of the English claim to the French throne.

Whereas the successful struggle had provided the English nobility with exceptional opportunities to enrich themselves, the war caused a profound economic crisis in France, partly as a result of a series of devaluations of coinage meant to cover some of the costs of the war. Even so, between 1369 and 1380 relatively small French armies succeeded in recovering most of the territory that had been lost during the previous decades.

Because of the failures to prevent this, and with a king, Richard II (1377–1399), who lent his ear to peace doves while not tolerating any opposition, tensions mounted in England too. The king's cousin, Duke Henry of Lancaster, engineered the deposition and execution of Richard, and then became king himself as Henry IV (1399–1413). He attempted to legitimise his usurpation by relaunching the offensive in France. This was continued with great success by his son and successor, Henry V (1413–1422), who inflicted defeat on the French at the field of Agincourt in 1415 and then occupied Normandy and Paris. The French ruling elite had brought part of this misfortune on itself, for after King Charles VI (1380–1422) had gone insane in 1392, a struggle for control of royal power had broken out. Soon, two parties stood out, one led by the king's uncle, Philip the Bold, duke of Burgundy, the other by the king's younger brother, Louis, duke of Orléans. France was plunged into civil war. When the crown prince or dauphin, Charles, had the duke of Burgundy assassinated, the latter's son, Philip the Good, decided to side with the English. He ensured that Charles was disinherited by his father in favour of Henry V of England, who also married the king's daughter, Catherine. The kingdom of France was now at rock bottom. After the death of Charles VI, the authority of the dauphin was recognised only south of the Loire: the north-west was in the hands of the English; the north-east in the hands of the duke of Burgundy.

What followed was the remarkable appearance of Joan of Arc, the seventeen-year-old daughter of a peasant from Lorraine who claimed to hear divine voices that called on her to liberate France. Through the agency of a nobleman (of the Armagnac party) living nearby she was moved to the dauphin's court in 1429. There it was decided to make use of the girl's charisma and to put her at the head of an army to relieve the town of Orléans that was besieged by the English. By taking over leadership of an army, Joan, or *la Pucelle* ('the virgin maiden') as she was called in documents of the time, broke through two privileges: one of male superiority, the other of the lofty position of noblemen, who by tradition held the command. But it worked: Orléans was relieved and after a daring *chevauchée* (cavalry march) through enemy territory the dauphin was crowned in the cathedral of Rheims as Charles VII (1422/1429–1461). One year later Joan was captured north of Paris by the Burgundians who sold her to their English allies. After a show trial she was burned at the stake in Rouen in May 1431.

In spite of this setback the French had regained self-confidence, which was expressed in various forms of national sentiment and underpinned by the introduction of permanent general taxation. The systematic recovery gave the king considerable prestige and new means of exercising power. In 1435, at Arras, he made a separate treaty with Duke Philip of Burgundy to whom important territories and rights were ceded. This ensured that the English lost their most important ally. In turn, the English now found themselves in trouble: changes in political fortunes brought their intense economic relations with the Low Countries under pressure. By 1453, the English had lost all of their French possessions except the port of Calais.

Almost immediately the control of the English crown became a matter of contention between the two main branches of the House of Plantagenet, York and Lancaster, and the baron factions that formed around them, and tensions started to

House of Plantagenet (from 1272) (direct line)

- Edward I (1272–1307)
- Edward II (1307–1327)
- Edward III (1327–1377)
- Richard II (1377–1399)

House of Plantagenet (Lancaster branch)

- Henry IV (1399–1413)
- Henry V (1413–1422)
- Henry VI (1422–1461; 1470–1471)

House of Plantagenet (York branch)

- Edward IV (1461–1470; 1471–1483)
- Richard III (1483–1485)

House of Tudor

- Henry VII (1485–1509)
- Henry VIII (1509–1547)

FIGURE 11.2 Kings of England, 1272–1547

build up. They boiled over in the Wars of the Roses (1455–1485), so called after the white and red roses of the Yorkist and Lancastrian coats of arms. The wars were devastating for the baronage rather than for English society as a whole, and only ended after three decades with the general recognition of Henry VII (1485–1509) of the Welsh House of Tudor, connected to the Lancasters. Henry had prevailed on the battlefield and was also acceptable as a compromise candidate because he had married the heiress to the York dynasty.

In the long term the Anglo-French dynastic struggle exhausted both sides, of course, although agricultural production was disrupted more severely in France simply because that was where the fighting occurred. Institutionally, the French monarchy emerged from the struggle stronger, as the saviour of the country, at the expense of the dukes and the Estates General, which were rarely summoned again after that. Louis XI (1461–1483) expanded the territory by 40,000 square kilometres by occupying Picardy, Artois, Burgundy, Provence and Roussillon. In England, the crown's efforts brought neither fame nor fortune, and

parliament and the barons continued to be formidable adversaries to the king.

The Holy Roman Empire and Italy: stalemate

From a historical point of view it may not be of great importance to know which house ruled the Holy Roman Empire after the Interregnum ended. For contemporaries, however, it did matter, because the emperor still enjoyed enormous prestige. In the late Middle Ages the emperorship certainly was not something to be scrambled for. In fact, for most of the time since 1273, the emperors came from only two families: the Austrian Habsburgs and the House of Luxemburg; the two exceptions, Louis IV (1314–1347) and Rupert (1400–1410) were both of the Bavarian Wittelsbach dynasty. Moreover, the election of Louis was heavily disputed, and he ran into serious conflict with successive popes in Avignon as soon as he tried to recover imperial rights in Italy. In a late echo of the papal claim to primacy of power, the popes pulled out all the stops

- Rudolf (1273–1291) (House of Habsburg)
- Adolf (1292–1298) (House of Nassau)
- Albert (1298–1308) (House of Habsburg)
- Henry VII (1308–1313) (House of Luxemburg)*
- Frederick the Fair (1314–1330) (House of Habsburg)
- Louis IV (1314–1347) (House of Bavaria–Wittelsbach)*
- Charles IV (1346–1378) (House of Luxemburg)*
- Wenceslaus (1378–1400) (House of Luxemburg)
- Rupert (1400–1410) (House of Bavaria–Wittelsbach)
- Sigismund (1410–1437) (House of Luxemburg)*
- Frederick III (1440–1493) (House of Habsburg)*
- Maximilian (1486–1519) (House of Habsburg)*
- Charles V (1519–1531; emperor until 1556) (House of Habsburg)*

* also crowned emperor

FIGURE 11.3 Kings of Germany, 1273–1531

against the recalcitrant Bavarian: excommunication, deposition, interdict, declaration of heresy, call for a crusade. Louis retaliated by marching on Rome where he installed an anti-pope who crowned him as emperor. His court in Munich became a centre of attraction for anti-papist intellectuals, among whom were Marsilius of Padua and William of Ockham. In 1338, mindful of Matthew 22:21 ('Render to Caesar the things that are Caesar's, and to God the things that are God's'), Louis issued a decree, labelled *Licet iuris*, which laid down that the German king, once elected, would automatically become Holy Roman Emperor; the pope's role was reduced to his ceremonial coronation. This would remain practice until the coronation of Charles V in 1530. Louis died in office in 1347, while Charles, the grandson of his predecessor Henry VII, of the House of Luxemburg, had already been elected and crowned. It shows how much further the conflict that had lasted for more than twenty years had undermined the German king's position.

Charles IV (1346–1378) was to reign in relative peace for thirty years, during which time he restored much of the prestige the German kings and emperors had lost since the decline of the Hohenstaufen dynasty, a century earlier. From his *Hausmacht* as king of Bohemia, he considerably expanded northward the territories under the direct rule of his own dynasty with Brandenburg and Silesia. Part of his success can be connected with the exploitation of the silver mine of Kutna Hora, 80 kilometres east from Prague, which had produced huge profits for the crown in the first decades after its discovery in 1298, and continued to be a sizeable source of income.

Charles' personal qualities prevailed, however. He clearly wanted to put an end to the disruptions that had caused so much damage during his predecessor's reign. He came to terms with the papacy and was crowned in Rome in 1355. He then felt sufficiently secure to issue one year later a fundamental law code called the Golden Bull which definitely restricted the number of electors of the German king – traditionally the preserve of

the highest-ranking princes – to seven. Three were ecclesiastical princes, the archbishops of Mainz, Trier and Cologne, and four were secular princes – the duke of Saxony, the count Palatine of the Rhine, the margrave of Brandenburg and the king of Bohemia (which had been part of the German Empire since 1158). Not only did the Golden Bull prevent further confusion over the election of the king/emperor, as had happened in 1314, it also excluded any interference by the pope. Notwithstanding the principle of election, Charles IV had surely in mind to be succeeded by his son, and establish a royal dynasty. But his son Wenceslas lacked his father's prestige and diplomacy; he was not crowned as emperor and he was even deposed in 1400. It would be the Habsburgs who effectively succeeded in manipulating the elections in favour of their House from 1438 until 1792.

All this did little to change the actual authority of the emperor, which remained largely symbolic if only because anything resembling a centralised bureaucracy was lacking. Until 1806, Germany was made up of many dozens of autonomous principalities with different statuses, such as archbishoprics, bishoprics, duchies, margraviates, counties and lordships, as well as numerous independent urban and rural communes (see Map 11.2). The further development of state institutions therefore occurred primarily at the level of the territorial principalities, not at that of the Empire. That also explains why, in spite of all the efforts made by the Habsburg emperor, Charles V, to uphold the unity of the Catholic Church, the outcome in the Augsburg Religious Peace of 1555 was that the Estates of territorial principalities and free imperial cities were entitled to decide themselves about the religious persuasion of their territory.

In northern and central Italy – the southern part of the Holy Roman Empire – autonomous city republics or 'communes' had emerged as the predominant type of government in the eleventh and twelfth centuries. A few of them were still fiefs held from the emperor, such as the vast duchy of Savoy-Piedmont, united since 1418, which

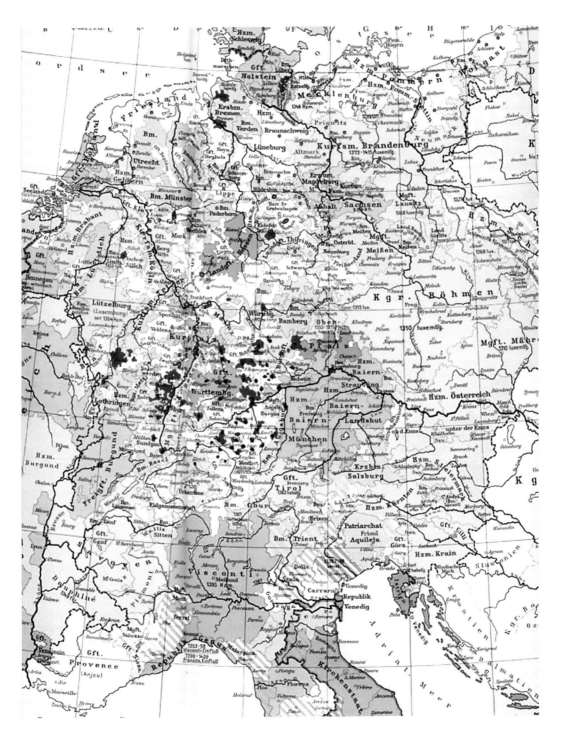

PLATE 11.1 Map of the Holy Roman Empire in the late Middle Ages taken from Westermann's *Grosser Atlas zur Weltgeschichte* (the 1978 edition), hence the German legend. The lands of the three dynasties that supplied all the German kings in the fourteenth and fifteenth centuries are clearly visible: those of the House of Bavaria in green, those of the House of Luxemburg in light green, and those of the House of Habsburg in light orange.

BOX 11.1 CHARLES IV, A CULTURED EMPEROR

Charles IV was elected German king on 11 July 1346, crowned in Aachen on 26 November, and crowned as king of Bohemia on 2 September 1347. His antagonist, Emperor Louis, died on 11 October of that year. Soon thereafter, the new king launched an extraordinary cultural programme which included the foundation of the University of Prague, which was the first in the Empire, the New Town of Prague, the Emmaus monastery where a Slavonic liturgy was celebrated, and the castle called Karlstein. Later on, he patronised the building of more castles named after him, he had the Royal Palace in Prague adapted and the St Vitus cathedral expanded. The famous bridge on the Moldau (Vltava) river, showing statues of Charles and his son and successor Wenceslas on the tower facing the Old Town, dates from 1357, two years after his imperial coronation in Rome. Interestingly, several of these building projects were realised under the leadership of Peter Parler along with his relatives and workshop. He was recruited from Swabia as a young talented architect, and created a particularly elegant late Gothic style in Bohemia.

Under the influence of his father John, count of Luxemburg and (by marriage) king of Bohemia, Charles was educated at the French royal court. At the age of thirteen, in 1329, he married Blanche of Valois, who belonged to the new royal dynasty. He was a true intellectual and polyglot who

Karlstein castle, Czech Republic.

encouraged the use of Latin, German and Czech for literary expression at court in Prague, which favoured the translation of the complete Bible into Czech shortly after the German version, around 1350. He wrote his autobiography up until his election as German king, and a Life of the Czech national saint Wenceslas, both in Latin. By character he was a cunning diplomat who restored good relations with the papacy and extensively used dynastic marriages to strengthen his position amidst the complex international relations of the Hundred Years War and the papacy in Avignon. In his endeavour to foster Prague's centrality, he failed to persuade Venetian merchants to prefer the overland route to Flanders via Linz, the Moldau and the Elbe to Hamburg, and further overseas. Effectively innovative was his support of the import of cotton from the Mediterranean into Swabia, where it was woven with local linen into fustian.

Charles's *monumentum aere perennius*, 'monument more robust than bronze' (Horace) was the castle at Karlstein, constructed within about ten years from 1348 onwards, on a remote mountain 30 kilometres south-west of Prague. This unassailable place comprised a residence for the viscount in charge of defence, an imperial palace, a tower with two chapels, and a second, specially protected, great tower, where the imperial and royal coronation jewels and Charles's personal relics would be kept. The graded scheme of the four buildings, dominated by the great tower, was inspired by the Temple Mountain in Jerusalem. Pilgrims would have to climb to reach the symbols of salvation in successive stages, the individual shrines being ordered in a precise way. The highest level was on the second floor of the great tower, attainable through a winding staircase and decorated with wall paintings representing the life of the Czech saints Wenceslas and Ludmila.

At Karlstein, Charles IV built his Holy Chapel, inspired by the Sainte Chapelle in Paris he knew so well. That had been constructed under King Louis IX as an architectural shrine for the preservation of the most precious relics of Christendom, including the Crown of Thorns. In Karlstein, a fragment of the Holy Rood would be kept, which King Charles V of France had offered to the emperor, with the coronation jewels. The chapel's walls are inlaid with semi-precious stones set in gilded plaster, where Charles's initials, the imperial crown, the Czech lion and the imperial eagle were moulded. The vaults are completely gilded and covered with lenses in Venetian glass and precious stones which made the whole look like a shrine, glowing in the sunlight. One hundred and thirty panel paintings showed saints, ordered in a strict hierarchy, as guardians of the deposited treasures. These were removed during the Hussite wars in the 1420s, and Karlstein lost its extraordinary symbolic role.

Source: Zoe Opacic (ed.), *Prague and Bohemia: Medieval Art, Architecture and Cultural Exchange in Central Europe* (Leeds: Maney Publishing, 2009).

stretched along both sides of the western Alps. Most of the communes, however, turned into *signorie* ('lordships') from the middle of the thirteenth century onwards when local noblemen or, more often, *condottieri*, mercenary captains in the service of cities, staged coups and constituted princely regimes. The most famous of these new lords acquired presumptuous titles such as duke or marquis and succeeded in establishing dynasties which sometimes remained in power for centuries. The Visconti family controlled Milan until 1450, followed by the Sforzas, while the Scaligeri ruled in Verona, the d'Este family in Ferrara, the Gonzagas in Mantua, the Malatestas in Rimini and the Montefeltros in Urbino. This pattern of ruling *signorie* was resisted by Venice,

Genoa and Siena, which maintained their republican forms of government run by councils. After a long struggle, Florence was forced to abandon its republican ambitions when it finally gave way in 1512 to the *signoria* of the Medici family, which had in fact governed the republic, with short interruptions, since 1434.

After the collapse of the Hohenstaufens, southern Italy continued to be governed by a monarchy, at first under the House of Anjou which enjoyed the support of the popes. During the Sicilian Vespers, a popular rising against the French occupation that broke out in 1282, the king of Aragon, Peter III, occupied the island of Sicily on the basis of a dubious claim to the succession. The Angevins stood firm in the kingdom of Naples, which comprised all of the Italian peninsula south of the Papal State, until 1442, when Aragon took the crown there as well. As a result of the personal union between Castile and Aragon (effective since 1504), southern Italy came under Spanish-Habsburg rule for a long period of time.

In the first half of the fifteenth century, the three major cities of northern and central Italy – Venice, Milan and Florence – conquered large territories in order to protect their economic interests and strengthen their position in the ongoing competition between states. In 1454, these three 'regional states' concluded a non-aggression pact: the Peace of Lodi. One year later, the Papal State, the kingdom of Naples and a number of smaller city-states were admitted to this new stable political order, which was then called the Italic League. The resulting balance of power would hold throughout the second half of the fifteenth century and was only disrupted by the invasions of the French kings, Charles VIII in 1494 and Louis XII in 1499, who laid claim to the crown of Naples and the duchy of Milan. They set in motion a whole new system of international alliances in which the Habsburgs, both as emperors and as kings of Spain, would play a major part. As a result, Italy became the main battleground of Europe for fifty years, though this did not lead to any essential change in the pattern of the regional division of power there until the nineteenth century.

Iberia: kings and cortes

State formation in Spain was affected dramatically by the progressive Reconquest – which in reality was as often a matter of negotiation with Muslim leaders as it was of military victory – and the vital issue of repopulation that followed in its wake. But the results were quite different in the two largest Christian kingdoms, Castile and Aragon, and these differences were only partly bridged when they were united under one dynasty. This occurred in 1469, when the rulers of Castile and Aragon, Isabella and Ferdinand II respectively, who were second cousins, became a royal couple, the so-called Catholic monarchs.

Despite the unity of interests between crown, nobility and towns that was visible in Castile during the thirteenth century and in spite of the early development of the Castilian cortes, a long-term tendency to absolutist royal power soon set in. Although the ability of the Castilian cortes to curb royal power was clearly back on the increase in the second half of the fourteenth century when a war of succession broke out between King Peter the Cruel and his illegitimate half-brother, Henry, count of Trastámara, there was a return to strong kingship soon afterwards. In the fifteenth century the Castilian cortes had less and less to say.

In Aragon, on the other hand, a contractual relationship remained intact between the king and the greater number of his subjects, with mutual obligations to be fulfilled. It fuelled a tendency that has been termed pactism between crown and people, whereby the exercise of royal power was conditional to the king's recognition of the customs and privileges of his subjects, also and especially against possible intrusions by feudal lords. A major reason was that Aragon was actually a confederacy of several older kingdoms (Aragon, Valencia, Mallorca) and a county (Barcelona-Catalonia), which were all keen to preserve their own customs and have their own cortes – with incidental meetings of the General Cortes, for the first time in 1289. Typically, in 1412 King Ferdinand I had to be formally elected by representatives of the cortes of Aragon and Catalonia, although he was the rightful successor. From early on in Aragon, all the monarch's major decisions, especially those relating to finance and taxation, were submitted to the cortes for approval, and the cortes were also involved in legislation. With the purpose of keeping an eye on the collection and spending of taxes the cortes, dominated by representatives of the wealthy merchant elite, set up a special agency, known as the *Generalitat*, which acquired permanency in the second half of the fourteenth century. In addition, the king was obliged to answer all grievances brought forward by the cortes, and there was no royal interference whatsoever with the appointment of representatives of the third estate. One of their main ideological spokesmen, Friar Francis Eiximenes (*c.*1340–1409), more than once expressed the idea of popular sovereignty.

It is clear that the third estate in the cortes of Catalonia and Valencia was dominated by the rich merchant elites of Barcelona and Valencia, Aragon's two most important cities. In addition to the cortes their interests were also, and jealously, guarded by the so-called *consulados del mar* ('consulates of the sea'). These were powerful merchants' guilds that came into existence around the middle of the thirteenth century and held important jurisdictional autonomy by the end of the fourteenth, making them virtually independent of the royal courts of justice. This resulted from the technicality of the methods used to solve specific problems of maritime trade, ranging from setting rules for exchange, mediation between foreign and indigenous partners, the application of maritime law and the protection of overseas relations.

Such large differences between Castile and Aragon in the development of kingship and representative institutions, besides going back to different experiences during the final stages of the Reconquest of Spain, were first and foremost a reflection of the huge contrast in their economic and social structures. To simplify, one could characterise Castile as a land of grain, olives and sheep, dominated by aristocratic and ecclesiastical large landowners, whereas Aragon was the heart of an overseas commercial empire that encompassed not only the eastern part of the Iberian peninsula, but also the Balearic islands (conquered around 1230), Sicily (from 1282), Sardinia, Corsica and for a while even stretches of Greece. However, Aragon's fortunes as a major sea power started to wane around 1400, when the Castilians and Portuguese excluded Catalan sailors from the new, burgeoning Atlantic trade, while in the Mediterranean Aragon experienced increasing commercial and military competition from the Genoese with whom it fought several costly wars.

Scandinavian dynastic unions

Scandinavian politics in the late Middle Ages were governed by the establishment of a number of personal unions that bound the Scandinavian kingdoms together. In 1319, Norway and Sweden were unified under the same Swedish royal dynasty. Denmark was drawn in some decades later. In 1387–1388, Margrete, the youngest daughter of the Danish king Waldemar Atterdag, and widow of King Håkon of Norway, was formally recognised as 'almighty lady and husband and guardian' of the kingdoms of Denmark, Norway and finally also Sweden. Margrete's appointment was the logical outcome of her self-assured action as mother-regent to her young son Oluf in the preceding years. After his death she did not act simply as a transitional figure, but rather revealed herself as the ruling monarch in all but name. Rather than trying to produce another heir herself, Margrete adopted her great-nephew, Bogeslav of Pomerania, who on that occasion received the Christian-Scandinavian name of Erik, and pushed through his designation as the royal heir. This was all the more remarkable since in both Denmark and Sweden kingship had always remained dependent on election; only in Norway was rightful hereditary succession sufficient. Margrete's appointment had not gone uncontested in Sweden because Oluf had never ruled there, whereas the actual king, Albrecht of Mecklenburg, was alive and well and had no intention of stepping down voluntarily. Worse still, Albrecht had equally good claims to the thrones of Norway and Denmark. But Margrete was not a person to allow anything or anyone stand in her way, so this meant war. Margrete had her adopted son Erik crowned king of Denmark, Norway and Sweden, in a ceremony at the royal castle of Kalmar in July 1397. At the same time, a document was drawn up, but never sealed, setting out the terms of this Union of Kalmar. The essence of it was that the three kingdoms would never again be separated, while at the same time each would be governed according to its own laws. Real power remained in the hands of Queen Margrete, who died in office in 1412. King Erik had far more difficulty than his stepmother had in fending off growing German influence in Scandinavian affairs. For instance, his introduction around 1425 of the so-called Sound Tolls, a tariff on all Baltic shipping trade, ensured the permanent enmity and meddling of the Hanseatic League. Nor did he succeed in producing any offspring. Only because of substantial juggling with the rules of inheritance was it possible for the Union of Kalmar to remain intact after Erik's death. After a bloody civil war, Sweden went its own way in 1523, but Norway remained united with Denmark until 1814.

Central Europe and the Baltic

In the fourteenth century three of the venerable royal dynasties that had ruled huge stretches of eastern Europe since the tenth century died out in the direct male line: first, in 1301, the Hungarian Árpáds, followed shortly afterwards, in

1306, by the Bohemian Premyslids, while the last king of Poland from the House of Piast died in 1370. All three were succeeded by prominent western European dynasties that were linked by marriage: the House of Anjou in Hungary and Poland, and the House of Luxemburg in Bohemia.

When the last king of the old Magyar dynasty of Árpád died in 1301, Hungary had grown into a most remarkable society that held the reputation of welcoming immigrants from all quarters. Hungary did indeed have a very ethnically mixed population, including substantial non-Christian minorities. Because of very low population density, medieval Hungary preserved for a long time a cellular character, in which the privileges of each group of *hospites* (guests or foreign settlers) was recognised. The Cuman was certainly the largest of the non-Christian minorities. It originated in the thirteenth century when, after the Mongol invasions of the western steppes, a substantial number of Cuman or Kipchak-Turk nomads were allowed to settle in Hungary in return for cavalry service against the Mongol threat. In the end, the Cuman minority may have constituted up to 8 per cent of the Hungarian population and the penultimate Árpád ruler of Hungary, László IV (1272–1290), was half-Cuman.

Hungary in László's time was much larger than the present-day state of the same name. After the beginning of the twelfth century it comprised Croatia and its Dalmatian coast, whereas the possession of Bosnia was constantly disputed between Hungary and the kingdom of Serbia. Only after Hungary came under Angevin rule (1310–1387) did it lose its hold on its Balkan-Slav territories with the exception of part of Croatia. The accession to power of the House of Anjou was not without problems. The first Angevin king, Charles-Robert, neatly shortened to Carobert, a grandson of an Árpád princess, had to be crowned three times in ten years before he was finally generally accepted. But Carobert succeeded in turning anarchy into order and stability, and the long reign of his son Louis (1342–1382), Lajos in Hungarian, radiated ambition. He gave shape to this ambition in the construction of sumptuous palaces and costly military expeditions into south Italy, the Dalmatian coast, the Balkans or to the north, in support of his Polish ally. More than by taxes, the costs of his expeditions were defrayed by the huge share the king could take from the revenues of several new gold and silver mines that had been discovered in northern Hungary. Although attempts to put his younger brother, Andrew, on the throne of Naples were shattered, Louis himself became king of Poland in 1370. But for all his ambitions, the days of the illustrious House of Anjou in eastern Europe were numbered when Louis died in 1382 without leaving a son. Now the way was clear for Sigismund of Luxemburg, a younger son of the Emperor Charles IV and married to Louis' daughter Maria, to take over – after having paid the staggering amount of 565,000 gold florins. Even then it would take Sigismund, who assumed the crown in 1387, another 15 years to smooth over the fierce opposition of the Hungarian nobility to the 'Czech swine'. Thereafter, his power and prestige began to rise, especially after he was elected Holy Roman Emperor in 1410.

When Sigismund died in 1437, after a long reign, Hungarian history repeated itself: since there was no living male heir, the kingdom became the plaything of the great dynasties of the age, in this case those of the Austrian Habsburgs and the Polish/Lithuanian Jagiellons. In the end, however, it would be a noble Hungarian family, the Hunyadi, which took the prize. This was all thanks to János Hunyadi who had a meteoric rise to power in the first half of the fifteenth century, starting as a rather obscure member of the lesser nobility and ending in around 1450 as the most powerful magnate in Hungary and the owner of a fortune beyond belief – his landed possessions alone comprised about 2.3 million hectares of land and included countless villages, towns and fortresses. However, what contributed most to the enhancement of Hunyadi's position, as well as to his virtuous reputation, which has remained untarnished right up to the present day, were his

relative successes as a military leader in the hopeless struggle against the Ottomans. It is a tale of lost but legendary battles, such as Kosovo's famous Field of the Blackbirds in 1448 – the second battle on that spot – where Hunyadi stood shoulder to shoulder with Vlad 'the Impaler' Dracula, the governor of Wallachia. Even if it did not bring victory, it eventually brought the Hunyadi the Hungarian crown, which in 1458 was placed on the head of János' younger son, Mathias Corvinus (meaning 'raven-like') (1458–1490), who, like his father, would attain legendary status. Mathias was in every respect made of the stuff of a great Renaissance prince: a great patron of the arts, a politician capable of reform and change, a talented diplomat and a dauntless warrior. Supported by his so-called 'black army' of 20,000 soldiers of fortune, Corvinus was able not only to keep the Ottomans at bay but also to form a serious military threat to Bohemia and Austria. Nevertheless, despite Corvinus' efforts to curb private violence, for example, Hungary remained a weak state by western European standards, simply because even Corvinus proved unable to extend the royal domain, that part of Hungary's territory in which the king could exercise direct lordship and display royal power to the full.

Poland enjoyed a revival under its last Piast kings, Wladislaw the Short (1320–1333) and his son Casimir III the Great (1333–1370). Even so there were territorial losses. Most of the old Polish dukedoms of Silesia were taken over by Bohemia, while Pomerelia, the rich rye-producing plains along the Vistula, with important towns such as Torun/Thorn and the harbour of Gdansk/Danzig, was annexed to the Prussian lands of the Teutonic Order. At the same time, relative peace in the north and west gave Casimir the opportunity to expand Polish territory in the east (Mazovia) and south (Ruthenia, which included Polish Galicia). This is often seen as a turning point in Polish history, because 'it firmly turned Poland's face to the east' (Knoll 1972). Besides, Polish expansionism to the east could always count on papal support, mainly because it could be seen as an extra defence against the non-Catholic world: together with its most loyal ally, Hungary, Poland extended and reinforced the Catholic barrier against pagans (Lithuanians, Mongols) and Christian schismatics (the Orthodox Russians).

Perhaps most astonishing in the later medieval history of central and eastern Europe was the rapid rise of the grand duchy of Lithuania. In western eyes, it emerges – not unlike medieval Russia – as a loose confederacy of numerous small lordships under the nominal leadership of princes who, at least as early as the thirteenth century, styled themselves grand dukes of upper Lithuania. Further unity and some degree of centralisation were reached under the grand-ducal dynasty of the Gediminids, so called after Gediminas, the younger of two brothers who successively ruled Lithuania between 1295 and 1342. They succeeded in consolidating Lithuanian power in a period when the brunt of Teutonic Order aggression had shifted from Prussia and Livonia, now conquered, towards the only area left in Europe that was not yet Christian and therefore formed the potential spoils of legitimate crusade. To that end the order repeatedly recruited western princes, who with substantial followings of knights came to 'hunt pagans' on a kind of crusade during wintertime – the only season when it was possible for armies to approach the impenetrable forests and marshes of western Lithuania.

The Gediminids stood their ground, however, and they continued to adhere to their native polytheistic religion. Even if there was a clear Christian presence in Lithuania from the thirteenth century on (friars were active as missionaries and the wives of many noblemen were Christians), the grand dukes only converted officially in 1387. This was the only occasion in medieval Europe when Christianity played no part in the formation of a state. Even so, Lithuania only reached the zenith of success after its conversion. Under Grand Duke Vytautas the Great (1392–1430) it grew into the most powerful principality in the east and in area was the largest state of late medieval Europe.

The extension of Lithuanian power from the late thirteenth century onwards – through military strength, clever marriages and forceful alliances – was set in motion by commercial interests and land hunger. It happened largely at the expense of the western and central Russian principalities of what is now north-west Russia (the Pskov district), White Russia and Ukraine – including the original Rus' capital of Kiev, first captured in 1323, and later again in 1362. In due course Lithuanian imperialism even threatened the stronger principalities farther to the east (Novgorod and Moscow), as well as the western fringes of the Golden Horde, the Mongolian power base in the vast steppe area to the north of the Black Sea and the Caspian Sea. Not until the beginning of the sixteenth century did the Lithuanian Empire start to crumble under Russian (Muscovite) pressure; the important town of Smolensk fell into Russian hands in 1514, for example. By that time, a long-lasting involvement in Russian affairs had left a deep and enduring Slav mark on Lithuanian society and culture.

On the frontier with Poland the Gediminids were not very successful; as we have seen, they lost the long struggle over Ruthenia. Expectations rose sharply again when, in 1386, Grand Duke Jagiello married Jadwiga, daughter of Louis of Anjou and heiress to the kingdom of Poland. But this first personal union of Poland and Lithuania did not lead to any real political association, since Jagiello soon had to cede the lordship over Lithuania to his cousin Vytautas. Only much later, in 1447, was a longer-lasting personal union of Poland and Lithuania effected, after Grand Duke Casimir (1440–1492) was recognised as king of Poland. Short as the first union had been, this second union was a happy one, but after Casimir's death the two kingdoms were once again separated and divided between his two sons. The Gediminid dynasty remained in power in Lithuania until 1572.

The remarkable expansion of Lithuania must have been supported by a well-organised, state-like society with a strong army and capable of mustering considerable resources. Such an impression is confirmed by rare historical documents which reveal many features of an early state under construction. Although the grand-ducal dynasty still had to rely heavily on its possession of land, organised in large estates, the Lithuanian nobility owed military service and was involved in public administration. In addition, trade was taxed in exchange for efficient protection of traders and trade routes. Military organisation had a high level of sophistication. Military strategy was aimed at avoiding pitched battles with clearly stronger enemies, such as the Teutonic knights and their allies. The Lithuanians preferred to counter them by making use of guerrilla tactics adapted to the difficult terrain, operating in relatively small but swiftly-moving intervention forces built round a core of light cavalry, by constructing fortresses, by excellent military intelligence work and the use of diplomatic skills, and by impeding enemy efforts to consolidate any military victory. Clearly there were substantial differences in political development with the most advanced principalities of the West, but they were not as profound as has too often been suggested.

Riurikid Russia

When speaking of medieval Russia we in fact refer to a confederation of principalities that emerged from the original Rus' or Viking principality around Kiev (see Chapter 3). Typically for eastern Europe, only male descendants of the quasi-legendary first Scandinavian ruler of Kiev, Riurik, could qualify for lording over one of the changing number of territorial units that were formed over the centuries in a combined process of territorial expansion, subdivision and loss. Hence the common denomination for medieval Russia was Riurikid Russia, which lasted uninterruptedly until 1598, when Feodor, the feeble-minded son of Tsar Ivan the Terrible, died without leaving any heirs. By that time, the original tradition of

collateral succession per generation had long been replaced by vertical succession in the male line. A certain measure of unity between the Riurikid principalities was maintained by the recognition of their dynastic leader as grand prince 'of All Rus', a title first connected to the lordship of Kiev, later of Vladimir in the Suzdal area, east of Moscow. This reallocation of the titular base of the grand principality was significant for the gradual northeastward shift of actual power in Riurikid Russia, a tendency further stressed after many of the western principalities became subject to Lithuania and the remainder came under Mongolian suzerainty. The latter development was the consequence of the conquest of the western steppe lands of central Asia by the Mongolian army of Chinggis Khan's grandson, Batu, who established an iron dominion over the entire area west of the Urals. This dominion, known as the Golden Horde, located its headquarters in the city of Sarai, near the mouth of the Volga, and was to last until the early fifteenth century. For the Russian principalities, even those which in due course were conquered by the Lithuanians, the Golden Horde hegemony meant that no prince could rule without a formal and written Mongolian consent (so-called *iarlyks* or permits to rule) and all were obliged to pay tribute to their Mongol masters in the form of money, goods or soldiers. Understandably, some Riurikid princes were more cooperative than others, but from a historical point of view cooperation paid off, because during the Golden Horde period the most trusted Riurikid allies of the Mongol khans emerged as the most powerful rulers of Russia: these were the princes of Moscow, until that moment an insignificant town.

A key factor in the rise of Moscow, apart from its unstinting allegiance to the Mongols, was its control of the southern trade routes from Novgorod. Novgorod was by far the most important commercial centre of Riurikid Russia: the axis in all trade between the Baltic on the one hand, and the Black Sea area, with its connections to the Italian and Byzantine markets of the

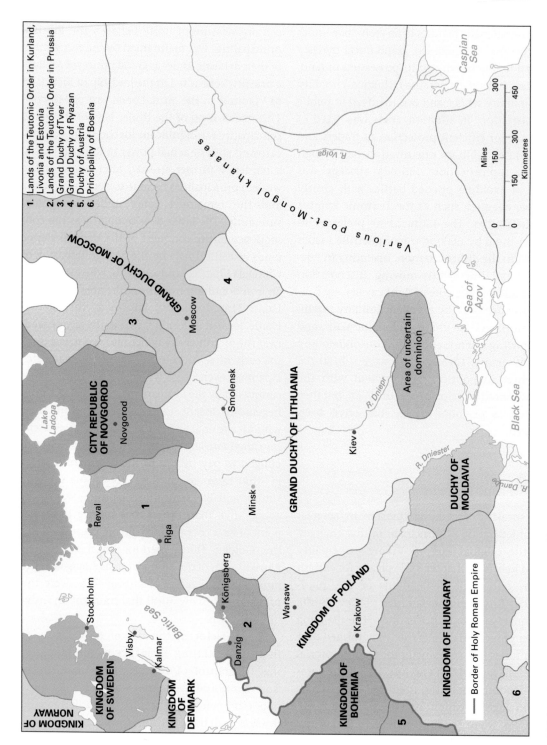

MAP 11.2 Eastern Europe around 1450

Map labels:

KINGDOM OF NORWAY

KINGDOM OF SWEDEN

KINGDOM OF DENMARK

Stockholm
Visby
Kalmar

Baltic Sea

Reval
Riga

CITY REPUBLIC OF NOVGOROD
Novgorod
Lake Ladoga

1

GRAND DUCHY OF MOSCOW
Moscow
3

4

Smolensk

Königsberg
Danzig
2

Warsaw

KINGDOM OF POLAND

Minsk

GRAND DUCHY OF LITHUANIA

Kiev

R. Dniepr

Area of uncertain dominion

KINGDOM OF BOHEMIA
Krakow
5

R. Dniester

DUCHY OF MOLDAVIA

R. Danube

KINGDOM OF HUNGARY

6

Black Sea

Sea of Azov

Caspian Sea

R. Volga

Various post-Mongol khanates

— Border of Holy Roman Empire

1. Lands of the Teutonic Order in Kurland, Livonia and Estonia
2. Lands of the Teutonic Order in Prussia
3. Grand Duchy of Tver
4. Grand Duchy of Ryazan
5. Duchy of Austria
6. Principality of Bosnia

Scale:
0   150   300   Miles
0   150   300   450   Kilometres

Mediterranean, the souks of the Muslim Middle East and the great silk route to China, on the other. Novgorod was also the capital of a vast northern territory, extending from the Gulf of Finland to the shores of the Arctic White Sea, and an eldorado for such prized forest products as squirrel furs, wood, honey and wax. Within the Russian confederation Novgorod had succeeded in taking an autonomous position; often it functioned essentially as an autonomous, quite oligarchic, city-state. During the fourteenth century, however, pressure on this autonomy started to build up, from both Muscovite and Lithuanian sides, until finally, in 1478, Novgorod was incorporated into the new Muscovite state, which was followed by large-scale confiscation and reassignment of landed property. In that crucial period, the Muscovite principality, as well as the title of Grand Prince of Vladimir, was already firmly in the hands of the Danilovich branch of the Riurikid dynasty, the first to have switched to vertical succession. The Danilovich took their name from Danil, a younger son of the famous prince of Novgorod, Alexander Nevsky who, in around 1240, halted Swedish and German expansionist ambitions in the Novgorod area.

It would take another two centuries, until after Mongolian dominance had declined and Lithuanian imperialism had lost its momentum, before the grand princes of Moscow could realise their own territorial ambitions. Around the middle of the sixteenth century the Muscovite-Russian Empire stretched from the Ob river in the northeast to within a short distance of the Sea of Azov in the south. After the Fall of Constantinople, in 1453, Moscow set itself up as its successor and as the new leader of the Orthodox Church. Grand Prince Ivan III (1462–1505) married the Byzantine princess Sofia Palaiologa. From the 1520s onwards, claims were elaborated into a full-blown Third Rome theory. In 1547 Ivan the Terrible was not the first Slav prince to be crowned with the title 'tsar' (*caesar*). He was preceded by several rulers of Bulgaria and Serbia who since the end of the twelfth century had wanted to express their

equality with the Byzantine emperor – but by taking on the same title, the first tsar of Russia clearly presented himself as the rightful heir and successor to the Roman emperors. His capital, Moscow, may have been a pale imitation of Constantinople at the pinnacle of its glory, but it was definitely a booming city, with probably well over 100,000 inhabitants at the beginning of the sixteenth century – certainly three times as many as Novgorod at the time.

Danilovich Moscow developed all the characteristics of an early modern state: there was some form of centralised, bureaucratic government with a high level of written documentation to support taxation and public administration; there was a clear jurisdictional hierarchy (with the grand prince himself acting as supreme judge); territorial principalities were replaced by provinces and rural districts led by appointed governors and district chiefs, who had their own small staffs; and officials were centrally appointed for special tasks. General taxes were levied and the army was gradually modernised by centralising recruitment and command, by assigning to the tsar greater control over military resources, and by reducing the importance of the private military retinues of princes and boyars (high noblemen). The core of the Muscovite army consisted of professional soldiers who, from Ivan III onwards, were increasingly rewarded with (confiscated) lands.

The most remarkable feature of the Muscovite political system, however, was undoubtedly its idea of loyalty to the state, according to which the entire elite was assumed to be ministerial in the literal sense of being a servant of the grand prince or tsar. In addition, a service hierarchy was devised and each member of the political elite had his place assigned via an intricate ranking system with meritocratic features, the so-called *mestnichestvo*. All members of the high nobility were appointed by the tsar; they occupied most court offices, while the tsar's council or *duma* consisted of ten to fifteen of the highest-ranking noblemen. This high nobility was partly recruited from old

Riurikid princely families, and also partly from untitled aristocratic families.

The end of Byzantium and the formation of the Ottoman Empire

In 1261 the so-called Latin Empire, founded in 1204 by a crusading army that had lost direction and conquered Constantinople, came to an end. One Greek reconnaissance patrol, led by a general about to retire, was all that was needed to enter the city deemed unassailable and re-occupy the empty imperial palace (the emperor and his bodyguard happened to be out of town). This nebulous event set the stage for the last episode of Byzantine history, which would prolong the life of the Empire by another 200 years, under the leadership of a new imperial dynasty, the Palaiologi. The splendour of its court ceremonies and the pompousness of its state rhetoric could not mask the paltry reality of the late Byzantine Empire. Its leading families did not care much for emperor or state; they had their own, quite autonomous, local or regional power bases, maintained by private armies. The Empire's territory around 1260 was confined to a shrinking part of western Asia Minor and the northern part of present-day Greece, including Constantinople and its surroundings. It would never even succeed in a lasting reconquest of the remainder of Greece, despite repeated campaigns. In all these regions Greek landlords (with unsteady loyalties towards Constantinople) had to share power and possession with a colourful and constantly changing international assemblage of competitors for land and lordship: western noblemen who had decided to stay after the fall of the Latin Empire; French, Slav and soon also Turkic princes; military orders such as the Hospitallers, which tried to make up for the loss of their bases in the Holy Land; Venice and Genoa, with huge commercial interests to protect in the eastern part of the Mediterranean; companies of foreign mercenaries in search of employment; the occasional

private adventurers, usually wealthy Florentines, Venetians and Genoese, greedy for greater fortune; and finally, but more difficult to picture, many thousands of Albanian immigrants, who settled in Epirus and the Peloponnese over the course of the fourteenth and fifteenth centuries. Any attempt at detailed historical reconstruction of the political situation in late medieval Greece is a recipe for a headache.

Overall, the Palaiologi emperors were not able to cope with such dazzling fragmentation of lordship, the more so because the dynasty was plagued by internal dissension, repeatedly leading to serious civil war, and because they constantly had to face new foreign invasions and intrusions. The threat first came from Charles of Anjou, the new master of Sicily, who tried to extend Angevin power over southern Greece and the Greek isles in the Adriatic. He had to lower his ambitions after the Aragonese take-over of Sicily in 1282, but his successors – now the Angevin kings of Naples – certainly did not disappear from the Greek scene. The Bulgarian tsars had often interfered in Greek policies during the Latin Empire, but their role was much reduced by the Mongol Golden Horde and its often unruly warlords. It suffered much from raiding, and for a while the Bulgar tsars even had to accept Mongol overlordship.

During the first half of the fourteenth century, the Serbs turned out to be the most dangerous enemy of the moribund Byzantine Empire. Largely responsible for this was the Serbian king, Stefan Dušan (1331–1355), who, measured in the surface of land he added to his kingdom by military conquest, probably was the greatest European conqueror of the late Middle Ages. Even before Dušan became king, there was a clear drive among the most powerful, land-hungry barons of Serbia to extend Serbian power to the south. Under Dušan, Serbian armies, within fifteen years, conquered all of Albania and Epirus, and the larger part of Macedonia, Thessaly and Chalkidiki. While doubling the size of his empire, Dušan halved that of the Byzantines. He gained these victories without delivering a single pitched

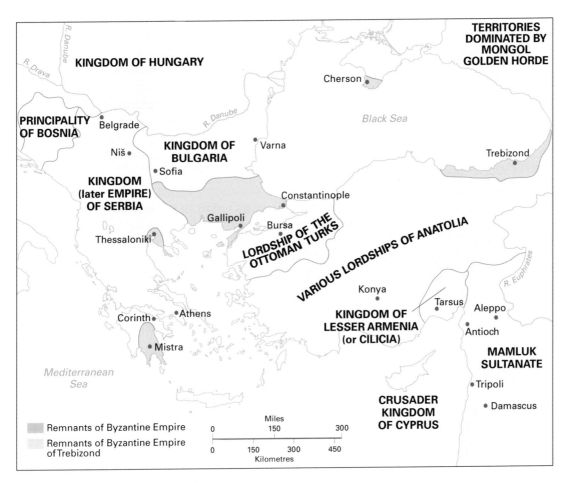

MAP 11.3 The Byzantine Empire, 1350

battle; his trademark was siege warfare, aimed at taking over fortresses and fortified towns. The rich silver mines of Serbia enabled him to pay for long campaigns or to buy support wherever it was for sale. To eternalise his military successes, and maybe also to express even higher ambitions, in 1346 Dušan had himself crowned 'tsar of the Serbs and the Romans'. In accordance with such a high honour, he started to present himself as a patron of culture and religious life, from which the famous monastic communities on Mount Athos profited most. Serbia fell prey to internal wars after his death in 1355, and Albania and many Greek territories were lost. At that infelicitous point in time, the Serbian armies had to confront

the last new enemy to enter the stage of late medieval Byzantine history: the Ottoman Turks.

The Ottomans are named after a quasi-legendary eponymous Turkic clan leader called Osman, who in the 1280s established a Turkic lordship or *beylik* in Bithynia, the north-western part of Asia Minor. For a long time, this dominion of the Osmanli dynasty would remain just one among a myriad of Greek and Turkic lordships and principalities as well as more or less autonomous coastal towns. In a sense, the Ottomans were lucky that the Byzantine emperors directed most of their attention and military effort to the west (Serbia) and south (Greece), while nourishing a viper in its backyard, so to speak. The

Ottoman lords in Bithynia proved to be as capable rulers as they were capable generals. Murad I (1362–1389) was the first to assume the title of sultan. He had a keen eye for developing governance, the organisation of border control, taxation and state bureaucracy (with both military and civil officials). During his reign Ottoman rule expanded over the western half of Asia Minor/Anatolia as well as over Bulgaria, northern Greece and the Balkans up to the Morawa river. Murad was assassinated during or shortly after the famous first battle against the Serbs and their allies on the Kosovo Polje (Field of the Blackbirds).

Murad's son and successor, Bayezid I (1389–1402), soon laid siege to Constantinople, which was now completely isolated.

Even so, the will to conquer Constantinople certainly had not been the only driving force behind Ottoman expansion into Europe. Rather, this was threefold. First, one has to remember that in the fourteenth century the Ottoman Turks were still nomads, with a pastoral economy based on transhumance of large herds of sheep between mountainous summer meadows and valleys with enough fodder to winter. Such thinly populated areas could be found in the Balkans, and that is

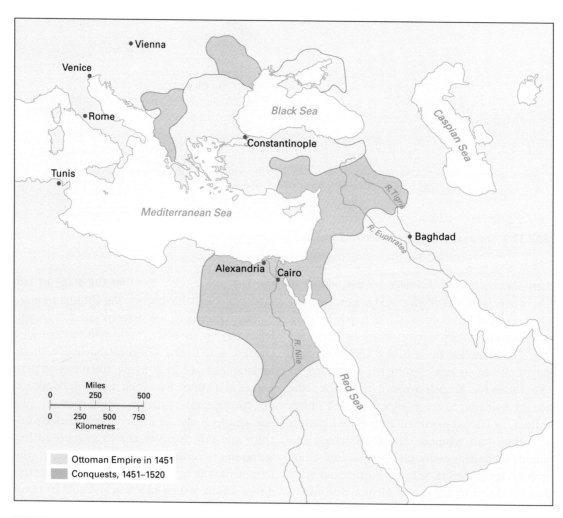

MAP 11.4 The rise of the Ottoman Empire

why the first major Ottoman raiding parties were directed towards Bulgaria, Macedonia and Serbia, not Greece proper. All three great battles that decided the fate of south-eastern Europe in the last quarter of the fourteenth century were fought in this area: against the Serbs and their allies at the Maritsa river in 1371 and at Kosovo Polje in 1389, and against an international crusading army led by the king of Hungary near the town of Nicopolis on the Danube in 1396.

The second major factor that attracted the Ottoman Turks to south-eastern Europe was the large and continuous demand for mercenaries in both the Balkans and Greece, and Turkish horsemen from Asia Minor – not just Ottoman Turks – were very much appreciated. By the 1260s Turkic mercenaries were active in Greece, and demand for them would remain high until the very end of the fourteenth century. Even in the 1380s and early 1390s, when the Ottoman Turks had left their true mark further north, Byzantine generals and pretenders continued to hire Ottoman mercenaries to fight internal wars, and more than once Turkish troops were actively present within the walls of Constantinople – in fact, Ottoman exiles were among the defenders of Constantinople in 1453!

The third often mentioned driving force behind Ottoman expansion into Europe is also the most debated: religious motivation. As fairly recent converts to Islam, the Ottoman Turks would have been especially sensitive to the religious duty of defending the faith by combining raiding with harming the infidel on the frontiers with Christendom. Be that as it may, it would be wrong to interpret Ottoman frontier warfare as merciless *jihad*; on the contrary, sources from the time underline the 'plasticity of identities' in such dynamic frontier environments (Kafadar 1995) and the acceptance of all kinds of accommodation and alliance, on both sides.

That Constantinople did not fall in around 1400, however, was only thanks to a new, redoubtable enemy, who crossed the Ottomans' path when they tried to extend their power over eastern Anatolia. This was Timur Lenk (Timur the Lame) or Tamerlane, the Turco-Mongol conqueror of a vast empire that reached from east Anatolia in the west to the Indus river in the east. In 1402, Timur beat the Ottomans in the battle of Ankara and military defeat was followed by civil war between the three sons of Sultan Bayezid, who died in Timur's captivity. These fateful events brought a halt to Ottoman expansion for some twenty years. Only under Murad II (1421–1451) did a new wave of conquests begin, first in Anatolia and then in the Balkans. Despite their fierce resistance, the Hungarians and Albanians suffered resounding defeats in 1444 and 1448 which paved the way for the incorporation of Serbia, Albania and the Peloponnese into the Ottoman Empire. Despite desperate attempts by the Byzantine emperor to get help from the West at the price of uniting the Byzantine and Roman churches, Constantinople was now lost. Deprived of its hinterland and surrounded by Turkish galleys, it could offer no more resistance when Sultan Mehmet II (1451–1481) laid siege in the spring of 1453 and after his artillery had breached the ancient walls. Constantine XI, the last emperor, fought to the death in the streets of the city named after his great homonymous forebear, while the victorious sultan added *kaysar* to his many titles. In the decades that followed the Ottomans took hold of the coasts of the Black Sea, including the Genoese trading colonies on the Crimea. But the Venetians would fight for their settlements on the islands and along the coasts of the Adriatic and Aegean for years to come. After taking the Mamluk territories, with the holy places of Islam in 1517, the Ottomans mounted a new offensive in the direction of central Europe. The king of Hungary was killed at the battle of Mohács in 1526, and Bosnia and the greater part of Hungary fell into Ottoman hands.

The systematic Ottoman conquests over two centuries had a spectacular result – the creation of an Islamic imperium that extended over an immense area and lasted for five centuries. Tight military organisation was the key to this success.

The sultans recruited a permanent, personal guard of footsoldiers, known as the janissaries (from the Turkish *yeni cheri* meaning 'new men'). They were levied through a system of enforced recruitment of young boys – in fact legalised kidnapping by the Ottoman state – from subjected Christian territories in the Balkans. Cavalrymen were mostly ethnic Turks. As remuneration for their service they were given the right to revenues from circumscribed units of land. The sultans recruited important civil servants from among their servants at court, often castrated slaves (eunuchs), who would remain loyal and did not immediately form a warrior aristocracy. They were also able to involve local people in government and war, through which their loyalty was assured. In their public appearance, the sultan and his household manifested themselves as religious leaders who kept a careful watch over every aspect of religious life. Mosques and Qur'anic schools were established everywhere; the subjected peoples were free to choose their religion, but by relating choice of religion to personal law (in legal dealings everybody was treated in accordance with the laws of his or her religious community) the Ottomans created a form of apartheid that made it possible at all times to identify non-Turks/non-Muslims. Most Ottoman sultans were born from female slaves, harem favourites who often originated from Greece or Georgia, and were provided with such official titles as *khatun* (± 'queen') or *sultana*.

Driving forces in the formation of states

Dynasties, territories, institutions, nations

Princes were constantly devising strategies to acquire new lands without much effort, either through marriage and succession, possibly through purchase or as security. The formula of the double marriage, by which a male and a female descendant of one dynasty were married to a female and male descendant of another dynasty, was designed to tie the bonds between two houses as tightly as possible. Bavaria and Burgundy were united in this way in 1385, so that later Hainaut, Holland and Zeeland (Bavarian possessions) came under the same ruler as Burgundian Flanders and Artois. In 1496 there was a double marriage between Spain and Habsburg, laying the foundations of the European empire of Charles V. By 1500 similar dynastic strategies had made the number of truly independent political units in Europe considerably smaller than three centuries previously. During the competition most 'winners' became larger and more powerful. The constant efforts of princes and feudal lords to expand their territories and the revenues they provided formed a driving force in this process. Dynastic continuity played a large part in systems that were focused so strongly on the person of the ruler. Problems arose when there was no direct adult, male and reasonably sound and competent successor at hand. More distant relatives could raise equally qualified claims, and subjects might see opportunities to strengthen their influence and privileges.

Dynastic ambitions and opportunities, however, cannot explain everything. Much depended on the geographical conditions and society in the territory involved. During the late Middle Ages society was no longer composed almost solely of peasants, serfs or otherwise; there was, as we have seen in Chapter 9, considerable differentiation through the development of the towns, communities of free peasants, the commercialisation and sometimes even the industrialisation of the countryside. Their interaction gave shape to the states that were formed out of the power struggle, in relation both to their territory and to their internal organisation. The enlarged scale of the competing units, the broadening of the resources at their disposal, and in particular the increase in the power of military destruction, made conflicts more drastic. The numbers of those fighting in wars increased, they caused greater and more lasting damage to the economy, and they had more victims. As state violence increased, subjects began to offer fiercer resistance as they became more conscious of their rights and organised themselves better. On the positive side, states could now suppress private and local violence more effectively.

It is obvious that late medieval states emerged in ways that could never have been so willed or planned. They were the results of the trials of strength between countless conflicting ambitions, interests and opposing forces or obstacles. In many cases, wars did not produce the results intended by the aggressors, but nevertheless they left deep marks. The Hundred Years War made a significant contribution to the formation of the French and English national consciousness. At the same time it created political affinities which steered relations between the kings and their subjects in both lands for many centuries to come, in particular the resounding voice of the English parliament in contrast with the virtual elimination of the French Estates General. The path trodden by a society in its confrontations between its members and with its rulers and neighbours gradually gave shape to the institutions which together formed the state; likewise it was imprinted in the collective memory of the communities concerned, which through their common fortunes, imperceptibly formed a national loyalty in addition to a local and dynastic one.

One of the characteristic state structures of the late Middle Ages was the development of a civil service apparatus, which expressed public authority in a more abstract sense and also more effectively than before. The king's person and his relations with powerful vassals were no longer the sole determinants of the fortunes of a state. Kings were bound by laws and institutions and in many cases by representation. They were obliged to create a hierarchical organisation of officials who would tie them to rules and procedures. The exercise of power became more complex and less personal.

Heraldic symbols, public ceremonial, mottos, emblems and genealogical histories strengthened the ties between princes and their subjects. Something as large and abstract as a state, the contours of which were not yet settled, only penetrated the collective consciousness very slowly. The differences between the Scots and the Irish on the one hand and the English on the other were fed by the repeated efforts made by the English to dominate. The Bohemians derived a strong sense of nationality from their opposition to continuing German expansion. Nation-building can thus be seen as an unplanned effect of foreign domination.

War

The American historical sociologist Charles Tilly (1990) once observed that 'wars made states and states made war', by which he meant that states, for both the demarcation of their territories and the growth of their institutions, were the product of continual competition between diverse political units. Conversely, by far the largest part of the resources – financial, material and services – which states had at their disposal was destined to make preparations for war, to wage it and to pay interest on the debts contracted for it. Indeed, it was precisely during those long periods of warfare that the state apparatuses managed to increase the tax burden on their subjects considerably and thus to enlarge the state resources. From the end of the thirteenth century onwards, rulers increasingly financed their wars by contracting debts that had to be paid back afterwards with substantial interest. Elite groups played an important role in this development: because they could profit from it or expect rewards from their state at war, they steered the decision process towards war. It is clear that the nobility, for whom armed conflict not only was a matter of honour but also gave them the opportunity to acquire land, take home booty or gain the favour of the king, continued to be a driving force behind the casual acceptance with which war was seen as a fixed part of continuing political competition.

Of course the great economic and demographic changes between the tenth and the thirteenth century were not without consequences for the art of war. During the thirteenth century more archers appeared on the battlefield, while footsoldiers were frequently hired from Wales. That was when the longbow and the crossbow came into use. In the course of the century these archers were often deployed as auxiliary troops, but by 1300 they were increasingly fighting for themselves. The Swiss peasants who defeated the Habsburg army of knights in 1291 and 1315 made history. On a much larger scale Flemish craftsmen and peasants cut the army of knights of the French king to pieces at the battle of the Golden Spurs in 1302. Such victories were a sign of the new power relations resulting from the growth of urban populations. In 1302 the Flemish force, 11,000 strong, fought 7,500 French – one-third of whom were heavily armed horsemen who were normally seen as equal in force to ten footsoldiers. Horses and equipment, and the attendants who were indispensable for them, were extremely expensive investments; considerable practice was needed to acquire the combative skills, moreover, and only the aristocracy could afford this. The Scots who defeated the English at Bannockburn in 1314 also fought for the most part on foot, armed with bows, pikes, and striking and stabbing weapons. They slashed away without fear or favour, clearly driven by a desire for liberation from what they saw as foreign domination.

In north and central Italy, ambitious military men from local noble families, but also foreign soldiers of fortune, took troops into their personal service in exchange for payment and hired themselves out with their companies to the highest bidder. This phenomenon of the *condottiere*, a commander of a mercenary company, was closely connected to the rivalry between the small but rich regional states in that part of Europe. The foot-soldiers in either paid or obligatory service were given more importance in the armies of princes. Welsh archers contributed substantially to the loss of 1,500 French knights at Crécy in 1346.

When towns built their walls they adopted the principle of the fortified castle on a larger scale. The assailant was vulnerable, while the defender was protected as long as his supplies lasted. The long circumference of towns made an effective blockade difficult, requiring a large number of troops over a long period of time, which often exhausted the financial resources and the morale of the besiegers. From the last decades of the fourteenth century, however, the cannon turned the towns' former advantage in siege warfare into a disadvantage. Town walls had been designed to face battering rams, not the force of cannon balls. They were built high to resist projectiles from catapults and siege-towers: it was difficult to breach the walls with trebuchets – at most the gates and parapets were damaged. When they were shot at by cannon, however, the walls became particularly vulnerable, especially if they were high. The effectiveness of the cannon on the battlefield was limited by its enormous weight, slowness and lack of accuracy and reach until the sixteenth century. But from the end of the four-teenth century, towns and castles were no longer safe from an army equipped with gunpowder artillery.

During the fifteenth century there was thus a discrepancy in military resources which gave the besiegers a considerable advantage as long as they could afford the high price of cannon. The new technique played into the hands of the largest competitors who were able to pay for the expensive innovations and the technically trained personnel to operate them. Besides, they could make far more effective use of them than the defenders could. Princes now saw the possibility of dealing a definitive blow against their most formidable rivals: local and regional rulers. Rebellions in France, the Low Countries and north Germany often gave princes the excuse to use their military supremacy to restrict the auton-omy of great aristocrats and large towns. The most spectacular example of this was the capture of Constantinople by the Ottomans in 1453: the legendary high walls which had withstood every siege since the sixth century were now shot to pieces by the Turkish artillery. In northern and central Italy there were few territorial monarchs apart from the pope who could afford to make use of the new military technology on a significant scale, so the advantage fell to the largest towns, which were thus able to enlarge the regions they controlled. Venice was the most successful: faced with losing part of its colonial empire to the Ottomans, it assured its domestic safety and prosperity by taking control of the eastern part of the Po valley.

On the battlefield, offensive action again gained the advantage at this time, providing military logistics adapted to new challenges. To offer some resistance to the significant power of footsoldiers, the most progressive princes turned their infantry into mobile phalanxes equipped with extremely long pikes. These were used to bring the enemy cavalry to a halt and force them back, or could lead the attack on the enemy infantry. The cavalry was now literally sidelined to the flanks, where it could carry out intermittent attacks. The initiative for this modern plan came from France, where for the first time in 1439 King Charles VII was allocated money to establish a standing army. In contrast to feudal practice, when the vassals were called up in the good season for campaigns of a limited length (40 days, for example), war had become a year-round business that required trained troops to be available permanently. The French king now took between 20,000 and 25,000 officers and men into permanent paid service as *gens d'armes* (men of arms), who used a combination of different weapons. The initiative coincided with the final offensive of the Hundred Years War and contributed to the definitive expulsion of the English.

As more subjects became involved in the business of war, and negotiations had to be undertaken with the parliament or assemblies of towns and estates for providing troops and subsidies, the necessity to justify these efforts grew. Religion provided an obvious legitimisation. It was the justification for the merciless war of exter-

mination against the Languedoc Cathars, which reached its most brutal stage with the dreadful massacre of Montségur in 1244. Declaring war a crusade was the most obvious form of religious legitimisation. Only the pope could do so, but often enough popes were prepared to be a secular ruler's tool. For example, when the papal client, Charles of Anjou, from the French royal house, lost his kingdom of Sicily to Peter III of Aragon during the Sicilian Vespers of 1282, the pope urged Charles' nephew, King Philip III of France, to undertake what he called a 'crusade against Aragon'. Much later, between 1420 and 1436, the war against Bohemian independence was waged by the German kings Wenceslas and Sigismund under the motto of a crusade against the heretical Hussites, the followers of the Church reformer, Jan Hus.

Kings could even use their personal bond with a saint as a legitimisation of their wars. The cult of a national saint was one means of achieving this: in France, for example, the saints Denis, the first bishop of Paris whose name resounded in the battle-cry '*Montjoie Saint-Denis*', Michael and (after 1297) Louis (IX). Military heroes had the privilege of being buried alongside the kings in the mausoleum of Saint-Denis, which also housed the *oriflamme*, the banner carried during the king's campaigns. As leaders of a war of liberation against foreign invaders, the kings of France could plead that they served a higher good than did the great territorial princes. In this way the king's war could be presented as the only one in the general interests of the kingdom, the only lawful and sacred one. The defence of the *patria*, fatherland, presented as a mystic body by analogy with the Church as the mystic body of Christ, was worth a courageous death, as the propaganda in fifteenth-century texts increasingly proclaimed. The kings stopped at nothing to give an exclusive justification to their wars, while those of the territorial princes under them were demoted to mere private conflicts, sometimes even to rebellions against the lawful authority.

State institutions and social order

Superior means of force was an essential condition for the long-term exercise of power, but not enough in itself. If large groups of subjects did not accept the legitimacy of the government imposed upon them, then it provoked internal resistance that forced up the costs of control for those in power, damaged their claims to provide protection for all subjects in their region and made their government vulnerable to coalitions between domestic and foreign foes. If we accept that, in addition to a healthy dose of aggression, every human community shows a fundamental need for peace and stability, then we can expect to see subjects and rulers make some attempt to reach long-term arrangements.

Supreme law courts

Kings and territorial princes attempted to establish their higher authority over the traditional forms of dispensing justice, but until the end of the eighteenth century they always had to take into account the large variety of legal systems and local customs within their territories. As the territories expanded, so did this variety. In general, they tried hard to reduce the autonomous action of foreign courts outside their own territories, especially ecclesiastical ones.

Princes made every effort to give their own laws and their own law courts precedence over local courts of justice in order to give their jurisdictional authority the highest validity – if not a monopoly. Such attempts at institutionalising supreme justice were anything but easy, in view of the conflicting interests. In England the law courts of the king enjoyed priority over all other courts as early as the twelfth century; in the course of the thirteenth century three central courts of justice emerged, among them the King's Bench which, apart from handling pleas to the crown, had the exclusive right to try serious

PLATE 11.2 James I, count of Barcelona and king of Aragon (1213–1276), sitting on his throne with the sword of justice upright, accompanied by two councillors and a soldier, oversees the justice rendered by a seated judge in a dialogue with two advocates holding written documents, and their female and male clients. Vidal Mayor, *Book of the Deeds*, late thirteenth century.

crimes. The French king found it far more difficult to reserve for himself certain 'royal cases' such as counterfeiting, *lèse-majesté* and appeals. The **parlement** of Paris, which King Louis IX had established around 1250 as the highest court of justice in the kingdom, had an increasing number of cases to deal with as confidence in the judges' independence grew.

The success of states' higher administration of justice over the many competing legal circles was based on several factors, above all of course on pure power relationships. Powerful local lords and rich towns offered effective opposition until well into the eighteenth century. Venice allowed all subordinate towns in the *Terraferma* to retain their own privileges and institutions, but made them subject to its political authority and fiscal discrimination. For the peasants, Venetian supremacy meant liberation from the class-based justice of the burghers in the smaller towns. Elsewhere, too, the possibility of appealing to a higher court of law offered new opportunities for parties who were economically or politically weak in relation to the main lords or towns. The princes tried to place their justice above local and regional law courts, and at the same time applied more general procedures and principles, often borrowed from learned law or jurisprudence. For instance, from the end of the fourteenth century Castilian peasants increasingly appealed to the crown to act as arbitrator in complaints against their exploitation by aristocratic landowners. To deal with the growing number of cases, royal judges (*alcaldes*) were appointed and a central court of justice, the *Audiencia*, was installed. In the long term the justice administered by the crowns of both Castile and Aragon strengthened the position of the peasants, and also that of the king as the highest guarantor of justice.

Both canon law, which had been extensively codified in the course of the twelfth and thirteenth centuries, and Roman law, which spread from Bologna and was studied intensively in the emergent universities (see Chapter 8), contained many elements that were of particular use to the princes in their efforts to justify their centralising activities. The surviving Roman law had a strongly centralistic and absolutist slant, with principles such as 'the prince is above the law' and 'what pleases the prince has the force of law'. Emperor Frederick Barbarossa made much use of these quotations after he defeated Milan in 1162, as did the king of Castile, much later, in the fifteenth century. In the thirteenth century lawyers close to the kings of France used formulas of the same type to justify decrees in which they claimed to serve the 'common interest'. This usage also aroused opposition, however, for example at the English court, which did not wish to consider itself subordinate to the emperor. Henry Bracton, a priest who served as judge on the King's Bench in the middle of the thirteenth century, wrote a treatise on the laws and customs of England, based on a collection of 2,000 judgements. He defended the superiority of the English jury system and natural law, for in his view Roman law favoured the king's interest. English law, on the other hand, defends the interests of the people, Bracton said. Outside England, Roman law certainly formed one of the basic subjects in the training of lawyers. Their thinking and their use of administrative language was permeated with concepts such as that of *res publica, la chose publique* (the republic) which, even without an exact equivalent at the time, sharpened state thinking and highlighted the distinction between public and private law.

Attempts to codify customary law at the level of kingdoms were exceptional in the Middle Ages. One was made in Castile, soon after the kingdom had experienced considerable growth at the expense of the Muslims: the *Fuero Real* of the early 1250s; another, the *Siete Partidas*, occurred in the 1260s. In similar circumstances of rapid territorial expansion a royal law code was produced in Poland in 1347. The breakthrough in the systematic recording of law at the level of the state did not occur until the sixteenth century, in a generally painstaking assessment of the many local, regional and national customary laws, most of which remained in force until the late eighteenth century. In France the royal order in the middle of the fifteenth century to provide an official, authorised record of the countless regional customary laws was carried out with painful slowness. A century later most of them had been published in the north and in central France, but not in the south, despite its much stronger Roman tradition. A real codification, a systematic collection and homogenisation on the authority of the central government never came about. Local judges continued to enjoy considerable freedom in the administration of justice.

The influence of canon law was felt in the administrative and judicial practices of the young states even earlier than Roman law. The rational investigation of the facts by a judge before a person was charged, in contrast to the early medieval customs of accusation and single combat, was modelled on the Church's *inquisitio*, the judicial inquiry. In 1215 the Fourth Lateran Council condemned trial by ordeal as a means of obtaining evidence because it was irrational and the outcome was often questionable. In the twelfth and thirteenth centuries both Church and secular authorities had progressed so far that they shunned the unpredictability of a trial by a publicly proclaimed ordeal and supported more rational methods of investigation.

It is of fundamental significance for Western thought that in the young universities law (Roman and canon law) was recognised as a separate discipline, independent of theology. Even if the universities were under ecclesiastical authority they still provided the opportunity for the development of non-dogmatic, rational juridical thinking, free of religious precepts. The technique of interpreting legal texts made continual renewal and adaptation to the changing reality possible. In this way the principles of Roman law were also absorbed in new jurisprudence.

University trained lawyers were given key positions in all public administrations, both at central and local levels of government, and in both state and Church. Government bodies and courts of law were increasingly often staffed with academically trained lawyers. Their activities contributed to the wider introduction of laws into public life, including principles from jurisprudence that protected private interests from governments, in particular the defence of private property, testamentary disposition, the freedom of contracting parties and the protection of widows and orphans. Notaries and solicitors took an increasing role in public life. The concept of the corporate legal entity, *universitas*, made its way into the towns

and communities in their associated and constituent organs, such as guilds. Like so many other matters, the spread of modern, rational legal thinking was closely connected to the urban environment, as well as, and in contrast to, that of the great royal courts.

However, the administration of justice according to old customary law played a larger part in legal practice than did legislation by princes. Local regulations were much closer to everyday life and could be more easily enforced by a combination of social control and common interest. We should not believe that the legislation of the French kings simply reflected the wishes, *le bon plaisir*, of the sovereign: the great majority of royal ordinances came into being in response to requests, via petitions from pressure groups. In this respect, the situation in England was rather different from that on the continent – on the one hand, because of the long tradition of trial by a jury of laymen, and on the other hand, because of the early (from the twelfth century) development of a system of professional royal courts of law with extensive powers. Common law, the growing part of customary law that was administered by royal judges according to uniform procedures only minimally influenced by jurisprudence and attaching much importance to legal precedent, remained intact in England, which meant that in fact it was the courts that made the law.

The establishment of the *Reichskammergericht*, the imperial high court, in 1495, itself the successor of the *Reichshofgericht* installed by Frederick II in 1235, offered opportunities for appeal throughout the German Empire, at least in theory. The weakness of the Empire was exposed, however, when the emperor was immediately compelled to allow powerful territorial princes exemption for their subjects, because the princes set up their own central courts. Regionalism was evident in France as well, where *parlements*, in this particular context meaning law courts, were set up in regions with a strong tradition of autonomy. The monarchy was able to adapt to this regional diversity and imposed its own model as far as the circumstances allowed.

It was a matter of pacification inside the borders and of creaming off resources for defence or imperialistic aims.

Bureaucratisation

As early as the twelfth century the emerging monarchies felt the need to surround themselves with growing numbers of experts in administrative matters. The growth into a civil service state can best be seen as a concentric development, beginning in the household of a territorial prince or king. The most elementary functions grew into differentiated court offices, whose structures remained fairly generally applied until the seventeenth century. To draw up and publish their written documents, the earliest princes called upon the services of nearby clerics, the only people who could read or write, and primarily so in Latin. This was common practice everywhere in the Catholic parts of Europe. As a result of help requested from the clerics by the illiterate ruffians who were the feudal lords to formulate their administrative activities, judicial pronouncements and agreements, Church Latin also became the administrative language of the early states all over Catholic Europe.

England was far ahead of the rest of Europe in matters of administrative and judicial organisation. This was the result of the centralisation of monarchy in later Anglo-Saxon England and the fact that after 1066 the Normans had to keep a tight grip on the land they had conquered. In the second half of the twelfth century two separate courts become recognisable, in two fields that required specific expertise: first, the Exchequer, the treasury where the king's financial officers had to justify their accounts, and then the Court of Common Pleas or Common Bench, the king's central court of justice for civil actions. This development can be seen as the beginning of a general European tendency towards progressive administrative specialisation and bureaucratisation, which came about at diverse times and to varying degrees depending on the social evolution of a particular region. Advisory functions were expanded and made permanent in separate institutions sustained by paid officials, who increasingly were professionally trained.

Around the middle of the thirteenth century, vernacular languages started to appear in official documents on the European continent. In England, Old English had been used for this purpose since the ninth century, although there had been a switch to Latin and French after the Norman Conquest. The new preference for the vernacular was connected to the growing role played by burghers in government, which helped to some extent to bridge the traditional gap between the knightly and urban worlds. One important result of this opening up of government circles to the vernacular and to officials of bourgeois or lower noble origin was that governments and subjects could communicate in the same language, hence the term 'parliament'. Government was no longer shrouded in a foreign, esoteric language and culture, keeping it remote from local authorities and the people. Use of the administrative language gained in social importance as government and judiciary increasingly relied on written procedures and reached more subjects directly. On several occasions during the fourteenth and fifteenth centuries, representatives of the Estates protested successfully against the use of a foreign language by their rulers: German in Bohemia or French in the Burgundian Low Countries. Administrative centres narrowed the gap with their subjects by using the vernacular, so that their language acquired a wider area of circulation than others, albeit often only in official documents.

Nevertheless, the lead enjoyed by the Church in the written culture of the West left its traces in the clerical status of the heads of the royal secretariats, the chancellors. The chancellors of the German kings were generally bishops, or were made bishops soon after their appointment. It was not until 1424 that a layman became chancellor in Germany. Between 1280 and 1332, all French chancellors were incumbents of the rich bishopric of Laon. However, secularisation set in from the middle of the fourteenth century onwards: chancellors from this point were laymen and, by 1500, only 8 per cent of royal secretaries were clerics.

Clerics had more to offer the princes than just their original monopoly of expertise. It was important that their ecclesiastical dignity provided them with their own substantial incomes, making them cheap employees for the princes. The Church freely granted dispensation to its clerics to enter such service, doubtless motivated by feelings of charity and concern for the good government of the faithful. As a result of providing such services the Church was in an excellent position to look after its own interests, directly and discreetly. No wonder then that the overwhelming majority of all surviving pre-1300 documents deal with Church property. On the other hand, it was important that princes could rely on the support of the Church, which was after all the largest landowner and very influential. Diplomacy was another field of activity much favoured by members of the higher clergy. Their internationally standardised education and knowledge of Latin were obvious reasons for this, together with the inviolability of their legal position and the trust radiating from their clerical status.

During the second half of the thirteenth century northern Italian financial specialists made their appearance in the princely courts of north-western Europe, no doubt in the pursuit of their activities as financiers and money-lenders. They held high positions in the service of princes as receivers, treasurers, tax-farmers or mint-masters until about the middle of the fourteenth century. In those capacities they rationalised the management of the rapidly growing princely finances, doubtless safeguarding their own interests at the same time.

An example of the numerical evolution of royal bureaucracy can be found in the central administration in France: at the beginning of the fourteenth century it had 8 master accountants,

19 by 1484; 10 notaries worked in the chancery in 1286, 59 in 1361, 79 in 1418 and 120 by the early sixteenth century. After that there was an enormous acceleration in bureaucratisation: by 1515 the French state in its entirety employed more than 4,000 officials. Around 1200, the king of England had 15 messengers in his service and in 1350 about 60, enabling the sheriffs of the counties to receive mail from the capital every week. In England there were probably fewer state officials per head of population, partly because several functions, such as that of justice of the peace (local judges), were unsalaried and exercised by local landowners.

Taxation

In those regions where there were enough silver coins in circulation, kings could generate a new form of revenue, levies in cash. The threat of invasion was an excuse for introducing general taxation. In order to pay for military defence against a new wave of Viking attacks, Danegeld, which had been levied at the time of the first invasions, was reintroduced in England in 991, but now on a permanent footing. It remained, under the name of *heregeld*, until the 1160s. It was based on a fixed assessment per area of land and was paid in silver coin, many more of which were minted during this period. *Heregeld* can thus be considered the oldest regular state tax in Europe.

Other general taxes were introduced in England far earlier than on the continent. In 1185, at the pope's dogged insistence, a tithe (10 per cent) was levied on personal property and incomes in preparation for the Third Crusade. It was a fiscal success, which is all the more remarkable because a similar attempt in France ran up against not only the immunities of the great territorial princes, who were powerful enough to refuse to cooperate, but also against the fundamental objection that the king by his own authority did not have the right to levy taxes on personal property or incomes. Soon afterwards the principle of the proportional tax on personal property was again applied in England, until the excesses of John Lackland led to a clause against arbitrary taxation in the Magna Carta in 1215.

In the long term, however, taxation proved to be the most successful method for enabling the English crown to centralise its power. In 1275 the English parliament approved indirect taxes for the first time. They mainly affected the export of wool. These taxes would form a permanent source of income for the crown and at the same time function as a political weapon against buyers on the continent, notably the Italians, Flemish and northern Germans. Parliament continued to determine the conditions of the tax, so a public discussion about great economic and political questions took place. When general taxation, both direct and indirect, was placed on a permanent footing in the thirteenth century, its level and frequency were determined by the rhythms of the war. Taxes were not levied during periods of peace with Scotland (1297–1306) and truces with France (1360–1369). By contrast, the intensive warfare of 1294–1298 and the beginning of the Hundred Years War caused explosive growth in the burden of taxation. The war enabled princes to ask for extra money and support from their subjects on the pretext of defending the country, which was after all the concern of every subject. The terms necessity and self-defence were brought out by learned advisers when the excuse of the Crusades could no longer be used. But which land had to be defended, and who was the aggressor? In 1297 the barons found that Edward's attack on Flanders could no longer be described as national defence, but his campaigns in Guyenne, Wales and Scotland did not attract such protest.

The collection of taxes required a widely ramified network of collectors, which kings and territorial princes could not build up easily, inevitably because all fiscal immunities, such as seignories, Church domains and towns, insisted upon maintaining their autonomy. They preferred to hand in a total amount for their whole area that was agreed upon beforehand, so that they could keep tax collection and thus control over the tax-bearing capacity of the population in their own hands. The system of levying export customs in the ports enabled the English kings to install their own collectors there: these duties were new crown rights mainly involving foreign buyers of wool. The introduction of general and permanent royal taxation, under the pressure of the Hundred Years War, gave the French king the opportunity to keep the collection of those taxes largely in his own hands.

The English crown was far more successful than the French in drastically increasing its revenues in a short time. Expressed in tonnes of fine silver, Edward III received 32 tonnes in 1336, 66 in 1337 and 92 in 1339. Loans then accounted for more than half the receipts; this was only possible if enough money-lenders were prepared to extend credit to the king. The French king's income was no more than 53 tonnes in 1339 and 56 in 1340. Clearly, at the beginning of the Hundred Years War, the English with their surprise attack had an enormous advantage over the French, who could not react adequately militarily, and certainly not logistically or financially. The disastrous course of the first phase of the war led to immense fiscal demands from the French crown, which was then granted permanent indirect taxes. These were easy to collect and did not require further negotiations but weighed disproportionately heavily on the lower income groups. They started in 1355 with the *gabelle*, a tax on salt, and a levy of one-thirtieth of the value of the merchandise; this ratio was raised to one-twentieth in 1435. A great opportunity came in 1440 with the introduction of a permanent annual tallage, *taille*, to be collected by officials of the king. Unlike the English parliament, the French Estates General and regional assemblies thus allowed themselves to be marginalised as a political body by surrendering the right to approve tax every year. In the long run, this had enormous consequences, leading to the supremacy of the crown in France as opposed to the supremacy of parliament in England.

In Castile, too, the expansion of the crown's powers by conquest at the expense of the Muslims gave it the right to appoint the *regidores* as collectors in the towns. In other parts of Europe, however, kings and princes encountered great difficulty in centralising the collection of taxes by their own officials over the whole territory. From 1292 onwards the *ayudas* (bids for help) rapidly followed each other in the lands under the Aragonese crown, as a result of the royal wars. The principle was that, outside the circumstances when as highest lord he could count on the services of his vassals, a prince must ask his free subjects for help. This meant negotiating with subjects, who could then set their conditions and wrest benefits or more autonomy from the prince. In 1363 the *Cortes Generales* of the four former kingdoms under the Crown of Aragon – Valencia, Aragon, Catalonia and Mallorca – agreed to introduce a tax on the production of cloth and the export of merchandise.

'Money is the sinew of war', wrote Cicero; by implication, it was also the touchstone of the relationships between those who made the decisions about war and lesser mortals. The more a prince was tempted to wage war, the more taxes he had to impose on or demand of his subjects. Now that princes asked for increasingly large taxes increasingly often, governments of towns and other representative bodies saw opportunities to negotiate about conditions for possible agreement. This development was one of extreme importance. It came to an end in many countries – France, but also Poland, Hungary, Sweden and Denmark – between the fifteenth and seventeenth centuries. The ability of princes to gain access to a tax system that could function independently of the approval of people's representatives played an essential role in this development.

The possibility for raising taxes again and again depended on the type of economy prevailing in a particular country. In England and Catalonia it was clear in the thirteenth and fourteenth centuries, respectively, that taxes could be levied on exports. An export-oriented economy could thus form the basis for a fiscal system that taxed not its own subjects but the foreign buyers. This functioned especially well when a unique selling point was at stake, such as English wool, oriental spices and wines. Even then, however, the level of taxation might put the competitiveness of a country's export trade at risk. Where the possibility of an export tax did not exist or did not exist sufficiently, the only recourse was to tax the subjects, with the risk of rebellion when the burden was felt to be unfair. There was a delicate relationship between increasing fiscal demands and strengthening opposition to them from people's representatives or even uprisings.

In England, the Low Countries, Catalonia and the Swiss Confederation, the supervision of the tax system by representative bodies put a brake on the increase of the tax burden to a level far above the capacity of the subjects. The ordinary burgher was closer to economic reality than princes and their advisers, who displayed aristocratic contempt for it. Lending for the public debt could be quite a profitable investment for members of the political elites, which might well have made them reflect favourably on the government's spending policy.

State budgets swelled under the growing pressure of the costs of wars, financed to a large extent by loans. But these loans meant there would be an additional tax increase in the long term. In the middle of the fourteenth century and the early fifteenth, the city-state of Florence was engaged in a series of wars against the Papal States, Milan and Pisa. At the beginning of the period the Republic's expenditure was 40,000 florins, but the wars cost 2.5, 7.5 and 4.5 million florins respectively. The difference had to be found in tax increases and in loans, for which the interest found its way into the pockets of the financiers, but was paid for by taxes on the everyday consumer goods of ordinary people. Government debts thus enriched the wealthy at the expense of simple tax payers.

If we look at fiscality as a means of exercising power then we are struck by the direct and continuing relationship between war and taxation. Wars stimulated new and higher taxation, and even active representative institutions could not really offer resistance. Princes were not guided by macro-economic considerations. They really could not know what results their activities might bring because there was no reliable statistical information available about their own finances or those of their subjects. Time and again the unplanned expenses for the purpose of war threw state finances into confusion. Once a conflict had broken out, expenses could not be kept under control because only victory counted in a war, not economic efficiency. Therefore a lot of money had to be spent and borrowed against high rates of interest, the repayment of which would have a snowball effect and continue to burden expenditure for decades thereafter. Only the states which seemed to be creditworthy could actually obtain credit. In other words, a well-functioning tax system increased the chances of obtaining credit, which then threatened the equilibrium of that system.

The economic system thus made a twofold difference in a state's chances of obtaining money: in a commercialised economy, surpluses could be syphoned off far more easily through indirect taxes, regardless of the level at which they were levied, than in an agrarian subsistence economy. Moreover, credit was cheaper and more easily available in a commercialised economy, making a rapid expansion of liquid assets possible, while the agrarian economy was mainly limited to the sluggish, restricted and barely flexible yields from demesnes. One result of this was that from the thirteenth century onwards a state's military opportunities were more and more determined by its access to the money market. The more commercialised regions could then achieve military superiority simply because they were able to hire as many soldiers as they needed. These mercenaries came predominantly from periphery regions which still had agricultural economies, such as Wales, Scotland, central France, Castile, the Swiss Confederation and central Germany. It

is thus quite conceivable that the agricultural regions not only produced fewer resources with which to resist the supremacy of the core regions, but that their own populations often also supplied the troops that would subject them.

The state's subjects

The initiative for the continual competition for more concentrated means of power which led to the formation of increasingly large and strongly equipped states naturally emanated from those persons and bodies which already were ahead in the power stakes: feudal lords, large landowners, princes, princes of the Church and urban oligarchies. Yet the outcome of this centuries-long struggle was not decided solely by these elites. People who became subordinated to more powerful states did not just sit and watch: communities had formed their own political systems in preceding centuries, which for a long time remained a weighty factor in resisting the centralising policies of monarchs and their councillors. The feudal lords, who were no match for their mightier rivals, sometimes formed alliances against their rulers and even sought the support of their natural opponents in the towns or ecclesiastical institutions. In short, the formation of stronger concentrations of power provoked counter-reactions in which losing parties formed coalitions that could turn the tide at the first sign of a ruler's weakness. This dialectical process created forms of representation and resistance that would make a unique contribution to world history: constitutional monarchies controlled by representative assemblies.

The formal recognition of a new ruler, analogous to a feudal contract, took the form of a reciprocal oath of loyalty in which first the future ruler promised to protect the rights of his subjects and the Church, and then his vassals and other representatives of his subjects swore an oath of faithful service to him. It was on the basis of this statutory extension of the feudal oath of homage, subject to the sanctions of breach of contract, that vassals and privileged urban and rural communities freely decided to accept a territorial lord and to hold him to the obligations he had assumed.

The appointment of a legitimate successor was a recurring problem, a consequence of the high mortality rate among the hardened warriors; disagreement generally arose because of the variety of legal rules for succession and complex family ramifications. Rules of succession, such as the right of the first-born (primogeniture) and the admission (England, Castile, Denmark) or exclusion (France, Holy Roman Empire, Aragon) of women, were pointers to the choice in theory but did not guarantee an unequivocal or good solution. Problems arose in one out of every two successions because there were several contenders with equally valid claims, or because the successor was a minor, incompetent or female. Even in those countries where a woman could succeed, there were always arguments about her husband and his claims. In those circumstances, subjects who were called to recognise a new ruler had the opportunity to assert their preference and to lay down conditions for their agreement. This applied even more strongly in those regions where kingship was by definition arranged by election, namely in the German Empire and its originally vassal kingdoms of Bohemia and Poland, as well as in Sweden. The election contest always stirred up intense rivalry among the most important princely houses so that the kingship itself remained weak, even after the Habsburgs succeeded in making the German kingship hereditary in practice after 1438. The heavily debated succession to Emperor Maximilian I led his grandson Charles V to accept a whole series of conditions and restrictions to his power in 1519.

From the twelfth century onwards evidence throughout Europe points to the representatives of different estates, including burghers, being involved in the recognition of a ruler and the formulation of the basic rules of his government. In 1135 Alfonso VII had himself proclaimed emperor of Spain before a solemn assembly made up of important spiritual dignitaries and great barons and 'judges' – the latter were probably elected representatives of the towns. This was certainly the case in 1187, when the governments of 50 towns took part in the meeting of the royal council of Castile, which affirmed Berenguela's right to the succession and her contract of marriage to Conrad of Hohenstaufen. One year later, after a much-disputed succession to the throne, Alfonso IX of León promised before 'the archbishops, bishops, religious orders, counts and other nobles of the kingdom together with elected burghers of the towns' to respect customary law and only to make decisions about war and peace after discussions with 'the bishops, nobles and good men'. The assembly in turn swore allegiance and to maintain the law and peace in the kingdom.

In the neighbouring kingdom of Aragon the cortes (assembly of the estates) met regularly from the mid-twelfth century onwards, with more than 100 members, some of them from the towns. The cortes dealt with political questions such as the maintenance of order, administration of justice, taxation and the minting of coinage. In 1214, the Aragonese cortes, consisting of 'barons, knights, burghers and vassals from the castles and villages', swore allegiance to the under-age king, James, in return for financial and judicial advantages. When the dynasty was in crisis, as happened in Castile-León between 1275 and 1325, the cortes formulated their grievances about a variety of matters in the kingdom and thus brought their influence to bear on the government to choose a rival claimant to the throne. The far-reaching rights which Spanish noblemen and towns had won in connection with the Reconquest gave them a stronger basis in their dealings with the crown than that of their colleagues elsewhere in Europe. In Aragon, where feudal institutions were fully developed, this tendency was even more outspoken than in Castile, where feudalism was largely absent in the structuring of power relations.

In Flanders representatives of the nobility and large towns had gone a step further as early as

1128 (see Box 5.1). This was the first time that the juridical form of an oath of homage was extended to a contract between a prince and the collectivity of his subjects. By doing this, the feudal right of resistance in case of infringement of the agreement became applicable to the government of the entire land. In other words: subjects were now entitled not to obey their ruler if he broke his promises. Consequently, in the event of violation, he would lose the allegiance not only of his vassals but of all his subjects, and therefore also his office. This principle would be further applied in Brabant in 1420 and in the Low Countries as a whole on the Act of Abjuration of Philip II of Spain in 1580–1581 and, via the English revolutions of the seventeenth century, would later be found as the impeachment process in the American constitution. In essence, the famous Magna Carta of 1215 was also a list of complaints that King John's vassals addressed to him for breaching feudal law. London was the only city mentioned. The deposition and execution of Edward II in 1327 and Richard II in 1399 were legally supported by similar procedures carried out in parliament.

In urbanised regions, towns did not wait until their princes had dynastic problems to introduce consultative structures on a regional and inter-regional scale. In this way they could take care of their own commercial interests with all the implications for coinage, tolls, administration of justice and security. If these interests were damaged by their own or foreign princes, then towns brought their grievances and requests to them as a collective body, compelling their compliance sometimes by means of financial concessions and, if necessary, through boycotts or reprisals. Since overseas and overland trading routes easily crossed borders, governments of trading towns operated in truly international associations. As long as princes showed no interest in economic politics, which was true of most of them until the fifteenth century, traders enjoyed much freedom in this. The attempts at territorialisation and expansion of state power set them on a collision course with princes. Typical points of friction were the harmful effects of dynastic wars on commercial relations, toll collections, the arrest of foreign merchants by a prince's officers of justice and devaluation of the currency. A typical conflict arose in Brabant around the death of Duke John II in 1312. As he fell ill leaving only a young son, he negotiated with the nobility and the towns to secure his succession. The towns complained that at that time many of their citizens were being arrested outside the duchy, kept as hostages and their goods confiscated, in order to enforce the repayment of the duke's debts. They managed to gain effective control over the duchy's finances by a regency council dominated by the seven major cities. This charter included a formula granting to *all citizens* the individual right to deny any support and obedience to the duke if he were to violate any of their privileges. This extension of the feudal right of resistance initiated a long tradition of constitutional charters in Brabant, limiting monarchical power.

With their associations, privileges, merchants' guilds and their own legal systems, trading towns had created solid structures that to a large extent functioned independently of the state. They could not be brushed aside easily by the new state apparatuses: after all, they had a great deal of specialist knowledge and contacts and were not inclined to give them up for nothing. States were thus obliged to negotiate with urban organisations with a long tradition of autonomous representation. That was where the money and financial competences were. The moment when their governments were incorporated into tighter state structures formed an excellent opportunity for this. Hence the emphatic role they played in purely political events, such as succession crises in regions like Aragon, Flanders and Brabant.

The survival of effectively functioning representative institutions depended on both external pressure and the social, economic and political structures of the regions concerned. The parliament in England owed its exceptional continuity

PLATE 11.3 Ceremonial session of the two Houses of Parliament in 1523. This highly ceremonial representation shows the king on his throne with three ecclesiastical councillors to his right and two laymen to his left. The seating order in quadrangles reflects this division: lords spiritual are seated on the king's right and lords secular in front and on the left. In the centre, officials are seated on four woolsacks and there are two scribes. The herald appears to allow the Commons to take their places.

(despite some interruptions of several years at the end of the fifteenth century) to the solid anchorage of its representation in the counties and boroughs, where the tradition of subjects' participation went back to the time of the Anglo-Saxon kings. Even the most centralised states could not completely eliminate the traditionally strong regional systems of representation. All the newly incorporated territories kept their traditional rights: for example, in France the Normans received their charter in 1315, Lorraine as late as

1766. Also in France, the estates' assemblies of Burgundy and of Languedoc functioned until the end of the eighteenth century.

A great deal depended then on how representative the representatives really were. For instance, if representatives of towns were purely private individuals with an eye on a noble title they ran the risk of their subjects sending a petition directly to the king or, even worse, of being brought down by revolt. Their role as intermediary between the centre and periphery in the state would then take a terrible blow. Two sorts of factors increased the pressure on such 'representatives' from the fifteenth century onwards: the expansion of monarchical authority limited their room for manoeuvre, and the escalation of war continually raised the fiscal and military expectations of the crown. Both these trends appeared at the same time, although the extreme lack of financial resources for war compelled states to give in and make concessions to local elites.

Balance of powers

In the competition between states described in this chapter there were naturally more losers than winners. Among the losers in the process of state-formation were countless local lords and territorial princes whose lands were swallowed up by more competitive units. In this we can see an increased efficiency within the same type of dominion. It was a different matter for the *cultural* losers, like the Welsh, Irish and Bohemians whose languages were banned from Church services, government and the law; Muslims who became second-class citizens in Castile, Portugal and the lands under the Crown of Aragon; and Christians in the Balkans after the Ottoman conquests. The German upper class in central European and Baltic towns and in the rural areas of Prussia was shameless in its discrimination against the Slav population. A great deal of urban autonomy was lost in the process of strengthening state power, because princes gained a tight hold on the composition of town government, the exercise of judicial powers and financial expenditure. There was naturally no question of independent military activity in the context of the state. Insurgency was repressed by superior strength.

No matter how strong the concentration of people and capital in towns was, they were still compelled to relinquish a large measure of autonomy to the monarchies because, apart from northern and central Italy, states gradually came to have more means of exercising power at their disposal. If the budgets of towns like Ghent and Louvain in the fourteenth century were more or less equal to the budgets of the count of Flanders and the duke of Brabant, respectively, territorial expansion and systematic tax levies would soon give the princes the advantage. Towns seldom managed to cooperate effectively for any length of time to form a counterbalance. Unions of German towns in regions like Swabia, Alsace and the upper Rhine, which contemplated protecting certain common interests of their burghers from the feudal powers, suffered from a lack of genuine solidarity. Even in the German Hanse, the great urban league, most of the time the interests of the regional groupings were deeply divergent, often even diametrically opposed. This made truly coordinated action only possible in exceptional circumstances. Certainly, members would not support each other in purely political conflicts with nearby princes.

The strengthening of state power was thus a predominant pattern of the late Middle Ages.

States continually occupied more territory, they concentrated a greater superiority of means of violence in relation to other power cores in society, and they built an apparatus of officials to maintain the law and collect taxes. Warfare and territorial acquisitions made a huge difference with regard to real state power, as expressed in the expenditure figures shown in Table 11.1. Note especially the weakness of the Empire vis-à-vis the major kingdoms as well as its constituent territories and even one single imperial city.

In the Holy Roman Empire territorial princes consolidated their positions at the expense of smaller contestants and towns, but continually changing coalitions among the dozens of 'states' prevented any real concentration from taking place for the time being. The Empire as a whole lost substantial areas because of the lack of cohesion in its periphery. The principalities in the Low Countries were combined into an exceptionally powerful complex under the Burgundian-Habsburg dynasty. Alsace, Lotharingia (Lorraine), Franche Comté, Dauphiné and Provence came into the French sphere of influence. The Swiss Confederation detached itself gradually, and in 1501 formally, from the Empire. Under the rule of Emperor Charles IV in 1373, after whom the famous bridge in Prague was named, the kingdom of Bohemia succeeded in stringing together vast areas of land that stretched from Brandenburg through Lausitz, Silesia, Moravia, Austria, Styria and Carinthia as far as the Tyrol. The Habsburg dynasty eventually supplanted the Luxemburg

TABLE 11.1 State expenditure, *c.*1500 (in tonnes of pure silver)

France	42–91	Habsburg Lands[b]	10
Venice	37	Brittany	7
England	17–44	Holy Roman Empire	5
Castile	12–76	Palatinate	3
Low Countries[a]	20–27	Bavaria	3
Naples	22	Nuremberg	2.7
Lombardy	22	Württemberg	2
Papal State	10	archbishopric of Cologne	1

Notes: [a] Franche Comté included. [b] Austria, Bohemia, Tyrol

Source: Martin Körner, 'Expenditure', in Richard Bonney (ed.), *Economic Systems and State Finance* (Oxford: Clarendon Press, 1995), p. 399.

house and, in 1526, brought all those regions back under imperial control through tactical marriages.

The enlargement of the monarchic states' power did not take place solely at the expense of local and territorial lords and princes and the towns. Church institutions also lost ground at every level during the fourteenth and fifteenth centuries. The ideal of the crusade was degraded in the thirteenth century to a purely political, internal-European weapon and disappeared into the realm of fiction. The popes' universalistic claims were stranded finally on French opposition, leading to a profound territorialisation of the Church (or rather nationalisation, such as the Gallican Church, a precedent for the Anglican Church founded in 1534), which came to depend on secular rulers and began to serve their interests more directly. Church property was thenceforth taxed regularly. Towns and states took over a growing number of functions that the Church had previously considered its own. Secular courts of law ruled on matters of marriage and heresy, and the organisation of poor relief and health care came increasingly into lay hands and was submitted to regulation by local authorities. Papal moral authority was diminished through the increasingly magnanimous application of the principle of granting indulgences and dispensations for illegitimate birth and the marriage of close relatives (see Chapter 12). As it became clear that it was increasingly possible to buy such favours, those who could afford to used them purely instrumentally. Although the role of the Church was in no way played out, it had lost its supremacy and even its independence in relation to the stronger secular rulers.

It must be clear from the above that in 1500 (just as in 1800) there still was no question of a single type of state in Europe. Expansion of territorial states in the German Empire and Italy was curbed by the balances of power existing between the countless political units. Incorporation into larger units rarely meant the abrogation of customary law and institutions. The stronger states could rely on a modern commercialised economy in which greater quantities of more flexible resources were available than in a traditional agrarian economy, such as that of Poland or Denmark. In Italy the commercial middle class ruled the cities directly during the so-called communal period, but, from the mid-thirteenth century onwards, the tendency towards investment in land and seigniorial rights underpinned the tendency towards the formation of *signorie*, or even outright monarchic rule. Commercial capital was not tied to a particular place or a particular territory. Should the lack of safety, non-repayment of royal debts, heavy tax burden or excessively high wages create unattractive conditions for investors in search of profits, then they sought refuge elsewhere and the local economy suffered. Princes could not control capitalists, and since they could not exist without their credit they had to allow them freedom in their activities. This mixed model would offer the best chances for the future.

Points to remember

■ Many late medieval states were expanded and transformed feudal kingdoms, others were built from the bottom (the seignories and territorial lordships) up through the expansion of the most powerful feudal lords.

■ Once a kind of equilibrium was reached in the power relations within a particular polity and in its relations with neighbouring states, that situation tended to be perpetuated (path dependency). The shape of consolidated states reflected the role of countervailing powers within the society.

■ Warfare was the most costly activity deployed by medieval and early modern states. As princes claimed that to be their exclusive prerogative, subjects were confronted with the damages and peaking taxation. These could offer opportunities for political participation, but more often princes successfully evaded this by seeking new sources of income such as tolls, loans and debasement of the currency.

■ Princely high courts of justice created opportunities for (wealthy) subjects to seek their right independent of local influences.

■ University training was valued for high clergymen, councillors, judges and lawyers; a practical training was preferred for financial agents.

■ Discontinuity of the monarchy, financial crises, lost wars and excessive violations of customary law by officials created typical incentives for representatives of subjects to raise their voice and claim constitutional rights as well as guarantees against future violations.

■ The right of resistance against arbitrary monarchical power was feudal in its origins, but in the most urbanised regions of Europe wealthier citizens succeeded in extending this right to all subjects by means of regular political representation and by enforcing constitutional covenants, in exchange for paying regular taxes.

Suggestions for further reading

Guenée, Bernard (1985), *States and Rulers in Later Medieval Europe* (Oxford: Blackwell) (orig. French, 1971). Classic and systematic analysis of the character of the late medieval state, its ideologies, resources, targets, and its relations to society.

Harding, Alan (2002), *Medieval Law and the Foundations of the State* (Oxford etc.: OUP, 2002). The need for social order, peace and justice is explored as the basis of systems of government from the centre, from the Frankish and Anglo-Saxon courts to the monarchic states.

Housley, Norman (2002), *Religious Warfare in Europe, 1400–1536* (Oxford: OUP). A bright analysis of the conflicts waged in God's name in the period from the later Crusades to the early Reformation.

Imber, Colin (2009), *The Ottoman Empire, 1300–1650*, 2nd edn (Basingstoke: Palgrave Macmillan). A chronological and institutional overview of the Empire's first centuries, focusing on the palace, the military, the law and taxation.

Watts, John (2009), *The Making of Polities: Europe, 1300–1500* (Cambridge etc.: CUP). An up-to-date and broad comparative overview of the course of political events, combined with the structural analysis of relevant processes and factors, with due attention given to the various forms of government and to political culture.

12 Crisis in the Church and the reorientation of the faithful

Who leads Christendom?

Towards the end of the thirteenth century it gradually became clear that the hierocratic aspirations of the popes would finally have to give way to a new type of caesaropapism, the formation of what has been called 'national churches', on which kings or other secular rulers had a strong hold. The history of the years around 1300 teaches us that the pope in Rome had not properly understood the signs of the times. We are indebted to his misunderstanding for some of the most fascinating politico-ideological documents of the Middle Ages, as the final act of the struggle between emperor and pope and between pope and French king was played out to the accompaniment of an unprecedented polemic barrage. The starting signal came in 1294 when Pope Celestine V abdicated after a pontificate of barely five months; the contest ended with the death of Emperor Louis in 1347.

In the entire history of the papacy there has never been such a difference in personality of two successive popes as there was between Celestine V (1294) and Boniface VIII (1294–1303). Both have been called a living anachronism, yet for totally different reasons. Celestine, an unworldly hermit, emerged as a compromise candidate whom nobody really wanted, when the papal throne had been vacant for a long period. Once he had become pope, so shocked was he by the moral laxity of the world he had entered that he could not retire quickly enough from his new dignity. Some reports say that a certain amount of pressure was brought to bear on him by his successor, Cardinal Benedetto Caetani, a brilliant lawyer who ascended the papal throne under the name Boniface VIII. Soon afterwards, the man of the world that Boniface had been became a man who wanted to be exalted above that world. And for the last time, a pope thundered from the Lateran that the highest power in the world

PLATE 12.1 Pope Boniface VIII, statue in copper and bronze on wood, 2.45 m high, *c*.1300 on show on the façade of the Palazzo Pubblico of Bologna.

belonged to him and him alone. Through his papal bulls and his legates he interfered in the high politics of temporal princes everywhere from Sicily to Denmark, only to be rebuffed everywhere.

Boniface's aggression was directed mainly at the French king, Philip IV the Fair, questioning his right to levy taxes on the French clergy and to try them in secular courts of law. Tensions mounted, and resulted in the publication of a series of radical bulls, the last of which, *Unam Sanctam* (1302), competes with the *Dictatus Papae* of 1075 for the prize of being the most extreme formulation ever of papal claims to temporal power (cf. Chapter 6). According to one contemporary satirical text, the French king would have laughed his head off 'when he heard that it had

been decreed by the Lord Pope Boniface that he himself [i.e. the pope] is and should be lord over all principalities and kingdoms.' In fact, King Philip, who suspected the pope of conspiring against him with the king of Aragon, decided to remove the Holy Father from the scene by constructing a charge of heresy against him and then having him kidnapped from Italy. The last part of the plan failed, although a Franco-Italian commando unit under the leadership of Philip's confidant, Guillaume de Nogaret, did manage to take Boniface prisoner in his summer residence at Anagni. The pope was released a day later, but died soon after his traumatic and humiliating arrest.

A combination of events led to the removal of the papal court to Avignon in 1309. Avignon was then a town divided by the river Rhône into the old, German-imperial part on the east bank, and a new, French, part on the west bank. The popes held the formal lordship over the German part, together with the small County of Venasque that surrounded the town, in fief of the counts of Provence who happened to be the kings of Naples from the French House of Anjou. In 1348, the popes bought these rights from the count – then countess, actually – after which Avignon and Venasque became a papal enclave between France and the Holy Roman Empire. The decision, in 1309, of Pope Clement V (1305–1314) to move to Provence was connected with the denouement of the Boniface VIII affair. Clement was anxious to prevent the French king from going ahead with his plan of having Boniface posthumously declared a heretic. He found it completely unacceptable that someone who had been invested with the keys of St Peter would ever be called an enemy of the faith, but he paid an outrageous price for Philip's acquiescence: he agreed to the persecution and eventual condemnation of the Knights Templar. After the fall of the last Christian bulwark in Palestine at the end of the thirteenth century this extremely wealthy military order had established its headquarters in Paris and successfully entered the banking business. The

French crown was one of its largest debtors. Philip IV and his advisers were mightily envious and looked for ways to destroy the order and confiscate its French possessions. Even after a thorough enquiry in the dioceses and a council held in Vienne in 1311–1312, mainly attended by French and Italian bishops, had voiced doubts, the Templars were 'unmasked' as a band of heretics and blasphemers given to homosexual practices and diabolic rituals. Many of them died as the result of terrible tortures or were burned at the stake.

Clement also witnessed the death of imperial universalism. It began in 1310 when the king of the Romans, Henry VII of Luxemburg, crossed the Alps with a small armed force to have himself crowned emperor and to impose his authority on the communes of northern and central Italy. The original enthusiasm of those who hoped that a powerful Roman king would put an end to the political conflicts in Italy rapidly faded away when Henry acted particularly harshly against the Lombard towns which refused to open their gates to him. At a tumultuous meeting, where he literally had to fight his way in, Henry was crowned emperor in Rome in 1312. He died the following year en route to southern Italy to take the kingdom of Naples.

The journey made to Italy in 1327 by his successor Louis was even more audacious. The pope had kept himself fairly aloof in 1311–1312, but now, from his palace in Avignon, John XXII (1316–1334) turned against the Roman king. In defiance, Louis had himself crowned emperor in Rome by the city's governor, Sciarra Colonna, who was not a prelate. It was a curious episode, stirring up memories from an already distant past, when pope and emperor regularly called each other heretic and deposed each other. Louis returned to Germany in 1330 without having accomplished very much in Italy.

Spiritual and secular power

The confrontations between Philip the Fair and Boniface VIII, and between Emperor Louis and John XXII, were conflicts between irreconcilable aspirations and also between powerful and obstinate personalities. All received the support of eminent intellectuals, most of them Italians, who were well able to cloak actions in ideology. For this reason the first three decades of the fourteenth century are a gold mine for those with an interest in the history of political thought.

The papal position was stated most clearly by James of Viterbo, Giles of Rome and Henry of Cremona, who were all three elevated, at some point, to archbishop or bishop. The American religious historian Steven Ozment once compared them to 'legal beavers' who 'labored methodically to construct a protective dam against the surging tide of secular power'. There was not much new to record, however. The most important of their hierocratic arguments were by now very well known: the pope, as Christ's only representative on earth, did not have to justify himself to any human authority. Equally, the pope could call every secular ruler to account, for papal power was higher than, and the source of, all secular power. In practice, it was best for the pope to leave the exercise of temporal power in the hands of princes, because sometimes it was necessary to use force. But the pope could certainly be involved in the drawing up of important policies. What was new was that the old arguments were underpinned by reasoning borrowed from Aristotle. This was especially the case in the work of James of Viterbo, who combined the Aristotelian idea of the state as the product of man's nature with the idea (inspired by Aquinas) that spiritual leadership of the Church was government informed by God's grace, and was therefore superior to, and institutive of, all forms of secular power. The same idea tempted Henry of Cremona to propose that the pope should have (final) temporal jurisdiction in all secular polities on this earth – which was less bizarre than the extremist claim by Giles of

Rome that all private property rights originated from the Church.

The position of King Philip the Fair of France was subtly defended by John Quidort, a theologian at the University of Paris and thus known as John of Paris. In his classical dualist proposition John recognised that spiritual power was indeed superior to temporal power, but only on a higher, metaphysical level. In the real world pope and secular princes were autonomous and supreme, each in his own well-defined sphere, because each had received his authority immediately from God. Quidort perceived with great clarity that in Christendom, as it had developed, with a Church emerging as a physical institution with all kinds of interests in the world, and with secular rulers who had the responsibility of the spiritual as well as temporal well-being of their subjects, the matters of Church and world by definition always intersected and overlapped. Consequently in extreme situations, but only then, pope and secular rulers were allowed to interfere in each other's spheres, for instance when a king proved to be heretical or a pope behaved scandalously. The implication was that, normally, the pope should not intervene in any way with the affairs of secular authority; the pope should only be heard when princes contravened the laws of the Holy Church.

Emperor Louis IV (nicknamed by Pope John XXII 'of Bavaria') could count on the formidable intellectual support of Marsilius of Padua (*c*.1275–1342), a physician who taught at the *artes* faculty in Paris and was in the service of the Visconti family, the pro-German rulers of Milan. Once he became known as the author of *Defensor Pacis* ('The Defender of the Peace'), which had been circulating since 1324, he fled to the Bavarian court, then at Nuremberg. He accompanied Louis on his journey to Rome where he was responsible for the coronation ceremony and the pro-imperial propaganda around it. *Defensor Pacis* is undoubtedly one of the most original politico-theoretical treatises of the entire Middle Ages. Its title refers directly to the emperor. His long experience with Italian politics had given Marsilius the deep conviction that the continuous interference of the Church in the exercise of secular power was the major cause of the long-lasting disruption of peace in Italy. Subsequently, he had extended this pessimistic view over the whole of Christendom. Not only did this situation prevent the well-being of man in this world, it also endangered his eternal salvation, because the conditions for achieving the latter could only be created in a society where peace reigned. Marsilius's radical solution was to deny every form of secular power to the clerical estate, whose only, and extremely important, task should be to take care of people's souls, to morally educate and spiritually guide them, and to administer the holy sacraments. In their turn, secular rulers, and the emperor first of all, should not take their temporal duty lightly, which was to provide good government. This meant preserving order, unity and social harmony within their realms, so that peace and prosperity would prevail.

Among political theorists the fame of *Defensor Pacis* largely rests on its restatement and adaptation of the Roman-republican idea of popular sovereignty, which vested legislative power in the people, to be taken as all (male, adult) members of a polity. For practical reasons, legislative power would always be delegated to a smaller body of people, in the *Defensor* called *pars valentior* ('the worthiest part'). But Marsilius's attachment to the cause of Emperor Louis makes any republican reading of his major work quite difficult. Therefore, most specialists agree that Marsilius advocated the identification of this legislative body with what he called the *principans* or *principatus*, meaning the executive power in general, or the secular ruler (prince) in particular.

By extending the principle of the sovereignty of the people over the Church, Marsilius blazed a second revolutionary trail. He argued that only the commune of the faithful (*universitas fidelium*) could be the fount of law-making and the exercisers of authority within the Church, including, for instance, the excommunication of heretics,

PLATE 12.2

The Seven Sacraments. This magnificent altarpiece by Rogier van der Weyden was commissioned between 1440 and 1445 by Jean Chevrot, bishop of Tournai and head of Duke Philip of Burgundy's Great Council. The triptych is framed as a church interior with the main sacrament, the Eucharist, in the nave, and the six others in the aisles, following the human life-cycle from left to right: baptism, confirmation, confession, ordination of a priest, marriage and anointing of the sick.

which in Marsilius's view was only an option when they threatened civil harmony. Again, for practical reasons, this fundamental competence could best be delegated to the civil authorities and not to the clerics, for the clergy should not hold any coercive power in the world. This also applied to general Church councils, which represented the community of the faithful at the highest level, but which should then leave secular princes to convert their pronouncements into enforceable laws. As if this was not enough, Marsilius delivered the *coup de grâce* to the Church hierarchy by pronouncing that Christ had not made any distinction in rank when he established the priesthood, so the pope was no higher than a village priest, let alone the holder of *plenitudo potestatis* (full powers)! Moreover, the Church should not have any worldly possessions, for Christ and the apostles had had none either.

Marsilius borrowed these trenchant views partly from John of Paris, and partly from the spiritual Franciscans who, after a century of varying success in their struggle to gain control inside the Franciscan Order and the acceptance of the

Church authorities, were silenced in 1323 when Pope John XXII declared the idea of the absolute poverty of Christ and the apostles to be heretical. Interestingly enough, the Franciscans, in their defence, were the first to explicitly advance a theory of papal infallibility. They pointed out that in 1279 Pope Nicholas III had endorsed the doctrine of apostolic poverty, so John XXII was not allowed to teach to the contrary because every pope was infallible in his doctrinal judgements. But at the time all this was to no avail – papal infallibility in doctrinal matters would not become the official teaching of the Catholic Church until 1870 – and several Franciscan leaders fled to Munich, which was rapidly becoming a meeting place for radical dissidents. Among them was the Franciscan friar William of Ockham, who shared many of Marsilius's ideas about the strict division of temporal and spiritual power (see Chapter 8).

Radical as the ideas of Marsilius and Ockham were, they could never have caused a reformation before the Reformation. Not that Marsilius and Ockham aimed to do so. The English theologian

John Wyclif (*c*.1325–1384), who worked at the University of Oxford and frequented the courts of Edward III and Richard II of England, came closer to such reformation. He developed pronounced views on the role of faith and the place of the Church in the world. He saw the visible Catholic Church as an artificial, unworthy shell sheltering the true Church, the invisible community of the faithful, which included only those who had been chosen by divine preordination. Since in earthly life it is not known who the chosen are, the visible Church must continue to exist, for want of anything better. That is why reforms were needed so urgently. The reforms should deal with three points. The first of these shows how much Wyclif was influenced by the spiritual Franciscans, for he believed that the visible Church should have no *dominium*, that is, no earthly possessions and no worldly power. In Wyclif's view, *dominium* was always the result of divine grace, so that lawful *dominium* could only rest on those whom God had chosen and who already lived in a state of grace on earth. As it was impossible to identify this elite body, Wyclif considered it best that Church property and rights should be confiscated by the king and managed by him. No wonder that Wyclif had many supporters in royal circles! Second, Wyclif believed that the whole truth of the faith lay enclosed in the Bible; every individual believer could thus have access to this truth, all the more so because Wyclif argued for a literal interpretation of the Bible and not the allegorical exegesis that was customary in the Middle Ages. The third point followed on from this: clerics were in fact superfluous as middlemen in the mediation of the truth, especially those who did not themselves live in the spirit of the Gospel.

Wyclif could count on the protection of the highest circles, but he also had many followers in the lower ranks of society. And yet there was no reformation before the Reformation in England. The main reason was that Wyclif's supporters, called the Lollards ('the mumblers'), radicalised soon after his death and lost the support of the elite, especially after an anti-royal revolt in 1414. Matters were different in Bohemia where Wyclif's works had been a great influence on Jan Hus, a dissident theologian at the University of Prague who linked his ideas on the reformation of the Church with an anti-German Bohemian nationalism. After the death of Hus at the stake in 1415, it looked for a long time as if Bohemia would break away from both the Empire and the Catholic Church. Widespread sympathy for the Hussite cause radicalised in 1419 when millenarian expectations arose and were mixed with social revolutionary ideas. It was thought that the victorious Second Coming of Christ on earth was imminent, and that this glorious event would take place in Bohemia, because God had chosen that land to restore the true faith and lay the foundation of the thousand-year reign of Christ on earth – hence millenarian – that had been foreseen in the Book of Revelations. To that end a cosmic landing stage was set by projecting the biblical geography of the Holy Land on Bohemia, with mounts Tabor (still the name of the town on that spot) and Horeb as the most conspicuous beacons. Emperor Sigismund (1410–1437) responded by organising, with papal consent, five extremely brutal crusades against the 'rebels', but all were very successfully repelled. In the end, the Bohemian case was undermined by internal dissension between radical-puritanist and moderate-conservative reformists (the latter based in Prague and at Prague University). However, it was not until 1436 that the emperor and the moderates reached a compromise which finally ended the Hussite wars.

The popes in Avignon and the bureaucratisation of the Curia

With the loss of its universalistic pretensions, the Catholic Church certainly lost much of the moral and spiritual leadership within Christian Europe. On the other hand, the Avignon popes were very successful in developing another thirteenth-century legacy: the attempts to centralise the exercise of papal authority within the Church. This process led inevitably to the strengthening of the bureaucracy in the Curia, the papal court, together with the consolidation of the position of the pope himself. The four permanent departments of the Curia established in the thirteenth century – chancery, *Camera Apostolica*, *Penitentiaria* and *Audientia* – were expanded and given new sections or wider powers. In the fourteenth century the chancery consisted of seven offices, each one with its own precisely defined tasks, which gave the treatment of incoming and outgoing documents an almost Prussian perfection. The enormous growth in chancery output was obviously closely connected with the expansion of the activities of the departments of finance and justice.

The basis for enlarging the financial scope of the Curia was laid during the papacy of Innocent III. He was the first pope to impose taxes on the clergy throughout Latin Christendom for 'urgent matters', such as crusades. In that way the popes became less dependent on their Italian possessions and occasional princely subsidies. A second new source of income, the collection of which was perfected during the Avignon papacy, was formed by the revenues from the granting of lower Church offices and the incomes attached to them (*beneficia*). Before the thirteenth century the popes had seldom intervened in appointments – only in exceptional circumstances or when conflicts arose. This changed gradually and in the bull *Licet ecclesiarum*, issued in 1265, Pope Clement IV laid down the basis in canon law for unrestrained papal intervention. The bull proclaimed that, as the holder of supreme authority in the Church, the pope could dispose of all ecclesiastical offices and their related benefices. Of course this did not bring an immediate end to the existing practices of canonical election that had been accepted since the Investiture Controversy. Popes could not afford to trample on the rights of others, but they systematically began to increase the number of occasions when their intervention was accepted. Their efforts reached a climax during the Avignon period. Pope John XXII, for example, issued some 3,000 dispositions relating to benefices in the first year of his pontificate, sometimes in the form of appointments in contested cases ('provisions'), sometimes in the form of firm allocations known as 'reservations', and sometimes in the form of promises concerning benefices which were expected to become free in a short time, hence 'expectancies'. This was partly the result of his fight against the widespread holding of plural benefices – a fight which the popes did not ultimately win. Not surprisingly, all these papal dispositions had to be paid for. Added to other new as well as existing sources of income, these proceeds from dispositions raised papal revenue during the Avignon period to between 166,000 and 481,000 gold florins per year. This did not make the popes as rich as the kings of France, England or Naples, but it certainly put them in the same league. No wonder that one of John's successors, Clement VI (1342–1352), had no trouble in finding the revenue to construct the magnificent new Palace of the Popes.

Clearly the whole machinery could only work with the assistance of a well-oiled bureaucratic apparatus. Altogether, the Curia employed between 5,000 and 6,000 people in 1350, more than double the number of a century earlier. This included the household staff and those involved with guard duties, but excluded the personal staffs of individual cardinals, which also comprised dozens of members, for the cardinals administered justice in a private capacity and were jointly responsible for the management of their revenues.

The Great Schism and the conciliar movement

Despite the fact that the papacy and the papal Curia stood under strong French influence during the Avignon period, almost all the popes continued to work towards a return to Rome. Peace in

Italy was one of the conditions for this. In 1319, Pope John XXII sent a legate to Italy, accompanied by a small armed force that would be complemented with mercenary troops on the spot, with instructions to get things organised in the papal territories, but the legate, Cardinal Bertrand du Poujet, was not always very adroit. The mission of Cardinal Gil Albornoz, archbishop of Toledo and a tough veteran from the later days of the Reconquest, reached Italy in 1350 and met with greater success, but Albornoz and his successors became caught up in the web of Italian politics. So it was that the popes did not return to Rome until Gregory XI (1370–1378). He arrived there in January 1377 only to die the following year.

Nobody could have foreseen the events that followed. The cardinals quickly voted for an apparently risk-free candidate, tried and tested in papal administration, in order to keep the papacy in Rome: Urban VI (1378–1389). However, the cardinals soon backtracked on their choice, probably fearing that the new pope would drastically reduce their influence in the Curia. To make matters worse, they then chose an anti-pope, Clement VII (1378–1394) who took up residence in the papal palace in Avignon while their first choice stayed in Rome. The Great Schism was a fact, although it was impossible then to surmise that this split within the Church – by no means the first! – would last for nearly forty years, from 1378 until 1417. The Schism immediately posed a major problem because the whole of Latin-Christian Europe had to choose one of the two popes. Not surprisingly, the main dividing lines in the field of international political power determined the composition of the two spheres of papal authority, or obediences: France and its allies (Naples, the great Spanish kingdoms, Scotland) chose Avignon; England, the German Empire, the Scandinavian kingdoms, Poland, Hungary and Portugal supported Rome. The obediences were by no means fixed; states changed sides as circumstances dictated.

From the very beginning, many on both sides made efforts to bring the Schism to an end. Since neither of the popes could oust the other by force of arms nor was prepared to abdicate or submit to arbitration, a general council was suggested after some time as being the appropriate means of ending the sordid discord within the Church. The idea of allowing a general council to pass judgement on a pope was not in itself new. We have seen how in the first half of the fourteenth century ideas about the role of general councils began to form a fixed part of the discourse on the relation between Church and state, as an almost natural counterweight to the growing centralism of the papacy.

Conciliarism developed further the longer the Great Schism lasted. It acquired, however, another, less divisive basis. Two French theologians appeared as its most eloquent exponents: Pierre d'Ailly (1350–1420), a gifted and versatile scholar, who was attached for many years to the University of Paris, was then bishop successively of Le Puy and Cambrai and was finally elevated to cardinal in 1411, and Jean Gerson (1363–1429), a fellow teacher from Paris. The basis of their conciliar thinking was that a general council could make a judgement over the pope and indeed had the duty to do so if the pope 'strayed from the faith' and threatened the continued existence of the Church, which a schism naturally did. This opinion, already outlined by earlier theorists, could still be supported with canon law. The more radical view that a pope was subordinate to a general council, whatever the circumstances, never prevailed.

The first attempt to put conciliar thinking into practice ended in a fiasco in 1409. The general council organised shortly thereafter by Emperor Sigismund proved an unqualified success, however. The Council of Constance (1414–1418) was the largest Church assembly in the Middle Ages; its sessions were public and attracted a steady stream of princes, nobles, members of the lower clergy and students; and all the ecclesiastics present were allowed to vote. The sitting popes were forced to resign and a new pope, Martin V (1417–1431), was elected and immediately accepted practically everywhere. At long last, the Great Schism was at an end.

It seemed as if the way was clear now for conciliar thinking to be transformed into a constitutional element in Church organisation. At Constance it had been decided to hold general councils at regular intervals, as had been the custom of the early Christian Church. For a while it looked as if this would indeed become standard practice. But things started to go wrong at the second convention after Constance, the Council of Basel in 1431. This was due mainly to the lack of cooperation by Pope Eugene IV (1431–1447), who refused to be browbeaten by the headstrong prelates; he felt far superior to them. At the end of 1437, he moved the meeting to Ferrara, a manoeuvre dividing those attending the council. The majority, including the most important spokesman for the conciliar movement at the time, Nicholas of Kues (1401–1465), made the best of the situation and joined the pope. Only a rump group of radicals remained in Basel, where they became rapidly marginalised. Bereft of significant support, the assembly finally adjourned in 1449. In hindsight the removal to Ferrara can be seen as a turning point – the beginning of the end of conciliarism as a mainstream movement within the Church, although it should be borne in mind that it persisted until at least the middle of the sixteenth century.

All things considered, two factors can be held responsible for the failure of conciliarism. In the first place, the conciliarists failed to create an institution or apparatus that would give their programme a firm basis and which would have looked after their interests between councils. Second, their criticism focused too much on the position of the pope inside the Church and too little on reforms in other segments of the Church.

The collapse of the conciliar movement opened the way to a powerful recovery of the papacy, but a high price had to be paid for the Great Schism and the conciliar period. It was precisely during this very critical phase that the forces opposing papal centralism had grown stronger. England and France, kingdoms constantly in need of money as a result of the Hundred Years War, were determined to prevent any drainage of ecclesiastical revenues to Rome. Their stance led to the formation of what have rightly been called 'national Churches', like the so-called Gallican Church in France, where as early as 1438 the king was able to re-establish his influence over the appointment of bishops, abbots and provosts.

Elsewhere, although the control exercised by kings and other rulers over the clerics was perhaps less strong, a new balance was found between papal and princely authority over Church and clergy within the boundaries of territorial principalities. The Renaissance popes fully understood this and even created a similar power base by further reinforcing the Papal State. The success of their policy was mirrored in the pomp of their court as well as in the new splendour they gave to Rome. The downside of this arrangement, however, was that after giving up the ideal of universal and unified Christendom under uncontested papal leadership, the head of the Catholic Church also surrendered the famous freedom of the Church, which had been so desperately fought for in the eleventh and twelfth centuries. The clergy became significantly dependent on the monarchs, who used the Church to support their policy and to provide an attractive income to many of their clients.

Religious life

The rich religious life of the late Middle Ages has fascinated many generations of historians. While some have looked primarily for the roots of the Reformation, others have stressed the very continuity with the past: religious sentiments underwent deep-seated change in the eleventh and twelfth centuries; the fourteenth and fifteenth centuries just continued the trends that had then been set in motion. At first glance, the evidence for the continuity view appears to be stronger, but this ignores two issues. First, it was not the forms in which religion found its expression as much as their profusion and the intensity of the faith experience that require attention. Second, the Reformation did not just happen: its prehistory must be placed in the late Middle Ages. We would like only to shift the emphasis. In the past, every critical attitude to wrongs in the Catholic Church, every expression of moral and religious reflection was seen as heralding the Reformation. Nowadays, the generally accepted view is that from the very beginning the reformers blamed the Church for demanding too much of the faithful rather than too little, and that criticism was rarely accompanied by a complete rejection of the Church, its ideology, institutions and rituals. This fits in with the image of a bipolar pluriformity in late medieval religious life. Between the two extremes of, on the one hand, a piety directed towards the internalisation of religious values and personal contact with the divine (introspective extreme) and, on the other hand, a popular faith accompanied by a great deal of external show (extrovert extreme) lay a broad grey area, full of rich forms of expression and offering something for everyone. One common element was the obsession with dying and death, which is hardly surprising in view of the high mortality of the period. It meant that the lists of souls to be remembered in prayer grew ever longer, and that religious poetry, songs, sermons, paintings and sculptures were full of motifs which made the reader, hearer or viewer grimly aware of the constant proximity of death.

Never before had Christian religious life shown such a wealth of Roman opulence, never before had individual involvement in religion been so great, and never before had there been such wide public support for the works of the Church. The Church had apparently succeeded more than ever before in reaching the faithful and in getting its most important religious and moral messages through to a broad spectrum of the people.

Observance and devotion

Calls for reformation inside monasticism were heard from time to time through the entire Middle Ages. Apparent weaknesses in the observance of the strict monastic rules provoked a reaction aimed at a return to basic principles. These reactionary aspirations, fed by the latent anti-clericalism of pious believers who expected regular clergy to behave virtuously, became known as observant reform (from *observare*, to comply with). This made itself felt from the second half of the fourteenth century onwards in all major orders, including the mendicants but with the notable exception of the Carthusians, who had never given up their original rigour and therefore would gain great popularity in the late Middle Ages. Observance in other orders was accompanied by a peculiar form of separateness, in which observant monasteries did not break with the order to which they belonged but differentiated themselves from the non-observant monasteries within the order. One dimension of this movement concerned the performance of the sacraments and liturgy. Both were important to the lay understanding of the Christian religion. Another was about the practical interpretation of monastic rules. Observant monasteries united in congregations which made communal agreements and carried out checks on their enforcement. An example of this is the *Congregatio Hollandiae*, a misleading name, because it comprised 75 observant monasteries of the Dominican Order in the area that extended from Brittany to Finland.

In addition to purifying monastic life, such efforts bore fruit in other ways. There existed in the late Middle Ages, even more than before, a basis for criticising monasticism in secular society, just as there was for anti-clericalism in general. Early signs of this criticism are found in satirical works – in Boccaccio's *Decameron*, for example, Franciscans are systematically portrayed as libertines and debauchees. No wonder then, that the number of entrants to some orders began to fall noticeably, and the size of gifts of money and goods to decrease drastically. Observance was able to reverse this negative trend to some extent. Orders such as the Carthusians, who mostly followed their rule without any need for correction, were richly rewarded with the result that the Carthusians flourished in the fifteenth century. However, their strict lifestyle never attracted as many brethren as the Franciscans. The years between about 1350 and 1500 saw the establishment of countless new convents and even the foundation of several new orders with long-forgotten names such as the Bridgettines, Colettines and Hieronymites. In urban areas especially, this gave rise to a richly varied monastic landscape. For example, the County of Holland had just a handful of monasteries in 1350, but within a century this number had risen to more than 200. All these new initiatives were only made possible through the financial support of prosperous laymen and secular clerics.

Some of these benefactors found that just giving donations was not enough, and they decided to live a regulated religious life themselves. Again the parallel with the twelfth and thirteenth centuries springs to mind. At that time the pressure to lead an authentically Christian life resulted in the foundation of mendicant orders and the formation of groups of laypeople who led a religious life, following a rule, but did not take a monastic vow or withdraw from life in the world – such as the Beguines and the third orders of the Franciscans and Dominicans. The Beguines were exceptionally successful in the southern Low Countries and the adjacent Rhineland but met with sustained suspicion elsewhere. In the Low Countries more than 200 beguinages and convents were founded between 1230 and 1320, each with an average of fifteen members. In 1350, there were 1,170 Beguines in Cologne living in 169 beguinages, forming 3.34 per cent of the urban population, with on average 7 inhabitants per house. The Beguines settled on the edges of the towns in small houses built in an enclosed courtyard with its own chapel or church. They

were supervised by a mistress or prioress and had rules for internal order. There were domestic quarters and larger buildings for communal activities. The Beguines supported themselves with their spinning and embroidery, often coming into conflict with the craft guilds which accused them of unfair competition.

A new devotional movement was launched in the fourteenth century by Geert Grote (1340–1384), the son of a cloth merchant from Deventer in the prince-bishopric of Utrecht who studied in Paris and then lived comfortably on the Church benefices that he held as a canon in minor orders, before repenting of his ways in about 1370. He was deeply inspired by the great Brabantine mystic John of Ruusbroec and his followers. Fiercely attacking the laxity of many clergy, he started to follow a strictly moral and ascetic way of life, and had himself ordained a deacon. His example led to the formation of a pious movement with three branches: first, the Brethren and Sisters of the Common Life (who were laypeople) and, second, an observant association of convents of Augustine canons and canonesses known as the Congregation of Windesheim. The third branch consisted of numerous convents of tertiaries (sisters of the third order of St Francis, see Chapter 6) that strongly sympathised with Grote's ideas, and adhered to observance. These three exponents positioned Grote's movement somewhere in between motivated laymen, secular clergy and observant monastics; what they shared was their craving for Modern (= 'contemporary') Devotion, the name Grote's movement soon acquired. Its success was conspicuous; the convents spread far beyond the Deventer region, in particular into the Rhineland and Westphalia.

Devotion was undoubtedly a key concept in the religious life of the late Middle Ages, but it is rather vague and difficult to explain. We have indicated earlier that an essential part of the religious revival in the centuries after 1000 consisted of a renewal of the spiritual tradition in the Christian perception of faith. The Modern Devotion continued and strengthened this tra-

PLATE 12.3 The Well of Life symbolises the Church, topped by God the Father, Mary and the Crucified Christ. The mystic winepress demonstrates how the blood of Christ's suffering is offered in the Eucharist by angels to the believers. These are represented here in the traditional hierarchy of the clergy in the forefront, the aristocracy led by the emperor, the third estate, and pilgrims. The original frame, decorated with the *Arma Christi*, the Instruments of the Passion, signifies that this painting served as the epitaph of a cleric from the northern Low Countries who died in 1511 and had himself portrayed kneeling with a chalice.

dition. It was focused on a strongly individual, inner spirituality and experience of God brought about through prayer and meditation. Seen from that perspective, Church rituals, above all the celebration of the mass, had first and foremost the task of priming an interior, rebirth-like transformation within the devout believer. An emphasis on ostentatious display, on the other hand, would only hinder spiritual worship, as would an excessive attachment to physical and material things. It was simplicity and silence, patience and penitence, austerity and restraint that were aimed for, the inner eye always turned towards the eternal light at the end of this world's vale of tears, which could only be reached by following Christ's example.

In addition to this stress on a pious, secluded life, aimed at transforming individual sinners into virtuous persons, the Modern Devotion saw an important mission in the writing, translating, copying and condensing of all kinds of devout texts into the vernacular, to help readers, both

from inside and outside the movement, in their personal prayers and meditations. The most popular texts were passages from the Bible, various Lives of Jesus that circulated at the time, *vitae* of appealing saints, prayers and edifying works, produced in simple, cheap books on a large scale. Three-quarters of all books preserved in Dutch from this period reproduced such devotional texts for individual reading.

If Geert Grote and his followers sometimes bordered on the unacceptable in the eyes of the Church authorities, other lay initiatives crossed the line and were declared heretic, just as had happened in the decades around 1200. One was the heresy of the Free Spirit, which seems to have sprouted from the Beguines (and their less numerous male counterparts, the Beghards) as a mystical branch. 'Free spirit' is a reference to the second letter of St Paul to the Corinthians: 'Where the Spirit of the Lord is, there is freedom.' It was used to support the claim that a mystical union of the human soul with the divine would completely free the former of any further will to sin. This led to suspicions of antinomianism, that is the conviction that one does not have to respect any human laws or any moral values.

Whether the Free Spirit was ever really a movement remains to be proved. One of its alleged leaders, the Beguine Marguerite Porete, author of the influential mystical tract *Mirror of Simple Souls*, died at the stake in Paris in 1310. Marguerite had also distinguished between an inferior outward Church and a superior internal-spiritual church, a theme that anticipated the ecclesiological theory of John Wyclif. Thanks to powerful protectors Wyclif had stayed out of the hands of the Inquisition; his followers, however, were accused of heresy soon after Wyclif's death. A central belief of these Lollards was the idea that within the Church there was a direct relationship between God and the faithful that had no need of the intervention of clerics, sacraments or even of saints. The Lollards laboured for an English translation of the Bible, the only source of Christian truth, and for Bible exegesis through sermons in the vernacular. This was by no means the first time that Holy Scripture had been translated into a vernacular language. In fact, there are already two examples from Late Antiquity: the Gothic Bible and the Vulgate (standard translation in Latin). In the thirteenth and fourteenth centuries, in spite of resistance from ecclesiastical authorities, these were followed by translations in French, Catalan, Castilian, Czech, High German and Low German (Dutch). However, the English-language Lollard Bible of *c*.1380 and other Christian key texts were duplicated on a scale and at a speed that would only be exceeded with the invention of printing. In this way, the Lollards clearly helped to promote literacy in England, as did the Modern Devoted in the Low Countries and the Rhineland.

As the Lollards received increasing support from members of the lower clergy and self-educated laypeople, so the movement became more radical. A virulent anti-clericalism, expressed in sharply-worded songs, began to predominate. After a revolt against the king the movement was forced underground and many Lollards met their end at the stake or on the gallows. It continued in south-eastern England until the Reformation, however, chiefly because of the continued sympathy of educated craftsmen. An interesting difference between the Modern Devotion and the Lollards was the dislike expressed by the latter for the new sort of piety that had a central role in the former.

Mysticism

Since St Paul, mysticism has always been an important current within Christendom. It can be described as a spiritual attempt to achieve a highly personal, emotional, often even ecstatic, union of the innermost soul with God in an intuitive, non-rational way through concentrated meditation. Often this attempt is described in terms of a mental journey along a difficult path, which leads in stages of increasing detachment from the transient world to the divine. From Late Antiquity on, ecclesiastical authorities had met mystics and mystical sects with sound suspicion, especially those that were active outside the closed walls of monasteries. They often accused them of disregarding the canonical teaching of the Church, even of pantheism, and of denying the grace-giving quality of sacraments and the necessities to have priests to administer them or to celebrate faith with outward ceremonies and liturgy. It was also thought that extreme forms of mystical exercise held the danger of deification, a state of mind in which the mystic felt him- (or her-)self completely united with God. The idea behind this was that, because Christ had been truly and completely human, every human being could truly become God through Christ.

As it happened, in the late Middle Ages mysticism flourished as never before. We can distinguish between a more intellectual current, directly inspired by fifth-century Christian neo-Platonism, and a non-intellectual trend, in which pure willpower, visions and an exaggerated affection for the suffering Christ were central. A group of German Dominican theologians at the end of the thirteenth and beginning of the fourteenth century, the best known of whom is Meister Eckhart (*c.*1260–1328), was typical of the first current. The second tendency had many practitioners in such lay movements as those of the Beghards and Beguines – we have already mentioned the heresy of the Free Spirit – as well as among individual female mystics who were not related to any order or movement in particular.

Meister Eckhart was a trained theologian who was also active in pastoral care and famous for his sermons in the vernacular. A key term in his works is 'ground' (*grunt* in Middle High German). It refers to the joining of God's essence with the most hidden part of the mystic's soul, which could only be reached after the outside world and all that binds the outer person and his will, desires and knowledge to it had been completely shut out, and every partition between the passive intellect and the inner soul had been breached. For Eckhart, this transcendence of the ego in a process of complete detachment from the world, of total self-denial and surrender, was the essence of the ideal imitation of Christ. Only after all the material environment created was stripped away and the individual was totally detached from everything, would the Word, which was already in the soul, became perceptible as a spark of God. This idea of a total immersion of the human soul into the divine made Eckhart's teaching controversial, because ecclesiastical authorities mistook it for pantheism. This mystical transition was an act of unknowing and amazement, because ultimately God remained unknowable, even if his presence was now felt all over. Not all of this could be concealed from the watchful eyes of ecclesiastical authorities, and at the end of his life Eckhart was tried before Inquisition tribunals at Cologne and Avignon.

Far more extreme than Meister Eckhart were female mystics who were active in the more visionary tradition of Bernard of Clairvaux. They re-transformed one well-known allegory – the mystical marriage of Christ with his Church – into a realistic personal and somatic experience. In feverish dreams they had intimate encounters either as brides of Christ or as his mother (as stand-in Marys, so to speak). In both cases, their relationship with Christ was intimate and imagined to be physical. They thought of themselves as breast-feeding the infant Jesus, giving him clean nappies or sucking the blood from his wounds at the cross, or they offered their flesh to be tortured instead of that of their beloved husband or son. The latter fantasy hits a deeper psychological level on which the extreme identification with Christ was focused on his suffering. According to the American historian Caroline Walker Bynum (1982), this was the result of a subtle manipulation of the medieval symbols for masculinity and femininity at a deeper psychological level. Because typically feminine qualities such as physical weakness and kindness were ascribed to men like Christ and St Francis in order to demonstrate how they had shown their humility by laying aside their male strength, religious women found it easy to empathise with them. Of the many extremist mystics in the later medieval period, who claimed to have been blessed with the stigmata – more than a hundred cases are known from the thirteenth to fifteenth century – by far the majority were women. One could say that this special physical and traumatic affinity with Christ made them equal to or even better than men.

The general admiration for the most remarkable of these devout women led to their recognition as saints or 'blessed' persons (a lesser category of sainthood). Their *vitae* (biographies and autobiographies) combined topoi from traditional saints' lives, especially from the eleventh and twelfth centuries, with not particularly subtle, populist descriptions of the most extreme forms of mortification and self-effacement, of ruthless penitence, of nauseating acts of self-humiliation, spiritual agony, quasi-erotic adoration, utter addiction to the Eucharist and endless prayer, all

PLATE 12.4 Episodes from the lives of hermits are shown in this rather enigmatic painting by Fra Angelico, which he named 'Tebaide', after the Egyptian city of Thebes. There, in the desert, St Pacome (296–346) founded the first Christian monastery with a rule. Angelico found his inspiration in anthologies of the lives of saints from the fourth to the tenth century, and in the *Golden Legend* by James of Voragine. Miracles performed by hermits and their encounters with devils are shown in a strange composition, possibly as a motivation for the new wave of eremitism at the time of the painting, around 1420.

of which, according to Richard Kieckhefer (1989), not only disturbed and shocked their readers, but were also intended to achieve that very effect. At the same time it is not always easy to determine the veracity of these 'lives', because most were (re)constructed and put on paper by their (male) confessors. For instance, in order to reconstruct the life and religious identity of Catherine of Siena (*c.*1347–1380) close to 400 letters, written or dictated by herself, and a visionary tract in her name have to be mixed with the detailed **hagiography**, written shortly after she died by her confessor, the leading Dominican Raymond of Capua. It becomes clear from these quite different testimonies that Catherine, who was already recognised as a saint during her lifetime, was a religious devout with two faces: besides being a renowned mystic, she was also active in Italian politics. Around 1375, when high tension between the governors of the Papal States and the leading Tuscan towns, Florence and Siena, ended in open warfare, Catherine became a valuable figurehead of the pro-papal/pro-Guelph side in the conflict. But, in the end, Catherine's personal political agenda was determined by her will to reconcile both parties in order to put them back together into spiritually more rewarding enterprises, such as a new crusade to the Holy

Land and the long-awaited return of the pope – whom she called *babbo* ('daddy') in her letters – to Rome.

The ordinary believers

The introverted and often fervent religious feelings just described were the realm of a small minority of highly motivated believers, both clerical and lay. Most believers gave expression to their faith through externals that were carefully orchestrated and controlled by the Church and clergy. This interaction can be described by the use of a well-known analysis model from communications theory, in which the two-way traffic between sender and receiver is central. The sender (the Church) had to make use of feedback procedures to find out whether its message (the faith) had reached the receiver (the believer) properly, and eventually to respond to popular reactions. Should this not be the case, then the sender had to correct itself, either by adapting the form in which the message was shaped or by improving the channels of communication through which the message was transmitted. This approach not only allows greater attention to be given to what the Church was thinking and wanting officially, but also and especially to the translation switch it had to make in order to instil the convictions and moral behaviour it desired, as well as to the demand made by the faithful and to the forms in which the faithful eventually made manifest their beliefs, their experience of the faith.

To reach the people the Church had above all to keep the message simple. Only a few of the faithful were able to read even the Bible in its entirety; most were only acquainted with selected parts of it through readings during mass or sermons. While we should remember that mass was said entirely in Latin, the practice of reciting common prayers was rather mixed: the vernacular was used next to Latin. The Christian message therefore had to be as succinct and simple as possible. It boiled down to five components:

1. Knowledge of the creed (from *credo* meaning 'I believe'), a short statement of the essential articles of the faith. The most usual creeds were those established at the Council of Nicaea in 325 and the Fourth Lateran Council in 1215. Every believer was required to be able to say the creed before confession and **communion**.
2. Knowledge of the most important prayers: the Lord's Prayer and Hail Mary were already standard prayers in the late Middle Ages. Well-to-do believers had special prayer books or Books of Hours made for their own use. Examples from the thirteenth century are still in existence, some of them illustrated with beautiful miniatures; in the fourteenth and fifteenth centuries, prayer books were extremely popular.
3. Knowledge of the most important moral precepts of Christianity – the Ten Commandments from the Old Testament and the three theological virtues (faith, hope and charity) from the New, with the four cardinal virtues from ancient philosophy (prudence, justice, fortitude and temperance) making up the seven capital virtues which were mirrored by the seven cardinal or deadly sins.

4. Some knowledge of the seven grace-giving sacraments (see Chapter 2).
5. Some knowledge of eschatology, the complex ideas on life after death. Central to this was the presentation of Purgatory, the temporary residence of the souls of Christians who had not been purged of their sins on earth. People were quite convinced that the length of the unpleasant stay in Purgatory could be shortened by indulgences (see Box 12.1), prayer, the practice of the seven works of charity or love (feeding the hungry, caring for the sick, etc.) and the works of spiritual comfort (such as granting forgiveness), of which there were also seven.

PLATE 12.5 Purgatory: angels rescue the souls of women who have fulfilled their penance and will be elevated to heaven. Note the head with a prelate's mitre and a couple of shaved monks' heads among those having to continue their penance. Miniature in the *Très riches heures du duc de Berry* (the illuminated Book of Hours), early fifteenth century.

Because the parish clergy were the people most clearly suited to deliver this message, the Fourth Lateran Council of 1215 decided upon a package of measures to raise their level of knowledge and their moral standards. In addition, the bishops were urged to instruct the clerics under their supervision by teaching and preaching. The effects of these measures were so promising that some historians speak of a pastoral revolution.

Later on, the first written instructions for spiritual care appeared, and by the end of the Middle Ages substantial numbers of parish clergy were likely to have been to university. At the same time bishops took greater pains with their periodical visitations to the parish clerics, partly to steal a march on anti-clerical voices. Apart from the usual complaints about poor education, suspect morality and simony, such criticism was directed chiefly towards a fault that resulted from the papal policy on benefices – pluralism (stacking up benefices) and the absenteeism inherent to it. This contemporary objection is shared by modern Church historians, who saw this policy as 'the rock upon which late-medieval attempts at church-wide reform were shipwrecked' (Oakley 2003).

From the thirteenth century onward, parish clergy had always been helped in carrying out their duties by preachers from the mendicant orders, a situation which did not always please them as shared tasks meant shared incomes. Top preachers, such as Bernardino of Siena of the Franciscan Order and the Dominicans Vincent Ferrer (c.1350–1419) and Girolamo Savonarola (d. 1498), for example, attracted enormous audiences for their sermons, or even weeks of sermons, especially during Lent, the period of fasting preceding Easter, when they might produce a lengthy sermon with a different theme every day for forty days. Ferrer, a Spaniard, was nicknamed 'the angel of the Last Judgement' because he constantly threatened his hearers with hell and damnation. It was not all innocent, however. With his inflammatory sermons, Ferrer must take a considerable share of the blame for the terrible persecution of Spanish Jews in 1391.

Preachers had a number of resources to help them when they were preparing their sermons. These included the first catechisms, which appeared after the Fourth Lateran Council; collections of summarised saints' lives, such as the *Legenda Aurea* ('Golden Legend'), compiled around 1265 by the Genoese Dominican, James of Voragine; various sets of *exempla* (examples, i.e. anecdotes and short tales with a moral message), and the *A, B, C des simples gens* (the 'ABC of Ordinary People') by John Gerson, which became very popular in the fifteenth century. The good examples were aimed primarily at the eradication of false beliefs and the persuasion of relief not only in the afterlife but also against all kinds of hazards in everyday life. Strong emphasis was laid on the sacrament of confession and penance; the reluctant were threatened with the most horrible torments. The larger churches supplied plenty of visual support in the form of paintings, sculptures, carvings and stained-glass windows, while liturgy was further adapted to satisfy both the spiritual sensibilities of the passionate believers and the theatrical expectations of the masses. Liturgical plays, representing biblical scenes, and stages in or before churches were the origins of a new kind of theatre which developed independently of the ancient tradition. The invention of printing made it possible for the first time to spread devotional and moralising texts and prints among the ordinary faithful on a large scale.

Of course, we cannot know exactly what was retained from the message spread through sermons and other channels. We have indicated in chapters 2 and 6 the survival into the Middle Ages of many superstitions which often had their roots in pre-Christian practices. Be that as it may, the religious life of the masses, with the traditional worship of saints at its centre, creates a rich, vital impression. Most notable was its clear move towards ever more emotion, to what Miri Rubin (2009) has termed 'the emergence of a European style of emotive devotion'.

Popular devotion

Central in this religious emotionality stood the devotion to Christ and the Virgin Mary that had grown up during the eleventh century and gained in popularity ever since. It had two clear thematic focal points: one the motherhood of Mary, the other the suffering and painful death of Christ. The deep interest in the Holy Virgin's motherhood was expressed in a preference for pictures and prayers which stressed the tender relationship between a mother and her son, and the broken heart of a mother who witnesses her child suffer and die. Most telling in this respect were paintings and sculptures of Jesus on his mother's lap, both as an infant and after his descent from the cross (so-called *pietàs*). Also very popular were other scenes from Jesus' infancy (Jesus in the manger and Jesus cradled in his mother's arms). Christ's suffering was commemorated in several new Church festivals – among them *Corpus Christi* (the feast of the body of Christ), the day of the Sacred Heart and the day of the Holy Cross. These were supported by pictures of the man of sorrows – images of the naked body of Christ with the wounds of the passion – and of exuberant crucifixion scenes on altar pieces and life-sized calvaries. Attentive prayer to the suffering Christ was stimulated by so-called *Andachtsbilder* (images that focus attention), rather crude vulgarisations of the 'man of sorrows', some with all the instruments of torture neatly depicted, others reduced to the five bleeding wounds of the crucified Jesus. All were intended to stir up empathy and inner reflection on the meaning of the Saviour's horrifying death. Pictures of this kind are at the end of a long iconographical evolution in the imaging of the Son of God, which runs from depicting Christ as the divine and majestic ruler of heaven to bringing him down to a completely helpless and deserted human wreck.

As before, devotion to saints, Christ and his holy mother was accompanied by the veneration of their relics. Rich people and wealthy religious institutions spent large amounts of silver and gold to expand and display their relic collections. At the top stood the French king Louis IX – Saint Louis – who in 1239 paid the incredible sum of 135,000 pounds to the Latin emperor of Constantinople, Baldwin II, for the purchase of about 30 relics from the Passion, with the Crown of Thorns as first prize. To have a worthy show-case for this religious treasure, the king spent another 40,000 pounds building a spectacular two-storey chapel on the premises of the royal palace on the Île de la Cité in the heart of Paris: the Sainte Chapelle (Holy Chapel). Louis' acquisition was a real assault on the market for this type of highly prized relic, because, as one can imagine, there were few physical leftovers of Christ and the Holy Virgin to be found on earth, although, quite remarkably, all that could possibly have been left had already been found: spilled drops of Mary's milk, the spilled blood of Jesus (to be admired in Bruges and even nowadays said to become fluid every Friday), his toenail clippings, imprints of his face and the Holy Prepuce, which was, of course, removed at the circumcision of the infant Jesus and which up to eighteen churches all over Europe claimed to have in their possession.

In addition to these bodily remains – with their inherent, for many believers unthinkable, problems of decay and putrefaction – there were so-called contact relics, objects that had been touched by Jesus and Mary. Most famous are the Holy Crucifix – or splinters of it, of which literally hundreds of specimens can be found in European reliquaries – and the Crown of Thorns just mentioned. But there were also less obvious objects. The Scala Santa in the Lateran Palace at Rome had originally been the stairs that Jesus had to climb to meet his judge, Pontius Pilate, in Jerusalem and the Casa Santa, the house in which the Holy Virgin had been born, which, almost incredible to believe, was – and still is – preserved in the Adriatic town of Loreto. In the Holy Land devout, and credulous, pilgrims could buy authentic footprints of Jesus, Mary, Joseph and the apostles. Objects like these saw their value (and attraction to crowds of pilgrims) rise when they generated miracles, something which also, and quite typically, occurred with another, but not perishable, central object of the Passion: the consecrated host, a holy replica of the bread Jesus broke at his Last Supper, while speaking the words 'this is my body'. The sophisticated theological handling of this mysterious transformation (see Chapter 8) did not prevent believers from conceiving of a literally physical presence of the body of Christ in the consecrated host. And when some hosts were seen to start bleeding, or to come unharmed out of blazing fires, this added to the belief in miracles and gave rise to an entirely new type of devotion, next to more traditional ones that were based on the adoration of statues of Jesus or Mary (or Mary with Jesus) which were supposed to be miracle working.

In any case, miracles remained important in popular belief throughout the later medieval period. However, according to specialists, several shifts in comparison with the earlier situation can be detected. For one, in the later Middle Ages there were more healing miracles as compared with the earlier Middle Ages, when there were more miracles of vengeance (God or a saint punishes the enemy of the person who prayed to them).

After Christ and his mother, other saints could count on their part of popular devotion: Mary's popularity led to the veneration of other impeccable virgins, who were preferably martyrs on top of that, such as the saints Catherine, Barbara, Lucia and Ursula and the 11,000 virgins from Cologne. More generally one can speak of a feminisation of holiness in the later Middle Ages that paralleled the increasing role of women in late medieval spirituality, mysticism and communal conventual life. Of the numerous local and regional saints who until the thirteenth century were acclaimed as saints by the faithful themselves or by the parish clergy, an increasing number were of the female sex and also of non-noble, at times even lowly, origins. The popes clamped down on the unrestrained growth of the whole business by making canonisation, preceded by a critical examination with a real 'devil's advocate', their prerogative, a step which effectively curbed the further proliferation of saints.

Not surprisingly, the late medieval period saw a new boost in pilgrimage. In addition to its devotional and penitential aims, pilgrimage could now also have a penitentiary purpose – the pilgrimage as a punishment imposed by an ecclesiastical or secular court of justice. By the late Middle Ages the pilgrimage also began to show holiday-like symptoms. Top destinations were obviously Jerusalem, Rome and Santiago de

BOX 12.1 INDULGENCES AND THE INDULGENCE TRADE

Among the odder expressions of Catholic belief is the granting of indulgences, defined in canon law as 'the remission of temporal punishment for sin, in response to certain prayers or good works'. So, strictly speaking, the indulgence (Latin, *indulgentia*) relates to the penitence, or that part of the Christian sacrament of confession which imposed a penalty on the sinner, and not to the part in which he had confessed his sins. That part was dealt with in the absolution ('remission [of guilt]') granted by the confessor. The granting of an indulgence has always been the exclusive right of popes, who saw themselves as the keepers of the so-called Treasury of Merit. This treasury can be seen as if it were a huge amount of credit in some heavenly account, earned by Christ and the saints, from which ordinary believers, under special circumstances were allowed to make a small withdrawal.

Popes Alexander II in 1063 and Urban II in 1095 first defined these circumstances as taking up arms against the Muslims in defence of the Holy Sepulchre. This was assigned the value of a 'plenary' indulgence, that is, a general remission of all temporal punishment for all sins. Later on, indulgences became more institutionalised: this happened with the crusade indulgence, for example, at the Fourth Lateran Council in 1215. In time, the number of occasions at which indulgences could be earned was expanded, first to include certain forms of church attendance, the accomplishment of a pilgrimage, the giving of alms or financial aid to build a new church, and later also intense and frequent prayer. After a while, and despite official Church opposition, the idea spread among the faithful that the bereaved could earn indulgences for their deceased relatives by remembering them frequently and at length in their prayers.

In sermons, the abstract idea of indulgence as a remittance or a mitigation of penitence soon came to be presented as a reduction of the time spent by sinners in Purgatory, the place where the souls of the departed suffer for a time until they are purged of their sins. Inflation inevitably set in, and the number of purgatory-free days soon reached astronomical levels. This illustrates how the system of indulgences gradually became commercialised. As early as the twelfth century, itinerant indulgence-preachers, commonly called pardoners, licensed by the pope, would preach a sermon and then hand out letters of indulgence in exchange for generous donations to all sorts of vague good works; the indulgence stated exactly how much remission the bearer could count on. With the advent of printing came the sale of indulgence prints, devout *Andachtsbilder* ('pictures to be watched with attention'), especially of the Passion of Christ, and produced in large numbers, bearing a simple prayer and noting an indulgence.

From early on there was opposition to such developments in the indulgence system, including from the new mendicant orders which had to make a living from preaching and alms – the Dominican Albertus Magnus, for example, railed against every form of trade in indulgences. In the run-up to the Reformation, such criticisms reached storm force and indulgences became one of the primary targets of the original reformers, above all because they were such a familiar phenomenon to every believer. The pardoners ran an increasing risk of being attacked, especially when reformation of the Catholic Church was under discussion, as it was during the *Bauernkrieg* in Germany in 1525.

Sources: *Lexicon für Theologie und Kirche, Band I* (Freiburg: Herder, 1993), s.v. 'Ablass', 'Ablassbilder' and 'Ablassprediger'; Robert W. Shaffern, *The Penitents' Treasury: Indulgences in Latin Christendom, 1175–1375* (Scranton PA/London: University of Scranton Press, 2007).

Compostela. Now they were joined by others: Rocamadour in the Dordogne, Canterbury, Mont-Saint-Michel and Wilsnack in Brandenburg, the hotspot for the new type of host miracles just mentioned.

This popular religious enthusiasm fostered the large increase of local social welfare institutions that were often closely connected to religious confraternities. The miraculous images of some saints, most generally Mary, became centres for such associations which exploited veneration and spent the proceeds on charitable works. Good examples are the Compagnia della Madonna di Orsanmichele in Florence and the Illustrious Confraternity of Our Beloved Lady in 's-Hertogenbosch in the duchy of Brabant (of which the painter Hieronymus Bosch was an esteemed member). Large cities like Florence and Ghent had dozens of such confraternities, but they were also to be found in smaller towns and even in villages. Sometimes they were primarily connected to the cult of a saint, sometimes associated with a craft guild or a particular age-group or social class. The richest of them had their own meeting house and chapel adorned with splendid altarpieces by famous artists. The simple ones just had an altar in a side aisle of a church. Their activities and numbers of members varied greatly. There were special confraternities of penitents who held collective flagellation sessions as well as simple prayer and choral societies. The

most common activities included funerals and memorial services for deceased members, sometimes financial support for widows and orphans and participation in local processions at which religious or morality plays were enacted – another new medium through which the Christian message could be relayed in a simplified form to a broad public.

However, just like in the centuries before, popular religious enthusiasm had its downsides as well, and in this respect the late Middle Ages must also be seen as a period in which religious

PLATE 12.6 A view of hell, from the scenes of the Last Judgement, fresco painted on the vaults of the imposing cathedral of Orvieto (Italy) by the Tuscan painter Luca Signorelli, *c.* 1500.

tendencies that had taken shape centuries before almost brimmed over in more extreme forms of expression. Most innocent were what the art historian Michael Camille has called the image explosion, and Caroline Walker Bynum (2011) the overbalancing of devotion on to material objects: reliquaries, paintings, sculptures, amulets, badges, books of prayer – all of them quite well known from Antiquity on, but now present in a superabundance never seen, and despite warnings of ecclesiastical authorities and protests by reformatory movements. Even more questionable was the increased belief in appearances of supernatural beings, especially when these were not sightings of Jesus, Mary or angels, but devils. The late Middle Ages saw the dawn of the witches' Sabbath. This was not just a thing of poor wretches. The first group of persons known from medieval sources to have been tried for witchcraft was led by a noble lady called Alice Kyteler of Kilkenny in Ireland. In 1324, she was accused of organising nightly gatherings, of repudiating Christ and his Church, of making horrifying potions, and of fornicating with the devil who sometimes took the shape of a black African (*Ethiops*). Alice herself luckily escaped but one of her maidservants was burned at the stake. The same fate was shared by Jews who were accused of the wilful desecration of hosts, poisoning of fountains or the butchering of Christian boys, tales that abounded in some regions of Europe in the fifteenth and sixteenth centuries and were often connected to host miracles.

Facing this emotional overdrive (and its negative excrescence), the Church acted with ambivalence – sometimes it poured oil on the flames of popular rage, but on many other occasions it was merely hesitant. On the one hand, ecclesiastical authorities, from high to low, could and would not deny the possibility of miracles and godly intervention. On the other hand, if ordinary believers could generate them and in that way have direct contact with the saintly and the divine, what role was left for clergy and Church? Willingly or not, masters of theology allowed narrow-minded pietism to enter scholarly discourse, while bishops and popes lent support to show trials against heretics or to the cult of saints, relics or miracles that had first won the hearts of common believers.

Ironically, the sentimental superstitions of the masses were grist to the mill of all kinds of dissenters and reformists, such as the Cathars and Waldensians of the twelfth and thirteenth centuries or the Lollards and Hussites of the fifteenth. One of their main objections against popular religious practice was the veneration of supposedly 'holy' material objects. The sixteenth-century reformers directed their criticism in general towards the outward display and superficial nature of this accumulative devotion, the most important aim of which seemed to be to gain as much quantifiable credit as possible with God and the saints, while the inner state of the believer scarcely seemed to matter. On the other hand, the Catholic Church was more successful in taking its message directly to the ordinary faithful in the late Middle Ages than previously. Through the variety of its institutions and rituals the Church offered the faithful a solid framework and support which gave meaning to their existence and provided them with mental and material succour in time of need. Had these ordinary believers not been so mobilised or their awareness so kindled, and without the critical approach to various aspects of Catholic life which was indeed the result, Luther, Zwingli and Calvin would never have found ground where their ideas could take root.

Points to remember

■ The years around 1300 saw the last, vain, attempt of the popes to be accepted as the undisputed leaders of Christendom. This gave rise to a polemic on the relationship between spiritual and temporal power, which paved the way for the incorporation of the Church and ecclesiastical matters into the state.

- The prolonged stay of the popes at Avignon (1309–1377) led to a successful extension and sophistication of the papal bureaucracy, which reinforced the pope's hold on the clergy.

- During the period of the Great Schism (1378–1417) there were two popes, one in Rome and one in Avignon. This situation gave rise to the further elaboration of conciliarist thought.

- *Imitatio Christi* remained the dominant ideal for religious reform movements such as Modern Devotion, while the penchant for a spiritual implementation of religious belief reinforced mysticism, among both clergy and laypeople.

- The religious perception of ordinary believers was characterised by emotionality and materiality.

- Thanks to a successful pastoral revolution lay believers in the later Middle Ages had a far better idea of the dogmatic and moral contents of the Christian religion than laypeople had had in the period before.

Suggestions for further reading

Bynum, Caroline Walker (2011), *Christian Materiality: An Essay on Religion in Late Medieval Europe* (New York: Zone Books). The eminent specialist of Christian spirituality and devotion describes miracles and discusses the problems they presented for both Church authorities and the ordinary faithful. Pointing to the proliferation of religious art, she argues that it called attention to its materiality in sophisticated ways that explain both the animation of images and the hostility to them on the part of iconoclasts.

Duffy, Eamon (2006), *Marking the Hours: English People and their Prayers, 1240–1570* (New Haven CT: Yale University Press). Books of Hours were unquestionably the most intimate and most widely used books of the later Middle Ages. They were used for private, domestic devotions, and in them people commonly left traces of their lives. Women feature very prominently among the identifiable owners and users. Duffy places these volumes in the context of religious and social change, and above all the Reformation.

Ozment, Steven (1980), *The Age of Reform, 1250–1550: An Intellectual and Religious History of Late Medieval and Reformation Europe* (New Haven: Yale University Press). This book grounds the great Protestant reformers firmly in the tradition of medieval scholastic, mystic, and ecclesio-political thought.

Tierney, Brian (1998), *Foundations of the Conciliar Theory: The Contribution of the Medieval Canonists from Gratian to the Great Schism* (Leiden: Brill) (orig. CUP, 1955). An account of canonistic theories of Church government that contributed to the growth of conciliar theory, as formulated before the Great Schism (1378). It is concerned particularly with the juristic development of fundamental conciliar doctrine, the assertion that the universal Church was superior to the Church of Rome, and of the denial of supreme papal authority.

Vauchez, André (1993), *The Laity in the Middle Ages: Religious Beliefs and Devotional Practices* (Notre Dame IN: University of Notre Dame Press) (orig. French, 1987). Based on various actual cases, the author demonstrates the tension between the clerical culture and that of the receivers of the message who had become increasingly self-conscious, especially laywomen.

Epilogue

As we saw in the introductory chapter it is difficult to draw a sharp line between 'Middle Ages' and 'early modern times'. No general 'historical' switch took place round any of the well-known symbolic dates (1453, 1492, 1498, 1517, let alone 1500). Each one of those dates deals with one particular aspect of the reality of the time (Ottoman expansion, the journeys of discovery and colonisation, the Reformation). Moreover, at least until the Industrial and the French Revolutions, the basic structures of the Middle Ages remained intact: a mainly agrarian class society, built on a locally particularistic foundation and monarchical concentration. Rather than engage in a pointless controversy about the demarcation of an era, we have chosen, as we did with the transition from Late Antiquity, to indicate the perspective of the historian who either believes he can detect the new very early on or continues to see the old for a long time. In reality, of course, both tendencies existed side by side in a relationship of creative tension.

Fernand Braudel (1902–1985), the renowned French historian, introduced the concept of the 'long sixteenth century', which he placed between 1450 and 1650. It was a time of growth, expansion and innovation in practically all of Europe. This view is supported by demographic and economic indicators: despite the sporadic outbursts of plague epidemics, their effect was less disastrous than between 1347 and 1440, and the population of Europe grew again. If the recurring epidemics had caused it to drop from 75 million to 50 million in about 1450, then by 1500 it had recovered to a total that – depending on the estimate and whether or not Russia and the Balkans are included – lay somewhere between 61 and 82 million, rising to between 78 and 106 million by 1600 – more than ever before, but nothing compared with Ming China, whose total population increased from an estimated 85 million in 1393 to an estimated 231 million in 1600. People had learnt to cope with contagious disease and could keep it under better control. This population growth was made possible primarily through the further introduction of intensive methods of agriculture, which had previously only been applied in the most advanced areas. Substantial growth in shipping capacity also facilitated the regular export of large quantities of grain to densely populated regions: 67,000 hectolitres were exported from Danzig/Gdansk to the West in 1470, growing to 1.2 million in 1562. The total volume of grain exported from all ports in Prussia between 1562 and 1569 is estimated at an average of 2.18 million hectolitres per year, sufficient to cover the demand for bread for 650,000 people.

A generalisation such as typifying the 'long sixteenth century' as a growth phase of course ignores the very considerable regional differences. The Balkans and Hungary suffered terribly under the Ottoman wars of conquest. After 1494 there was a grave crisis in Italy as the great powers continued to wage their wars there during half a century. It was one of the causes of the shift of economic leadership – Italy had been the undisputed leader since the growth phase beginning in the tenth century – to the North Sea area, to Antwerp in particular. Should one share Braudel's view of the unity of the period between 1450 and 1650, the economic perspective is crucial. We shall summarise here some of the trends discernible in the fifteenth century and first half of the sixteenth which resulted directly from developments in the late Middle Ages.

Acceleration

From the perspective of the Middle Ages the innovations of the late fifteenth and the sixteenth century can be better described as progressive accelerations than as radical breaks. This is even true of the invention of printing. From the thirteenth century, government, trade, the Church, education and literature made increasing use of the written word. At the same time there was a swing towards the use of vernacular languages for all these purposes, so that much larger segments of the population took part in the culture of writing. Parchment soon became a scarce item, reserved for luxury books. Cheaper paper made the continued growth of literacy possible. In the Low Countries and the Rhineland, the religious reform movement of the Modern Devotion, which rapidly won large numbers of followers in the last decades of the fourteenth century, is a typical example. Among its aims was the dissemination of pious literature in the Dutch language

in the form of cheap pamphlets which could be read by everyone 'in a corner', as Geert Grote expressed it.

Growing demand for the written word explains the search for methods to reproduce it more quickly and on a larger scale. When Gutenberg printed his first Bible in Mainz around 1455, he set in motion a process that would quickly be imitated and improved. There is no doubt that printing was a considerable help in spreading new political, religious and scientific ideas. Yet it was not technology that was initially responsible for this media revolution, but the strongly increasing demand for devotional literature for quiet personal reading that met the need for a more individual perception of religion. The German historian Uwe Neddermeyer has calculated that in the German Empire the production of handwritten books increased by roughly 25 per cent per decade between 1370 and 1470, from 20,000 annually in 1370 to 200,000 by 1460. No wonder that efforts were made to find more efficient methods of reproduction. Two million books were printed in the decade around 1500.

Overseas colonisation got into its stride around the Mediterranean, Black, Baltic and Irish seas from the twelfth century. European travellers started searching for overland routes to the Far East from the mid-thirteenth century, and soon afterwards for sea routes as well. The voyages of discovery along the coast of Africa and later across the oceans lie in the continuation of the dynamic that had been growing for centuries, although it must be recognised that Columbus and Vasco da Gama gave an impetus to qualitative leaps. For several years, however, these discoveries had only marginal effects on the European economy. The economic growth of the sixteenth and seventeenth centuries did not imply a breakthrough to a totally different system, only a very advanced state of pre-industrial society. Nor should it be assumed that at this time Europe had achieved a higher level of economic, cultural and political development than China, Japan or the princely states of India. Until industrialisation, western

Europe was no more than one of the world's more highly developed agricultural societies, but it was the one that took more initiatives towards other continents; whether this is a sign of progress or relative failure is still a matter of debate.

The European voyages of discovery certainly changed the view of the world, in both senses, very quickly. Geographical insights, as visualised in maps, grew on the basis of the wider knowledge and experience of the seafarers. The atlases published in Antwerp by Abraham Ortelius in 1570 and Gerard Mercator between 1585 and 1589 took many of their new facts and insights from the descriptions of coasts that had been collected gradually and handed on piecemeal by generations of sailors whose maps have been preserved since the thirteenth century. In this way people's view of their planet grew in a few generations into the globe that we know today.

Chapter 8 described how fourteenth- and fifteenth-century Italian humanists refined their knowledge of ancient sources, brought the study of classical languages and literature to a higher level and, above all, how they forged a new educational concept from them. The Latin school was the dominant pedagogic model until the 1960s, propagating its own methods as fundamentally innovative. Both Counter-Reformation schools, notably those run by the Jesuits, and the grammar schools and high schools in Protestant countries were powerful forces in spreading this image of a fundamental Renaissance. But both systems make the mistake of overestimating themselves. There was interest in and admiration for the culture of Antiquity throughout the Middle Ages. Although the humanists examined more and older manuscripts of ancient and early Christian texts and became more critical in their search for sources, it was not until the nineteenth century that scientific philology actually reached a level that still meets current standards. That being said, without the assiduous copying of diligent medieval monks, the continuous flow of translations from Greek and Arabic and the intellectual curiosity of Franciscans and Dominicans, a substantial part of the writings of Antiquity would never have been preserved for us.

Medieval methods and concepts were still followed at the universities. Medical education was based on the ancient Greeks' teachings of the four body fluids until the seventeenth century, and was far removed from the sickbed, while theology focused on the authority of the teachers of Late Antiquity. In 1543 the founder of modern anatomy, Andreas Vesalius of Brussels, published a huge and richly illustrated empirical study of human anatomy, pointing out the mistakes in Galen's second-century theory. He dissected bodies in front of his students, confronting them with inconsistencies between these empirical observations and Galen's outdated ideas. He met with so much opposition from supporters of traditional teachings that he had to resign from the universities of Louvain, Padua and Pisa where he taught consecutively. Innovative as Vesalius's findings were, he followed in a surgical tradition that had been active at the universities of Paris and Montpellier until about 1300.

In 1920 no less a scholar than Max Weber advanced the proposition that commercial capitalism's rational pursuit of profit could only truly flourish in those lands where the Protestant ethic of austerity held sway. By this he meant that commercial capitalism could not have existed in the Middle Ages. Nevertheless, it must be remembered here too that after a more thorough study of medieval commercial and other sources specialists are in agreement that merchants and entrepreneurs in Italian, southern French, Catalan and Flemish cities in particular consistently displayed a capitalist mentality from the twelfth century onwards: they made rationalised efforts to make as much profit as possible, which was then reinvested in the business to make it grow. Other considerations, religious or ethical, for example, were subordinated to their pursuit of profit. Forms of vertical integration and of partnerships based on shareholdings were seen in growing numbers from the thirteenth century, particularly in Italy. Here, too, it must be stressed that the great sixteenth-century capitalist firms, such as the Fuggers and Welsers of Augsburg, were larger than their medieval predecessors, but essentially no different.

Just like book production, colonisation, cartography, surgery and commercial capitalism, the Reformation was not a fundamentally new phenomenon. In many respects – his political and social principles, for example – Luther was more conservative than the so-called Cathar heretics, the Franciscan spirituals or John Wyclif. Criticism of the clergy echoed through the works of John of Leeuwen, the 'good cook' of the priory of Groenendaal in the Sonian Forest just south of Brussels between 1355 and 1370, no less sharply than in those of Erasmus. The Modern Devoteds' emphasis on simplicity, austerity and sincere personal devotion based on readings in the vernacular joined a long line of reformers in a call for Church reformation that had been made at regular intervals since the tenth century. Some were given their place within the Church, sometimes after difficult negotiations, concessions and secessions, such as Francis of Assisi and his followers. Others, especially those who exposed the socio-political order, such as the Cathars, Lollards and Hussites, and the Lutherans and Anabaptists in the sixteenth century, were condemned as heretics and burned without mercy.

The criticisms levelled by the early sixteenth-century reformers closely resembled those made by the critics of previous centuries. They spoke out against the love of luxury and the worldly conduct of the clergy, against the purely formal character of Church ritual; they pleaded for the Bible and private reading matter in the vernacular, and for the role of the individual conscience, and translations of the complete Bible were made in several languages from the thirteenth century. The great differences between the situation in the first half of the sixteenth century and in the earlier movements for reform lay in the combination of a Church lacking moral authority and incapable of incorporating criticism positively, the strong interrelation between the authority of the state and the hierarchy of the Church, and the enormous spread of reformist thinking made possible by the printing press. The effects of the sixteenth-century Reformation were of course more lasting than those of the earlier reform movements: these, however, had created the breeding ground.

Martin Luther, as an Augustinian friar and theology professor at the University of Wittenberg in Saxony, was deeply embedded in medieval, particularly Augustinian theology. He was also a gifted preacher and a sharp polemic writer, of whose works more than half a million copies had been disseminated in the years 1516 to 1521 in the form of hundreds of pamphlets and also substantial books. He enjoyed the protection of Duke Frederick the Wise, elector of Saxony. Much of his criticism against the Church had already been expressed by numerous reformers since the thirteenth century, and in 1417 the German participants in the Council of Constance had agreed upon an extensive list of abuses. They mainly concerned papal interference in the appointments of prelates in the Empire, in their jurisdiction and in financial matters. In France, England and elsewhere, similar complaints had led to royal legislation and concordats with the papacy, but the multi-layered political structure of the Empire and the emperor's unique position vis-à-vis the pope had prevented any action. In the Imperial Diet held at Worms in 1521, Emperor Charles V felt that, after Luther's excommunication by Pope Leo X, he as 'defender and protector of the Catholic faith' had no choice but to extend his imperial ban on Luther and to order the complete destruction and burning of all his works. The authorities were evidently unaware of how widely these works had already been disseminated and of the enormous public interest in reformist thought. Indeed, at the same Diet of Worms, 102 articles of 'Complaints of the German Nation against the Holy See' were discussed in line with the list of 1417; the issue returned to the agenda of several assemblies, but the violence against Church property during the Peasants' War impeded a resolution. The emperor urged successive popes to convene a general council, but they had reason enough to view any reformation of the Church 'in head and members' with the greatest suspicion; moreover, they were far too much involved in the rivalries between the west European monarchies to help with solving a problem which they saw primarily as a problem in the Empire. There matters evolved in practice: at the Diet of Speyer in 1529, the evangelically minded estates declared that a majority decision could not be binding on 'matters concerning the honour of God and our spiritual welfare and salvation'. This 'protest' led by the elector of Saxony and the landgrave of Hesse and supported by scores of autonomous towns, mainly in south Germany, was the impulse for the formation of a political alliance to protect reformist beliefs. The Empire's complex political structure had hindered reforms from being implemented for more than a century, but it also enabled the breakthrough of Protestantism.

Finally, 'early modern' times are often associated with the age of the 'modern state'. Even when a precise description of this term is adhered to, in the sense of a centralised government organisation which shows itself to be an effective supreme power in its own territory, early examples can be seen – in England from the twelfth century – next to late developers, in particular Castile and Poland in the seventeenth and eighteenth centuries. Here, too, we must emphasise the differences were those of degree and not of fundamental importance, and there are considerable variations between the regions in every period. Expansion did indeed take place in the prominent monarchies of the West from the twelfth century onwards, in a development which was not always direct but was continuous in the long term.

The territories of France, England, the Spanish kingdoms, the principalities of the Low Countries and the Italian regional states expanded and integrated steadily, and their resources grew more than proportionally. Their destructive power far exceeded that of lesser princes, local lords or towns, who were thus fatally deprived of their power. The autonomy of local bodies and their political voice in the form of parliaments and state assemblies suffered. This again was a process that was set in motion in the central Middle Ages, sometimes accelerating, sometimes encountering setbacks. The so-called medieval particularist state model, based on the autonomous rights of local communities and regions, existed until the end of the eighteenth century in some of Europe's most progressive states – the Dutch Republic, northern Italy and Switzerland. Monarchical states became larger and stronger as a result of constant and continual fighting between each other, especially if they were in a position to draw off commercial profits, such as England. The threat of the Ottoman Empire was ever present, especially for the Habsburgs.

The medieval roots of modern culture

In conclusion, we would like to examine which characteristics of our own culture can be traced back directly to medieval origins. Many fundamental characteristics of what Europe is today evolved out of developments occurring during the Middle Ages.

Europe is characterised by its cultural diversity: the multiplicity of peoples, languages and customs form the basis of a consciousness that in certain periods has been fanned into an aggressive nationalism. During the early Middle Ages linguistic areas were consolidated as the result of migration and acculturation. This diversity now forms a marked contrast with continents where, although there is a great variety of cultures, a common language and a set of common values provide an integrating framework. Such a culture was provided in China by the Empire, in Islamic regions by religion and law in the Arabic language. This unifying cultural pattern was completely absent in Europe. The Catholic Church provided something of the sort, and Latin – the language of the Church – also operated as a universal language for government until the thirteenth century, functioning in Europe rather as Mandarin did in China. In diplomacy and scholarship Latin even remained the common language much longer. But the Church, just like the emperors, failed in its ambition to become the supreme universal power. Political fragmentation formed a barrier to cultural homogenisation, gradually even reinforcing the national identity.

Throughout the ages, the Church has been an exceptionally influential institution. It was the most important medium for the transfer of classical culture, to which it added specifically Christian values that in many cases were diametrically opposed to those of Antiquity. In principle the Church defended every human soul and was thus obligated to oppose slavery and arbitrary killing. It defended, again in theory, spiritual values over material values, poverty over riches, the weak over the mighty, and it encouraged charity and love of one's neighbour. However much and however often these principles may have been set aside, reformers and zealots could still revitalise the message and pass it on. The Church is the oldest and most all-encompassing medieval institution and, in the long term, was thus able to assert its message in relative independence. Slavery disappeared among European Christians in the course of the Middle Ages. Rulers could no longer apply violence indiscriminately: sooner or later they would have to render account to the clerics. The institutional division between Church and secular power, which had grown gradually out of the realities of the late Roman Empire and been shaped by the doctrine of the two swords, was unprecedented in world history. It allowed breakthroughs in Europe that had either never taken place elsewhere or never produced such long-lasting results: autonomous forms of rationality in the fields of religion, government, economic activity and scientific thought.

During the Middle Ages feudalism gradually took shape as a system of feudo-vassalic relations aimed at warranting military power and some sort of public government through a controlled redistribution of land and lordship. Strictly organised and carefully managed lordships and principal-

ities were created out of small units through a process of continuous competition and struggle. This was followed by the elimination of weaker rivals and the expansion of the surviving entities, forming the basis of monarchic states. It is impossible to imagine European history without the basic units upon which it was built: political fragmentation was added to cultural diversity. The two categories that make up nations – peoples and polities – did not overlap each other, for they had grown out of differing dynamics. Despite the strong trend towards homogenisation over the past few hundred years, most European states are still made up of more than one ethnic group. Diversity of cultures and states, with all the concomitant tensions, conflicts and creativity, is the European characteristic par excellence. A coordinated empire had no chance of surviving there because of the cohesiveness of the older political and cultural patterns. Empires with an effective power could not last for long in the West. In later centuries the Ottoman, Habsburg and Russian empires were only able to survive in the less progressive and more thinly populated parts of the continent by using superior physical violence. They all disintegrated after the First World War, in part under pressures from national cultures dating from the Middle Ages.

The multiplicity of political and cultural entities was an impediment to the monolithic exercise of power, a situation that was reinforced by the separate organisation of Church and state. In Europe there was no single central authority that could intervene in every field of human activity throughout a very extensive territory, as there was in China, for example. The relatively short distances made it possible for dissidents and other persecuted people to move to other areas of authority. Inside the monarchic states central authority again encountered many areas that governed themselves to a large extent. Religious institutions and noble lords held considerable domains where rulers were unable to exercise direct control. Large commercial cities continued to enjoy a great degree of self-government and could administer their own laws. This autonomy forced rulers to consult with influential subjects and their representatives, from which constitutional constraints on the monarchy grew up and a parliamentary tradition could develop. No single European prince could function as an absolute ruler during the Middle Ages; he was accountable both to his father confessor and to subjects who had their own means of exercising power and could eventually oppose his policy. Europe was therefore the only continent where representative institutions came into being which controlled the purse strings on behalf of specific categories of subjects – the estates: clergy, nobles, burghers, free peasants – and at crucial moments had the power to curb the arbitrary designs of princes.

A civic culture grew up in the towns which, together with the chivalric culture, gave shape to the pattern of values and the imagination of Europeans for many centuries. There are substantial differences between them. The culture of chivalry valued bravery and skill with weapons, valorous deeds, brilliant physical accomplishments. It continued to prevail as a model of masculine and aggressive behaviour. At the same time, however, it also advocated selfless assistance to widows, orphans, clerics and other people in need, the willingness to serve one's lord and the Christian faith actively, generosity in sharing booty and gifts with followers, indifference to material gain – except land linked to lordship. In its romanticised version this grew into the cult of courtly love, a literary construct that survives in today's popular literature.

The cultural horizon of urban patriciates, on the other hand, was determined by a businesslike attitude, the desire for material gain, but also the ability to deal with and learn from other cultures and other social categories. The inhabitants of the great seaports, in particular, were very open in their outlook. Townspeople had had to fight for their place in a world that was controlled by landed aristocracy and were therefore readier to make compromises. The calculation of risk, not physical conflict, offered the means of success.

Certain elements from the chivalric culture gradually filtered through into the civic culture via the patrician elite. Yet what distinguished the latter was that it allowed neither Church nor prince or aristocrat to impose their laws on it, even though its members were anxious to do business with all of them. This was the context for the emergence of civil and property rights, and of commercial capitalism, which became the driving force behind the western economy.

The Middle Ages saw the creation of the universities, centres which reproduced and commented on the knowledge from the ancient authorities. It was at the universities that efforts were made to harmonise Christian doctrines with ideas from pagan Antiquity that were considered valuable. Here, too, the initial impetus was given to test ancient theories against Arabic empirical knowledge and personal observations. In theory, universities were under papal authority. In practice this meant that they enjoyed far-reaching independence from the clergy and temporal rulers in the immediate vicinity. The weakening of the papacy in the late Middle Ages allowed critical intellectuals to emerge and develop, who formulated new ideological foundations attuned to the radically changing social realities.

The Christian West originally grew up completely aware that it trailed behind its great neighbours, the Byzantine Empire and the Arabic world. The relationship with the latter was often discordant, but it never prevented intensive commercial dealings or frequent cultural exchanges. The close contact enabled the West to borrow much and to evolve further, gradually becoming emancipated. As the Ottoman Empire swept the Byzantine Empire off the map it formed an enormous military and cultural challenge for the West. This friction dominated the sixteenth and seventeenth centuries in central Europe and the Mediterranean. Here again we thus encounter continuity with the Middle Ages. Europe evolved during these distinctive centuries into an entity that has made a radical contribution to world history.

	Roman and Byzantine empires	The Church	Islamic world	Iberia	Italy
300	306–337 Emperor Constantine the Great 379–395 Emperor Theodosius I 395 Partition of the Empire	325 Council of Nicaea 381–392 Christianity recognised as state religion 354–430 Augustine of Hippo			
400	410 Goths plunder Rome c.440 *Codex Theodosianus* 476 Dethroning of the last emperor in the western Empire	451 Council of Chalcedon 492–496 Pope Gelasius I		409 Settlement of Vandals, Sueves, Alans 429 Vandals move to North Africa	476–493 Odoacer king of Italy 493–526 Theoderic king of the Ostrogoths
500	527–565 Emperor Justinian 530 *Corpus Iuris Civilis* 532–537 Construction of the Hagia Sophia	c.529 Monastic rule of Benedict of Norcia c.560 Irish missions on the continent 590–604 Pope Gregory I	c.570–632 Mohammed	589 Visigoths forswear Arianism	535–552 Gothic wars c.550 Mosaics in Ravenna 568 Langobard invasion 568–774 Langobard kingdom
600	610–641 Emperor Heraclius 636 Syria conquered by Muslims 641–668 Emperor Constans II	649 First Lateran Council	622 Mohammed's flight to Medina 636–637 Muslims occupy Syria and Persia 661–750 Umayyad dynasty in Damascus		
700	717–741 Emperor Leo the Isaurian 730–843 Iconoclasm	c.710–754 Boniface, missionary and archbishop of Mainz	750–1055 Abbasid dynasty in Baghdad	711 Invasion of Muslims, battle of Jerez de la Frontera 756 Foundation of the Umayyad emirate Córdoba	c.700–750 Formation of the 'Papal State' 756 Pippin the Short acknowledges the Papal State

Gaul, Frankish kingdoms	Britain	Central and eastern Europe	German Empire	Eastern Europe
341 Salian Franks recognized as *foederati*		c.340 Conversion of the Goths		
		376 Goths cross the Danube		
		378 Battle of Adrianople		
418 Visigothic kingdom in Aquitaine recognized as *foederatus*	c.400 St Patrick in Ireland			
440–534 Kingdom of the Burgundians	407 Withdrawal of regular Roman legions			
481–511 Clovis king of the Franks				
507 Battle of Vouillé				
		c.550 Invasion of Avars		
	563 Columbanus on Iona	c.570 Start of Slav migrations to Balkans and Greece		
	597–604 Mission of Augustine of Canterbury			
	600 Formation of seven Anglo–Saxon kingdoms			
	c.672–735 The Venerable Bede	c.680 Invasion of Bulgars		
687 Pippin, mayor of the palace in Austrasia, defeats Neustrians	698 Gospels of Lindisfarne			
719 Charles Martel mayor of the palace				
719/751 Carolingian dynasty, until 911 in Germany, until 987 in France				
733/734 Battle of Tours				
751 Mayor of the palace Pippin III, 'the Short', crowned as king of the Franks Pippin I	757–796 Offa king of Mercia			
768–814 Charlemagne				

	Byzantine empire	The Church	Islamic world	Iberia	Italy
700					774 Charlemagne king of the Langobards
800		817 Monastic reform by Benedict of Aniane			800 Charlemagne crowned as Emperor
				844 Normans conquer Lisbon	
	867–1056 Macedonian dynasty				878 Muslims occupy Sicily
900		910 Foundation of the abbey of Cluny	909 Fatimid dynasty established in north-western Africa	929 Umayyad caliphate of Córdoba	
					951 Otto I king of Italy
	963–1025 Emperor Basil II		961–967 Caliph al-Hakim II		962 Otto I Roman emperor
			969 Fatimids conquer Egypt, caliphate of Cairo		
		989 Council of Charroux: Peace of God			
		999–1001 Pope Silvester II			
1000					
	c.1015 The Bulgarian Empire under Byzantine protectorate			1031 Overthrow of caliphate of Córdoba	
		1049–1054 Pope Leo IX	c.1050 Turkmen expansion	1031–1086 *Taifa* kingdoms	

Gaul, Frankish kingdoms	Britain	Central and eastern Europe	German Empire
772–804 Wars against the Saxons	793 First Viking attacks		
814–840 Emperor Louis the Pious		c.800 Disintegration of the Avar Empire	800 Charlemagne crowned as (Roman) emperor
834 Danish invasion along the North Sea coast of the Frankish Empire	836–841 Viking invasions in Scotland and Ireland		814–840 Emperor Louis the Pious
			817/840–855 Emperor Lothar
840–877 Emperor Charles the Bald			840–877 Emperor Charles the Bald
842 Oaths of Strasbourg			843 Treaty of Verdun
855–892 Viking invasions in West Francia			
876/881–888 Charles the Fat, last Carolingian emperor, king of Italy, East and West Francia	871–899 Alfred the Great, king of Wessex	c.861–864 Mission to Bulgars and their conversion	876/881–888 Charles the Fat, last Carolingian emperor, king of Italy, East and West Francia
		893–927 Bulgar khan Symeon	
888–895 Odo 'duke' of West Francia		895 Magyar invasion	
911 Danish warlord Rollo count of Rouen, core of duchy of Normandy	c.900–950 Integration of the seven kingdoms	10th century Dissemination of Cyrillic script	919–1024 Saxon (Ottonian) dynasty
			936/962–973 Emperor Otto I
			955 Battle of Lechfeld
		966 Conversion of the Polish Prince Mieszko	967/973–983 Emperor Otto II
		976 Foundation of the bishopric of Bohemia in Prague	
987–996 Hugh Capet, king of France	991 Imposition of Danegeld	989 Conversion of Prince Vladimir of Kiev	983/996–1002 Emperor Otto III
987–1328 Capetian royal dynasty		992–1024 Bolesław first king of Poland	
		997–1001 Waik/Stephan of Hungary	
	1016–1035 Cnut of Denmark, king of England	1001 Kingdom of Hungary recognized by Emperor Otto III	1002/1014–1024 Emperor Henry II
		c.1015–1185 Bulgarian Empire Byzantine protectorate	1024–1125 Salian dynasty
			1024/1027–1039 Emperor Conrad II

	Byzantine empire	The Church	Islamic world	Iberia	Italy
1000		1054 Schism between Greek and Latin Church	1055 Seljuks conquer Baghdad		1061–1091 Sicily occupied by Normans
	1071 Battle of Manzikert: most of Asia Minor lost to the Seljuk Turks	1073–1085 Pope Gregory VII	1071 Seljuks conquer most of Asia Minor		1071 Bari under Norman rule
	1081 Dynasty of Comnenus	1090–1153 Bernard of Clairvaux		1085 Christian conquest of Toledo	1082 Venice receives free trade privileges in Byzantine Empire
		1096–1099 First Crusade		1086–1147 Berber dynasty of Almoravids	
		1098 Foundation of the abbey of Cîteaux			
1100		1101 Foundation of the abbey of Fontevraud			
		1120 Foundation of the abbey of Prémontré			
		1128 Foundation of the Templars' Order		1137 Union of kingdom of Aragon with County of Barcelona	1130–1154 Roger II king of Sicily
		1147–1149 Second Crusade	1146 Turkish conquest of Edessa	1147 Foundation of kingdom of Portugal	1130 Sicily and southern Italy under papal suzerainty
		1159–1181 Pope Alexander III	1171 Nur ed-Din dislodges Fatimids from Egypt	1172–1212 Almohad rule	1167–1183 Lombard League
	1176 Battle of Myriokephalon: Seljuk victory	1179 Third Lateran Council	1174 Kurdish vizir Saladin rules over Egypt and Syria		c.1188 Foundation of the University of Bologna
		1189–1192 Third crusade	1187 Saladin chases crusaders out of Jerusalem		1197–1250 Frederick II king of Sicily, 1212 Roman king and emperor
		1198–1216 Pope Innocent III			
1200	1204 Constantinople occupied by crusaders	1202–1204 Fourth Crusade			
	1204–1261 Latin Empire	1209–1229 Albigensian Crusade			
		1210 Pope Innocent III approves the Franciscan Order			
		1215 Fourth Lateran Council		1212 Battle of Las Navas de Tolosa	
		1216 Approval of the Dominican Order			
		1217–1221 Fifth Crusade	1220 Chinggis Khan overruns Iran		

France	Britain	Central and eastern Europe	German Empire
	1066 Battle of Hastings	1025 Kingdom of Poland recognised by Emperor Conrad II	
	1066–1087 William of Normandy, the Conqueror, king of England		1075–1122 Investiture Controversy
	1086 Domesday Book		
1144 Abbot Suger initiates the construction of 'Gothic' church at Saint–Denis			1132–1254 Hohenstaufen dynasty
1157–1191 Philip of Alsace, count of Flanders	1154–1485 Royal House of Plantagenet		1152/1157–1190 Emperor Frederick I, Barbarossa
	1154–1189 King Henry II		1159 Formation of regional hanse leagues
	1170 Murder of Thomas Becket		
1180–1223 King Philip II Augustus	1171–1172 First expedition in Ireland		
	1189–1199 King Richard I, the Lionhearted		
Early 13th century Foundation of the universities of Paris and Montpellier	Early 13th century Foundation of the universities of Oxford and Cambridge		
1204 Conquest of Normandy			
1208–1229 Albigensian Crusade			
1214 Battle of Bouvines	1215 Magna Carta		1212/1220–1250 Emperor Frederick II
1226–1270 King Louis IX, the Saint			1228 Frederick II king of Jerusalem

	Byzantine empire	The Church	Islamic world	Iberia	Italy
1200				1230 Dynastic union Castile and León	1228 Ten years' peace between Emperor Frederick II and the sultan of Egypt
				1235–1248 Christian Reconquest of Seville and Córdoba	
		1243–1254 Pope Innocent IV			
		1248–1252 Crusade to Egypt and Palestine	1250–1517 Mamluk rule over Egypt, Syria, Palestine		
			1253 Iran and Iraq taken by Mongols		
	1261–1453 Dynasty of Palaiologi		1258 Baghdad captured by Mongols		1265–1321 Dante Alighieri
					1266 Charles of Anjou king of Naples and Sicily
		1291 Loss of Acre. End of crusades to Middle East	1291 Conquest of Acre, the last crusader base		1282 Sicilian Vespers: Sicily under Aragonese rule
		1294–1303 Pope Boniface VIII			
1300		1309–1377 Popes reside in Avignon			1304–1374 Petrarch
		c.1325–1384 John Wyclif	1326 Ottoman Turks conquer Bursa (Asia Minor)		
		1340–1384 Geert Grote			
			1361 Ottomans conquer Adrianople and push into the Balkans	1369 Trastámara dynasty in Castile	

France	Britain	Central and eastern Europe	German Empire	Eastern Europe
		1237–1242 Mongol invasion of Russian principalities and Hungary		
		1241 Battles of Liegnitz and the Sajó river		
			1254–1272 Interregnum	
	1272–1307 King Edward I			
1285–1314 King Philip IV, the Fair	1282–1284 Conquest of Wales		1291 Beginnings of the Swiss Confederation	
	1295 Model parliament			
	1296–1314 Wars with Scotland			
1302 Estates General summoned about taxation of ecclesiastical property				
1302 Battle of the Golden Spurs	1314 Battle of Bannockburn			
1323–1328 Peasants' War in Flanders	1327 King Edward II dethroned and executed	1320 Unification of Poland		
1328 Controversy about succession, decision based on Salian law	1327–1377 King Edward III			
1328–1589 Valois royal dynasty				
1337–1453 Hundred Years War	1337–1453 Hundred Years War		1346–1378 Emperor Charles IV, of Luxemburg	
1346, 1356 Battles of Crécy and Poitiers			1348 Foundation of the University of Prague	
1358 Jacquerie			1356 Golden Bull	
1364–1380 King Charles V			1358 German Hanse reforms from merchants' association to an encompassing urban league	

	Byzantine empire	The Church	Islamic world	Iberia	Italy
1300		1378–1415 Great (western) Schism			1378 Ciompi revolt in Florence
					1395 Gian Galeazzo Visconti duke of Milan
1400		1414–1418 Council of Constance	1405 Death of Timur Lenk (Tamerlane)		
		1415 Jan Hus dies at the stake			
		1431–1449 Council of Basel			1434 Cosimo de' Medici, signore of Florence
		1439 Council of Florence			1449–1492 Lorenzo de' Medici, il Magnifico
	1453 Ottoman conquest of Constantinople, actual end of Byzantine Empire		1453 Ottoman conquest of Constantinople	1479 Marriage of 'the Catholic kings' Isabel of Castile and Ferdinand of Aragon	1454 Peace of Lodi
		c.1467–1536 Desiderius Erasmus		1492 Columbus discovers the New World	
			1492 Christian conquest of Granada, the last Muslim stronghold in Iberia	1492 Christian conquest of Granada, the last Muslim stronghold in Iberia	1494–1529 French invasion and wars between the houses of Valois and Habsburg
				1498 Vasco da Gama reaches India by sea	
1500		1517 Martin Luther's 95 Theses		1516–1556 Charles (V) of Habsburg king of Castile and Aragon	

France	Britain	Central and eastern Europe	German Empire
1380–1422 King Charles VI, mentally ill since 1392, regency by the dukes; dynastic war between Armagnacs and Bourguignons	1381 Peasants' Revolt	1386 Personal Union Poland and Lithuania	
		1389 First battle on the Field of the Blackbirds, Kosovo: Ottoman victory over Great Serbia	
1384–1404 Philip the Bold, duke of Burgundy, count of Flanders	1399 King Richard II dethroned and executed		
	1399–1461 Lancaster royal dynasty		
1415 Battle of Agincourt			1410–1437 Emperor Sigismund
1419–1467 Duke Philip of Burgundy, the Good			1419–1436 War against Hussites
1420 Treaty of Troyes			
1429 King Charles VII crowned in Rheims			
1431 Joan of Arc dies at the stake			
1435 Peace of Arras			
1450–1453 French victories reduce the English possessions to Calais			1438–1806 Habsburg imperial dynasty
			1440–1493 Emperor Frederick III
1461–1483 King Louis XI	1461–1485 Wars of the Roses	1466 Poland incorporates Prussia, until then ruled by the Teutonic Order	
1465–1559 Wars between the houses of Valois and Burgundy-Habsburg	1485–1603 Tudor royal dynasty	1478 Great Prince Ivan III of Moscow conquers Novgorod	1486/1493–1519 Emperor Maximilian I
1477 Conquest of the duchy of Burgundy			1495 Constitutional reform
1515–1547 King Francis I	1509–1547 King Henry VIII		1501 Secession of the Swiss Confederation
			1520–1556 Emperor Charles V
1529 Cession of the sovereignty over Flanders and Artois			1521 Diet of Worms
	1534 Act of Royal Supremacy over the Church of England	1526 Ottomans conquer most of Hungary in the battle of Mohács	1525–1526 Peasants' War
	1536–1539 Dissolution of the monasteries		

Glossary

Abbey monastery, or closed community of nuns or monks, led by an abbot (which means 'father') or abbess ('mother'). Monks and nuns took vows of (personal) poverty, chastity and obedience, and they led a life of contemplation and prayer for the salvation of souls.

Al-Andalus Arab name for the part of the Iberian peninsula that was under Muslim rule. Now, the general term for southern Spain.

Artes liberales 'liberal' (free) arts taught at schools for higher education which took their name from the fact that their practice was free from manual labour, in contrast to 'mechanical' arts, which included medicine and architecture. Traditionally the seven liberal arts were divided into the trivium, the linguistic arts connected with the spoken and written word, and the quadrivium, the collective name for the four mathematical disciplines.

Bailiffs, baillis officials appointed in Flanders in 1170, salaried and dismissible at will. Their main tasks were to maintain the count's prerogatives, to collect revenues on his behalf and to organise the administration of justice. Similar officials were soon afterwards appointed in France.

Banal lordship, seigneurie local lordship based not primarily on the possession of land and of peasants living on that land, but on the local appropriation and exercise of bannus and other regal rights by local strongmen who were not accountable to either kings or counts.

Banlieu a town's jurisdiction extending a few miles surrounding the walls.

Bannus, bannum in the Carolingian Empire, royal prerogative to coerce and to command each and everybody (actually, the early medieval equivalent of sovereign power), which was delegated at regional level to counts, and at local level to the counts' representatives (vice-counts, etc.). Later, 'banal' rights formed the basis of banal lordships.

Benefice a source of income, mostly land along with its workers, given as a conditional tenure (as a fief) in exchange for services rendered to the lord.

Bishop, bishopric (from the Greek epi-scopus, overseer) the head of the Christian community within a territory, originally around a Roman civitas or city. Responsible for the appointment of priests and the conduct of the community. In the early Middle Ages bishops were usually involved in local government and jurisdiction.

Bull papal ordinance, authenticated by a leaden seal (Latin bulla).

Caesaropapism a form of rule in which the

secular head of state ('*caesar*') is also the religious leader ('pope').

Canon law laws of the Church, codified systematically in the twelfth century. Resolutions taken by councils are also called canons.

Canon, canoness canons were originally priests who strictly followed the rules of the Church and formed a religious association called 'chapter'. Secular canons were attached to important churches, in particular cathedrals; they lived individually and they did not follow a monastic rule. Regular canons, however, lived in monasteries and followed a monastic rule, usually that of St Augustine. There were also female canons or canonesses who could not of course be priests and always lived in monasteries. Depending on whether or not they followed a monastic rule, they were called secular or regular canonesses.

Canonisation official proclamation of sainthood of a person having lived as an exemplary Christian; the formal procedure was established only in the thirteenth century.

Cardinal senior title in the Catholic Church, awarded to the principal clergy within the city of Rome and its vicinity, where cardinals hold the seven bishoprics. Cardinals occupy the main offices at the Curia, and since 1059 cardinals have elected the pope.

Castellanus local official holding a castle for a superior lord (king, count, banal lord).

Catholic originally this Greek word signified 'universal [Christian]'; since the Schism of 1054, Latin Christians became labelled as 'the' Catholics.

Chancellor the head of a ruler's administration, originally responsible for the emission of public acts. Increasingly the chief councillor or prime minister.

Chapter the formal association of secular canons.

Chiefdom small-scale polity headed by a warlord and his personal retinue of armed followers (also called *Gefolgschaft* in German).

Chivalry cultural and moral encasement of knighthood, cultivating a code of values and behaviour, such as courage, loyalty, fellowship, charity and generosity.

Commune sworn community of citizens, mentioned in northern Italy from the late eleventh century, claiming self-government and particular privileges.

Communion the culmination of the holy mass, the consecration of bread and wine as the body and blood of Christ, is believed to make Christ present. The host (consecrated wafer) is offered to the believers; cf. excommunication.

Complexio specific mixture of bodily fluids which, according to medieval medicine, determined a person's temperament and health condition.

Convent house or community of friars or nuns belonging to one of the mendicant orders, headed by a prior or prioress.

Conversi lay brothers primarily drawn from popular classes, employed as manual labourers in the monastic orders of Cistercians and Premonstratensians.

Copyhold written contract whereby English landlords gave out parts of their demesne to their bondsmen for the possession of their holdings in a form of hereditary lease.

Council or synod; in the Christian Church: assembly of bishops with decisive authority about dogmatic issues. In the early Middle Ages, councils were held at the ecumenical level (all of Christendom) as well as at the regional level, and they were mostly summoned and presided over by lay rulers.

Count, county, Latin *comes, comitatus* in the late Roman period, a military commander and his soldiers; in the early Middle Ages, regional representative of the king and his territory.

Curia court of a prince, or more likely that of the pope. Any court was a centre of decision-making, administration and jurisdiction.

Danegeld land tax to be paid in silver coin as tribute to Danish invaders from 991, which was maintained – as a general land tax – in England until 1162.

Danelaw the area of England north-east of the old Roman road from London to Chester, where numerous Danish farmers settled from the late ninth century onwards. Danish law and institutions survived for centuries even after English reconquest.

Demesne, domain 1) landed estate, parts of which – also called 2) 'demesne' or 'reserve' – were reserved for direct exploitation by the landlord using the labour services of his dependent tenants. 3) As in 'royal domain': that part of a kingdom over which the king himself directly exercised full royal (public) authority.

Denarius penny, silver coin first struck at the end of the seventh century, worth one-twelfth of a *solidus*, the standard Roman gold coin.

Diet *Reichstag*, assembly of territorial princes in the (German) Empire, along with the German king or emperor. From 1470 onwards, cities were also represented.

Disputatio oral debate as a didactic art in the teaching of rhetoric, initiated just before 1000.

Doom customary law in Anglo-Saxon England.

Duke, dukedom, duchy in the barbarian kingdoms dukes were governors with military powers over large territories that were supposed to be inhabited by distinct peoples; later they were the highest-ranking princes in the Empire or kingdom.

Emperor the east Roman emperors in Constantinople saw themselves as the only true successors to the Roman emperors. They considered Charlemagne's imperial coronation and that of his Carolingian successors as usurpation. Otto II created the tradition of the coronation by the pope of the elected German king as 'Roman emperor'.

Enfeoffment the act of conferring a fief on a vassal.

Estates term derived from Latin *status* (state, condition) and French *état*; in English, apart from referring to large landownership, it means representative assemblies on the scale of principalities and kingdoms, also called parliaments. In the latter meaning, the plural refers to the composition of several social classes, mostly clergy, nobility, citizens and in some territories also rural communities.

Ethnogenesis the process by which highly dynamic multi-ethnic confederations over the course of time grew into peoples with a new identity, which was grafted on to the culture of the dominant, often name-giving, group.

Eucharist collective commemoration (in holy mass) by a Church community of the Last Supper that Christ shared with his apostles.

Exchequer financial department of the kings of England since the twelfth century, composed of the treasury and an accounting office. Sheriffs had to submit their accounts for control on a chequered tablecloth, hence exchequer.

Excommunication ecclesiastical censure barring a person from receiving the communion (Eucharist), which meant exclusion from the Christian community until repentance.

Exemption the whole or partial release of an ecclesiastical person, corporation or institution from the authority of the ecclesiastical superior next highest in rank. In particular: direct subordination of a religious institution (e.g. an abbey) to the authority of the pope.

Feudal mode of production (neo)Marxist shibboleth to define medieval society as a social order in which a substantial share of agrarian surpluses is transferred from peasants to aristocratic lords under non-economic (i.e. non-market) pressure.

Feudal society medieval society could qualify as a feudal society when feudal-vassalic relations were extended, and applied more systematically, to such crucial elements of society as public governance (mediatisation), public defence (feudal levies/armies) and the aristocratic land market. This was the case for large parts of western Europe from the twelfth century onwards.

Feudal-vassalic relation contractual, asymmetric relationship between a higher- and a lower-placed person, called lord and vassal, respectively, aimed at exchanging political and military support for protection and maintenance, ensured by the grant of a fief.

Fief see benefice.

Fondaco, funduq trading post in Islamic cities where blocks of houses were designated to foreign traders to store their goods and so they could live according to their own customs, with their own churches, bath-houses, ovens, administrative and court buildings; imitated by Venice for German traders.

Gefolgschaft the armed followers or military retinue of a barbarian warlord.

God's peace, God's truce peace agreement designed by bishops, abbots, but also secular lords from the late tenth century to protect vulnerable people (peasants, women, travellers, etc.) against excessive violence perpetrated by aristocrats; the restrictions were agreed within a defined territory and for particular days and periods, the sanction was religious.

Grundherrschaft type of aristocratic lordship in which a large landowner exercises (to a certain degree) what we would call public authority over the peasants who lived on his estate.

Guild association of a professional group; merchant guilds organised the trade in their home town, and the regulation and protection of the members' trade in foreign countries. Craft guilds were compulsory local organizations regulating a particular craft.

Hagiography the description of the life of exemplary Christians, often written to support the claim to their sainthood by the demonstration of miracles.

Hanse originally a regional association of merchants to secure their regular trade routes and mediate or adjudicate conflicts. The German Hanse grew in the thirteenth century as a conglomerate of regional associations, and transformed itself in 1358 into a league of nearly two hundred towns.

Hausmacht the resources of a German king in the territories (duchy, county, margraviate, etc.) under the direct rule of his dynasty.

Hierocracy conception of religious leaders (e.g. popes in Christendom) who claim a superior authority over secular heads of state.

Holy Roman Empire the coronation of Charlemagne as emperor in 800 was presented as the 'transfer' of the ancient Roman Empire. The qualification of the Empire as 'Holy' first appeared in an imperial charter of 1157, with the intention of stressing the Empire's equality with the Church; the title *Sacrum Imperium Romanum* was first used in 1254, during the Interregnum – the period in German medieval history when there was not a generally recognised German king – and remained until 1806.

Homagium homage or *commendatio*, i.e. becoming a lord's man, symbolised by the ritual of joining hands with the lord. Homage became a standard part of the ceremony in which someone became a vassal.

Humanism in general the intellectual effort to trace, copy and study (narrative) texts from classical (Greek and Roman) Antiquity – which by itself generates a larger interest in secular culture and human action (hence: humanism). In particular: the flourishing of this effort in the fourteenth and fifteenth centuries, first in Italy, then also north of the Alps. The new Italian brand of humanism is called 'civic humanism' because it was closely linked to a new educational ideal aimed at creating virtuous and politically active citizens. Another current, 'biblical humanism', was more widespread. Its aim was to reconstruct by philological means the original text of the Bible. See also Renaissance.

Hundred subdivision of a county or (in England) shire; in England since the early tenth century: local district of originally one hundred homesteads, administered by a royal reeve who summoned the hundred's law court.

Immunity freedom of Church institutions from administrative or judicial interference by secular authorities.

Inquisition literally 'inquiry', in particular about someone's religious orthodoxy. From the early thirteenth century on, popes started to use 'inquiries' systematically in their attempt to eradicate groups of supposed heretics in southern France, northern Italy and the mid-Rhineland. Inquisitors often belonged to the Dominican Order. Suspects and witnesses were interrogated, if need be under torture; sanctions could be imprisonment and, more rarely, burning at the stake. In 1478, the 'Catholic kings' of Castile and Aragon created their own Inquisition to detect *conversos* or 'crypto-Jews'.

Interdict papal ban or 'interdict[ion]' on the administration of holy sacraments in a particular territory, sometimes an entire kingdom or principality.

Investiture the conferment of the symbols of spiritual power to bishops and abbots; the fact that investiture was done by secular rulers who chose incumbents gave rise to a serious conflict (the Investiture Controversy), especially between the pope and the emperor, because bishops were closely involved in the Empire's secular administration (*Reichskirche*).

Knight, knighthood the social order of heavily armoured elite warriors on horseback, formed from the tenth century onwards by men of various social origins. In the long run, the knighthood in many parts of Europe became difficult to distinguish from the nobility.

Konigsnähe German, proximity to the king.

Landfriede German, in analogy with the God's peace, princes and kings in the German Empire tended to make voluntarily agreed arrangements between prominent parties to foster peaceful relations within their territory.

Liege the preferred lord of a vassal.

Ligesse French, preferential fealty of a vassal to one particular lord, the liege.

Maior domus head of a ruler's household.

Mamluk or ghulam-system (literally 'slave' or 'page'). Recruitment system, introduced by Abbasid caliphs in the ninth century, to use mounted slave soldiers of non-Arabic, in particular Turkic, origin as elite household troops.

Manorial system the system of exploitation of large estates (called *villae* or *curtes* in the early and central Middle Ages on the continent, and manors in England after 1066) based on unfree labour services and deliverables in kind to the landlord.

March, *Mark* border region of the Carolingian Empire with a strong military administration, ruled by a margrave.

Mediatisation devolution of government whereby a king or comparable prince leaves the effective exercise of public authority on the regional and/or local level to vassals.

Miles Latin, knight, mounted warrior on horseback.

Ministerial knight of unfree status or origin (in the German Empire).

Missi dominici emissary counts and bishops sent in pairs as inspectors in the Carolingian Empire.

Monophysitism the Christian dogma that the union of the divine and the human in the historical incarnation, Jesus Christ, as the incarnation of the Word of God, had only a single 'nature' which was either divine or a synthesis of divine and human.

Mozarab Christians in al-Andalus who adapted their way of life, their language and manner of dress, but not their religion, to the dominant Arabic culture.

Natural philosophy medieval equivalent of modern (natural) science – especially physics, cosmology and biology – which was mainly based on the works of Aristotle.

Orthodox, orthodoxy Greek for 'the right belief'. Since the Schism of 1054, applied to eastern Christianity.

Ostkolonisation, eastward colonisation long-term and massive migration movement of west European settlers into central Europe.

Pair, peer literally in French: 'equal' (to the king). In late medieval France, six bishops and six dukes formed the twelve *pairs*; in England, the dukes, earls, viscounts and barons are seen as peers.

Parlement French supreme court, developed from 1261 as the judicial section of the royal court, formally organised in 1345. In England, parliament in the early thirteenth century also referred to extended assemblies assisting the king in the exercise of justice; later, taxation and petitions were also dealt with. The social basis of the representation was gradually broadened to the shires and boroughs, and meetings became more regular; a 'model parliament' was summoned in 1295.

Patrician, patriciate term applied by modern historians to the social elite in medieval towns, defined by more or less formal contemporary criteria such as membership of the merchants' guild or ownership of land in the city centre.

Popolo political organisation of affluent middle classes in Italian city-states.

Purgatory the state of purification of the soul during the time interval between death and the Final Judgement; in the Middle Ages often conceived as a period of temporary punishment for minor sins. The duration of the stay in the Purgatory was thought to be proportional to the virtues and devotion of the deceased as well as to prayers for his/her soul. A full-blown doctrine of Purgatory was established in the Council of Lyon in 1245.

Quaestio Latin, literally 'question': a fixed teaching method in higher education from the twelfth century on. The pros and cons of possible answers to often complicated questions are weighed up systematically using the technique of logical analysis, before a balanced conclusion is drawn.

Reconquest, Reconquista piecemeal occupation by Christian warriors, from the late tenth century to 1492, of those parts of the Iberian peninsula that had been in Muslim hands since 711.

Regalia Latin, the rights immanently belonging to the king.

Reichskirche, imperial Church the policy of German emperors – systematic after the beginning of the eleventh century – to confer the secular office of count or duke on (arch-) bishops, thereby integrating the highest clergy closely in secular policies and making their selection dependent on the emperor.

Renaissance literally 'rebirth', referring to the restoration of classical forms and ideals as these were evoked in imitations of classical literature or of (supposedly) classical models in buildings, paintings and sculptures. Modern medieval historians distinguish renaissances in the Carolingian period, in the twelfth, and in the fourteenth to sixteenth centuries.

Réserve see demesne.

Sacrament ceremonial and performative acts, instituted by the Church and to be administered by priests, by which divine grace is dispensed to the worthy believers. The Church gradually formalised seven sacraments, the most relevant being baptism, confession and the Eucharist.

Scholasticism shorthand for the teaching in schools for higher education and universities from the twelfth century onwards. Scholasticism was characterised by its optimism about the power of human reason, especially in seeing into theological mysteries.

Seigneur, seigneurial, seignory see banal lordship.

Sénéchal, pl. *sénéchaux* royal official in southern France, responsible for maintaining the king's prerogatives, to collect revenues on his behalf and to organise the administration of justice (cf. bailli).

Serf, serfdom a shorthand for all sorts of legally unfree peasants. The typical serf lived on a small farm on the estate of a large landowner; he owed labour service and was subjected to his landlord's jurisdiction (cf. *Grundherrschaft*).

Sheriff administrative and judicial official of the English king in a shire.

Shire administrative unit of land in Anglo-Saxon England, from the Norman Conquest equivalent to county, common on the continent.

Signoria, pl. *signorie* tyrannical regimes constituted since the middle of the thirteenth century in Italian cities by local noblemen or mercenary captains in the service of cities.

Simony the practice of the buying and selling of clerical offices.

Sovereign the highest power, not recognising any superior.

Suzerain the highest feudal lord.

Syncretism functional fusion of old and new religious representations and practices.

Synod regional assembly of bishops (cf. [church] council).

Templar member of the religious military Order of the Temple (in Jerusalem).

Tenant-in-chief holder of a royal fief in England after 1066. Most fiefs consisted of a bigger or smaller number of manors (estates), never of public offices (as on the continent).

Tithe share of the harvest, traditionally one-tenth, contributed to the Church for the maintenance of the local priest, local church building and the relief of the local poor.

Universitas Latin for guild or corporation, including that of teachers and students in schools for higher education that were called *studia generalia* at the time but which modern historians describe as universities.

Vassalage see feudal-vassalic relation, *homagium*.

Villein another word for serf, especially in England.

Wergeld in Germanic law codes the compensation money that had to be paid for killing or severely injuring a person in order to avoid a blood feud.

Bibliography of secondary literature

This bibliography of secondary literature is a selection of books (monographs and edited volumes) that is biased in two important respects: year of publication and language. What we want to offer is a sampling of new, often thought-provoking works rather than a bouquet of classics. This means that hardly any titles that appeared before 1990 have been entered in our list. Moreover, because this is a textbook aimed at undergraduates who have English as their first language and only limited knowledge of foreign languages, the bibliography contains only English titles. We fully recognise that by this decision we do grave injustice to the many, many authors, editors and publishers of high-quality books on medieval history in other languages – French, German, Italian and Spanish for a start.

Students who want to further explore any theme or subject of medieval history are recommended not to stop at our bibliography, but also to consult general reference works that have not been included. The first that spring to mind are the awe-inspiring, multi-volume series of 'Histories of (. . .)', published by Cambridge University Press. Several of these are entirely dedicated to the Middle Ages, not just the *New Cambridge Medieval History*, but also for example the *Cambridge History of the Byzantine Empire*, of *Medieval Political Thought*, or of *Medieval Philosophy*, while various other series extend over the medieval period, e.g. the last volumes of the *Cambridge Ancient History*. The easiest way to find and select articles in journals and edited volumes on medieval history is to make use of the fully digitalised *International Medieval Bibliography*, edited by the medieval history department of the University of Leeds. It has to be consulted via Brepolis, the website for all online projects of Brepols Publishers. Finally, to get a quick idea of the supply, content and quality of major new publications in the field of medieval history, one should consult the review pages of top journals, such as *Speculum*, or the free internet review site of growing importance, *The Medieval Review*, hosted by Indiana University, Bloomington.

In our bibliography, title descriptions are by chapter and in alphabetical order of the authors. Titles appear only once in the bibliography, even if their content ranges over more than one chapter. In these cases we chose the most fitting chapter for a title, so readers should be aware of this limitation. Furthermore to save space we used UP as a general abbreviation for 'University Press', while the two greatest suppliers of titles, Cambridge University Press and Oxford University Press, were shortened to CUP and OUP, respectively.

Introduction

Biddick, Kathleen (1998), *The Shock of Medievalism* (Durham NC: Duke UP).

Bildhauer, Bettina (2011), *Filming the Middle Ages* (London: Reaktion Books).

Cantor, Norman F. (1991), *Inventing the Middle Ages: The Lives, Works, and Ideas of the Great Medievalists of the Twentieth Century* (New York: Quill – William Morrow).

Chazelle, Celia, Simon Doubleday, Felice Lifshitz and Amy G. Remensnyder (eds) (2012), *Why the Middle Ages Matter: Medieval Light on Modern Injustice* (Abingdon/ New York: Routledge).

Cohen, Jeffrey Jerome (ed.) (2000), *The Postcolonial Middle Ages* (New York/Basingstoke: Palgrave).

Davis, Kathleen (2008), *Periodization and Sovereignty: How Ideas of Feudalism and Secularization Govern the Politics of Time* (Philadelphia: University of Pennsylvania Press).

Davis, Kathleen and Nadia Altschul (eds) (2010), *Medievalisms in the Postcolonial World: The Idea of 'The Middle Ages' outside Europe* (Baltimore: the Johns Hopkins UP).

Dinshaw, Carolyn (1999), *Getting Medieval: Sexualities and Communities, Pre- and Postmodern* (Durham NC: Duke UP).

Dreyer, Edward L. (2006), *Zheng He: China and the Oceans in the Early Ming Dynasty, 1405–1433* (Harlow: Pearson).

Finke, Laurie and Martin B. Schichtman (2009), *Cinematic Illuminations: The Middle Ages on Film* (Baltimore: the Johns Hopkins UP).

Harris, Stephen J. and Bryon L. Grigsby (eds) (2008), *Misconceptions about the Middle Ages* (New York/ London: Routledge).

Hinde, John R. (2000), *Jacob Burckhardt and the Crisis of Modernity* (Montreal: McGill-Queens UP).

Holsinger, Bruce (2005), *The Premodern Condition: Medievalism and the Making of Theory* (Chicago: University of Chicago Press).

Humphrey, Chris and W.M. Ormrod (eds) (2001), *Time in the Medieval World* (York: York Medieval Press).

Kabir, Ananya and Deanne Williams (eds) (2005), *Postcolonial Approaches to the Middle Ages: Translating Cultures* (Cambridge: CUP).

Kemp, Anthony (1991), *The Estrangement of the Past: A Study in the Origins of Modern Historical Consciousness* (New York/Oxford: OUP).

Little, Lester K. and Barbara H. Rosenwein (eds) (1998), *Debating the Middle Ages: Issues and Readings* (Malden MA/Oxford: Blackwell).

Marshall, David W. (ed.) (2007), *Mass Market Medieval: Essays on the Middle Ages in Popular Culture* (Jefferson NC: McFarland).

Mazzotta, Giuseppe (1993), *The Worlds of Petrarch* (Durham NC: Duke UP).

Ortenberg, Veronica (2007), *In Search of the Holy Grail: The Quest for the Middle Ages* (London/New York: Continuum).

Otterspeer, Willem (2011), *Reading Huizinga* (Amsterdam: Amsterdam UP).

Pugh, Tison and Susan Aronstein (eds) (2012), *The Disney Middle Ages: A Fairy-tale and Fantasy Past* (New York: Palgrave Macmillan).

Pugh, Tison, Susan Aronstein and Angela Jane Weisl (eds) (2013), *Medievalisms: Making the Past in the Present* (New York/London: Routledge).

Rubin, Patricia Lee (1995), *Giorgio Vasari: Art and History* (New Haven/London: Yale UP).

Stahuljak, Zrinka (2013), *Pornographic Archaeology: Medicine, Medievalism, and the Invention of the French Nation* (Philadelphia: University of Pennsylvania Press).

Subrahmanyam, Sanjay (1997), *The Career and Legend of Vasco da Gama* (Cambridge: CUP).

Wilcox, Donald J. (1989), *The Measure of Times Past: Pre-Newtonian Chronologies and the Rhetoric of Relative Time* (Chicago/London: University of Chicago Press).

Chapter 1

Amory, Patrick (1997), *People and Identity in Ostrogothic Italy, 489–554* (Cambridge: CUP).

Banaji, Jairus (2001), *Agrarian Change in Late Antiquity: Gold, Labour, and Aristocratic Dominance* (Oxford: OUP).

Barbero, Alessandro (2007), *The Day of the Barbarians: The Battle that Led to the Fall of the Roman Empire* (New York: Walker & Company) (orig. Italian, 2005).

Barnes, Timothy (2011), *Constantine: Dynasty, Religion and Power in the Later Roman Empire* (Malden MA/Oxford: Blackwell).

Barnwell, Peter (1997), *Kings, Courtiers, and Imperium: The Barbarian West, 565–725* (Bristol: Bristol Classical Press).

Bell, Peter (2013), *Social Conflict in the Age of Justinian: Its Nature, Management and Mediation* (Oxford: OUP).

Blair, Peter Hunter (2003), *An Introduction to Anglo-Saxon England* (Cambridge: CUP).

Brogiolo, G.P. and Bryan Ward-Perkins (eds) (1999), *The Idea and Ideal of the Town between Late Antiquity and the Early Middle Ages* (Leiden: Brill).

Brubaker, Leslie and John Haldon (2011), *Byzantium in the Iconoclast Era, c.680–850: A History* (Cambridge: CUP).

Cameron, Averil (2005), *The Later Roman Empire* (Cambridge MA/London: Harvard UP).

Christie, Neil (1995), *The Lombards* (Oxford: Blackwell).

Curta, Florin (ed.) (2005), *Borders, Barriers, and Ethnogenesis: Frontiers in Late Antiquity and the Middle Ages* (Turnhout: Brepols).

— (2006), *Southeastern Europe in the Middle Ages, 500–1250* (Cambridge: CUP).

— (ed.) (2010), *Neglected Barbarians* (Turnhout: Brepols).

Evans, J.A.S. (1996), *The Age of Justinian: The Circumstances of Imperial Power* (London/New York: Routledge).

Garnsey, Peter, and Caroline Humfress (2001), *The Evolution of the Late Antique World* (Cambridge: Orchard Academic).

Geary, Patrick J. (2002), *The Myth of Nations: The Medieval Origins of Europe* (Princeton/Oxford: Princeton UP).

Gillett, Andrew (ed.) (2002), *On Barbarian Identity: Critical Approaches to Ethnicity in the Early Middle Ages* (Turnhout: Brepols).

— (2003), *Envoys and Political Communication in the Late Antique West, 411–533* (Cambridge: CUP).

Goetz, Hans-Werner, Jörg Jarnut and Walter Pohl (eds) (2003), *Regna and Gentes: The Relationship between Late Antiquity and Early Medieval Peoples and Kingdoms in the Transformation of the Roman World* (Leiden/Boston: Brill).

Goffart, Walter (2006), *Barbarian Tides: The Migration Age and the Later Roman Empire* (Philadelphia: University of Pennsylvania Press).

Gregory, Timothy (2010), *A History of Byzantium*, 2nd edn (Malden MA/Oxford: Blackwell).

Gwynn, David M. (ed.) (2008), *A.H.M. Jones and the Later Roman Empire* (Leiden/Boston: Brill).

Haldon, John F. (1990), *Byzantium in the Seventh Century: The Transformation of a Culture*, 2nd edn (Cambridge: CUP).

— (1999), *Warfare, State and Society in the Byzantine World 565–1204* (London: UCL Press).

Harries, J. (1994), *Sidonius Apollinaris and the Fall of Rome, AD 407–485* (Oxford: Clarendon Press).

Heather, Peter (2005), *The Fall of the Roman Empire: A New History of Rome and the Barbarians* (Oxford: OUP).

— (2009), *Empires and Barbarians: The Fall of Rome and the Birth of Europe* (Oxford: OUP).

Hen, Yitzhak (2007), *Roman Barbarians: The Royal Court and Culture in the Early Medieval West* (Basingstoke: Palgrave Macmillan).

Henning, Joachim (ed.) (2007), *Post-Roman Towns, Trade and Settlement in Europe and Byzantium*. 2 vols. (Berlin: Walter de Gruyter).

Herrin, Judith (2010), *Byzantium: The Surprising Life of a Medieval Empire* (Princeton: Princeton UP).

— (2013), *Margins and Metropolis: Authority across the Byzantine Empire* (Princeton: Princeton UP).

Holmes, Catherine (2005), *Basil II and the Governance of Empire, 976–1025* (Oxford: OUP).

Jones, Allen E. (2009), *Social Mobility in Late Antique Gaul: Strategies and Opportunities for the Non-Elite* (Cambridge: CUP).

Kaegi, Walter E. Jr. (1992), *Byzantium and the Early Islamic Conquests* (Cambridge: CUP).

— (2003), *Heraclius, Emperor of Byzantium* (Cambridge: CUP).

— (2010), *Muslim Expansion and Byzantine Collapse in North Africa* (Cambridge: CUP).

Kaldellis, Anthony (2007), *Hellenism in Byzantium: The Transformation of Greek Identity and the Reception of the Classical Tradition* (Cambridge: CUP).

Kelly, Christopher (2004), *Ruling the Later Roman Empire* (Cambridge MA: Belknap Press of Harvard UP).

Kulikowski, Michael (2007), *Rome's Gothic Wars from the Third Century to Alaric* (Cambridge: CUP).

Liebeschuetz, J.H.W.G. (2001), *The Decline and Fall of the Roman City* (Oxford/New York: OUP).

Little, Lester K. (ed.) (2007), *Plague and the End of Antiquity: The Pandemic of 541–750* (Cambridge: CUP).

Matthews, John (2007), *The Roman Empire of Ammianus*, 2nd edn (Ann Arbor: Michigan Classical Press).

Merrills, A.H. and R. Miles (2010), *The Vandals* (Oxford: Wiley-Blackwell).

Mitchell, Stephen (2007), *A History of the Later Roman Empire, AD 284–641* (Oxford/Malden MA: Blackwell).

Murray, Alexander Callander (ed.) (1998), *After Rome's Fall: Narrators and Sources of Early Medieval History. Essays Presented to Walter Goffart* (Toronto: University of Toronto Press).

Noble, Thomas F.X. (ed.) (2006), *From Roman Provinces to Medieval Kingdoms* (London/New York: Routledge).

Pohl, Walter and Helmut Reimitz (eds) (1998), *Strategies of Distinction: The Construction of Ethnic Communities, 300–800* (Leiden: Brill).

Pohl, Walter, Clemens Gantner and Richard Payne (eds) (2012), *Visions of Community in the Post-Roman World: The West, Byzantium and the Islamic World, 300–1100* (Farnham/Burlington VT: Ashgate).

Potter, David S. (2004), *The Roman Empire at Bay, AD 180–395* (London/New York: Routledge).

Rollason, David (2003), *Northumbria, 500–1100: Creation and Destruction of a Kingdom* (Cambridge: CUP).

Salzman, Michelle Renee (2002), *The Making of a Christian Aristocracy: Social and Religious Change in the Western Roman Empire* (Cambridge MA/London: Harvard UP).

Sarris, Peter (2006), *Economy and Society in the Age of Justinian* (Cambridge: CUP).

— (2011), *Empires of Faith: The Fall of Rome to the Rise of Islam, 500–700* (Oxford: OUP).

Smith, Julia M.H. (2005), *Europe after Rome: A New Cultural History 500–1000* (Oxford: OUP).

Stephenson, Paul (2003), *The Legend of Basil the Bulgar-Slayer* (Cambridge: CUP).

— (2010), *Constantine: Roman Emperor, Christian Victor* (New York: The Overlook Press).

Treadgold, Warren T. (1997), *A History of the Byzantine State and Society* (Stanford: Stanford UP).

Van Dam, Raymond (2010), *Rome and Constantinople: Rewriting Roman History during Late Antiquity* (Waco TX: Baylor UP).

Ward-Perkins, Bryan (2005), *The Fall of the Roman Empire and the End of Civilization* (Oxford: OUP).

Whittaker, C.R. (1994), *Frontiers of the Roman Empire: A Social and Economic Study* (Baltimore/London: the Johns Hopkins UP).

Wickham, Chris (2009), *The Inheritance of Rome: Illuminating the Dark Ages, 400–1000* (New York: Penguin).

Williams, Stephen (1985), *Diocletian and the Roman Recovery* (New York: Methuen).

Williams, Stephen and Gerard Friell (1999), *The Rome That Did Not Fall: The Survival of the East in the Fifth Century* (London/New York: Routledge).

Wolfram, Herwig (2005), *The Roman Empire and its Germanic Peoples* (Berkeley: University of California Press) (orig. German, 1990).

Chapter 2

Arnold, John H. (2005), *Belief and Unbelief in Medieval Europe* (London: Hodder Arnold).

Ayres, Lewis (2004), *Nicaea and its Legacy: An Approach of Fourth-Century Trinitarian Theology* (Oxford: OUP).

Bachrach, David S. (2003), *Religion and the Conduct of War, c.300–1215* (Woodbridge/Rochester NY: Boydell & Brewer).

Bagnoli, Martina, Holger A. Klein, C. Griffith Man and James Robinson (eds) (2010), *Treasures of Heaven: Saints, Relics, and Devotion in Medieval Europe* (New Haven/London: Yale UP).

Biller, P. and A. Minnis (eds) (1998), *Handling Sin: Confession in the Middle Ages* (Woodbridge: Boydell & Brewer).

Boynton, S. and D.J. Reilly (eds) (2011), *The Practice of the Bible in the Middle Ages: Production, Reception and Performance in Western Christianity* (New York: Columbia UP).

Brown, Peter (1995), *Authority and the Sacred. Aspects of the Christianisation of the Roman World* (Cambridge: CUP).

— (2000), *Augustine of Hippo. A Biography*, 2nd edn (Berkeley: University of California Press).

— (2003), *The Rise of Western Christendom. Triumph and Diversity AD 200–1000*, 2nd edn (Oxford: Blackwell).

— (2012), *Through the Eye of a Needle: Wealth, the Fall of Rome, and the Making of Christianity in The West, 350–550 AD* (Princeton/Oxford: Princeton UP).

Brubaker, Leslie (2012), *Inventing Byzantine Iconoclasm* (Bristol: Bristol Classical Press).

Burton-Christie, Douglas (1993), *The Word in the Desert: Scripture and Quest for Holiness in Early Christian Monasticism* (Oxford: OUP).

Cameron, Alan (2011), *The Last Pagans of Rome* (Oxford: OUP).

Chadwick, Henry (2001), *The Church in Ancient Society: From Galilee to Gregory the Great* (Oxford: OUP).

Chareyron, Nicole (2005), *Pilgrims to Jerusalem in the Middle Ages* (New York: Columbia UP).

Clark, James G. (2011), *The Benedictines in the Middle Ages* (Woodbridge: Boydell).

Clay, John-Henry (2010), *In the Shadow of Death: Saint Boniface and the Conversion of Hessia, 721–754* (Turnhout: Brepols).

Collins, Roger (2009), *Keepers of the Keys of Heaven: A History of the Papacy* (New York: Basic Books).

Cooper, Kate and Julia Hillner (eds) (2007), *Religion, Dynasty, and Patronage in Early Christian Rome* (Cambridge: CUP).

Crone, Patricia (2004), *Meccan Trade and the Rise of Islam*, 2nd edn (Princeton: Gorgias Press of Princeton UP).

— (2004), *God's Rule: Government and Islam. Six Centuries of Medieval Islamic Political Thought* (New York: Columbia UP).

Dietz, Maribel (2005), *Wandering Monks, Virgins, and Pilgrims: Ascetic Travel in the Mediterranean World, AD 300–800* (University Park PA: Penn State Press).

Dunn, Marilyn, *The Emergence of Monasticism: From the Desert Fathers to the Early Middle Ages* (Oxford/Malden MA: Blackwell).

Esler, Philip F. (ed.) (2000), *The Early Christian World* (London/New York: Routledge).

Evans, G.R. (ed.) (2001), *The Medieval Theologians: An Introduction to Theology in the Medieval Period* (Oxford: Blackwell).

Fassler, Margot E. and Rebecca A. Baltzer (eds) (2000), *The Divine Office in the Latin Middle Ages: Methodology and Source Studies, Regional Developments, Hagiography* (Oxford: OUP).

Fletcher, Richard (1997), *The Conversion of Europe: From Paganism to Christianity 371–1386 AD* (London: Harper Collins).

Flint, Valerie I.J. (1991), *The Rise of Magic in Early Medieval Europe* (Princeton: Princeton UP).

Gaddis, Michael E. (2005), *There Is No Crime for Those Who Have Christ: Religious Violence in the Christian Roman Empire* (Berkeley/Los Angeles: University of California Press).

George, Karen (2009), *Gildas' De Excidio Britonum and the Early British Church* (Woodbridge: D.S. Brewer).

Gurevitch, Aron (1988), *Medieval Popular Culture: Problems of Belief and Perception* (Cambridge: CUP).

Harrison, Carol (2000), *Augustine: Christian Truth and Fractured Humanity* (Oxford: OUP).

Hopkins, Keith (1999), *A World Full of Gods: Pagans, Jews and Christians in the Roman Empire* (London: Weidenfeld & Nicholson).

Howard-Johnston, J., P.A. Hayward, and R.A. Markus (eds) (1999), *The Cult of Saints in Late Antiquity and the Middle Ages: Essays on the Contribution of Peter Brown* (Oxford: OUP).

Humphreys, R. Stephen (1991), *Islamic History: A Framework for Inquiry* [revised edition] (Princeton: Princeton UP).

Jacobs, Andrew S. (2012), *Christ Circumcised: A Study in Early Christian History and Difference* (Philadelphia: University of Pennsylvania Press).

Kennedy, Hugh (2004), *The Prophet and the Age of the Caliphates: The Islamic Near East from the Sixth to the Eleventh Century*, 2nd edn (Harlow: Pearson).

— (2004), *When Baghdad Ruled the Muslim World: The Rise and Fall of Islam's Greatest Dynasty* (Philadelphia PA: Da Capo Press).

— (2007), *The Great Arab Conquests: How the Spread of Islam Changed the World We Live In* (Philadelphia PA: Da Capo Press).

Klingshirn, William E. (1994), *Caesarius of Arles: The Making of a Christian Community in Late Antique Gaul* (Cambridge: CUP).

Lawrence, C.H. (2001), *Medieval Monasticism. Forms of Religious Life in Western Europe in the Middle Ages*, 3rd edn (Harlow: Pearson Education).

Levy, Ian Christopher, Gary Macy and Kristen Van Ausdall (eds) (2012), *A Companion to the Eucharist in the Middle Ages* (Leiden/Boston: Brill 2012).

McGuire, Brian Patrick (2010), *Friendship and Community: The Monastic Experience, 350–1250*, 2nd edn (Ithaca NY: Cornell UP).

Macmullen, Ramsay (1984), *Christianizing the Roman Empire (AD 100–400)* (New Haven/London: Yale UP).

— (1997), *Christianity and Paganism in the Fourth to Eighth Centuries* (New Haven/London: Yale UP).

Markus, R.A. (1990), *The End of Ancient Christianity* (Cambridge: CUP).

— (1997), *Gregory the Great and His World* (Cambridge: CUP).

Mathisen, Ralph W. and Danuta Shanzer (eds) (2011), *Romans, Barbarians, and the Transformation of the Roman World: Cultural Interaction and the Creation of Identity in Late Antiquity* (Farnham/Burlington VT: Ashgate).

Melville, Gert, and Anne Müller (eds) (2011), *Female Vita Religiosa between Late Antiquity and the High Middle Ages: Structures, Developments, and Spatial Contexts* (Münster: LIT Verlag).

Mitchell, Stephen and Peter van Nuffelen (eds) (2010), *One God: Pagan Monotheism in the Roman Empire* (Cambridge: CUP).

Moorhead, John (1999), *Ambrose: Church and Society in the Late Roman World* (London: Longman).

— (2005), *Gregory the Great* (London/New York: Routledge).

Noble, Thomas F.X. (1984), *The Republic of St Peter: The Birth of the Papal State, 680–825* (Philadelphia: University of Pennsylvania Press).

Pelikan, Jaroslav (2003), *Credo: Historical and Theological Guide to Creeds and Confessions of Faith in the Christian Tradition* (New Haven: Yale UP).

— (2005), *Whose Bible Is It? A History of Scriptures through the Ages* (London: Penguin).

Petts, David (2011), *Pagan and Christian: Religious Change in Early Medieval Europe* (Bristol: Bristol Classical Press).

Rees, B.R. (1988), *Pelagius, A Reluctant Heretic* (Woodbridge: Boydell).

Ridyard, Susan J. (1988), *The Royal Saints of Anglo-Saxon England: A Study of West Saxon and East Anglian Cults* (Cambridge: CUP).

Rollason, David (1989), *Saints and Relics in Anglo-Saxon England* (Oxford/Cambridge MA: Blackwell).

Rosenwein, Barbara H. (1999), *Negotiating Space: Power, Restraint, and Privileges of Immunity in Early Medieval Europe* (Manchester: Manchester UP).

— (2006), *Emotional Communities in the Early Middle Ages* (Ithaca NY: Cornell UP).

Russell, James C. (1994), *The Germanization of Early Medieval Christianity: A Sociohistorical Approach to Religious Transformation* (Oxford: OUP).

Sarris, Peter, Matthew dal Santo, and Phil Booth (eds) (2011), *An Age of Saints? Power, Conflict and Dissent in Early Medieval Christianity* (Leiden/Boston: Brill).

Schulenberg, Jane Tibbetts (1998), *Forgetful of their Sex: Female Sanctity and Society, c.500–1000* (Chicago: Chicago UP).

Sessa, Kristina (2012), *The Formation of Papal Authority in Late Antique Rome: Roman Bishops and the Domestic Sphere* (Cambridge: CUP).

Shaw, Brent (2011), *Sacred Violence: African Christians and Sectarian Hatred in the Age of Augustine* (Cambridge: CUP).

Simonsohn, Uriel (2011), *A Common Justice: The Legal Allegiances of Christians and Jews under Early Islam* (Philadelphia: University of Pennsylvania Press).

Stowasser, Barbara Freyer (1994), *Women in the Qu'ran: Traditions and Commentaries* (Oxford: OUP).

Thacker, Alan, and Richard Sharpe (eds) (2002), *Local Saints and Local Churches in the Early Medieval West* (Oxford: OUP).

Thibodeaux, Jennifer D. (ed.) (2010), *Negotiating Clerical Identities: Priests, Monks and Masculinity in the Middle Ages* (New York: Palgrave Macmillan).

Tilley, Maureen A. (1997), *The Bible in Christian North-Africa: The Donatist World* (Minneapolis: Fortress Press).

Tronzo, William (ed.) (2005), *St Peter's in the Vatican* (Cambridge: CUP).

Van Dam, Raymond (1993), *Saints and their Miracles in Late Antique Gaul* (Princeton: Princeton UP).

Walsh, Christine (2007), *The Cult of St Katherine of Alexandria in Early Medieval Europe* (Aldershot/ Burlington VT: Ashgate).

Weaver, Rebecca Harden (1996), *Divine Grace and Human Agency: A Study of the Semi-Pelagian Controversy* (Washington DC: The Catholic University of America Press).

Winroth, Anders (2012), *The Conversion of Scandinavia: Vikings, Merchants, and Missionaries in the Remaking of Northern Europe* (New Haven/London: Yale UP).

Wood, Ian (2001), *The Missionary Life: Saints and the Evangelisation of Europe, 400–1000* (Harlow: Longman).

Wood, Susan (2006), *The Proprietary Church in the Medieval West* (Oxford: OUP).

Chapter 3

Abels, Richard (1988), *Lordship and Military Obligation in Anglo-Saxon England* (Berkeley/Los Angeles: University of California Press).

— (1998), *Alfred the Great: War, Kingship and Culture in Anglo-Saxon England* (London: Longman).

Abun-Nasr, Jamil M. (1987), *A History of the Maghrib in the Islamic Period* (Cambridge: CUP).

Algazi, Gadi, Valentin Groebner and Bernhard Jussen (eds) (2003), *Negotiating the Gift: Pre-modern Figurations of Exchange* (Göttingen: Vandenhoeck & Ruprecht).

Althoff, Gerd (2004), *Family, Friends, and Followers: Political and Social Bonds in Early Medieval Europe* (Cambridge: CUP) (orig. German, 1990).

Bachrach, Bernard S. (2001), *Early Carolingian Warfare: Prelude to Empire* (Philadelphia: University of Pennsylvania Press).

Bagge, Sverre, Michael H. Gelting and Thomas Lindkvist (eds) (2011), *Feudalism: New Landscapes of Debate* (Turnhout: Brepols).

Barbero, Alessandro (2004), *Charlemagne: Father of a Continent* (Berkeley: University of California Press) (orig. Italian, 2000).

Barford, P.M. (2001), *The Early Slavs: Culture and Society in Early Medieval Eastern Europe* (London: The British Museum Press).

Bazelmans, Jos (1999), *By Weapons Made Worthy: Lords, Retainers and their Relationship in Beowulf* (Amsterdam: Amsterdam UP).

Becher, Matthias (2003), *Charlemagne* (New Haven: Yale UP) (orig. German, 1999).

Bitel, Lisa M. (2002), *Women in Early Medieval Europe, 400–1100* (Cambridge: CUP).

Booker, Courtney (2009), *Past Convictions: The Penance of Louis the Pious and the Decline of the Carolingians* (Philadelphia: University of Pennsylvania Press).

Boone, James L. (2009), *Lost Civilization: The Contested Islamic Past in Spain and Portugal* (London: Duckworth).

Brink, Stefan [in collaboration with Neil Price] (eds) (2008), *The Viking World* (London/New York: Routledge).

Buc, Philippe (2001), *The Dangers of Ritual: Between Early Medieval Texts and Social Scientific Theory* (Princeton: Princeton UP).

Byock, Jesse (2001), *Viking Age Iceland* (London: Penguin Books).

Christiansen, Eric (2002), *The Norsemen in the Viking Age* (Oxford/Malden MA: Blackwell).

Clarke, Catherine A.M. (2012), *Writing Power in Anglo-Saxon England: Texts, Hierarchies, Economies* (Cambridge: D.S. Brewer).

Collins, Roger (1998), *Charlemagne* (Basingstoke: Macmillan).

Costambeys, Marios (2007), *Power and Patronage in Early Medieval Italy: Local Society, Italian Politics and the Abbey of Farfa, c.700–900* (Cambridge: CUP).

Costambeys, Marios, Matthew Innes and Simon MacLean (2011), *The Carolingian World* (Cambridge: CUP).

Curta, Florin (2006), *Southeastern Europe in the Middle Ages, 500–1250* (Cambridge: CUP).

Curta, Florin and Roman Kovalev (eds) (2008), *The Other Europe in the Middle Ages: Avars, Bulgars, Khazars, and Cumans* (Leiden: Brill).

Davies, Wendy and Paul Fouracre (eds) (2010), *The Languages of Gift in the Early Middle Ages* (Cambridge: CUP).

Davis, Jennifer R. and Michael McCormick (eds), *The Long Morning of Medieval Europe. New Directions in Early Medieval Studies* (Aldershot/Burlington VT: Ashgate).

Duggan, Anne J. (ed.) (2003), *Nobles and Nobility in Medieval Europe* (Rochester NY/Woodbridge: Boydell & Brewer).

Evans, Stephen S. (1997), *The Lords of Battle: Image and Reality of the 'Comitatus' in Dark-Age Britain* (Woodbridge: Boydell).

Fletcher, Richard (1992), *Moorish Spain* (London: Weidenfield & Nicholson).

Foot, Sarah (2011), *Aethelstan: The First King of England* (New Haven/London: Yale UP).

Fouracre, Paul (2000), *The Age of Charles Martel* (London: Longman).

Fouracre, Paul and Richard Gerberding (1996), *Late Merovingian France: History and Historiography, 640–720* (Manchester: Manchester UP).

Gabriele, Matthew (2011), *An Empire of Memory: The Legend of Charlemagne, the Franks, and Jerusalem before the First Crusade* (Oxford: OUP).

Gabriele, Matthew and Jace Stuckey (eds) (2008), *The Legend of Charlemagne in the Middle Ages: Power, Faith, and Crusade* (New York: Palgrave Macmillan).

Garver, Valerie L. (2009), *Women and Aristocratic Culture in the Carolingian World* (Ithaca NY: Cornell UP).

Glick, Thomas F. (2005), *Islamic and Christian Spain in the Early Middle Ages*, 2nd edn (Leiden: Brill).

Goldberg, Eric J. (2006), *Struggle for Empire: Kingship and Conflict under Louis the German, 817–876* (Ithaca/London: Cornell UP).

Hadley, D.M. (2000) *The Northern Danelaw: Its Social Structure, c.800–1100* (London/New York: Continuum).

Hadley, Dawn M. and Julian D. Richards (eds) (2000), *Cultures in Contact: Scandinavian Settlements in England in the Ninth and Tenth Centuries* (Turnhout: Brepols).

Halsall, Guy (2003), *Warfare and Society in the Barbarian West, 450–900* (London/New York: Routledge).

Hammer, Carl I. (2002), *A Large-Scale Slave Society of the Early Middle Ages: Slaves and their Families in Early Medieval Bavaria* (Aldershot/Burlington VT: Ashgate).

Hedeager, Lotte (2011), *Iron Age Myth and Materiality: An Archaeology of Scandinavia AD 400–1000* (Abingdon/New York: Routledge).

Hodges, Richard (2000), *Towns and Trade in the Age of Charlemagne* (London: Duckworth).

Hodges, Richard and David B. Whitehouse (1983), *Mohammed, Charlemagne, and the Origins of Europe: Archaeology and the Pirenne Thesis* (London: Duckworth).

Hodges, Richard, David B. Whitehouse and William Bowden (eds) (1998), *The Sixth Century: Production, Distribution and Demand* (Leiden: Brill).

Hummer, H. (2005), *Politics and Power in Early Medieval Europe: Alsace in the Frankish Realms, 600–1000* (Cambridge: CUP).

Innes, Matthew (2000), *State and Society in the Early Middle Ages: The Middle Rhine Valley 400–1000* (Cambridge: CUP).

— (2007), *An Introduction to Early Medieval Western Europe, 300–900: The Sword, the Plough and the Book* (London/New York: Routledge).

Jong, Mayke de (2009), *The Penitential State: Authority and Atonement in the Age of Louis the Pious, 814–840* (Cambridge: CUP).

Jong, M. de, and F. Theuws [with C. van Rhijn] (eds) (2001), *Topographies of Power in the Early Middle Ages* (Leiden: Brill).

Koziol, Geoffrey (1992), *Begging Pardon and Favor: Ritual and Political Order in Early Medieval France* (Ithaca NY: Cornell UP).

Logan, F. Donald (2005), *The Vikings in History*, 3rd edn (Abingdon/New York: Routledge).

McCormick, Michael (2001), *Origins of the European Economy: Communications and Commerce, AD 300–900* (Cambridge: CUP).

MacLean, Simon (2003), *Kingship and Politics in the Late Ninth Century: Charles the Fat and the End of the Carolingian Empire* (Cambridge: CUP).

McKitterick, Rosamond (1983), *The Frankish Kingdoms under the Carolingians, 751–987* (London/New York: Longman);

— (1989), *The Carolingians and the Written Word* (Cambridge: CUP).

— (1994), *Carolingian Culture: Emulation and Innovation* (Cambridge: CUP).

— (2004), *History and Meaning in the Carolingian World* (Cambridge: CUP).

— (2008), *Charlemagne: The Formation of a European Identity* (Cambridge: CUP).

Mitterauer, Michael (2010), *Why Europe: The Medieval Origins of its Special Path* (Chicago: University of Chicago Press) (orig. German, 2003).

Nelson, Janet L. (1992), *Charles the Bald* (London: Longman).

— (2003), *The Frankish World, 750–900* (London/New York: Continuum).

Pelteret, David A.E. (1995), *Slavery in Early Mediaeval England: From the Reign of King Alfred until the Twelfth Century* (Woodbridge: Boydell).

Pestell, Tim, and Katharina Ulmschneider (eds) (2003), *Markets in Early Medieval Europe: Trading and 'Productive' Sites, 650–850* (Macclesfield: Windgather Press).

Poulsen, Björn and Søren Michael Sindbæk (eds) (2011), *Settlement and Lordship in Viking and Early Medieval Scandinavia* (Turnhout: Brepols).

Randsborg, Klavs (1991), *The First Millennium AD in Europe and the Mediterranean: An Archaeological Essay* (Cambridge: CUP).

Reuter, Timothy (1991), *Germany in the Early Middle Ages 800–1056* (London/New York: Longman).

Reynolds, Susan (1994), *Fiefs and Vassals: The Medieval Evidence Reinterpreted* (Oxford: OUP).

Riché, Pierre (1993), *The Carolingians: A Family Who Forged Europe* (Philadelphia: University of Pennsylvania Press) (orig. French, 1983).

Roesdahl, Else (1998), *The Vikings*, 2nd edn (London: Penguin Books).

Rotman, Youval (2009), *Byzantine Slavery and the Mediterranean World* (Cambridge MA: Harvard UP).

Russo, Daniel G. (1998), *Town Origins and Development in Early England, c.400–950* (Westport CT/London: Praeger).

Scragg, Donald (ed.) (2008), *Edgar, King of the English, 959–975: New Interpretations* (Woodbridge: Boydell).

Smith, Julia M.H. (2005), *Europe after Rome: A New Cultural History 500–1000* (Oxford: OUP).

Stanton, Robert (2002), *The Culture of Translation in Anglo-Saxon England* (Woodbridge/Rochester NY: Boydell & Brewer).

Story, Joanna (2003), *Carolingian Connections: Anglo-Saxon England and Carolingian Francia, c.750–870* (Aldershot/Burlington: Ashgate).

— (ed.) (2005), *Charlemagne: Empire and Society* (Manchester/New York: Manchester UP).

Verhulst, Adriaan (2002), *The Carolingian Economy* (Cambridge: CUP).

West, Charles (2013), *Reframing the Feudal Revolution: Political and Social Transformation between Marne and Moselle, c.800–c.1100* (Cambridge: CUP).

Wickham, Chris (2005), *Framing the Early Middle Ages: Europe and the Mediterranean, 400–800* (Oxford: OUP).

Willemsen, Annemarieke and Hanneke Kik (eds) (2010), *Dorestad in an International Framework: New Research on Centres of Trade and Coinage in Carolingian Times* (Turnhout: Brepols).

Williams, Ann (1999), *Kingship and Government in Pre-Conquest England, c.500–1066* (Basingstoke/New York: Macmillan/St Martin's Press).

Wood, Ian (1994), *The Merovingian Kingdoms 450–751* (London/New York: Longman).

Chapter 4

Aberth, John (2012), *An Environmental History of the Middle Ages: The Crucible of Nature* (London/New York: Routledge).

Arnold, Benjamin (2004), *Power and Property in Medieval Germany: Economic and Social Change, c.900–1300* (Oxford: OUP).

Astill, Grenville and John Langdon (eds) (1997), *Medieval Farming and Technology: The Impact of Agricultural Change in Northwest Europe* (Leiden: Brill).

Bagge, Sverre, Michael H. Gelting and Thomas Lindkvist (eds) (2011), *Feudalism: New Landscapes of Debate* (Turnhout: Brepols).

Barber, Malcolm (1994), *The New Knighthood: A History of the Order of the Temple* (Cambridge: CUP).

Barthélemy, Dominique (2009), *The Serf, the Knight and the Historian* (Ithaca/London: Cornell UP) (orig. French, 1997).

Bartlett, Robert (1993), *The Making of Europe: Conquest, Colonization and Cultural Change 950–1350* (London: Allen Lane).

Barton, Richard E. (2004), *Lordship in the County of Maine, c.890–1160* (Woodbridge/Rochester NY: Boydell & Brewer).

Berkhofer, Robert F., Alan Cooper and Adam J. Kosto (eds) (2005), *The Experience of Power in Medieval Europe, 950–1350* (Aldershot: Ashgate).

Bisson, Thomas N. (1998), *Tormented Voices: Power, Crisis, and Humanity in Rural Catalonia, 1140–1200* (Cambridge MA/London: Harvard UP).

— (2009), *The Crisis of the Twelfth Century: Power, Lordship, and the Origins of European Government* (Princeton/Oxford: Princeton UP).

Bloch, R. Howard (1991), *Medieval Misogyny and the Invention of Western Romantic Love* (Chicago/London: University of Chicago Press).

Bouchard, Constance Britten (1998), *'Strong of Body, Brave and Noble': Chivalry and Society in Medieval France* (Ithaca NY/London: Cornell UP).

Bowman, Jeffrey (2004), *Shifting Landmarks: Property, Proof, and Dispute in Catalonia around the Year 1000* (Ithaca NY: Cornell UP).

Brown, Warren C. (2011), *Violence in Medieval Europe* (Harlow: Pearson Education).

Brown, Warren C. and Piotr Górecki (eds) (2003), *Conflict in Medieval Europe: Changing Perspectives on Society and Culture* (Aldershot: Ashgate).

Bumke, Joachim (1991), *Courtly Culture: Literature and Society in the High Middle Ages* (Berkley/Los Angeles/Oxford: University of California Press) (orig. German, 1986).

Cheyette, Fredric L. (2001), *Ermengard of Narbonne and the World of the Troubadours* (Ithaca NY: Cornell UP).

Coss, Peter (1991), *Lordship, Knighthood and Locality: A Study in English Society, c.1180–c.1280* (Cambridge: CUP).

— (1993), *The Knight in Medieval England 1000–1400* (Stroud: Alan Sutton Publishing).

Crouch, David (2005), *The Birth of Nobility: Constructing Aristocracy in England and France, 900–1300* (Harlow: Pearson).

— (2005), *Tournament* (London/New York: Hambledon).

— (2011), *The English Aristocracy, 1070–1272: A Social Transformation* (New Haven/London: Yale UP).

Doran, Linda and James Lyttleton (eds) (2007), *Lordship in Medieval Ireland: Image and Reality* (Dublin: Four Courts Press).

Epstein, Stephen A. (2012), *The Medieval Discovery of Nature* (Cambridge: CUP).

Faith, Rosamond (1997), *The English Peasantry and the Growth of Lordship* (London/Washington: Leicester UP).

Fossier, Robert (1988), *Peasant Life in the Medieval West* (Oxford: Blackwell) (orig. French, 1984).

Freedman, Paul (1999), *Images of the Medieval Peasant* (Stanford/Cambridge: Stanford UP).

Genicot, Léopold (1990), *Rural Communities in the Medieval West* (Baltimore/London: the Johns Hopkins UP).

Glick, Thomas F. (1995), *From Muslim Fortress to Christian Castle: Social and Cultural Change in Medieval Spain* (Manchester/New York: Manchester UP).

Harvey, Alan (1989), *Economic Expansion in the Byzantine Empire 900–1200* (Cambridge: CUP).

Jaeger, C. Stephen (1985), *The Origins of Courtliness: Civilizing Trends and the Formation of Courtly Ideals 923–1210* (Philadelphia: University of Pennsylvania Press).

Jones, Richard and Mark Page (2006), *Medieval Villages in an English Landscape: Beginnings and Ends* (Macclesfield: Windgather Press).

Kaeuper, Richard W. (1999), *Chivalry and Violence in Medieval Europe* (Oxford: OUP).

— (2009), *Holy Warriors: The Religious Ideology of Chivalry* (Philadelphia: University of Pennsylvania Press).

Keen, Maurice (1984), *Chivalry* (New Haven/London: Yale UP).

Keiser, Elizabeth B. (1997), *Courtly Desire and Medieval Homophobia: The Legitimation of Sexual Pleasure in 'Cleanness' and its Contexts* (New Haven/London: Yale UP).

Knight, Stephen (2003), *Robin Hood: A Mythic Biography* (Ithaca NY/London: Cornell UP).

Laiou, Angeliki E. and Cécile Morisson (2007), *The Byzantine Economy* (Cambridge: CUP).

Moore, Robert I. (2000), *The First European Revolution, c.970–1215* (Oxford/Malden MA: Blackwell).

Muir, Lynette R. (1985), *Literature and Society in Medieval France: The Mirror and the Image, 1100–1500* (London/New York: Macmillan/St Martin's Press).

Nicholson, Helen (1995), *Templars, Hospitallers and Teutonic Knights: Images of the Military Orders 1128–1291* (Leicester: Leicester UP).

— (2010), *The Knights Templar: A Brief History of the Warrior Order*, 2nd edn (London: Running Press).

Noble, Thomas F.X. and John van Engen (eds) (2012), *European Transformations: The Long Twelfth Century* (Notre Dame: University of Notre Dame Press).

North, Michael (2012), *The Expansion of Europe, 1250–1500* (Manchester: Manchester UP) [orig. German 2007].

Paterson, Linda (1993), *The World of the Troubadours: Medieval Occitan Society, c.1100–c.1300* (Cambridge: CUP).

Philips, J.R.S. (1998) *The Medieval Expansion of Europe*, 2nd edn (Oxford: OUP).

Rösener, Werner, *Peasants in the Middle Ages* (Champaign IL: University of Illinois Press) (orig. German 1985).

Rosenwein, Barbara (ed.) (1998), *Anger's Past: The Social Uses of Emotion in the Middle Ages* (Ithaca NY: Cornell UP).

Saul, Nigel (2011), *Chivalry in England* (Cambridge MA: Harvard UP).

Schofield, Philipp (2003), *Peasant and Community in Medieval England* (Basingstoke: Palgrave Macmillan).

Stafford, Pauline (1989), *Unification and Conquest: A Political and Social History of England in the Tenth and Eleventh Centuries* (London: Edwin Arnold).

Stahuljak, Zrinka, Virginia Greene, Sarah Kay, Sharon Kinoshita and Peggy McCracken (2011), *Thinking Through Chrétien de Troyes* (Cambridge: D.S. Brewer).

Teuscher, Simon (2012), *Lords' Rights and Peasant Stories: Writing and the Formation of Tradition in the Later Middle Ages* (Philadelphia: University of Pennsylvania Press) (orig. German, 2007).

Thompson, Kathleen (2002), *Power and Border Lordship in Medieval France: The County of the Perche, 1000–1226* (Woodbridge/Rochester NY: Boydell & Brewer).

Williamson, Tom (2003), *Shaping Medieval Landscapes: Settlement, Society, Environment* (Macclesfield: Windgather Press).

Chapter 5

Abulafia, David (1988), *Frederick II: Medieval Emperor* (London: Allen Lane/Penguin).

— (1997), *The Western Mediterranean Kingdoms, 1200–1500: The Struggle for Dominion* (Boston: Addison Wesley).

— (2004), *Italy in the Central Middle Ages, 1000–1300* (Oxford: OUP) (Short Oxford History of Italy).

Adams, Jonathan, and Katherine Holman (eds) (2004), *Scandinavia and Europe, 800–1350: Contact, Conflict, and Coexistence* (Turnhout: Brepols).

Althoff, Gerd (2003), *Otto III* (University Park PA: Penn State Press) (orig. German, 1996).

Arnold, Benjamin (1997) *Medieval Germany, 500–1300:*

A Political Interpretation (Basingstoke/London: Macmillan).

Aurell, Martin (2007), *The Plantagenet Empire 1154–1224* (Harlow: Pearson) (orig. French, 2003).

Bachrach, Bernard S. (1993), *Fulk Nerra, the Neo-Roman Consul, 987–1040: A Political Biography of the Angevin Count* (Berkeley: University of California Press).

Bagge, Sverre (2002), *Kings, Politics, and the Right Order of the World in German Historiography, c.950–1150* (Leiden: Brill).

Baldwin, John W. (1986), *The Government of Philip Augustus: Foundations of French Royal Power in the Middle Ages* (Berkeley/London: University of California Press).

Barber, Richard (2001), *Henry Plantagenet: A Biography of Henry II of England*, 2nd edn (Rochester NY: Boydell & Brewer).

Barlow, Frank (1986) *Thomas Becket* (London: Weidenfeld & Nicolson).

— (2000), *William Rufus*, 2nd edn (New Haven/London: Yale UP).

— (2003), *The Godwins: Rise and Fall of a Noble Dynasty* (London: Longman).

Bartlett, Robert (2000), *England under the Norman and Angevin Kings, 1075–1225* (Oxford: OUP).

Bates, David (2001), *William the Conqueror* (Stroud: Tempus).

Benham, Jenny (2011), *Peacemaking in the Middle Ages: Principles and Practice* (Manchester: Manchester UP).

Berend, Nora (2001), *At the Gate of Christendom: Jews, Muslims and 'Pagans' in Medieval Hungary, c.1000–c.1300* (Cambridge: CUP).

Berkhofer, Robert F. III (2004), *Day of Reckoning: Power and Accountability in Medieval France* (Philadelphia: Pennsylvania State UP).

Bernardt, John W. (2002), *Itinerant Kingship and Royal Monasteries in Early Medieval Germany, c.936–1075*, 2nd edn (Cambridge: CUP).

Bertelli, Sergio (2001), *The King's Body: Sacred Rituals of Power in Medieval and Early Modern Europe* (University Park PA: Penn State Press) (orig. Italian, 1990).

Bianchini, Janna C. (2012), *The Queen's Hand: Power and Authority in the Reign of Berenguela of Castile* (Philadelphia: University of Philadelphia Press).

Bradbury, Jim (1998), *Philip Augustus, King of France, 1180–1223* (London: Longman).

— (2007), *The Capetians: Kings of France, 987–1328* (London/New York: Hambledon Continuum).

Breay, Claire (2002), *Magna Carta: Manuscripts and Myths* (London: British Library).

Bridgeford, Andrew (2005), *1066: The Hidden History in the Bayeux Tapestry* (London: Fourth Estate).

Brink, Stefan, and Neil Price (eds) (2011), *The Viking World* (London/New York: Routledge).

Brown, Reginald Allen (2000), *The Normans and the Norman Conquest*, 2nd edn (Woodbridge: Boydell).

Bull, Marcus (ed.) (2003), *France in the Central Middle Ages, 900–1200* (Oxford: OUP).

Burt, Caroline (2013), *Edward I and the Governance of England, 1272–1307* (Cambridge: CUP).

Catlos, Brian A. (2004), *The Victors and the Vanquished: Christians and Muslims of Catalonia and Aragon, 1050–1300* (Cambridge: CUP).

Chibnall, Marjorie (1984), *The World of Orderic Vitalis: Norman Monks and Norman Knights* (Oxford: Clarendon).

— (1986), *Anglo-Norman England 1066–1166* (Oxford: Blackwell).

— (1999), *The Debate on the Norman Conquest* (Manchester/New York: Manchester UP).

Clanchy, M.T. (1993), *From Memory to Written Record: England 1066–1307*, 2nd edn (Oxford: Blackwell).

Collins, Paul (2013), *The Birth of the West: Rome, Germany, France and the Creation of Europe in the Tenth Century* (Philadelphia: PublicAffairs).

Crouch, David (1986), *The Beaumont Twins: The Roots and Branches of Power in the Twelfth Century* (Cambridge: CUP).

— (1990), *William Marshal: Court, Career and Chivalry in the Angevin Empire, 1147–1219* (London/New York: Longman).

— (2000), *The Reign of King Stephen, 1135–1154* (Harlow: Longman).

Curta, Florin (2006), *Southeastern Europe in the Middle Ages, 500–1250* (Cambridge: CUP).

Dalton, Paul and Graeme J. White (eds) (2008), *King Stephen's Reign (1135–1154)* (Woodbridge: Boydell).

Danziger, Danny and John Gillingham (2004), *1215: The Year of Magna Carta* (New York: Touchstone).

Davies, R.R. (2000), *The First English Empire: Power and Identities in the British Isles, 1093–1343* (Oxford: OUP).

Delogu, Daisy (2008), *Theorizing the Ideal Sovereign: The Rise of the French Vernacular Royal Biography* (Toronto: University of Toronto Press).

Drell, Joanna H. (2002), *Kinship and Conquest: Family Strategies in the Principality of Salerno during the Norman Period, 1077–1194* (Ithaca NY: Cornell UP).

Duggan, Anne (2004), *Thomas Becket* (London: Arnold).

Dunbabin, Jean (1998), *Charles of Anjou: Power, Kingship and State-making in Thirteenth-century Europe* (London: Longman).

— (2000), *France in the Making, 843–1180*, 2nd edn (Oxford: OUP).

— (2011), *The French in the Kingdom of Sicily, 1266–1305* (Cambridge: CUP).

Fleming, Robin (1998), *Domesday Book and the Law: Society and Legal Custom in Early Medieval England* (Cambridge: CUP).

Foote, David (2004), *Lordship, Reform, and the Development of Civil Society in Medieval Italy: The Bishopric of Orvieto, 1100–1250* (Notre Dame IN: University of Notre Dame Press).

Frame, Robin (1995), *The Political Development of the British Isles, 1100–1400* (Oxford: OUP).

Fuhrmann, Horst (1986), *Germany in the High Middle Ages, c.1050–1200* (Cambridge: CUP).

Gaposchkin, M. Cecilia (2008), *The Making of Saint Louis: Kingship, Sanctity, and Crusade in the Later Middle Ages* (Ithaca/London: Cornell UP).

Garcia-Oliver, Ferran (2011), *The Valley of the Six Mosques: Work and Life in Medieval Valldigna* (Turnhout: Brepols).

Gillingham, John (1999), *Richard I* (New Haven/London: Yale UP).

Glenn, Jason (2004), *Politics and History in the Tenth Century: The Work and World of Richer of Reims* (Cambridge: CUP).

Gorecki, Piotr (1993), *Economy, Society and Lordship in Medieval Poland, 1100–1250* (New York: Holmes & Meier).

Graham-Leigh, Elaine (2005), *The Southern French Nobility and the Albigensian Crusade* (Woodbridge/ Rochester NY: Boydell & Brewer).

Green, Judith (1989), *The Government of England under Henry I* (Cambridge: CUP).

— (1997), *The Aristocracy of Norman England* (Cambridge: CUP).

Guy, John (2012), *Thomas Becket: Warrior, Priest, Rebel* (New York: Random House).

Hagger, Mark S. (2001), *The Fortunes of a Norman Family: The De Verduns in England, Ireland and Wales, 1066–1316* (Dublin/Portland: Four Courts Press).

Hamilton, J.S. (2010), *The Plantagenets: History of a Dynasty* (London/New York: Continuum).

Harper-Bill, Christopher and Nicholas Vincent (eds) (2007), *Henry II: New Interpretations* (Woodbridge: Boydell).

Haverkamp, Alfred (1992), *Medieval Germany, 1056–1273*, 2nd edn (Oxford: OUP).

Higham, N.J. (2002), *King Arthur: Myth-Making and History* (London/New York: Routledge).

Hitchcock, Richard (2008), *Mozarabs in Medieval and Early Modern Spain: Identities and Influences* (Aldershot: Ashgate).

Hollister, C. Warren, and Amanda Clark Frost (2003), *Henry I* (New Haven/London: Yale UP).

Hosler, John D. (2007), *Henry II: A Medieval Soldier at War, 1147–1189* (Leiden: Brill).

Howard, Ian (2003), *Swein Forkbeard's Invasions and the Danish Conquest of England, 991–1017* (Woodbridge/ Rochester NY: Boydell & Brewer).

Hudson, John (1996), *The Formation of the English Common Law: Law and Society in England from the Norman Conquest to Magna Carta* (London: Longman).

Huffman, Joseph P. (2000), *The Social Politics of Medieval Diplomacy: Anglo-German Relations 1066–1307* (Ann Arbor: University of Michigan Press).

Ingham, Patricia Clare (2001), *Sovereign Fantasies: Arthurian Romance and the Making of Britain* (Philadelphia: University of Pennsylvania Press).

Jayyusi, Salma Khadra (ed.) (1994), *The Legacy of Muslim Spain*. 2 vols. (Leiden: Brill).

Jones, Dan (2012), *The Plantagenets: The Warrior Kings and Queens Who Made England* (New York: Penguin).

Jones, Philip (1997), *The Italian City-State: From Commune to Signoria* (Oxford: Clarendon).

Klaniczay, Gábor (2002), *Holy Rulers and Blessed Princesses: Dynastic Cults in Medieval Central Europe* (Cambridge: CUP) (orig. Hungarian, 2000).

Kosto, Adam J. (2001), *Making Agreements in Medieval Catalonia: Power, Order and the Written Word, 1000–1200* (Cambridge: CUP).

Lawson, M.K. (2004), *Cnut*, 2nd edn (London: Longman).

Le Goff, Jacques (2009), *Saint Louis* (Notre Dame IN: University of Notre Dame Press) (orig. French, 1996).

Maddicott, J.R. (2010), *The Origins of the English Parliament, 924–1327* (Oxford: OUP).

Marvin, Laurence W. (2008), *The Occitan War: A Military and Political History of the Albigensian Crusade, 1209–1218* (Cambridge: CUP).

Matthew, Donald (1992), *The Norman Kingdom of Sicily* (Cambridge: CUP).

— (2002), *King Stephen* (London: Hambledon).

Mortimer, Richard (ed.) (2009), *Edward the Confessor: The Man and the Legend* (Woodbridge: Boydell).

O'Callaghan, Joseph F. (2003), *Reconquest and Crusade in Medieval Spain* (Philadelphia: University of Pennsylvania Press).

Oksanen, Eljas (2012), *Flanders and the Anglo-Norman World, 1066–1216* (Cambridge: CUP).

Pleszczynski, Andrezej (2011), *The Birth of a Stereotype: Polish Rulers and their Country in German Writings c.1000 AD* (Leiden/Boston: Brill).

Prestwich, Michael (2005), *Plantagenet England, 1225–1360* (Oxford: OUP) (New Oxford History of England).

Rady, Martyn (2001), *Nobility, Land and Service in Medieval Hungary* (Basingstoke: Palgrave Macmillan).

Reilly, Bernard F. (1993), *The Medieval Spains* (Cambridge: CUP).

Reuter, Timothy and Janet L. Nelson (eds) (2006), *Medieval Polities and Modern Mentalities* (Cambridge: CUP).

Reynolds, Susan (1997), *Kingdoms and Communities in Western Europe 900–1300*, 2nd edn (Oxford: Clarendon Press).

Rider, Jeff and Alan V. Murray (eds) (2009), *Galbert of Bruges and the Historiography of Medieval Flanders* (Washington DC: The Catholic University of America Press).

Robinson, I.S. (1999), *Henry IV of Germany, 1056–1106* (Cambridge: CUP).

Scott, Robert A. (2003), *The Gothic Enterprise: A Guide to Understanding the Medieval Cathedral* (Berkeley/Los Angeles: University of California Press).

Smith, Damian J. (2010), *Crusade, Heresy and Inquisition in the Lands of the Crown of Aragon (c.1167–1276)* (Leiden/Boston: Brill).

Stih, Peter (2010), *The Middle Ages between the Eastern Alps and the Northern Adriatic: Select Papers on Slovene Historiography and Medieval History* (Leiden: Brill).

Thomas, Hugh M. (2003), *The English and the Normans: Ethnic Hostility, Assimilation and Identity, 1066–c.1220* (Oxford/New York: OUP).

— (2008), *The Norman Conquest: England after William the Conqueror* (Lanham: Rowman & Littlefield).

Turner, Ralph and Richard R. Heiser (2000), *The Reign of Richard Lionheart: Ruler of the Angevin Empire, 1189–1199* (Harlow: Pearson).

Turner, Ralph V. (2005), *King John: England's Evil King?* (Stroud: Tempus).

— (2009), *Eleanor of Aquitaine: Queen of France, Queen of England* (New Haven: Yale UP).

Waley, Daniel (2010), *The Italian City Republics*, 4th edn (Harlow: Pearson).

Warren, Michelle (2000), *History on the Edge: Excalibur and the Borders of Britain (1100–1300)* (Minneapolis: University of Minnesota Press).

Warren, W.L. (1973), *Henry II* (Berkeley: University of California Press).

Webber, Nick (2005), *The Evolution of Norman Identity, 911–1154* (Woodbridge/Rochester NY: Boydell & Brewer).

Weinfurter, Stefan (1999), *The Salian Century: Main Currents in an Age of Transition* (Philadelphia: University of Pennsylvania Press) (orig. German, 1992).

Wilson, David MacKenzie (2004), *The Bayeux Tapestry*, 2nd edn (London: Thames & Hudson).

Chapter 6

Abou-el-Haj, Barbara (1995), *The Medieval Cult of Saints* (Cambridge: CUP).

Andrews, Frances (1999), *The Early Humiliati* (Cambridge: CUP).

Arnold, John H. (2001), *Inquisition and Power: Catharism and the Confessing Subject in Medieval Languedoc* (Philadelphia: University of Pennsylvania Press).

Ashley, Kathleen and Marilyn Deegan (2009), *Being a Pilgrim: Art and Ritual on the Medieval Routes to Santiago* (Farnham/Burlington VT: Ashgate).

Astell, Ann W. (2006), *Eating Beauty: The Eucharist and the Spiritual Arts of the Middle Ages* (Ithaca NY/London: Cornell UP).

Audrisio, Gabriel (1999), *The Waldensian Dissent: Persecution and Survival, c.1170–c.1570* (Cambridge: CUP) (orig. French, 1989).

Barber, Malcolm (2000), *The Cathars: Dualist Heretics in Languedoc in the High Middle Ages* (London: Longman).

Barber, Richard (1991), *Pilgrimages* (Woodbridge: Boydell).

Berman, Constance Hoffman (2000), *The Cistercian Evolution: The Invention of a Religious Order in Twelfth-Century Europe* (Philadelphia: University of Pennsylvania Press).

— (ed.) (2005), *Medieval Religion: New Approaches* (London/New York: Routledge).

Bijsterveld, Arnoud-Jan A. (2007), *Do Ut Des: Gift Giving, Memoria, and Conflict Management in the Medieval Low Countries* (Hilversum: Verloren).

Biller, Peter (2001) *The Waldenses, 1170–1530: Between a Religious Order and a Church* (Aldershot: Ashgate) (Variorum Collected Studies Series; 676).

Biller, Peter and Anne Hudson (eds) (1994), *Heresy and Literacy, 1000–1500* (Cambridge: CUP).

Blumenthal, Uta-Renate (1988), *The Investiture Controversy: Church and Monarchy from the Ninth to the Twelfth Century* (Philadelphia: University of Pennsylvania Press) (orig. German, 1982).

Brasher, Sally Mayall (2003), *Women of the Humiliati: A Lay Religious Order in Medieval Civic Life* (London/New York: Routledge).

Burger, Michael (2012), *Bishops, Clerks and Diocesan Governance in Thirteenth-Century England: Reward and Punishment* (Cambridge: CUP).

Burr, David (2001), *The Spiritual Franciscans: From Protest to Persecution in the Century after Saint Francis* (Philadelphia: Pennsylvania State UP).

Burton, Janet and Julie Kerr (2011), *The Cistercians in the Middle Ages* (Woodbridge/Rochester NY: Boydell & Brewer).

Bynum, Caroline Walker (1982), *Jesus as Mother: Studies in the Spirituality of the High Middle Ages* (Berkeley: University of California Press).

— (1987), *Holy Feast and Holy Fast: The Religious Significance of Food to Medieval Women* (Berkeley: University of California Press).

— (1995), *The Resurrection of the Body in Western Christianity, 200–1336* (New York: Columbia UP).

Cameron, Euan (2000), *Waldenses: Rejections of Holy Church in Medieval Europe* (Oxford: Blackwell).

Carville, Geraldine (2003), *The Impact of the Cistercians on the Landscape of Ireland 1142–1541* (Ashford: KB Publications)

Chazan, Robert (2010), *Reassessing Jewish Life in Medieval Europe* (Cambridge: CUP).

Constable, Giles (1995), *Three Studies in Medieval Religious and Social Thought: The Interpretation of Mary and Martha, the Ideal of the Imitation of Christ, the Orders of Society* (Cambridge: CUP).

— (1996), *The Reformation of the Twelfth Century* (Cambridge: CUP).

Costen, Michael (1997), *The Cathars and the Albigensian Crusade* (Manchester: Manchester UP).

Drury, John (1999), *Painting the Word: Christian Pictures and their Meanings* (New Haven/London: Yale UP).

Evans, G.R. (2000), *Bernard of Clairvaux* (Oxford: OUP).

France, James (2012), *Separate but Equal: Cistercian Lay Brothers, 1120–1350* (Collegeville MN: Liturgical Press).

France, John (2005), *The Crusades and the Expansion of Catholic Christendom, 1000–1714* (London/New York: Routledge).

Frugoni, Chiara (1998), *Francis of Assisi: A Life* (London: Continuum) (orig. Italian, 1995).

Fulton, Rachel (2002), *From Judgment to Passion: Devotion to Christ and the Virgin Mary, 800–1200* (New York; Columbia UP).

Given, James B. (1997), *Inquisition and Medieval Society: Power, Discipline, and Resistance in Languedoc* (Ithaca NY: Cornell UP).

Head, Thomas, and Richard Landes (eds) (1992), *The Peace of God: Social Violence and Religious Response in France around the Year 1000* (Ithaca NY/London: Cornell UP).

Hiscock, Nigel (ed.) (2003), *The White Mantle of Churches: Architecture, Liturgy and Art around the Millennium* (Turnhout: Brepols).

Hugo, William R. (1996), *Studying the Life of St Francis of Assisi: A Beginner's Workbook* (Quincy: Franciscan Press).

Hunter, Ian, John Christian Laursen and Cary J. Nederman (eds) (2005), *Heresy in Transition: Transforming Ideas of Heresy in Medieval and Early Modern Europe* (Aldershot: Ashgate).

Iogna-Prat, Dominique (2002), *Order and Exclusion: Cluny and Christendom Face Heresy, Judaism, and Islam (1000–1150)* (Ithaca NY/London: Cornell UP) (orig. French, 1998).

Jamroziak, Emilia (2011), *Survival and Success on Medieval Borders: Cistercian Houses in Medieval Scotland and Pomerania from the Twelfth to the Late Fourteenth Century* (Turnhout: Brepols).

Jones, Anna Trumbore (2009), *Noble Lord, Good Sheperd: Episcopal Power and Piety in Aquitaine, 877–1050* (Leiden: Brill).

Kieckhefer, Richard (1989), *Magic in the Middle Ages* (Cambridge: CUP).

Kienzle, Beverly Mayne (2001), *Cistercians, Heresy and Crusade in Occitania, 1145–1229: Preaching in the Lord's Vineyard* (York: York Medieval Press).

Koopmans, Rachel (2011), *Wonderful to Relate: Miracle Stories and Miracle Collecting in High Medieval England* (Philadelphia: University of Pennsylvania Press).

Lambert, Malcolm (1992), *Medieval Heresy: Popular Movements from the Gregorian Reform to the Reformation*, 2nd edn (Oxford: Blackwell).

Landes, Richard (1995), *Relics, Apocalypse, and the Deceits of History: Ademar of Chabannes, 989–1034* (Cambridge MA: Harvard UP).

Landes, Richard, Andrew Gow and David C. Van Meter (eds) (2003), *The Apocalyptic Year 1000: Religious Expectation and Social Change, 950–1050* (Oxford: OUP).

Lawrence, C.H. (1994), *The Friars: The Impact of the Early Mendicant Movement on Western Society* (London/New York: Longman).

Le Goff, Jacques (1986), *The Birth of Purgatory* (Chicago: University of Chicago Press) (orig. French, 1981).

Lerner, Robert E. (2001), *The Feast of Saint Abraham: Medieval Millenarians and the Jews* (Philadelphia: Pennsylvania State UP).

Lester, Anne E. (2011), *Creating Cistercian Nuns: The Women's Religious Movement and its Reform in Thirteenth-Century Champagne* (Ithaca NY: Cornell UP).

Little, Lester K. (1978), *Religious Poverty and the Profit Economy in Medieval Europe* (Ithaca NY/London: Cornell UP).

Loud, G.A. (2007), *The Latin Church in Norman Italy* (Cambridge: CUP).

McGuire, Brian Patrick (2002), *Friendship and Faith: Cistercian Men, Women, and their Stories, 1100–1250* (Aldershot: Ashgate) (Variorum Collected Studies Series; 742).

McNamer, Sarah (2010), *Affective Meditation and the Invention of Medieval Compassion* (Philadelphia: University of Pennsylvania Press).

Madden, Thomas F. (1999), *A Concise History of the Crusades* (Lanham: Rowman & Littlefield).

Malegam, Jehangir Yezdi (2013), *The Sleep of Behemoth: Disputing Peace and Violence in Medieval Europe, 1000–1200* (Ithaca NY: Cornell UP).

Mews, Constant J. and Claire Renkin (eds) (2010),

Interpreting Francis and Clare from the Middle Ages to the Present (Mulgrave: Broughton Publishing).

Minnis, Alastair and Rosalynn Voaden (eds) (2010), *Medieval Holy Women in the Christian Tradition, c.1100–c.1500* (Turnhout: Brepols).

Moore, John C. (2009), *Pope Innocent III (1160/61–1216): To Root up and to Plant* (Notre Dame IN: University of Notre Dame Press).

Moore, R.I. (2007), *The Formation of a Persecuting Society: Power and Deviance in Western Europe, 950–1250*, 2nd edn (Oxford: Blackwell).

— (2012), *The War on Heresy* (Cambridge MA: The Belknap Press of Harvard UP).

Nederman, Cary J. (2000), *Worlds of Difference: European Discourses of Toleration* (University Park: Pennsylvania State UP).

Newhauser, Richard G. and Susan J. Ridyard (eds) (2012), *Sin in Medieval and Early Modern Culture* (Woodbridge: Boydell & Brewer).

Nirenberg, David (1996), *Communities of Violence: Persecution of Minorities in the Middle Ages* (Princeton: Princeton UP).

Nyberg, Tore (2000), *Monasticism in North-Western Europe, 800–1200* (Aldershot/Burlington VT: Ashgate).

Pegg, Mark Gregory (2005), *The Corruption of Angels: The Great Inquisition of 1245–1246* (Princeton: Princeton UP).

— (2008), *A Most Holy War: The Albigensian Crusade and the Battle for Christendom* (Oxford: OUP).

Peltzer, Jörg (2008), *Canon Law, Careers, and Conquest: Episcopal Elections in Normandy and Greater Anjou: c.1140–c. 1230* (Cambridge: CUP).

Prudlo, Donald S. (ed.) (2011), *The Origin, Development and Refinement of Medieval Religious Mendicancies* (Leiden: Brill).

Rivard, Derek A. (2009), *Blessing the World: Ritual and Lay Piety in Medieval Religion* (Washington DC: The Catholic University of America Press).

Robinson, I.S. (1990), *The Papacy 1073–1198: Continuity and Innovation* (Cambridge: CUP).

Rosenwein, Barbara H. (1982), *Rhinoceros Bound: Cluny in the Tenth Century* (Philadelphia: University of Pennsylvania Press).

— (1989), *To Be the Neighbor of Saint Peter: The Social Meaning of Cluny's Property, 909–1049* (Ithaca NY/London: Cornell UP).

Rudolph, Conrad (2004), *Pilgrimage to the End of the World: The Road to Santiago de Compostela* (Chicago: University of Chicago Press).

Russell, Jeffrey Burton (1997), *A History of Heaven: The Singing Silence* (Princeton: Princeton UP).

Sayers, Jane (1994), *Innocent III: Leader of Europe 1198–1216* (London: Longman).

Shepkaru, Shmuel (2006), *Jewish Martyrs in the Pagan and Christian Worlds* (Cambridge: CUP).

Smith, Damian J. (2004), *Innocent III and the Crown of Aragon: The Limits of Papal Authority* (Aldershot/Burlington VT: Ashgate).

Spoto, Donald (2003), *Reluctant Saint: The Life of Francis of Assisi* (New York: Penguin).

Stow, Kenneth R. (1992), *Alienated Minority: The Jews of Medieval Latin Europe* (Cambridge MA/London: Harvard UP).

Stroll, Mary (2012), *Popes and Antipopes: The Politics of Eleventh-Century Church Reform* (Leiden/Boston: Brill).

Taylor, Claire (2005), *Heresy in Medieval France: Dualism in Aquitaine and the Agenais, 1000–1249* (Woodbridge/Rochester NY: Boydell & Brewer).

Tellenbach, Gert (1993), *The Church in Western Europe from the Tenth to the Early Twelfth Century* (Cambridge: CUP) (orig. German, 1988).

Vauchez, André (1993), *Spirituality in the Medieval West* (Kalamazoo: Liturgical Press) (orig. French, 1975).

— (2012), *Francis of Assisi: The Life and Afterlife of a Medieval Saint* (New Haven/London: Yale UP) (orig. French, 2009).

Vose, Robin (2009), *Dominicans, Muslims and Jews in the Medieval Crown of Aragon* (Cambridge: CUP).

Waugh, Scott L., and Pieter Diehl (eds) (1996), *Christendom and its Discontents: Exclusion, Persecution and Rebellion, 1000–1500* (Cambridge: CUP).

Webb, Diana (1999), *Pilgrims and Pilgrimage in the Medieval West* (London/New York: I.B. Tauris).

— (2002), *Medieval European Pilgrimage, c.700–c.1500* (Basingstoke: Palgrave).

Wolf, Kenneth Baxter (2003), *The Poverty of Riches: St Francis of Assisi Reconsidered* (Oxford: OUP).

Chapter 7

Abu-Lughod, Janet L. (1989), *Before European Hegemony: The World System AD 1250–1350* (Oxford: OUP).

Akbari, Suzanne Conklin and Amilcare A. Iannucci (eds) (2008), *Marco Polo and the Encounter of East and West* (Toronto: University of Toronto Press).

Amitai-Preiss, Reuven (1995), *Mongols and Mamluks: The Mamluk–Ilkhanid War, 1260–1281* (Cambridge: CUP).

Angold, Michael (2003), *The Fourth Crusade: Event and Context* (Harlow: Pearson).

Bolton, J.L. (2012), *Money in the English Economy, 973–1489* (Manchester: Manchester UP).

Brand, Hanno (ed.) (2007), *The German Hanse in Past and Present Europe: A Medieval League as a Model for Modern Interregional Cooperation?* (Groningen: Hanse Passage/Castel International Publishers).

Britnell, R.H. (1993), *The Commercialisation of English Society 1000–1500* (Cambridge: CUP).

Britnell, R.H. and B.M.S. Campbell (eds) (1995), *A Commercializing Economy: England 1086–1300* (Manchester: Manchester UP).

Bronstein, Judith (2005), *The Hospitallers and the Holy Land: Financing the Latin East, 1187–1274* (Woodbridge/Rochester NY: Boydell & Brewer).

Cahen, Claude (2001), *The Formation of Turkey: The Seljukid Sultanate of Rum, Eleventh to Fourteenth Century* (London: Longman) (orig. French, 1988).

Cardini, Franco (2000), *Europe and Islam: History of a Misunderstanding* (Oxford: Blackwell) (orig. Italian, 2000).

Chazan, Robert (1987), *European Jewry and the First Crusade* (Berkeley/Los Angeles: University of California Press).

Chrissis, Nikolaos G. (2012), *Crusading in Frankish Greece: A Study of Byzantine-Western Relations and Attitudes, 1204–1282* (Turnhout: Brepols).

Christian, David (1998), *A History of Russia, Central Asia, and Mongolia: Volume 1. Inner Eurasia from Prehistory to the Mongol Empire* (Malden MA/Oxford: Blackwell).

Christiansen, Eric (1980), *The Northern Crusades: The Baltic and the Catholic Frontier 1100–1525* (London/ Basingstoke: Macmillan).

Dodds, Ben and Christian D. Liddy (eds) (2011), *Commercial Activity, Markets and Entrepreneurs in the Middle Ages: Essays in Honour of Richard Britnell* (Woodbridge: Boydell).

Doosselaere, Quentin van (2009), *Commercial Agreements and Social Dynamics in Medieval Genoa* (Cambridge: CUP).

Ellenblum, Ronnie (1998), *Frankish Rural Settlement in the Latin Kingdom of Jerusalem* (Cambridge: CUP).

Epstein, Stephan R. (1992), *An Island for Itself: Economic Development and Social Change in Late Medieval Sicily* (Cambridge: CUP).

Farber, Lianna (2006), *An Anatomy of Trade in Medieval Writing: Value, Consent, and Community* (Ithaca NY/London: Cornell UP).

Favier, Jean (1998) *Gold and Spices: The Rise of Commerce in the Middle Ages* (New York: Holmes & Meier) (orig. French, 1987).

Frakes, Jerold C. (ed.) (2011), *Contextualizing the Muslim Other in Medieval Christian Discourse* (New York: Palgrave Macmillan).

France, John (2005), *The Crusades and the Expansion of Catholic Christendom, 1000–1714* (London/New York: Routledge).

Greif, Avner (2006), *Institutions and the Path to the Modern Economy: Lessons from Medieval Trade* (Cambridge: CUP).

Hansen, Valerie (2012), *The Silk Road: A New History* (Oxford: OUP).

Hillenbrand, Carole (1999) *The Crusades: Islamic Perspectives* (Edinburgh: Edinburgh UP).

— (2008), *Turkish Myth and Muslim Symbol: The Battle of Manzikert* (Edinburgh: Edinburgh UP).

Hodgson, Marshall G.S. (2005), *The Secret Order of Assassins: The Struggle of the Early Nizari Ismailis against the Islamic World* (Philadelphia: University of Pennsylvania Press).

Houben, Hubert (2002), *Roger II of Sicily: A Ruler between East and West* (Cambridge: CUP) (orig. German, 1997).

Housley, Norman (1982), *The Italian Crusades: The Papal-Angevin Alliance and the Crusades against Christian Lay Powers, 1254–1343* (Oxford: Clarendon).

— (1992), *The Later Crusades, 1274–1580: From Lyons to Alcázar* (Oxford: OUP).

— (2006), *Contesting the Crusades* (Malden MA/Oxford: Blackwell).

Howell, Martha C. (2010), *Commerce before Capitalism in Europe, 1300–1600* (Cambridge: CUP).

Hunt, E.S. (1994), *The Medieval Super-Companies: A Study of the Peruzzi Company of Florence* (Cambridge: CUP).

Hunt, E.S. and James M. Murray (1999), *A History of Business in Medieval Europe, 1200–1550* (Cambridge: CUP).

Irwin, Robert (1986), *The Middle East in the Middle Ages: The Early Mamluk Sultanate, 1250–1382* (Carbondale IL: Southern Illinois UP).

Jackson, Peter (2005), *The Mongols and the West, 1221–1410* (Harlow: Pearson).

Jacoby, David (2005), *Commercial Exchange across the Mediterranean: Byzantium, the Crusader Levant, Egypt and Italy* (Aldershot: Ashgate) (Variorum Collected Studies).

Kedar, Benjamin Z. (1988), *Crusade and Mission: European Approaches toward the Muslims* (Princeton: Princeton UP).

— (1994), *The Franks in the Levant, 11th to 14th Centuries* (Aldershot: Ashgate) (Variorum Collected Studies).

Kostick, Conor (2008), *The Social Structure of the First Crusade* (Leiden/Boston: Brill).

Ladd, Roger A. (2010), *Antimercantilism in Late Medieval English Literature* (New York: Palgrave Macmillan).

Larner, John (1999), *Marco Polo and the Discovery of the World* (New Haven/London: Yale UP).

Leopold, Antony (2001), *How to Recover the Holy Land: Crusading Proposals of the Late 13th and Early 14th Centuries* (Aldershot: Ashgate).

Liu, Xinru (2010), *The Silk Road in World History* (Oxford: OUP).

Lock, Peter (1995), *The Franks in the Aegean 1204–1500* (London/New York: Longman).

— (2006), *The Routledge Companion to the Crusades* (London/New York: Routledge).

Lopez, Roberto S. (1976), *The Commercial Revolution of the Middle Ages, 950–1350* (Cambridge: CUP).

Loud, Graham A. (2000), *The Age of Robert Guiscard: Southern Italy and Northern Conquest* (London/New York: Longman).

MacEvitt, Christopher (2008), *The Crusades and the Christian World of the East: Rough Tolerance* (Philadelphia: University of Pennsylvania Press).

Madden, Thomas F. (2003), *Enrico Dandolo and the Rise of Venice* (Baltimore/London: the Johns Hopkins UP).

— (gen. ed.) (2004), *Crusades: The Illustrated History: Christendom, Islam, Pilgrimage, War* (Ann Arbor: University of Michigan Press).

— (2012), *Venice: A New History* (New York: Viking Penguin).

Masschaele, James (1997), *Peasants, Merchants, and Markets: Inland Trade in Medieval England, 1150–1350* (New York: St Martin's Press).

Moore, Ellen Wedemeyer (1985), *The Fairs of Medieval England: An Introductory Study* (Toronto: Pontifical Institute of Mediaeval Studies).

Morgan, David (1986), *The Mongols* (Cambridge MA/Oxford: Blackwell).

Mueller, Reinhold C. (1997), *The Venetian Money Market: Banks, Panics, and the Public Debt, 1200–1500* (Baltimore: the Johns Hopkins UP).

Ohler, Norbert (1989), *The Medieval Traveller* (Woodbridge: Boydell) (orig. German, 1986).

Peacock, Andrew (2010), *Early Seljuq History: A New Interpretation* (Abingdon/New York: Routledge).

Peacock, Andrew and Sara Nur Yildiz (eds) (2013), *The Seljuks of Anatolia: Court and Society in the Medieval Middle East* (London/New York: I.B. Tauris).

Philipp, Thomas, and Ulrich Haarmann (eds) (1998), *The Mamluks in Egyptian Politics and Society* (Cambridge: CUP).

Powell, James M. (ed.), *Muslims under Latin Rule, 1100–1300* (Princeton: Princeton UP).

Purkis, William J. (2008), *Crusading Spirituality in the Holy Land and Iberia, c.1095–c.1187* (Rochester NY/Woodbridge: Boydell).

Riley-Smith, Jonathan (2002), *What Were the Crusades?* 3rd edn (Basingstoke/London: Macmillan).

— (2012), *The Knights Hospitaller in the Levant, c. 1070–1309* (New York: Palgrave Macmillan).

Rouighi, Ramzi (2011), *The Making of a Mediterranean Emirate: Ifriqiya and its Andalusis, 1200–1400* (Philadelphia: University of Pennsylvania Press).

Rubenstein, Jay (2011), *Armies of Heaven: The First Crusade and the Quest for the Apocalypse* (New York: Basic Books).

Ruffini, Giovanni R. (2012), *Medieval Nubia: A Social and Economic History* (New York/Oxford: OUP).

Schildhauer, Johannes (1985), *The Hansa: History and Culture* (Leipzig: Edition Leipzig).

Skinner, Patricia (2013), *Medieval Amalfi and its Diaspora, 800–1250* (Oxford: OUP).

Spufford, Peter (1988) *Money and its Use in Medieval Europe* (Cambridge: CUP).

— (2002), *Power and Profit: The Merchant in Medieval Europe* (London: Thames & Hudson).

Tolan, John V. (2002), *Saracens: Islam in the Medieval European Imagination* (New York: Columbia UP).

Tyerman, Christopher (2008), *God's War: A New History of the Crusades* (Cambridge MA: The Belknap Press of Harvard UP).

Ward, Robin (2009), *The World of the Medieval Shipmaster: Law, Business, and the Sea, c.1350–1450* (Woodbridge: Boydell).

Winter, Michael, and Amalia Levanoni (eds) (2004), *The Mamluks in Egyptian and Syrian Politics and Society* (Leiden/Boston: Brill).

Wubs-Mrozewicz, Justyna and Stuart Jenks (eds) (2012), *The Hanse in Medieval and Early Modern Europe* (Leiden: Brill).

Chapter 8

Bartlett, Robert (2008), *The Natural and the Supernatural in the Middle Ages* (Cambridge: CUP) (The Wiles Lectures).

Brooke, Christopher (1989), *The Medieval Idea of Marriage* (Oxford: Clarendon).

Brundage, James A. (1995), *Medieval Canon Law* (London/New York: Longman).

Clanchy, M.T. (1997), *Abelard: A Medieval Life* (Oxford: Blackwell).

Coene, Karen de, Martine de Reu and Philippe de Maeyer (2011), *Liber Floridus 1121: The World in a Book* (Tielt: Lannoo Publishers).

Colish, Marcia L. (1994), *Peter Lombard*. 2 vols (Leiden: Brill).

— (1997), *Medieval Foundations of the Western Intellectual Tradition, 400–1400* (New Haven/London: Yale UP).

Copeland, Rita and Ineke Sluiter (eds) (2010), *Medieval Grammar and Rhetoric: Language Arts and Literary Theory, AD 300–1475* (Oxford: OUP).

Cotts, John D. (2009), *The Clerical Dilemma: Peter of Blois and Literate Culture in the Twelfth Century* (Washington DC: The Catholic University of America Press).

Courtenay, William J. (1987), *Schools and Scholars in Fourteenth-Century England* (Princeton: Princeton UP).

Cowdrey, H.E.J. (2003), *Lanfranc: Scholar, Monk, and Archbishop* (Oxford: OUP).

Crosby, Alfred W. (1997), *The Measure of Reality: Quantification and Western Society, 1250–1600* (Cambridge: CUP).

Cross, Richard (1999), *Duns Scotus* (Oxford: OUP).

DeGregorio, Scott (ed.) (2010), *The Cambridge Companion to Bede* (Cambridge: CUP).

Edson, Evelyn (1997), *Mapping Time and Space: How Medieval Mapmakers Viewed their World* (London: British Library).

Edson, Evelyn and E. Savage-Smith (2004), *Medieval Views of the Cosmos* (Chicago: University of Chicago Press).

Ferruolo, Stephen (1985), *The Origins of the University: The Schools of Paris and their Critics, 1100–1215* (Stanford CA: Stanford UP).

French, Roger (2003), *Medicine before Science: The Business of Medicine from the Middle Ages to the Enlightenment* (Cambridge: CUP).

Gaukroger, Stephen (2006), *The Emergence of a Scientific Culture: Science and the Shaping of Modernity, 1200–1685* (Oxford: Clarendon Press).

Gimpel, Jean (1976), *The Medieval Machine: The Industrial Revolution of the Middle Ages* (New York: Holt, Rinehart & Winston) (orig. French, 1975).

Godman, Peter (2009), *Paradoxes of Conscience in the High Middle Ages: Abelard, Heloise, and the Archpoet* (Cambridge: CUP).

Grant, Edward (1996), *The Foundations of Science in the Middle Ages: Their Religious, Institutional and Intellectual Contexts* (Cambridge: CUP).

— (2004) *Science and Religion, 400 BC to AD 1550: From Aristotle to Copernicus* (Baltimore: the Johns Hopkins UP).

Grendler, Paul F. (1989), *Schooling in Renaissance Italy: Literacy and Learning, 1300–1600* (Baltimore: the Johns Hopkins UP).

— (2002), *The Universities of the Italian Renaissance* (Baltimore/London: the Johns Hopkins UP).

Hannam, James (2009), *God's Philosophers: How the Medieval World Laid the Foundations of Modern Science* (London: Icon Books).

Harvey, P.D.A. (1991), *Medieval Maps* (London: British Library).

Houston, Jason M. (2010), *Building a Monument to Dante: Boccaccio as Dantista* (Toronto: University of Toronto Press).

Huff, Toby E. (2003), *The Rise of Early Modern Science: Islam, China and the West*, 2nd edn (Cambridge: CUP).

Jaeger, C. Stephen (2000), *The Envy of Angels: Cathedral Schools and Social Ideals in Medieval Europe, 950–1200* (Philadelphia: University of Pennsylvania Press).

Jardine, Lisa (1994), *Erasmus, Man of Letters* (Princeton: Princeton UP).

Kline, Naomi Reed (2001), *Maps of Medieval Thought: The Hereford Paradigm* (Woodbridge: Boydell).

Kuskin, William (2008), *Symbolic Caxton: Literary Culture and Print Capitalism* (Notre Dame IN: University of Notre Dame Press).

Lindberg, David C. (2007), *The Beginnings of Western Science: The European Scientific Tradition in Philosophical, Religious, and Institutional Context, Prehistory to AD 1450*, 2nd edn (Chicago/London: University of Chicago Press).

Long, Pamela O. (2001), *Openness, Secrecy, Authorship: Technical Arts and the Culture of Knowledge from Antiquity to the Renaissance* (Baltimore/London: the Johns Hopkins UP).

— (2003), *Technology and Society in the Medieval Centuries: Byzantium, Islam and the West, 500–1300* (Washington DC: American Historical Association).

Lozovsky, Natalia (2000), *The Earth Is Our Book: Geographical Knowledge in the Latin West, ca. 400–1000* (Ann Arbor: University of Michigan Press).

Luscombe, David (1997), *Medieval Thought* (Oxford: OUP).

McGrade, Arthur Stephen (2002), *The Political Thought of William Ockham: Personal and Institutional Principles*, 2nd edn (Cambridge: CUP).

McKitterick, Rosamond (1990), *The Uses of Literacy in Early Medieval Europe* (Cambridge: CUP).

Marenbon, John (1997), *The Philosophy of Peter Abelard* (Cambridge: CUP).

— (2003), *Boethius* (Oxford/New York: OUP).

— (2007), *Medieval Philosophy: An Historical and Philosophical Introduction* (Milton Park/New York: Routledge).

Martin, John Jeffries (ed.) (2002), *The Renaissance: Italy and Abroad* (London/New York: Routledge).

Matthews, Gareth B. (1998), *The Augustinian Tradition* (Berkeley: University of California Press).

Mews, Constant J. and John N. Crossley (eds) (2011), *Communities of Learning: Networks and the Shaping of Intellectual identity in Europe, 1100–1500* (Turnhout: Brepols).

Nauert, Charles J. Jr. (2006), *Humanism and the Culture of Renaissance Europe*, 2nd edn (Cambridge: CUP).

Nauta, Lodi (2009), *In Defense of Common Sense: Lorenzo Valla's Humanist Critique of Scholastic Philosophy* (Cambridge MA: Harvard UP).

O'Boyle, Cornelius (1998), *The Art of Medicine: Medical Teaching at the University of Paris, 1250–1400* (Leiden: Brill).

Pedersen, Olaf (1997), *The First Universities: Studium*

Generale *and the Origins of University Education in Europe* (Cambridge: CUP).

Pormann, Peter E. and Emilie Savage-Smith (2007), *Medieval Islamic Medicine* (Washington DC: Georgetown UP).

Power, Amanda (2012), *Roger Bacon and the Defence of Christendom* (Cambridge: CUP).

Rosemann, Philipp W. (2004), *Peter Lombard* (Oxford: OUP).

Saliba, George (2007), *Islamic Science and the Making of the European Renaissance* (Cambridge MA/London: The MIT Press).

Schoek, Richard J. (1990–1993), *Erasmus of Europe*. 2 vols (Edinburgh: Edinburgh UP).

Simek, Rudolf (1996), *Heaven and Earth in the Middle Ages: The Physical World before Columbus* (Woodbridge: Boydell) (orig. German, 1992).

Siraisi, Nancy G. (1990), *Medieval and Early Renaissance Medicine: An Introduction to Knowledge and Practice* (Chicago: University of Chicago Press).

— (2001), *Medicine and the Italian Universities 1250–1600* (Leiden: Brill).

Southern, Richard W. (1988), *Robert Grosseteste: The Growth of an English Mind in Medieval Europe* (Oxford: OUP).

— (1990), *Saint Anselm: A Portrait in a Landscape* (Cambridge: CUP).

— (1995–2001), *Scholastic Humanism and the Unification of Europe*. 2 vols (Oxford: Blackwell).

Stiefel, Tina (1985), *The Intellectual Revolution in Twelfth-Century Europe* (New York: St Martin's Press).

Swanson, R.N. (1999), *The Twelfth-Century Renaissance* (Manchester: Manchester UP).

Sweeney, Eileen C. (2012), *Anselm of Canterbury and the Desire for the Word* (Washington DC: Catholic University of America Press).

Tracy, James D. (1996), *Erasmus of the Low Countries* (Berkeley: University of California Press).

Trinkaus, Charles (1979) *The Poet as Philosopher: Petrarch and the Formation of Renaissance Consciousness* (New Haven/London: Yale UP).

— (1983), *The Scope of Renaissance Humanism* (Ann Arbor: University of Michigan Press).

Wei, Ian P. (2012), *Intellectual Culture in Medieval Paris: Theologians and the University, c. 1100–1330* (Cambridge: CUP).

Weisheipl, James A., O.P. (1975), *Friar Thomas d'Aquino: His Life, Thought, and Works* (Oxford: Blackwell).

— (1980), *Thomas d'Aquino and Albert his Teacher* (Toronto: Pontifical Institute of Mediaeval Studies).

Witt, Ronald G. (2000), *In the Footsteps of the Ancients: The Origins of Humanism from Lovato to Bruni* (Leiden: Brill).

Zak, Gur (2010), *Petrarch's Humanism and the Care of the Self* (Cambridge: CUP).

Zupko, Jack (2003), *John Buridan: Portrait of a Fourteenth-Century Arts Master* (Notre Dame IN: University of Notre Dame Press).

Chapter 9

Arnade, Peter (1996), *Realms of Ritual: Burgundian Ceremony and Civic Life in Late Medieval Ghent* (Ithaca NY: Cornell UP).

Barron, Caroline M. (2004), *London in the Later Middle Ages: Government and People, 1200–1500* (Oxford: OUP).

Black, Anthony (1984), *Guilds and Civil Society in European Political Thought from the Twelfth Century to the Present* (London/New York: Methuen).

Boffey, Julia and Pamela King (eds) (1995), *London and Europe in the Later Middle Ages* (Turnhout: Brepols).

Dean, Trevor, and Chris Wickham (eds) (2003), *City and Countryside in Late Medieval and Renaissance Italy: Essays Presented to Philip Jones* (London: Hambledon).

de Vries, Jan (1984) *European Urbanization, 1500–1800* (Cambridge MA: Harvard UP/London: Methuen).

Edwards, John (1982), *Christian Córdoba: The City and its Region in the Late Middle Ages* (Cambridge: CUP).

Epstein, Steven A. (1991), *Wage Labor and Guilds in Medieval Europe* (Chapel Hill: University of North Carolina Press).

Epstein, S.R. (ed.) (2004), *Town and Country in Europe, 1300–1800* (Cambridge: CUP).

Farmer, Sharon A. (2002), *Surviving Poverty in Medieval Paris: Gender, Ideology, and the Daily Lives of the Poor* (Ithaca NY: Cornell UP).

Frugoni, Chiara (1991), *A Distant City: Images of Urban Experience in the Medieval World* (Princeton: Princeton UP) (orig. Italian, 1983).

Frugoni, Chiara and Arsenio Frugoni (2005), *A Day in a Medieval City* (Chicago: University of Chicago Press) (orig. Italian, 1997).

Goldthwaite, Richard A. (1980), *The Building of Renaissance Florence: A Social and Economic History* (Baltimore: the Johns Hopkins UP).

Goodson, Caroline, Anne E. Lester and Carol Symes (eds) (2010), *Cities, Texts and Social Networks, 400–1500: Experiences and Perceptions of Medieval Urban Space* (Farnham/Burlington VT: Ashgate).

Hall, Derek (2002), *Burgess, Merchant and Priest: The Medieval Scottish Town* (Edinburgh: Birlinn Publishers).

Hanawalt, Barbara A. (1993), *Growing Up in Medieval London: The Experience of Childhood in History* (Oxford: OUP).

Hanawalt, Barbara, and Kathryn L. Reyerson (eds) (1994), *City and Spectacle in Medieval Europe* (Minneapolis: University of Minnesota Press).

Hilton, Rodney (1992), *English and French Towns in Feudal Society* (Cambridge: CUP).

Hohenberg, P.M., and L.H. Lees (1995), *The Making of Urban Europe, 1000–1994*, 2nd edn (Cambridge MA: Harvard UP).

Howell, Martha C. (1998), *The Marriage Exchange: Property, Social Place, and Gender in Cities of the Low Countries, 1300–1550* (Chicago: University of Chicago Press).

Huffman, Joseph P. (1998), *Family, Commerce and Religion in London and Cologne: Anglo-German Emigrants, c.1000–c.1300* (Cambridge: CUP).

Jones, Philip (1997), *The Italian City-State: From Commune to Signoria* (Oxford: Clarendon).

Le Goff, Jacques (1980), *Time, Work and Culture in the Middle Ages* (Chicago/London: University of Chicago Press) (orig. French, 1978).

Lilley, Keith D. (2002), *Urban Life in the Middle Ages, 1000–1450* (Basingstoke: Palgrave).

— (2009), *City and Cosmos: The Medieval World in Urban Form* (London: Reaktion Books).

Lynch, Katherine A. (2003), *Individuals, Families, and Communities in Europe, 1200–1800: The Urban Foundations of Western Society* (Cambridge: CUP).

Miller, Edward, and John Hatcher (1995), *Medieval England: Towns, Commerce and Crafts 1086–1348*, 2nd edn (London: Longman).

Murray, J.M. (2005), *Bruges, Cradle of Capitalism, 1280–1390* (Cambridge: CUP).

Najemy, John M. (2007) *A History of Florence, 1200–1575* (Malden MA/Oxford: Blackwell).

Nicholas, D.M. (1997), *The Growth of the Medieval City from Late Antiquity to the Early Fourteenth Century* (London/New York: Longman)

— (1997), *The Later Medieval City 1300–1500* (London/New York: Longman).

— (2003), *Urban Europe, 1100–1700* (Basingstoke: Palgrave Macmillan).

Ogilvie, Sheilagh (2011), *Institutions and European Trade: Merchant Guilds, 1000–1800* (Cambridge: CUP).

Oldfield, Paul (2009), *City and Community in Norman Italy* (Cambridge: CUP).

Palliser, David M. (2006), *Towns and Local Communities in Medieval and Early Modern England* (Aldershot: Ashgate).

Pounds, Norman (2005), *The Medieval City* (Westport CT: Greenwood Press).

Ricciardelli, Fabrizio (2007), *The Politics of Exclusion in Early Renaissance Florence* (Turnhout: Brepols).

Stabel, Peter (1997), *Dwarfs among Giants: The Flemish Urban Network in the Late Middle Ages* (Apeldoorn: Garant).

Titone, Fabrizio (2009), *Governments of the Universitates: Urban Communities of Sicily in the Fourteenth and Fifteenth Centuries* (Turnhout: Brepols).

Vance, James E. Jr (1990), *The Continuing City: Urban Morphology in Western Civilization* (Baltimore: the Johns Hopkins UP).

Verhulst, Adriaan (1999) *The Rise of Cities in North-West Europe* (Cambridge: CUP).

Webb, Diana (1996), *Patrons and Defenders: The Saints in the Italian City State* (London/New York: I.B. Tauris).

Chapter 10

Bailey, Mark and Stephen Rigby (eds) (2012), *Town and Countryside in the Age of the Black Death: Essays in Honour of John Hatcher* (Turnhout: Brepols).

Bartlett, Robert (2004), *The Hanged Man: A Story of Miracle, Memory, and Colonialism in the Middle Ages* (Princeton: Princeton UP).

Benedictow, Ole J. (2004), *The Black Death 1346–1353: The Complete History* (Woodbridge: Boydell & Brewer).

Biller, Peter (2001), *The Measure of Multitude: Population in Medieval Thought* (Oxford: OUP).

Bisson, Lillian M. (1998), *Chaucer and the Late Medieval World* (New York: St Martin's Press).

Blamires, Alcuin (1997) *The Case for Women in Medieval Culture* (Oxford: Clarendon).

Blickle, Peter (1985), *The Revolution of 1525: The German Peasants' War from a New Perspective*, 2nd edn (Baltimore: the Johns Hopkins UP) (orig. German, 1975).

— (1998), *From the Communal Reformation to the Revolution of the Common Man* (Leiden: Brill) (orig. German, 1993).

Borsch, Stuart J. (2005), *The Black Death in Egypt and England: A Comparative Study* (Austin: University of Texas Press).

Bothwell, J.S. (2008), *Falling from Grace: Reversal of Fortune and the English Nobility* (Manchester: Manchester UP).

Brown-Grant, Rosalind (1999), *Christine de Pizan and the Moral Defence of Women: Reading beyond Gender* (Cambridge: CUP).

Campbell, Bruce M.S. (ed.) (1991), *Before the Black Death: Studies in the 'Crisis' of the Early Fourteenth Century* (Manchester: Manchester UP).

— (2000), *English Seignorial Agriculture 1250–1450* (Cambridge: CUP).

Cantor, Norman F. (2001), *In the Wake of the Plague: The*

Black Death and the World it Made (New York/ London: The Free Press/Simon & Schuster).

Cohn, Samuel K. Jr (1992), *The Cult of Remembrance and the Black Death: Six Renaissance Cities in Central Italy* (Baltimore: the Johns Hopkins UP).

— (2002), *The Black Death Transformed: Disease and Culture in Early Renaissance Europe* (London/New York: Arnold/OUP).

— (2006), *Lust for Liberty: The Politics of Social Revolt in Medieval Europe, 1200–1425* (Cambridge MA: Harvard UP).

Coss, Peter (2003), *The Origins of the English Gentry* (Cambridge: CUP).

Crassons, Kate (2010), *The Claims of Poverty: Literature, Culture, and Ideology in Late Medieval England* (Notre Dame IN: University of Notre Dame Press).

Davis, James (2012), *Medieval Market Morality: Life, Law and Ethics in the English Marketplace, 1200–1500* (Cambridge: CUP).

Denton, Jeffrey Howard (ed.) (1999), *Orders and Hierarchies in Late Medieval and Renaissance Europe* (Basingstoke: Palgrave Macmillan).

Dyer, Christopher (1998), *Standards of Living in the Later Middle Ages. Social Change in England, c.1200–1520*, 2nd edn (Cambridge: CUP).

Eckstein, Nicholas A. and Nicholas Terpstra (eds) (2009), *Sociability and its Discontents: Civil Society, Social Capital, and their Alternatives in Late Medieval and Early Modern Europe* (Turnhout: Brepols).

Farmer, Sharon (2002), *Surviving Poverty in Medieval Paris: Gender, Ideology and the Daily Lives of the Poor* (Ithaca NY: Cornell UP).

Freedman, Paul (1991), *The Origins of Peasant Servitude in Medieval Catalonia* (Cambridge: CUP).

Goldberg, P.J.P. (1992) *Women, Work and Life-Cycle in a Medieval Economy: Women in York and Yorkshire* (Oxford: Clarendon).

Goodich, Michael E. (1995), *Violence and Miracle in the Fourteenth Century: Private Grief and Public Salvation* (Chicago/London: University of Chicago Press).

Hatcher, John (1977), *Plague, Population and the English Economy 1348–1530* (London/Basingstoke: Macmillan).

Hatcher, John and Mark Bailey (2001), *Modelling The Middle Ages: The History and Theory of England's Economic Development* (Oxford: OUP).

Hewlett, Cecilia (2008), *Rural Communities in Renaissance Tuscany: Religious Identities and Local Loyalties* (Turnhout: Brepols).

Hilton, Rodney (2003), *Bond Men Made Free: Medieval Peasant Movements and the English Rising of 1381*, 2nd edn (London/New York: Routledge).

Jordan, William Chester (1996), *The Great Famine:*

Northern Europe in the Early Fourteenth Century (Princeton: Princeton UP).

Kaye, Joel (1998), *Economy and Nature in the Fourteenth Century: Money, Market Exchange, and the Emergence of Scientific Thought* (Cambridge: CUP).

Kelleher, Marie A. (2010), *The Measure of Woman. Law and Female Identity in the Crown of Aragon* (Philadelphia: University of Pennsylvania Press).

Kitsikopoulos, Harry (ed.) (2012), *Agrarian Change and Crisis in Europe, 1200–1500* (London/New York: Routledge).

Langholm, Odd (1992), *Economics in the Medieval Schools: Wealth, Exchange, Value, Money, and Usury According to the Paris Theological Tradition 1200–1350* (Leiden: Brill).

— (2003), *The Merchant in the Confessional: Trade and Price in the Pre-Reformation Penitential Handbooks* (Leiden: Brill).

L'Estrange, Elizabeth (2008), *Holy Motherhood: Gender, Dynasty and Visual Culture in the Later Middle Ages* (Manchester: Manchester UP).

Margolis, Nadia (2011), *An Introduction to Christine de Pizan* (Gainesville: University Press of Florida).

Martines, Lauro (2001), *Strong Words: Writing and Social Strain in the Italian Renaissance* (Baltimore: the Johns Hopkins UP).

— (2006), *Fire in the City: Savonarola and the Struggle for the Soul of Renaissance Florence* (Oxford: OUP).

Mate, Mavis E. (1998), *Daughters, Wives and Widows after the Black Death: Women in Sussex, 1350–1535* (Woodbridge: Boydell).

Meyerson, Mark D. (2004), *Jews in an Iberian Frontier Kingdom: Society, Economy and Politics in Morvedre, 1248–1391* (Leiden: Brill).

— (2004), *A Jewish Renaissance in Fifteenth-Century Spain* (Princeton: Princeton UP).

Mollat, Michel (1987) *The Poor in the Middle Ages: An Essay in Social History* (New Haven: Yale UP) (orig. French, 1979).

Montanari, Massimo (1996), *The Culture of Food* (Oxford: Blackwell) (orig. Italian, 1993).

Mormando, Franco (1999), *The Preacher's Demons: Bernardino of Siena and the Social Underworld of Early Renaissance Italy* (Chicago: University of Chicago Press).

Mullett, Michael (1987), *Popular Culture and Popular Protest in Late Medieval and Early Modern Europe* (London: Croom Helm).

Munro, J.H. (1992), *Bullion Flows and Monetary Policies in England and the Low Countries* (Aldershot: Variorum) (Variorum Collected Studies; 335).

Noble, Elizabeth (2009), *The World of the Stonors: A Gentry Society* (Woodbridge: Boydell).

Platt, Colin (1996) *King Death: The Black Death and its Aftermath in Late Medieval England* (London: UCL Press).

Pleij, Herman (2001), *Dreaming of Cockaigne: Medieval Phantasies of the Perfect Life* (New York: Columbia UP) (orig. Dutch, 1997).

Polecritti, Cynthia L. (2000), *Preaching Peace in Renaissance Italy: Bernardino of Siena and his Audience* (Washington DC: Catholic University of America Press).

Rigby, S.H. (1995), *English Society in the Later Middle Ages: Class, Status and Gender* (Basingstoke/London: Macmillan).

Shahar, Shulamith (2003), *The Fourth Estate: A History of Women in the Middle Ages*, 2nd edn (London/New York: Routledge).

TeBrake, William H. (1993), *A Plague of Insurrection: Popular Politics and Peasant Revolt in Flanders, 1323–1328* (Philadelphia: University of Pennsylvania Press).

Vivanco, Laura (2004), *Death in Fifteenth-Century Castile: Ideologies of the Elites* (Woodbridge: Boydell & Brewer).

Willard, Charity Cannon (1984), *Christine de Pizan: Her Life and Works* (New York: Persea Books).

Wright, Nicholas (1998), *Knights and Peasants: The Hundred Years War in the French Countryside* (Woodbridge: Boydell).

Chapter 11

Allmand, Christopher, (1992), *Henry V* (Berkeley: University of California Press).

— (2001), *The Hundred Years War: England and France at War c.1300–c.1450*, 2nd edn (Cambridge: CUP).

— (ed.) (2001), *War, Government and Society in Late Medieval France* (Liverpool: Liverpool UP).

Armstrong, Lawrin and Julius Kirshner (eds) (2011), *The Politics of Law in Late Medieval and Renaissance Italy* (Toronto: University of Toronto Press).

Arnold, Benjamin (1991), *Princes and Territories in Medieval Germany* (Cambridge: CUP).

Bartusis, Mark C. (1992), *The Late Byzantine Army: Arms and Society, 1204–1453* (Philadelphia: Pennsylvania State UP).

Bean, J.M.W. (1989), *From Lord to Patron: Lordship in Late Medieval England* (Manchester: Manchester UP).

Black, J. (2009), *Absolutism in Renaissance Milan: Plenitude of Power under the Visconti and the Sforza, 1329–1535* (Oxford: OUP).

Blockmans, Wim and Walter Prevenier (1999), *The Promised Lands: The Low Countries under Burgundian Rule, 1369–1530* (Philadelphia: University of Pennsylvania Press) (orig. Dutch, 1997).

Bratchel, Michael E. (2009), *Medieval Lucca and the Evolution of the Renaissance State* (Oxford: OUP).

Brundage, James A. (2008), *The Medieval Origins of the Legal Profession: Canonists, Civilians and Courts* (Chicago/London: University of Chicago Press).

Burns, J. H. (1992), *Lordship, Kingship, and Empire: The Idea of Monarchy, 1400–1525* (Oxford: Clarendon) (Carlyle Lectures).

Caferro, William (2006), *John Hawkwood: An English Mercenary in Fourteenth-Century Italy* (Baltimore: the Johns Hopkins UP).

Carpenter, Christine (1997), *The Wars of the Roses: Politics and the Constitution in England, c.1477–1509* (Cambridge: CUP).

Chrimes, S.B. (1999), *Henry VII* (New Haven/London: Yale UP).

Connell, William J. and Andrea Zorzi (eds) (2000), *Florentine Tuscany: Structures and Practices of Power* (Cambridge: CUP).

DeVries, Kelly (1996), *Infantry Warfare in the Early Fourteenth Century: Disipline, Tactics and Technology* (Woodbridge: Boydell).

Earenfight, Theresa (2009), *The King's Other Body: María of Castile and the Crown of Aragon* (Philadelphia: University of Pennsylvania Press).

Echevarría, Ana (1999), *The Fortress of Faith: The Attitudes toward Muslims in Fifteenth-Century Spain* (Leiden: Brill).

Engel, Pal (2005), *The Realm of St Stephen: A History of Medieval Hungary*, 2nd edn (London/New York: I.B. Tauris).

Etting, Vivian (2004), *Queen Margrete I (1353–1412) and the Founding of the Nordic Union* (Leiden: Brill).

Fine, John V.A. Jr. (1987), *The Late Medieval Balkans: A Critical Survey from the Late Twelfth Century to the Ottoman Conquest* (Ann Arbor: The University of Michigan Press).

Franklin, Simon, and Jonathan Shepard (1996), *The Emergence of Rus, 750–1200* (London/New York: Longman).

Giancarlo, Matthew (2007), *Parliament and Literature in Late Medieval England* (Cambridge: CUP).

Given-Wilson, Chris (1987), *The English Nobility in the Late Middle Ages: The Fourteenth-Century Political Community* (London/New York: Routledge).

Gomes, Rita Costa (2003), *The Making of a Court Society: Kings and Nobles in Late Medieval Portugal* (Cambridge: CUP).

Guenée, Bernard (1985), *States and Rulers in Later Medieval Europe* (Oxford: Blackwell) (orig. French, 1971).

Harding, Alan (2002), *Medieval Law and the Foundations of the State* (Oxford: OUP).

Harriss, Gerald (2005), *Shaping the Nation: England 1360–1461* (Oxford: OUP) (New Oxford History of England).

Heer, Friedrich (1995), *The Holy Roman Empire* (London: Phoenix Press) (orig. German, 1967).

Hicks, Michael (1995), *Bastard Feudalism* (London: Longman).

— (2010), *The Wars of the Roses* (New Haven/London: Yale UP).

Horrox, Rosemary (1989), *Richard III: A Study of Service* (Cambridge: CUP).

Housley, Norman (2002), *Religious Warfare in Europe, 1400–1536* (Oxford: OUP).

— (ed.) (2004), *Crusading in the Fifteenth Century: Message and Impact* (Basingstoke: Palgrave Macmillan).

— (2013), *Crusading and the Ottoman Threat, 1453–1505* (Oxford: OUP).

Imber, Colin (2009), *The Ottoman Empire, 1300–1650: The Structure of Power*, 2nd edn (Basingstoke: Palgrave Macmillan).

Inalcik, Halil (1997), *An Economic and Social History of the Ottoman Empire: Volume 1: 1300–1600* (Cambridge: CUP).

Kaeuper, Richard W. (1988), *War, Justice and Public Order: England and France in the Later Middle Ages* (Oxford: Clarendon).

Kafadar, Cemal (1995), *Between Two Worlds: The Construction of the Ottoman State* (Berkeley: University of California Press).

Kelly, Samantha (2003), *The New Solomon: Robert of Naples (1309–1343) and Fourteenth-Century Kingship* (Leiden/Boston: Brill).

King, Andy and Michael Penman (eds) (2007), *England and Scotland in the Fourteenth Century: New Perspectives* (Woodbridge: Boydell).

Kirshner, Julius (ed.) (1995), *The Origins of the State in Italy 1300–1600* (Chicago/London: University of Chicago Press).

Knecht, Robert (2004), *The Valois Kings of France, 1328–1589* (Basingstoke: Palgrave Macmillan).

Knoll, Paul W. (1972), *The Rise of the Polish Monarchy: Piast Poland in East Central Europe, 1320–1370* (Chicago/London: Chicago UP).

Law, John E. and Bernadette Paton (eds) (2010), *Communes and Despots in Medieval and Renaissance Italy* (Farnham: Ashgate).

Lowry, Heath W. (2003), *The Nature of the Early Ottoman State* (Albany: State University of New York Press).

Martin, Janet L.B. (1995), *Medieval Russia, 980–1584* (Cambridge: CUP).

Martines, Lauro (2002), *Power and Imagination: City-States in Renaissance Italy* (London: Pimlico).

— (2003), *April Blood: Florence and the Plot against the Medici* (Oxford: OUP).

Matthews, David (2010), *Writing to the King: Nation, Kingship and Literature in England, 1250–1350* (Cambridge: CUP).

Meserve, Margaret (2008), *Empires of Islam in Renaissance Historical Thought* (Cambridge MA: Harvard UP).

Necipoglu, Nevra (2009), *Byzantium between the Ottomans and the Latins* (Cambridge: CUP).

Nicholas, David (2009), *The Northern Lands: Germanic Europe, c.1270–c.1500* (Malden MA: Wiley-Blackwell).

Nicol, D.M. (1993), *The Last Centuries of Byzantium, 1261–1453*, 2nd edn (Cambridge: CUP).

Nuttall, Jenni (2007), *The Creation of Lancastrian England: Literature, Language and Politics in Late Medieval England* (Cambridge: CUP).

Ormrod, W.M. (1990), *The Reign of Edward III: Crown and Political Society in England 1327–1377* (New Haven/London: Yale UP).

— (1995), *Political Life in Medieval England, 1300–1450* (Basingstoke/New York: Macmillan/St Martin's Press).

Ostrowski, Donald (1998), *Muscovy and the Mongols: Cross-cultural Influences on the Steppe Frontier, 1304–1589* (Cambridge: CUP).

Palmer, Alan (2006), *The Baltic: A New History of the Region and its People* (New York/London: Overlook Press).

Pernoud, Régine, and Marie-Véronique Clin (2000), *Joan of Arc: Her Story*, 2nd edn (London: Weidenfeld & Nicholson).

Phillips, Seymour (2010), *Edward II* (New Haven/London: Yale UP).

Potter, David (1995), *A History of France, 1460–1560: The Emergence of a Nation-State* (Oxford: OUP).

— (2008), *Renaissance France at War: Armies, Culture and Society, c.1480–1560* (Woodbridge: Boydell).

Prestwich, Michael (1996), *Armies and Warfare in the Middle Ages: The English Experience* (New Haven/London: Yale UP).

— (1997), *Edward I* (New Haven/London: Yale UP).

— (2003), *The Three Edwards: War and State in England 1272–1377*, 2nd edn (London/New York: Routledge).

Raban, Sandra (2000), *England under Edward I and Edward II, 1259–1327* (Oxford: Blackwell).

Raffensperger, Christian (2012), *Reimagining Europe: Kievan Rus' in the Medieval World* (Cambridge MA: Harvard UP).

Rowell, S.C. (1994), *Lithuania Ascending: A Pagan Empire within East-Central Europe, 1295–1345* (Cambridge: CUP).

Saul, Nigel (1997) *Richard II* (New Haven/London: Yale UP).

Scase, Wendy (2007), *Literature and Complaint in England, 1272–1553* (Oxford: OUP).

Sedlar, Jean W. (1994), *East Central Europe in the Middle Ages, 1000–1500* (Seattle: University of Washington Press).

Sugar, Peter F. (1977), *Southeastern Europe under Ottoman Rule, 1354–1804* (Seattle/London: University of Washington Press).

Tilly, Charles (1990), *Coercion, Capital and European States, 990–1990* (Cambridge MA: Blackwell).

Tuck, Anthony (1999), *Crown and Nobility: England 1272–1461*, 2nd edn (Oxford: Blackwell).

Vale, Malcolm (1981), *War and Chivalry: Warfare and Aristocratic Culture in England, France and Burgundy at the End of the Middle Ages* (London: Duckworth).

— (2001), *The Princely Court: Medieval Courts and Culture in North-West Europe (1270–1380)* (Oxford: OUP).

Vaughan, Richard (2004), *Philip the Good: The Apogee of Burgundy*, 2nd edn (Woodbridge: Boydell).

— (2004), *Charles the Bold: The Last Valois Duke of Burgundy*, 2nd edn (Woodbridge: Boydell).

— (2005a), *Philip the Bold: The Foundation of the Burgundian State*, 2nd edn (Woodbridge: Boydell).

— (2005b), *John the Fearless: The Growth of Burgundian Power*, 2nd edn (Woodbridge: Boydell).

Vernier, Richard (2003), *The Flower of Chivalry: Bertrand du Guesclin and the Hundred Years War* (Woodbridge: Boydell).

— (2008), *Lord of the Pyrenees: Gaston Fébus, Count of Foix (1331–1391)* (Woodbridge: Boydell).

Watts, John (1996), *Henry VI and the Politics of Kingship* (Cambridge: CUP).

— (2009), *The Making of Polities: Europe, 1300–1500* (Cambridge: CUP).

Wheeler, Bonnie, and Charles T. Woods (eds) (1996), *Fresh Verdicts on Joan of Arc* (New York: Garland).

Wolffe, Bertram (2001), *Henry VI* (New Haven/London: Yale UP).

Wood, Charles T. (1988), *Joan of Arc and Richard III: Sex, Saints and Government in the Middle Ages* (Oxford: OUP).

Woolgar, C.M. (1999), *The Great Household in Late Medieval England* (New Haven/London: Yale UP).

Chapter 12

Anderson, Wendy Love (2011), *The Discernment of Spirits: Assessing Visions and Visionaries in the Late Middle Ages* (Tübingen: Mohr Siebeck).

Barr, Beth Allen (2008), *The Pastoral Care of Women in Late Medieval England* (Woodbridge: Boydell).

Barr, Jessica (2010), *Willing to Know God: Dreamers and Visionaries in the Later Middle Ages* (Columbus OH: Ohio State UP).

Bernard, G.W. (2012), *The Late Medieval English Church: Vitality and Vulnerability before the Break with Rome* (New Haven: Yale UP).

Black, Anthony (1992), *Political Thought in Europe 1250–1450* (Cambridge: CUP).

— (2003), *Church, State and Community: Historical and Comparative Perspectives* (Aldershot/Burlington VT: Ashgate) (Variorum Collected Studies).

— (2008), *The West and Islam: Religion and Political Thought in World History* (Oxford: OUP).

Bossy, John (1985), *Christianity in the West, 1400–1700* (Oxford: OUP).

Boureau, Alain (2006), *Satan the Heretic: The Birth of Demonology in the Medieval West* (Chicago/London: University of Chicago Press) (orig. French, 2004).

Bryan, Jennifer (2008), *Looking Inward: Devotional Reading and the Private Self in Late Medieval England* (Philadelphia: University of Pennsylvania Press).

Burgtorf, Jochen, Paul F. Crawford and Helen J. Nicholson (eds) (2010), *The Debate on the Trial of the Templars (1307–1314)* (Burlington VT: Ashgate).

Bynum, Caroline Walker (2007), *Wonderful Blood: Theology and Practice in Late Medieval Northern Germany and Beyond* (Philadelphia: University of Pennsylvania Press).

— (2011), *Christian Materiality: An Essay on Religion in Late Medieval Europe* (New York: Zone Books).

Caciola, Nancy (2003), *Discerning Spirits: Divine and Demonic Possession in the Middle Ages* (Ithaca NY: Cornell UP).

Canning, Joseph (2011), *Ideas of Power in the Late Middle Ages, 1296–1417* (Cambridge: CUP).

Collins, Amanda (2002), *Greater than Emperor: Cola di Rienzo (c.1313–54) and the World of Fourteenth-Century Rome* (Ann Arbor: University of Michigan Press).

Collins, David J. (2008), *Reforming Saints: Saints' Lives and their Authors in Germany, 1470–1530* (Oxford: OUP).

Craun, Edwin D. (2010), *Ethics and Power in Medieval English Reform Writing* (Cambridge: CUP).

Dove, Mary (2007), *The First English Bible: The Text and Context of the Wycliffite Versions* (Cambridge: CUP).

Duffy, Eamon (1992), *The Stripping of the Altars: Traditional Religion in England, 1400–1580* (New Haven CT: Yale UP).

— (2006), *Marking the Hours: English People and their Prayers, 1240–1570* (New Haven CT: Yale UP).

Elliott, Dyan (2004), *Proving Woman: Female Spirituality and Inquisitional Culture in the Later Middle Ages* (Princeton: Princeton UP).

Engen, John van (2008), *Sisters and Brothers of the Common Life: The Devotio Moderna and the World of the Later Middle Ages* (Philadelphia: University of Pennsylvania Press).

Fudge, Thomas A. (1998), *The Magnificent Ride: The First Reformation in Hussite Bohemia* (Aldershot: Ashgate).

Garnett, George (2006), *Marsilius of Padua and 'the Truth of History'* (Oxford: OUP).

Heft, James (1986), *John XXII and Papal Teaching Authority* (Lewiston NY: Edwin Mellen Press).

Herwaarden, Jan van (2003), *Between Saint James and Erasmus: Studies in Late-Medieval Religious Life: Devotion and Pilgrimage in the Netherlands* (Leiden: Brill).

Housley, Norman (2002), *Religious Warfare in Europe, 1400–1536* (Oxford: OUP).

Jansen, Katherine Ludwig (2000), *The Making of the Magdalen: Preaching and Popular Devotion in the Later Middle Ages* (Princeton: Princeton UP).

Jordan, William Chester (2005), *Unceasing Strife, Unending Fear: Jacques de Thérines and the Freedom of the Church in the Age of the Last Capetians* (Princeton: Princeton UP).

Kamerick, Kathleen (2002), *Popular Piety and Art in the Late Middle Ages: Image Worship and Idolatry in England, 1350–1500* (Basingstoke: Palgrave).

Kleinberg, Aviad M. (1992), *Prophets in their Own Country: Living Saints and the Making of Sainthood in the Later Middle Ages* (Chicago: University of Chicago Press).

Lahey, Stephen E. (2003), *Philosophy and Politics in the Thought of John Wyclif* (Cambridge: CUP).

Lesnick, Daniel R. (1989), *Preaching in Medieval Florence: The Social World of Franciscan and Dominican Spirituality* (Athens GA: University of Georgia Press).

Linder, Amnon (2003), *Raising Arms: Liturgy in the Struggle to Liberate Jerusalem in the Late Middle Ages* (Turnhout: Brepols).

Lindgren, Erika Lauren (2009), *Sensual Encounters: Monastic Women and Spirituality in Medieval Germany* (New York: Columbia UP).

Luongo, F. Thomas (2006), *The Saintly Politics of Catherine of Siena* (Ithaca NY/London: Cornell UP).

MacCulloch, Diarmaid (2003), *The Reformation: A History* (New York: Penguin).

McDougall, Sara (2012), *Bigamy and Christian Identity in Late Medieval Champagne* (Philadelphia: University of Pennsylvania Press).

McGinn, Bernard (1991–2012), *The Presence of God: A History of Western Mysticism*. 6 vols (New York: Crossroad).

— (ed.) (1994), *Meister Eckhart and the Beguine Mystics: Hadewijch of Brabant, Mechteld of Magdeburg and Marguerite Porete* (New York: Continuum).

Mansfield, Mary C. (2005), *The Humiliation of Sinners: Public Penance in Thirteenth-Century France* (Ithaca NY: Cornell UP).

Marks, Richard (2004), *Image and Devotion in Late Medieval England* (Stroud: Sutton).

Menache, Sophia (1998), *Clement V* (Cambridge: CUP).

Meuthen, Erich (2010), *Nicholas of Cusa: A Sketch for a Biography* (Washington DC: Catholic University of America Press) (orig. German, 1992).

Miller, Kathryn A. (2008), *Guardians of Islam: Religious Authority and Muslim Communities of Late Medieval Spain* (New York: Columbia UP).

Mixson, James (2009), *Poverty's Proprietors: Ownership and Mortal Sin at the Origins of the Observant Movement* (Leiden: Brill).

Moreno-Riaño, Gerson and Cary J. Nederman (eds) (2012), *A Companion to Marsilius* (Leiden: Brill).

Mossman, Stephen (2010), *Marquard von Lindau and the Challenges of Religious Life in Late Medieval Germany* (Oxford: OUP).

Murdoch, Brian (2003), *The Medieval Popular Bible: Expansions of Genesis in the Middle Ages* (Rochester NY/Woodbridge: Boydell & Brewer).

Musto, Ronald G. (2003), *Apocalypse in Rome: Cola di Rienzo and the Politics of the New Age* (Berkeley: University of California Press).

Nieuwenhove, Rik van (2003), *Jan van Ruusbroec: Mystical Theologian of the Trinity* (Notre Dame IN: University of Notre Dame Press).

Nixon, Virginia (2004), *Mary's Mother: Saint Anne in Late Medieval Europe* (University Park PA: Penn State Press).

Oakley, Francis (2003), *The Conciliarist Tradition: Constitutionalism in the Catholic Church, 1300–1870* (Oxford: OUP).

Ozment, Steven (1980), *The Age of Reform, 1250–1550: An Intellectual and Religious History of Late Medieval and Reformation Europe* (New Haven: Yale UP).

Palmer, Robert C. (2002), *Selling the Church: The English Parish in Law, Commerce, and Religion, 1350–1550* (Chapel Hill NC/London: University of North Carolina Press).

Phillips, Helen (ed.) (2010), *Chaucer and Religion* (Cambridge: D.S. Brewer).

Rex, Richard (2002), *The Lollards* (Basingstoke/New York: Palgrave).

Rollo-Koster, Joëlle (2008), *Raiding Saint Peter: Empty Sees, Violence and the Initiation of the Great Western Schism (1378)* (Leiden: Brill).

Rubin, Miri (1991), *Corpus Christi: The Eucharist in Late Medieval Culture* (Cambridge: CUP).

— (1999), *Gentile Tales: The Narrative Assault on Late Medieval Jews* (New Haven/London: Yale UP).

— (2009), *Emotion and Devotion: The Meaning of Mary in Medieval Religious Cultures* (Budapest/New York: Central European University Press) (The Natalie Zemon Davis Annual Lectures).

Saak, Eric L. (2002), *High Way to Heaven: The Augustinian Platform between Reform and Reformation, 1292–1524* (Leiden: Brill).

Scheepsma, Wybren (2004), *Medieval Religious Women in the Low Countries: The 'Modern Devotion', the Canonesses of Windesheim and their Writings* (Woodbridge: Boydell) (orig. Dutch, 1997).

Simons, Walter (2001), *Cities of Ladies: Beguine Communities in the Medieval Low Countries, 1200–1565* (Philadelphia: University of Pennsylvania Press).

Somerset, Fiona, Jill C. Havens and Derrick G. Pitard (eds) (2003), *Lollards and their Influence in Late Medieval England* (Woodbridge: Boydell & Brewer).

Stansbury, Ronald J. (ed.) (2010), *A Companion to Pastoral Care in the Late Middle Ages (1200–1500)* (Leiden: Brill).

Stephens, Walter (2002), *Demon Lovers: Witchcraft, Sex, and the Crisis of Belief* (Chicago/London: University of Chicago Press).

Stinger, Charles L. (1985), *The Renaissance in Rome* (Bloomington IN: Indiana UP).

Swanson, R.N. (1995), *Religion and Devotion in Europe, c.1215–c.1515* (Cambridge: CUP).

— (2007), *Indulgences in Late Medieval England: Passports to Paradise?* (Cambridge: CUP).

Tierney, Brian (1998), *Foundations of the Conciliar Theory: The Contribution of the Medieval Canonists from Gratian to the Great Schism* (Leiden: Brill) (orig. CUP, 1955).

Tinsley, David F. (2010), *The Scourge and the Cross: Ascetic Mentalities of the Later Middle Ages* (Leuven: Peeters).

Van Dussen, Michael (2012), *From England to Bohemia: Heresy and Communication in the Later Middle Ages* (Cambridge: CUP).

Vauchez, André (1993), *The Laity in the Middle Ages: Religious Beliefs and Devotional Practices* (Notre Dame IN: University of Notre Dame Press) (orig. French, 1987).

— (1997), *Sainthood in the Later Middle Ages* (Cambridge: CUP) (orig. French, 1981).

Vroom, Wim (2010), *Financing Cathedral Building in the Middle Ages: The Generosity of the Faithful* (Amsterdam: Amsterdam UP).

Warnar, Geert (2007), *Ruusbroec: Literature and Mysticism in the Fourteenth Century* (Leiden/Boston: Brill) (orig. Dutch, 2003).

Waters, Claire (2004), *Angels and Earthly Creatures: Preaching, Performance, and Gender in the Later Middle Ages* (Philadelphia: University of Pennsylvania Press).

Epilogue

Blumenberg, Hans (1983), *The Legitimacy of the Modern Age* (Cambridge MA: MIT Press) (orig. German, 1966).

— (1987), *The Genesis of the Copernican World* (Cambridge MA: MIT Press) (orig. German, 1975).

Chakrabarty, Dipesh (2008), *Provincializing Europe: Postcolonial Thought and Historical Difference*, 2nd edn (Princeton: Princeton UP).

Cole, Andrew and D. Vance Smith (eds) [with an afterword by Fredric Jameson] (2010), *The Legitimacy of the Middle Ages* (Durham NC: Duke UP).

Fernández-Armesto, Felipe (2006), *Pathfinders: A Global History of Exploration* (Cambridge: CUP).

Grafton, Anthony [with April Shelford and Nancy Siraisi] (1992), *New Worlds, Ancient Texts: The Power of Tradition and the Shock of Discovery* (Cambridge MA: The Belknap Press of Harvard UP).

McMullan, Gordon and David Matthews (eds) (2007), *Reading the Medieval in Early Modern England* (Cambridge: CUP).

Mignolo, Walter D. (2011), *The Darker Side of Western Modernity: Global Futures, Decolonial Options* (Durham NC: Duke UP).

Russell, Jeffrey Burton (1991), *Inventing the Flat Earth: Columbus and Modern Historians* (New York: Praeger).

Index

ROUTLEDGE

Forthcoming...

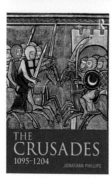

The Crusades, 1095-1204

2nd Edition

By Jonathan Phillips

This new and considerably expanded edition of *The Crusades, 1095-1204* couples vivid narrative with a clear and accessible analysis of the key ideas that prompted the conquest and settlement of the Holy Land between the First and the Fourth Crusade.

This edition now covers the Fourth Crusade and the Sack of Constantinople, along with greater coverage of the Muslim response to the crusades from the capture of Jerusalem in 1099 down through Saladin's leadership of the counter-crusade, culminating in his struggle with Richard the Lionheart during the Third Crusade. It also examines the complex motives of the Italian city states during the conquest of the Levant, as well as relations between the Frankish settlers and the indigenous population, both Eastern Christian and Muslim, in times of war and peace. Extended treatment of the events of the First Crusade, the failure of the Second Crusade, and the prominent role of female rulers in the Latin East feature too.

2014 | 280 Pages | PB: 978-1-405-87293-5| HB: 978-0-415-73636-7
Learn more at: http://www.routledge.com/books/details/9781405872935/

Available from all good bookshops